PATERNOSTER THEOLOGICAL MONOGRAPHS

Beyond Salvation

Eastern Orthodoxy and Classical Pentecostalism on Becoming Like Christ

PATERNOSTER THEOLOGICAL MONOGRAPHS

Full listings of all titles in both Paternoster Biblical and
Theological Monographs appear at the close of this book

PATERNOSTER THEOLOGICAL MONOGRAPHS

Beyond Salvation

Eastern Orthodoxy and Classical Pentecostalism on Becoming Like Christ

Edmund J. Rybarczyk

Foreword by

Cecil M. Robeck, Jr.

Wipf & Stock
PUBLISHERS
Eugene, Oregon

Wipf and Stock Publishers
199 W 8th Ave, Suite 3
Eugene, OR 97401

Beyond Salvation
Eastern Orthodoxy and Classical Pentecostalism on Becoming Like Christ
By Rybarczyk, Edmund J.
Copyright©2004 Paternoster
ISBN: 1-59752-732-7
Publication date 6/5/2006
Previously published by Paternoster, 2004

This Edition published by Wipf and Stock Publishers
by arrangement with Paternoster

Paternoster
9 Holdom Avenue
Bletchley
Milton Keyes, MK1 1QR
PATERNOSTER Great Britain

Series Preface

In the West the churches may be declining, but theology—serious, academic (mostly doctoral level) and mainstream orthodox in evaluative commitment—shows no sign of withering on the vine. This series of *Paternoster Theological Monographs* extends the expertise of the Press especially to first-time authors whose work stands broadly within the parameters created by fidelity to Scripture and has satisfied the critical scrutiny of respected assessors in the academy. Such theology may come in several distinct intellectual disciplines—historical, dogmatic, pastoral, apologetic, missional, aesthetic and no doubt others also. The series will be particularly hospitable to promising constructive theology within an evangelical frame, for it is of this that the church's need seems to be greatest. Quality writing will be published across the confessions—Anabaptist, Episcopalian, Reformed, Arminian and Orthodox—across the ages—patristic, medieval, reformation, modern and counter-modern—and across the continents. The aim of the series is theology written in the twofold conviction that the church needs theology and theology needs the church—which in reality means theology done for the glory of God.

Series Editors

David F. Wright, Emeritus Professor of Patristic and Reformed Christianity, University of Edinburgh, Scotland, UK

Trevor A. Hart, Head of School and Principal of St Mary's College School of Divinity, University of St Andrews, Scotland, UK

Anthony N.S. Lane, Professor of Historical Theology and Director of Research, London School of Theology, UK

Anthony C. Thiselton, Emeritus Professor of Christian Theology, University of Nottingham, Research Professor in Christian Theology, University College Chester, and Canon Theologian of Leicester Cathedral and Southwell Minster, UK

Kevin J. Vanhoozer, Research Professor of Systematic Theology, Trinity Evangelical Divinity School, Deerfield, Illinois, USA

For Tawnya, God's gift to me

CONTENTS

Foreword

The relationship between Pentecostal Christians and Orthodox Christians has seldom been a comfortable one. Orthodoxy is an ancient, Eastern Christian tradition. Pentecostalism is a recent, Western Christian tradition. Orthodoxy is steeped in Tradition, rites, symbols, liturgy, and a way of life that are centuries old. Pentecostalism is primitive, pragmatic, and spontaneous in its orientation. It is marked by its chameleon-like adaptability, its innovation, and its vitality. There are few places in the world where Orthodoxy and Pentecostalism have been practiced in close proximity to one another to the extent that they are genuine competitors. For the most part they have been strangers. As a result, each of them has frequently looked askance at the other, not quite sure how they should react. In some cases, there has been outright animosity between them.

When Pentecostals look at the Orthodox, they often see only ancient Greek culture, worship in a language they cannot understand, long black robes, stovepipe hats, a bearded clergy, Byzantine music often badly sung, people kissing icons, the smell of incense, doctrinal legalism, and domed churches. When the Orthodox look at Pentecostals, they often see only the American culture of the "Bible Belt" complete with southern accent, worship in a language they cannot understand (*glossolalia*), flashy suits, women's decorative hats, fire-breathing televangelists with long hair, raucous music with keyboards, guitars, and drums, people kissing one another, the smell of sweat, extravagant doctrinal claims, and no consistent church architecture.

Orthodoxy finds its strength in places like Greece and in Middle Eastern countries such as Lebanon, Syria, Turkey, and Israel. For millennia it has been a vital church in northeastern Africa, in Egypt and Ethiopia. It has been present for a thousand years in Central and Eastern Europe, countries like Bulgaria, Romania, Albania, Armenia, Georgia, the Ukraine, and Russia. It is even an ancient presence in India, having arrived there by trade routes from the Middle East during the middle of the first millennium A.D.

On the other hand, Pentecostalism is strong in the western hemisphere. It is present in significant numbers in North, Central and South America. It is burgeoning in sub-Saharan Africa, where it has contributed not only to the development of Classical Pentecostal denominations, but to a plethora of African Independent or indigenous churches. It has fared less well in Europe, though there are clearly exceptions in places like the Scandinavian countries of Northern Europe, and in Italy. It is also strong in parts of Southern and Eastern Asia, places like Singapore, the Philippines, and most notably in the massive churches of Korea.

While in Alaska the presence of the Orthodox predates that of Pentecostals by over a century, on the whole their worlds, the worlds of Orthodoxy and Pentecostalism do not seem to overlap very much. And yet they do.

As early as 1909, that began to change on the historical scene, as Pentecostalism spread from Germany through Poland and into Estonia, Latvia, Lithuania, Belarus, and Russia. By 1911 the Finns were sending Pentecostal workers to Russia's northern cities. By the onset of World War I in 1914, Pentecostalism was present from St. Petersburg in the north of Russia, to Saratov on the Volga River in South Central Russia, in large part the results of a missionary named Eleanor Patrick, working under the auspices of the German Pentecostal movement. By 1916 they were found in the Caucuses, the mountain range that borders on Russia, Turkey, Armenia, Georgia, Azerbaijan, and Iran, initially introduced by a Swiss Mennonite turned Pentecostal missionary named Maria Gerber, and extended by the work of Andrew bar David Urshan. By 1918 Pentecostalism had arrived in Romania. By 1921, it had arrived in the Ukraine and Bulgaria through the work of Ivan Voronaev.

Technically, the Pentecostal movement operated on the fringes of society in these areas, largely concentrating its efforts on the many German and other western European immigrants who had found their way to Russia. These young Pentecostal churches were subject to regional persecution by the "Secret Police," acting on behalf of the government and the Orthodox Church, and were often forced to conduct their meetings secretly.

The arrival of the Russian Revolution in 1917 brought turmoil to the region that surprisingly, through the 1920s, aided the small but growing Pentecostal churches to flourish. For over 900 years, Orthodoxy had functioned as the spiritual arm of the Russian State. As the Bolsheviks took over the Russian empire, however, Orthodoxy found itself in for a long period of persecution and Pentecostal churches became pawns in the Bolshevik attempt to destabilize the Russian Orthodox Church and decrease its influence among the Russian people as the Bolsheviks dispersed Pentecostals and then looked the other way while they planted new congregations. This helped to establish the influence of the Pentecostal movement as far, east as Siberia.

Many Russian Orthodox priests and bishops were arrested, imprisoned in the gulags, or murdered. When in 1929 the Soviets passed repressive anti-religious legislation, Pentecostals were treated like the rest. Thousands of churches of all kinds were closed. In exchange for their tolerated existence, Christians were required to register with the State. Many chose to go underground and were regularly pursued and imprisoned. Millions of Christians, Orthodox, Mennonite, Baptist, Pentecostals and others, especially from the times of Joseph Stalin (1929-1953) through that of Nikita Khruchev (1953-1964), were imprisoned or martyred.

I can well remember the many prayers that were offered for the persecuted Christians of the Soviet Union in the Pentecostal churches in the United States that I attended during the 1950s, 60s, 70s, and even through 80s. We didn't make distinctions between Christians who were Pentecostals and Orthodox Christians. Our intercessory prayers, a genuine manifestation of our Pentecostal spirituality, were offered regardless of their denominational titles. We considered them all to be our sisters and brothers with whom we wanted to stand in solidarity. Our hearts went out to them in their suffering. And ultimately those prayers were answered when in 1989 the walls of hostility came crashing down between the east and west, and the following year Russia granted its people "freedom of religion".

Since that time, however, new walls have been constructed between Orthodox and Pentecostal Christians in a number of places. In Greece, for instance, several Pentecostals, among them Don Stevens, with whom my wife and I attended college in the 1960s were arrested and placed on trial in 1982/3 on highly publicized charges of "proselytism", fueled by the fears and anger of Orthodox leaders. While Stevens and two friends were convicted in the lower court and sentenced to 3 years in prison, the appeal of their conviction in a higher court, ultimately freed them.

In Russia, Armenia, Bulgaria, and elsewhere in the traditionally "Orthodox" countries that were formerly part of the Soviet Union, Pentecostals have found it very difficult to operate with the implementation of new and restrictive laws. They have had difficulty with the registration of their churches and properties. They have had problems obtaining building permits, encountered limitations placed upon their publications, and in some cases, endured outright persecution in the form of intimidation, protests, and vandalism. Only in Romania, where Pentecostals have prospered, does there seem to be a level of respect offered each other by people in the two communities.

Even in the United States, the Orthodox, as late as September 1994, moved to undercut the influence of Pentecostals throughout the Americas. At that time His Eminence Archbishop Iakovos, Archbishop of the Greek Orthodox Church of North and South America issued an encyclical to the pastors and priests of his archdiocese that declared the Assemblies of God and other Pentecostals as "religious groups which are not of the Christian tradition."[1] Only when he received vigorous protests, providing clear evidence to the contrary, was that statement changed to read that "most congregations" of the Assemblies of God and other Pentecostal churches "*are* of the Christian Tradition."[2] I still wonder

---

[1] Iakovos, Archbishop of the Greek Orthodox Church of North & South America to the Pastors and Reverend Priests of the Greek Orthodox Archdiocese of North & South America (September 1994), 2 pages. The subject was "Interfaith Marriages".
[2] On May 22, 1995, operating on the authority granted to him by Archbishop Iakovos, the Reverend Dr.Milton B. Efthimiou issued a two page document knownas Protocol 13 to the Reverend Fathers of the Greek Orthodox Archdiocese of North and South America, in which this new position was announced. Emphasis his.

where those congregations that are *not* part of the designation "most congregations" exist.

As a Pentecostal, I could wish that all the errors had been committed by the Orthodox. But that is not the case. The early Pentecostal gadfly Frank Bartleman, writing in his book *Two Years Mission Work* (1924), accused the Orthodox of writing "intolerant religious laws," that repressed Pentecostals. Pentecostals still chafe at the kinds of laws recently implemented in Russia, the Ukraine, and Belarus. But that has never stopped them. Their independent spirit has sometimes been read as the Holy Spirit, and often it has been used as an excuse to act, regardless of the consequences. Pentecostals have never waited to be invited to minister in "Orthodox" countries; they have simply gone there. Partly because of the resistance they have felt upon their arrival, and partly because of the strangeness with which they regard Orthodox ritual and culture, Pentecostals have all too often lumped the Orthodox together with the unbelievers of the region, sometimes targeting them for conversion. All too often, Pentecostals have treated the Orthodox as theologically errant at best, and worse, as idolaters who worship hand painted wooden gods (icons). With the implementation of newer laws that favor the Orthodox Church and appear to penalize all others in Russia and elsewhere, Pentecostals have strongly criticized the Orthodox, crying "Foul".

Unfortunately, few in the west have any knowledge of or appreciation for how Christianity came to be present in these many "Orthodox" lands. They are generally ignorant of the Slavic history, languages, and culture. They have never heard of St Cyril and St. Methodius, who were invited to bring the Gospel to the Slavic people in the first place. They know nothing of the 6th Century Emperor Justinian's theory of *symphonia*, which stands behind much of the Orthodox concept of "territoriality," that conceives of Orthodoxy as the national/territorial church, whose territory should be recognized as inviolable by representatives of all other Christian traditions, a position to which the Orthodox cling so tightly. Furthermore, few Pentecostals acknowledge the enormous price that the Orthodox paid for faithfulness to the Gospel from the time of the crusades to the Muslim rule of the Ottoman Empire, or during the Communist era. All too often, Pentecostals have rushed to judgment and painted all Orthodox believers in the former Soviet Union as compromisers and Communist supporters.

Clearly, there is a need for greater understanding between these two enormous traditions that together may number as many as three quarters of a billion people. But history is not the only place where Pentecostals and the Orthodox do not understand one another. If one were to look only at their worship services, one would think that their theological positions were poles apart. And in one sense they are. On the other hand, they hold far more in common than they realize, far more in common than either of them would believe without a deeper look.

Edmund Rybarczyk is the first Pentecostal to help us in this regard. He is eminently suited for the task. His father is a Pentecostal, a member of the Assemblies of God. His mother is Russian Orthodox. Thus, this groundbreaking study is actually an ecumenical experiment that recognizes the legitimate contribution of each member of the same Christian family. One need not read very far into this work to understand the love and respect that he brings to both traditions. He clearly understands the richness of each tradition, and he is fearless in lifting up the strengths and the weaknesses of each tradition and showing in what way(s) they are alike and/or differ from each other.

Coming as it does from Greece, Central, and Eastern Europe, Orthodoxy rejected many of the ways of thinking and working that Western Europe and much of North America embraced from the time of the 18th Century onward. In some ways, Orthodoxy is still somewhat Pre-Modern in its worldview. Pentecostals rejected much of what the Modern world brought to bear upon their lives, and also have been described as Pre-Modern in their worldview. Certainly they have been critical of much of Modernity, though some want to argue that they are more Post-Modern than they are Pre-Modern. Regardless of the position adopted in this debate, it can be said that while their worldviews have some significant differences, they are much closer to one another than either of them are to Modern and Post-Modern Protestant worldviews, especially when one considers the worldview of the Pentecostal majority who come not from North America, but from the Two-thirds world.

As for the ancient doctrines of the Church, the Orthodox and Pentecostals share much in common. The Orthodox have long been strong defenders of classical Trinitarianism. Pentecostals have had their deepest disagreements with one another over the doctrine of the Trinity, but 80% of them would side with the Orthodox articulation of this doctrine. Unlike the western Christian tradition as it is represented by Roman Catholics and historic Protestants, the Orthodox have been champions of the Holy Spirit, a point shared by Pentecostals. It was, after all, the Cappadocian, and therefore, Eastern Father, Basil the Great, who first made it clear to his contemporaries that the Holy Spirit was, in fact, a Person of the Divine Trinity. And Basil's friend, Gregory of Nazianzus convinced many of his peers for the first time that the Holy Spirit could, therefore, rightfully be worshipped together with the Father and the Son. And both traditions acknowledge that it is through the Holy Spirit that the Lord, Jesus Christ, the Son of God, makes Himself known to us today.

The "Desert Fathers" especially in Egypt, from St. Antony to Pachomius, were no strangers to such charisms as the words of wisdom and knowledge, visions, prophecy and the discernment of spirits, miracles and healings, including exorcisms. They viewed monastic life, not as an escape from the real world, but as loving abandonment to God. As my friend, Patristic scholar Roberta Bondi has observed, it was an act of love with all their heart soul, strength, and mind, the Great Commandment (Luke 10:27) being lived out that formed the basis for their lives of prayer.

What may surprise Pentecostals is that John Wesley, through whose line Pentecostalism ultimately came into being, drank deeply from the spirituality but drew sparingly from the theology that was present in the well dug by these Desert Fathers and others within the Orthodox tradition. Therefore, it should not surprise us to note that the Pentecostal tradition, a tradition which places a high value upon prayer, especially prayer "in the Spirit," would also find a deep spiritual ally in the life of prayer so evident in the Orthodox tradition. Both traditions know something of the "Holy," the ineffable, the glory, the inexpressible, and the sense of awe that enfolds them in times of prayer and worship. Both traditions, then, embrace the Divine-human encounter as an essential and anticipated facet of the Christian walk. And, perhaps as a result of their shared experience of the presence of God, they take the value of life very seriously. Their concerns for ethics and morality have much in common.

In this book, Dr Rybarczyk brings into dialogue both Orthodox and Pentecostal discussions on the philosophy, history, theology, and spirituality of a very important aspect of the Christian life, the theme of transformation. Pentecostal and Orthodox Christians share the concern that entry into the Christian life should bring about a spiritual transformation of the person, which results in a transformed life. The ways they conceive of this transformation are very different, but the goal to be achieved is surprisingly similar. While the Orthodox view all of life as a whole, and the movement into Christ with its transformative process known as *theosis* as essentially being an ontological reality, Pentecostals tend to view the transformative process in terms of "sanctification." It is essentially described first in juridical rather than ontological terms, and then lived out in pragmatic and existential terms. In spite of such enormous differences on the surface, they are after much the same result.

What Dr Rybarczyk's insightful work illustrates for us is how to understand the core of what each tradition has to say on the theme of spiritual transformation through the use of a common language. In the end, he also provides a series of challenges to both traditions that could bring them into a unique relationship with one another, if they would only take the time to engage one another directly in some kind of conversation.

It was in 1920 that the Ecumenical Patriarchate issued a call to the Christians of the world inviting them to seek a way to develop an ongoing ecumenical conversation through some formal organization. This call, along with others from the Protestant missionary community beginning in the famous Conference on World Mission convened by John R. Mott in Edinburgh, Scotland in 1910, ultimately paved the way for the founding of the World Council of Churches in 1948. When the World Council of Churches met in New Delhi, India in 1961, many of the Orthodox churches joined the Council. Three small, autochthonous, Pentecostal churches from Chile joined the Council that same year. In the intervening years, however, nothing more has transpired between the Orthodox and Pentecostal communities that would facilitate further conversation.

During the past decade, a growing number of Pentecostal scholars have added their voices to the call for some kind of Dialogue to begin to explore the similarities and differences that obviously exist between Orthodox and Pentecostal Christians. Several obstacles may yet need to be removed before such a discussion can be considered. The differences between the Eastern and Oriental Orthodox churches may need to be resolved. The struggle for power between the acknowledged leader of the Orthodox, the Ecumenical Patriarchate, and the Patriarch of Moscow may need to be settled. The differences between Rome and Constantinople and especially the differences between Rome and Moscow that currently take such a toll on Orthodox energies in the regions of the former Soviet Union may need to reach a stage in which the Orthodox leadership feels that it can turn its primary energies elsewhere. The struggle for an American Patriarchate may need to be resolved. And the lack of trust, even the fear that many Russian and Bulgarian Orthodox have toward ecumenism clearly needs to be addressed before the Orthodox feel that they can enter wholeheartedly into talks with Pentecostals.

On the Pentecostal side, the situation is not that different. While it is the case that there are now a half-dozen Pentecostal groups that hold membership in the World Council of Churches, these groups are small, Latin American or African groups that are often not as representative of the global Pentecostal movement as one might hope. On the other hand, they represent a not so obvious link between the missionary sending churches in North America and Europe and the missionary receiving churches of the two-thirds world.

Recent years have seen an enormous increase in the size and the restlessness for independence being expressed by many of the missionary churches around the world. Some of them are increasingly interested in pursuing ecumenical contacts, much to the chagrin of the North American and European Pentecostals who gave them their birth. It is only a matter of time before these newer Pentecostal bodies become completely independent of the controls currently in place by the various missionary sending churches. When the inevitable break comes, they will find Pentecostal churches with nearly a half-century of ecumenical experience from whom they can learn.

The bigger problem lies in the reluctance of certain North American and European Pentecostal groups to allow the others to become truly independent, and to pursue their ecumenical dreams. This is particularly true because the General Council of the Assemblies of God in the United States has chosen to enshrine its anti-ecumenical biases within its Bylaws. As a result, it continues to try to control the ecumenical actions of the now 95% of its constituency that do not share either its history or its culture. One example of this is the protest raised by Assemblies of God leaders in the United States when Dr. David Yonggi Cho led the Yoido Full Gospel Church into membership in the Korean National Council of Churches, and the pressure applied to Pastor Cho through the International Fellowship of the Assemblies of God when he showed a desire to establish a relationship with the World Council of Churches. The lack of trust and the fears that certain Russian and Bulgarian Orthodox Christians have embraced regarding ecumenism in recent years are thus identical to those embraced by their North American and European Pentecostal counterparts.

What would be most helpful for Pentecostals is for them to dig deeply into their Pentecostal spirituality where they have offered prayer for decades for Orthodox and other Christians who face persecution. Today, especially in places like Egypt, Ethiopia, Syria, Israel, Lebanon, Turkey, Iraq, Iran, Azerbaijan, and other States where Islam is the majority faith, they continue to need Pentecostal prayers. It simply makes no sense to pray for someone and then refuse to talk with them.

At the moment, the separation between Orthodox and Pentecostal Christians may seem intractable to many. But if both traditions pursue their experience of God within eyesight of the other, if both traditions reach out and think about the places where there may be convergences in their doctrine and life, if both traditions are willing to acknowledge that they have both common concerns and common approaches to life, they may ultimately come to some form of common recognition and common witness.

Dr Rybarczyk's work *Beyond Salvation* provides a first step in this discussion. Those who follow him in this study will find a firm foundation from which to begin further discovery. I am deeply encouraged about the potential for the ultimate transformation of Orthodox-Pentecostal relations, through the thoughtful example he provides. If his work is taken seriously, the Church cannot help but be edified in the process, and the missionary and evangelistic vision that Pentecostals hold dear to their hearts may reach new levels of fulfilment.

Cecil M. Robeck, Jr.
Professor of Church History and Ecumenics
Fuller Theological Seminary

Preface

One never knows exactly what lies within the horizon of one's future, but inevitably it involves some sort of change. It is almost a given that journeys of immense distance can alter one's perceptions both about life and one's own immediate environment. But short trips are viewed as commonplace and mundane. My own conceptual horizon began to be impacted in 1992 when, upon my mother's invitation, I took a short ferry-ride across Puget Sound into Seattle, Washington. It was then that I attended my first Orthodox Liturgy.

Standing amid the congregation of Russian Americans in St. Spiridon's Russian Orthodox Cathedral, I was overwhelmed by the number of icons that surrounded me. Not only was the iconostasis positioned between the altar and the nave, but along either side of the sanctuary a multitude of icons gazed at me with holy austerity. I stood in silence not only because it was an unfamiliar and uncertain experience, but because I felt that something holy, immense even, was silently being shouted at me. It was an immensity of holy community. As strange as that was, what struck me as even more odd was the familiar atmosphere of the Holy Spirit that surrounded me. I was reared in a Pentecostal church, so an awareness of the Spirit's presence in itself was nothing novel. What was new was that He was there, marvelously there, in a setting entirely foreign to me! In lieu of my own church's shouts of praise there were reverent prayers for mercy. In lieu of hands thrusting upward people reverently crossed themselves. Instead of the cacophonous sound of people praying in tongues, there were corporate prayers and Scripture readings. In contrast to the audible character of my own church, my very nose was made to be a participant in the service as the aroma of burning incense filled the church. Something familiar - the presence of God's Holy Spirit - had impacted me through very unfamiliar vehicles.

I had taken the ferry-ride to the Liturgy with my mother, in part, because Orthodoxy comprises the religious tradition of her family's own Russian heritage. I wanted to know something about what my grandparents, and their parents before them, held in their religious experience and practice. Little did I expect that my experience among the ancient and routinized ways of the Orthodox would put me on a long exploratory path whereby I would re-examine my own Pentecostal background's assumptions and beliefs. This exploration and re-examination produced in me the conviction that, as one scholar aptly put it, "an encounter with Eastern-Orthodoxy in its contemporary form is not an optional extra for a Western Christian in search for the fulness and integrity of Christian faith."[1]

Over the years it has become my growing belief that it is no mere accident that Pentecostalism and Eastern Orthodoxy - when each mirrors its authentic identity - share very mystical and vibrant characteristics. Though the two are dramatically different in many ways (culture, ecclesiology, styles of worship, and missiological strategies, to name a few), they share several beliefs which historically have facilitated a dynamic and often inexpressible Christian experience. First among these beliefs is that both groups hold that God has made Himself known through His Son, Jesus Christ, and that He continues to make Himself known by the presence of His Spirit. Both hold that He wants to be known by those who will seek Him. Both resolutely assert that this knowledge of Him is by no means limited to the intellectual domain of human existence, but that the human person can feel, and sense, and hear God in visceral and profound ways. And finally, perhaps most importantly, both maintain that salvation, in its fullest biblical sense, involves communion with God; to be a Christian is far more than having one's legal slate in heaven wiped clean.

Sometimes the horizon of our understanding is cloudy because things are unfamiliar to us. One can fairly surmise that some of the disdain many Orthodox folks feel for Pentecostals (and their reciprocated disdain) stems from the fog of misunderstanding residing between them. For my part, I admittedly write as a Westerner who is physically removed from the strife and political turmoil that too often exists between Pentecostals and the Orthodox in Eastern Europe. A government officer, spurred by an Orthodox church official, is not telling my tiny Pentecostal church that our worship services are illegal, or that we have no right to pass out evangelistic tracts in our neighborhood. Conversely, my beloved homeland has not experienced the dissolution of its government with the result that my fellow-citizens are quizzical about the future of our religion at best, or desperately fearful at worst. No, I do not live in Eastern Europe where such tensions and problems exist. But this distance does not make me apathetic. True enough, I was taught to love my country. My grandfather was enlisted in the U.S. army during World War 1, my uncle fought in World War 2, and my father served in the U.S. military. But it is also the case that I have an affinity

---

[1] A.M. Allchin, "The Epworth-Canterbury-Constantinople Axis," *Wesleyan Theological Journal,* 26:1 (Spring 1991), 35.

for Eastern European peoples. My father's family came from Poland, and I had Russian relatives who were starved and frozen to death in Leningrad (St. Petersburg) behind Hitler's military blockade. All to say, although I am indeed a Western Pentecostal, I have written this study with empathy for both sides as well as with a critical eye toward both sides.

If sometimes unfamiliarity clouds our horizon, at other times our horizon is hard to discern precisely because we are too much a part of the immediate environment. We can be naîve regarding our own vista if only because we assume we are in the right. By way of analogy, it is easy to be like the frog in a pot, who, as the water got increasingly hotter, failed to jump out and eventually died in the boiling water. The frog was initially so comfortable he failed to see that he was gradually being turned into froggy stew! This study, in more ways than I could ever have imagined, made me realize how much my own Pentecostal heritage is - and is becoming - a product of its own cultural pot. In inevitable but nonetheless alarming ways, the Pentecostal movement (in the U.S., anyway) is markedly resembling the cultural pot of stew around it. Furthermore, the nature of this study, a theological comparison of two Traditions which are drastically separated by cultural and epistemological distinctions, has caused me to see how each's own historical-cultural context has rather forced each one to accept some of the assumptions and values of that context.

This study will take the theological issue of Christian transformation as its focus. I will not examine the political, ecclesial, geographical or economic issues confronting these two traditions, or even begin to address how it is that those issues impinge upon each's doctrine of transformation (they likely do impinge upon each's theology). Accordingly, each reader will have to determine the accuracy of the following assessment from her own, or his own, vantage point (and thereby determine for herself or himself whether it is my lenses that are warped!). Whatever the reader's vantage point, it is hoped that this study might help both Traditions recognize Christ when and where He is present in the other. Most of all it is hoped that this dissertation can somehow help both Traditions better reflect the person and nature of Christ to the world He created.

Acknowledgements

This study has provided me with many enjoyable and rewarding conversations with my family about theology, philosophy, and life's broad constructs. To them all, I owe a great deal of thanks. My mother, Valerie Tenney, not only encouraged me to take this study as my dissertation topic, she has also been a kind of soul-mate in pondering some of the assumptions and latent mechanisms residing beneath and behind both Orthodoxy and Pentecostalism. My children - John, Kareese, and Lucy - have not only been patient in allowing me to research and write this study ("Dad, are you going to go to school your whole life?"), they have filled my life with joy and laughter that enabled me to press onward. They have also, in unspoken ways, reminded me that it is the little things in life which enable us to do the big things.

There are other family members to whom I owe more than I can repay. My now deceased mother-in-law, Charlotte McNutt, babysat (and fed!) our kids countless times, and enabled me to write even when my wife was at work. The daily prayers of my step-mother, DyAnn Rybarczyk, were an unseen and invaluable source of strength for me, even when she didn't always know as much. Dennis McNutt, my father-in-law, both encouraged me along the way and served as a sage sounding-board for any number of wild and weird ideas which trespassed through my mind and across my lips! Frank and Denise Heinrichs gave so much of their own time, both in terms of caring for our children upon occasion and in their being invaluable resources regarding computer technology. Additionally, I must thank David and Rachel McNutt (my uncle and aunt-in-law, who are more like a brother and sister to me) who, while requiring no recompense, initially allowed me to work for them as I pleased (in accord with my academic schedule) and who subsequently offered me an opportunity to help provide for my family.

Another person deserving my acknowledgment is Dean Langis, Pastoral Assistant at St. Paul's Greek Orthodox Church in Irvine, California. Dean both gave me advice about my Orthodox bibliography and graciously loaned me books from his own library. Furthermore, not only was he was not offended by some of the questions and ideas about Orthodoxy which I ran past him through the course of this study, he warmly welcomed them and helped me think through them. In the best sense of the word, Dean manifested Orthodox *ekstasis* toward me.

Contrary to what many holding ecclesial power may believe, one simultaneously can be thoroughly committed to, and critically minded about, one's own Christian tradition. Because he not only taught me that truth in the academy, but also because he embodies that tension in his very life and ministry, my own mentor, Cecil Robeck, Jr., also deserves my sincerest gratitude. Not only has he offered me wise guidance, invaluable encouragement, and many of his own bibliographic resources, Dr. Robeck - through his prevalent attitude of hope, through his submission to the larger body of Christ, and through his courage to speak prophetically - has taught me much about life in the "now but not yet" of the Kingdom.

Dr. James Bradley made a scrutinizing and critical examination of my work. To no small extent, he saved me from a "multitude of sins"! It was my honor to have Bishop Kallistos Ware read and evaluate this study. Sincere appreciation goes to Dr. Richard Muller who played an integral role during my years of study at Fuller Seminary. Desmond Cartwright, the faculty, and the staff all at Mattersey Hall in England also deserve my public thanks. Not only did they graciously allow me to peruse their rich collection of early British Pentecostal literature, they were also most hospitable during my stay there.

Lastly, I want to publicly thank my faithful wife, Tawnya. She not only worked 20 and 30 hours a week outside our home while I completed my studies, she both managed our home and also unfailingly encouraged me to continue onward with my studies. Not once in eight years did she say anything negative about my study's time demands, my academic pursuits, or my own abilities, even when on all those fronts I was utterly convinced otherwise! If anyone ever deserved to be canonized as a saint, it is Tawnya. She bore "all things, believed all things, hoped all things, and endured all things." Apart from the empirical fact (as I will develop in this study, something which is so dear in Western epistemologies!) that I could never have completed my studies without her, she typifies what it means to be authentically Christian. In that light, I dedicate this study to her.

Abbreviations

D P C M   *Dictionary of Pentecostal and Charismatic Movements.* Stanley M. Burgess and Gary B. McGee, Eds. Grand Rapids, Michigan: Zondervan Publishing House, 1988.

E D T   *Evangelical Dictionary of Theology.* 10th ed. Walter A. Elwell, Ed. Grand Rapids, Michigan: Baker Book House, 1994.

NASB   *New American Standard Bible.* La Habra, California: The Lockman Foundation, 1977.

NPNF   *A Select Library of Nicene and Post-Nicene Fathers of the Christian Church.* Vol. 4, 2nd series. Trans. Philip Schaff and Henry Wace. Archibald Robertson, Ed. Grand Rapids, Michigan: William B. Eerdmans Publishing Company.

PE   *Pentecostal Evangel: The Weekly Magazine of the Assemblies of God.* In the United States.

PG   *Patrologiae Cursus Completus, Series Graecae.* Migne, I. P., Ed. 168 vols. Reprint, Turnholti, Belgium: Typographi Brepols, 1978.

RT   *Redemption Tidings.* A Weekly Publication of the Assemblies of God in Great Britain and Ireland.

TOHFC   Robert E. Sinkewicz, *Saint Gregory Palamas: The One Hundred and Fifty Chapters.* Toronto: Pontifical Institute of Mediaeval Studies, 1988.

1

Eastern Orthodoxy and Classical Pentecostalism: Similarities and Suspicions

Mysticism. Say the word and images of smoke, crystal balls, catatonic trances, and the paranormal spring to mind. Television networks love to produce exposés about it. Novelists and screenwriters employ it in order to entice their audiences. Surpassing those media, the religious New Age movement in the United States has made use of mystical practices and teachings in order to generate an annual multi-million dollar business. Even interested scientists are trying to determine what goes on in the minds of religious mystics.[1] But mention the word mysticism with regard to Christianity in some circles and eyes will begin to roll. Of course, many folks know that church history has been interspersed with mystics. Usually they formed numerically small bands and existed on the heterodox fringe. They were sects of disenfranchised peoples who either could not, or would not, fit in with the larger church and its structures of authority. But mysticism has never been an element within thoughtful, rational, or circumspect Christianity. Or, so it would seem.

For nearly two thousand years, millions of Christians in Eastern Europe and the Middle East have practiced what is by Western standards a very mystical form of Christianity. These Christians call themselves the Eastern Orthodox church. Many Western Christians would be surprised to know that despite Orthodoxy's traditional Eastern mooring, the Orthodox have been in the Western Hemisphere since 1794,[2] and in the continental United States since 1820.[3] In the United States alone there are 5.6 million Orthodox adherents,

---

[1] Robert Lee Hotz, "Seeking the Biology of Spirituality," *Los Angeles Times,* April 26, 1998, A1 and A28.

[2] The Russian-American Company, a dealer in animal furs, sponsored ten Russian Orthodox missionaries who went to Alaska in 1794. The Russian Orthodox moved their episcopal see from Alaska to San Francisco in 1872. Barbara Smith, *Orthodoxy and Native Americans: The Alaskan Mission.* Occasional Paper #1 for the Department of History and Archives, Historical Society (Crestwood, NY: St. Vladimir's, 1980).

[3] Economically pressured, Greek Orthodox laypersons began to immigrate to the U.S. in 1820. Between 1820 and 1890 fewer than 5000 Greeks came to the U.S. The first Greek Orthodox parish was founded in New Orleans in 1864. Between 1900 and 1910 167,500 Greeks, 95% of whom were male, immigrated to America. Many of these came thinking they would only be here temporarily, and so they sent money

while around the world there are more than 215 million.[4] However, another
rather mystical group of Christians, a group from the West, today comprises the
second largest segment (the Roman Catholics are the largest) of Christianity in
the world: The Pentecostals. These Christians number more than 22 million in
North America, and over 410 million around the globe.[5] As of 1988 there were
sizeable groups of Pentecostals on every continent in the world, and they could
be found in 230 countries.[6] Together the Eastern Orthodox and the Pentecostals
comprise more than 600 million of the roughly 2 billion who call themselves
Christians. And together, these two represent very mystical manifestations of
Christianity.

Initial Comparisons

Curious by evangelical Christian standards, neither the Orthodox nor the
Pentecostals have *traditionally* been concerned about rebutting any attacks on
their respective experiential characters. In fact, it is clear that both groups have
flourished because of - and not in spite of - their mystical character. However,
whereas the Orthodox celebrate their mysticism as an element which they
believe even the apostles enjoyed, *contemporary* North American Pentecostals
(and this is a more recent phenomenon) would undoubtedly dismiss the charge
that they themselves ever were, or are, mystical. Many of Pentecostalism's
denominational officials ardently present their denominations to the larger
evangelical milieu as being mainstream, conservative, and even rational. To no
small extent their endeavors seem to have succeeded. A recent historical-cultural
survey of mysticism fails to even mention Pentecostals among the ranks of the

back to their families. But with the outbreak of the Balkan Wars and World War I,
many stayed permanently. Alexander Doumouras, "Greek Orthodox Communities in
America Before World War I, " *St. Vladimir's*, 11:4 (1967), 172-192.
[4]Daniel B. Clendenin, "Did You Know, Little-known or fascinating facts about
Eastern Orthodoxy," *Christian History*, 54:2 (1997), 2-3.
[5] Harvey Cox, *Fire From Heaven: The Rise of Pentecostal Spirituality and the
Reshaping of Religion in the Twenty-first Century* (Reading, Massachusetts:
Addison-Wesley, 1995), xv.
[6] D. B. Barrett, "Global Statistics," in *DPCM*, 810-830. For more on Pentecostalism's
growth also see Cecil M. Robeck, Jr., "Pentecostal Origins in Global Perspective," in
Harold D. Hunter and P. D. Hocken (eds.), *All Together in One Place: Theological
Papers from the Brighton Conference on World Evangelization* (Sheffield, England:
Sheffield Academic Press, 1993), 166-180.

mystical.[7] When one examines them and their history more closely, however, one cannot help but notice that they exhibit tendencies and characteristics which by most any measure would be deemed mystical. Pentecostals employ the following practices in their spirituality: in public meetings they ecstatically speak and sing aloud in unknown tongues, they fall backwards in trance-like states, they sit or stand or kneel stone-silent for extended periods, they pray aloud together in cacophonous ways, they exuberantly shout to God and one another, they believe that praying in an unknown tongue accomplishes untold things in the realm of the invisible, and - to take their grand doctrinal distinctive as an example - they encourage an encounter with God that leaves one's entire being both suffused and sated with the divine presence. In these various ways, the Pentecostals both manifest their subjective experience of, and facilitate their mutual experience of, God. In all of these ways they are mystical, at least by more rational and stolid standards, and their recent qualifications to the contrary ring hollow.

Despite the mystical nature that characterizes them both, these two groups know little to nothing about the other. North American Pentecostal ministers and parishioners, if they know anything at all about the Orthodox church, tend to view it as the twin-sister of the Roman Catholic church; Orthodoxy might still contain a remnant of Christian truth, but it is too mired in ancient culture, too caught up in icons and a static liturgical form of worship to be of any consequence to the modern person. Worse, to take Russia as an example of a traditionally Orthodox country, Pentecostals have dismissed altogether the idea that people living in Eastern Europe, apart from the influence of Western missionaries, could ever be Christian. Predisposed by their own eschatological hermeneutic (Russia is the great anti-Christian nation "Gog and Magog" of Ezek. 38-9 and Rev. 16:12), and equally predisposed by the cold-war between the United States and Russia (xenophobia plays no small part in many eschatological schemes), Pentecostals tend to view Russians as godless pagans, as though the entire country had accepted Marxist Socialism's atheism *in toto*.[8] Conversely, Orthodox priests and parishioners, if they know anything at all about Pentecostals, lump them in with the larger pools of evangelicals[9] or

---

[7] Denise Lardner Carmody and John Tully Carmody, *Mysticism* (Oxford University Press, 1996).

[8] See Dwight J. Wilson, "Pentecostal Perspectives on Eschatology," in *DPCM,* 264-268.

[9] Evangelicals are generally characterized by the following beliefs: God as the sovereign One; the universality of human sin and the concomitant need of forgiveness; Jesus as the only means of salvation, and that apart from human works;

charismatics.[10] One deceased eminent Orthodox theologian pejoratively
dismissed Pentecostals as Holy Rollers.[11] Another leader, a foreign Orthodox
patriarch, lumped Pentecostals together with other non-Christian religions (he
subsequently retracted his statement when the understandable outcry arose).[12]
Pentecostals might proffer a semblance of Christ's presence, but lacking

---

the Bible as the inspired, and therefore authoritative, revelation of God; and, a deep
commitment to proclaiming the gospel. Charismatics are Christians who have had a
personal experience of the Holy Spirit and who affirm/encourage the operation of
the Spirit's gifts (the charismata). They do not necessarily deny evangelical tenets,
but they are different in that they variously emphasize praising God, Bible reading,
hearing God speak, Christ's imminent return, and spiritual power in the Christian's
life. Classical Pentecostals, when Pentecostalism erupted, formed their own
denominations. Since their rise in the 1960s, charismatics have conversely tended
to stay in their original denominations (representing the entire rainbow of Christian
traditions) with the hope of renewing them spiritually. The Orthodox too, for their
part, have been impacted by the charismatic movement but the official hierarchies
have staunchly opposed this as a solely Protestant phenomenon. Timothy P. Weber,
"Evangelicalism," in *EDT*, 382-384; George M. Marsden, *Reforming
Fundamentalism: Fuller Seminary and The New Evangelicalism* (Grand Rapids:
Eerdmans, 1987); Peter D. Hocken, "Charismatic Movement," in *DPCM*, 130-160.
The Orthodox church also has been impacted by the charismatic movement. See
especially *Theosis: Newsletter for Orthodox Charismatic Renewal East Lansing:
Service Committee For Orthodox Charismatic Renewal* (first published in 1978);
Kallistos Ware, "Orthodoxy and the Charismatic Movement," *Eastern Churches
Review*, 4 (1973), 182-186; and, Stanley M. Burgess, "Stephanou, Eusebius A.," in
DPCM, 831-832.
[10] Ware, "Orthodoxy and the Charismatic Movement," 183-185.
[11] Sergius Bulgakov as quoted by John Warren Morris, "The Charismatic
Movement: An Orthodox Evaluation," *The Greek Orthodox Theological Review*,
28:2 (Summer 1983), 110; and Bulgakov, *The Orthodox Church*, L. Kesich (tr.)
(Crestwood, NY: St. Vladimir's, 1988) 110-111.
[12] Archbishop Iakovos asserted that Seventh-day Adventists, the Assemblies of
God, and Pentecostals were "religious groups which are not of the Christian
tradition." Cf. "Encyclical Letter of Archbishop Iakovos to the Pastors and Reverend
Priests of the Greek Orthodox Archdiocese of North and South America," September
1994, 1, reported in "Archbishop Calls Pentecostals Non-Christian," *Christianity
Today*, 39:1 (January 9, 1995), 42. Following the aforementioned groups' outcry,
Reverend Dr. Milton B. Efthimiou, on behalf of the Archbishop's Office, proclaimed
that most of the congregations within these groups "are of the Christian Tradition.
Some are not." See, *Protocol* 13, to the Reverend Fathers of the Greek Orthodox
Archdiocese of North and South America, May 22, 1995.

Christ's apostolic priesthood and "the fulness of Orthodoxy," as the Orthodox like to state it, they are relegated to a shallow emotionalism which can never produce lasting change.

These generally antagonistic and mutual sentiments aside, there are many characteristics which the Orthodox and Pentecostals share. Obviously, but not unimportantly, both are not Roman Catholic, neither answers to the pope in Rome; in this regard both traditions like to present their respective churches as being organically structured, and not "top heavy" concerning authority or polity (whether such is the actual case with either tradition would be its own dissertation).[13] Furthermore, both like to emphasize the laity's role and importance in the life, thought, and work of the church. Secondly, both Traditions allow and encourage their local ministers/priests to marry and have children; ordained Christian service is the privilege of married persons and parents, and not just a select or celibate few. Thirdly, both perceive themselves as the great defenders of pneumatology. The Pentecostals, in light of their own experiential spirituality, believe they are re-introducing and re-familiarizing the universal church to the Holy Spirit. The Orthodox, conversely, believe that they are the true pneumatologists, especially in light of their historical rejection of the *Filioque* clause into ancient church creeds.[14] Fourthly, especially when compared with some contemporary Protestant denominations, and some Roman Catholic scholars, both are theologically quite conservative. They share the following dogmatic assertions: both believe that Jesus Christ is God's only means of salvation, and that he was born of the virgin Mary; both argue that the Christian canon is inspired of the Holy Spirit and is therefore the primary and authoritative source for a Christian epistemology; and, both maintain a Nicene-Constantinopolitan Christology (that Jesus was fully human and fully divine)

---

[13] Presently the Greek Orthodox church in America is wrestling with the role and voice the laity should have in relation to that of the Archbishop. See Shelly Houston, "Growing Unrest: Greek Church says laity lamentations are groundless," *Christianity Today*, 42:10 (September 7, 1998), 28. Pentecostals also struggle with involving the laity in important ways. Cf. Editorial, "Ask the Superintendent: An Interview with Thomas E. Trask," *Enrichment*, 3:4 (Fall 1998), 8-10.
[14] Athanasios F. S. Emmert, "Charismatic Developments in the Eastern Orthodox Church," in Russell P. Spittler (ed.), *Perspectives on the New Pentecostalism* (Grand Rapids: Baker, 1976) 37-39, discusses Orthodoxy and reception of the Spirit. More will be said about *Filioque* in this study's fifth chapter.

and Trinity (three persons in one being).[15] Furthermore, both traditions censure their clergymembers for denying these beliefs.

Each of the above theological features are important and deserve their own careful comparative study. Yet, there is another feature shared by both Traditions, and it is one that is central to both groups' Christian identity. This is the issue of worldview. That is, both view the human person, God, and creation in a fascinatingly similar manner. When one considers the historical, cultural, and philosophical differences which separate the two, this similarity of worldview is nothing short of incredible. The Orthodox have existed for more than 19 centuries, the Pentecostals for one. Orthodoxy has dramatically impacted and shaped the world of Eastern Europe and North Africa. Pentecostalism initially impacted the Western hemisphere, but today it is impacting and shaping the entire globe with tremendous force. Orthodoxy primarily works from, but also qualifies, the philosophical constructs of ancient Greece, constructs which have made themselves felt around the world for most of 2500 years. North American Pentecostalism arose within its own philosophical milieu to be sure, but for reasons which will be noted later it has proven itself to be incredibly amorphous and able to adapt itself within the indigenous environment in which it moves.[16]

The key for this study is that for both groups Christianity is - indeed life is - comprised of experience. This holds true for each not only as it concerns Christian living but for both groups' theology as well. Neither Tradition is much interested in doing theology for the sake of intellectual exercise. Neither automatically makes the brightest of its thinkers into saints or heroes, and neither has much use for those who want to reduce Christianity to the realm of the abstract. To be a Christian, as both express it, is to live for, and in, Christ. How one explains that life, or even more starkly *whether* one bothers to explain that life, is always secondary to the Christian life itself. Alexander Schmemann, an Orthodox historical-theologian, expressed the experiential sentiment of both camps well when he said, "all genuine theology is mystical at the root, since it is primarily evidence of religious experience." Christianity that is merely theoretical is dead. Christianity that is learned but not lived is meaningless.[17]

Though each of these Traditions see the experiential realm as necessary, neither group makes the experiential realm to be the first principle in its

[15] The topics of Christology and the Trinity will be dealt with more carefully in our text.
[16] The impact of the North American milieu on Pentecostals will be developed later.
[17] Alexander Schmemann. *The Historical Road of Eastern Orthodoxy,* L. Kesich (tr.) (Crestwood, NY: St. Vladimir's, 1992), 235.

Christian epistemology, nor is either side ambivalent about the precise ways in which Christianity should be understood. In words that accurately summarize both Traditions' sentiments in this regard, John Meyendorff said, "The lack of concern for systematization, however, does not mean a lack of interest in the true content of the faith or an inability to produce exact theological definitions."[18] Pentecostals, for their part, have also attempted to produce exact theological definitions and doctrines, but they have historically limited their efforts to the core issues of their spirituality: Spirit-baptism, charismatic gifts, and eschatology.[19] What this experiential thrust does do for both camps, however, is color every dimension of their life, practice, and theology. At both the individual and communal levels, the important thing is one's experience of God. Faith as intellectual assent to Christian truths is important, and disciplined duty in light of one's commitment to Christ is necessary, but if one really wants to understand Orthodoxy or Pentecostalism one must feel and know God in one's gut in the way that these two do. It is that visceral-existential knowledge which simultaneously brings alive the otherwise merely intellectual truths, and which makes the otherwise rigorous duty of discipline an inspired work of love.

Still another feature which both groups share regarding theology is the ad hoc and narrative way that both tend to express their own respective positions. One can read either group's theological treatises and be unsure whether one is reading an anecdotal anthology, an extended personal testimony, a collection of devotional poetry, or a systematic theology. Vladimir Lossky said that Orthodox systematic presentations are written to edify the church, not to make dogmatically pointed assertions about a given system.[20] Historically driven by

---

[18] John Meyendorff, *Byzantine Theology: Historical Trends and Doctrinal Themes* (NY: Fordham Press, 1974), 5.

[19] Pentecostals have assumed the broader church's thought on the issues of Christology, Trinity, Creation, and the atonement - issues which have comprised the bulk of Christendom's history of theology.

[20] Vladimir Lossky, *Orthodox Theology: An Introduction* (Crestwood, NY: St. Vladimir's, 1978), 15, illustrated this discomfort with systematic theology, "Theology that constitutes itself into a system is always dangerous. It imprisons in the enclosed sphere of thought the reality to which it must open thought." For Lossky, and the Orthodox in general, Christian faith (or better, knowledge of God) is not constituted simply in the mere mental assent to precise descriptions of truth. Lossky, 15, further clarifies that Christian faith is "adherence to a presence which confers certitude, in such a way that certitude, here, is first. What one quests is already present, precedes us, makes possible our questing itself. It is an ontological

evangelism, Pentecostals have been little interested to write or defend precise theological systems. Indeed, when they do discuss or write theology, they consistently do so using personal and anecdotal items in order to bring the reader to an evangelistic, or a truth-claim, decision. Should one begin to study the Orthodox "system" of theology, and should one in turn attempt to re-present it in an orderly fashion (as is being attempted here), one will be simultaneously confronted by the whole (the "fulness," again) of Orthodoxy. For example, one cannot study Christology apart from studying iconography, one cannot study iconography apart from studying ecclesiology, and one cannot study ecclesiology without an education in anthropology, the latter of which will bring one full-circle back to Christology. In this regard the Orthodox are most Platonic (in the sense that the individual categories are parts of the whole). Conversely, although Pentecostals make cleaner distinctions between these categories, and thereby reveal their own western orientation toward life, they have been little interested in formal theology per se. Again, this narrative and ad hoc similarity stems from both sides' experiential orientation.

The experiential realm - accurately defined as the mystical realm because it incorporates ineffable and mysterious elements - is affirmed by both traditions, but there are distinctions. Anglicanism, because it severed its ties from Rome but continued to maintain the latter's sacramental and ecclesial system, understands itself to be a *via media* between Catholicism and Protestantism; the sacramental model is sustained, but faith - so important for the Reformers - is also emphasized. In light of each's respective experiential-mystical thrust, it is fair to interpret Pentecostalism as a *via media* between Orthodoxy and the more rational branches of Protestantism. Obviously, the institutional character shared by Anglicanism and Catholicism is not analogous for the Orthodox and Pentecostals, and without question, most Pentecostals do not hold the precise sacramental, or iconic, understandings of the Orthodox (although the distance between them in this regard is not so great as it appears at the onset, as will become apparent within this study). Additionally, neither do these two interpret apostolicity or ecclesiology in the same way. But, as this study will develop, the two emphasize an experiential participation in the triune God to a degree unlike most other sub-groups within Christendom. Moreover, it is this experiential - not just symbolic or sacramental or invisible, though it may include these three and more - participation that connotes the meaning of

---

relationship between God and man. . . ." My conviction is that the modern Pentecostal layperson would resonate to such a statement of faith but might restate it in terms like, "I know that I know that my redeemer lives!"

mysticism intended herein. To reiterate, both traditions teach that there is a real presence of God which can be apprehended and sensed in the visceral regions of the human person. One distinction between the two is that whereas Orthodoxy emphasizes mystical dimensions throughout the entirety of its theology and spirituality, Pentecostalism facilitates Christian mysticism at a mostly individual level. In light of its own historical-cultural locale, Pentecostalism does not extend its mystical bent into the farther reaches of its theology. (Spirituality is distinguished here as being the subjective and lived response to the perceived reality. Following Assemblies of God scholar Simon Chan, theology, for its part, is distinguished here as "the systematic reflection and formalization of that reality.")[21]

Because of their experiential emphasis, neither group is simply content with getting people saved, although contemporary Pentecostals have leaned in that direction. Both are emphatic that to be a Christian is to experience Christ and his Holy Spirit - not only at conversion, but throughout one's Christian life - in the deepest recesses of one's being. There is more. While they use different terminologies to express it, both are clear that the human person is comprised of mysterious and nearly ineffable qualities, which, far from being relegated to a subordinate place in human existence (as more rationally oriented Christian groups emphasize it), comprise a critical dimension of what it means to be human. Both traditions are also quite clear that it is within this mystical human core that the Spirit of Christ seeks to have communion with human persons and thereby transform them into his image. All this similarity despite the fact that there is no apparent historical connection.

John Wesley: Pentecostalism's Historical Bridge to Orthodoxy?

In recent decades scholars have been intrigued with the historical connection between, and theological similarities shared by, some of the patristic Orthodox fathers and the Anglican-turned-Methodist minister, John Wesley (1703-

---

[21] Simon Chan, *Spiritual Theology: A Systematic Study of the Christian Life* (Downers Grove, Illinois: InterVarsity Press, 1998), 16. Chan represents a significant historical shift in Pentecostal scholarship in that he discusses spirituality - lived out Christianity - precisely in light of theology. See also his "Sharing the Trinitarian Life: John 17:20-26, 1 John 1:1-4," in Thomas F. Best and Günther Gassmann (eds.), *On the Way to Fuller Koinonia* (Geneva: WCC Publications; Faith and Order Paper no. 166, 1994), 85-90.

1791).[22] Wesley is important for understanding the historical antecedents to Pentecostalism because the latter built upon Wesley's experiential foundations, even though those foundations themselves had been modified by the time of Pentecostalism's advent.[23] Educated at Oxford, where he associated with a pietistic group known as the Manchester Non-Jurors, and motivated by his belief that Constantine's conversion to Christianity had corrupted the church (in light of church-state issues),[24] Wesley studied several of the Eastern Orthodox fathers and even preferred to read them over the Western fathers.[25] Quite clearly Wesley borrowed from the early Greek fathers in developing both his own anthropological understandings and the ensuing experientially oriented doctrine of entire sanctification (something he also described as perfection).[26] However, because he was either wary of, or ignorant of (the latter is more likely given that Wesley consistently studied the Greek fathers through the writings of other

---

[22] Albert C. Outler was the first one to posit the connection between Wesley and Orthodoxy. *John Wesley* (NY: Oxford University Press, 1964) n. 26, pp. 9-10; and, "John Wesley's Interest in the Early Father's of the Church," *Bulletin of the United Church of Canada Committee on Archives and History*, 29:2 (1980), 5-17.

[23] Wesley's own nomenclature for this experiential life of Christianity was rather flexible and imprecise. Methodists and Holiness proponents (John Fletcher, Asa Mahan, and Phoebe Palmer) after him took his categories and gave them narrower definitions. It was these definitions which partially formed the theological milieu for Pentecostalism. Cf., Donald Dayton, *Theological Roots of Pentecostalism* (Peabody, Massachusetts: Hendrickson, 1987), 51-54, 63-84, 92-100; William Arnett, "The Role of the Holy Spirit in Entire Sanctification in the Writings of John Wesley," *Wesleyan Theological Journal*, 14:2 (Fall 1979), 15-30; W. Stanley Johnson, "Christian Perfection as Love for God," *Wesleyan Theological Journal*, 18:1 (Spring 1983), 50-60.

[24] Ted Campbell, "Wesley's Use of the Church Fathers," *Asbury Theological Journal*, 50:2 and 51:1 (Fall 1995 and Spring 1996), 47-51, 60. See also Campbell's *John Wesley and Christian Antiquity* (Nashville, TN: Kingswood Books, 1991), 23-33.

[25] These included Athanasius, Basil, John Chrysostom, Clement of Alexandria, Clement of Rome, Dionysius the Areopagite (Pseudo-), Gregory of Nazianzus, Ephraem Syrus, Ignatius, Irenaeus, Justin Martyr, Origen, Polycarp, and (Pseudo-)Macarius. Cf. Campbell, *John Wesley and Christian Antiquity*, Appendix 2, 125-134.

[26] Maddox, "John Wesley and Eastern Orthodoxy: Influences, Convergences and Differences," *Asbury Theological Journal*, 45:2 (1990), 38-40.

Anglican scholars, and not the fathers themselves)[27] the ramifications of the Greek fathers' own philosophical constructs (constructs which themselves relied heavily upon ancient Greek neo-platonism), and because he criticized the Eastern Orthodoxy of his own day, it is more accurate to say Wesley borrowed the implications of those fathers' teachings than their precise terminology or constructs per se. For example, in describing how the Christian is to grow in Christ-likeness, he used the words holiness, entire sanctification and perfection, but avoided the Greek word *theosis* (deification or divinization in English); in describing the Christian's interior life, Wesley generally omitted the East's teaching on *apatheia* (passionlessness),[28] and even warned his followers against being apathetic.[29] And, along with other vocabulary omissions or transformations,[30] whereas the Greek fathers tended to describe this deification in ontological terms (as will be delineated more fully in my chapters on Orthodoxy), Wesley preferred to describe this transformation using affective terms. When the Christian is living as Scripture instructs, as Wesley understood it, he or she will be filled with, and living from, perfect love. He did not deny that Christian transformation ultimately would even involve the human's body, but he believed such would only happen in the afterlife.[31]

Together with his experiential emphasis, Wesley preferred to center the Christian life around sanctification rather than justification (though he did not deny the latter).[32] This life of sanctification involved ascetic activities and disciplines such as fasting on Wednesdays, Fridays, and the prescribed days of the ancient church, attending catechetical classes, and penance. Moreover, those disciplines were necessary for all Christians, not just the clergy. Since the early Greek fathers practiced asceticism, and since, in Wesley's opinion, they so clearly lived out a life of Christian holiness, he, in turn, encouraged ascetic activities as a way to repristinate eighteenth century British and American Christianity. Asceticism aided believers in the restoration of the original image

---

[27] David Bundy, "Christian Virtue: John Wesley and The Alexandrian Tradition," *Wesleyan Theological Journal*, 26:1 (Spring 1991), 139-155.

[28] Campbell, *John Wesley and Christian Antiquity,* 42.

[29] David Bundy, "Christian Virtue," 150.

[30] Bundy, "Christian Virtue," 143-150, notes that Wesley did not employ *gnosis* (knowledge), teachings about the contemplation of the divine, prayer, or Christian character in the same way as did the Alexandrian fathers.

[31] Maddox, "John Wesley and Eastern Orthodoxy," 40.

[32] Maddox, "John Wesley and Eastern Orthodoxy," 39; and, K. Steve McCormick, "Theosis in Chrysostom and Wesley: An Eastern Paradigm on Faith and Love," *Wesleyan Theological Journal*, 26:1 (Spring 1991), 44-48.

of God (*imago dei*) which, in Wesley's theology, had been lost in the fall. Like the ancient Greek Christian ascetics, Wesley believed that the soul's therapy could be facilitated through ascetic cures. In this regard, Ted Campbell says, "Wesley considered himself to be something of a scientist of the religious life." The result was that Wesley, Campbell continued, "developed something like a scientific taxonomy of spiritual problems" which his own Methodist ministers could diagnose and cure.[33] But, and this distinction is important, Wesley's asceticism was not as quietistic or withdrawn as that of the ancient Greek fathers, and it very little resembled the teachings and practices of the still later Orthodox monks known as hesychasts.[34] These later Orthodox monk-theologians included Maximus the Confessor, Symeon the New Theologian, and Gregory Palamas; theologians to whom Wesley did not have access.[35]

Wesley's lasting effects on Pentecostalism lie along anthropological and soteriological lines. The Christian life, for him, was not just a matter of judicial pardon, although human beings certainly needed God's pardon. Because human beings' identities were marred and corrupted, Christ had also come to restore the image of God in humanity.[36] By participating in the life of grace, a life given by and through the Holy Spirit, the Christian is enabled to love God, other people, and the whole of creation with a perfect love.[37] Wesley's gospel was, A. M. Allchin said, "empowered by an optimism of grace, not by the threat of judgment; it is a gospel which sees the fulfillment of God's purposes not in the redemption of humankind alone but in the redemption of the whole creation."[38] In Wesley's theological model, we are pardoned, according to

---

[33] Campbell, "Wesley's Use of the Church Fathers," 62-66, quotes taken from p. 65.
[34] A. M. Allchin, "The Epworth-Canterbury-Constantinople Axis," *Wesleyan Theological Journal*, 26:1 (Spring 1991), 28; Campbell, *John Wesley and Christian Antiquity*, 41-42.
[35] Maddox, "John Wesley and Eastern Orthodoxy," 32.
[36] Alexander Knox, one of Wesley's friends said, "But what has John Wesley done? In my mind, in a manner unprecedented, he has not overlooked the forgiveness of sins, but he has, indeed, looked much above it, and beyond it. . . . The faith, therefore, which my friend urged his hearers to implore from God, had not one great fact only for its object. It did not merely relate to the propitiation of our sins, but it was an influential, vital apprehension of all the Divine facts which are placed before us in the Gospel." *Remains of Alexander Knox, Esq.* (London: Duncan and Malcom, 1844), 3:162-164, quoted in McCormick, "Theosis in Chrysostom and Wesley," 47.
[37] Allchin, "The Epworth-Canterbury-Constantinople Axis," 32-33.
[38] Allchin, "The Epworth-Canterbury-Constantinople Axis," 35.

Albert Outler, "in order to participate."[39] Wesley's own existential Aldersgate experience,[40] and his ensuing experiential theology more specifically - a theology very much colored by his primitivistic motivations - set him on a path which Pentecostals are still walking today.

A few qualifications about this divine-human participation are in order. Like Wesley, Pentecostals tend to avoid the ontological language of the Greek fathers in their discussions of participation. Distinguishing themselves from Wesley, most Pentecostals describe their path using a different vocabulary than he did, even though their experiential and primitivistic bent is much the same as his.[41] While both Pentecostals and Wesley differentiate themselves from Orthodoxy by avoiding ontological language, both Pentecostals and Wesley are deeply concerned with what happens in the Christian and not just what happens for the Christian; in this regard Orthodoxy shimmers within both Wesley and Pentecostalism. Pentecostals, like both the Orthodox and Wesley, urge a divine-human communion, a coinhering communion which extends far beyond the moment of conversion. The ontological implications of such a communion have quite naturally come to the fore, and that is the case for the Orthodox, Wesleyans, and Pentecostals.[42]

Critical for our comparison of Pentecostalism and Orthodoxy, John Wesley represents an exegetical shift which has had a tremendous impact on the Pentecostal movement. He moved away from both the traditional Protestant

---

[39] Albert Outler, "The Place of Wesley in the Christian Tradition," in Kenneth E. Rowe (ed.), *The Place of Wesley in the Christian Tradition* (Metuchen, New Jersey: Scarecrow Press, 1976), 29-32.

[40] On the morning of his great Aldersgate experience, Wesley had been reading a Biblical text of great prominence in Orthodoxy, 2 Peter 1:4, ". . . whereby are given to us exceeding great and precious promises that by these ye might be partakers of the divine nature." Allchin, "The Epworth-Canterbury-Constantinople Axis," 29.

[41] Campbell, *John Wesley and Christian Antiquity*, in chapter 3, "Primitive Christianity in the Wilderness," and in his conclusion, develops Wesley's primitivistic-restorationistic impulses at length.

[42] That is, those who followed Wesley had to carefully clarify what perfection (entire sanctification) was, what is was not, and how it occurred. Similarly, Pentecostals today are continually having to answer questions about *glossolalia* and the charismatic gifts. Recently, a Christian friend wanted me to answer both of these questions: "Do you control your tongue when you exercise *glossolalia*? To what extent is it you, and to what extent is it the Holy Spirit in you, when a charismatic gift is exercised?" All to say, the ontological issues and questions which are not at all in vogue among western theologians seem never to disappear, and that even for laypersons.

(Lutheran) exegetical method which especially emphasized the literal meaning
of Scripture and the traditional Catholic (and Orthodox) method whereby church
tradition was granted great authority. Instead, Wesley, clearly influenced by
Enlightenment thought, allowed that human reason had a role to play in
hermeneutics. He neither believed human reason to be superior to Biblical
revelation, nor did he believe the Scriptures were antithetical to human reason.
Rather, he believed, the human soul has a faculty denoted as reason. Reason
alone cannot produce faith - this is the Holy Spirit's role, in concert with
Scriptures - nor can reason alone disprove faith.[43] But, this faculty, aided by the
Holy Spirit, could perceive, as an internal sensation or discernment, the truths
of God's revelation, and thereby have faith in spiritual things. The Scriptures
are necessary to convey the message of salvation, but they only provide
absolute certainty regarding the essentials of salvation, and not about the non-
essentials of the physical-scientific world.[44] He thus sided with the
soteriological sufficiency of Scripture, but he did not attempt to make the Bible
more than it was.[45]

   In his exegetical methods in specific, and his epistemological framework in
general, Wesley was clearly a Western Christian, despite his frequent reliance
upon the ancient Eastern fathers. While the later North American Pentecostals
would initially be cautious to admit that human reason should play a role in the
Christian epistemology, and while they were even more cautious to grant
church tradition a role in that epistemology (both of which Wesley granted),
they did in fact include those elements into their worldview, even though it is
hard to make them admit as much. As will become evident in my later

---

[43] In its original doctrinal proclamation, the Assemblies of God echoed Wesley in
this regard, "The Bible is the inspired Word of God, a revelation from God to man,
the infallible rule of faith and conduct, and is superior to conscience and reason, but
not contrary to reason." *A Statement of Fundamental Truths Approved By The
General Council of the Assemblies of God*, October 2-7, 1916, 10.
[44] Troy W. Martin, "John Wesley's Exegetical Orientation: East or West?" *Wesleyan
Theological Journal*, 26:1 (Spring 1991), 104-121.
[45] That is, as Martin put it, "Scripture needs no other authority to establish doctrine
or duty, but other authorities, such as reason, tradition, or experience, can be used to
ascertain and confirm the Scriptural position." Experience, Martin continued by
quoting Wesley, "is not sufficient to prove a doctrine unsupported by Scripture,"
but it is "'sufficient to support a doctrine which is grounded on Scripture.'"
"Wesley's Exegetical Orientation" 105, quoting Wesley, "The Witness of the Spirit,"
The Works of John Wesley, 14 vols. (London: Wesleyan Conference Office, 1872;
reprint Kansas City: Beacon Hill Press, 1978), 5:132-133.

delineation of them, their theological model, like that of Wesley, is acutely attuned to the framework of their own meta-context - that complex package of history, epistemology, philosophy, and culture within which one lives, thinks, and serves. The Pentecostals' meta-context differs dramatically from that of historical Eastern Orthodoxy. Important about Wesley and his epistemological model for Pentecostalism is its Western orientation. The Pentecostals, like Wesley, even when they exhibit Eastern Orthodox elements, are emphatically Western.

In all of the above Wesley is an important historical figure, but it is not accurate to interpret him as the bridge between Orthodoxy and Pentecostalism. Even though he appreciated and studied the Greek patristic theologians, Wesley by no means promulgated the whole of Eastern Orthodox thought. Instead, in good pragmatic fashion - a feature itself which will be manifestly important in our delineation of the Pentecostal movement - he took what he found beneficial from the Greek fathers, modified it, and re-presented it to the world in which he lived. In all of this, Wesley is better understood as the historical sieve through which early Eastern Orthodoxy passed. Thus, if and when one sees the anthropological, soteriological, and pneumatological understandings of Eastern Orthodoxy shimmering within Pentecostalism - understandings which will be more carefully exposed in this study - one must realize that they have been reprocessed and reconfigured with regard to an entirely new set of cultural, philosophical, and epistemological tenets. That is, not only did Wesley filter some of Orthodoxy's theology, the Pentecostal movement, following him as it did by roughly 120 years, in turn filtered Wesley's understandings. In the end, none of the Pentecostal movement's founding figures would even know they were impacted by Orthodoxy as such.

No, John Wesley does not alone account for the remarkable similarities between contemporary Orthodoxy and Pentecostalism. There are, I will posit, other and better reasons that account for the rather odd similarities shared by these two Christian tributaries. They are reasons which are much older than Wesley, reasons which are as old as the human race itself. However, in order to analyze and compare these two great traditions in one study our focus must be narrow. To that focus, with its underlying motivations and methodology, we now turn.

This Study's Purposes, Presuppositions, and Method Clarified

This study's primary task will be to delineate and compare the doctrine of Christian transformation as both Orthodoxy and Pentecostalism present it. The topic of Christian transformation has been chosen because it is an issue around which each side's theology is acutely oriented. Put another way, for both Orthodoxy and Pentecostalism, theology is always soteriological, and always has precise anthropological implications. Jaroslav Pelikan, the eminent historical theologian at Yale, once said that *theosis* was the chief idea in Eastern Orthodoxy.[46] Similarly, if Pentecostalism is concerned about anything, it is concerned about the human person's transformation. However, rather than just looking at how each believes the human person is transformed into the image of Christ, an enterprise so narrow that it would produce truncated understandings of both Pentecostalism and Orthodoxy, we will also examine some issues foundational to both groups' understandings of transformation. Firstly, because history has tremendous force in how each group concludes theologically, pertinent issues and/or theologians within each's history will be noted. Secondly, in order to understand "how" each believes the human person is transformed, one needs also to understand "what" each believes about anthropology. Thirdly, and again for reasons of clarification, the theological foundations for facilitating one's Christian transformation will be examined. That is, on what theological basis or bases can one hope to be transformed? Fourthly, each tradition's specific means will be delineated; these are the "how" of a believer becomes like Christ. It is hoped that by making a narrow but detailed focus - the doctrine of Christian transformation - we will have evoked and revealed important elements of both the Orthodox and the Pentecostal identities.

Within these four heuristic categories - history, anthropology, theological foundations, and means - it will become apparent that each group's meta-context has tremendous import for understanding each's respective theological position. Failing to understand that each reflects, to employ an Orthodox term, its own respective meta-context will result in understandings of both Pentecostalism and Orthodoxy filled with gaping holes. We not only want to trace out each's respective theology of transformation, we want to push the reader toward a consideration of the broader framework and how that framework impinged upon, and continues to impinge upon, these two Christian traditions. Simply stated, until both groups can appreciate something of the other's religious womb - that organic vehicle of intricately intertwined values, beliefs,

---

[46] Jaroslav Pelikan, *The Spirit of Eastern Christendom (600-1700), The Christian Tradition: A History of the Development of Doctrine*, 5 vols. (University of Chicago Press, 1989). 10.

philosophical underpinnings, and historical features - there will be no mutual appreciation for the other as authentically Christian.

The Orthodox discuss their doctrine of Christian transformation as a process involving *theosis* or *theopoiesis*; because the former is regularly used by the Orthodox it will be consistently employed throughout this study. The word *theosis* itself, as well as the Orthodox doctrine about it more broadly, connotes the belief that in the process of becoming Christ-like the believer undergoes an ontological change. United to Christ in Orthodox water baptism and the *mysteries* (as the Orthodox prefer to call them, in contrast to the Catholic use of sacraments),[47] one is not only transformed so one can live like Christ, in terms of morality, and one is not only transformed so that one can exist in harmony with God, in terms of attitudes and affections, one's very being is deified. The Christian is, quite literally, made to be a new creation (2 Cor. 5:17). He or she does not become a god, but, in keeping with the Scriptural teaching,[48] he or she is renewed in Christ's image. Within the Orthodox' own model, salvation involves organic union, not just forensic pardon.

The Pentecostals, for their part, have consistently discussed their doctrine of transformation using the word sanctification. The moment of conversion is critical in the *ordo salutis*, but a progressive process of transformation is also necessary. That is, whereas the believer is cleansed and forgiven at conversion, the life *in Christ* - something expressed by Pentecostals as the life *in Christ's Spirit* - involves far more. Indeed, as they express it, the Christian who is satisfied with conversion alone will likely lead a muted and listless Christian life. Yes, one is indeed cleansed and consecrated at conversion, but one must both also live a life in keeping with that initial moment in one's own salvation history and subsequently allow the Holy Spirit to transform oneself in the depths of one's being. Additionally, the vibrant and dynamic Christian walk which Pentecostals so typically describe is not at all limited to their distinctive doctrine of Spirit-baptism, even if Spirit-baptism gives rise to their typical discussions. In all of this, and like their Orthodox counterparts, the

---

[47] The Greek Patristic church did not distinguish the sacraments "as a specific category of Church acts." Instead, the word *musterion* had to do more broadly with the "mystery of salvation," so that the sacraments were understood more as "aspects of a unique mystery of the Church" which share in God's divine life. Meyendorff, *Byzantine Theology*, 191.

[48] Ware believes the Orthodox doctrine of *theosis* is rooted in Scripture and says, "the idea of personal and organic union between God and humans is a constant theme" in John's gospel, Paul's Epistles, and 2 Peter 1:4. *The Orthodox Church* (Baltimore, Maryland: Penguin Books, 1964), 231.

Pentecostals believe the Christian walk is comprised of far more than repentance and faith.

As I noted above, there are many areas where Eastern Orthodoxy and Pentecostalism could be compared, if only because the two have not, with few exceptions, been so compared.[49] Outside the immediate pale of Pentecostalism, scholars of evangelicalism and Orthodoxy themselves have begun to explore their own respective similarities and divergences. Theological emphases, guiding theological principles, favored Scriptural passages, and various church teachings are lined up beside one another, clarified and contrasted. However, because both insist upon different historical eras as being normative for Christian theology - the Patristic era for the Orthodox, and the Reformation era for the evangelicals - and, because both work from entirely different set of presuppositions, both the Orthodox and evangelicals conclude, more often than not, by disregarding the other for not measuring up to each's respective standards and formulations. Too often these studies fail to clarify each respective side's important underlying presuppositions (historical, philosophical, epistemological, and hermeneutical), and rarely are attempts made toward convergence or synthesis.[50] (I should clarify that there are indeed some writers who have proposed, for reasons of mutual edification, some kind of dialogue between the Orthodox and the Pentecostals. However, these writers have not attempted any kind of convergence or synthesis between the two.)[51]

---

[49] Stanley M. Burgess, "Implications of Eastern Christian Pneumatology for Western Pentecostal Doctrine and Practice," in *Experiences of the Spirit: Conference on Pentecostal and Charismatic Research in Europe at Utrecht University,* 1989 Studies in the Intercultural History of Christianity, 68 (Frankfurt am Main: Peter Lang, 1991), 23-34.

[50] Daniel B. Clendenin, "Why I'm Not Orthodox." *Christianity Today,* 41:1 (January 6, 1997), 32-35; *Eastern Orthodoxy: A Western Perspective* (Grand Rapids: Baker, 1997). The most outstanding historical-theological explications of Orthodoxy, from a Western vantage point, are Pelikan's *The Spirit of Eastern Christendom (600-1700),* and his *Christian Doctrine and Modern Culture (since 1700),* vols. 2 and 5, respectively, in The Christian Tradition: A History of the Development of Doctrine. 5 vols. (The University of Chicago Press, 1989). Two of the finest Orthodox pieces, in terms of presenting Orthodoxy to the West, are Anthony Ugolnik's, *The Illuminating Icon* (Grand Rapids: Eerdmans, 1989), and Alexander Schmemann's, *Church, World, Mission: Reflections on Orthodoxy in the West* (Crestwood, NY: St. Vladimir's, 1979).

[51] Claire Randall, "The Importance of the Pentecostal and Holiness Churches in the Ecumenical Movement," *One in Christ,* 23:1-2 (1987), 83-92; Efsthathios V.

One can surmise that the glaring cultural and ecclesiological differences between Pentecostalism and Orthodoxy account for the lack of any comparative studies in the academy, but it is also necessary to clarify that Pentecostal studies have only been conducted for the past 40 years or so. These studies have consistently been intramural examinations, discussions among Pentecostals (and scholars of Pentecostalism) themselves about the movement's distinctives, roots, motivations, and theological orthodoxy; beneficial, necessary, and deserved studies to be sure, but studies that have only infrequently looked beyond the borders of their own camp.[52] These reasons aside, there is a more insidious reason that such comparative studies are lacking within Pentecostalism. Stemming from their reaction to the mainline Christian traditions and denominations, Pentecostals have been wary to involve themselves in trans-denominational or inter-traditional discussions or studies, this even though they have steadily and consistently been impacted and transformed through their ecumenical interaction with evangelicals.[53] Many North American Pentecostal denominational hierarchies warn their ministers against such outside fellowship or interaction. Such involvement, they fear, will compromise any constituent so involved and lead him or her down the inevitable and slippery slope of theological liberalism.[54] One can only surmise the extent to which this fear of causing displeasure at the official and denominational levels has limited the scope of not only Pentecostal study but also Pentecostal praxis, and it seems likely that Pentecostalism's larger and more sweeping impacts - at many levels of the Christian life - will only occur

Mylonas, "Towards The Common Expression of the Apostolic Faith Today: An Orthodox Reply," *One in Christ*, 23:1-2 (1987), 131-137.

[52] Stanley M. Burgess, *The Holy Spirit: Eastern Christian Traditions* (Peabody, Massachusetts: Hendrickson, 1989); Cecil M. Robeck, Jr. (see his numerous articles in my bibliography); and Frank Macchia, "Tongues as a Sign: Towards a Sacramental Understanding of Pentecostal Experience," *Pneuma*, 15:1 (Spring, 1993), 61-76, all exemplify recent Pentecostal attempts to look beyond the traditional borders.

[53] Cecil M. Robeck, Jr., "National Association of Evangelicals," in *DPCM*, 634-636; "Pentecostals and the Apostolic Faith: Implications for Ecumenism," *One in Christ*, 23:1-2 (1987), 110-130; "Name and Glory: the Ecumenical Challenge," Paper presented to the Society for Pentecostal Studies, 1983.

[54] Not only does this position belie their fearful and defensive attitude, it also reveals something of the theological insecurity Pentecostals feel in general. It is as if a thoroughly convinced Pentecostal would only stand to lose, and as if the outsiders would never have anything to gain, in such encounters.

when future generations of foreign and indigenous Pentecostals, themselves
having received educations and matured theologically, begin to interact with the
farther reaches of Christendom.[55]

The Orthodox, for their, part are quite willing to dialogue with other
Christian traditions and denominations.[56] Unfortunately, their dialogue is
consistently a "top-down" venture, one whereby the Orthodox eagerly share the
truths, beauty, and effectiveness of their own heritage, but seem unable - or
unwilling - to recognize the truths, beauty, or effectiveness resident within
others. Sergius Bulgakov typified the Orthodox' sentiments in this regard when
he said, "Orthodoxy is present at such [ecumenical] conferences to testify to the
truth." "The Christian peoples of the world," "heterodox" though they are,
Bulgakov continued, "are now seeking Orthodoxy, often without knowing it."[57]
The Orthodox tend to involve themselves in such dialogues and studies in order
to bear witness to the fullness of Orthodoxy, something quite obviously absent
in all who are not Orthodox (though to be fair, all Christian traditions and
denominations assert that they themselves possess the catholic fullness of
Christianity).[58] The Orthodox too, like their theologically conservative
Pentecostal siblings, are wary of considering or accommodating non-
homogenized theology, but it is much more a matter that they are capital "O"
Orthodox, and therefore believe they have little or nothing to learn from the
West.

This study is written with the conviction that both Orthodoxy and
Pentecostalism have a great deal to learn from one another. As my earlier
comments implied, because Pentecostals exhibit Orthodox-like characteristics
and tendencies they would do well to understand that portion of the church

---

[55] Indeed, an example of a more inclusive openness to other denominations is
evident in the World Assemblies of God Fellowship (WAGF), a trans-global AG
fellowship organized in 1989. Currently chaired by David Yonggi Cho of Seoul,
Korea, the WAGF does not prohibit membership in ecumenical or national church
fellowships even though it discourages its own members from joining the World
Council of Churches (WCC). Cf. *WorldLink*, A Quarterly Communique Linking The
World Assemblies of God Fellowship, 4:3 (July 1998), 8, 16.
[56] The Orthodox were one of the original and founding members of the World
Council of Churches.
[57] Bulgakov, *The Orthodox Church,* 191-192.
[58] Himself a Pentecostal, Frank Macchia, "The Tongues of Pentecost: A Pentecostal
Perspective on the Promise and Challenge of Pentecostal/Roman Catholic
Dialogue," *JES*, 35:1 (Winter 1998), 9-10, notes that Pentecostals too are guilty of
speaking as though they possessed the "fulness" of what it means to be Christian.

which comprised a critical dimension of Christendom - for the entire Roman Empire - for 1000 years, and the primary, if not sole, dimension of Christendom in Eastern Europe for roughly 1800 years.[59] Conversely, the Orthodox would do well to understand a movement which itself facilitates a mystical-existential encounter with the triune God. The Orthodox need to carefully consider why Pentecostalism is quite literally transforming huge areas of the globe, areas increasingly encroaching on formerly Orthodox territory. The

---

[59] That is, excluding the first and the twentieth centuries. The Roman Catholics and Eastern Orthodox saw themselves as one church until the year 1054, when they mutually excommunicated one another. The Catholics believed the Orthodox had separated themselves from the church (and therefore authentic Christianity) because they refused to submit to the Roman Pope's authority. The Orthodox believed the Catholics had separated themselves from the church (and therefore authentic Christianity) because the Roman Pope had attempted to usurp for himself the formerly collegial structures of authority. While power was indeed a central problem, it is also the case that the two had begun to grow apart along cultural, linguistic, and theological lines as early as the 5th-7th centuries. The theological crucible - and as it turned out, the final straw - between these two was the West's unilateral insertion of the *Filioque* clause (that the Spirit proceeds from the Father "and the Son") into the Nicene Creed. Whereas *Filioque* may have been assumed in the West as early as the 3rd century with Tertullian, and whereas it was certainly being advocated by Augustine early in the 5th century, it was not until the 7th century (in part due to the language barriers) that there was an awareness of the difference in the use of doxological and theological terms in the East and West to describe the inner-Trinitarian life of the Godhead and the procession of the Spirit. At the local councils of Toledo (446-447, 589, and 633) the Franks in the West relied on the mis-named Athanasian Creed, also known as the *Quicunque Vult* (from the opening words of the Creed *Quicunque vult salvus esse*, literally "Whoever will be saved") in its battle with Arianism. The Franks insisted that the Son was in no way inferior to the Father, and the *Quicunque* aided them in this because it said that the Spirit proceeds from the Father and the Son. Although the Toledo councils did not prompt an official (ecumenical) alteration of the Nicene Creed to include *Filioque*, they made evident its acceptance in the West. The bibliography in this regard is extensive. For starters see Mary Ann Fatula, "The Holy Spirit in East and West: Two Irreducible Traditions," *One in Christ: A Catholic Ecumenical Review*, 19:4 (1983), 379-386; Michael Fahey, "Son and Spirit: Divergent Theologies between Constantinople and the West," in *Conflicts about the Holy Spirit*, eds. Hans Küng and Jürgen Moltmann (NY: The Seabury Press, 1979); Francis Dvornik, *The Photian Schism* (Cambridge: At The University Press, 1970); and, Dvornik's *The Ecumenical Councils. Twentieth Century Encyclopedia of Catholicism* (NY: Hawthorn Books, 1961), Vol. 82.

issue of mutual understanding is important as its own topic, however, for the enhancement of Christian witness (on this point I unabashedly reveal my own pragmatic Western character!) the two must begin to learn something of one another. For the sake of revealing Christ to the world (John 17:23; 1 John 1:7-11; 4:11-21), it simply will not do for each camp to refer to the other as quasi-Christians at best, or heretics at worst.

To so clarify my presuppositions, or indeed to undertake a study such as this, does not at all mean that I believe "all paths lead to God." All is *not* relative. Christ *is* the only means of salvation. And yet, the Holy Spirit - from the time of Scripture's writing onward - seems eager to allow God's people to have an important role in conveying the good news about God's Kingdom, even to the extent that the church's own character impacts and shapes the message itself. This, then, is my study's *secondary* purpose: to note how and where the church's culture - that of Orthodox and Pentecostals alike - has crept in and usurped the content of the Gospel. If the Kingdom is like yeast (Mt. 13:33; Lk. 13:21), penetrating and transforming cultures, it is also the case that those cultures regularly subsume the yeast and color it with their own identity. Subsequently, and here the Orthodox and Pentecostals represent marvelous cases studies, each respective tradition then dogmatically insists that all other yeast-penetrated-traditions look just like itself. Throughout this study, at each chapter's end, I will critique areas where the loaf of culture, or in some cases more specifically where each tradition's own character, seems to have subsumed the yeast of the Kingdom; the result is that the Kingdom itself gets obfuscated.

By suggesting some of the features of these two traditions' meta-contexts, I do not want to give the impression that either tradition is simply, or solely, the logical or necessitated product of said context. To hold such would be to affirm determinism and rule out both God's immanence and human creativity. Instead, I believe that God is not only sovereignly - if usually mysteriously - reigning over History, he also providentially and personally works within History. But, as with the case of his incarnation, his tools of choice consistently have been people. Hence, from the onset it is herein affirmed that both the Orthodox and the Pentecostals have been used mightily of God for his higher and ultimate purposes. It is just that sometimes God's tools get dirty. Sometimes they become so stained by their work-place's environment that they begin to look just like one more element within it. I want to expose, to some extent, the degree to which those work-places have soiled and stained each tradition's identity.

Throughout this study I will be comparing these two traditions as though each is a unified whole. This is generally the case, but along with the political and administrative divisions which characterize both traditions, it is also the case that within each camp there are theological and practical nuances which are debated among its members, issues which have caused divisions within each group.[60] To remedy this multi-faceted characteristic on the Pentecostal side, I have selected one denomination, the Assemblies of God, and will use it to model Pentecostal theology. On the Chalcedonian Orthodox side, I will usually present their doctrine as though the fourteen autocephalous (self-ruling) churches[61] represent a unified front (although some disagreements will be noted), when in fact there is a fair amount of debate as to the level of individual mysticism normative for *theosis.*[62] By so defining my subjects, East and West, I admit that some mutually internal intricacies and nuances will be glossed over on both fronts, but in the course of a broader comparison and analysis of these two, those intricacies and nuances will not have played an important role.

Both Orthodoxy and Pentecostalism - rooted as they are in the worldwide body of Christ, and building upon the Scriptural witness - will regularly exhibit features shared by many within that larger body. However, I consistently will *not* be making comparisons between either Orthodoxy or

---

[60] On the Orthodox side, these divisions have consistently arisen over power, who has it, or who should have it. To no small extent the various ethnic divisions within Orthodoxy are attributable to the issue of power. For example, the extent to which each ethnic church answers to the Patriarch in Constantinople (generally recognized as the universal patriarch of Orthodoxy) is a source of constant friction. See Alexander Webster, *The Price of Prophecy: Orthodox Churches on Peace, Freedom, and Security.* (Grand Rapids: Eerdmans, 1995[2]). On the Pentecostal side, there was, generations ago, a raging debate about the definition and place of sanctification. This debate will be noted more fully in my chapter on the Assemblies of God's history.

[61] The autocephalous Chalcedonians (affirming Christ's human and divine natures) consist of the churches of Constantinople, Alexandria, Antioch, Jerusalem, Russia, Georgia, Serbia, Romania, Bulgaria, Cyprus, Greece, Albania, Poland, and Carpatho-Russia (Czech and Slovak). Autonomous Chalcedonian churches include those of Sinai, Finland, Japan, and the Ukraine. Still other Chalcedonians include the Chaldaean Catholic church, the Malabar Catholic church, the Maronite Catholic church, and the Malankara Catholic church. Non-Chalcedonians (believing in a single nature in Christ - the divine/human) consist of the Coptics (Egyptians), the Syrian Orthodox, and the Indians. Lastly, the Assyrians are also Orthodox. Orthodoxy is as characterized by political and jurisdictional fragmentation as Protestantism. Each geographical church wants autonomy. And the emigrés of each geographical church, in turn, eventually want autonomy from their mother church.

[62] Orthodoxy has historically been characterized by a tension between the sacramental and mystical means of *theosis.*

Pentecostalism and the broader sweep of Christendom. Any specific comparisons between Orthodoxy and Pentecostalism made herein should not be taken as excluding the larger church, unless it is explicitly stated otherwise.

The reader is also reminded that one's analytical framework and methodology (whether along historical, apologetic, or hermeneutical lines) can itself predispose, or even force, a particular outcome. That is, how one defines the perimeter of one's study can itself limit the ultimate and concluding vantage point. I will indeed follow a rather traditional and time-sequential order, but as much as possible, I want to present each tradition's model as it stands on its own. For example, when I present Orthodoxy's Christology I will delineate some important events in Orthodox history. However, because Pentecostalism's doctrine of transformation is not primarily founded upon Christology, I will not attempt to similarly delineate any events in Pentecostal history. To take another example, the Orthodox are quite sacramental in their transformational model, but when the Pentecostals prove to be other than sacramental I will do little to explain why this is so or what they say about the sacramental model. To take still another example, the Pentecostals are quite pragmatic, along both theological and transformational lines, but I will not look for instances where the Orthodox are pragmatic or impugn them for not so being, especially when it is foreign to their epistemology.

The features and factors of each tradition will be examined for their own internal importance, and as much as possible they will not be analyzed with foreign standards. To make an analogy, these two traditions have many theological apples in common. What differentiates them is first the fruit stand upon which each places its apples, and second how each then stacks its apples. To no small extent this analogy holds well for the whole of Eastern and Western Christianity.

2

Orthodox Theologians and *Theosis* – Athanasius and Palamas

For He was made man that we might be made God.[1]

When contemporary Orthodox theologians discuss *theosis* they do so in light of Orthodox tradition. Tradition, as the Orthodox believe, "is the life of the Church in the Holy Spirit."[2] Or, as another scholar put it, tradition is "the natural and essential 'term of reference' in Orthodoxy."[3] In fulfilment of Jesus' prophecy (Jn. 14:26), the Orthodox believe the Spirit guides the church into truth in at least three ways: through Ecumenical councils, by the wisdom of the Fathers, and especially within the context of the divine liturgy. In each of these the church's truth is to be respected as authoritative for Christian belief and practice, and in each of these there is an acute sense of awareness regarding historical continuity. Accordingly, before we examine more contemporary Orthodox theologians on *theosis*, it behooves us to note their historical forebears. We will limit our historical inspection to the teachings of two theologians critical for understanding Orthodoxy: Athanasius and Gregory Palamas.[4] These two are developed herein as representing the advent of, and synthesis of, Orthodox theology; as such these two are pillars of the Orthodox' teaching on *theosis*. As will be shown, Athanasius initiated Orthodoxy's modification of Platonic constraints, and Palamas synthesized those who preceded him.

---

[1] Athanasius, "The Incarnation of the Word of God," 54, in *PG*, XXV, col. 192.

[2] Vladimir Lossky, *The Mystical Theology of the Eastern Church* (Crestwood, N.Y.: St. Vladimir's, 1991³), 188.

[3] Alexander Schmemann, *Church, World, Mission: Reflections on Orthodoxy in the West* (Crestwood, NY: St. Vladimir's, 1979), 87.

[4] For more extensive historical treatments of Orthodox spirituality see Vladimir Lossky, *The Vision of God*, A. Moorhouse (tr.) (Great Britain: The Faith Press, 1973²); and, John D. Zizioulas, *Being as Communion* (Crestwood, N.Y.: St. Vladimir's, 1985), especially his second chapter, "Truth and Communion," where he analyzes the Patristic fathers' thought concerning ontology.

Athanasius (AD 293-373)

Athanasius is most famous for being the chief opponent of Arianism at the Council of Nicea (325). But he is also deeply respected among the Orthodox for his theological writings. Gregory of Nazianzus called Athanasius "the law of Orthodoxy" and the "cornerstone of the Fathers."[5] Athanasius' writings were occasional documents - not systematic treatises - which primarily addressed the Christological and philosophical questions of his day. This caveat about the nature of Athanasius' own writings is an important one because it typifies the arbitrary nature of our study: we are highlighting and systematizing a specific topic. We are doing this even though the Orthodox rarely systematize their theological presentations, and instead tend to present their theology as an organic whole. In Athanasius' teachings on *theosis*,[6] three foundational issues are noteworthy: 1) the importance of the incarnation for soteriology, 2) the relationship between the church and Scripture, 3) and his Platonic influences.

The Incarnation and Soteriology

THE INCARNATION AND THE CROSS
In his soteriological understanding, Athanasius emphasized the incarnation over the cross, just as he more generally emphasized Christ's person over Christ's work.[7] Athanasius primarily viewed the cross as satisfying the law's demand for death because of sin, "for the death which [his enemies] thought to inflict as a

---

[5] George Dragas, "Holy Spirit and Tradition: The Writings of St. Athanasius," *Sobornost* 1:1 (1979), 55.

[6] Thomas F. Torrance, *The Trinitarian Faith: The Evangelical Theology of the Ancient Catholic Church* (Edinburgh: T. and T. Clark, 1988), 139, n.101, says that although the word θέωσις does not occur in Athanasius' writings, it nonetheless does express his use of the verb θεοποιέω.

[7] *Orationes contra Arianos* IV 2:51; in *NPNF*, 4:376. E. P. Meijering, *Orthodoxy and Platonism in Athanasius: Synthesis or Antithesis?* (Leiden: E. J. Brill, 1968), 101, 136, and 186, holds that the motive for Athanasius' ontological theology was his desire to safeguard the doctrine of God's immutability and consequently his faithfullness to humanity. A doctrine of God wherein being is pre-eminent to doing guards against the problem of God's identity changing in the course of his doing. Such an ontic foundation also protects the identity of the Son as *homoousion* with the Father. Even more specifically, it deflects Arius' notion that the Logos was capable of sinning.

disgrace, was actually a monument of victory against death itself."[8] Athanasius, unlike Anselm, did not portray Christ's death as a vicarious sacrifice, rather he portrayed it as the method for dealing with physical death.[9] Those persons who share in Christ's death will indeed suffer physical death, but they will no longer suffer the penalty or corruption of death.[10] Both the crucifixion and the incarnation were acts of divine condescension whereby God, motivated by love for his creation, humbled himself.[11] Clearly then, Athanasius discusses the necessity of Christ's cross, but it is the incarnation, as is evident in voluminous number of passages throughout his works, which was the crucial dimension of Christology concerning *theosis*.[12]

THE INCARNATION AND CREATION

Athansius' teaching on the incarnation was interspersed with qualifications regarding the creator and creation. Following Scripture, he taught that the Father created through the Word. Contrary to Arianism, the Son of God was not to be confused as one of the Father's creations.[13] To make such an error, even if the Son's origin was posited to have occurred in eternity, was to make the Son a creature nonetheless.[14]

God transcends his creation because matter was not, and is not, eternal. Athanasius said, "Rather, from nothing, and from no prior existence, God called forth creation through His Word."[15] (This belief in creation *ex nihilo* starkly contrasted with the ancient Greek position that matter eternally coexisted with Being [God]. Athanasius' position on creation also revealed that he rejected

---

[8] *De Incarnatione Verbi Dei* 24.4; in *NPNF*, 49. Cf. *De Incarnatione* 10; 13:9; 22:3; 23. *De Incarnatione*, together with *Contra Gentes*, is traditionally understood to have been written around AD 318, and thus before the Arian controversy broke out.

[9] Robertson's comments in *NPNF*, 4:lxx.

[10] *De Incarnatione* 8:4; and 10:5; in *NPNF*, 40-41.

[11] *De Decretis Nicaenae Synodi* (Defense of The Nicene Definition) 3:14; in *NPNF*, 159.

[12] Again, one can surmise that his emphasis in this regard was due to the Christological controversies of the day. Not only did the teachings of Arius seriously threaten normative Christian doctrine, those of Paul of Samosata (dynamic monarchianism) were still extant.

[13] The Arians had supposed that because the Son was begotten of the Father (μονογενής θεός, 1 Jn. 4:9), there must have been a time when He did not exist.

[14] Thus in the Nicene formula Athanasius employed homoousion (ὁμοούσιον) to denote that the Son shares a common essence with the Father. The nature of the Son's eternal begottenness is mysterious and unknown.

[15] "ἀλλ' ἐξ οὐκ ὄντων καὶ μηδαμῶς ὑπάρχοντα τά ὅλα εἰς τό εἶναι πεποιηκέναι τό θεὸν διὰ τοῦ Λόγου οἶδεν. " Athanasius, *De Incarnatione* 3; in *PG*, XXV:101. Cf. *De Decretis Nicaenae Synodi III*, 11; in *NPNF*, 157.

Platonism's hierarchy of being, as well as the various emanations of being.)[16] Importantly, God continued to be immanent within his creation even after the fall.[17] Conversely stated, creation subsisted in and through the Word of God, even after the fall, because of the goodness, kindness and power of God. The relationship between God and creation has always been one of *giving and receiving*: the creator gives, and the creation receives, existence.[18] Throughout Athanasius' discussions about creation and soteriology the ontological dimension figures prominently. It is a dimension that characterizes all subsequent Orthodox theology.

When God created Adam he, "made him according to His own image."[19] Athanasius understood humanity's image to be, "a kind of shadow of the Word,"[20] engendering a "life in correspondence with God."[21] We may summarize him by saying that as the Word of God reflects the identity of the Father, so also Adam reflected, and had the responsibility to reflect, the identity of the Word.[22] Athanasius believed the Word of God was the prototype for human beings: just as the Word of God enjoys fellowship with the Father, humans were created for fellowship with God; just as the Word of God is a perfect reflection of the Father, humans were created to reflect the image of the Word to all creation.[23]

---

[16] For a survey of ancient Greek thought on creation and matter see Frederick Copleston, S. J., *A History of Philosophy* (Westminster, Maryland: The Newman Press; rpt. NY: Image, 1985), vol. I.

[17] *Contra Gentes*, 26; 27; 29; 41; and 42; in *NPNF*, 17-19, and 26-27 . *De Incarnatione*, 43.6; in *NPNF*, 60.

[18] Khaled Anatolios, "The Soteriological Significance of Christ's Humanity in St. Athanasius," *St. Vladimir's*, 40:4 (1996), 265-286, my emphasis. Anatolios draws out the reciprocal relationship, the giving and receiving dimensions, between God and creation in Athanasius' writings.

[19] "ἀλλὰ κατὰ τὴν ἑαυτοῦ εἰκόνα ἐποίησεν αὐτούς. " *De Incarnatione* 3; in *PG*, XXV, col. 101.

[20] "ἵνα ὥσπερ σκιάς τινας ἔχοντες τοῦ Λόγου, " *De Incarnatione* 3; in *PG*, XXV, col. 101.

[21] *De Incarnatione* 5:1; in *NPNF*, 38.

[22] *Contra Gentes* 31; 41:1; 46:8; and, 47:2; in *NPNF*, pages 20, 26, and 29, respectively. *De Incarnatione* 13:7; in *NPNF*, 43.

[23] *De Incarnatione* 4; and 5; in *NPNF*, 38-39. Cf. *Contra Gentes* 4, where Athanasius, discussing the human soul, said the good that the soul contemplates and chooses is a παράδειγμα, an idea of God Himself. So that to contemplate and choose the paradigm, is to contemplate and choose God. Plato posited that the παραδείγματα existed outside of God, space, and time. His followers (e.g., Albinus and Atticus) used the notion of παραδείγματα to differentiate between God and the sensible world. Cf. Meijering,

For Athanasius, Adam and Eve did not exist in a state of perfection in Eden. The very fact of their being made out of finite matter meant that by nature (φύσις) they were mortal and corruptible.[24] Adam and Eve were created in the image of God, and were created for fellowship with God. As long as they lived in fellowship with God via *theoria* (θεωρία τῶν θείων),[25] and by obedience partook of the grace of the Word of God, they were promised a life free from pain and sorrow and could ultimately attain immortality.[26] Thus, they were created with the potential for incorruptibility.[27] However, when they listened to the devil, sinned, and turned toward corruptible things, they became their own source of corruption and death and introduced the same into creation.[28] The image of God can be effaced by sin, but because the human identity was rooted in the image for God's glory[29] it cannot be erased.[30]

THE INCARNATION AS THERAPEUTIC

Following Irenaeus, Athanasius said, "For he was made human so that we might be made divine. And he revealed himself through a body so that we might receive an understanding of the invisible Father. And he endured the mistreatment

---

Orthodoxy and Platonism, 10-13. This theme of paradigms (ideas) reflecting the mind of God (but having a kind of existence) will be important for later iconographical, and coincidingly anthropological, developments.

[24] Meijering, *Orthodoxy and Platonism,* 43, clarifies that for Athanasius Adam and Eve's nature (φύσις) was mortal in the sense that because it had a beginning it necessarily would have an end (i.e., their finitude), but not that it was by nature destined to sin. Athanasius thus opposed the Platonic notion that humanity's physical nature constituted its fall from full spirituality.

[25] *Theoria* is defined as the participatory contemplation of God, involving "a certain participation in the incorruptible state, a stability of the being participating in the creative nature of the Logos." Lossky, *The Vision,* 59. Mere intellectual apprehension of, or mere intellectualization about, God was hereby ruled insufficient for Christian theology. Moreover, mysticism, defined here as participation in and communion with God, began to be normative in the East as early as Origen and the Alexandrian school. Addressing this notion of participation with the divine, Anatolios, "Soteriological Significance," 27, said that in Alexandrian theology humanity was not defined merely by moral categories, the quality of receptivity of the divine also constituted what it meant to be human.

[26] *De Incarnatione* 4:6; in *NPNF,* 38.

[27] *De Incarnatione* 3:3-5; 4; and 5; in *NPNF,* 37-38.

[28] *De Incarnatione* 5:2; and 6; in *NPNF,* 38-39.

[29] "καὶ κατ᾽ εἰκόνα γεγόναμεν, καὶ εἰκὼν καὶ δόξα θεοῦ ἐχρματίσαμεν, " *Orationes contra Arianos IV* 3:10; in *PG,* XXVI, col. 344.

[30] *De Incarnatione* 14:1; in *NPNF,* 43.

of humans, so that we might inherit immortality."[31] Elsewhere he said, "For He has become Man, that He might deify us in Himself."[32] As noted above, the Word of God did not take on flesh solely to suffer upon the cross and nullify the sting of death, as important as that was. His broader purpose was to restore human beings to the fullness of the image of God, and thereby restore them to fellowship with and knowledge of God.[33] "The Word," Athanasius said, "loved His creation, and because His own goodness could not bear to see it suffer corruption, He entered into a human body in order to save us."[34] Through the incarnation, the image of God in humanity is restored to a state surpassing Adam's original state. Because the prototype (Christ) has, in human flesh, wed himself to his creation, suffered in it, and raised it from the dead, the new image of God surpasses the original.[35]

THE INCARNATION: APPLYING ITS BENEFITS

In contrast to later Protestant presentations of the *ordo salutis*, faith was not the first point of departure for human transformation in Athanasius' theology. As mentioned above, and as is implied throughout Athanasius' writings about the incarnation and its applications for soteriology, ontology was of the utmost importance. In order for the transforming work of the Word's incarnation to be effective one must receive the Holy Spirit.

When he lost the gift of grace that had enabled him to enjoy incorruptibility and fellowship (θεωρία) with God, Adam proved, all to well, that humans lose God's gracious gifts. But Jesus Christ received the gift of the Spirit (at the Jordan river)[36] for humanity in such a manner that it could never again be lost. Discussing Athanasius, Khaled Anatolios observed, "Thus it is precisely in the Incarnation, through Christ's human receptivity on our behalf, that our reception of the grace of the Spirit finally becomes securely united within our

---

[31] "Αὐτὸς γὰρ ἐνηνθρώπησεν, ἵνα ἡμεῖς θεωποιθῶμεν. Καὶ αὐτὸς ἐφανέρωσεν ἑαυτὸν διὰ σώματος, ἵνα ἡμεῖς τοῦ ἀοράτου Πατρὸς ἔννοιαν λάβωμεν. Καὶ αὐτὸς ὑπέμεινε τὴν παρ᾿ ἀνθρώπων ὕβριν, ἵνα ἡμεις ἀθανασίαν κληρο-νομήσωμεν. " *De Incarnatione* 54, in *PG*, XXV, col. 192.

[32] *Ad Adelphium* 4; in *NPNF*, 576.

[33] *De Incarnatione* 11:3; 13:7-9; 16:5; 19:1; *passim*.

[34] "καὶ Λόγος... διὰ τὴν ἡμῶν σωτηρίαν ἐν ἀνθρωπίνῳ σώματι ἡμῖν πε-φανέρωται, " *De Incarnatione* 1, in *PG*, XXV, col. 97. Cf. DI 6:10; and 43:6; in *NPNF*, pages 39 and 60 respectively.

[35] *Orationes contra Arianos IV* 2:67; in *NPNF*, 385.

[36] *Orationes contra Arianos IV* 1:47; in *NPNF*, 334. In this section Athansius teaches that it was Christ's humanity that received the Spirit, not his divinity. As the Word, He is sender of the Spirit.

flesh."[37] For Athanasius, because Christ took on humanity and received the necessary gift which humanity was no longer in itself able to secure, "the Incarnation [is] the supreme instance of grace."[38]

The Word was incarnated on behalf of all humanity, but individuals only appropriate the benefits of the incarnation upon their reception of the Spirit. Individuals receive the Holy Spirit's grace at their (water) baptism.[39] People maintain the Spirit's indwelling through the confession that Jesus is the Son of God,[40] and live moral and spiritual lives in correspondence to the Spirit's indwelling grace.[41] But as to how the benefits of Christ are applied (apart from water baptism), or as to how the sacraments convey grace, Athansius said little (though his sacramental lacuna may be the simple result of his having assumed their existence and use).[42]

The Church and Scripture

Athanasius believed that Scripture, holy and inspired,[43] was the most authoritative source of Christian truth.[44] Nonetheless, he was also adamant that church tradition was also authoritative. It was, he said, "An anchor for the faith."[45] His appeals to the authority of church teaching and doctrine were usually made in his anti-schismatic documents.[46]

For Athanasius, church doctrine was founded upon Scripture. Throughout his writings he implied both that the church was founded on Scripture, and that

---

[37] Anatolios, "Soteriological Significance," 284. Anatolios followed Athanasius in *Orationes contra Arianos IV* 3:38.

[38] Anatolios, "Soteriological Significance," 284.

[39] *Orationes contra Arianos IV* 3:33; in *NPNF*, 412.

[40] *Orationes contra Arianos IV* 3:24; in *NPNF*, 407.

[41] Peter Widdicombe, "Adoption, Salvation, and Life of Unity," in *The Fatherhood of God from Origen to Athanasius* (Oxford University Press, 1993), 247. Widdicombe summarizes Athanasius on this point.

[42] Robertson, *NPNF*, lxxix. Athanasius discusses water baptism in *Orationes contra Arianos IV* 3:33.

[43] *Contra Gentes* 1; in *NPNF*, 4. *De Incarnatione* 37:2-3; in *NPNF*, 56.

[44] *De Decretis Nicaenae Synodi* 32; in *NPNF*, 172.

[45] "τόν τε σκοπὸν τὸν ἐκκλησιαστικὸν ὡς ἄγκυραν τῆς πίστεως. " *Orationes contra Arianos IV* 3:58; in *PG*, XXVI, col. 445.

[46] E.g., *Contra Gentes* 6:3; 7:3; and 33:1; in *NPNF*, pages 6-7, and 21, respectively. *De Synodis* 6; in *NPNF*, 453. *Ad Episcopos Aegypti* 4; in *NPNF*, 224-225, where he scolded Marcion, Manichaeus, Paul of Samosata and the Arians for rejecting portions of Scripture.

Scripture was properly interpreted by the church. Those who failed to interpret Scripture correctly proved themselves to be beyond the walls of normative Christendom. Robertson, the translator of Athanasius' writings for *A Select Library of Nicene and Post-Nicene Fathers of the Christian Church,* may have been correct to assert that church tradition, for Athanasius, was only founded upon the written documents of the Fathers and not upon a "secret unwritten body of teaching handed down orally." But Robertson erred when he asserted that Athanasius did not understand church tradition as "*supplementing* Scripture."[47] Athanasius not only understood that tradition supplemented Scripture, he saw it as necessarily doing so. In the first chapter of *Contra Gentes,* one of his earliest documents, Athanasius referred to his Christian teachers and believed his teaching was in accord with theirs.[48] Even a quick scan of *De Decretis or Orationes contra Arianos IV* will show that for Athanasius the church's doctrine and doctrinal rulings were terribly important for both a proper understanding of Scripture and the life and truth of the church.

The above qualification about Athanasius' view of church tradition as authoritative is necessary because it clarifies one of the points of departure for his theology. Middle-Platonism provided the philosophic point of departure for Athanasius' theology, and to it we now turn.

Platonic Influences

Athanasius simultaneously challenged and criticized both the Greek philosophers and the Christian heretics. As he did this he freely interwove arguments from reason and revelation; and, we must clarify, those two were not so distinct for him as they are for Christians today. Though he did not consider himself a philosopher,[49] he interwove philosophical terminology and Scriptural sources. His ability to synthesize philosophy and Scripture stemmed both from his education and his ability to freely quote Greek philosophers and Scripture from memory. Thus, while Athanasius was a product of his own Hellenistic environment, he maintained a commitment to Biblical expressions of Christian truth. In the end he both adapted and altered Hellenistic thought as he related

---

[47] Robertson's editorial comments, *NPNF,* lxxiv. Emphasis his.

[48] Meijering, *Orthodoxy and Platonism,* 105, said these teachers were likely those from the Alexandrian school: Origen, Dionysius, Pierius, Theognostus, Serapion, Peter, and Alexander.

[49] Hans Von Campenhausen, *The Fathers of the Greek Church.* L. A. Garrard (tr.) (London: Adam and Charles Black, 1963), 81.

his theology to the scholars of his day.[50] For our purposes we will note some features which he either modified or borrowed from Platonism,[51] features which have prevailed within Orthodoxy into the present day.

ONTOLOGY: CREATION AND ANTHROPOLOGY

The decisive Greek philosophical questions of Athanasius' day pertained to the question of being. Specifically, what is the relationship between the material realm and God? Consequently, and quite naturally, the ontological issues raised similar questions for Christians. Origen shaped his theology within the structures of Alexandrian Platonic thought. So heavily committed to the assumptions of Platonic philosophy, some of Origen's teachings were eventually branded either heterodox or unorthodox.[52] Athanasius, however, broke away from Platonic teaching when he asserted that whereas God is eternal, immutable, and incorruptible, the created realm is finite, mutable, and corruptible. The created realm only has order and existence because of the Divine *Logos*. Not only was the universe called forth *ex nihilo*, it continued to exist only by the action and will of the *Logos*. In making distinctions between God's inner Being and God's economy *ad extra*, Athanasius was a pioneer.[53] For Athanasius, it must be emphasized, God's Being was, "an absolute ontological priority over God's action and will."[54]

---

[50] Meijering, *Orthodoxy and Platonism,* carefully details the degree to which Athanasius borrowed from and modified Platonism. Georges Florovsky, "St. Athanasius' Concept of Creation," *Aspects of Church History*, in the Collected Works of Georges Florovsky (Belmont, Mass.: Nordland, 1975), 4:41, says that the Patristic writers were not always aware of the tensions and ambiguities which their use of Greek categories caused.

[51] I will not attempt to resolve the debate here about whether Athanasius borrowed from Middle or Neo-Platonism (Meijering held to the former, Zizioulas said Athanasius reflected both).

[52] Florovsky, "Athanasius' Concept of Creation," 42-45, showed that for Origen God is whom He always is; that is, because He existed eternally as the creator (to believe otherwise violated God's immutability) matter, as a paradigm or *logikos* (divine thought), also must have existed eternally.

[53] This distinction between God as He is and God as He reveals himself in the economy of salvation is an important element in the *Filioque* controversy (a topic discussed more fully in my fifth chapter). Cyril of Alexandria, following Athanasius on generation and creation, was one of the first who used "divine energy" to describe God's external workings (Basil had also used this terminology, *Letter* 234). Florovsky, "Athanasius' Concept of Creation," 60.

[54] Florovsky, "Athanasius' Concept of Creation," 49-52. Quote drawn from p. 52. Florovsky clarifies that for Athanasius this was a logical order, but not one of temporal sequence.

The aforementioned discussion on creation is important as it applies to *theosis* because for Athanasius, in the fall humans acted against their very ontological identity: they were beings whose immortality was contingent upon the contemplation of (via *theoria*), and obedience to, the Word of God. To reiterate a previous comment,[55] humans were uniquely created with the potential to live eternally with God and to reflect him to all of creation. Their violation of God's law thrust them into corruption and necessitated their restoration (*theosis*). The incarnation, and our adoption into God's family through the person and work of Christ, was God's answer for the ontological demise of humanity (whereas we become children of God by grace, Christ remains the Son of God by nature). For Athanasius, as Peter Widdicombe said, "The incarnation is the objective guarantee of our salvation."[56]

ONTOLOGY: THE IMAGE AND IMAGES

Athanasius discussed the human image in a manner that would be repeated and developed throughout Orthodox history. Consistent with his writings' overarching theme, this topic was one very much rooted in ontology. Moreover, he was more consistent with Plato on this topic than he was concerning creation. Indeed, on this point he Christianizes Plato's position regarding *Logos* and *nous*.

God's creation, Athanasius believed, is specifically good because it contains *nous*. The *Logos* (Reason, Wisdom, Word, or Son) of God created the universe using, and pervaded his creation with, *nous*. Thus, human beings, as creations of the *Logos*, have *nous* which is an εἰκών (icon, reflection, mirror) of the divine Reason. The human image must not be misunderstood as co-equal to that of the *Logos*, who was of the same essence (ὁμοούσιος) as God the Father. Nonetheless, because we are images of the Divine Reason, Athanasius believed we are "capable of receiving revelation and knowing God."[57]

For Athanasius, human beings can only be properly understood within their reciprocal relationship to God. We are only authentically human, and we only authentically exercise our human nature, as we have fellowship with God and

---

[55] See my earlier comments about Adam and Eve in the garden under "The incarnation and creation."

[56] Widdicombe, "Adoption, Salvation, and Life of Unity," 225.

[57] Meijering, *Orthodoxy and Platonism,* 117-120. Quote drawn from p. 118. Meijering follows Athanasius here in *Contra Arianos* 2:78-79; and, *Contra Gentes* 2. Meijering also shows that Athanasius parallels Plato's *Timaeus* on this topic. Everett Ferguson, *Backgrounds of Early Christianity* (Grand Rapids: Eerdmans, 1993[2]), 313, said that Plato's "*Timaeus* provided the starting point for the Hellenistic and later Platonic worldview."

then reflect the dimensions of that fellowship to his creation. As will be more extensively developed later, for all subsequent Orthodox theologians this theo-centric understanding of humanity predominates: anthropology divorced from its divine moorings is both fallacious and idolatrous. To be created in the image of God meant more than that something (soul or *nous*) was added to human nature which was not added to that of the animals.[58] It meant that being fully human could only be expressed within the relationship to, and reflection of, God.

The incarnation, an event wherein the Word of God took on flesh and thereby sanctified it, provided the means of our *theosis*, a process which restores our knowledge of, and participation in, God. The incarnation, furthermore, has initiated a new ontological stage in the economy of salvation: contemplation of and fellowship with God is once again possible through the incarnate Word who "was made a bearer of the flesh (σαρκοφόρος), in order that men might become bearers of the Spirit (πνευματοφόροι)."[59]

ONTOLOGY: SPIRIT VS FLESH

Lastly, it deserves qualification that despite Athanasius' modification of and reliance upon Platonic terminology, salvation is *not* a matter of delivering humanity from the physical realm. The Word did not take on a physical body because the material realm itself was the problem. To the contrary, God had pervaded creation with order and harmony so that humans might gain knowledge of him through his works.[60] It *was* the case that humans, by substituting the physical realm (themselves and their own idolatrous interests) for the intelligible realm of God, sinned and fell. The fall caused corruption to become attached to their bodies,[61] but sin originated in their will, not their bodies. As will be developed below, Orthodox soteriology from Athanasius unto the present, is far too cosmologically concerned to denigrate the material realm as the source of evil.

---

[58] Some clarification is deserved here. The Orthodox were not unique in developing the notion of the image of God in humans. Thomas Aquinas, the great Roman Catholic theologian, also emphasized this idea and as such was foundational for Western doctrines of human rights.

[59] Lossky, "Alexandria," in *The Vision*, 59.

[60] *Contra Gentes* 35-45; in *NPNF*, 22-28.

[61] *De Incarnatione* 44:4-5; in *NPNF*, 60.

Gregory Palamas (AD 1296-1359)

As it was with Athanasius, the primary theological preoccupation of the Orthodox, until the final defeat of the iconoclasts in the eighth century,[62] was Christology. After the Christological epoch reached its end the new theological concerns were pneumatology and grace.[63] Symeon the New Theologian (c. 949-
1022)[64] emphasized that *theosis* occurred through the human person's participation with, and in, the Holy Spirit. In a very personal manner, he discussed the
experience of the divine light.[65] Symeon was also important for pushing the
Orthodox position on *theosis* in a more individualistic and mystical direction.[66]
But there was another who stands out as the eminent mystical theologian of the
Spirit.

Gregory Palamas, a monk and theologian at the monastic center of Mount
Athos, developed the understanding of Christ's incarnation and the corollary effects for redemption beyond all previous theologians. Palamas taught that the
Logos took on flesh for the following reasons: to teach us the heights to which
God would raise us, to keep us from exalting ourselves as the answer to the sinful fall, to join together the divine and human natures, to break the chain of sin,
to purify us, to show us God's love, to be an example of humility and remedy

---

[62] Ambrosios Giakalis, *Images of the Divine: The Theology of Icons at the Seventh Ecumenical Council* (NY: E. J. Brill, 1994) provides a detailed analysis of the iconoclastic
controversy. He notes that the iconoclasts primarily consisted of Christian leaders who
believed that the successive invasions of the Muslims and a severe earthquake were
God's judgments on the Byzantine empire for allowing and encouraging iconography. At
a more theological level, the debate was specifically about the avenues of deification.
The iconodules (or iconophiles as Giakalis calls them) believed God's grace was communicated through the sacraments, monks, holy men, wonder working relics, and icons.
Conversely, the iconoclasts believed that God's grace was communicated solely through
the sacraments and the clergy. The Seventh Ecumenical Council of 787 pronounced
victory for the iconodules, with the outcome that icons were affirmed as normative for
Christianity (though the patriarchs of Rome, Alexandria, Antioch, and Jerusalem expressed reservations), while the Eucharist was maintained to be more than an icon.

[63] Lossky, *The Vision*, 124.

[64] So called because of his new pneumatological emphasis. Gregory of Nazianzus was
called The Theologian.

[65] John Meyendorff, "Symeon the New Theologian," *St. Gregory Palamas and Orthodox
Spirituality* (Crestwood, N.Y.: St. Vladimir's, 1974), 48, said that whereas most Eastern
mystical writings were often impersonally expressed, Simeon intimately presented the
mystical life.

[66] To be accurate, Simeon also emphasized the sacramental element in one's experience
of God. Lossky, *The Vision*, 120.

for pride, to show how our created nature is good, to destroy the despairing of death, to make us children of God, and to honor our mortal flesh in light of proud spirits (angels and demons).[67] In all of this Palamas synthesized the thought of the fathers,[68] and, like Symeon three centuries earlier, he emphasized an existential knowledge of God. Clearly, Palamas' understanding of *theosis* was manifold, however we will limit our examination of him to three primary features: 1) his emphasis upon an existential knowledge of God; 2) his position regarding the essence and energies of God; and, 3) his developments in relation to philosophy.[69]

The Existential Knowledge of God

At the age of twenty Palamas left Constantinople and joined a monastic community, the Great Lavra of St. Athanasius, at Mount Athos. For eight years there he practiced unceasing prayer, and for ten more in a mountain cave away from Athos he lived a hermitic life and practiced hesychasm (prayerful silence and stillness in God's presence). His monastic diligence and his influential writings, especially his defense of hesychasm, eventually caused others to recognize him as an important spiritual leader. It was during his debates with Barlaam, an Italian Greek monk and philosopher, that Palamas developed the important existentialist foundations for the Orthodox doctrine of *theosis*.[70]

In 1327 Barlaam went to Constantinople and debated with Palamas about the Latin insertion of the *Filioque* into the Nicene-Constantinopolitan Creed. Barlaam believed that because God could not directly be apprehended by the human mind, appeals to Scripture and the patristic writings were the only suffi-

---

[67] Georgios I. Mantzaridis, *The Deification of Man: St. Gregory Palamas and the Orthodox Tradition* (Crestwood, NY: St. Vladimir's, 1984), 27.

[68] John Meyendorff, *Gregory Palamas: The Triads*, Nicholas Gendle (tr.) (NY: Paulist Press, 1983), 13, said Palamas cited Maximus the Confessor and Pseudo-Dionysius more than any other fathers. *The Triads* is a translation of Meyendorff's original *Grégoire Palamas, Défense des saints hésychastes, Spicilegium Sacrum Lovaniense, études et documents, fascicules 30 and 31, Louvain* 1973²). *The Triads* was a defense of hesychasm.

[69] I will base this three-fold examination of Palamas primarily upon: 1) Meyendorff's *The Triads*; 2) Palamas' Greek text, *De Hesychastis*,in Migne's *PG*, vol. CL; and, 3) Robert E. Sinkewicz, *Saint Gregory Palamas: The One Hundred and Fifty Chapters* (Toronto: Pontifical Institute of Mediaeval Studies, 1988). Like *The Triads*, The *Capita 150* was partly a polemical work against the Barlaamite heresy. Sinkewicz' work (hereafter *TOHFC*) reproduces the Greek text found in *PG*, CL, cols. 1121-1225.

[70] Meyendorff, *"Les Débuts de la Controverse Hésychaste,"* in *Byzantine Hesychasm: Historical, Theological, and Social Problems* (London: Variorum Reprints, 1974), 90-102.

cient doctrinal foundations. Palamas, for his part, accepted those two sources of truth but also defended the realm of Christian experience, especially the experience of the divine within the human body.[71] Even further, Palamas believed *theosis*, becoming like God, is the goal for every Christian believer, and his writings reflect that, as John Meyendorff said, "the entire Greek patristic tradition can be seen as an affirmation of the goal of *theosis*."[72] Alarmed by such mystical notions, Barlaam opposed the hesychastic practices, believed they were nonsensical and erroneous, and held that they circumvented the accepted sacramental system.[73] Rebuked by two Orthodox church councils in 1341, Barlaam returned to Italy. Until recently in the twentieth century, Barlaam's own polemic writings caused Palamas' position to be misunderstood.[74] In 1347 and again in 1351 Orthodox church councils at Constantinople vindicated Palamas' hesychastic position. More importantly, his theology greatly impacted successive generations of Eastern Orthodox believers.

In light of Palamas' hesychastic background, it can be said that he was very much an mystic/existentialist in his Christian practice. Because the term mysticism is too often viewed pejoratively, I will consistently refer to this element as existentialism: that element of human existence and experience which is not always precisely described or understood in rational terms. Additionally, existentialism, as it is being used herein, is *not* to be equated with its individualistic and subjective models as prefigured in nineteenth century (Kierkegaard) and

---

[71] Meyendorff, *"Les Débuts de la Controverse Hésychaste,"* 119, explained the difference between Barlaam and Palamas on experiencing the divine. "Barlaam's attack, stemming from his humanistic and dialectical agnosticism, tended to eliminate the direct role of grace upon Christian understanding from theological formulations" *("Ce qu'il attaquera en Barlaam, ce sera toujours son agnosticisme d'humaniste et de dialecticien, qui tendait a eliminer de la pensée théologique le role direct de la grace sur l'intelligence du chrétien").* "In this regard, even Palamas' personality was examined, he was not in the least a mystical person, like Simeon the New Theologian, and even less a visionary, but a speculative and dogmatic theologian" *("Cet aspect de la question nous éclaire sur la personnalité meme de Palamas, qui ne fut aucunement un mystique personnel, comme Syméon le Nouveau Théologien, et encore moins un visionnaire, mais un spéculatif et un dogmaticien").* More simply, Barlaam leaned toward philosophical positivism, while Palamas favored the contemplative and existentialist approaches.

[72] Meyendorff, *The Triads,* 8. Pelikan, *The Spirit of Eastern Christendom (600-1700),* 10, said the sum of "all of Eastern theology [was] the idea of deification."

[73] Meyendorff, *The Triads,* 6-8, 12. Barlaam was the first to call the hesychasts *omphalopsychoi,* "people-whose-soul-is-in-their-navel" (a.k.a., navel-gazers), because of their practice of resting their beards on their chests, looking toward their bellies, and entering into profound and silent prayer *(hesychia).*

[74] Pelikan, *The Spirit of Eastern Christendom,* 263, 271.

exemplified in twentieth century (Heidegger, Sartre, Jaspers) existentialists. Although Orthodoxy would share with those philosophers the belief that existence cannot be reduced to rational concepts, contemporary Orthodox existentialism (and like it, Pentecostal existentialism) would generally differ with those philosophers on at least two important points: 1) the existential nature of human existence (psyche, soul, will, affections) is most authentic when experienced as a communal participation in, and sharing of, God's Kingdom, and not in an individualized manner; and, 2) the human person does not answer only to himself, but to both the Christian community and the living God. When the words existential and existentialism are being used in the modern philosophic sense the reader will be notified.[75]

Hesychasm, from ἡσυχία (hesychia), is the ascetic practice of being silent and still in the presence of God. Based on New Testament teaching regarding prayer without ceasing,[76] hesychasm dates to the fourth-century asceticism of Evagrius of Pontus (d. 399), but it was made famous especially by Symeon in the eleventh century.[77] Simultaneously called spiritual, true, pure, or interior prayer, hesychasm encouraged perpetual prayer and perpetual awareness (θεωρία, contemplation) of God's presence via co-operation with the Holy Spirit.

To the hesychast, the heart was the seat of the soul. As such the heart must be perpetually guarded and watched over (a practice called *nepsis*), lest the passions[78] rule over the person and distract one from the contemplative experience.

---

[75] Eastern Orthodoxy is more mystical (more expressly oriented around the invisible, non-measurable, and eternal) than most Western models of Christianity, but it is precisely the existential root of a human being's identity that both Orthodoxy and Pentecostalism are attuned to and able to impact tremendously. Such impacting, in both traditions, may result in fantastic or mystical experiences (visions of divine light, or glossolalic outpourings, respectively). Often such impacting will stir one's affections and produce Christian works and fruit. Sometimes it results in the shedding of a quiet tear. All of this is herein classified as existential experience, but not all of it need be classified as mystical.

[76] Lk. 18:1; 1 Thes. 5:17.

[77] Martin Jugie, "Palamas Grégoire," *Dictionnaire de théologie catholique*, vol. XI, 2 (Paris, 1932), col. 1735-1776, develops the historical background of hesychasm. Meyendorff also does this in *A Study of Gregory Palamas*, George Lawrence (tr.) (The Faith Press, 1974²).

[78] We may summarize Palamas by describing the passions as the sinful inclinations, movements, or energies within a human. They lead one to anger, lust, anxiety, hatred, and the like. As such they easily distract and prevent one from internally experiencing the grace of the Holy Spirit.

Apatheia, the state of dispassion,[79] could be achieved through the ascetic practices of fasting and vigils, and together with hesychia it readied the hesychast to
participate in the grace of the Spirit. *Apatheia*, enabled one to give oneself entirely to God.[80] Palamas encouraged the hesychast to enter into *hesychia*, or
contemplative prayer, in order to grow in the knowledge and grace of Christ,
"Therefore, I urge you not to separate your heart from God, but continually
guard it above all with the memory of our Lord Jesus Christ. And while you
implant the Lord's name in your heart, consider nothing else, so that Christ may
show great mercy upon you."[81] This contemplative prayer had two primary
features. Firstly, the hesychast focused himself on the act of breathing. This
concentration on breathing would facilitate the gathering of the *nous* within
oneself, and apart from such existential stillness the divine would rarely be
contemplated.[82] Secondly, amid his breathing, the hesychast would pray the
"Jesus prayer," "Κύριε Ἰησοῦ Χριστὲ Υἱὲ τοῦ θεοῦ, ἐλέσον [με]."[83]

Palamas believed that God had created the human mind in such a way that it
alone of God's creations could transcend itself and participate in the divine.[84]

---

[79] *Apatheia*, Palamas said, "does not consist in mortifying the passionate part of the soul,
but in removing it from evil to good, and directing its energies toward divine things."
The one who achieves *apatheia* has "tamed his irascible and concupiscent appetites. . . to
the faculties of knowledge, judgement and reason in the soul." Meyendorff, *The Triads*,
54.

[80] Meyendorff, *The Triads*, 69.

[81] "Παρακαλῶ οὖν ὕμας, μὴ χωριζέτε τὰς καρδίας ὑμῶν ἀπὸ τοῦ θεοῦ, ἀλλὰ
προσμένετε καὶ φυλάττετε αὐτὴν μετὰ τῆς μνήμης τοῦ κυρίου ἡμῶν Ἰησοῦ Χρισ—
τοῦ πάντοτε, ἕως οὗ ἐμφυτευθῇ τὸ ὄνομα τοῦ κυρίου ἔσω ἐν τῇ καρδία, καὶ μηδέν
ἕτερον ἐννοεῖτε, ἢ ἵνα μεγαλονθῇ χριστὸς εν ὑμῖν." *Contra Barlaam et Acindynum*,
PG, CL, col. 689.

[82] "τοῦτο δ᾽ ἴδει τις ἄν καὶ αὐτομάτως ἑπόμενον τῇ προσοχῇ τοῦ νοῦ. Ἡρέμα γάρ
εἴσεσι τε καὶ ἕξεισι τουτὶ τὸ πνεῦμα, κἀπὶ πάστις ἐναγωνίου σκέψεως. μάλιστα
δὲ ἐπὶ τῶν ἡσυγαζόντων σώματι καὶ διανοία, " ("This specific [process of unifica-
tion] is secondarily spontaneous in the attention of the mind. For the gentle inhaling and
exhaling of the breath is tranquil for those seeking internal observation, especially those
who are hesychasts in body and mind.") *Contra Barlaam et Acindynum*, *PG*, CL, cols.
1109-1112. One focused one's eyes upon the belly so that just as one's gaze was being
stilled and concentrated, so also one's mind was being stilled and concentrated within
one's body. Focussing upon one's breathing was taught earlier by pseudo-Simeon and
Nicephorus. In the middle ages some believed that the powers of concupiscence were
concentrated in the belly, so that to focus on it was to do battle with evil precisely where
it was centered. Meyendorff, *The Triads*, 46, endnotes 50, 59, and 60 on pp. 127-128.

[83] *Contra Barlaam et Acindynum*, *PG*, CL, cols. 689-690.

[84] Meyendorff, *The Triads*, 32.

Human beings, created in the image of God, have an *"organ of vision"* which, when it receives divine grace, is able to transcend itself and commune with God.[85] (Meyendorff said Palamas was little concerned to enter the physiological debates about where the mind [*nous*] was precisely located.)[86] The apostle Paul himself was caught up (ἁρπαγέντα)[87] amid a mystical experience of God, and knew not whether it occurred while he was within or without his body (2 Cor. 12:2). Additionally, based on Scripture, the believers' bodies were held to be the temples of the Holy Spirit (Τὰ σώματα ἡμῶν ναὸς τοῦ ἐν ἡμῖν ἁγίου Πνεύματός ἐστι), and the dwelling places of God (ὅτι ὁ Οἶκος τοῦ θεοῦ ἡμῶν ἐσμεν). The human body so described, Palamas held that one should not think it unusual that God would take up his abode within a person.[88] In this respect Palamas said, "The Kingdom of God is inside us."[89]

For Palamas, the experience of the divine was ineffable, but it was nonetheless real.[90] It often produced "a fountain of holy joy" which caused one to despise things opposed to God.[91] Explaining this existential knowledge of God, Meyendorff said, "The vision of God for Palamas is not an intellectual grasp of an external object, but *an interior participation* in the life of the Holy Spirit: to see God is to share in this life, i.e., become divinised. This involves a complete transfiguration of the whole person, body and soul together."[92]

Most often Palamas likened the experience to a vision of light, though he also described it as transcending physical vision.[93] "This mysterious light," he said, "inaccessible, immaterial, uncreated, deifying, eternal, this radiance of the Divine Nature. . . is at once accessible to sense perception and yet transcends it."[94] This vision is possible for the worthy, but they themselves do not make it happen; it is neither a work of their imagination, a sensation, a product of rea-

---

[85] Meyendorff, *The Triads*, 35. My emphasis.

[86] Meyendorff, *The Triads*, 16.

[87] Gendle, Meyendorff's translator of *The Triads*, repeatedly translated this as "ravished" (34, 38, 53), so as to convey the mystical element (as against the physical notion of transportation) of Paul's and the hesychast's experiences.

[88] *De Hesychastis*, in *PG*, CL, col. 1104; Meyendorff, *The Triads*, 41. *PG* supplied the Scriptural references of 1 Cor. 6:19 and Heb. 3:6.

[89] "ἡ Βασιλεία τῶν οὐρανῶν ἐντὸς ἡμῶν ἐστι. " *De Hesychastis*, in *PG*, CL, col. 1108.

[90] Meyendorff, *The Triads*, 33.

[91] Meyendorff, *The Triads*, 50-51.

[92] Meyendorff, *The Triads*, endnote 11, 121. My emphasis.

[93] Meyendorff, *The Triads*, 33, 37, 39, 63, 100.

[94] Meyendorff, *The Triads*, 80.

son, nor an opinion reached by syllogistic argument. Instead, it only happens by virtue of the Holy Spirit's grace visited upon the one in prayer.[95]

The details of hesychasm's ascetic and mystical prayer as a means of *theosis* may seem rather removed from Athanasius' original, and mostly Christological, formulations. Nonetheless hesychasm did have a Christological orientation, albeit one expressed within the confines of Neo-Platonism. Palamas said, "The hesychast is he who seeks to circumscribe the non-physical in his body."[96] The hesychast, by circumscribing the non-physical (his *nous*) in his body, patterns himself after Christ who earlier had circumscribed himself in a body. Just as the Word, through his incarnation, initiated a new economy in God's workings with humanity and made it possible for matter to become a vehicle for the Spirit, so also the hesychast, by attaining *apatheia*, calming himself and drawing his *nous* into the center of his being, makes his body an avenue for participation in the Spirit. The human's union with the divine not only suffuses the soul with the grace of the Holy Spirit, it also penetrates and divinizes the human body.[97] Palamas held that some of the saints' bodies were so suffused with divinity, or so divinized (having so thoroughly participated in *theosis*), that their very relics continued to be the source of miracles.[98]

In his defense of hesychasm, Palamas made mystical asceticism critical to the contemplation (*theoria*) and experience of God. Indeed, he took Orthodox asceticism, codified it, and gave it a central role in *theosis*.

The aforementioned hesychastic prayer methods must not be misunderstood as directly facilitating an encounter between the Holy Spirit and the image of God (especially the *nous*, yet transcending it) within humanity, as though there could be a simple, if nonetheless rigorous, appropriation of the divine by a human. Rather, Palamas' hesychastic way of life presupposed, and then qualified, the long accepted Orthodox practice of apophatic theology (Η ἀποφατικὴ θεολογία), that is, negative theology.[99] The church had used apophaticism for

---

[95] Meyendorff, *The Triads*, 35, 50. Palamas was not exclusive about receiving grace in hesychia. One could receive grace through the sacraments, and through the laying on of hands. *The Triads*, 53.

[96] "ὡς ἡσυχαστής ἐστιν, ὁ τὸ ἀσώματον ἐν σώματι περιορίζειν σπεύδων." *De Hesychastis*, in *PG*, CL, col. 1109. He referred to John Climacus' ladder of divine ascent.

[97] Meyendorff, *The Triads*, 51, and endnotes 47 and 48 on pp. 126-127.

[98] Meyendorff, *The Triads*, 52.

[99] Zizioulas, 89-92, clarified that apophaticism is not a kind of theological agnosticism, instead it is a way to reorient epistemological foundations away from the human *nous* (as the connection point for knowledge of God) and toward the transcendent God's self-revelation.

centuries to express God's transcendence.[100] The cloud of thick darkness (Ex. 20:21), a cloud simultaneously visible and mysterious, was referred to repeatedly in apophatic teachings to convey the God's transcendence. Pseudo-Dionysius held that the created mind knows only creatures, and therefore "can conceive of God only by the method of exclusion."[101] Palamas similarly taught that God's nature, "since it is the cause of all things. . . and since it is prior to all things, and since the divine nature has conceived all things within itself beforehand in a general and indeterminate manner, its name must be derived from all things inexactly and not in a proper sense."[102]

Palamas noted the importance of apophaticism for intellectual formulations, but then throughout his defense of hesychasm qualified that the *via negativa* could indeed be surpassed through union with the divine. Even though one experienced the incomprehensibility (darkness) of God, one did not understand it, nor could one express it. In order to know and experience the transcendent God genuinely, one must be transformed by the Holy Spirit. Meyendorff summarized Palamas, "Revelation always remains a free and sovereign act of God, by which the Transcendent comes down from his transcendence and the Unknowable makes himself known; therefore the knowledge we have of him is always the knowledge 'through grace' (χάριτι), subject to his will (θελήσει), and dependent on an act (ἐνέργειαι) of condescension (συγκαταβάσει) of Almighty God."[103]

Apophaticism signifies the inability to know God apart from such divine aid.[104] Moreover, the vision of the divine did not result in a positive, or cataphatic,[105] theology because it was a vision of God made possible only by the energies of God.

---

[100] Meyendorff, *A Study of Gregory Palamas*, 203-208, showed that apophaticism especially became prominent in the Neo-Platonic writings of (Pseudo-) Dionysius late in the fifth century.

[101] Meyendorff, *The Triads,* 13.

[102] Capita 106, *The One Hundred and Fifty Chapters*, 203.

[103] Meyendorff, *A Study of Palamas*, 209.

[104] Meyendorff, *The Triads*, 14.

[105] Theology wherein things can be asserted to be positively provable. Barlaam had charged the hesychasts with practicing Messalianism: the belief and practice of attempting to see the divine essence with physical eyes. Palamas, with his distinction between God's essence and energies, denied this accusation.

The Essence and Energies of God

"God, while remaining entirely in Himself," Palamas said, "dwells entirely in us by His superessential power; and communicates to us not His nature, but His proper glory and splendour."[106] Palamas agreed with Orthodox tradition that it was blasphemous to suppose that God's transcendent and unknowable essence could be known or seen. But he nonetheless believed God himself could be both known and seen. To illustrate this dichotomy, Palamas presented Jesus' transfiguration as a model. When the disciples witnessed Christ's transfiguration they in fact saw it with their physical eyes. But they could not have seen God's essence, because Scripture is clear that no one had ever seen God. Certainly the light that shone forth from Christ was no part of his human nature. What they saw, Palamas taught, was the uncreated light, simultaneously called the energies (ἐνέργειαι), grace, or illumination (glory) of God [107]

Prior to creation and time, ideas (παραδείγματα) existed in the mind of God. God thought about creation, his providential exercise over creation, his will, and even about himself. None of these ideas could rightly be called God himself,[108] even though they were without beginning in the mind of God. They are more properly understood as energies of God, having existence within his mind. Furthermore the virtues (attributes) of God are also without beginning in God, even though they are not properly called God's essence. Nonetheless, Palamas believed that because these un-originate works of God stem from

---

[106] Meyendorff, *The Triads*, 39.

[107] Capitae 146, 148, 149, in *TOHFC*, pages 251 and 255 respectively. Jugie, "Palamas Grégoire," 1753, showed that Barlaam refused to admit that the Transfiguration revealed anything about God's divine identity. Barlaam, holding to his rather empirical framework, believed the Transfiguration was a phenomenon of the material realm which immediately afterward dissipated and returned to nothingness ("*la lumiere du Thabor avait été a phénomene d'ordre matériel et passager, produit miraculeusement, au moment meme de la transfiguration, et aussitot apres dissipé et retourné au néant*"). Furthermore, the disciples had not been transformed by this encounter with the divine glory, as the hesychasts so claimed. Instead they were left with imperfect strength, but not full cleansing ("*et les apotres qui en avaient joui étaient encore fort-imparfaits et non pleinement purifiés*").

[108] It must be clarified that Palamas, like Orthodoxy as a whole, emphasizes God's *prosopon* (person) over his essence. Cf. Meyendorff, *A Study of Palamas*, 212-216. In contradistinction to Roman Catholicism, God is not a *quidditas* within which exist three *hypostases*. For the Orthodox He is an ineffable Being whose *quidditas* is defined by the mutual perichoresis of the three *hypostases*.

within God himself, we cannot call them anything other than God himself.[109] Saint Paul himself, Palamas argued, discussed the parts (energies) of the Holy Spirit in such a manner that the Spirit himself was not divided.[110] Palamas quoted Maximus, "God infinitely transcends these participable virtues an infinite number of times."[111] Despite these qualifications between God's essence and energies,[112] Palamas maintained that "God is entirely present in each of the divine energies."[113]

Applying Palamas' theology to our study of *theosis*, it is through one's participation in the divine energies (eternally created graces, illuminations, or attributes) of God, freely given through the Holy Spirit to those who seek God earnestly, that one becomes divinized. Palamas said that the grace and power of divinization is, "bestowed proportionately upon those who participate and, and according to the capacity of those who receive it, it instills the divinizing radiance to a greater or lesser degree."[114] Elsewhere he quoted Paul the apostle and said, "He who clings to the Lord is one spirit with him."[115] These energies of the Holy Spirit are only given to those in Christ. Because both the giver of the graces (the Spirit) and the ontological foundation for their being given (Christ incarnate) are divine *hypostases*, the divine energies must not be misunderstood as mere metaphysical powers. Instead, because the divine energies (graces) are personalized (ἐνυπόστατοι, enhypostasized) - without themselves being the divine *hypostases*[116] - they are the personal God himself raining down to, and into, people who were created after his image. Discussing this process of becoming Christ-like he said, "They became living icons of Christ (ζῶσαι τινες

---

[109] In Capita 68. In *TOHFC*, 163, Palamas said God, the transcendent being, should never be named in the plural, but the graces and energies of God, which enlighten many, and give life to His creation, are called "not only one but also many."

[110] Meyendorff, *The Triads*, 99. Capitae 68 and 74; in *TOHFC* 163, 170-171.

[111] Meyendorff, *The Triads*, 95-96.

[112] These energies, because they are unoriginate in God's mind, are God. But they are not his essence.

[113] Meyendorff, *The Triads*, 95. Thus, Palamas denied that the uncreated energies of God where somehow lesser or inferior manifestations of the divine. God is such that he cannot be partitioned. Meyendorff, *A Study of Palamas*, 214.

[114] ". . .ἀναλόγως τοῖς μετέχουσι χορηγουμένη καὶ κατὰ τὴν ἐπιτηδειότητα τῶν ὑποδεχομένων ἐπὶ μᾶλλον καὶ ἧττον ἐνιεῖσα τὴν θεοποιὸν λαμπρότητα. " Sinkewicz's translation, Capita 69; in *TOHFC*, 165.

[115] "ὁ δὲ κολλώμενος τῷ κυρίῳ ἓν πνεῦμα ἐστιν. " Capita 75; in *TOHFC*, 171. Quoting 1 Cor. 6:17.

[116] Which would result in polytheism and/or pantheism. Cf. Capita 75; in *TOHFC*, 171.

ἐικόνες χριστοῦ) and the same as He is, more by grace than by assimilation."[117]

Whereas Athanasius had focused his Christological discussions upon the incarnation and its ontological role in redemption, Palamas believed that Christ's work (crucifixion and resurrection) was critical for humanity's redemption. Adam's sin had plunged humanity into corruption and mortality, but "by a single death," Palamas said, "he has healed us from a double death and delivered us from a double captivity, that of our soul [corrupted] and that of our body [sentenced to mortality]."[118] Having so redeemed us, our deification is now possible through communion with Christ. (It is noteworthy that the notion of Christ's double-cure, a phrase dear to Wesleyans and many Pentecostals, can be seen within Palamas in the fourteenth century!)

Philosophical Developments

The fourteenth-century Byzantine theological milieu was one wherein apophaticism predominated. Founded upon Neo-Platonism, apophaticism taught that the gulf between humanity and the divine was not so much the result of God's transcendence as it was the result of humanity's limitations. Subsequently, Neo-Platonism held that the human body was a critical part of the problem, and it taught that one must "go beyond oneself," "become detached from created things," and "unify oneself" in order to attain the knowledge of God.[119] Palamas modified Neo-Platonism in the following ways. Firstly, he insisted that the dividing gulf was in fact God's transcendence, not the finitude of the human person or the human mind. Secondly, he taught that even though God, when he chooses to reveal himself by virtue of his energies, can be experienced, it is only on the basis of God's own free choice; thus, even though silence is the appropriate response with respect to God's transcendence, no amount of personal detachment can force God to reveal himself.[120] Thirdly, because a new economy of the knowledge of God was initiated in Christ's incarnation, the human body itself is no longer to be understood as separated from communion with God; the dualism of Platonic thought had finally been vanquished.[121] Fourthly, Palamas insisted that God, as he is (in his transcendent essence), is imparticipatory, but

---

[117] Sinkewicz's translation, Capita 76; in *TOHFC*, 171. Palamas quoted Maximus.

[118] Meyendorff, *A Study of Palamas*, 158.

[119] Dionysius' neo-platonism was devoid of Christological moorings, which allowed it to be interpreted variously. Meyendorff, *A Study of Palamas*, 209.

[120] Meyendorff, *A Study of Palamas*, 203.

[121] Lossky, *The Vision*, 132-133.

God as he relates to us in his energies is intimately participatory; God's dialectic nature consisting of transcendence and immanence was thus sustained. Like Athanasius a millennium before, Palamas, in each of the above mentioned modifications, took existing philosophic paradigms and modified them for Orthodox theology.[122]

Summary

Although Athanasius and Palamas are foundational for understanding the Orthodox doctrine of *theosis*, this brief examination of them has by no means exhausted the historical development of the topic. There were many others who contributed to, and helped develop, the doctrine of *theosis*: Irenaeus, Clement of Alexandria, Origen, The Cappadocians, Pseudo-Macarius, Evagrius of Ponticus, (Pseudo-) Dionysius the Areopagite, Maximus the Confessor, John Climacus, John of Damascus, and Symeon the New Theologian are just a few of those to be named. The brevity of our treatment here notwithstanding, Athanasius and Palamas represent some important features which contemporary Orthodox writers both build upon and openly restate. I will note these features below.

---

[122] Jugie ultimately charged the Palamites with gross heresy, " If Palamas and his followers accused their opponents with errors of the imagination, they themselves were blameworthy of innovatively resurrecting nearly every ancient heresy, and they did not have too much trouble demonstrating it without needing to dress up their thought," ("*Si Palamas et les siens accusaient leurs adversaires d'erreurs imaginaires, ces derniers reprochaient aux novateurs de ressusciter a peu pres toutes les anciennes hérésies, et ils n'avaient pas trop de peine a le démontrer sans avoir besoin de travestir leur pensée*"), "Palamas Grégoire," 1763. But Jugie pressed Palamas' terminology regarding God as He is and God as He relates to creation too far when he said, "As we have already said, the fundamental error in his system is that he admits in God a composition of nature and person, of substance and accidents, of essence and of physical properties following the essence, of a primary and secondary element," ("*Comme nous l'avons déja dit, l'erreur fondamentale du systeme est d'admettre en Dieu une composition de nature et de personnes, de substance et d'accidents, d'essence et de propriétés physiques découlant de l'essence, d'élément primaire et d'élément secondaire*"). We may summarize Palamas by saying that there are ways to speak about God which maintain necessary tensions, but which nonetheless can be asserted as not being cataphatic.

Christology

Both men stressed the ontological dimensions of Christology. Athanasius believed Christology was the objective ontological foundation for *theosis*, even if he said little about how to subjectively appropriate the benefits of Christ (it is quite likely this was assumed by both himself and his audiences). For Athanasius, the incarnation provided the means for our own deification. Palamas agreed that the incarnation was critical, but his emphasis was on subjectively appropriating its ontological benefits. Palamas' subjective appropriation was neither a matter of mere mechanical ritualism, as though the hesychastic practices themselves could produce a state of union with Christ, nor did it advocate the abdication of human personality, as is evident in Eastern religious practices such as yoga.[123] Contrary to both mechanical ritualism and the erasing of human personality, Palamas argued that the contemplative union with God required God's freewill (revealing himself amid *theoria*), and that such union fully engaged the human being (according to one's measure) in an encounter with Christ.[124]

Despite both theologian's Christological emphasis, both men developed their theology within sacramental boundaries. That is, Athanasius' view of Christ as the objective basis of *theosis* in no way contradicted his being subjectively received in the Eucharist. Similarly, while for Palamas Christ could be mystically encountered outside the walls of the church, such existential encounters did not cancel Orthodoxy's sacramental structure.

Salvation

Throughout this examination of Athanasius and Palamas, the Western judicial framework wherein salvation is portrayed as matter of settling a legal debt was almost non-existent. The issues of corruption and death were indeed central to these two men's understandings of salvation, but they were issues primarily overcome through divine healing, not divine fiat. We may summarize them by describing sin as a corrosive and deadly infection within humans which will ultimately prevent us from entering the Kingdom of God. Our internal infection engendered God's humble condescension and mercy, resulting in his incarnation and movement toward us. The Orthodox doctrine of *theosis* involves com-

---

[123] Palamas, believed that causing the mind to go out of the body was "the greatest of the Hellenic errors." *The Triads*, 44.
[124] Meyendorff, *A Study of Palamas*, 210.

munion with God at the deepest levels of human existence, but it is little concerned with expunging one's legal record. For both Athanasius and Palamas, salvation is a critical issue between persons. Whereas restoring the divine-human relationship is critical, salvation is further or more deeply personal in that it emphatically involves restoring the human person so that he or she may be all he or she was intended to be.

The Human Body

Both men affirmed the physical realm. Firstly, Athanasius did so in his emphasis upon Christ's incarnation within, and concomitant sanctification of, human nature. Secondly, Palamas affirmed the physical realm by arguing that it provides an avenue of existential encounter with the divine, even if such an encounter transcends physical definitions. The human person has an organ of vision, an organ which is able to "see" (visibly or existentially), and thereby participate in, God. Neither theologian believed the human body itself was the problem, although both men moved perilously close to such a position if only because they were working within the strictures and vocabulary of Greek philosophy, an ontic philosophy which presupposed that matter is less than spirit.[125]

Transcendence vs Immanence

Both Athanasius and Palamas strongly asserted God's transcendence. This aspect of their theology was clearly in response to the Greek philosophic discussions of the day, and both men believed that the Greeks were correct to assert God's supreme unknowability. However, because both men held Scripture to be an epistemological foundation, both nonetheless believed that God desires for his creations to know him. For them, the God of the old economy (Old Testament) had immanently revealed himself in the new economy (Christ's incarnation and the sacred record of it).

---

[125] Meyendorff, *St. Gregory Palamas and Orthodox Spirituality*, A. Fiske (tr.) (Crestwood, N. Y. : St. Vladimir's, 1974), 96-99, said that Byzantine theology, in contradistinction to Catholic theology, was often suffused with Greek philosophy and was constantly attempting to incorporate it into its epistemology. "The Greek Fathers," Meyendorff said, "could allow no human activity - and especially no intellectual activity - outside the essential Christian experience of life in Jesus Christ," 98.

Both Athanasius and Palamas maintained the tension between God's transcendence and immanence. Athanasius did so as he used ontological categories pertaining to God and his creation, Christ's own incarnation, and human beings having been created in God's image. Palamas affirmed these polarities when he distinguished between the essence and energies of God, and when he simultaneously affirmed God's transcendence and Christ's personal immanence in the incarnation. Both theologians believed that people can, by the grace of the Holy Spirit which is founded upon the incarnation of Christ, become deified. Nonetheless both men affirmed that we are transformed by grace; we cannot thereby become sons of God in the same matter as the eternal Word. God can be *intimately* known and experienced, but he remains *ultimately* known only to himself. As we proceed, this dialectical tension will become important for understanding the contemporary Orthodox on *theosis*.

Church Tradition

Finally, it deserves reasserting that for both Athanasius and Palamas, the writings of the Fathers carried great significance for their own doctrinal formulations. The Fathers comprised and conveyed the ever growing body of knowledge - church tradition - which informed each theologian as he wrote about *theosis*. Athanasius borrowed from and refashioned Origen and the Alexandrian school. Palamas built upon the foundation of many fathers, but especially emphasized the teachings of (Pseudo-) Dionysius and Maximus. Both Athanasius and Palamas believed church tradition supplemented, and guided the interpretation of, Scripture. Additionally, because of their commitment to the Spirit's teaching throughout church history, they increasingly built upon and nuanced the terminology of Greek philosophy.

3

Orthodoxy's Anthropology

'Tell us about the visions that you see,' a monk once said to St.
Pachomius (286-346). 'A sinner like me does not expect to see
visions from God,' Pachomius replied, 'But let me tell you about
a great vision. If you see a holy and humble man, that is a great
vision. For what greater vision can there be than this: to see the
invisible God revealed in his temple, a visible human person?'[1]

The doctrinal differences between the Eastern half and the Western half of
Christendom cannot be accounted for solely by the issues of history,
hermeneutics, or philosophical influences, as crucial as each of those are.
Equally important are the epistemological foundations, the *a priori* assumptions,
that each tradition builds upon. North American evangelicals - and for now we
will include Pentecostals among them - historically have made the salvation of
souls their focus. As both our previous chapter and the above quote typify, the
Eastern Orthodox historically have made the transformation of human beings
their focus. The root cause for this difference of emphasis lies, to a large extent,
with how each tradition understands anthropology. In this chapter we will
develop the Orthodox understanding of the human person, first at creation and
then after the fall.

Human Beings at Creation

Adam in Eden: Communal Presuppositions

"Then God said, 'Let Us make man in Our image, according to Our likeness. . .'
And God created man in His own image, in the image of God He created them,"

---

[1] *First Greek Life of Pachomius* 48 (Halkin, ed.), quoted in Kallistos Ware, "The
Mystery of the Human Person," *Sobornost*, 3:1 (1981), 62.

(Gen. 1:26, 27).[2] The point of departure for Orthodox anthropology is not the human person, it is instead God himself. The applied sciences and the humanities can reveal important data about the human person's makeup and environment, and they can discern processes of cause and effect. But when they are applied apart from the spiritual and communal dimensions of anthropology, they can easily result in myopic, and ultimately idolatrous, views of humanity.[3] Lossky said that secularized and scientific anthropology, defined as analyses of humans based upon observing measurable facts, "can have only an accidental value for theology." For him, Christian theology always works from the Trinitarian and Christological doctrines downward.[4] This ambivalence toward the empirical sciences also stems from their understanding of the fall and its effects on the inner-workings of the human soul.[5] In all of this, the Orthodox believe their anthropological view is not only epistemologically accurate, they believe it is authentically Christian.[6]

---

[2] New American Standard Bible, hereafter referred to as *NASB*. The Orthodox interpret this passage as an inner-Trinitarian conversation. Cf. Vladimir Lossky, *In the Image and Likeness of God*, John H. Erickson and T. E. Bird (eds.) (Crestwood, N.Y.: St. Vladimir's, 1974), 123. Lossky, in his historical survey of the doctrine of image, 125-39, admits that the Hebrew expressions of *selem* and *demut* originally referred to the dominion granted to humans, and were used especially (perhaps) in contradistinction to Egyptian religion where animals were accorded divine status. Nonetheless, Lossky argues that because of the incarnation - because Jesus the Christ revealed God himself - and because the New Testament Christians reinterpreted Scripture in light of Christ's person and work, an argument for Christian progressive revelation must be made. This issue will be addressed further in my chapter on Orthodox Christology.

[3] Ware, *The Orthodox Way*, 46.

[4] Lossky, *Image and Likeness*, 185.

[5] Hierotheos Vlachos, *Orthodox Psychotherapy: The Science of the Fathers*, E. Williams (tr.) (Levadia, Greece: Birth of the Theotokos Monastery, 1994[2]), 206-207. Orthodoxy's ambivalence respecting the empirical sciences will be developed more fully in our chapter on the means of *theosis*.

[6] Indeed, Orthodoxy's epistemological presuppositions raise appropriate challenges for Western Christians. That is, amid our increasingly secularized society, we are plunged into the tension of how much we allow science (and it seems clear that science is increasingly becoming society's religion of preference) to become *the* standard and measure for truth. We may agree or disagree with Orthodoxy's final anthropological definitions, and we may even agree or disagree with their hermeneutical methods, but we must ask ourselves what are our own epistemological presuppositions? Their anthropological presuppositions are unabashedly formulated with regard to God.

Prior to creation, the Triune Godhead existed eternally and enjoyed divine communion within himself. As we saw earlier with Gregory Palamas, the Trinity is not understood by the Orthodox as a substance within which three *hypostases* exist.[7] Rather God is an eternal communion of three divine *hypostases*: the ἀρχή, first cause, and source of being for the other two *hypostases* - the Father; the μονογενή and eternal expression of the Father - the Son; and, the πνεῦμα (divine breath) of God, eternally spirated from the Father - the Spirit. The three exist not by virtue of their sharing a divine substance (which would make divine personhood contingent upon non-personal substance), but by the free willing of the Father. John Zizioulas said, "The substance of God, 'God,' has no ontological content, no true being, apart from communion."[8] God does not exist as an ontological necessity, rather he exists because of his free will. "And," Zizioulas said, "it is precisely His trinitarian existence that constitutes this confirmation: the Father out of love - that is, freely - begets the Son and brings forth the Spirit."[9]

Thus, from eternity God's very identity is one characterized by inter-hypostatic communion and the transcending of individualistic categories. The Father's love is eternally ecstatic (from *ekstasis*, out-going, transcending) in that He freely willed to establish the being and communion of the Son and Spirit, *hypostases* who are "outside Himself."[10] The Father, from his own love, was pleased (but not constrained) to generate and spirate the other two divine *hypostases*. The result is that God's very being, contended Zizioulas, "is identical with an act of communion."[11]

Similarly, the act of creation is also understood by the Orthodox as an act of God's ecstatic love. "The circle of divine love," Kallistos Ware said, "has not remained closed." God wanted beings beside himself, Ware continued, "to participate in the life and love that are his."[12] The universe, like human beings,

---

[7] In keeping with Orthodox preferences, I will describe the threeness of God using *hypostasis* (ὑπόστασις) and not person. Each of the *hypostases* contain all divine attributes of the Godhead, but each is nonetheless irreducible to a divine essence (οὐσία). Cf. Lossky, *Image and Likeness*, 112-113.

[8] Zizioulas, *Being As Communion*, 17.

[9] Zizioulas, *Being As Communion*, 41.

[10] Zizioulas, *Being As Communion*, 91, consistent with Orthodox tradition, denied that this ecstatic movement should be in any way understood as an emanation of the divine.

[11] Zizioulas, *Being As Communion*, 44.

[12] Kallistos Ware, *The Orthodox Way* (Crestwood, N.Y.: St. Vladimir's, 1995, rev. ed.), 44.

is perpetually contingent upon God for its existence and is therefore a participant in God's love. Ware said, "Existence is always a gift from God - a free *gift* of his love, a gift that is never taken back, but a gift none the less [sic], not something that we possess by our own power."[13] Because God is this source of existence for every created thing (but is himself not every created thing),[14] and because God created it "good,"[15] the universe images (shines forth, reflects) God's identity. In the end, even God's creation reflects the communitarian nature of the Triune God.

Applying the aforementioned to anthropology, when God created human beings he made them so that they would image (reflect, from e0ikw\n) his very ontology as one who transcends himself. They were created to transcend themselves through their participation in, and spiritual perception of (via *theoria*), God as well as through their mutual communion of love with one another. In the same way that each member of the Trinity is who he is by virtue of his ecstatic relationship to the others, human beings can only be authentically human persons when they are in communion with one another. In fact, Zizioulas says, "There is no true being without communion."[16] "The genuinely human person," says Ware, "faithful to the image of God the Trinity, is always the one who says, not 'me' but 'us', not 'mine' but 'ours'."[17]

This communal dimension, noted here with respect to anthropology, is a characteristic that manifests itself throughout Orthodox theology, whether it concerns Christology, Pneumatology, Ecclesiology or Eschatology. From its explications of Eden to those concerning the New Jerusalem, Orthodox thought incorporates a corporate dimension. This is a decisive difference of *theological* emphasis between Pentecostals (as well as contemporary evangelicals) and the Orthodox. Whether this emphasis produces a *practical* result which is not surpassed in either evangelicalism or Pentecostalism is doubtful.

---

[13] Ware, *The Orthodox Way*, 45. Emphasis his.
[14] Ware, *The Orthodox Way*, 46, affirms panentheism.
[15] Following Gen. 1:31. The goodness of God's creation reflects His absolute goodness. The Orthodox understand creation's goodness not only in an aesthetic sense, and clearly not only in a moral sense, but in an ontological sense. Cf. Ware, *The Orthodox Way*, 45-46.
[16] Zizioulas, *Being As Communion*, 18.
[17] Ware, "The Mystery of the Human Person," 67.

Adam in Eden: Defining Characteristics

As was implicit in the aforementioned discussion, Orthodoxy primarily makes its anthropological formulations based on humans as they existed *before* the Fall. They believe that if we are to understand fully what constitutes a human person today, we must understand what God originally created the human person to be. To take either the human person as one's subject (for example, through physiology or psychology), or the individual human person as distinct from societal dimensions, to be one's point of departure for anthropological definition is to reproduce the fall itself. That is, the fall occurred when humans determined to make themselves the ultimate point of reference.[18]

That Adam and Eve were created in such a way that they were to reflect and participate in the communitarian likeness of God is widely accepted among the Orthodox. Concerning how the human's image and likeness of God is to be precisely understood there is less unanimity. We will more fully explicate the theology of image and likeness in our chapter on Orthodox Christology below.[19] For now we will limit ourselves to an examination of unfallen humans through the characteristics of *nous*, free will, and potential for growth.

NOUS

As was apparent in our observation of Athanasius and Palamas, both the universe and human beings were created by the Divine Logos (Self-Expression, Reason) of God. The Logos' act of creation was not one whereby he, like a master craftsman, simply constructed the universe and then left it to run on its own. His creative act suffused creation with his own identity as a loving, rational, and ordering Being. Indeed, he marked creation with a kind of divine seal which placed each created thing into a personal relationship with God. Vladimir Lossky said, "The very being of God is reflected in the creature and calls it to share in His divinity."[20] The human person who is himself attuned to the voice of the Logos as he speaks from within his creations can perceive the

---

[18] Zizioulas, *Being As Communion*, 101-102.

[19] We will wait until then because Christology is precisely where the theology of the image surfaces in Orthodox history and theology. For them the issue of image and likeness is firstly a matter of progressive revelation, and secondly a matter of eschatology.

[20] Lossky, *Orthodox Theology*, 53.

world, Lossky said, "as 'musical arrangement': in each thing he hears a word of the Word."[21]

Explaining how it is that creatures participate in God, Lossky quoted John of Damascus, "God contemplated all things before their existence, formulating them in His mind; and each being received its existence at a particular moment, according to His eternal thought and will. . . which is a predestination (προορισμός), an image (εἰκών) and a model (παράδειγμα)."[22] These divine ideas, as we saw earlier in Palamas, are neither God's essence himself, nor are they identical with the created things themselves. Instead they are located in the energies of God, things that Lossky described as "that which is after the essence."[23] The energies are of a dynamic character and stem from God's will. These divine ideas foreordain the creatures' levels of participation in God's energies, with the result that each creature cooperates with God in a manner analogous to its nature. Stated differently, all of creation can share this communion with God, but some beings/things are capable of more intimately sharing it than others. The end result is a carefully defined panentheism wherein God is simultaneously affirmed as ontologically transcendent *and* immanent.[24]

More specifically pertaining to humanity, this aforementioned divine seal is frequently referred to by the Orthodox as the *nous*: a superior faculty through which humans enter into communion with God.[25] Because Orthodoxy is less concerned with acute theological definitions, and more concerned that the believer apprehend the life of the Spirit in the church,[26] *nous* is not uniformly understood. For the Orthodox fathers, *nous* was usually understood to be the defining feature that constituted human persons as having been fashioned in the

---

[21] Lossky, *Orthodox Theology*, 58.

[22] Lossky, *Mystical Theology*, 94. He follows Damascene in *De fide Orth.*, II, 2, *PG*, XCIV, 865A.

[23] Lossky, *Mystical Theology*, 95.

[24] The Orthodox position in this regard, as noted earlier with Palamas, developed within and in response to Greek philosophy. Contrary to Platonism, neither the mind (ideas) of God nor the will of God constitute a superior reality of which the physical world is but a poor reflection.

[25] Lossky, *Mystical Theology*, 127; Ware, *The Orthodox Way*, 48-49.

[26] We must clarify. As it concerns conciliar theology, that is the theology of the ecumenical councils, the Orthodox are extremely dogmatic. But as it concerns the remaining bulk of theological discussion, the Orthodox are rather flexible regarding theological presentation.

image of God.[27] Often this superior faculty is described as the rational aspect of humanity, though even therein it usually connotes a spiritual dimension.[28] Sometimes it is described as the spirit or *pneuma*, by which a person, Ware said, "understands eternal truth about God or about the logoi or inner essences of created things, not through deductive reasoning, but by direct apprehension or spiritual perception . . . a kind of intuition that St. Isaac the Syrian calls 'simple cognition.'"[29] Furthermore, it is also the case that individual authors themselves will describe this feature in a variety of manners.[30] Zizioulas, with his more thoroughgoing ontology, ignored a discussion of the *nous* altogether. These variations aside, there is agreement that the *nous*, or the image, is not something added to human nature; the dichotomy between nature and grace found in some Western models is largely non-existent in Eastern ones.[31] The Orthodox maintain that the *nous* was something God imprinted on, or within, human nature at creation which constituted people as uniquely positioned for relationship with God.[32]

---

[27] The early church especially tended to locate the image of God within the human nous. Lars Thunberg, "The Human Person as Image of God," in *Christian Spirituality, I, Origins to the Twelfth Century*, Bernard McGinn, J. Meyendorff, and J. Leclercq (eds.) (NY: Crossroad, 1988), 295. The early church aside, the "image of God" is understood by the Orthodox alternatively as immortality, potentiality, freedom, and more generally as God-likeness. Maximos Aghiorgoussis, "Sin in Orthodox Dogmatics," *St. Vladimir's*, 21:4 (1977), 180-181. Vlachos, *Orthodox Psychotherapy*, 41, 118-121, also shows the difficulty that the Orthodox fathers had in defining the image. John Meyendorff, *Christ in Eastern Christian Thought,* Y. Dubois (tr.) (Crestwood, NY: St. Vladimir's, 1987²), 114, said there is no consensus among the Orthodox fathers as to the exegesis of Gen. 1:26-27 and the meaning of image. Lossky, *Orthodox Theology*, 123, followed the teaching of Gregory of Nyssa and said that the image of God in people is "necessarily unknowable, for, reflecting the plenitude of its prototype, it too must possess the unknowability of the divine being."

[28] Lossky, *Mystical Theology*, 127.

[29] Ware, *The Orthodox Way*, 48.

[30] Cf. Mantzaridis, *The Deification of Man*, 16, where he shows that Clement of Alexandria, Gregory of Nyssa, and Epiphanius of Cyprus each explained it in a variety of ways.

[31] Lossky, *Orthodox Theology*, 134-125. Meyendorff, *Christ in Eastern Christian Thought*, 124-127, 136.

[32] Lossky, *Mystical Theology*, 126-127. Contrary to pagan Greek portrayals, the human soul (*nous*) was not pre-existent in God. It was created by God and breathed into dust so as to constitute human identity. Lossky, *Orthodox Theology*, 69, said that the act of

Because the *Logos'* own *nous* defined, in an important manner, what it meant to be a human being, and because humankind as the image of God also carried with it relational-communitarian dimensions, the Orthodox do not believe that the fall destroyed or erased the image of God. At Orthodox funerals a hymn is sung containing the words, "I am the image of Your inexpressible glory, even though I bear the wounds of sin."[33] The permanent nature of the *imago dei* is an important distinguishing feature of Orthodoxy not only because it stands in contradistinction to the doctrine of total depravity that characterizes some Protestant theological models (for example, Wesley) but also because it has important ramifications for understanding the Orthodox on the fall and Christian transformation (*theosis*). As will be developed more fully below, Adam's sin truly did introduce a powerful phenomenon into the universe and human existence, but it did not cause Adam to altogether cease being whom God had created him to be. This aspect alone helps account for the fact that the Orthodox view fallen humans more positively than do the Christians of the West.

FREE WILL

The *Logos* not only fashioned Adam and Eve with *nous* - the reflection of his being - he created them with the ability to exercise their wills as they pleased. As had been the case with both his act of creation and his act of facilitating participation in and with him (the granting of *nous*, and/or fashioning human beings after himself), God ecstatically (again with reference to *ekstasis*) created humans with full being. The Triune God did not need created beings to share in, or worship, him.[34] Instead he delighted in creating beings who would participate in him, share in his Being, and thereby transcend themselves. This they could only authentically do through the assent of their free wills. Those creatures without free will cannot transcend themselves, cannot move beyond their own created identity. But those with free will, those who not only know themselves but know those with whom they have fellowship, are able to affirm ecstatic (out-going, transcending) choices which result in not only their own transformation but those with whom they fellowship as well.[35]

God's breathing the soul, provides an analogy for the hesychastic practice of breathing to focus one's *nous* within oneself.

[33] Ware, *The Orthodox Church* (Baltimore: Penguin Books, 1993, rev. ed.), 224.

[34] Lossky, *Orthodox Theology*, 52-53.

[35] Ware, *The Orthodox Way*, 35, shows how it was that the Logos' incarnation was dependent upon the exercise of Mary's free will. Had Mary refused, she would not have been the *theotokos*, the mother of the incarnate God.

Zizioulas described human free will in ontological terms, and in the same way he described the characteristic of communion, he founded it in the Trinity.[36] From eternity the Father freely caused the Word and the Spirit to be. And because the latter two are authentic *hypostases*, they have free will.[37] Each freely participates in loving communion with the other. Each is eternally and freely yielding preference to the other: the Father sends his Word to become the Messiah and King of all; the Word teaches that he came to glorify his Father; and the Spirit comes to bear witness not to himself, but to the Father's Word.[38]

Similarly, when God created Adam and Eve he granted them full being: an ontological existence which not only presupposed their ability (and desire) for communion, but their ability (and allowance) for free willing. The difference between their free will and that of God's own free will, and indeed the more encompassing difference between God and humanity, was one of ontology: whereas God himself is the cause of his being, human persons are not their own cause for being. Because they are creations, people cannot "escape the 'necessity' of [their] existence."[39] Thus, they could only choose between freedom as love (for God and others, which ultimately would facilitate immortal life for themselves) and freedom as negation (the kind of choices that immediately or eventually would terminate their own existence, and which thereby would end their freedom).[40] Had Adam and Eve continued, with the help of God's grace, to make free and loving choices for others persons (in their case, choosing God himself), they would have eventually transcended themselves and participated in God's eternal personhood (*not* substance);[41] the

---

[36] The reader is again referred to the first two chapters of Zizioulas' *Being As Communion*.

[37] Though it must be clarified that because of God's ontology - one characterized by perfect mutual love, perfect mutual freedom, and perfect mutual existence - the three share one will. There are not three wills in God.

[38] The Orthodox believe that the economy of salvation - God's workings *ad extra* - reveal that God's very nature and identity is one of humility and condescension. The Triune God is eternally granting existence, communion, free-will, and glory to the "others" in His being.

[39] Zizioulas, *Being As Communion*, 43.

[40] Thus, *nihilism* is indeed an ultimate and free will decision on the part of a full being. It just does not last very long.

[41] Zizioulas, *Being As Communion*, 49-50. As I stated in my introduction, I will use *theosis* instead of divinization precisely because the latter is too easily misunderstood as a kind of metaphysical fusion with divinity, or with the divine substance; the latter resulting in a kind of dualistic notion whereby the spiritual realm is superior to the

result of which would have resulted in their becoming like God, that is, their *theosis*.

Thus far we have portrayed the Orthodox view of human free will in the sense of choosing others over themselves and in the sense of choosing to commune with others - both of which reflect the ontology of the Trinity.[42] Orthodoxy also clearly describes human free will in moral categories. The human person is distinguished from all other creatures by virtue of the will: one's self-consciousness, voice of conscience, and ability to make moral decisions.[43] When Adam and Eve violated God's command, they deliberately and freely chose to turn away from God and unto themselves. Accordingly, it was through the human will that sin entered the universe. When God created the first humans and gave them free will, he took a risk, Ware said, "Without freedom there would be no sin. But without freedom. . . man would not be capable of entering into communion with God in a relationship of love."[44]

POTENTIAL FOR GROWTH

Humans were the most unique of all God's creations. Unlike the angels, they had a physical body. But like the angels they participated in the noetic (intellectual, spiritual) level of existence. Alone of all God's creations, humans existed at both the physical and noetic levels. Situated as they were among God's creations, human beings thus stood at the ontological center of God's creation. Ware said, "Participating as he does in both the noetic and material

---

physical realm. *Theosis* is *not* a matter of transforming the human body with the divine substance, but a matter of communion with (mutual interpenetration) and participation in (volitionally, existentially, and ontologically) God's person. In its worst forms, Orthodoxy has indeed been guilty of the kind of dualistic notions whereby the physical realm is in need of a metaphysical fusion with the divine. The latter understanding often results in superstitious activities.

[42] Though Zizioulas represents the viewpoint wherein ontology and communion are critical for anthropological definitions, the Orthodox are equally aware of the moral dimensions of human free will (as will be shown herein). I have arbitrarily highlighted the former Orthodox views because I believe they have captured a very Jesus-Christ-ian view of religion which can be helpful for we Pentecostals who almost entirely discuss human free will in morally laden terms. That is, while Jesus was clearly attuned to moral categories, he was equally attuned to the relational dimensions of existence; indeed, the latter were as much a cause for his crucifixion as the former. Or more accurately, for Jesus the two were thoroughly integrated.

[43] Ware, "The Mystery of the Human Person," 62.

[44] Ware, *The Orthodox Way*, 58-59.

realms, [man] is an image or mirror of the whole creation, an *imago mundi*, a 'little universe' or microcosm. All created things have their meeting place in him."[45] Similarly, Lossky taught, "man, penetrating the indefiniteness of the visible to bind it again to the invisible, is the central being of creation, the being who reunites in himself the sensible and the intelligible and thus participates, richer than the angels, in all the orders of 'earth' and of 'heaven.'"[46] Along with their ontological makeup (*nous*, free will, noetic apprehension and physicality), humans were also unique in that God had created them to move beyond themselves, as noted earlier, and have fellowship with God.

The Orthodox, despite their high view of humans at creation (as the above has shown) do not teach that Adam was a perfect human being. He was not created with a perfect knowledge of God or the universe. He was not formed out of dust with perfect wisdom for living. Neither was he created with perfect holiness, though this does not mean he was in anyway sinful.[47] He was not like, said Eusebius Stephanou, "a manufactured article that leaves the factory as a finished commodity."[48] Instead he was created with αὐτεξοψσία (inner self-determination); he could choose to grow in godliness, knowledge, and wisdom, or he could choose to pursue his own desires and interests.[49] Adam was like an infant, said Ware, "perfect not so much in an actual as in a potential sense." "God the creator," Ware continued, "set Adam's feet upon the right path, but Adam had in front of him a long road to traverse between reaching his journey's

---

[45] Ware, *The Orthodox Way*, 49.

[46] Lossky, *Orthodox Theology*, 64. Thunberg, "The Human Person as Image of God," 295-297, said that the notion of people as microcosms can be traced back into Greek antiquity to Democritus and Plato. The early Christian fathers probably borrowed from Philo, the Jewish philosopher and theologian, as they developed this position. It was especially the three Cappadocians who especially made the notion prevalent.

[47] Zizioulas, *Being As Communion*, 100, said the position wherein "perfection [belonged] to the original state of things" originated with Plato, and was then adopted by Origen and Augustine (the latter so influential for the West).

[48] Eusebius Stephanou, *Man: Body, Soul and Spirit* (Fort Wayne, Indiana: Logos Ministry for Orthodox Renewal, 1974), 4.

[49] Lossky, *Orthodox Theology*, 135. Thunberg, "The Human Person as Image of God," 297, contended that Irenaeus was the first to develop the idea that the first humans existed in a state of immaturity.

end."[50] The long road before him was traversable only if he, of his own free will, cooperated with God's grace.[51]

The Orthodox describe this cooperation between the human and divine as synergy (*synergeia*, in Greek): the working together of the human person's energies and those of God.[52] People were, and are, unable by themselves to raise themselves to God's level of existence. God, respecting the free will of human beings, would never force fellowship with himself (salvation, in strictly Augustinian models) upon anyone. Accordingly, there could be no plan of divine fiat whereby God predetermined the saved and the damned. God is perpetually reaching out (moving beyond himself in *ekstasis*) for fellowship with humans, but only when human persons respond to God's grace and thereby enjoy communion with him can synergy occur.

Orthodox anthropology is peerless in the sense that it incorporates a cosmic dimension.[53] Man, uniquely the microcosm of creation, is understood to be the *hypostasis* of the cosmos. Man is the personalization of God's created order. Contrary to pagan Greek philosophy and the far-Eastern religions, man is not saved through the universe. Neither is he to become depersonalized, or dis-individualized, into the larger cosmic existence. Instead, the created universe becomes "personalized" and finds its meaning through man's *theosis*. Lossky said, "To the universe, man is the hope of receiving grace and uniting with God, and also the danger of failure and fallenness. 'Creation anxiously awaits this revelation of the sons of God,' writes St. Paul."[54] The unique position among creation enjoyed by the first humans was not for their benefit alone. They were created as they were in order to present God to creation and creation back to

---

[50] Ware, "The Mystery of the Human Person," 69.

[51] Ware, *The Orthodox Way*, 52, appropriately clarified that while the theory of evolution is not necessarily implied within Orthodox formulations of *theosis*, neither are the two incompatible.

[52] The precise word is used repeatedly in Paul's New Testament letters. Therein it refers to the work of the Gospel, or the work of the Kingdom, which people share with God. The Orthodox personalize it so that the individual is understood to cooperate with God's work of personal transformation.

[53] I use the word "man" instead of "man and woman" (or "humanity," "mankind," et al) here because it conveys the singular dimension in contrast with the plurality of the cosmic order. The plural forms here are also quite burdensome regarding the use of "*hypostasis*" in the discussion; and, the use of "*hypostases*" opens up avenues of thought which are problematic for the issue.

[54] Lossky, *Orthodox Theology*, 71. He refers to Rom. 8:19-21.

God; this they could accomplish in their ecstatic and free loving of God, one another, and God's creation. Concerning mankind's ultimate purpose Lossky said:

> Finally, this cosmic Adam, by giving himself without return to God, would give Him back all His creation, and would receive from Him, by the mutuality of love, that is to say by grace, all that God possesses by virtue of His nature. Thus, in the overcoming of the primordial separation of the created and the uncreated, there would be accomplished man's deification, and by him, of the whole universe.[55]

Positing humanity to be the nexus and apex of the universe is an unpopular, and often perceived as arrogant, position in today's North American society, an increasingly secular society where human beings are frequently portrayed as just one more of the earth's creations. Often it is maintained that we are animals with more reason than the others, but nevertheless we are just one more species in a world of species. Such views have not gone without impact among the churches, Protestant ones especially. But the lofty anthropological views of the Orthodox should ultimately prosper the earth, not injure it. That is, if human beings are indeed responsible to God to be priests who lovingly care for, nurture, and personalize creation they cannot violate it for their own gain.[56]

It stands to reason that if the Orthodox view Adam and Eve in their Edenic state somewhat differently from Western Christians, so too must they view them differently in their fallen state. Again, if Adam and Eve were not established with perfect knowledge, wisdom, or mature holiness then how do the Orthodox describe the fall? To that issue we now turn.

Human Passions and the Fall

The fall, as noted above, occurred when Adam and Eve chose to break fellowship with God and posited themselves as their own point of reference: they became their own gods. In all of this their will played the critical role.

---

[55] Lossky, *Orthodox Theology*, 74.

[56] The applications for such a microcosmic *cum* macrocosmic worldview are enormous and range from the simple issues of pet ownership and home gardening, to the larger issues of agriculture, forestry, and transportation. The view that humans are just one species among the animal kingdom will ultimately justify horrific attitudes and practices, both for humans and the earth.

Lossky said, "the origin of evil lives in the liberty of creatures."[57] Alongside the human will it is necessary to add the dimension of the passions. There is a Patristic stream, initiated especially by Clement and Origen at the Alexandrian school, and then fortified by the monastic leader Evagrius of Pontus (d. 399), which holds that the human passions played, and continue to play, a critical role in the human will's move toward sin. Not all Orthodox theologians accept the precise Alexandrian ideas in this regard,[58] others modify them.[59] But because the themes of passion and *apatheia* are prevalent in Orthodoxy, we will treat them briefly here.[60]

Adam and Eve sinned by *desiring* to taste the fruit of the knowledge of good and evil. It was not just their choosing to sin that constituted original sin, but the desire - the passion - that motivated their wills to choose disobedience that constituted original sin. Adam and Eve were created with a disposition to naturally know and love God. As was noted in the former chapter, Adam and Eve's *theoria* of God involved a participatory knowing. It then follows that their knowledge of God was not simply through intellectual apprehension.[61] Despite their created disposition for communion with God, Adam and Eve allowed the tempter to entice their passions and offer the illusion of good: the "taste" of autonomous knowledge. Their knowledge was founded *in* God, but the tempter

---

[57] Lossky, *Orthodox Theology*, 80.

[58] Lossky, *The Vision of God*, 38-60, shows how the Alexandrians adopted and modified Platonic ideas of perfection. The result was that the Patristic fathers after them either had to ignore (as in the case of Athanasius) or modify their position that perfection (*theosis*) is gained by a kind of philosophic spirituality. Orthodox theologians generally avoid Origen's ideas (excluding Gregory of Nyssa who was indeed an Origenist).

[59] Ware, *The Orthodox Way*, 116-117, shows how some modify the original position.

[60] The topic of the passions and apatheia are dealt with in a vast array of Orthodox writings, whether theological (like those examined herein) or spiritual in nature. As an example of the latter see, Dumitru Staniloae, *Prayer and Holiness: The Icon of Man Renewed in God*, A. M. Allchin (tr.) (Oxford: The Sisters of the Love of God, 1982); Lorenzo Scupoli, *Unseen Warfare*, Nicodemus of the Holy Mountain (ed.), Theophan the Recluse (rev.), E. Kadloubovsky and G. E. H. Palmer (tr.) (Crestwood, N.Y.: St. Vladimir's, 1995). Scupoli was a Roman Catholic priest, but upon Nicodemus' translation of Scupoli into Greek the work became a classic for Orthodox asceticism.

[61] That Adam and Eve's enjoyed a knowledge of God which was communal, that is participatory, only heightens the scandal of their fall. They not only knew God via his instructions to them, they had enjoyed communion with him; and still they chose to disobey.

offered knowledge *apart from* God.[62] Instead of wrestling against the temptation to sin, Adam and Eve participated in the tempter's idea of sinning: they contemplated the "'thoughts' (λογισμοὶ) or images" that rose up within their souls and subconsciousnesses, and they allowed themselves to entertain the seduction (προσβολή) of alien thoughts, thoughts that tempter introduced into their consciousnesses. Thus, original sin was born when they allowed their minds to become united with the tempter's thoughts.[63]

Although they were the icons (images) of God who were created to reflect God in their minds and wills, they became like broken mirrors, taught Lossky, reflecting the image of formless matter (sin as non-being). They allowed the passions to violate their created disposition. Ever after Adam and Eve, the passions have easily served to obstruct communion with God.[64] All of Adam and Eve's progeny are thus, quoted Lossky, "offspring of a tarnished race."[65]

The passions impact the person and his or her needs, ranging from food to self-interest. From the Greek verb *pascho* (to suffer), passions are those energies or influences that cause sickness within the human soul. The passions are not necessarily sins. Sins are things which the mind or body manifests. Passions are the movements within the soul, the influences that lurk within the soul and, because of sin, cause it disease. One author, Hierotheos Vlachos, described the passions as "the wounds of the soul." When a temptation enters the human soul and is therein acted upon it becomes sin. When this same sin, Vlachos continued, "is repeated many times and the organism acquires a habit, passion comes into being." The passions are neither essences nor *hypostases*. Instead, like sin itself, the passions feed on being. They could not exist apart from a person, and they feed on, or live within, the naturally created powers of the soul which were to engender virtue.[66] Moreover, there is a perceived existential hierarchy among the passions, a hierarchy which moves from the simplest forms of sin toward the more demonic: "gluttony, fornication, avarice, grief, wrath,

---

[62] Again, the general Orthodox antipathy toward science will be addressed more fully later, but they tend to view scientific knowledge as knowledge apart from God.

[63] Lossky, *Orthodox Theology*, 133.

[64] Lossky, *Orthodox Theology*, 135. Lossky took the mirror analogy from Gregory of Nyssa, *On the Structure of Man*, XII, in *PG* 44, col. 164.

[65] Lossky, *Orthodox Theology*, 136. Lossky quoted St. Macarius of Egypt, *Spiritual Homilies* XXIV, 2, XLIII, 79 in *PG* 34, col. 664, 776-777.

[66] Vlachos, *Orthodox Psychotherapy*, 217-252. The quote is from p. 220.

weariness, vainglory, and pride." Each of these passions, John Meyendorff said, "imply interest in sensible things and distraction from God."[67]

Ware qualified that the passions need not be understood as intrinsically evil. Neither must they be understood as "inward diseases alien to man's true nature." Instead they can be understood as "dynamic impulses originally placed in man by God." Because they were created by God, these impulses were good, but because of sin's presence they have been distorted. The older Alexandrian tradition held that the passions must be rooted out, until a state of *apatheia* (dispassion) is reached. Ware, who represents a more progressive position, taught that these passions can be redirected in Christ so that, "uncontrolled rage [is] turned into righteous indignation, spiteful jealousy into zeal for the truth, sexual lust into an eros that is pure in its fervor." He continued, "the passions, then, are to be purified, not killed; to be educated, not eradicated; to be used positively, not negatively."[68]

Apatheia is not the passive indifference or open ambivalence of Stoicism. Rather, it is simultaneously the freedom from being ruled by the passions and the process of becoming so united to God that one's appetites are thereby altered. As the Orthodox consistently argue it, *apatheia* is gained primarily through prayer (especially hesychastic versions) and asceticism. Evagrius taught that dispassion and love were two sides of the same coin. Following him Ware said, "If you lust, you cannot love. Dispassion means that we are no longer dominated by selfishness and uncontrolled desire, and so we become capable of true love."[69]

Additionally, concerning the passions, the issue of *eros* consistently comes to the fore in Orthodox explications. *Eros*, understood specifically in regard to human sexuality, is generally viewed by the Orthodox as an evil passion. Maximus the Confessor especially made this view prominent. He was heavily influenced by monastic and ascetic thought,[70] but his position regarding *eros* continues to be followed because he interwove ascetic views with a brilliant - if

---

[67] Meyendorff, *Byzantine Theology*, 67.

[68] Ware, *The Orthodox Way*, 116-117. The quotes are found on p. 116. Vlachos, *Orthodox Psychotherapy*, 249, similarly agreed that the passions are the soul's stirrings which have been perverted.

[69] Ware, *The Orthodox Way*, 117.

[70] One only needs to survey the literature on Orthodox spirituality and prayer, or recall that one must be celibate to be either an Orthodox patriarch or an Orthodox bishop, to know that the influence of monasticism and asceticism have not faded on the contemporary scene.

curious - theological scheme. It was necessary for Adam, Lossky said summarizing Maximus, to "suppress in his own nature the division into the two sexes, in his following of the impassible life according to the divine archetype." But, Maximus believed, God knew *man* (the gender exclusivity is intended here by the Orthodox) would fall, and thereby incur death. Because God did not want his supreme creation - man - to stop existing with Adam's death, he created Eve. The duality of human gender was a division which has, Lossky said, "no relation to the divine Archetype, but which, as we have said, is in agreement with irrational [fallen] nature." The division into two sexes only became definitive after the fall.[71]

Unlike Ware or Lossky, Zizioulas portrayed the passions in ontological terms, rather than in visceral terms. For Zizioulas, the human passions are rooted in our very fallen biology. He believed there are two "passions"[72] which plague humanity, and both of them derive from our biological constitution. The first passion is our ontological necessity: the human *hypostasis* is "inevitably tied to the natural instinct, to an impulse which is 'necessary; and not subject to the control of freedom."[73] The second is, Zizioulas said, "*individualism*, of the separation of the hypostases." God's intention was the communion of unique human *hypostases*, not their rabid individualization where each is only able to "affirm their identity as *separation* from other unities or 'hypostases.'" Both of these passions (ontological necessity and individualism) result in death, and human nature (what it means to be human, the nature shared by all people) is only perpetuated through the creation of other human beings. But alas, those human beings too are limited by both of the aforementioned passions, they too are limited by a nature that, Zizioulas stated, "precedes the person and dictates its laws (by 'instinct')."[74] "This 'failure' of the survival of the biological hypostasis is not the result of some acquired fault of a moral kind (a transgression)," continued Zizioulas, "but of the very *constitutional make-up* of the hypostasis, that is, of the biological act of the perpetuation of the species."[75]

---

[71] Lossky, *Mystical Theology*, 108-109. The quotes are from p. 109. Lossky follows Maximus *in De hominis opificio*, XVI, *PG,* 44, col. 181-185.

[72] Again, the things we suffer.

[73] Zizioulas, *Being As Communion*, 50. By this necessary impulse he means that we have an instinct whereby we *must* live. Existing via this instinct means we do not exist freely, that is without contingency (only God, or deified beings, exist thusly).

[74] Zizioulas, *Being As Communion*, 51. The former quote was also from p. 51. Original emphasis.

[75] Zizioulas, *Being As Communion*, 52. His emphasis.

Because of our passionate nature[76] we are figures of tragedy. Positively, we are fashioned as the result of ecstatic love: erotic love. Negatively, this ecstatic act is interwoven with the aforementioned natural instinct, and implies our ontological contingency. Positively, we are born having *"hypostatic* fact."[77] Negatively, this hypostatic factuality is part and parcel of having a human body, the very characteristics of which are individuality and death. The body can be used to have communion with others (for example, physical touch, conversation, artistic expression). But the body can be used both to conceal hypocrisy and to serve as a "fortress of individualism," so that even the saints cry, "Wretched man that I am! Who will deliver me from this body of death?" (Rom. 7:24). Continuing, Zizioulas said, "The tragedy of the biological constitution of man's hypostasis does not lie in his being a person because of it; it lies in his tending towards becoming a person through it and failing."[78]

Maximus maintained, said Zizioulas, that "the true 'being' of man is found only in his eschatological state."[79] That is, to understand God's purpose for mankind most accurately, we must look to the eschaton. For it is in the eschaton that the division of the sexes will no longer be definitive. It is in the eschaton that the human body and eros will no longer be "bearers of death." The human body and human passions will not be abandoned, but they will change their activity and become participants in love, freedom, and life, all without contingency.[80]

---

[76] The nature that we endure.

[77] The Orthodox distinguish between individuality and personhood. We were created to be persons, not starkly distinct automatons. Following the doctrine of the Trinity (which, I reiterate, is the Orthodox' point of departure for anthropology), to be an *hypostasis* (person) is to participate in the common nature shared by all *hypostases*. To be an *hypostasis* is not to insist that one's own *hypostasis* is the definitive measure for the common nature shared by the community.

[78] Zizioulas, *Being As Communion*, 52.

[79] Zizioulas, *Being As Communion*, n. 46. Zizioulas also followed Maximus in *De hominis opificio*, XVI, *PG,* 44.

[80] Zizioulas, *Being As Communion*, 53. Zizioulas believes that we can realize our true hypostatic existence in the church, so that our ecclesial existence (as he defines it) prefigures, and participates in, the eschatological existence of the eschaton.

Human Beings after the Fall

Death and Corruption

As the Orthodox consistently present it, the primary consequence of the fall was death. When Adam and Eve were tempted by "the ruler of the world"[81] (the one "who was a murderer from the beginning,")[82] they chose to follow their own interests above God's. That free-willing privilege was indeed theirs. The problem was, that by rejecting God's intent and purpose for them, they rejected their previous ontological existence as those with the potential of unhindered fellowship with God and its resultant immortality. They knew that God's desire for them was their own *theosis*: that they might become deified. Accordingly, when the serpent said, "you will be like God," he was not speaking concepts unfamiliar to them. Rather, he was luring them toward making a shortcut, albeit a vain and perverse one, toward their own deification. Whereas God wanted to transform them through participation in himself, the tempter wanted to transform them as he had transformed himself: by becoming autonomous against God, a god apart from God. In their vain attempt to circumvent God, they failed to achieve their very destiny, their *theosis*.[83]

Western theology, especially as it follows Tertullian, Augustine and Anselm, holds that Adam's sin violated God's command and incurred his punishment of death. Indeed, because of Adam's status as humankind's federal head, the entire human race was plunged into original sin and thereby became deserving of the verdict of death.[84] As Augustine put it, the human race is a *"massa damnata*, a

---

[81] Jn. 12:31; 14:30; 16:11.

[82] Jn. 8:44.

[83] Lossky, *Orthodox Theology*, 81-82. See also, Aghiorgoussis, "Sin in Orthodox Dogmatics," 182.

[84] Reinhold Seeberg, *Text-book of the History of Doctrines*, C. Hay (tr.) (Grand Rapids: Baker, 1954), 1:132-4, reveals that Tertullian's (f. 195-220) soteriology was characterized by legal formulations whereby "the fundamental relation of man to God is that of fear;" satisfaction must be paid to God in response to His wrath. In the theology of Augustine (354-430), just as Adam's sin becomes ours through procreation, so also his guilt becomes ours; cf. Seeberg, 1:342-343. Even babies are born guilty of Adam's sin. Anselm (d. 1109), in his *Cur deus homo?*, took theological formulations and wove them together with "juristic principles," especially the notion of "punishment or satisfaction (*poena aut satisfactio*)." Seeberg, 2:66-70, rightly points out that Anselm, despite his

horde fated for hellfire."[85] Western systematic theology is thus laden with legal and judicial terminology. However, Eastern theology, as has been repeatedly noted, takes an ontological vista concerning sin and redemption (though to be fair, Western theology is also familiar with, and employs, ontological categories; the sacramental doctrine of the eucharist is just one example of Western ontology). The original sin was the introduction of death (non-being, or perhaps also fairly understood as the principle of contra-being) into God's creation. Put more simply, original death resulted in sin. Adam and Eve's ancestors thus receive a "congenital inheritance" which leads them to sin. Since Adam and Eve, the human race is, Meyendorff said, "involved in a sort of vicious circle of death and sin." What all human beings receive from Adam and Eve is death, not guilt (Rom. 5:12). Each human person is thus responsible - and will only be judged - for his or her own sins, sins which result from the death passed on from Adam. (This does not mean the Orthodox believe anyone could live a sinless life apart from Christ.)[86]

As Orthodoxy argues it, the original sin did not cause God to bring the punishment of death, instead the original sin naturally resulted in death.[87] God's

---

having done well to assert the importance of Christ's atoning death, overemphasized the relationship between God and humanity as "that of a subject to his legal ruler." Anselm's portrayal underemphasized both Jesus Christ's life (in contrast to his death) and the dimension of intimate communion between the divine and human.

[85] Denise L. Carmody and J. T. Carmody, *Mysticisn,* 199. See also Meyendorff, *Catholicity and the Church* (Crestwood, NY: St. Vladimir's, 1983), 67.

[86] Meyendorff quoted in Boris Bobrinskoy, "The Adamic Heritage According to Fr. John Meyendorff," *St. Vladimir's,* 42:1 (1998), 38. Meyendorff's position is based upon a study of Augustine in contrast to Cyril of Alexandria, Theodoret of Cyrus, and Gregory Palamas. Cyril and Theodoret, despite the fact that the two represented conflicting schools of interpretation (Alexandria and Antioch), both agreed that the *eph' ho* of Rom. 5:12 referred to death so that death, not guilt, is passed on to all humans. Augustine, for his part, based his interpretation upon a Latin version of the text wherein the *in quo* was understood to mean that "in Adam" all have sinned and thereby deserve God's wrath and punishment. Babies, in Orthodoxy, are not born guilty of sin, but because the principle of non-being (death, sin, $\phi\theta o\rho\acute{\alpha}$-the latter linking the former two) is at work in them from the beginning they will (and indeed all eventually do) sin. The horrific issue (both pastorally, and in the sense of God's justice) of unborn (aborted, miscarried, et al) babies being cast into eternal hellfire because of Adam's sin, which by necessity holds in Augustinian models, is not a factor in Orthodox theology.

[87] It deserves qualification that both Lossky and Ware hold that physical death is ultimately a merciful act on God's part because it prevents our eternal existence in

instruction to Adam and Eve, "do not eat or you will die,"[88] is not interpreted by the Orthodox as a threat against affronting the divine. It is interpreted as a warning: God was not going to kill them for their disobedience, they would quite naturally die by separating themselves from his being, purpose and intent. The "murderer from the beginning" murdered humanity when he enticed them to introduce death into the universe.[89]

Adam and Eve's corrupting act infected the created realm's ontological structure with the corrupting power of non-being (φθορα/). By an act of free willing, they made themselves to become living contradictions, Zizioulas said, "in the absurdest terms," because they had become, "dying beings."[90] As was noted earlier, Adam and Eve's existence was contingent upon another source - God - which Itself was without contingency. When they chose to separate themselves from their source of being, they actualized within themselves the potential for non-being. Their sin did not *create* something new within the universe, because evil (non-being) has no creative power. Instead, their sin actualized, Zizioulas said, "*the limitations and potential dangers inherent in creaturehood, if creation is left to itself.*" He continued, "For since the fall results from the claim of created man to be the ultimate point of reference in existence (to be God), it is, in the final analysis, the state of existence whereby the created world tends to posit its being ultimately with reference to itself and not to an uncreated being, God."[91] Adam and Eve placed their own being (existence) prior to the truth of communion with God, and thus the communion was shattered. No longer were they defined by their relationship with God. Usurping the divine-human relationship, the human self was posited as supreme.

Because sin irrupted through personality (both the tempter's and human's), and because, like a parasite, it feeds on personal being, sin manifests itself in very personal ways. It is, Lossky instructed, "revolt against God, that is to say, a personal attitude."[92] The irruption of death and corruption occurred personally

---

corrupted and decaying bodies. Lossky, *Orthodox Theology*, 83, 113; Ware, *The Orthodox Way*, 60.

[88] Gen. 2:17. My paraphrase.

[89] John Meyendorff, "Theosis in the Eastern Christian Tradition," in *Christian Spirituality, III, Post-Reformation and Modern*, 471-472. This position also implies that the murderer of humanity himself had been previously corrupted. Cf. Ware, *The Orthodox Way*, 57.

[90] Zizioulas, *Being As Communion*, 105.

[91] Zizioulas, *Being As Communion*, 102. Earlier emphasis his.

[92] Lossky, *Orthodox Theology*, 80.

within the human will, or as the Orthodox would say, in the noetic dimension of human existence. Nevertheless, sin's corrupting power (or perhaps sin's corrupting non-power) equally pervades the physical realm. People are subject to physical pain and disease. We have to cope with the debilitating effects and physical disintegration of aging. The whole of human suffering is ultimately attributable to the introduction of sin onto the plane of human existence.

Sin as Fragmentation

Individualism, a notion so cherished and championed in the United States, *is*, say the Orthodox, *the result of the fall*.[93] People are born into existence as beings whose interests are separated from those of God. Quite naturally, one's focus becomes oneself. One's struggle for survival in a fallen world pervaded by death, corruption, and fragmentation, quite naturally occurs at the expense of one's neighbor and becomes, said Meyendorff, "a struggle for *my* property, *my* security, and *my* interests."[94]

Lossky contrasted the fall's resultant selfishness with God's intended order. God had created people in such a way that they were supposed to share - by authentically affirming each other and each other's unique identity - what it meant to be human. Lossky said, "each person is an absolutely original and unique aspect of the nature common to all." However, the fall caused humans to believe that each one now owns, he taught, "a portion of human nature for himself, so that 'my' will contrasts 'myself' with all that is 'not I.'" The result is that while individualism is championed, personhood is denigrated. "In our habitual experience," continued Lossky, "we know neither true personal

---

[93] My emphasis. I refer here to contexts and emphases, not entire theological frameworks. Western (evangelical) models of theology and spirituality, for too long shackled by the phrase, "a personal relationship with Jesus," are increasingly becoming aware of the corporate dimensions of Christianity. Eastern models, as was noted earlier concerning human free will and ontology, and as will be apparent in this subsection, never deny the hypostatic uniqueness of each human. The latter issue of individuality will also be developed more fully in the next chapter on Orthodox Christology.

[94] Meyendorff, "Theosis in the Eastern Christian Tradition," 472. Original emphasis.

diversity nor true unity of nature. We see on the one hand human individuals, and on the other hand human collective totalities, in perpetual conflict."[95]

To the above levels of fragmentation, the Orthodox also add *existential fragmentation:* the human person is even divided against himself. At the moral level, one is, "weakened in will," Ware said. As the apostle Paul described it, one struggles with whether to choose goodness or evil. Often one is even, continued Ware, "morally paralyzed. . . we find ourselves caught in a situation where all our choices result in evil."[96]

When a person cooperates with sin,[97] one becomes increasingly depraved, darkened in character, puffed up with pride, numbed with indifference to others, and blinded by avarice and sensual pleasure.[98] The harmonic order which God intended for a person's *nous*, heart, and intelligence are cast headlong into chaos by the presence of sin. Because of sin, the heart - the seat of the soul - no longer governs the *nous* and the intelligence as it should. Instead, as is especially made evident in Western civilization,[99] the intelligence is exalted to a place not properly its own (here Vlachos paints in unfairly stereotypical strokes and would have us also broadly characterize Western Christianity).[100] Because mankind is less able to know God with the *nous* and heart, the intelligence has been exalted as the supreme epistemological avenue. And, because it cannot find empirical reasons to believe in God, the human intelligence concludes that there is no God.[101]

As is evident in the aforementioned, selfishness is a multi-edged sword. It severs oneself from one's true source of life and being (God). It severs the whole of humanity from itself; each insists on his or her own autonomy. Selfishness cleaves persons in the above-mentioned existential fashion. But selfishness does not stop at the personal dimensions of existence, it also cuts

---

[95] Lossky, *Image and Likeness*, 107.

[96] Ware, *The Orthodox Way*, 61. He follows Paul in Rom. 7:18-24.

[97] So that just as there is synergy with God's grace (shown later herein), there is also synergy with sin.

[98] Vlachos, *Orthodox Psychotherapy*, 134-135.

[99] Vlachos, *Orthodox Psychotherapy*, 212.

[100] Vlachos, *Orthodox Psychotherapy*, 121-123, 205. Vlachos follows Maximus, Palamas, and the Desert Fathers in presenting the intricate psycho-somatic structure of the human person. I will touch on this further in my chapter on the Orthodox means of *theosis*, but because Vlachos' discussion in this regard is very extensive the reader is referred to see Vlachos himself, 97-241.

[101] Vlachos, *Orthodox Psychotherapy,* 207-208.

away a proper understanding of all of life. A sinful person no longer looks, Ware said, "upon the world and other human beings in a eucharistic way, as a sacrament of communion with God." Sin causes one to stop regarding God's creation and other people as God's gifts which can be, Ware continued, "offered back in thanksgiving to the Giver." Instead the others, and God's creation, are treated as objects to be possessed. They become mere means for one's self pleasure and satisfaction. They become things, Ware said, "to be grasped, exploited and devoured." Athanasius believed God's creation reflected the personality and love of God, but the fall made it so that one can no longer gaze upon God through his creation. The formerly transparent window of creation was, because of sin's marring power, made to be opaque.[102]

The fall, perhaps better understood in Orthodox terms as the rupture, introduced chaos into God's created order. Chaos is all that is contrary to God's being himself: death, corruption, fragmentation, selfishness, deceitfulness, and so on. The unity and order that existed upon the completion of God's creative act, the unity and order that characterized Adam and Eve's initial relationship with God, was thrown into disorder. The harmony and mutual penetration of diversity (God's creations) with unity (God's irreducible self) was fractured. *Theosis*, as will be increasingly developed, is the process which re-unifies the whole.[103]

Sin and the Imago Dei

Contrary to Augustinian formulations, the Orthodox do not assert that the fall caused human beings to become totally depraved,[104] but neither do they assert

---

[102] Ware, *The Orthodox Way*, 59-60. Incidentally, John Calvin used the same metaphor in his discussion of the Fall's effects.

[103] For years now I have been taken back by the Orthodox' consistent, and insistent, movements toward monism. There are many catalysts for this, including eschatology (the end for the Orthodox prophetically judges the present and calls it toward itself), Christology (the Orthodox see Christ incarnate as the recapitulation and recreation of all creation), and Trinity (as was noted earlier). Though it seems clear that those theological catalysts are primary, a secondary catalyst is Orthodoxy's reliance upon and modification of Greek philosophical constructs (if only because their theology is often in response to those). Zizioulas, *Being As Communion*, 16, 68-70, clarifies that the Greeks (pre-Christian and non-Christian) viewed life through monistic lenses, whether it pertained to the universe and God; matter, thought and being; or, truth and beauty.

[104] Seeberg, *Text-book of the History of Doctrines*, 1:338, shows that Augustine believed that the human race was a "mass of sin." Seeberg, 1:343, said, "that nothing good and no

that human beings can ever do anything to save themselves. It is worth reiterating here that the Orthodox do not make the distinctions between nature and grace which characterize some Western views of humanity.[105] Yet, for the Orthodox, it is true that in the fall human beings chose to sever themselves from unhindered fellowship with the divine, so that, as Lossky said, "Man has closed up within himself the springs of divine grace."[106] Accordingly, the Orthodox - like many Western theologians - do not hold that human beings ceased to be the images of God. Rather, the Orthodox believe that which reflected God (to other human beings and to creation) - the image - has been perverted.

Again, despite the fact that human beings are fallen, the divine-reflective dimension of their identity remains. "All men are made in the image of God," Ware said, "and however corrupt their lives may be, the divine image within them is merely obscured and crusted over, yet never altogether lost."[107] Similarly Lossky taught that the faculty within humans for communing with God has been obfuscated.[108] The flame that formerly burned brightly within humans prior to the fall has been reduced to a spark, instructed Stephanou, but it remains nonetheless.[109]

For those who respond to and cooperate with God's gracious and ecstatic (again, from ekstasis) offers of grace, via the energies of the Holy Spirit, this image or flame can be made to increase in stature and influence. But because of the corrupting power of sin, which insidiously works within every facet of human existence, no one is able to save himself or herself, no one can become like God apart from Him. Summing up humanity's post-fallen identity and situation, Lossky said:

> Adam did not fulfil his vocation. He was unable to attain to union with God, and
> the deification of the created order. That which he failed to realize when he used
> the fullness of his liberty became impossible to him from the moment at which he
> willingly became the slave of an external power. From the fall until the day of

---

salvation can be found except in Christ was the thought impressed upon the church" by Augustine's discussions.

[105] Western explications wherein the fall cut humans off from God's grace is a moot issue for the East.

[106] Lossky, *Image and Likeness*, 131. Lossky quoted Philaret of Moscow, *Discours et sermons*, I, 5.

[107] Ware, *The Orthodox Way*, 52.

[108] Lossky, *Image and Likeness*, 132.

[109] Stephanou, *Man: Body, Soul and Spirit*, 5.

Pentecost, the divine energy, deifying and uncreated grace, was foreign to our human nature, acting on it only from outside and producing created effects in the soul. The prophets and righteous men of the Old Testament were the instruments of grace. Grace acted upon them, but did not become their own, as their personal strength. Deification, union with God by grace, had become impossible.[110]

It will become more obvious as we proceed, but the Orthodox' explication of *theosis* encompasses their doctrine of salvation. Even the first people, sinless as they were, were in need of divine fellowship and cooperation with God's grace if they were to realize God's intention and purpose for them as his ultimate creations. So that *theosis*, apart from being a means of healing and redemption, was God's intention for human beings from the moment of their creation. Salvation - freedom from sin and mortality - is the negative dimension of *theosis*. Said Lossky, "After the Fall, human history is a long shipwreck awaiting rescue. but the port of salvation is not the goal; it is the possibility for the shipwrecked to resume his journey whose sole goal is union with God."[111]

Summary and Analysis

In the eyes of Pentecostals, and North American evangelicals more broadly, the Orthodox present and define anthropology, and therefore spirituality, in a disquieting manner. The primary reason for this dissonance is the issue of context. The Orthodox view anthropology with dramatically different interpretational lenses than those who are located in an individualistic-pragmatic milieu (discussed later in the Pentecostal section). Clearly the Orthodox have their own philosophical milieu deserving of careful analysis, but because our broader purpose is to compare the Orthodox and Pentecostals on the topic of Christian transformation, we cannot exhaustively analyze the Orthodox' backgrounds. Nonetheless, it will be helpful to make some general observations about their framework.

---

[110] Lossky, *Mystical Theology*, 133.
[111] Lossky, *Orthodox Theology*, 84.

Essentialism

As has been delineated in our first two chapters, Orthodox anthropology is suffused with ontological dimensions. Human beings cannot be rightly understood apart from their ontological makeup as reflections of God's own Trinitarian identity. This identity manifests itself through the ecstatic love shared between persons, so that human beings can only be fully human when they are involved in authentic communion with God and one another. This God-reflective identity also manifests itself in that humans have *nous*, free will, and the potential to grow. The *nous* and free will, if exercised in cooperation with God's grace, can enable the human person to traverse the path of God-likeness (since Jesus' life, this is ever after defined as Christ-likeness). Concomitant with their communal and noetic dimensions, human beings were created to share what it means to be human - the personified intersection of the material and spiritual realms - with the rest of God's creation. We were meant to be priests unto God, one another, and the material realm. Just as there is symmetry between the divine *hypostases*, so was there supposed to be between humans, God, and creation.

Orthodox theology is so suffused with ontology that it is fair to characterize their entire model as an ontological one. Even humanity's fall is cast in ontological categories: human beings, by allowing their passions to run unchecked, shattered the ontological harmony and position that was theirs upon creation. By choosing the autonomous, albeit illusory, knowledge offered to them by the tempter, they forsook the participatory knowledge they had of God and made themselves their own reference point of existence. Because they were contingent beings, beings whose identity and life was necessarily reliant upon God himself, the natural result of their choice was death, separation (from God and one another), and fragmentation. The chasm that erupted between human beings and God was not so much a juridical problem needing pardon as it was an ontological one needing healing. But they could neither remedy the new disease called death, nor could they heal the existential fragmentation running deep within their souls. In the end they were in need of someone to reunite and restore the divine order.

The Orthodox' position regarding the fall is rich and touches upon the fractured existence that typifies much of life on earth. The categories of ontology serve well to develop some of the intricacies of sin's effects. However, the Orthodox' ontological emphasis regarding the fall does not reflect the full biblical picture. Adam and Eve clearly did suffer God's judgment. The apostle

Paul very distinctly portrayed sin as having juridical ramifications which included guilt, pardon, ransom, and forgiveness. We human persons do not only suffer ontologically from sin, in our consciences (indeed, in our bodies) we also experience the guilt of sin, and concomitantly yearn for the liberating proclamation of the Gospel. In all of this, the Protestant emphasis upon salvation (itself very much a juridical concept) by faith in Christ's redemptive work can never be compromised.

Implicit throughout Orthodox anthropology is the tenet that people are most accurately understood in an essential, rather than an existential (in the modern philosophical sense)[112] manner. That is, the Orthodox believe if one wants to understand the human person one must know what she is. In this case, the human person is a being with *nous*, free-will, a soul, a body, and so forth; all of which variously reflect something of God's own identity. The Orthodox' essentialist viewpoint is part and parcel of their having developed their theology in light of Greek philosophical issues, most specifically the issue of being and non-being. Motivated by the primary issue of what is it that constitutes a person's being, less emphasis is placed upon what a person does, experiences, or believes. The essentialist viewpoint also assumes that human nature is consistently the same, from culture to culture and from historic era to historic era; neither sociology, economics, nor politics are recognized as having significance in understanding the human person.

Because the Orthodox cast their theology in light of Greek philosophical terms, they must constantly wrestle with the tension that the Greek dualism about spirit and matter presents for them. We noted this tension in our examination of Athanasius and Palamas, but it was especially apparent in this chapter's delineation of Zizioulas and Lossky where the human body and passions (especially eros) are both transmitters of death. As much as they qualify that the material realm, or more properly the human body, is not the root problem for human existence, their model of salvation remains one whereby the human body will ultimately be delivered from its limitations.

The essentialist characteristic of Orthodox anthropology will be most fully evinced in our later chapter on the means of *theosis*. This is because in their striving to become Christ-like they emphasize the role which asceticism plays in

---

[112] Modern existentialism is the view which holds that one's existence is more important than one's essence, and that one's uniqueness (and the numerous and varied factors which give rise to such uniqueness) is more important than an assigned category to which one belongs. Millard Erickson, *Christian Theology* (Grand Rapids, Michigan: Baker, 1994[11]), 45-48, 467-468; Colin Brown, "Existentialism," in *EDT,* 395-396.

order to tame the passions. Through ascetic practices the Christian is supposed to unify himself or herself. The desert fathers held to an essentialist viewpoint and wrote extensively about the need, and method, to subdue the passionate appetites. They believed the process of deification involves an internal struggle, more accurately understood as an internal spiritual war, wherein the body, the passions, and the mind must be brought into humble subjugation to the *nous*. Having achieved such subjugation, one may then most fully participate in an authentic encounter with God. This essentialist anthropology will also be implicit in our next chapter as we examine Orthodox Christology: Christ is the one in whom human nature - including the human body and passions - is deified.

The Orthodox' essentialist view also implies that human beings' identity *can be* accurately understood. Within their own model this is a liberating feature. Although descriptions about God himself are always qualified with apophatic statements, Scripture and especially church tradition have made it such that human beings can be understood with a great deal of certainty. In light of Scripture and the teachings of the fathers, it is clear that humans are persons with spiritual and material dimensions. As will be shown in our chapter on the means of *theosis*, the dimensions of the heart, soul, and mind are carefully analyzed and presented in Orthodox models. Humanity's problem is identified (ontological corruption), as is the solution (*theosis* via cooperation and communion with God). Whereas human beings *can be* identified in their model, the Orthodox also tend toward dogmatism because human beings must be understood within the Orthodox' essentialist framework. That is, if the Holy Spirit, through the teachings of the fathers and the decisions of the ecumenical councils, has guided the church into all truth (Jn. 16:13), then the church's tradition (the life of the church in the Holy Spirit) must be accepted. And, as this study is delineating, Orthodox church tradition is very precise in adhering to an essentialist model.

Orthodox Tradition and its Cultural Context

As the above has illustrated, it is impossible to analyze or critique Orthodoxy apart from a discussion of church tradition. Though there are variations within Orthodox theology, especially as it concerns issues not ratified by ecumenical councils,[113] all Orthodox theologians present their own studies with a mindful eye toward the past. One will not find Orthodox theologians heralding *sola scriptura* as *the* grand epistemological anthem. There are several reasons for this. Firstly, the Orthodox believe that Scripture was written by the church upon the inspiration of the Holy Spirit. Thus, only the authentic church - the one guided by the Holy Spirit - can properly interpret its book.[114] Secondly, the Orthodox view Scripture neither as a kind of static embodiment of Christian truth nor as the only Christian document against which truth claims can be measured. The Bible is indeed the supreme record of God's revelation, but it is better understood as a dynamic witness to the life of that inspired truth. Thus, any and all witnesses to the truth of God's revelation can be consulted in theological formulations. Thirdly, the Orthodox do not herald *sola scriptura* because they have not experienced a Reformation the likes of which the West has undergone; for this they are grateful. They variously believe the Reformation was either God's judgment upon the Catholics because the Roman Pope usurped authority from the other four bishops in the pentarchy, or the natural consequence visited upon a recalcitrant family (a rebellious parent naturally produces rebellious children).[115] Fourthly, and perhaps most importantly, the Orthodox do not herald *sola scriptura* because they believe that the teachings of the Orthodox fathers accurately contain and present the truth of Christian doctrine. Though it is usually only implicit, this epistemological affirmation is simultaneously an affirmation of God's workings within the church through the course of Eastern Orthodox history. In fact, we may fairly say that as it is presented within the Orthodox understanding of dogma, the Holy Spirit's workings in and through the Orthodox church provide a subtle affirmation of Orthodox culture and history itself. That the Holy Spirit would choose to reveal the truths of the Godhead and clarify the meanings of Scripture most especially to the Chalcedonian Christians of the East cannot, in Orthodox dogma, be understood otherwise. Lest this analysis seem unfair, John Meyendorff personified this very sentiment when he said, "An Orthodox believes that there is essential unity between the biblical view of God and the

---

[113] The most obvious examples are eschatology and descriptions of human existence in the after life.

[114] Veselin Kesich, *The Gospel Image of Christ* (Crestwood, NY: St. Vladimir's, 1991, rev. ed.), 49-53. Daniel Clendenin, "What the Orthodox Believe: Four key differences between the Orthodox and Protestants," *Christian History*, 54:2 (1997), 34-35.

[115] Meyendorff, *Catholicity and the Church*, 49, 76.

Greek patristic synthesis, and this is why for him the Fathers are 'The Fathers.'"[116]

Despite their qualifications to the contrary, it is the case that Orthodoxy's Hellenistic context, together with its belief that Christianity is firstly the experience of God's life and secondly a body of truth claims,[117] has sometimes caused it to read foreign meanings into the biblical texts.[118] Specifically, the teaching that Adam and Eve were created with the ability to become God-like is simply untenable. The Jews were far too acutely aware of the distance between God and his creation to have ever affirmed that we can become like him, however such likeness might be qualified. The terms image and likeness (*selem* and *demut*) were synonyms in the Hebrew text, and, as was noted earlier, they only appeared as distinct words in the Septuagint and Vulgate. The Old Testament passages[119] that use image and/or image and likeness were indeed teaching the uniqueness of human beings *vis-a-vis* God; thus, the Orthodox correctly assert that human beings reflect something of God's identity.[120] But they go too far when they dogmatically assert that this identity must be

---

[116] Meyendorff, *Catholicity and the Church*, 79. His emphasis.

[117] For the Orthodox there has historically been less concern about practicing biblical *eisegesis* because they believe that authentic Christian living is to share in the same life which the biblical writers themselves experienced. Thus, if one reads one's own life into the life of the Scripture one is nonetheless remaining loyal to Scripture's essence. We cannot here make an extensive study of the Orthodox' hermeneutic, but theirs clearly is not simply an allegorically driven hermeneutic as too many scholars have purported. Such conclusions are the result of analyzing the Orthodox through the lenses of twentieth-century philosophic constructs without attempting to understand the essence, or drive, of their hermeneutic.

[118] This is a striking feature which the Orthodox share with Pentecostals. The latter have been charged as practicing a subjectivizing hermeneutic. Cf. Dayton, *Theological Roots of Pentecostalism*, 23-6; Gary B. McGee, "Early Pentecostal Hermeneutics: Tongues as Evidence in the Book of Acts," in *Initial Evidence: Historical and Biblical Perspectives on the Pentecostal Doctrine of Spirit Baptism*, G. McGee (ed.) (Peabody, Massachusetts: Hendrickson, 1991), 96. The fact of the matter is that no Christian tradition is devoid of this contextual problem, some are just more willing to admit it than others. The Orthodox' own use and modification of Greek constructs exhibits the widespread phenomenon whereby the filter through which one processes Scripture is as important for how one understands Scripture as are the biblical texts themselves.

[119] These are Gen. 1:27-28; 5:1-3; 9:6; and, Ps. 8.

[120] Anthony A. Hoekema, *Created in God's Image* (Grand Rapids: Eerdmans, 1986), 11-19.

understood in ontological terms. Because the Old Testament is vague at best respecting ontology, the Orthodox err to read their own philosophical context back into the text. The Old Testament's *imago dei* texts themselves, apart from God's words regarding dominion over creation (Gen. 1:26) and his statement pertaining to Adam and Eve's prosperity and procreation (Gen. 1:28-30), only minimally record God's expectations of them as persons in general, and reveal nothing about the supposed divine intent for their ontological transformation in particular.

Admittedly there are a greater number of texts which teach about, or are implicit concerning, image-terminology in the New Testament. Many of these texts witness to the new identity believers share with Christ, still others bear witness to the unprecedented union of the divine and human in Jesus of Nazareth. While too much Protestant biblical interpretation, overcome by philosophical biases antithetical to the life of primitive Christianity, has skirted around the mystical dimensions of what it means to be "in Christ," it nonetheless remains the case that most of the New Testament passages should not be interpreted as one-for-one equivalents with Hellenistic ontological formulations. At most, these New Testament texts incorporate a kind of nascent ontology which the inspired writers themselves did not develop. Contrastingly, Anthony Hoekema cogently argues that many, if not all, of the New Testament passages concerning image can be interpreted in reference to human action, not ontology. We become like Christ by the things we do, so that image can be understood "not as a noun but as a verb."[121]

Concerning human passions, we must clarify that the Old Testament accounts have little to substantiate the Orthodox' position. However, in light of Peter's teaching and Paul's frequent teachings about the inner struggle of a person's flesh (carnal desires) and spirit (upright motives), and the resultant need to live according to the latter, it seems that the Orthodox' doctrine of the passions is not without some kind of Biblical warrant, even if that warrant is mostly implicit. The problem occurs when that which is implicit is made explicit and then dogmatized. For example, Vlachos argued that the apostle Paul, in Galatians 5:19-21, Romans 1:28-31, and 2 Timothy 3:1-5, addressed the issue of the passions. Vlachos correctly asserted that these passages pertain to

---

[121] Hoekema, *Created in God's Image*, 19-32. The quote is taken from p. 28. Hoekema contends that the indicative-imperative dialectic of the Gospel is much better understood in terms of action than it is in terms of essence. He does affirm that we are images of God both as nouns and verbs, so that we are both uniquely who we are as well as what we do, 65, 69-101. But his emphasis is upon our action , 73.

those persons governed by carnal desires, but his position that Paul herein described the energies or impulses of the soul (to the extent and detail that Vlachos himself presented them) is clearly the result of *eisegesis*. That Vlachos spent one page discussing the passions as noted in Paul's writings, and fourteen pages discussing the passions as noted in the Orthodox fathers reveals the extent to which the doctrine of the passions is rooted primarily in Orthodox tradition, and not Scripture. More will be said about the passions in a later chapter, for now it deserves qualifying that Paul clearly did not describe these with the depth or nuance that Orthodoxy's fathers did.[122]

Orthodoxy's specific teaching about the human *nous* has little biblical substantiation. To be sure, the word itself occurs repeatedly in the New Testament (mostly in Pauline literature), but it therein conveys the meanings of understanding, thought, and/or mind. Nowhere does it imply the existential meaning which the Orthodox see in it. Even though there is a tremendous amount of prayerful insight concerning *nous* and the passions that can be genuinely edifying for the church universal, it remains the case that neither finds its point of departure in Scripture. Instead both arose amid the early church's discussions with and formulations within Hellenistic philosophy, especially Stoicism.

Stoicism flourished between 300 BC and AD 100, but its effect upon the doctrinal formulations of the early Christian theologians was enormous.[123] The Stoics, following Socrates, Plato, and Aristotle believed human beings were characterized by *nous*, something they more narrowly defined as intelligence.[124] They also maintained a philosophical system wherein *Logos* was something that pervaded the entire universe. Human beings shared in this *Logos*-existence by

---

[122] Vlachos, *Orthodox Psychotherapy*, 253 (regarding Scripture), 254-267 (regarding Orthodox fathers).

[123] A. A. Long, *Hellenistic Philosophy: Stoics, Epicureans, Sceptics* (London: Duckworth, 1974), 107. The Greek Stoics, traditionally sought to harmonize their philosophy with the pantheon of Greek and Roman Gods. However, later Roman Stoics were, Long said, "practically if not formally monotheist." While the Orthodox fathers were doubtlessly attempting to "demonstrate the superiority of Christianity to Greek philosophy," they also made positive uses of "Stoic and Platonic doctrines." Clement of Alexandria (c. AD 150-216) used the Stoics' logos synonymously with the 'word of God,' taught the suppression of emotional impulses, and emphasized the rational nature of Christianity. Long, *Stoics, Epicureans, Sceptics*, 235-236.

[124] Julia Annas, *Hellenistic Philosophy of Mind* (Berkeley and Los Angeles: University of California Press, 1992), 51. Long, *Stoics, Epicureans, Sceptics*, 110.

virtue of their rational characteristic (*nous*), and the more a person acted
according to reason (*logos*) the more one acted in harmony with nature. Ethical
practice was thus encouraged so that the harmony and order of creation would
be sustained.[125] The Stoics' philosophy additionally prefigured Orthodox
theology in that human beings were understood to be microcosms of the larger
universe.[126] The Orthodox' language about the intended unity of human
existence - as individuals, with each other, and with the universe - and its polar
opposite of fragmentation at every level of human existence was also prefigured
in Stoicism.[127] The views about, and ascetic practices regarding, the passions
similarly had been an important feature of Stoic thought. The passions (*pathe*)
in themselves were understood as amoral, but it remained true that they easily
devolved into excessive and immoral behavior. The Stoics believed the passions
could be, and should be, educated and tamed.[128]

Similarly, Orthodoxy's use of, and development with respect to, Neo-
Platonism also deserves mention. Plotinus, an eminent Neo-Platonist, believed
the following: 1) there were three basic *hypostases* in the universe, the One (or
the First), the World Mind (*Nous*), and the World Soul; 2) the physical cosmos
reflected the divine Being; 3) the human soul could become too attached to the
human body and thus be harmed. Cornelia De Vogel quoted Porphyry who said,
"Plotinus seemed to be ashamed of being in a body."[129] Clearly, the asceticism
of the fourth-century Christian monks, and their teaching concerning the
passions, had certifiable ties to the kinds of ideas put forth by Plotinus.[130]
Additionally, the ontological categories of being and non-being, *hypostasis*, and
prosopon, are traceable to Plato and his pupils through history.[131]

---

[125] Long, *Stoics, Epicureans, Sceptics,* 108.

[126] Long, *Stoics, Epicureans, Sceptics,* 125.

[127] Annas, *Hellenistic Philosophy of Mind,* 115; Long, *Stoics, Epicureans, Sceptics,* 164.

[128] Annas *Hellenistic Philosophy of Mind,* 103-120.

[129] Cornelia J. De Vogel, "Plotinus' Image of Man: Its Relationship to Plato as well as to
later NeoPlatonism" in *Images of Man in Ancient and Medieval Thought,* Gerardo
Verbeke (ed.) (Louvain, Belgium: Leuven University Press, 1976), 167. The
Cappadocians made use of Plotinus model concerning the human soul.

[130] De Vogel, "Plotinus' Image of Man," 167.

[131] Zizioulas, *Being as Communion,* 27-41. There is such a deep appreciation for Plato
that some within Eastern Orthodoxy believe he should be understood as one of the
apostles or church fathers. John and D. L. Carmody, *Interpreting the Religious
Experience: A Worldview* (Englewood Cliffs, New Jersey: Prentice-Hall, 1987), 179.

Because both Stoicism and Neo-Platonism were pantheistic philosophies, an exact one-for-one transfer of their principles into Orthodox theology is absolutely not being put forth here.[132] The patristic synthesis, as noted above with Meyendorff, was precisely the fusion of a Christian biblical understanding with a Hellenic philosophical framework.[133] Nonetheless it is undeniable that a syncretistic mix of religion, culture, and philosophy occurred within the Orthodox church. To be sure it was a biblically oriented, thoughtful, prayerful, and learned form of syncretism, but it was syncretism all the same. This had a very pragmatic and beneficial effect: for roughly fifteen hundred years it enabled the Orthodox church to present the Gospel to the inhabitants of Eastern Europe through an incredibly rich (at both the theological and aesthetic levels) vehicle that fit the historical-cultural climate's context. Whether or not this synthesis of Christianity and Greek thought remains as pragmatically effective today, or whether this synthesis is one maintained by the masses or the ecclesiastical elite alone, are both debatable.

These two prominent dimensions of Orthodox theology - essentialism and church tradition - will reappear as we progress onward in our examination of *theosis*, because they are bulwarks in the Orthodox' epistemology. Next we will turn to the Orthodox doctrine of Christology, because it is there that *theosis* receives it most foundational theological treatment.

---

[132] For that matter, the historical issue is even more complex. After the reign of Constantine the church was given numerous freedoms and privileges with the result that the empire was increasingly becoming a religious-philosophic melting pot. G. B. Kerferd, "The Image of the Wise Man in Greece in the Period before Plato," in *Images of Man in Ancient and Medieval Thought*, 17-19, showed that even prior to Plato there was no single primitive, concrete, understanding of wisdom, or philosophy, from which the varied Greek philosophical systems had spun off. Gerardo further muddies the historical picture by arguing that it is mythical to argue that in Greek philosophy what we see is the progressive evolution of *Geist* (Mind or the Spiritual) from a humble to an advanced level. I note this to argue that from Greek philosophy's beginning, or even prior to its beginning, the historical situation was filled with ambiguity and complexity.

[133] Hans Von Campenhausen, *The Fathers of the Greek Church*. 27, argues that for Clement of Alexandria Plato was the Greek philosopher who came closest to the truth of Christianity. Thomas F. Torrance, *Space, Time, and Incarnation* (Oxford University Press, 1969), in his chapter, "The Problem of Spatial Concepts in Nicene Theology," sketches the patristic reliance upon, and modification of, Hellenic thought. Torrance concludes by affirming the Patristic synthesis because it preserved an understanding of God who is simultaneously immanent and transcendent with regard to space and time.

4

Theosis' Theological Foundation: Christology

> So also is the resurrection of the dead. It is sown a perishable
> body, it is raised an imperishable body; it is sown in dishonor, it
> is raised in glory; it is sown in weakness, it is raised in power; it
> is sown a natural body, it is raised a spiritual body. If there is a
> natural body, there is also a spiritual body. So also it is written,
> 'The first Man, Adam, became a living soul.' The last Adam
> became a life-giving spirit. However, the spiritual is not first,
> but the natural; then the spiritual. The first man is from the
> earth, earthy; the second man is from heaven. As is the earthy,
> so also are those who are earthy; and as is the heavenly, so also
> are those who are heavenly (1 Cor. 15:42-49).

Whereas some Protestant theologians since the Enlightenment have, in their
quests for Jesus of Nazareth as he was apart from the faith claims of the
Christian community, emphasized the humanity of Jesus, the Orthodox have
historically emphasized His divinity. Quests for an historical Jesus divorced
from the historical Christian faith, to the Orthodox mind, only belie the
unorthodox identity of those so searching.[1] The image of the invisible God must
not be understood apart from His true theandric (divine-human) nature. That
some Protestants have erroneously depicted him only sustains the Orthodox
critique that humanity's intelligence has indeed emerged victorious over its
noetic nature in the epistemological struggle. As was noted in our examination
of Athanasius, Christology is a matter of soteriology for the Orthodox; correct
understandings of Christ are necessary for proper formulations concerning
theosis. But, as will be developed in this chapter, Christology is also a matter of
anthropology; who Christ is has important ramifications for understanding what
human beings are.

It is not our purpose to exhaust the history of Orthodox Christology, nor will
we attempt to comprehensively delineate the Orthodox' position regarding the

---

[1] Kesich, *The Gospel Image of Christ*, 13-46, surveys and critiques the Protestants who
have quested for the historical Jesus. He is one of the initial Orthodox scholars to
respond to the critical methods of biblical study.

metaphysical nature of Christ,[2] nonetheless both the history of the doctrine and metaphysics will be addressed. The focus here, in keeping with our study, will be an examination of Jesus Christ and His role in *theosis*. In accord with that focus we will show why it is that the Orthodox believe Christ is the one for the many, how and why it is that Christ is the archetypical image of God, and how and why the theology of the image is important both for Orthodox religious art and its role in the transformation of human beings.

Christ the One, We the Many

As we noted earlier, the Orthodox do not view the totality of Christ (His incarnation, life, work, death, and resurrection) in a juridical framework whereby both God's law concerning, and anger toward, sin are thus appeased. Instead Jesus' person and work make it possible for us both to be healed of sin's morally obfuscating - and existentially fragmenting - power, and to realize God's original purpose for us: that we might become divinized. The Orthodox model of Christian transformation is thus one of healing, not legal pardon. Given their therapeutic, rather than juridical model, the following questions arise for those of us holding the Western model. Firstly, how did Jesus' becoming an human person open the door for the entire human race to become like God? Secondly, if Jesus is not the legal payment for sin, is it simply the case that the substitutionary framework becomes ontological rather than juridical, so that he, in all of His perfection, now stands before God on our behalf? As we proceed, it will be our purpose to answer these questions.

The Importance of Metaphysics

At creation God gave human beings a mission. Just because Adam and Eve plunged the human race into corruption and fragmentation did not mean that somehow God had rescinded that mission. It is true that the last Adam - the image of God, as expressed in the 1 Corinthian passage above - fulfilled the mission which God gave to humanity, but His success did not alleviate us from completing the mission ourselves. Echoing the teachings of Athanasius, Lossky taught that God the Father did not substitute Christ for human beings because, as he said, "the infinite love of God would not replace the bond of human

---

[2] For such studies see Meyendorff, *Christ in Eastern Christian Thought*; and "Christ as Savior in the East," *in Christian Spirituality, I, Origins to the Twelfth Century*, 231-251.

freedom, but [He gave Christ] in order to return man to the possibility of accomplishing his task, to reopen for him the path to deification, this supreme synthesis, through man, of God and the created cosmos, wherein rests the meaning of all of Christian anthropology." Because of sin, God became human so that humans could fulfil their vocation of becoming like God.[3] *Jesus became an ontological doorway.* All who pass through him, all who participate in His identity as the theandric one, can share in His likeness and complete God's mission for themselves.

Despite the fact that the entire Trinity was involved in the Christ-event, the incarnation itself is properly a work of the Word alone. And it was the Patristic church that took as its task exactly how the Word's incarnation was to be properly understood. Early in the fifth century tensions existed between the theologies of Antioch and Alexandria. The Antiochenes (Diodore of Tarsus, Theodore of Mopsuestia, and Theodoret) were "anthropological maximalists" who studied the gospels literally and their examination upon the historical Jesus. They held that Jesus' humanity maintained its free will, and that His humanity merited salvation for humans because of its cooperation with the Word. In keeping with their understanding of Christ, the Antiochenes taught that by imitating Jesus we can similarly cooperate with God through asceticism and moral effort. The Antiochenes did not deny Christ's divinity, but they tended to see it less fully coinhered by His humanity. The result was that Christ was viewed in terms of two entities: the human ("assumed by the Word") and the divine ("the Word assuming"). Jesus' actions thus could be attributed to either one of His natures, depending upon the interpretation.[4]

The Alexandrians, represented especially by Cyril, tended to read Scripture allegorically and emphasized God's role in salvation. Whereas the Alexandrian school did teach that there was a union between the two natures in Christ, so that Jesus' actions were always attributed to the one person, "it did not preserve," said Meyendorff, "the necessary role played by the human nature in the work of salvation." The result was a kind of "anthropological minimalism" which the Monophysites defend to this day.[5] Cyril believed he was being faithful to the teachings of Athanasius, but unwittingly he followed a text

---

[3] Lossky, *Orthodox Theology,* 75.

[4] Meyendorff, *Eastern Christian Thought,* 15-18.

[5] Meyendorff, *Eastern Christian Thought,* 18-19. Meyendorff follows Georges Florovsky (source uncited) in using the phrases anthropological maximalism and minimalism. The Monophysites are located today especially within Egypt as the Coptic church. It is their emphasis that the "Word became flesh," and that the humanity of Christ was drowned in His divinity, "like a drop of wine in the ocean." Lossky, *Orthodox Theology,* 97.

written by Apollinarius and employed Apollinarian vocabulary (even though he staunchly opposed the latter's position).[6] The result was that in Alexandrian theology Christ's divinity was championed over His humanity, even though a union of the two natures was asserted. Furthermore, Cyril, in his Christological definitions, did not employ the terms φύσις, ουσία, or υπόστασις which the Cappadocians had used in their Trinitarian delineations.[7]

The Chalcedonian formula managed a synthesis between the emphases of Antioch and Alexandria, as well as between the Orthodox and Catholics more broadly.[8] Christ, it was asserted, was perfect concerning both His divinity and His humanity. He had a human body and a human soul, and was in all ways like us apart from sin. More specifically, his two natures existed in communion without confusion or change; each nature maintained its own distinctiveness.

Critical for our study was Chalcedon's confession that while Christ had two natures, only one *hypostasis* existed: that of the divine Logos. Lossky said, "the humanity of Christ, by which He is 'consubstantial with us,' never had any other *hypostasis* than that of the Son of God."[9] The Logos of God, Lossky continued, "became an *hypostasis* of human nature without transforming Himself into the *hypostasis* of a human person."[10] Following and developing the teaching of Chalcedon, Maximus the Confessor (d. 662), similarly held that Jesus' *hypostasis* was that of the divine Logos. Maximus asserted that, "communion with the Logos is precisely the natural state (λόγος φυσικὸς) of true humanity."[11] Jesus' *hypostasis* was that of the Logos, but His humanity

---

[6] Meyendorff, *Eastern Christian Thought*, 19-20. Apollinarius rejected the idea that the Logos was of the same substance as the Father. Instead he held that Christ brought with him from heaven a kind of heavenly flesh (a flesh not received from Mary). There was not, in Apollinarius' mind, two natures in Christ, but one: that of the *Logos*. Furthermore, Apollinarius posited that whereas Christ had a heavenly flesh, he did not assume a human spirit (νοῦς); the Logos himself took the place of the *nous*. In all of this Christ's divinity was emphasized over His humanity. Cf. Seeberg, *Text-book of the History of Doctrines*, 1:245; Bengt Hagglund, *History of Theology*, Gene J. Lund (tr.) (St. Louis, MO: Concordia, 1968), 111.

[7] Meyendorff, *Eastern Christian Thought*, 22.

[8] In the West terminological distinctions were being made between nature and *hypostasis*. Neither Antioch nor Alexandria had made these careful distinctions by the time of Chalcedon. Meyendorff, *Eastern Christian Thought*, 24-25. Lossky, *Orthodox Theology*, 95-104, also recounts the issues between Antioch and Alexandria heading toward Chalcedon.

[9] Lossky, *Image and Likeness*, 117. He quoted from the Chalcedonian Creed.

[10] Lossky, *Image and Likeness*, 118.

[11] Meyendorff, *Eastern Christian Thought*, 210.

was not passive because it was restored to its authentic human activity.[12] Chalcedon's Christology is thus interpreted by the Orthodox not only as a careful statement of how Christ's divinity and humanity should be understood, it is also the church's assertion that Jesus Christ was the theandric one who, in His own being, united all of humanity to God's divinity.

The Logos was enfleshed with all that it meant to be human, excluding sin and an human *hypostasis*. There are in Christ, Lossky said, "two wills, two intellects, two ways of acting, but always united in a single person."[13] Jesus Christ took on human nature (body, soul, mind, and will) but His *hypostasis* remained that of the Logos. The incarnate Word of God "enhypostasized" human nature. Just as the three hypostases of the Trinity interpenetrate each other, yet remain distinct, the two natures in Christ interpenetrated each other. "'The flesh became Word without losing what it had, while identifying with the Word according to the *hypostasis*,'" said Lossky quoting John of Damascus.[14]

In Orthodox theology, Christ has thus become the archetypical model for all human beings, and this in two ways. Firstly, he is the archetypical model for all people because he divinized human nature. In so doing, Christ became the last Adam, the prototype for all who seek to fulfil God's mission. The first Adam made it so all those after him were like him: corrupted, fragmented, and destined for death.[15] The last Adam was like the first Adam in that those who incorporate His nature will receive His effects, but the effects of the last Adam are: healing, unity, and eternal life. Secondly, Christ is the archetypical model for all humans because of the necessary definitional terms (*hypostasis* and nature) pertaining to His existence; in this way Christ has also opened new understandings of the human being. Lossky illustrated the connection between Christology and anthropology, "this refusal to admit two distinct personal beings in Christ means at the same time that one must also distinguish in human

---

[12] Meyendorff, *Eastern Christian Thought*, 79. It is recalled that to be fully and authentically human, in Orthodox theology, is to be in communion with God. Jesus, because of the perfect union of His two natures, therefore personally actualized this divine-human communion within himself.

[13] Lossky, *Orthodox Theology*, 99.

[14] Lossky, *Orthodox Theology*, 99. Lossky did not cite the Damascene's text. This mutual penetration is also known as *perichoresis* in Greek, and *communicatio idiomatum* in Latin.

[15] The Orthodox generally deny that Adam plunged the entire human race into a state of guilt. John Meyendorff, "Salvation in Orthodox Theology," in *Rome, Constantinople, Moscow: Historical and Theological Studies* (Crestwood, NY: St. Vladimir's, 1996), 162.

beings the person or *hypostasis* from the nature or the individual substance."[16] It is in light of Christ that the church now knows that humans are beings who, like God, have an *hypostasis* and a nature. Humans were created with the ability to transcend themselves, to participate in the nature of God, as well as that of others.[17] Reflecting God's identity, human personhood "implies the idea of freedom in relation to nature," said Lossky.[18] Fashioned after our maker, each person, Lossky taught, "potentially includes the whole, having in himself the whole of the earthly cosmos, of which he is the *hypostasis*." So that, continued Lossky, "each person is an absolutely original and unique aspect of the nature common to all."[19]

---

[16] Lossky, *Image and Likeness*, 118.

[17] The Orthodox have a very fluid view of the human person, yet in their writings it seems less developed than it might be. Absent not only in every Orthodox theological treatise, but also in their ascetic writings, were the psychological ramifications of such an anthropology. To be sure, they did discuss this as it pertains to the transcending power of Christ and the Holy Spirit. But in all of my research, they did not discuss how human persons transcend themselves and impact and/or transform other human persons. That is, if we were created to transcend ourselves one would expect discussions of how this occurs at the inter-personal level. Pertinent to this study (for Pentecostals), is the dimension of human charisma: is it the case that something is being transferred between a charismatic individual and his or her audience? Might one say that charismatic persons are especially adept at transcending themselves and participating in the nature of others? The same questions could be asked regarding families: are familial characteristics simply the result of the transference of DNA and a shared environment? Or, is something of the parents' hypostatic identities being transferred to, and/or inculcated in, the children? Though they do not develop it as fully as they might, the Orthodox' view of anthropology presents some interesting avenues for exploring the mystery of human persons.

[18] Lossky, *Orthodox Theology*, 126. Christos Yannaras, *The Freedom of Morality*, Elizabeth Briere (tr.) (Crestwood, N.Y.: St. Vladimir's, 1984), 21, similarly develops the notion of the human person.

[19] Lossky, *Image and Likeness*, 107. In the same way that the local church is not a part of the universal church, but is the universal church, so also each human person is not simply a part of human nature, but is human nature. This monism, or we may properly say this mysticism, characterizes the whole of Orthodox theology. There are not neat and clean distinctions between the various dimensions of theological knowledge; theirs is a wholistic understanding. In light of this, the Orthodox do not attempt to systematize their theology. God they say, and His immanence within creation and history, cannot be systematized. Cf. Meyendorff, *Byzantine Theology*, 5.

In light of the previous metaphysical clarifications, it is evident why the Logos' incarnation is as important for the Orthodox, if not more important,[20] than Jesus Christ's death and resurrection: the Logos' perfect communion with human nature was that which divinized humanity. "The Son of God," Lossky said, "by a prodigious humbling, by the mystery of His kenosis (κένωσις), descends into a self-annihilating condition. . . paradoxically, He unites to the integral fullness of His divine nature the unfullness no less integral to fallen human nature."[21] Thomas Torrance summarized the patristic teaching in this regard, "If what Christ has done for us is not the work of God become man, but only of a man who as a reward for his service to other human beings has been designated 'Son of God', then he does not embody for mankind the saving grace (χάρις) of God, and is utterly incapable of divine activity (θεοποίησις)."[22]

To answer this subsection's introductory questions about Orthodox Christology, Jesus Christ's life was not a substitution for our own, not even in an ontological sense. Instead, through the mutual interpenetration of humanity and divinity within Christ's person the great ontological abyss that separated humanity from God was bridged. To be sure, he did not automatically, or necessarily, bridge that abyss for every human *hypostases*; such a position would violate the freewill God granted to each human *hypostasis* (person). But what he did do was provide a potential bridge for all who participate in His theandric nature.

Because of Christ's incarnation of human nature and the meaning of that for human existence, we are brought full-circle back to the doctrine of the Trinity.[23]

---

[20] This was made evident in our earlier study of Athanasius. Christ's death did two things: Firstly, it exemplified the full extent to which he entered our nature as mortal beings; secondly, it conquered death itself, removing death's sting and corruption for all those found in Christ. Lossky, *Image and Likeness*, 104.

[21] Lossky, *Orthodox Theology*, 100. He follows Phil. 2:5-11.

[22] Torrance, *The Trinitarian Faith,* 138.

[23] This must be emphasized because it is where Orthodoxy and Western Christendom begin to part company concerning anthropological definitions. The West, following Thomas Aquinas' lead, tended to follow an Aristotelian philosophical framework wherein empirical measures, and distinctions between form and essence caused the very definitions to be narrowed. But it was especially following the Enlightenment's emphasis upon human reason and the concomitant challenges to the authority of the church and tradition that the notion of the autonomous individual took root. In contrast, the East tended to follow a Platonic framework where monism prevailed. Moreover, the East (especially Russia which had in the seventeenth and eighteenth centuries become the practical, if not official, stronghold of Orthodoxy) was not impacted by either the Reformation or the Enlightenment, and instead continued to maintain its Trinitarian, and

Just as the three *hypostases* of the Trinity share their existence in common, so also human beings share a common nature. To reiterate an earlier point, Christ's incarnation accomplished the task originally given to Adam and Eve so that human nature is now enabled to participate in the transcendent nature of God. The *Logos' hypostasis* took on human nature and divinized it. Thus, the *Logos'* incarnation makes it possible for those who participate in him to share in the divine life of the Trinity. This *shared life* - this *theosis* - *is the ultimate reason God created humans.* God did *not* create humans so that he could test them as to whether or not they could, or would, live sinless lives. He wanted persons who would share in His eternal life and fellowship - the *sobornost'* (as the Russian Orthodox call it)[24] - of what it meant to be God.

That the Eastern Orthodox make their anthropological formulations based upon Christology and the Trinity presents us with different points of departure than are usually employed in Western formulations. Orthodoxy's formulation is decidedly a spiritual understanding of human persons, and it is one not based on the empirical sciences, the humanities, or modern philosophical considerations. Today, Orthodox theologians are aware of the newer philosophic models and questions. They are equally aware of the effect of the empirical sciences and the humanities on anthropological formulations in western models. But, as Lossky made so evident, the Orthodox are decidedly ambivalent with regard to both philosophy and science.[25] This ambivalence, coupled with the fact that Orthodoxy's epistemological foundations incorporate the noetic dimension of human existence, helps to exemplify why the Eastern and Western views of anthropology are so different. That the West alone has experienced philosophical revolutions in the last few centuries does not by itself explain the differences between the two halves of Christendom: it is clearly also a matter that each has its own epistemological points of departure.

---

therefore corporate, view of humanity. Despite Peter the Great's (tsar, 1682-1725) attempts to westernize Russia, the common people, and thus the great majority of the Orthodox church, were unaffected by the cataclysmic philosophical shifts of the West. In fact, Peter's attempts to westernize Russia caused great numbers among the Orthodox to react defensively and solidify the older Russian ways of thinking and believing. Schmemann, *The Historical Road of Eastern Orthodoxy*, 300-339.

[24] *Sobornost'* will be developed further in the next chapter.

[25] Lossky, *Image and Likeness*, 185. The Orthodox' ambivalence is also tied to the consequences of the fall for human identity. We will note this further in our chapter on the means of *theosis*.

The Archetypal Human: Image and Likeness

The biblical doctrine of anthropology prior to Christ's coming was cloudy at best, but since His coming, and since God's mission for humanity was fulfilled in Christ, the Orthodox hold to a more precise and aesthetic understanding of the image of God in man.[26] As was previously noted, the Orthodox admit that the Hebrew words *selem* and *demut*, (Gen. 1:26-27) did not originally imply the full theological meaning the Orthodox now see in it. Furthermore, Lossky instructed, the early Orthodox fathers themselves did not have a highly developed anthropological understanding, nor could they have: they were not asking the same questions that later Orthodox theologians asked. The fathers were neither confronted with the rather recent questions about the nature of human beings, nor did they have a centuries-old philosophical Christian tradition to rely upon.[27] But with Christ's coming, and with the progressive revelation that he initiated in his person and then furthered when he sent the Holy Spirit, the church was able to reflect and make careful theological statements about people and the image of God. This precise understanding regarding progressive revelation was exemplified by Lossky who said, "'Theology' in the proper sense, as the Fathers of the Church were to understand it, remains a closed book to Israel until the Incarnation of the Word." Lossky continued, "It is in the context of the Incarnation. . . that the creation of man in the image of God receives all its theological value, which remained unperceived (or somewhat impoverished) in the letter of sacerdotal narrative of the creation as seen by critical exegesis."[28] Because of Christ, and the additional revelation given via him, we are to understand human beings as images of God in a fuller sense. For the Orthodox, this fuller sense is reflected in the New Testament.

Scriptural passages like that of Paul's comments in 1 Corinthians 15 (quoted at this chapter's beginning), with its physical-spiritual duality and its "image" phraseology, helped initiate the patristic reflection on the nature and existence of human beings. Paul was following the Septuagint wherein the words *selem* and *demut* are rendered as *kat' eikona, kat' homoiosin* (according to the image

---

[26] In our previous chapter we intentionally did not discuss image and likeness precisely because the terms find their definitive locus in Christology.

[27] Lossky, *Image and Likeness*, 111-112, and 129. Thunberg, "The Human Person as Image of God," 300, avers the same. Although Thunberg focuses upon the patristic church in his study, he qualifies their views in light of some modern issues.

[28] Lossky, *Image and Likeness*, 136. Lossky repeatedly criticized modern critical methods of biblical study as being devoid of Christian faith in its theological formulas, 132, 136-137.

and the likeness). These two words, juxtaposed as they are, seem to imply, Lars Thunberg said, "a distance between what is given at the outset and what could be realized within the category of time." Examined with respect to the Greek philosophical questions about ontology, and especially regarding the biblical doctrine of humanity's fall and sinfulness, the two terms, continued Thunberg, "might lead to an understanding of humans as in tension between their 'ontological' image character and their 'moral' similitude."[29] For Clement of Alexandria (d. ca. 215), Origen (d. ca. 254) and the three Cappadocians (fourth century), a distinction was indeed made between the image (that which is given) and likeness (that which is to be realized) of God in humans.[30] Lossky said the Septuagint's translation of *selem* and *demut* laid the foundation for a future - Christian - theology and prepared for a brighter light of revelation, so that when Christ, the God-Man, came the notion of image could be favorably connected to anthropology. Aided by this progressive revelation, the church could then look within the Old Testament and find a latent image theology therein.[31] Not all Orthodox theologians agree with this exegesis.[32] Some of the early Christian fathers rejected it because it was perceived as an excessive Scriptural interpretation and because it tended to be ensnared in the Platonic web wherein the human mind must overcome the human body via ascetic effort.[33] These exceptions notwithstanding, the notions of potentiality and realization (image and likeness) are prominent features within the Orthodox' doctrine of *theosis*.[34]

Paul referred to Jesus Christ as the "image of the invisible God," (Col. 1:15; 2 Cor. 4:4). Especially as qualified by the Greek patristic context of person (ὑπόστασις) and nature (φύσις), Christ, the image of God, could only reflect the nature, not the person (which by definition is a distinction), of the Father. The Son is consubstantial (ὁμοούσιος) with the Father as to nature, but the Son is nevertheless not the person of the Father (whose *hypostasis*, the Orthodox

---

[29] Thunberg, "The Human Person," 293.

[30] Aghiorgoussis, "Sin in Orthodox Dogmatics," 180-181. Thunberg, "The Human Person," 298.

[31] Lossky, *Image and Likeness*, 137.

[32] Ware, *The Orthodox Way*, 51.

[33] Thunberg, "The Human Person," 295, 298. Later in Christian history Maximus the Confessor would argue for the distinction, but he rejected Origen's Platonic anthropological model (the soul as pre-existent). The majority of Latin fathers as well as Cyril of Alexandria did not make the distinction between image and likeness.

[34] Contrastingly, Catholic medieval theologians also interpreted "image and likeness" as being distinct, but believed godly likeness only resulted when one received a *donum super-additum* ("a divine gift added to human nature"). Erickson, *Christian Theology*, 500. Again, the Orthodox deny such a bifurcation between nature and grace.

maintain, is unknowable in itself to humans).[35] A human child is, said Lossky who made an analogy, "'the picture of his father' by the family characteristics which he has in common with him, not by the personal qualities which distinguish his father." Similarly, the *Logos* is an ἐικών φυσική, completely like the Father, "excepting the characteristics of unbegottenness and fatherhood."[36] By becoming a human being, the Son made the Father's nature visible to those humans who are aided by the grace of the Holy Spirit.[37]

Whereas the *Logos* is the precise image of the Father, the ἐικών φυσική, human persons as images of God do not, and cannot, so perfectly reflect their creator, the Logos. This is because of the infinite distance between the uncreated nature of God and the created nature of humans. While there is not the precise correspondence between humans and the *Logos* that there is between the *Logos* and the Father, there is nonetheless an analogy between human images and the divine Image they reflect. This analogous existence is understood by the fact that humans, like the persons of the Trinity, are not just participants in a common nature but they are also persons created with liberty with regard to themselves.[38] As persons with liberty, humans are able to achieve the likeness of God by becoming assimilated to him.[39]

Thunberg followed Maximus the Confessor in teaching that the image of God in which human persons are created is better understood as a kind of dynamism and not a kind of static identity. In accord with what was stated in my previous chapter about human freedom and *potentia*, the image of God is a kind of potentiality that blossoms, Thunberg said, "only when human beings are set free from enslavement to sin and are able to develop the potential capacities given at creation to their full maturity."[40] Thus, humans are created in the image of God so that they might become like him. Whereas God's image is the *common property* of all human beings, taught Georgios Mantzaridis, likeness unto God is the *goal* of existence for every human being. "By submitting himself freely to God's will," said Mantzaridis, "and being constantly guided by

---

[35] Just to qualify, Western theology, following the Ecumenical statement at Chalcedon, agrees with this.

[36] Lossky, *Image and Likeness*, 133-135. He quoted John Damascene, *De imaginibus III*, 18; *PG*, 94, col. 1340AB.

[37] Paul said, "No one can say 'Jesus is Lord' except by the Holy Spirit," 1 Cor. 12:3b.

[38] It must be admitted that here we are also diverging from Zizioulas' presentation of the Trinity as a shared existence, rather than a shared nature.

[39] Lossky, *Image and Likeness*, 137-138.

[40] Thunberg, "The Human Person," 298.

His grace, man can cultivate and develop the gift of the 'image,' making it a possession individual, secure and dynamic, and so coming to resemble God."[41]

Even though God created every person in His image, and even though it remains the task of each person to be transformed into God's likeness, it is not the case that every person is therefore the same. "Uniqueness," Zizioulas said, "is something absolute for the person." Thus, each person, continued Zizioulas, "does not permit itself to be regarded as an arithmetical concept, to be set alongside other beings, to be combined with other objects, or to be used as a means, even for the most sacred goal. The goal is the person itself; personhood is the total fulfilment [sic] of being, the catholic expression of its nature."[42] Similarly, Lossky affirmed the unique identity of each human person, "what is for us most dear in some human being, what precisely makes him 'himself,' remains undefinable, for in his nature there is nothing that would belong properly to his own person, always unique, incomparable, having none other like itself."[43] This belief in the unique quality of each person (founded on the distinct, yet ineffable, *hypostases* of God himself) guards against both the Platonic notion that somehow God will ultimately absorb all within himself, and the notion that every Christian, whether in the process of *theosis* or having attained that goal, will somehow become identical. The Father's goal that we become like His Son includes the notion that each of us will fulfil that goal according to our own unique person.

As was noted in our examination of Orthodox anthropology, many Orthodox fathers believed the image of God was especially located in the human *nous*. Contrastingly, contemporary Orthodox theologians tend to argue that the whole of human identity constitutes the image.[44] Humans do not *have* an image of God, they *are* an image of God. Similar to the corporate dimensions of anthropology as developed in the previous chapter, the image of God, though personally located within each human being, also incorporates broader ramifications. Thunberg said, "this likeness is both their own maturity as human beings and their fulfillment of a microcosmic and mediating task within the created universe."[45] To be created in the image, Thunberg developed, did not only incorporate issues pertinent to humanity, it also included the created realm. Created after God's image, humans were given dominion over creation. The dominion given to human beings at creation was, Thunberg instructed, qualified

---

[41] Mantzaridis, *The Deification of Man,* 22.

[42] Zizioulas, *Being as Communion*, 47.

[43] Lossky, *Orthodox Theology*, 126.

[44] Mantzaridis, *The Deification of Man*, 16. Thunberg, "The Human Person," 299. Lossky, *Orthodox Theology*, 124.

[45] Thunberg, "The Human Person," 298-300.

by their relationship to God. It was not God's intention to give humans dominion which could be either arbitrarily or capriciously exercised; rather they were to rule creation in the same way that God himself exercised dominion. They were always to rule it in light of their own relationship to God himself. In this way their dominion was like that given to viceroys. In addition to their relationship to God, dominion over creation by human beings was contingent upon their exercising dominion over themselves. In this regard the Alexandrian tradition of the passions and the concomitant need for dispassion developed. Human beings share the passions with the animal kingdom, but because they were created *as* more than the animals they were expected *to be* more than the animals and control themselves.[46] In the end, even the characteristic of dominion within the *imago dei*, in Orthodox delineations, contains an ontological dimension not usually found in the West.

As has been evident throughout, people are created in the image of the Logos, but they are also called to reflect that image. Even those Orthodox theologians who do not accept that *selem* and *demut* imply the human endowments of *position* and *potential* accept the fact that humans nonetheless need to be transformed by the grace of the Holy Spirit into conformity with the archetypal image of God - Jesus Christ. The Word became flesh, divinized that flesh, and bridged the ontological gulf that separated humankind from God. Because Christ's person is the necessary antidote to sin and its fragmenting effects, participation in him via His Holy Spirit is the means for our ontological healing and wholeness. We will develop how such participation is facilitated in our next chapter, but because the notion of Christ as the perfect icon took on great importance for the religious art and worship of the East we will now examine Orthodox iconography. This is because the most dramatic portrayal of Christ as God's image appears in iconography.

Christology and Anthropology: From Image to Icon

The Orthodox believe that painted icons embody and reflect both the divine ethical and aesthetical ideals. Christians of the West who are sympathetic toward Orthodoxy might agree that icons reflect the holiness and purity of those so depicted. They might even agree that they convey something about the mysterious nature of God; something about God is conveyed in the icon, yet we do not see God himself. But the Orthodox go further. They *believe iconography is critical for a proper understanding of Christ, as well as for the spiritual life*

---

[46] Thunberg, "The Human Person," 300-304.

of the Church. Leonid Ouspensky said, "the icon belongs to the *esse* or essential being of the church; it is a vital part of that general order of human activity within the church that serves to express Christian revelation." "Through its content and meaning," Ouspensky continued, "the icon conveys the same truth that is expressed by other essential elements of the church's life and faith, *including Holy Scripture.*"[47] Michel Quenot similarly stated, "'Theology in imagery,' the icon expresses through colors what the Gospel proclaims in words. Consequently, the icon is one of the aspects of divine revelation and of our communion with God."[48]

For the Orthodox, the icon visually symbolizes and expresses the supernatural in a way that spoken or written words cannot.[49] Orthodoxy teaches that both Scripture and icons, if they are to be recognized as revelatory, require a person's faith and the enlightenment of the Holy Spirit.[50] Scripture provides a means of symbolism so that the believer's intellect can understand the divine, but a painted icon provides the believer's eyes with a visible picture of the divine. The icon is described as a means, a bridge, a window, and a gate by which to glimpse, and participate in, the divine life. Additionally, though the icon is motionless it must not be understood as something static; beyond their emotive effect, several icons are purported even to have effected miracles.[51]

Iconography is far more than just a kind of stylized religious art. Behind iconography lies a deeply rooted history and theology. Ouspensky held that icons existed since the beginning of Christianity; St. Luke himself, Orthodox tradition holds, painted icons of the Theotokos, the Mother of God. Ouspensky said that as important as external documents and historical evidence are for substantiating iconography, it is equally founded in the life, faith, and content of

---

[47] Leonid Ouspensky, "Icon and Art," in *Christian Spirituality, I,* 382. My emphasis.

[48] Michel Quenot, *The Icon: Window on the Kingdom,* A Carthusian Monk (tr.) (Crestwood, NY: St. Vladimir's, 1991), 12.

[49] Leonid Ouspensky and Vladimir Lossky, *The Meaning of Icons* (Crestwood, NY: St. Vladimir's, 1982, rev. ed.), 22.

[50] With regard to the actualization and transmission of the sacramental grace or divine energy the Orthodox express the principle of synergy - both the divine and the human are involved; both *ex opere operato* and *ex opere operantis* are valid understandings of the sacrament. But the presence of God in the sacramental element or action is not dependent on the faith or participation of the believer. Bobrinskoy, "The Icon: Sacrament of the Kingdom," *St. Vladimir's,* 31:4 (1987), 294.

[51] For example, Ambrosios Giakalis, *Images of the Divine: The Theology of Icons at the Seventh Ecumenical Council* (NY: E. J. Brill, 1994), 46-50, notes that people have been healed of leprosy and sickness, as well as set free from demon possession through icons. The icons most often cited as having caused wonders (e.g., the weeping or spilling of blood) and miracles are those depicting Mary, Jesus' mother.

Christian revelation.[52] Quenot more modestly argued that while religious art was immediately present in church history within the catacombs, iconography seems to have been well established early in the fifth century. On the heels of Constantine's having made Christianity the state religion, "Christian art burst forth from the catacombs and replaced art themes of pagan inspiration."[53]

During Christendom's first few centuries the cult of icons was opposed in three primary ways. First there was the church's own struggle against the pagan culture and its rampant idolatry. But as the pagan culture receded into the background in light of Christianity's political gains, so did the debate about idolatry. Secondly, there were the Old Testament prohibitions against graven images and idols. But the prohibitions of the Old covenant were understood to have been put to an end by virtue of Christ's incarnation. Because of Christ, believers can have a true knowledge of God, one liberated from the old tendencies toward idolatry.[54] The third catalyst for opposition to the icons was neo-Platonism and its dualistic framework wherein matter was inferior and spirit (or idea) was superior. Regarding this framework the neo-Platonist Christians were forced to consider why they defended material images (icons) when their philosophy predisposed them against the material realm. They responded that the image provided the human mind a means of access to the divine prototype, but that the prototype remained veiled by our own material limitations.[55]

As the empire entered the eighth century there were additional factors that contributed to the iconoclastic tendencies. Firstly, emperors of Semitic, and not

---

[52] He cited a passage from the Seventh Ecumenical Council (Nicea II, 787) which stated that iconography was being practiced in the apostolic era. Ouspensky, "Icon and Art," 383.

[53] Quenot said Christian art served a didactic purpose, whether practiced publicly after Constantine's era, or within the catacombs privately before. The catacombs were adorned as they were because the early Christians venerated their dead there. Quenot, *The Icon*, 15-20.

[54] Quenot, *The Icon*, 39. Pelikan, *Imago Dei: The Byzantine Apology for Icons* (Princeton University Press, 1990), 39-40, noted one way the icon defenders overcame the Old Testament passages that condemned images. In the Septuagint, the prohibition (Deut. 27:15-17) against images was immediately followed "by a curse upon anyone who 'dishonors father or mother' or who 'removes the landmarks [*horia*] of his neighbor.'" The latter was restated as, "'Cursed is he that removes his father's landmarks,'" and subsequently reinterpreted as a defense of church tradition. Moreover, it was the case that the ecumenical councils of the first several centuries neither condemned nor vilified icons, this despite the fact that numerous practical questions about the church's everyday life had been addressed therein.

[55] Meyendorff, *Eastern Christian Thought*, 174-176.

Hellenic, backgrounds acceded to the Byzantine throne; so that culture and nationalism contributed to the debate. Secondly, the Byzantine empire was forced to endure the Muslims' criticism that the use of holy images was idolatrous; the war Byzantium waged against the Islamic invaders caused the Byzantines to consider their enemies' views warily. Thirdly, the iconoclastic emperors tended to hold "caesaropapist" pretensions which caused them to fight monasticism; monasticism had always presented a challenge to the institutionalized church, and the monks held their icons dearly.[56] Thus, according to Meyendorff, the iconoclasts' arguments were less theological than might be expected. Furthermore, the iconoclasts, Meyendorff said, "lacked patristic references directly condemning the veneration of images."[57]

The Quinisext Council (AD 692) made Christology the primary factor in the debate when it declared that Christ should no longer be depicted as a lamb, a figure entrapped in the Old Testament law, but rather in his human form, according to the grace and truth given the church. Nonetheless, by 730 the iconoclasts were destroying uncountable icons, both within churches and private homes. The iconodules (also known as iconophiles; that is, icon-defenders/lovers), mostly monks, who attempted to defend the icons were persecuted, thrown in prison, and maimed. Quenot said, "their monasteries were sacked and burned, their lands and possessions confiscated."[58]

Despite the aforementioned historical lack of theological argumentation, the iconoclasts eventually did formulate a theological argument.[59] Harkening back to Chalcedonian Christology, they believed that if Christ's humanity was being depicted in an icon apart from His divinity, Nestorianism resulted: God and

---

[56] Meyendorff, *Eastern Christian Thought*, 174-176. We will develop how it is that monasticism holds a challenge for the institution in our next chapter. Meyendorff, *The Orthodox Church: Its Past and Its Role in the World Today*, J. Chapin (tr.) (Pantheon, 1962), in his chapter, "The Orthodox Church and Islam," also added to the iconoclasts' motives the factor that the Byzantine emperor wanted Christianity to be more easily accepted by the surrounding Moslem culture. Pelikan, *Imago Dei*, 7-39, developed the relationship between politics, art, and ecclesiology in the iconoclastic controversies. Clearly, the historical debate over icons was as much rooted in politics and a specific zeitgeist as it was in theology per se. The political context is further and fascinatingly elucidated by Bat Ye'or, *The Decline of Eastern Christianity under Islam: From Jihad to Dhimmitude* Mariam Kochan and D. Littman (tr.) (Fairleigh Dickinson University Press, 1996).

[57] Meyendorff, *Eastern Christian Thought*, 176. Meyendorff also reviews the iconoclastic controversy in *Byzantine Theology*, 42-53.

[58] Quenot, *The Icon*, 26.

[59] This originated during the reign of Constantine V, Copronymos (741-775). Meyendorff, *Eastern Christian Thought*, 180.

man are thus separated in Christ. If Christ, in the fullness of both His humanity and divinity, was being depicted then the iconographer was assuming that God can be circumscribed and was therefore committing an absurd blasphemy. Meyendorff said the iconoclasts wanted to maintain the full sense of "the Chalcedonian apophaticism that had defined the hypostatic union in negative terms."[60]

The iconodules similarly founded their arguments in Christology. They held that the hypostatic union of Christ, also formerly affirmed at Chalcedon, deified His humanity. The iconodules quoted John of Damascus (d. 749) in their apologies:

> In former times, God, without body or form, could in no way be represented. But today, since God has appeared in the flesh and lived among men, I can represent what is visible in God (εἰκονίζω θεοῦ τὸ ὁρώμενον). I do not venerate matter, but I venerate the Creator of matter, who became matter for my sake, who assumed life in the flesh and who, through matter, accomplished my salvation.[61]

The iconodules made a distinction between the prototype and the image it reflects, a distinction made centuries earlier by the Neo-platonist Christians, and they were thus protected from the charge of idolatry: they argued that they were not worshipping matter (the object of art), they were worshipping the subject reflected by the matter. The object, because it reflects someone holy, may be venerated, but true worship (*latreia*) is "reserved for God alone."[62] An ancient Orthodox iconodule, Leontius of Neapolis, made the defense against idolatry even stronger, "We do not make obeisance to the nature of wood, but we revere and do obeisance to Him who was crucified on the Cross. . . . When the two beams of the Cross are joined together I adore the figure because of Christ who on the Cross was crucified, but if the beams are separated, I throw them away and burn them."[63]

To summarize the iconodule's position, when the archetypal image of God, took on flesh and circumscribed His identity in a human body, he not only redeemed humanity, he also sanctified the entirety of created matter. Because of

---

[60] Meyendorff, *Eastern Christian Thought*, 181. Meyendorff provides a more extensive view of iconoclastic theology on 181-187. For more on apophaticism, see this study's second chapter.

[61] Meyendorff, *Eastern Christian Thought*, 179, quoting Damascus in *Or.* I, *PG*, 94, col. 1245a.

[62] Meyendorff, *Eastern Christian Thought*, 182-184. Quote from p. 183. Neither Mary nor the saints may be worshipped.

[63] Ware, *The Orthodox Church*, 40, quoting Leontius in *PG*, XCIV, 1384D.

Christ's matter-sanctifying work, the church is now free to depict him by using His creation.[64]

If Christology serves as the foundation for the theology of icons, anthropology is its counterpart. Despite the fall, the image of God in humans was not destroyed. Thus, to a lesser or greater extent, depending upon the person's relationship with and participation in God, each person is an icon. "Humans 'image forth' their Creator," Anthony Ugolnik said, "and in that process they become icons of Christ, conveyors of the 'sacred image.'"[65] Just as a living person is an icon and reflects the image (icon or *paradigma*) of God, so also does a painted icon. Because of humanity's iconographic nature God views each human person as infinitely precious. And, because God holds a deep respect and love for each human icon, we are exhorted to love each one as though he or she were God himself.[66] Whereas human beings, microcosms of the physical and spiritual universe, reflect something of God's identity, so also do icons.

Finally, as it pertains to theological foundations, iconography, because it is linked to Christology, also has sacramental ramifications. In the same manner that a painted icon represents the *communicatio idiomatum* of Christ's divinity and humanity, the eucharist presents the reality of Christ's body and blood. Meyendorff argued that icons testify to the reality of the Eucharist.[67] Christ not only sanctified created matter when he "enhypostasized" human nature, he also made His body to be the source of deification. Meyendorff said, "the real

---

[64] Meyendorff, *Eastern Christian Thought*, 191. Pelikan, *Imago Dei*, 1:67-96, showed that the iconophiles' defense of iconography was also tied to their Scriptural hermeneutic. The Council of Ephesus (431) had ruled that it was erroneous to interpret the New Testament passages about Christ as referring to only His divinity or only His humanity; rather, they always referred to His single and entire person. Because Christ could be represented in the words of Scripture, he could also be represented in the artistic works of the church. The new order that Jesus Christ's incarnation had initiated (2 Cor. 5:17) included the aesthetic realm. Before Christ, similitudes (likenesses) of God were forbidden (Ex. 20:4). In Christ, the ultimate similitude of God had appeared (Rom. 1:23; 5:14; 6:5; 8:3; Phil. 2:7), and he thus could be depicted. He who wanted to be seen (ergo the incarnation), should be seen (ergo iconography). Additionally, iconography was defended for didactic reasons: icons provided the illiterate a means of receiving the gospel.

[65] Ugolnik, *Illuminating Icon*, 78. Ugolnik, though he is an ordained deacon in the Greek Orthodox church, is not a theologian. Perhaps because he is an English professor, and not a theologian, he is able to present iconography in a way that takes into account post-modernism and its language about texts.

[66] Ware, *The Orthodox Church*, 221.

[67] Meyendorff, *Eastern Christian Thought*, 189.

theological dimensions of the iconoclastic controversy thus appear clearly: the image of Christ is the visible and necessary witness to the reality of humanity of Christ. If that witness is impossible, the Eucharist itself loses its reality."[68]

Again, an icon is not the divine itself, nor is the idea of transubstantiation involved. But neither is the icon simply paint, canvas, or wood. Moshe Barasch says, "The icon suggests the divine without fully unveiling it."[69]

Though the Second Council of Nicea in 787 declared in favor of iconography, another iconoclastic phase broke out again early in the ninth century. In 843 the cult of the icons was established once and for all in Orthodox theology and practice.[70] This brief history is recounted not only to provide an historical foundation for understanding Orthodox iconography, it is also recounted to exemplify how dear the Orthodox hold their icons. That monks and laypersons would rather be persecuted, tortured, and killed, as well as persecute, torture, and kill, all for the sake of icons reveals how essential icons are for the Orthodox' theology and their doctrine of *theosis*.[71] If we are unable to say that Christ became fully human while remaining fully God, if we are unable to say that Christ sanctified His creation when he became incarnate, then we are equally unable to say that there is any hope for our salvation. In this brief survey we can see that the theology of the image progressed from its latent forms in the Old Testament, through the revelation of the archetypal image - Jesus Christ, into a dogmatic assertion of the necessity of icons.

---

[68] Meyendorff, *Eastern Christian Thought*, 190.

[69] Moshe Barasch, *Icon: Studies in the History of an Idea* (NY University Press, 1991), 217. Although Barasch is not Orthodox (he is Jewish), his examination carefully traces out the development of iconography. Especially insightful is his analysis of *The Ladder of Divine Ascent*, written near the beginning of the seventh century by John Climacus. John of Damascus (called by some the Aquinas of the East) was probably the greatest iconographical theologian ever. He took the Ladder, reworked it with the help of Dionysius the Areopogite's Neoplatonic philosophical framework, and used it as a model for his defense of icons. For John of Damascus, icons have tremendous force in Christian piety because of their visual characteristics. This is tied to the understanding that God in His pre-creation mind (his foreknowledge) knew what kind of things were to be created by looking at their image in His divine mind. *"Looking - that is, the visual experience taking place within God's mind—is a primary form of knowledge,"* said Barasch, 224 (my emphasis). It logically followed for John of Damascus to teach that looking likewise is a form of true knowledge for the believer.

[70] As important as the theological arguments were, it was also the case that the emperors in 787 and 843 were iconodules.

[71] Thousands of iconodule monks were killed in these conflicts. Bradley Nassif, "Kissers and Smashers: Why the Orthodox killed one another over icons." *Christian History*, 54 (1997, no. 2), 21.

Jaroslav Pelikan has insightfully developed how it is that the difference of emphasis between Western Christian (most specifically Catholic) and Eastern Christian (Orthodox) religious art is very much a matter rooted in Christology. Pelikan said:

> In the West it was - and is - the Passion and Crucifixion that was seen as having achieved the reconciliation between God and fallen humanity, with the Resurrection seen as the divine attestation that the Atonement achieved on the cross had been accepted by God the Father and that divine justice had been satisfied. Iconographically, that emphasis led to the almost universal distribution of the crucifix in the medieval Latin Church as the distinctive symbol of the Atonement.[72]

Christ's incarnation enabled him to be crucified in the place of sinful humanity. The result was that the violation of God's justice was thereby atoned. Pelikan described this soteriological view as an "upward" one: God himself has been appeased. Even though the Catholic crucifix was replaced with a bare cross by the bulk of Protestantism, the latter nonetheless remains affixed near the altar of most Protestant churches.[73]

In the East, Pelikan argued, a "downward" view of Christology and soteriology resulted: Christ, as God incarnate, descended into Hades, "bound the strong man" (Luke 11:21-22) and stripped him of his spoils (the souls imprisoned there).[74] To Pelikan's analysis we can add that not only is the East's view a "downward" one by virtue of Christ's defeat of Satan, it is also a downward one because of its emphasis upon the incarnation of the Logos. The Logos, in an act of supreme condescension, humbled himself and took on flesh. God descended and took on human nature so that human beings may ascend and partake of His nature. Clearly, in the Orthodox model salvation is always initiated by God himself. Thus, Orthodoxy denies that people can gain God's grace or energies apart from Christ. Moreover, despite their high view of human persons as the beings created to reflect God's identity, they do not accept that persons can achieve God's purpose apart from the person of Christ.[75]

To the aforementioned theological issues, the issue of the Orthodox' love of beauty must be added in order to accurately understand Orthodox

---

[72] Pelikan, *Imago Dei*, 96.

[73] Pelikan, *Imago Dei*, 96-97.

[74] Pelikan, *Imago Dei*, 97-98.

[75] Ware, *The Orthodox Church*, 226-229, also described the differences between the East and the West. His conclusion was much like Pelikan's.

iconography.[76] This aesthetic dimension of Orthodoxy stems from its appropriation of ancient Hellenistic culture, a culture which held that beauty reveals something of ultimate truth.[77] Orthodoxy made inroads into Russia as early as AD 987 precisely because of its aesthetic and ceremonial beauty. The cultural antecedent is clear, but unique to the Orthodox is their conviction that that which is truly beautiful is something which is recognized as such by the Christian community, and not just by an individual. Something is not beautiful solely because it produces an emotional response in the eye of the beholder. Something is authentically beautiful when the community recognizes something in the object that signifies a shared communal value. True beauty, Ugolnik asserted, is not a product or achievement of artistic genius, rather it is something that "radiates from the Godhead itself," and causes a kinetic effect on those who participate in it. Additionally, the thrust of beauty is to effect a bridge between the object and the audience; a luminous experience is the desired result, not a system of didactic facts which can be broken down into parts and rationally understood.[78] And, lest it seem that we are straying from the topic, it is reiterated that iconography is only possible, and only has its role in *theosis*, because of Christ's incarnation and the subsequent ramifications for the transformation of the entire cosmos.

Finally, while iconography is motivated by theology and aesthetics, it is also true that the contemporary Orthodox believe icons serve a very central role in the believer's spiritual life. Quenot rightly argued that we are influenced by society's symbols. Whether they come at us from the media or Madison

---

[76] For a very detailed presentation of beauty and mysticism see Vladimir Sergeyevich Solovyov, "Beauty, Sexuality, and Love," in *Ultimate Questions: An Anthology of Modern Russian Religious Thought*, A. Schmemann (ed.) (Crestwood, NY: St. Vladimir's, 1977), 73-134. The use of aesthetics is something precious to Catholics and the Orthodox alike, but the Orthodox are more intent in arguing that aesthetics are central in Christian living. The arena of aesthetics is very critical in understanding the differences between Sacramental churches and Protestant "free" or "low" churches such as Baptists or the Pentecostals.

[77] Philip Sherrard, "The Revival of Hesychast Spirituality," in *Christian Spirituality*, III, *Post-Reformation and Modern*, 418-419.

[78] Meyendorff, *Rome, Constantinople, Moscow*, 113. Ugolnik, *Illuminating Icon*, 181-190. Quote drawn from p. 187. The parallels between iconography and Jesus' method of parabolic speaking are fascinating. Neither is concerned with empirical facts. Neither is primarily concerned with systems of epistemology or truth. Both have as their goal the participatory response of the audience whereby the audience affirms that which is being conveyed and causes them to draw closer to God.

Avenue, we are greatly impacted by the images which constantly bombard us.[79] "Images and pictures manage to worm their way into the very depths of our souls by their highly suggestive, symbolic force; their impact on our sensibilities at the same [time] threatens our interior life," Quenot said. Icons, not only of Christ but also those of angels and the saints, represent to the believer, continued Quenot, "a world transformed, transfigured, rendered transparent by a spiritualization which embraces the entire cosmos." Because icons reflect the life and purity of those depicted, they are images which help to sanctify the believer's soul.[80] The believer is not changed, and does not experience something of the divine, by passively standing in front of icons or by simply having them in one's home; thus, the Orthodox deny superstitious transference. But by actively participating in the life of Christ (through contemplation, prayer, confession, and veneration) that is reflected in the icon, the believer's faith and courage are strengthened, and the believer's interior life is purified. Expressing the dynamism of this kind of experience Lossky said, "An icon or a cross does not exist simply to direct our imagination during our prayers. It is a material centre [sic] in which there reposes an energy, a divine force, which unites itself to human art." The believer's active participation via contemplation (*anamnesis*) avails the believer "an initiation into a mystery," the mystery of Christ's incarnation and the deifying union made possible via His Holy Spirit.[81]

Paul Evdokimov, a Russian Orthodox philosopher-theologian, taught that simple signs do not participate in the reality of their subject. For example, a stop sign or an algebraic sign are only arbitrary symbols, they only have meaning because civilization agrees that they do. Religious symbols, on the other hand, do participate in the reality of their subject. The icon, Evdokimov said, "performs the function of revealing the 'meaning' and at the same time it is the expressive receptacle of the 'presence.'"[82] The icon, in itself, has no ontological existence. But because it participates in the subject reflected, it becomes sacramental and participates in the subject's existence. The icon's purpose is not to arouse an emotional response in the believer, instead it is

---

[79] American Protestant Christians openly affirm political and cultural symbolism, but deny nearly all religious symbolism. Clearly, this is neither necessary nor healthy. Should evangelical Christians nullify all symbolism, or should they more carefully employ edifying religious symbols in an attempt to level the existing imbalance?

[80] Quenot, *The Icon*, 147. The iconographical ramifications for Orthodox spirituality are manifold and cannot be exhausted here.

[81] Lossky, *Mystical Theology*, 189-191. Quotes are from p. 189.

[82] Peter C. Phan, *Culture and Eschatology: The Iconographical Vision of Paul Evdokimov* (NY: Peter Lang, 1985), 276.

painted in order to evoke within the believer a mystical feeling, a sense of the mysterium tremendum.[83]

Summary and Analysis

Orthodoxy's Christology and iconography are both so theologically complex that we cannot give either of these two facets of Orthodoxy the detailed analysis they deserve. Nonetheless because these declarative chapters establish the foundation for the later conclusion, some comment is both appropriate and necessary.

Christology

As this chapter has shown, the Orthodox' doctrine of *theosis* rests firmly upon Christology. For the Orthodox, the decisions of the early church, such as that rendered at Chalcedon, were not simply clarifications of extremely complex doctrinal issues, they were foundational for a proper understanding of humankind's salvation. Because of their Hellenistic philosophical context, the early church quite naturally asked these questions: How could it be simultaneously affirmed that God is one and Jesus is God? If Jesus is truly God how then can it be said he is fully human? These were largely resolved by employing the philosophical terms of *hypostasis, physis,* and *homoousios,* respectively. The Western church increasingly tended to interpret these ontological terms within a juridical framework whereby Jesus was able to satisfy the demands of the law because he was human; he had the ability to forgive sins and send the Holy Spirit because he was God. Contrastingly, the Eastern church increasingly developed the church fathers' decisions within its original ontological framework: God's becoming something new (human) had a plethora of ramifications for both humans and the entire cosmos. First and foremost, Jesus Christ's taking on of human nature opened the door of possibility for human persons to take on God's nature. As the above has shown, the church believed that this matter of transformation was not only motivated by God's desire that we become like him, it was also motivated by God's desire to share His existence with us. Through and in Christ's being, it is now possible

---

[83] Phan, *Culture and Eschatology,* 277. My emphasis.

that we can enjoy the very life of the Triune God (though this will ultimately be realized in eternity).

In this chapter we have clarified that the foundation for the Orthodox' anthropological essentialism is Christ himself. Simply stated, the Orthodox believe Christology has shed new light on anthropology. The church experienced its progressive theological realization not only through Jesus' teachings or the Scriptural testimony, but through reflection about the person of Jesus himself. Because of the fathers' Christological reflections, we know that each person has an *hypostasis* unique to himself or herself, even though each person shares a common nature with all other human beings. Just as Christ has been revealed as the archetypical image of God who reflects God's very nature, it is similarly argued that human beings both are, and are called to be, images of God, though by grace and not nature. In an analogous manner to that of Christ's kenosis, humans are able to transcend their own nature and move in greater accord with the divine nature.

Clearly both the fathers' Christological reflections and the subsequent formulations for anthropology stemmed more from the fathers' historical context than it did from Scripture. The terms *hypostasis, physis*, and *homoousios* find their definitional locus in the patristic modification of Greek philosophy, not Scripture.[84] That the fathers sought to understand Christ primarily regarding the categories of being, space, and time is the result of the historical context which pressed down heavily upon them, though the Orthodox themselves would view this as the providence of God working for the edification of the church. That the very word "theology" for the Orthodox is not an intellectual enterprise but an experience of the Triune God's being,[85] makes evident their reliance upon the Greek ontological context. We dare not fault them for this; they were not in control of the cultural-philosophical milieu or historical climate any more than we are today. Instead, they are to be admired for their commitment to the Gospel, their spiritual zeal, and their intellectual genius. Furthermore, it is here asserted that they were being guided by the Holy Spirit as they sought to define and present Christ within their historical context.

---

[84] Υπόστασις (2 Cor. 9:4; 11:17, and Heb. 3:14) and φύσις (Rom. 11:21, 24; 1 Cor. 11:14; Gal. 2:15; Eph. 2:3; Jas. 3:7; 2 Pet. 1:4) do appear in Scripture. The former is best interpreted as confidence, assurance, or frame of mind. The latter is variously interpreted as one's condition, one's characteristics, one's disposition, or the natural order. Walter Bauer, *A Greek-English Lexicon of the New Testament and Other Early Christian Literature*, W. F. Arndt and F. W. Bauer (tr.) (The University of Chicago Press, 1979). 2 Pet. 1:4 is the passage closest to the patristic ontological themes, and for that reason is a shibboleth in Orthodox theology.

[85] Lossky, *Mystical Theology*, 9, 38, 43, 65, et al.

Indeed, the church will forever be indebted to their witness to the truth and life of Christ's person. All this notwithstanding, there are at least three problems with Orthodox Christology: an historical one, a hermeneutical one, and an issue of inconsistency.

AN HISTORICAL CRITICISM

The Orthodox do not believe that the *charismata* of the Spirit have ceased being present or irrupting on to the plane of human existence (though, like the Catholics, the Orthodox believe the Spirit's activity occurs primarily, but not exclusively, within a sacramental structure). However, the Orthodox do believe that Spirit-guided and inspired doctrinal formulation, especially as it concerns Christian dogma, ceased (for all intent and purpose) with the Orthodox fathers. It remains for each subsequent generation of the church to reflect back upon the fathers' formulations. Those formulations may be recontextualized, but the core of their truths may be neither abandoned nor altered. In this the Orthodox view of history and doctrinal formulation is unique: the *sine qua non* is the patristic era. John Meyendorff said, "The Church is apostolic indeed, but the Church is also patristic." He continued:

> There is no way in which one can remain faithful to the original gospel without learning how the Fathers defended it, and without sharing in their struggle to formulate it in a way accessible to their contemporaries. Indeed, it is *their* victory over heresies that the Church endorsed at its ecumenical councils. They are the 'Fathers' because the Church recognized them. . . as having taken the right positions on issues of faith.

> There is no way in which that [patristic] truth can be known and understood except by entering the 'mind' of the Fathers, becoming their contemporaries in spirit and, therefore, allowing oneself to become as Greek as they were. Our theology today must maintain *consistency* with their positions: all Orthodox theologians must therefore become 'Greek' in that sense.[86]

In light of such sentiments, it is clear that Orthodoxy's Christology is not the chief problematic issue for non-Orthodox theologians, or non-Orthodox Christians, in general. But the Orthodox' rather insistent position wherein doctrinal formulation - for all intent and purpose - froze with the end of the patristic era, their belief that all subsequent Christological formulations and

---

[86] Meyendorff, *Catholicity and the Church*, 46-47. Meyendorff was initially quoting from Georges Florovsky, *Bible, Church, Tradition: An Eastern Orthodox View* (Belmont, Mass.: Nordland, 1972), 107. Emphases are Meyendorff's.

reflections must be consistent with that of the Greek fathers, and their belief that all theologians - if they are to be consistent with the true church - must somehow become Greek, results in a parochial definition of both church history and Christian theology which segregates those who are not Orthodox as somehow being heterodox.

The crucible for Orthodox' continued influence is not Christology, it is history. God is immutable, but history is forever changing. The Orthodox are correct to assert the necessity of historical continuity for Christianity. God became human in time and space. Those people who bore witness to that event, and who in turn wrote down that witness, lived in time and space. We are sinners who live in time and space, and we need a Savior who impacts time and space. Ever confronted by the issues of time and space, we must - as the Orthodox do - carefully reflect on the ramifications which the Christ-event continues to have on each subsequent historical generation. The Orthodox' theological strength in that regard notwithstanding, the problem confronting the Orthodox' model is that since the demise of the Byzantine era (c. fifteenth century)[87] the historical-philosophical-cultural context, for the West anyway, has changed with great regularity. Today the Orthodox are experiencing unprecedented philosophical and cultural changes within nations that were largely, though far from exclusively, their own domain. The danger that such contextual shifts holds for Orthodoxy is that the genius and beauty of its Christology (presenting Christ in terms of ontology, time, and space) will be disregarded altogether, and this for two coterminous reasons. Firstly, the Orthodox argue adamantly that authentic Christological dogma must be preeminently expressed in Greek terms, as Meyendorff exemplified above. Those who do not accept this Greek framework (though it is clear each national Orthodox church slightly modifies it) are told that they do not enjoy the fullness of what it means to be Christian. The sheer triumphalism of such a claim unquestionably presents a stumbling block, not only to the billions of non-Christians who happen to find themselves situated on the other 80% of the earth, but also to the other Christians who were either so unfortunate as to be born in non-Orthodox countries, or born into a historic context where Greek philosophy no longer reigns or never did.[88] Secondly, and vastly more

---

[87] The Byzantine empire's fall coincidentally occurred at approximately the same time as the Renaissance and Reformation of Western Europe. Schmemann, *The Historical Road of Eastern Orthodoxy*, 271.

[88] One must ask, is God sovereign over the whole of human history, or over the Greek patristic and Byzantine eras alone? That is, what is the standard for determining when God is providentially guiding human history and when he is not? Because the Byzantine empire fell around the same time of the Renaissance should we hold that God

important, is the Orthodox' insistence to hold to, and purport, a philosophical context that is being eaten away by the winds of time and forces of modernity.[89] Jesus Christ must be presented within the various philosophical constructs of each culture and age. Each Christian generation is given the task to present Christ to the milieu in which it finds itself. The apostle Paul did not say, "all people must become like me," but instead said, "I have become all things to all people, that I might by all means save some," (1 Cor. 9:19-23). The apostle Peter initially resisted, but then accepted, God's revelation in this regard (Acts 10:9-16). The failure to so re-contextualize the good news about Christ will potentially render the Orthodox church irrelevant, and the entire church will suffer for it.[90]

A HERMENEUTICAL CRITICISM
The second critique of Orthodox Christology concerns biblical hermeneutics (though admittedly, this is part and parcel of their historical view). As was noted in our critique of Orthodox anthropology, the Bible need not be necessarily understood via ontological lenses. Within their own historical-cultural context, the Jewish writers of the Old Testament and the Christians of the New were as concerned with the function and actions of the messiah, if not more so, than his being. One way to understand Jesus' historical-cultural context is through a study of His titles.[91] There are a multitude of titles which could be noted, but because they are foundational for Orthodoxy's Christology and anthropology we will briefly note the titles of Son of God, Son of Man, and Image. Furthermore, it is asserted here that the chief and initial historical

providentially wanted to change the course of human history? These are huge problems needing delicate and careful treatment.

[89] That is, Western capitalism and its underpinning pragmatic-individualistic-existential philosophy which is pervading the entire globe. Newspaper and magazine articles are printed every week journaling the spread of Western values and commercialism into formerly non-impacted geographic locations, especially within the former Communist bloc. Schmemann, *Church, World, Mission: Reflections on Orthodoxy in the West* (Crestwood, NY: St. Vladimir's, 1979) makes similar criticisms of Orthodoxy throughout his book.

[90] Indeed, we can say that the entire church has suffered for it, not only at the level of shared missiological activity, or at the level of national cooperation, but even theologically and spiritually. I am here especially thinking of the corporate dimensions of Orthodox spirituality which have largely been ignored in the West.

[91] There are several other avenues which could similarly be employed (e.g., His miracles, His resurrection, the early Christian kerygma, and the higher critical methods).

context for understanding Jesus' identity lies with Judaism first, and Hellenism only secondarily.[92]

In the Old Testament divine sonship was ascribed to angels, the nation of Israel, and - most importantly for understanding Jesus - kings. A king's sonship was characterized functionally in that he belonged in a unique way to God, was a special servant of God, and was the benefactor of God's blessings. The king was called God's son because of his authority over the people and because of God's covenant with David. In the Old Testament, Son of God is not used with reference to the messiah.[93] When Jesus used the title for himself, or when we read it on the lips of others, we do well to understand the phrase with the Old Testament context in mind. Jesus uniquely belonged to God, was indeed God's special servant, and uniquely enjoyed the blessings of God.

In the Synoptic Gospels Jesus only refers to himself explicitly as the Son of God five times.[94] Each of these five, as well as those instances where others call him the Son of God, can be understood in terms of His unique relationship to God the Father. He was unique in His belonging, His appointed status, and His blessing. Moreover, Jesus' temptation as the Son of God was precisely directed at his messianic role, and not His messianic nature.[95] Taken together, the Son of

---

[92] That is, while the apostles - the eyewitnesses of Jesus - likely spoke Greek, they were firstly Jews. This is especially evident in Acts, where the shift in the church's identity, from a Jewish to a Gentile organism, takes place only with great difficulty (and the aid of divine visions).

[93] D. R. Bauer, "Son of God," in *Dictionary of Jesus and the Gospels*, Joel B. Green, S. McKnight, I. H. Marshall (eds.) (Grand Rapids: InterVarsity Press, 1992), 769-775. Hereafter this Dictionary will be referred to as *DJG*.

[94] Lk. 22:70 where he indirectly says so by answering a question; in John's gospel Jesus refers to himself as the Son of God four times (5:25; 9:35; 10:36; 11:4). I hold that John the evangelist is speaking in 3:18. Other manuscripts have Son of Man at Jn. 9:35. Throughout the Gospels, Son of God is used almost exclusively by those addressing Jesus (exorcised demons or those confessing His identity).

[95] Mt. 4:1-11; Lk. 4:1-13. It is fascinating how Jesus' contemporaries reacted to him. His opponents did not reject him because of his metaphysical claims, they primarily rejected him because of His words and actions. According to their understanding of the Old Testament and in light of their nationalistic pride, he was not doing the things they expected of the messiah. Though the examples are numerous, we will note just a few. He eliminated the notion that God would exact vengeance upon the Gentiles and taught that salvation/the Kingdom of God included the Gentiles (Lk. 4:16-29; 9:51-56; Mk. 4:30-32). He taught that humans were more important than the sabbath, and that he was lord over the sabbath (Mk. 2:27-28; Lk. 13:10-17). He performed miracles which garnered a large popular following, but he taught in an unorthodox manner at best, and an heretical one at worst; in this he was perceived as a false prophet, the likes of which were warned

God passages imply a relationship that was marked by intimacy, obedience -
especially as it concerned His suffering and death - and a task to glorify the
Father.[96] Taken together, the Son of God passages imply the unprecedented
functional role that belonged to Jesus of Nazareth.[97]

Son of Man was Jesus' preferred manner of self-designation. Of the eighty-
two instances where it occurs in the Gospels, only once does someone else
address him as such.[98] Regarding the title's historical background, scholars are
fairly unanimous that there is a direct correspondence with its Old Testament
usage in Daniel (7:13), but that Jesus and/or the evangelists modified it with the
"rejected stone" of the Psalms (22; 69; 118:22) and the "Servant of Yahweh" in
Isaiah (52:13-53:12). In each case the figure is one who suffers, is vindicated by
God, and given authority. Thus, when Jesus is referring to himself as the Son of
Man, he is revealing something about His function as God's chosen one: he has
been chosen by God to suffer, be vindicated, and retain God's authority. Again,
the title is not employed by Jesus to indicate His human nature (few of his
contemporaries would have doubted that), but to indicate His function as God's
chosen agent.[99]

---

about in Deut. 13. Similarly, John the Baptist had proclaimed Jesus as the lamb of God
(Jn. 1:29,36), had been present at His baptism, had seen the Holy Spirit in the form of a
dove descend upon Jesus, and perhaps had heard the heavenly voice of approval (Mt. 3;
Mk. 1; Lk. 3). And yet John still doubted, in part, because Jesus wasn't doing the kinds
of Messianic things he expected (Mt. 11:2-6; Lk. 7:18-23). After His resurrection we
would expect that the disciples would have had a better understanding of Jesus,
nonetheless they were still hoping he would do the things they expected the Messiah to
do (Acts 1:6). Because of his teachings and actions he was ultimately crucified. Scot
McKnight, "Gentiles," in *DJG*, 259-265; Stephen Westerholm, "Sabbath," in *Dictionary
of Jesus and the Gospels*, 716-19; Gary M. Burge, "'I Am' Sayings," in *DJG*, 354-356;
Colin Brown, *Miracles and the Critical Mind* (Grand Rapids: Eerdmans, 1984); Larry
W. Hurtado, "Christ," in *DJG*, 106-117.
[96] Bauer, "Son of God," 772-775.
[97] James D. G. Dunn, *Christology in the Making: An Inquiry into the Origins of the
Doctrine of the Incarnation* (London: SCM, 1989[2]), 12-64, offers a thorough
examination of the historical context for Son of God. Dunn carefully examines the
various functional ways the Synoptic evangelists use the phrase in their gospels, rejects
John's use of Son of God in a pre-existent sense as an interpolation, and ultimately
concludes that, "we cannot say with any confidence that Jesus knew himself to be divine,
the pre-existent Son of God," 32.
[98] Jn. 12:34 where the people quote Jesus' phrase back to him and inquire about its
messianic meaning.
[99] I. Howard Marshall, "Son of Man," in *DJG*, 775-781, believes that alongside these
functional meanings for the title, it may have indicated both Jesus' divinity (because,

The word image is never used for Jesus in the Gospels. This does not at all mean it is not authentically Christian, but it does mean it was not a vehicle used by Jesus to express either His identity or function. We cannot here exhaust each of the six New Testament passages (each of which is found in Pauline literature)[100] related to Jesus Christ as God's image, but we can make a few summary points. In none of these six is the notion of the divinization of human nature explicitly taught, and this true whether Jesus and/or believers are the subject(s) of the passage. It is true that in five of these Jesus' incarnate nature is a presupposition for the believer's own transformation,[101] but not one of these five gives any detail as to how the believer can increasingly become divine in this life.[102] Instead, the clear emphasis in each of these five is the action of God in and upon the believer.[103] The passage quoted at this chapter's onset (1 Cor. 15:42-49) is a passage that, upon first glance, may seem to be forcefully arguing for the divinization of human nature; indeed, it is a theological explanation of the transformation of human persons. However, in this passage Paul founded

---

like the figure in Daniel 7, he comes from heaven) and His humanity (though he thinks it doubtful the ancient Greek reader would catch this sense from the phrase). Dunn, *Christology in the Making*, 65-97, ascribes much functional meaning to the phrase, but categorically denies that Son of Man initially (with Jesus or His disciples) denoted the idea of pre-existence, 95.

[100] Εἰκὼν: Rom. 8:29; 1 Cor. 15:49; 2 Cor. 3:18; 4:4; Col. 1:15; 3:10. Heb. 1:3 uses χαρακτὴρ τῆς ὑποστάσεως αὐτοῦ (the exact representation of God's nature/being/reality).

[101] Rom. 8:29; 2 Cor. 3:18; 4:4; Col. 1:15; 3:10.

[102] Though the argument could be made that to be divine is to *do* the things Christ did and does.

[103] In Rom. 8:29 God foreknew and predestined those who would be conformed to His Son's image. The emphasis upon God's action is continued in 8:30 where God calls, justifies, and glorifies. John Murray, *The Epistle to the Romans*, The New International Commentary on The New Testament (Grand Rapids: Eerdmans, 1980[11]), 303-321. In 2 Cor. 3:18-4:4 the emphasis is upon God's work of transformation, a work which occurs via the knowledge of the Gospel. In Col. 1:15 nothing is mentioned about how humans must become divine like Christ. Instead Christ is presented, F. F. Bruce said, "as the agent of God in the whole range of His gracious purpose towards men, from the primaeval work of creation through the redemption accomplished at history's mid-point on to the new creation in which God's purpose will be consummated." *Commentary on the Epistle to the Colossians*. The New International Commentary on The New Testament (Grand Rapids: Eerdmans, 1980[11]), 193. Col. 3:10 sits within a pericope where Paul compares the ways and attitudes of the old life with those of the new; but none of the new characteristics have to do with the divinization of human nature. Instead, we are to become like Christ our creator in the mundane ways described in 3:11-4:6. Cf., Bruce, *Colossians*, 266-274.

the ultimate transformation of the believer's body upon Jesus Christ's *resurrection*, not His incarnation. Moreover, Paul does not teach that we have a part to play in this final and glorious transformation, but rather that God will cause it to occur at our resurrection.[104]

The image language in the New Testament is sparse at best. When it does occur it has more to do with behaviors and attitudes, both those of Christ and His followers, than it does with precise metaphysical delineations. The latter are not altogether excluded, but each passage does not find its force, or emphasis, in the metaphysical realm. It is only when one approaches these passages within a Greek philosophical context that the metaphysical dimensions leap out, as it were, from the biblical context.

By no means is it here denied that the various titles of Christ imply and/or reveal something of His metaphysical identity. Jesus' own self-understanding, His teaching, the fullness of the Spirit upon him, His deeds, and His resurrection all imply that there were unique characteristics about the one whom the primitive church would call creator and Lord. What is being argued is that the Christological titles themselves are as much about function as they are about nature.[105] If one exclusively interprets these titles within an ontological framework, as the Orthodox tend to, it is easy to overlook the function and action unique to Christ. Within the Orthodox' hermeneutic, Jesus' life, teaching, atoning work and resurrection become secondary to His incarnation. But this interpretation is not harmonious with the full apostolic witness. Admittedly, we are critiquing the degree of emphasis in Orthodox Christology. Nonetheless, to uncritically read Nicene-Constantinopolitan Christology back into the biblical record is to work an anachronistic Scriptural hermeneutic.

A CRITICISM OF INCONSISTENCY

My last critique of Orthodox Christology is its inconsistency regarding the implications of Christ's incarnation. The Orthodox teach that Christ took on the fullness of human nature, though he did so without assuming an human *hypostasis*. Nonetheless, the Orthodox teach that although he became a man, the

---

[104] Gordon D. Fee, *The First Epistle to the Corinthians*. The New International Commentary on The New Testament. F. F. Bruce (ed.),(Grand Rapids: Eerdmans, 1987) 784-801. F. F. Bruce, *I and II Corinthians*. The New Century Bible Commentary, Ronald E. Clements and M. Black (eds.) (Grand Rapids: Eerdmans, 1984), 151-153.

[105] Bauer, "Son of God," in *DJG*, 769-775. Bauer notes that the debates about Jesus' titles are complex and varied. We must also look to the Epistles in order to understand the early church's beliefs about Jesus. It is in the latter that what was formerly rather implicit regarding Christ's nature in the Gospels becomes more explicit (E.g., Rom. 1:3-4; 1 Cor. 15:42-49; Phil. 2:5-11; Col. 1:15-20, et al.).

implications of His incarnation are not limited to maleness. Instead, Christ took on human nature and enhypostasized it in a way that all of humanity was included in himself (again, because to be human is to share in the reality and existence of the entire human race). This enhypostasization sanctified every facet of human nature. It would seem logically to follow that this sanctification included the dimension of gender. That is, either these gender dimensions were pronounced null and void in Christ with respect to life in the Kingdom, or they were not.[106]

Despite both Christ's incarnational affirmation of creation and His enhypostasization of humanity, each of the fourteen autocephalous branches of Eastern Orthodoxy prohibits women from significant leadership within the church.[107] Is this not spurious? Put differently, those churches which do not make such a forceful ontological argument for the all-encompassing character of Christ's incarnation may be somewhat justified, on the basis of some Scripture verses, in maintaining distinctions between men and women in Christian leadership. However, despite the Orthodox' ontology of Christ and its ramifications upon eschatological living (life in the Kingdom), they deny the most culturally and socially radical implication of Christ's incarnation: that men and women are equal - but not the same - in God's Kingdom. Despite their intricately developed Christology, and despite the ramifications for the sexes implicit in their doctrine of the incarnation, the contemporary Orthodox have clearly fallen prey to the patriarchal milieu from which they originated.[108]

---

[106] One writer who addressed Christ's maleness and its implications for ontology (human and divine) was Nonna Verna Harrison, "The Maleness of Christ." *St. Vladimir's*, 42:2 (1998), 111-151. Harrison made a fascinating survey of Greek patristic discussions about male and femaleness and the implications for theological and iconic language. However, she did not at all address the ecclesial issues, issues that went begging despite her study's implications.

[107] Women are not allowed to be hierarchical officials or priests. In most Orthodox national churches abroad, women have no role to play in the liturgical services. Many Orthodox churches in the United States have begun to more effectively enjoin the service of women, but the Greek Orthodox Archbishop of the United States, Spyridon, had strongly urging the churches to return to the old ways. To the disdain of many U.S. Orthodox, he had even opposed having women sing in church choirs. Paul Glastris, "An American-born archbishop, Old World values," in *U. S. News and World Report*, 123:15 (October 20, 1997), 62-63.

[108] Ware, *The Orthodox Church*, 292-4, said that in the ancient (patristic) Orthodox church women were ordained as deacons. Whereas women baptized other women and performed pastoral duties among female members of the church they did not preach or help administer the eucharist. Women's roles in this regard began to diminish in the sixth and seventh centuries, and was completely gone by the eleventh century. Ware

The New Testament contains a few specific statements limiting women's roles in the church, but it may well be that those were intended for specific audiences and their particular historical issues.[109] Those exclusionary passages need to be taken together with the numerous New Testament passages which favor women and their ministerial roles. Jesus, culturally iconoclastic as he was, practiced a radical inclusiveness, numbering women among his disciples.[110] He healed women, accepted them, and forgave them. And, especially as Luke portrays it, women played a critical proclamatory role, both at Christ's coming and resurrection.[111] Several passages in the epistles denote women's key roles, their service, and their exercise of the charismata.[112] Paul made what were then revolutionary sociological statements about the mutuality and reciprocity of husbands and wives.[113] His statement, "There is neither Jew nor Greek, there is neither slave nor free man, there is neither male nor female; for you are all one in Christ Jesus," was an incredible comment regarding the implications of Christ's life and atoning work.[114] In light of all these passages affirming both women and their ministerial roles, it seems that the few passages limiting women's churchly roles only evince how difficult it was for the primitive church itself to break from its own patriarchal culture. With regard to Scripture's implications, can one fairly argue that whereas women had a critical role in salvation history (carrying the Saviour in utero, as well as the above mentioned examples) - that is pertaining to Christ in the flesh - they must nonetheless be excluded from those roles pertaining to the resurrected Christ? The Orthodox, in effect, seem to be saying, "Women and salvation history? Yes! But, in the past, not now."

Additionally, Maximus' position that God created Eve in light of the fall, so that the human race would be thus enabled to survive their death as mortals, directly contradicts the passage's very context wherein God pronounces the

---

argued that the Orthodox needed to carefully reconsider the arguments pertaining to women's service.

[109] 1 Cor. 14:34-35; 1 Tim. 2:12.
[110] Lk. 8:1-3; 10:38-42; Jn. 2:5; 19:26-67; Acts 1:15; 2:17; 9:36; 12:12.
[111] For his coming see Lk. 1:5-2:40. On the resurrection see Lk. 24:1-10; par. Mt. 28:1-8; Mk. 16:1-8; Jn. 20:1-13. See, David M. Scholer, "Women," in *DJG*, 880-887.
[112] Acts 1:14 (women numbered among the disciples); Rom. 16:1-15 (among the several women noted here is Phoebe, a lady deacon); 1 Cor. 11:5 (women prophesying); 1 Cor. 16:19 (Priscilla, Paul's co-worker); Phi. 4:3 (women as Paul's co-workers).
[113] 1 Cor. 7: 2-6; Eph. 5:22-33.
[114] Gal. 3:28.

entirety of His creation as good (Gen. 1:31).[115] In light of the Genesis accounts, the very definition of what it means to be created in the image of God implies this orientation toward the other. That is, the distinctions between maleness and femaleness reflect the similarity-but-otherness of the three divine *hypostases*.[116] Thus, *the imago dei* must itself be understood in light of the male and female distinctions. The Orthodox rightly assert that humans, created in God's image, were created with the need for fellowship with others. But, I would assert that this otherness is not just a distinction between human *hypostases*, it is precisely a God-intended distinction between the genders. We must indeed transcend ourselves to be fully human; in this the Orthodox prod us in very Christian directions. But to realize fully our potential as humans, we need even to transcend our own sexual identity and enjoy the fellowship of those sexually different from ourselves.[117] Ultimately, this recognition of the genuine goodness of God's creating humans as male and female, coupled with both Christ's own radical teaching and His sanctification of the entire human race, can never stand in harmony with teachings that limit and exclude one or the other gender from full Christian service.

Iconography

Into the eighth and ninth centuries, a multifaceted theology developed regarding sacred images - icons. Whereas the earliest Christians employed religious art for didactic reasons and reasons of veneration, later theologians, especially when provoked by the iconoclasts, wrought a very detailed and intricate defense on the basis of Christ's incarnation. Ultimately the iconophiles' apology was

---

[115] John Behr, Assistant Professor of Patristics at St. Vladimir's Seminary, argues that neither the creation narratives nor Christ himself (Mt. 19:3-7) attributed sexual differentiation to the Fall. "A Note On The 'Ontology of Gender," *St. Vladimir's*, 42:3-4 (1998), 365-366.

[116] Hoekema, *Created in God's Image*, 75-82.

[117] Dennis Praeger, a Jewish philosopher-theologian and talk-radio show host, argues that homosexual relationships fall short of God's full intent for humans precisely because they do not transcend this gender gap. For the same reason, he believes we are to marry strangers and not extended family members. Homosexual sex is ultimately a very selfish kind of sex because it does not move one beyond one's own sexual identity. Praeger voiced his opinion on this as recently as 10/24/97. For a compendium of his thought, see, *Think A Second Time* (NY: ReganBooks, 1995). Racism, and the fostering of racial homogeneity, similarly falls short of God's intent that we transcend our own definitional boundaries.

one rooted in the Greek categories of ontology: if Christ genuinely took on created matter and located himself within space and time, if the ineffable and transcendent God had genuinely circumscribed himself in human flesh, then it could be cogently argued that God had both sanctified His creation by entering into it and allowed himself to be seen in the flesh. Whereas the invisible God formerly made himself known through the prophets and angels, he - the second *hypostasis* of the Trinity - had permitted himself to be seen in Christ. Whereas the holy and ineffable God had formerly forbidden images, Christ - the very image of the Father - fulfilled the law and liberated the church to use created matter to reflect His identity. Eventually icons were understood to be essential to the life of the church; and, the reasoning again was that the Logos had not only appeared to be a man, he had in fact become a man. Icons testify to and reflect this coinherence of the divine and the material in Christ. If we refuse to use art to reflect Christ's identity, the Orthodox argue, then we are simultaneously refusing to admit that God became man, that he sanctified his creation, and that he wants us to make those things known. Just as Scripture employs written symbols to express God's self-revelation, so too can the church's use of art. Just as faith is necessary to understand and acknowledge the Scriptural message, so too is faith necessary to understand and acknowledge the iconographical message.

Iconography deserves its own careful analysis, both at the theological and aesthetic levels, but because of our broader purpose only a few comments will be made. The following remarks are qualified as those of a Westerner looking East. I am a neophyte to Orthodoxy who sees tremendous beauty in Orthodox theology, generally, and the icons, more specifically. However, I do not share the Orthodox' conviction that icons are essential for Christian faith (pedagogically or theologically), nor would I establish their being warranted on the basis of Christ's incarnation (but rather on the goodness of God's creation, and our cultural mandate in Gen. 1:28).

AESTHETICS AND AFFECTIVE SPIRITUALITY

Whether icons ontologically participate in the reality (*hypostasis* or *ousia*) of those depicted (the prototypes) is largely an issue of faith. As such, icons' metaphysical participation can either be believed or rejected. There is neither a favorable biblical foundation for a thoroughgoing philosophy of sacred images, nor can the empirical sciences sustain the Orthodox' belief that icons share in the reality of those depicted. Icons are artwork plain and simple. Having said that, there is little plain or simple about them. They are quite simply, and quite powerfully, effective tools for shaping a precise spiritual atmosphere. There are many features about iconography deserving comment, but, in keeping with the functional character of this study, I will focus on their effect.

Especially within an Orthodox church, amid the smell of incense and the drama of the Liturgy, icons can indeed cause a perceptible affective response within one observing them. Without words, icons convey something of the numinous. Silently, they represent something of the transcendence and imminence of God and eternity. Icons capture and portray something of the mysterious nature of God. Icons remind one that God is the One who exists and moves in ways that surpass our rational capacities. Even more, icons remind the observer that the church is not only comprised of those alive on earth, it also consists of those in Christ's presence as well. In the midst of a bevy of icons one *feels* something. What one feels stems from at least two sources. First, it is clear that the believer experiences what the Orthodox community intends for one to experience: the shared spiritual ethos embraced by that community. A numinous atmosphere, a reverence for God's holiness, and a pervasive sense of the inbreaking of God's kingdom into the realm of this world are all intentionally reflected and portrayed through the icons. Secondly, one feels one's own affective response to the icons. That is, to borrow from Orthodox theology itself, there is a synergistic dynamic which occurs: the believer experiences the community's shared ethos with the result that one's own existential core is stirred. Or, put more simply, one can be made to be a participant in the symbol simply by observing it.[118]

Icons can cause effects resembling those intended by Jesus' use of parables: their purpose is not to convey didactically a rational tenet of God's truth,[119] but an existential-affective response to the reality of God's presence. I am intentionally employing the phrase existential-affective response regarding icons in contradistinction to the words emotional or intellectual response(s). One is not merely stirred emotionally, that is, one does not only feel awe, reverence, hope, or peace. But, neither is one merely stirred intellectually, that

---

[118] This communitarian-individual dynamic is likely one reflected (at the sociological and psycho-somatic levels) within many religions. There is much that could be done concerning a comparison of Pentecostal and Orthodox worship services and the role of symbol. One Pentecostal who interprets the Pentecostal doctrine of Spirit baptism and the manifestation of tongues at a symbolic/sacramental level is Frank Macchia, "Tongues as a Sign: Towards a Sacramental Understanding of Pentecostal Experience," *Pneuma*, 15:1 (Spring, 1993), 61-76.

[119] Gordon Fee, "The Parables: Do You Get the Point?" in Fee and D. Stuart, *How to Read the Bible for All Its Worth*, (Grand Rapids: Zondervan, 1993), 135-148. See Ugolnik, 181-190, and Kesich, *The Gospel Image of Christ*, 196, for Orthodox comments in this regard.

is, one does not simply begin to ponder afresh the doctrines of the incarnation, Trinity, ecclesiology, or the like. Instead one can be stirred in the core of one's being, with the result that one's emotions move one toward rational contemplation, and conversely so that one's intellectual contemplation causes one to desire to draw closer to the divine reality. Icons are purposefully intended to cause a response in the depths of one's being. This response, the Orthodox assert, can enable a person to progress in the process of *theosis*.

Fascinatingly, the existential-affective response wrought by the aesthetic dimensions of icons resembles the affective response wrought by the kinesthetic dimensions of Pentecostal worship.[120] In light of the vast cultural and philosophical differences between North American Pentecostals and Eastern European Orthodox Christians, this similarity is remarkable. It is a similarity that will be explored further in this dissertation's concluding section. For now I will posit that both the Orthodox and the Pentecostals are very attuned to the existential dimensions of human identity and existence. Knowledge is critical in Christian theology and transformation, but intellectual apprehension can never supplant the existential-affective dimensions of authentic Christian experience. In all of this, to be a Christian is not just to know the truth about Christ, it is also to know him experientially.

One danger posed by the powerful effect of icons, and one too often manifested within countries deemed as Orthodox, is the resultant tendency toward superstition. The Orthodox, in their theological discussions, are careful to make the distinction between veneration and true worship (*latreia*), however, if surveys are accurate, the average Orthodox layperson may not always be so mindful. Too often the image itself is seen as the source of answered prayer, or blessing, or forgiveness.[121] A second danger is that the icons are so beautiful and so existentially and affectively powerful that believers may turn to them instead of seeking Christ directly. This would seem to move icon veneration perilously close to the worship of images forbidden in the Old Testament, an issue which brings us to my second observation about iconography.

---

[120] There are indeed kinesthetic dimensions to Orthodox worship - kneeling, crossing oneself, the entry of the eucharistic elements, the priest's blessings, the lighting of candles - that I will not discuss here.

[121] Eleanor Randolph, *Waking the Tempests: Ordinary Life in the New Russia* (NY: Simon and Schuster, 1996), 144, 177-178. Sergei Filatov and Liudmila Vorontsova, "New Russia in Search of an Identity," in *Remaking Russia*, Heyward Isham (ed.) (Armonk, NY, 1995), 283, said that 67 per cent of the Russian population believe in evil spells, 66 per cent in mental telepathy, 56 per cent in astrology, and 46 per cent in UFOs. Many of these surveyed were Russian Orthodox.

A THEOLOGICAL-CONTEXTUAL INQUIRY

Together with Jesus himself,[122] the writers of the New Testament were clearly opposed to idol worship.[123] Located within their Jewish context and the surrounding rampant Gentile worship of idols, the first-century Christians would have certainly been opposed to full-fledged iconography (this despite the fact that they decorated the catacombs of the dead with Christian art to honor them).[124] But since that time the cultural and philosophical milieu has shifted so dramatically - in many non third-world countries, anyway - it seems fair to ask whether the danger of blatant idol worship is as insidious as it once was. Thus, is it fair, or accurate, to unilaterally label icons as idols?

The Orthodox are right to hold that Christ fulfilled the old covenant's laws, with the result that the Jewish religious laws therefore cease to govern our lives.[125] We are not thereby made free to practice antinomianism, because sin is still sin, and sin is antithetical to the righteousness that is ours in Christ. Thus, if some worship icons, they are in fact committing idolatry and sinning. But, if it is indeed the case that with Christ's person and work a new epoch in the history of salvation is upon us, we may indeed ask whether we are free to use His creation (physical material) to depict him. If either the paintings of Christ for sale in every Christian bookstore in the United States or if the movies regularly made about him are indications, the answer is yes. Yes, with a distinction. We do not worship those images, we use them to establish a context for our spiritual lives. We use them to aid our understanding of him, and to evoke due respect and awe for him. Similarly, the Orthodox say they are not worshipping icons, but are employing them to establish a context for their spiritual lives and their understanding of him.[126]

Protestants may disagree that icons are essential to Christian theology, or that they participate in their subject's reality, but they need to at least recognize that icons shape the worship experience of Orthodoxy's believers in important ways, ways that reflect the shared values of the larger community. We can either believe or disbelieve the Orthodox when they say they are not

---

[122] Mt. 4:8-10; Lk. 4:5-8.

[123] 1 Cor. 5:11; Gal. 5:20; 1 Pet. 4:3; 1 Jn. 5:21.

[124] Quenot, *The Icon*, 15-20.

[125] Mt. 5:17; par. Lk. 16:16-17. I would make a distinction from the Orthodox' emphasis on Christ's incarnation as the event that fulfilled the law (and thereby divinizes human nature), and instead hold that the fulfilment occurred in Christ's coming and fulfilling of the Old Testament promises about salvation-history. See Douglas J. Moo, "Law," in *DJG*, 450-461. Nonetheless, both the Orthodox and evangelicals would hold that in Christ the Jewish law has been surpassed as a means of covenant.

[126] Ugolnik, *Illuminating Icon*, 46-7.

worshipping icons. But we would do well to learn from them that every culture has its icons, some just admit it more readily than others.[127]

The issue of spiritual context, or spiritual atmosphere, and its impact on Christian transformation is an important one because the individual believer is very much shaped by the Christian community and its values. In our next chapter we will examine the atmospheres, together with some of Orthodoxy's values, as we study the means of Orthodox *theosis*.

---

[127] In part, because the use of religious objects and religious art was abusive and excessive heading into the Reformation, Protestants (especially low, or free, churches like Pentecostals) traditionally have shied away from using religious objects and art. Ugolnik, *Illuminating Icon*, 8, 48, 57, 67, and 263, exposes North American evangelicals who openly affirm and defend value indicators - icons - that are not religious but cultural. These include political icons (e.g., the president's office and the US flag, the latter of which stands in the position of honor - instead of the Christian flag - within many evangelical churches in the USA), personal icons (charismatic preachers), and materialistic icons (cars, homes, clothing, and the right to own each without limit). Ugolnik, 48, said, "Americans are like any other cultural group in that they exempt their own image-making from suspicion because they understand its context." Evangelicals will use and honor non-religious symbols, but not religious ones. What irony!

5

The Means of *Theosis*

> Do not say that it is impossible to receive the Spirit of God. Do
> not say that it is possible to be made whole without Him. Do not
> say that one can possess Him without knowing it. Do not say that
> God does not manifest Himself to man. Do not say that men
> cannot perceive the divine light, or that it is impossible in this
> age! Never is it found to be impossible, my friends. On the
> contrary, it is entirely possible when one desires it.
> Symeon the New Theologian, (AD 949-1022)[1]

Thus far we have established the historical and theological foundations for, as
well as the necessary anthropological presuppositions for, the Orthodox doctrine
of *theosis*. We saw that those foundations very much rely upon both church
tradition, especially as it was developed regarding Greek ontological constructs,
and Christology. But we have not discussed the means by which the believer is
transformed into the image of Christ. Although it is the case that the doctrine of
theosis is rooted in the belief that God is always the first mover,[2] it is also very
much the case that the individual believer has a role, a responsibility, in his or
her own transformation. It must be emphasized, the Orthodox unequivocally
affirm that salvation is through Christ Jesus alone, no one can save himself or
herself.[3] Nonetheless, as Symeon's quote above indicates, one must both desire
encounter with the divine and the resultant transformation, and one must
cooperate with the Holy Spirit in that process. The Orthodox call this mutual
cooperation synergy (from συνεργός, working together). This mutual
cooperation between the human and the divine is usually cast by the Orthodox
in ontological terms as a fusion of the divine and human natures, and not so

---

[1] Symeon the New Theologian, Hymn 27, 125-132, quoted in Basil Krivocheine, *In the
Light of Christ: St Symeon the New Theologian*, A. Gythiel (tr.) (Crestwood, NY: St.
Vladimir's, 1986), Foreword.

[2] He created us, became incarnate, sent his redeeming Holy Spirit, chooses us, and
lovingly draws us to himself. We cannot approach him without his aid.

[3] Ware, *The Orthodox Church*, 222.

much in the cooperation of the divine will and the human will, though the latter is not excluded.[4]

The Orthodox spend little effort explaining either the psychological element (the role of, or the importance of, the human will and affections) or the element of faith (its role, or the level of faith one must have to be saved and/or transformed) in the synergistic process.[5] One reason for these glaring defects, as many in the West would see them, is that the East has been largely unaffected by the growth and development of the humanities in the West (so that as understandings of the human person developed, so also did the subsequent understandings of the human person's role in salvation/spirituality). We have already examined the Orthodox' understanding of anthropology, but it deserves reiteration here that their anthropology is a very spiritual one, one not nearly as concerned with the empirical sciences. Another reason for this apparent psychological lacuna is *that Orthodoxy is more concerned with Christ's role in salvation than with the human role.*[6] If one is concerned enough to participate with Christ in his salvific role (a way of speaking which more accurately reflects Orthodoxy's understanding of salvation), one has implicitly manifested faith.[7] No one is coerced to live in light of the grace of his or her water baptism, indeed, that grace can even be lost.[8] No one is forced to love Christ. While it is true that God rewards those who diligently seek him (Heb. 11:6), no one is forced to want to become like him. Christian salvation and spirituality, reflecting the ineffable nature of the divine life itself, are not always easily understood, so that the level of one's faith is not nearly as important as the degree of one's submission to the life in Christ.[9] There are indeed ways to involve oneself in the life of Christ.

---

[4] Meyendorff, *Byzantine Theology,* 206-207.

[5] Although it should be clarified that even Athanasius recognized the necessity of faith and repentance. Constantine N. Tsirpanlis, *Introduction to Eastern Patristic Thought and Orthodox Theology* (Collegeville, Minnesota: The Liturgical Press, 1991), 68. Moreover, in Orthodoxy, repentance receives a greater emphasis than faith, both in the corporate liturgy and personal spirituality.

[6] Meyendorff rightly asserted that this focus on Christ's role in salvation was the similar thrust of both Luther and Calvin. *Catholicity,* 66-70. My emphasis.

[7] See Meyendorff, *Catholicity,* 75-76, where he discusses the human will acting in Christ.

[8] Tsirpanlis, *Eastern Patristic Thought,* 68.

[9] Thus, when a Westerner studies the Orthodox on salvation and *theosis,* and hears them expressing the Christian life in terms of involving oneself in Christ through various activities, it is tempting to charge them with a kind of works-righteousness. The irony is

In Orthodox history there have been two general approaches, two schools of thought regarding the means of *theosis*. The first is the ecclesiastical one. This includes not only the church's sacramental system (though that is essential), but also the entirety of life in the formal Christian community.[10] The second is the unmediated. This approach does not necessarily occur apart from the church (though it may), but it is generally understood as a means of encounter with the living God in a personal, and especially hesychastic, manner. Although most Orthodox theologians emphasize one of these over the other, in the history of Orthodox theology and practice it is the case that both approaches have been affirmed as having value. Moreover, the two are more accurately understood as intermingled and suffusing one another.[11] In this chapter we will examine these two means of *theosis*.

The Ecclesiastical Means of *Theosis*

The Mysteries

The sacraments, or the mysteries (from μυστήριον) in Greek,[12] are physical transmitters of God's invisible and spiritual grace. The Orthodox prefer to call them mysteries rather than sacraments because, as John Meyendorff said, the Patristic church did not distinguish the sacraments "as a specific category of Church acts." Instead, the word *musterion* had more broadly to do with the "mystery of salvation," so that the mysteries were understood more as "aspects of a unique mystery of the Church" which shares in God's divine life. These mysteries, themselves thus participating in the divine life, are the primary means

---

that this is the very charge they level against the Protestant West for its emphasis upon the human role - faith - in salvation! This reciprocal practice of libel surely reveals much about the mutual ignorance between East and West.

[10] Authentic Christian community, in the Orthodox' understanding, is one served by a priest. A church building is not necessary for the reception of the Holy Spirit's grace, but it is preferable.

[11] Meyendorff, *Byzantine Theology*, 226; Tsirpanlis, *Eastern Patristic Thought*, 150-151.

[12] Meyendorff, *Byzantine Theology*, 191. Tsirpanlis, *Eastern Patristic Thought*, 117-118, in his study of the Didache (AD 70-110) described the eucharistic sacrament as a rite of confession. Through this rite the early Christians bound themselves to Christian purity and fellowship.

for facilitating unity with God.[13] (Because the use of "mysteries" in the plural is often grammatically cumbersome, I will usually denote these as "sacraments," although the reader is urged to keep their participatory dimension in mind.) Like the church itself, the sacraments mysteriously, but orderly and objectively, contain and dispense God's grace. Sergius Bulgakov said that unlike the "disordered, unformed, [and] hysterical ecstasy" of the Holy Rollers and other sects, "the Holy Spirit is conferred. . . in a manner regulated by the Church." The sacraments are the vehicles which repeat the event of Pentecost for and in each believer, bestowing the Spirit's grace upon each according to each believer's own person. Moreover, the sacraments do not have to be understood, nor does one have to be aware of their effect, in order for grace to be transmitted.[14] So critical are they to the believer's transformational process that Nicholas Cabasilas (fourteenth century) called the sacraments "the Gates of Heaven."[15]

As was noted in our earlier discussion of Gregory Palamas, in Orthodoxy God's grace is not primarily understood as judicial pardon, but rather as the created energies of God which transform and imbue the believer with God's life.[16] Through the grace available in the sacraments, human beings are regenerated, brought into communion with God, and divinized.[17] And, while we will herein examine the sacraments as means of *theosis* (in keeping with the focus of our study), they are not simply understood as conduits of grace. They also incorporate an eschatological dimension not usually taught among the Western Christians who maintain sacramental views. The sacraments enable one to participate in, and live according to, the presence of God's Kingdom.[18] *Participation, not pardon, epitomizes Orthodox spirituality.*

---

[13] Stanley S. Harakas, *Living the Liturgy* (Minneapolis: Light and Life, 1974), 20.

[14] Sergius Bulgakov, *The Orthodox Church*, 110-111. The position that one does not have to be aware of the sacraments' effect, or understand them, in order for grace to be transmitted, is traced at least as early to Augustine and his struggles with the Donatists. Cf. Hagglund, *History of Theology*, 124-127. Nonetheless, the Orthodox tend to assert that authentic sacramental grace is only transmitted within apostolic - that is Orthodox - Christianity.

[15] Nicholas Cabasilas. *The Life in Christ*, C. J. de Catanzaro (tr.) (NY: St. Vladimir's, 1974), 51-53, 56-57.

[16] See my chapter 2, especially Palamas on God's essence and energies.

[17] Mantzaridis, *Deification*, 41-43.

[18] Meyendorff, *Byzantine Theology*, 191.

The Orthodox teach that the incarnate Word of God initiated sacramental participation in his divinity when he gave the disciples bread and said, "Take, eat; this is my body."[19] The arguments of the seventh and eighth centuries in Byzantium regarding the views of the human body, created matter, and the spiritual realm provided philosophical grist for the theological development of both iconography and the sacramental system. The iconophiles refused to acquiesce to the dualism which they believed resulted if Christ, in his incarnation, had not genuinely consecrated created matter. Christ did not symbolically take on flesh, neither did he intend his words of institution (regarding the sacraments) to be taken symbolically. The iconoclasts, for their part, did not deny Christ's incarnation, but some of them did argue against the sacraments. As was shown in our last chapter, the conservative iconophiles prevailed: Christ was understood to have sanctified created matter so that it might participate in his identity (hence iconography) and so that it might manifest his created grace (hence sacraments).[20]

As was implicit in our examination of iconography, Orthodox worship and spirituality is replete with symbolism. The various symbols used to present and represent the divine life to the church are multiple and *are utilized to impact the person's physical senses*, Lossky said, "in order to remind us of spiritual realities." The sacraments, because the Holy Spirit is conveyed through them, also represent and present the divine life to the believer, but *they are also tools of anamnesis*: they move the believer beyond simple commemoration of Christ and instead facilitate participation into a mystery, the mystery of the divine reality within the church.[21] Again, by participating in the sacraments one is not simply remembering the grace that is made available on behalf of Christ's redemptive work, one is participating in Christ's very presence.[22] In this way the sacraments are tools of the Kingdom of God. They signify and manifest the presence of God's Kingdom. Through them the Orthodox receive and participate in the Kingdom.

As has been said repeatedly, both sacraments and icons are rooted in incarnational Christology, but they are not therefore the same. Icons signify and portray something of Christ's identity, but the sacraments participate in God's

---

[19] Mt. 26:26. Par. Mk. 14:22; Lk. 22:19; 1 Cor. 11:24.
[20] Pelikan, *The Spirit of Eastern Christendom,* 225-227. The parties asserting a symbolic position on the sacraments were the Paulicians and the Bogomils.
[21] Lossky, *Mystical Theology,* 189.
[22] Zizioulas, *Being As Communion,* 161.

divinity as active instruments. Thus, while icons are venerated and honored, sacraments (especially the eucharist) are adored because the Lord himself is present in them.[23]

In Orthodoxy there is a hierarchy among the sacraments, especially as they are expressed regarding *theosis*.[24] As in Roman Catholicism, the eucharist is preeminent, but it is followed in importance by water baptism (a person may not receive the Orthodox eucharist unless one has been first baptized into Orthodoxy; a fact which is a tremendous barrier between the Orthodox and the non-Orthodox, including Catholics). Unlike the Catholics, the Orthodox are not generally precise about the number of sacraments. They do affirm the traditional seven:[25] baptism, chrismation (confirmation), penitence, the eucharist, the laying on of hands (ordination), marriage, and anointing the sick. However, the Orthodox do not dogmatically limit the number of sacraments and maintain that God uses many other things to share his grace with us. These others include priestly blessings (upon churches, water, bread, homes, etc.), funerals, monastic vows, and the consecration of icons and crosses.[26] Others, holding to panentheistic views, have begun to consider whether the entire creation, together with the whole of life, may be viewed as sacramental. God's means of grace are clearly established in the ecclesiastical sacraments, but he may very well use the everyday events of our lives to confer his grace upon us. Sacramental living is as much a matter of our own attitudes and understandings as it is God's institutionalized methods.[27]

---

[23] For a further comparison of icons and sacraments see Meyendorff, *Byzantine Theology*, 203-206.

[24] Bulgakov, *The Orthodox Church*, 111; Ware, *The Orthodox Church*, 275.

[25] The number seven was made at the suggestion of Peter Lombard in the twelfth century. The medievals believed seven was a sacred number. J. C. Lambert, "Sacraments," in *The International Standard Bible Encyclopaedia* (Grand Rapids: Eerdmans, 1955), 4:263; Meyendorff, *Byzantine Theology*, 192.

[26] Bulgakov, *The Orthodox Church*, 111-112. Bulgakov revealed that since the twelfth century it has been traditionally understood within Orthodoxy that there are seven sacraments. Cf., Ware, *The Orthodox Church*, 276.

[27] Schmemann, *Church, World, Mission*, in his chapter, "The World as Sacrament," 217-227. See also Ware, *The Orthodox Way*, 43-46; and, Meyendorff, *Eastern Christian Thought*, 138-140.

Baptism and the eucharist were specifically instituted by Christ and so they receive greater emphasis than the other sacraments.[28] Palamas said of the eucharist and baptism, "From these two acts depends our entire salvation, for in them is recapitulated the whole of the divine-human economy."[29] Baptism is the new birth, the moment when the person enters God's Kingdom. Unlike Protestant formulations, baptism's effect is not contingent upon the person's comprehension or faith. Salvation is a free gift from God, and so ineffable and mysterious is this gift that, instructed John Meyendorff, "The ultimate eschatological goal of new life cannot be fully comprehended even by the 'conscious adult.'"[30] Baptism washes the filth of sin and wickedness from the catechumen, and unites the believer's nature to Christ. Baptism is immediately followed by chrismation (anointing with oil) which activates the energies of the Holy Spirit. Together baptism and chrismation begin the transformation process and bestow divinity upon the initiate.[31] Those two notwithstanding, it is the eucharist (simultaneously known as holy communion, the Lord's supper, the mystical banquet, or the "medicine of immortality")[32] that is especially held to have transformational power. Emphasizing the eucharist's importance Cabasilas said, "It is therefore the final Mystery. . . since it is not possible to go beyond it or add anything to it."[33] "So perfect is this Mystery," continued Cabasilas, "so

---

[28] In the seventeenth century Metrophanes Critopoulos argued that the eucharist, baptism, and penance were paramount in rank over the other sacraments because they were instituted by Christ. Critopoulos did not attain much success among the Orthodox in this regard. Pelikan, *The Spirit of Eastern Christendom*, p. 291. Christoforos Stavropoulos does indeed assert the primacy of eucharist, baptism, and penance. Stavropoulos, *Partakers of the Divine Nature*, S. Harakas (tr.) (Minneapolis: Light and Life, 1976), 37-38.

[29] John Meyendorff, *Gregory Palamas*, 160, quoting Palamas from *Homilies* 62, Oikonomos (ed.), 250.

[30] Meyendorff, *Byzantine Theology*, 193.

[31] Lossky, *Mystical Theology*, 170-171. Baptism marks the moment when one becomes a Christian and is thereby saved (though, again, the Orthodox do not tend to express this in the legal format of the West). Baptismal ceremonies often include the exorcism of Satan from the catechumen who cannot reside in both the realm of Satan and that of Christ. Bulgakov, *The Orthodox Church*, 112, said, "Baptism is the only sacrament which may be administered by the layman (man or woman) by virtue of the universal Christian priesthood."

[32] Harakas, *Living the Liturgy*, 19. For the last phrase see Tsirpanlis, *Eastern Patristic Thought*, 120.

[33] Cabasilas, *The Life in Christ*, 114.

far does it excel every other sacred rite that it leads to the very summit of good things. It assists the initiates after their initiation, when the ray of light derived from the Mysteries must be revived after having been obscured by the darkness of sins."[34] It is the eucharist which both makes a human community become the church of God and is the raison d'être of the episcopal ministry.[35] The liturgical service itself is a service of purification and preparation for the reception of the eucharist.[36] Indeed, because the entire liturgical service is one which anticipates, builds toward, and crescendos towards the eucharist, the Orthodox speak of the liturgy and the eucharist as almost synonymous. All other sacraments either anticipate the eucharist or flow from it.[37]

Each of the sacraments convey the Spirit's energies, but, as noted above, the eucharist is the main source for the believer's *theosis*. This is the case because while other sacraments convey God's grace, Christ himself is encountered in the eucharist. For the Orthodox, the eucharist is not just a memorial rite, it is a personal and real participation in Jesus Christ. Anthony Coniaris, an Orthodox priest, said, "[it] is where we meet Christ and invite Him into our soul. The eucharist is a divine blood transfusion."[38] Through the eucharist, the Christian's "body is interpenetrated with the eternal substance of Christ's body," said Constantine Tsirpanlis. Through the eucharist, Tsirpanlis continued, "the Christian bears the 'flesh of the Lord' in his body."[39] Meyendorff similarly exalted the eucharist when he said, "The Eucharist is, indeed, the *ultimate* manifestation of God in Christ."[40] Alexander Schmemann expressed the unique nature of the eucharist, "in Christ, life - life in all its totality - was returned to man, given again as sacrament and communion, [and] made Eucharist."[41] The eucharist strengthens the believer's spiritual life, unites the believer with the

---

[34] Cabasilas, *The Life in Christ*, 116-117.
[35] Meyendorff, *Catholicity*, 118.
[36] Meyendorff, *Byzantine Theology*, 206-210.
[37] Panagiotis Bratsiotis, *The Greek Orthodox Church*, Joseph Blenkinsopp (tr.) (London: The University of Notre Dame Press, 1968), 50.
[38] Anthony Coniaris, *Introducing The Orthodox Church: Its Faith and Life* (Minneapolis: Light and Life, 1982), 134.
[39] Tsirpanlis, *Eastern Patristic Thought*, 120, following Ignatius of Antioch (f. AD 110). John of Damascus (d. AD 754) is very important for Orthodoxy's sacramental doctrine. The Damascene held to a mystical, rather than physical, interpretation of how a human's soul is nourished by the eucharist. Tsirpanlis, 135-139.
[40] Meyendorff, *Byzantine Theology*, 210. Original emphasis.
[41] Schmemann, *For the Life of the World*, 20.

triune God, enables the believer to fight off sin, and helps the believer to obey God's will. In light of such blessings St. Basil encouraged his congregation to receive the eucharist four times a week.[42] Cabasilas emphasized the need to eat the eucharist regularly because of our sinfulness and need of cleansing.[43] There are limits though. Daily celebration of the eucharist is not normal, and a priest may not celebrate the eucharist more than once per day.[44]

In the eucharistic ritual the Orthodox offer the elements back to God who freely gave them in his Son.[45] In this way they symbolically offer themselves, and their obedience, back to God. God freely gives life. God freely gave Jesus Christ and through him God freely gives salvation. In response to God's benevolence Schmemann said, "There is nothing we can do, yet we become all that God wanted us to be from eternity, when we are *eucharistic*."[46]

As the above evinces, the Orthodox do believe in a real presence in the mysteries, but they are less concerned with how that presence occurs. Only as the Orthodox came into contact with Protestants in the seventeenth century and needed to articulate their doctrines against the Westerners did their use of transubstantiation, respecting the eucharist, arise.[47] Transubstantiation is not dogmatically or universally accepted by the Orthodox.[48] Meyendorff held that transubstantiation pressed the "how" of the eucharist too far. He preferred to speak of Christ's eucharistic presence in terms of consubstantiality. The food and drink of the ceremony constitute a physical meal, but they are correctly understood as sacramental types of Christ's humanity. Meyendorff used the terms "trans-elementation" or "re-ordination" to describe Christ's presence in

---

[42] George Nicozisin, *Born Again Christians, Charismatics, Gifts of the Holy Spirit: An Orthodox Perspective* (Greek Orthodox Archdiocese of North and South America, undated), 7.

[43] Cabasilas, *The Life in Christ*, 121. Harakas, *Living the Liturgy*, p. 23, echoed the same.

[44] Meyendorff, *Byzantine Theology*, 117.

[45] Tsirpanlis, *Eastern Patristic Thought*, 120-123, showed that as early as the Didache the eucharist was understood as involving the element of sacrifice unto God.

[46] Schmemann, *For the Life of the World*, 45. Original emphasis.

[47] Pelikan, *The Spirit of Eastern Christendom*, 291-292. Pelikan said the Orthodox borrowed transubstantiation from the Catholics.

[48] The Orthodox' use of transubstantiation dates back to 1672 when the Council of Jerusalem accepted the Latin term and then added clauses which qualified that the elemental change was mysterious and incomprehensible. In 1838 the Russian church translated the 1672 Jerusalem Council's words but left out the technical terms "accident" and "substance." Ware, *The Orthodox Church*, 284.

the eucharist.[49] Dan-Ilie Ciobotea similarly illustrated this reticence when he noted that the issues of what happens to the elements, or how it happens (for example, epiclesis versus words of institution), are not nearly as important as what happens to us and what God wants to happen in us. The "empirical," "scientific," or "abstract" examinations of the eucharist, and Orthodox theology in general, is, Ciobotea said, the result of "Western, post-patristic theology" and only leads to an unfortunate fragmentation of theology.[50] Schmemann, despite being an Orthodox liturgical theologian, was equally reticent to discuss the eucharist in the Western categories of cause and effect, essential and non-essential elements, validity, accidental qualities, or the sacraments' exact number. All of these, Schmemann said, are categories of time, substance, and causality, "the very categories of 'this world.'" These categories are not the categories of the divine presence of Christ, nor are they categories of the Kingdom of God from whence the eucharist was given.[51]

The "how" of sacramental transformation is a mystery, and this makes the Orthodox generally hesitant to be dogmatic.[52] Vladimir Lossky affirmed that the church participates in Christ via the sacraments, but he did not explain how this is so in either phenomenological or philosophical language. Lossky simply quoted church tradition and said, "That which was visible in our Redeemer now has passed into the sacraments."[53] Schmemann, in yet another book, reflected the Orthodox sentiment that the mystery of sacramental reality is obscured by lengthy definitions.[54] In all of this the Orthodox exhibit, Jaroslav Pelikan said,

---

[49] Meyendorff, *Byzantine Theology*, 201-205.

[50] Dan-Ilie Ciobotea, "The Role of the Liturgy in Orthodox Theological Education," *St. Vladimir's*, 31:2 (1987), 104. Ciobotea's comment in this regard needs to be seen as the polemical one it is: western categories regarding transubstantiation are rooted in Aquinas' rediscovery of Aristotelian thought. Aristotle was no more, or less, Western than was Plato.

[51] Alexander Schmemann, *For the Life of the World* (Crestwood, NY: St. Vladimir's, 1973), 48. In his chapter entitled "Worship in a Secular Age," 125-134, he lamented the modern theological preoccupation with semantics. He was also distressed by the modern person's ability to talk at length about God without simultaneously worshipping and experiencing God; both worship and experience find their zenith in Orthodoxys Liturgy.

[52] Coniaris, *Introducing The Orthodox Church*, 136.

[53] Lossky, *Image and Likeness*, 104. Lossky quoted Leo the Great, *Sermon* 74, 2; *PL* 54, col. 398.

[54] Schmemann, *Church, World, Mission*, 217.

"a certain 'reverential reserve' about the metaphysical details" of the sacraments.[55]

Whereas the Orthodox are hesitant to explain the "how" of the sacraments' participation in, and conveyance of, God's grace, they are most willing to explain the "who" of the sacraments. As was noted earlier, Christ is the objective basis for the divinization of human nature, but it is the Holy Spirit who actualizes Christ within each believing person. Because the Holy Spirit is one of the *hypostases*, one of the persons, of the Trinity, it can thus be said that God *personally* conveys his grace to each believer. The Orthodox are emphatic on the personhood of the Spirit, and this is an emphasis that they believe stands in contradistinction to Roman Catholic teaching.

Augustine (354-430), the famous Latin bishop, expressed God's unity in terms of the divine essence. The result was that while he had developed a logical and cogent model of God he de-emphasized God's triune character. Among the three persons, for Augustine, there was no subordination because each of the persons shared the divine essence. In light of this equanimity, Augustine had difficulty explaining the procession of the Spirit and viewed him as the mutual love which bonded together the Father and Son.[56] Thomas Aquinas (1224-1274) similarly held that God's unity resides with God's essence. Between the two persons - the Father and the Son - there existed a "relation of opposition" which shared the divine characteristics of both the Father and the Son, and which spirated from them both. Thomas held that the Spirit was this "relation of opposition" shared between the Father and the Son.[57]

Many Orthodox are vehemently opposed to Augustine's and Thomas' impersonal notions of either the Trinity or the Holy Spirit, and this is so because of their adamant belief that salvation is by virtue of God's person, not his substance or nature.[58] We cannot delve into the history or ramifications of the

---

[55] Pelikan, *The Spirit of Eastern Christendom*, 292.

[56] William G. Rusch (ed.), *The Trinitarian Controversy*, Sources of Early Christian Thought Series (Philadelphia: Fortress Press, 1980), 26-27.

[57] Lossky, *Image and Likeness*, 76, follows Aquinas from his *Summa Theologica*, I, qu. 28 and qu. 36. Meyendorff also made an historical analysis of Augustine and Aquinas, and their respective positions about God and salvation, in *Catholicity*, 65-70. Like Lossky, Meyendorff believed that the West's overarching theological problems were rooted in the doctrine of God.

[58] This criticism of Catholicism was not limited to the ancient past. Zizioulas, *Being as Communion*, 123, said the Catholics of Vatican II continued to denigrate the importance of Pneumatology.

Filioque clause at this point, however we can summarize its scandalous nature, in the perception of many Orthodox theologians,[59] by noting that it *is held to be heretical precisely because it has to do with the means of salvation.* For the Orthodox, the doctrine of the Trinity is not merely an abstract intellection reserved for a subsection of theology, *the Trinity is salvation itself.* In Orthodox trinitarian theology the Father is the cause *(aition)* of the other two *hypostases,* and this from eternity. The Orthodox take God's oneness for granted and insist upon the mysterious diversity of the Trinity. We may summarize the varying positions of the West and the East by noting that whereas the West tends to describe the Trinity in light of the unity of the divine *quidditas* (essence, substance), the East tends to describe the Trinity in light of the mutual relations of three distinct *hypostases.* Lossky said, "personal diversity in God presents itself as a primordial fact," a fact to be confessed by faith.[60] "Eastern theology," Lossky said elsewhere, "refuses to ascribe to the divine nature the character of an essence locked within itself. God - one essence in three persons - is more than an essence." He continued, "God overflows His essence."[61] Similarly Meyendorff taught that God is not imprisoned or secluded within his transcendence.[62] Lossky asserted that the (initially Catholic) West moved away from authentic Christian doctrine specifically because of its aberrant views of the Holy Spirit as a power and not a person.[63] While it is true, Lossky reasoned, that the very name "Spirit" conjures a certain degree of anonymity, and while it is also true that, as he said, "all that we know of the Holy Spirit refers to his economy," it nonetheless remains undeniably true that he is a person.[64]

---

[59] Ware, *The Orthodox Church*, 213-217, clarified that there are varied opinions among the Orthodox about the degree of the *Filioque* clause's heresy.

[60] Lossky, *Image and Likeness*, 80. The Spirit is the *hypostasis* of God who enables us to participate in God (Christ's) own person. Nearly every Orthodox theological treatise expounds upon the errors of the Latins' insertion of the *Filioque* clause into the Nicene-Constantinopolitan creed so that a bibliographic list at this point would be too extensive. However, for brief treatments see Lossky's chapter, "The Procession of the Holy Spirit in Orthodox Trinitarian Doctrine," 71-96; and, Ware, *The Orthodox Church*, 210-218. For more on the *Filioque* see my bibliography.

[61] Lossky, *Mystical Theology*, 240. Here he made reference to the doctrine of God's created energies.

[62] Meyendorff, *Catholicity*, 72.

[63] Lossky, *Image and Likeness*, 103, 105.

[64] Lossky, *Image and Likeness*, 75. By this he meant that we know nothing about the Spirit from Scripture pertaining to his inner-Trinitarian role or identity. When Scripture

The Spirit is the hidden and mysterious person of the Trinity who does not seek to make himself known. Instead, he seeks to glorify Christ and Christ's Father. Lossky said the Spirit is, *"par excellence* the hypostasis of manifestation, the Person in whom we know God the Trinity. His Person is hidden from us by the very profusion of the Divinity which He manifests." The Spirit exhibits a kind of "personal kenosis," in terms of self-revelation and the economy of salvation.[65] Dumitru Staniloae taught that because the Holy Spirit points not to himself but Christ, there is a self-effacing quality about the Spirit that constantly draws us toward others. The Spirit's very nature is one oriented toward otherness.[66]

Whereas one might see this brief foray into Trinitarian theology as having only incidental application to the means of Christian transformation, the Orthodox hold that authentic Christian transformation - *theosis* - is extremely problematic apart from a correct view of both the Trinity and the Holy Spirit. Humans are not divinized by the infinitely transcendent and wholly-other essence of God (in this way the Neo-Platonic notions of pantheism are rendered null and void); only God knows his transcendent existence. However, humans can be transformed by the life and grace of God. To this end, the Spirit kenotically works to present, not himself, but the person of Christ to human beings through the eternally created energies which are transmitted in the sacraments. These energies are not to be understood as contrary, or in opposition, to human nature; the Orthodox model is not one wherein human nature and God's divinity are in violent tension with one another.[67] Instead human beings, though now corrupted by sin, were nonetheless created in the image of God and still continue to reflect God's being. The Holy Spirit's grace cooperates with human nature, infuses it, and transforms it so that it reflects God, communes with God, and becomes divinized. Meyendorff, discussing Maximus' theology, described this synergistic work between the divine and human and said, "This essentially dynamic doctrine of salvation supposes a double movement: a divine movement toward man consisting of making God

---

describes Christ's sending of the Spirit it is speaking of the economy of salvation, not the inner-trinitarian relations.

[65] Lossky, *Image and Likeness*, 92. Original emphasis.

[66] Dumitru Staniloae, "The Holy Spirit and the Sobornicity of the Church," in his *Theology and the Church*, R. Barringer (tr.) (Crestwood, NY: St. Vladimir's, 1980), 62.

[67] Lossky, *Orthodox Theology*, 134-135. Meyendorff, *Eastern Christian Thought*, 124-127, 136.

partakable [sic] of by creation, and a human movement toward God, willed from the beginning by the Creator and restored in Christ."[68]

Orthodoxy's synergism is not a resurrection of Pelagian's position of meritorious salvation. Not only do the Orthodox not view human nature in the same manner as did Pelagius,[69] they believe that *salvation is only possible with God's grace*, and not something attainable by man's own willing. In contrast to Pelagius, the Orthodox maintain that authentic human existence, and authentic human freedom, occurs when the human person cooperates with God's grace. "Man is called to participate in God," said Meyendorff, "without there ever being any confusion between his nature and that of God, without any diminution of his freedom; on the contrary, it is in this communion that he finds, 'in a total feeling of certainty in his heart'. . . his own destiny, while continuing to fight against Satan."[70]

Because the Holy Spirit is divine, because he is one of the *hypostases* of the Trinity, he is able to unite believers to God in Christ. If Christ had not been both human and divine he could not effect our salvation. Similarly, if the Holy Spirit were just another of God's creations he too would be powerless to effect our transformation. We noted in our earlier chapters that soteriology is inextricably woven into Orthodox Christology. Similarly, it deserves clarification that the Orthodox' pneumatology is also inextricably woven with the fabric of soteriology. This reiterates an earlier point that the whole of Orthodox theology can be said to pertain to *theosis*. Participation in Christ and transformation by the Holy Spirit's grace are to be understood as a way of life, and as essential to life. Christology and pneumatology are not properly or primarily understood as subsections of a broader system of theology. As has been noted repeatedly, the Orthodox believe they are not nearly as interested to dissect theology or epistemology - even for the sake of understanding or clarification - as they are to live it and participate in it. If theology cannot be lived, if it is only an abstraction for the sake of theory, or an explanation for what otherwise is unexplainable, the Orthodox reject it as spurious. To no small extent this

---

[68] Meyendorff, *Eastern Christian Thought*, 143-144.

[69] Pelagius believed humans had the capacity to choose the good on their own. Sin, for him, was not passed on through nature, but through the human will. God's grace facilitates a person's ability to willingly choose and attain the good. Thus, even though he was modifying the Western model of salvation, Pelagius continued to view grace as a benefit of nature (*bonum naturae*). Hagglund, *History of Theology*, 132-136.

[70] Meyendorff, *Eastern Christian Thought*, 126. Cf. Ware, *The Orthodox Church*, 221-222.

approach to religion explains their ambivalence about science and the scientific method.[71] Apart from the fact that the mysterious life of God is just that - mysterious and inexplicably life giving - attempts to painstakingly describe and detail the life in Christ are viewed as somewhat antithetical to its very nature. That is, one must not be nearly as concerned to describe it, or even understand it, as to live it.[72] Furthermore, the Orthodox believe that one of Satan's greatest temptation is to lure humans toward a love of knowledge in lieu of a love for God.[73] Discussing the necessary aspect of living one's theology Schmemann said, "The appearance of ecclesiology as a separate theological discipline is the fruit of *doubt*, of that need for justification which is inevitable, indeed 'normal,' in a theology which is itself conceived as a 'justification' - rational, or philosophical, legal or practical - of the Christian faith." Although he was specifically discussing ecclesiology, Schmemann's sentiments reflect the Orthodox attitude about theology in general.[74] We may reiterate that it is this attitude, or approach to theological method, which typifies the Orthodox' narrative and ad hoc character.[75] In light of Orthodoxy's lengthy and manifestly technical theological history, it is very clear that this emphasis on living versus understanding is not a mere turn to fideism amid a world that craves knowledge and understanding. It is an assertion of an experience in God - one made possible by Christ and actualized by the Holy Spirit - that is necessary for the life of fullness. Again, this experiential emphasis is an notable characteristic which the Orthodox share with Pentecostals.

---

[71] Christos Yannaras, *Elements of Faith: An Introduction to Orthodox Theology*, K. Schram (tr.) (Edinburgh: T and T Clark, 1991), 37-42, echoes this ambivalence toward the empirical sciences, but does so with a full understanding of said sciences' epistemological presuppositions.

[72] Schmemann, *Church, World, Mission*, 16-22.

[73] Cuttat, Jacques-Albert. *The Encounter of Religions: A Dialogue between the West and the Orient with an Essay on the Prayer of Jesus*. P. De Fontnouvelle and E. McGrew (tr.) (NY: Desclée, 1960), 109.

[74] Schmemann, *Church, World, Mission*, 21. Emphasis his.

[75] The Orthodox use narrative in the sense that they include anecdotes amid technical discussions, and their theological method can be characterized as rather ad hoc in the sense that they break away from stated purposes or discussions with little apparent concern.

The Liturgy

In many ways, much of what was already mentioned about the sacraments can be applied to the Orthodox' corporate worship service - the divine liturgy.[76] Like the sacraments, the liturgy does not just teach about Christ's person and work, it presents Christ to the believer; more accurately it establishes Christ's presence which surrounds and suffuses the believer. Like the sacraments, the liturgy has divinizing power because of the person and energies of the Holy Spirit. Like the sacraments, the liturgy is not simply an opportunity to receive from God, but also present an opportunity to give (thanks and praise) back to God. Like the sacraments, the liturgy provides the believer an opportunity to participate in Christ's presence. However, the sacraments and the liturgy are not understood as distinct from one another, even though we are examining them as distinct means of *theosis*. The liturgy is in large part what it is because of the sacraments, and the sacraments find their fullest expression within the liturgy. These similarities and connections notwithstanding, we will nonetheless note a few elements about the liturgy which are important for the doctrine and experience of *theosis*.

Unlike much of North American evangelicalism today, the Orthodox worship service is not simply for the sake of edification or even corporate Christian prayer and worship. The single focal point, and purpose, of the liturgy is that God may fill his temple and therein be glorified.[77] In this regard the Orthodox have a much greater affinity with Old Testament Judaism and the characteristic of mystery than does much of Protestantism. The Orthodox believe that just as the church longs for Christ, Christ longs to be with his people. This mutual longing is fulfilled within the liturgy. It is within the liturgical service that the infinite God dwells in time and space.

The Orthodox not only affirm the mystery of the transcendent God's presence in the liturgy, they believe that the characteristic of mystery is a central element for both the corporate and individual Christian life. Anthony Ugolnik explained to his Western readership the role and necessity of mystery in the Orthodox liturgy, as well as the traditional aversion which the West has felt toward mystery.

---

[76] There are several forms of the Orthodox liturgy. The one practiced on nearly every Sunday and nearly every weekday feast is that of St. John Chrysostom (d. 408). Harakas, *Living the Liturgy*, 22. Others include St. Basil's (d. 379), and St. James' (the apostle). Meyendorff, *Byzantine Theology*, 117.

[77] Bulgakov, *The Orthodox Church*, 129.

Partly because the history of the intellect in the West has Christian roots, and partly because Christians wish to remain in dialogue with the secular mind, we in the West fail to satisfy the hunger of those who come and stare at the feast. Living among those utilitarian rationalists who control the world and with whom we seek to communicate, we Christians can forget the nature of Christian perception. We confess to doctrines profoundly mysterious by their nature - that a man should be God, that one God should be at the same time three persons, that we of corruptible flesh should also be temples of the living God. So we believe, but so we cannot comfortably think. For as 'thoughts,' these are in essence mystery. Mystery is what many contemporary minds are hungry for; it is what they seek far afield, in the non-Christian realms and such Eastern, Asiatic sources as the Bhagavad Gita and the Tibetan Book of the Dead. We Christians in the West have not shared what we possess. We have mystery in plenty, yet our discourse averts it, avoids it as if in embarrassment. For mystery is what we have been taught through our education to relentlessly extinguish. . . . Our continual impulse is not to 'apprehend' mystery but to render it extinct.[78]

Because they believe that the bride of Christ, the church, is mysteriously united to and in Christ, the Orthodox do not view life in this world and life in Christ's eternal presence as so radically distinct as do most Protestant Christians. Christ united time and eternity in himself with the result that the deceased in Christ are not nearly as removed from the living as one might suppose.[79] Indeed, Christ became the bridge that spans the chasm between this life and the afterlife. The Orthodox community, as it glorifies God and participates in his presence within the liturgy, shares and re-enacts their belief in the mysterious unity of the body of Christ: a plethora of icons reminds the gathered believers that they are part of a heavenly community, a community which transcends time and finite existence.[80] Additionally, this fusion of time

---

[78] Ugolnik, *The Illuminating Icon,* 93-94.

[79] Zizioulas, *Being As Communion,* 64-65, in his ontological framework, said, "When the eucharistic community keeps alive the memory of our loved ones - living as well as dead - it does not just preserve a psychological recollection; it proceeds to an act of ontology, to the assurance that the person has the final word over nature, in the same way that God the Creator as person and not as nature had the very first word."

[80] The bibliography in this regard is extensive, but one could consult most any Orthodox treatise on the liturgy or eschatology. For example, Bulgakov, *The Orthodox Church,* 1-35; Coniaris, *Introducing the Orthodox Church,* 97-100, 183-7. Zizioulas said, "there is

and eternity is further fostered in their belief that the liturgical service is an earthly participation in, and manifestation of, the heavenly worship service (Rev. 5).

Recognizing that the human body has a critical part to fulfil in the drama of liturgical worship, the Orthodox actively stimulate and use the entire human body to glorify God. They cross themselves, Peter Gillquist said, "as a way to physically express their allegiance to Christ,"[81] to invoke the power of the cross against temptation, to glorify God in their bodies, and to remind themselves of God's triune nature.[82] They burn incense to stimulate their olfactory sense - it helps them to focus themselves during the liturgy, and points them toward Isaiah's vision of the heavenly temple.[83] They kneel on the church floor or use kneelers (if the church has them) as a way to reverence the triune God and Holy Scripture. They light candles during their pre-liturgy prayers. They use architecture and art as a means to seize the participants' attention, to assist their worshipping of God, and to attempt to circumscribe the indescribable transcendence of eternity.[84] They variously employ music in order to express their love and worship of the Trinity, to sing the Scriptures (it helps make the written word come alive in the participants' hearts and minds), and to remind themselves that there is, and will be, singing in heaven.[85] Each of the

---

no room for the slightest distinction between the worshipping eucharistic community on earth and the actual worship in front of God's throne," 232. Despite the fact that Orthodoxy rejects the doctrine of purgatory, the dead are prayed for in the Liturgy as well as in special services. Meyendorff, *Byzantine Theology*, 96, 110-111, 220-221.

[81] Peter E. Gillquist, *Becoming Orthodox: A Journey to the Ancient Christian Faith* (Ben Lomond, California: Conciliar, 1992[2]), 121. Gillquist was formerly a leader in Campus Crusade for Christ.

[82]To further support the practice of crossing oneself, Gillquist, 124, quoted Jack Sparks, "The Sign of the Cross," *New Oxford Review* (January-February, 1982), "We freely use the symbol of the cross atop our church buildings, our lecterns, altars, bulletins, and imprinted on our Bibles. Why not use it on ourselves - the people for whom Christ died - as well? We use our voices and lips to tell others of the cross. Why should we withhold our hands and arms, which God has also given us, from doing the same?"

[83]Gillquist, *Becoming Orthodox,* 86-88.

[84]Quenot, *The Icon*. Though his book is devoted to the subject of icons, he discusses Orthodox architecture on 43-45.

[85]Gillquist, *Becoming Orthodox,* 81-84. The degree to which the congregation sings can vary depending upon the ethnicity of the , and the service itself. It is also true that many Orthodox churches do not use instruments for fear that it make the service artificial and/or worldly. Bulgakov, *The Orthodox Church*, 135-136.

aforementioned acts is also intended to stimulate the participants' awareness of Christ's mysterious and holy presence.

Because Christ's incarnation is continued on earth through the life of the church, the Orthodox believe that Christ himself may be experienced within the church's services. Thus, when the Orthodox receive a sacrament, or participate in a New Testament reading, they are not just commemorating Christ, but re-enacting him in their midst. If this seems bizarre to the Western mind, Ugolnik clarified, it is because of the fundamentally different ways that the West and the East define their experience of Christianity. The West tends to define this within a textual frame of understanding, so that in order to experience orthodox Western Christianity, as Ugolnik said, "one must read the right books correctly."[86] Even the very word "symbol," in the West, is perceived literarily, so that words are the primary symbols and conveyors of truth, and means of worship, among Protestants (thus, the centrality of the sermon). Among the Orthodox the liturgical experience is also expressed through symbols, but their symbols are not so much linguistic as they are dramatic, that is, acted out.[87] Christ is understood to be in their midst not so much because of the words that are being spoken and read, but because of the drama that is being enacted (one might more accurately say re-enacted) within the liturgy. The focal point of the drama, as was mentioned earlier, is the eucharist, but the entirety of the liturgy contributes to the re-enactment of the Christian drama: Christ's entering history, and then his dwelling with and in his people.

The Orthodox maintain that the eucharistic celebration by the corporate body is the richest experience of Christ's presence here on earth. This is the case not only because Christ is manifested therein, but because the Orthodox believe that heaven and the entire cosmos themselves are, because of Christ's incarnational presence, united in the liturgy. Through the iconographical art, the architecture, and the drama of re-enactment Bulgakov said, "The vision of spiritual beauty is joined to that of the beauty of this world."[88] The service is directed not only to the individual believers who are present, but to the entire cosmos as well. This orientation reminds the believer that his own transformation is part and parcel of Christ's cosmic sanctification.[89]

---

[86]Ugolnik, *The Illuminating Icon*, 88.

[87]The Orthodox do include a brief sermon within the course of the Liturgy.

[88]Bulgakov, *The Orthodox Church*, 129.

[89]Bulgakov, *The Orthodox Church*, 136-137. This echoes our previous delineation that humans are microcosms of the entire cosmos.

The Church

Although the church will be herein presented as a distinct means of *theosis* we need to qualify that the Orthodox do not make such a clean distinction between the church and the liturgy or the mysteries (sacraments). At her core the church is both liturgical and sacramental. Nonetheless, I want to focus specifically upon the corporate dimensions of the church and its impact on *theosis*. In light of our specific focus we will not examine the ecclesiastical structure, nor the issues of legal or jurisdictional polity.[90] However, we will note how it is that *theosis*, the process of being transformed into the image of Christ, is not something understood as limited to the individual alone. This dimension of Orthodoxy stands in stark contrast to the standard evangelical formulations wherein salvation is a personal relationship between Jesus and a believer. The Orthodox view such formulations as truncated understandings of what it means to be Christ-like.

The church, in the Orthodox mind, is not the organism that she is because of her multi-ethnicity, her gender inclusiveness, or any other socially constructed characteristic.[91] The church is who she is because of God himself, and because she participates in the very life of God. She shares in this life specifically when she gathers in Christ's name. Individual Christians, including bishops and priests, are individually sinners, Meyendorff taught, "whose prayers are not necessarily heard." But when these gather together in Christ, they become participants in the New Covenant and share in the grace and life of the Son and Spirit.[92] Again, whereas Christians are sinners, the church is holy. The blood of Christ sanctifies the church. The presence of the Spirit indwells the church and makes it to be the house of God. The church does not derive its holiness from the sanctification of the gathered individual members, rather, the members are sanctified because of their inclusion within the church. In all of this, the

---

[90]Neither will we be examining how it is that the is either one, holy, apostolic, or catholic.

[91]We could include in this the characteristics of a social ethos (worship, joy, peace, love, compassion, consolation, and shared values). To be fair, the Orthodox are indeed aware of such characteristics. E.g., Meyendorff, *Catholicity*, 117.

[92] Meyendorff, *Byzantine Theology*, 207; Zizioulas, *Being as Communion*, 209-212.

Orthodox will not admit that the church in anyway incorporates sin in its essence.[93]

The Trinity is a communion of persons existing in perfect union. Similarly, the church is a communion of persons united in Christ; and, the church is perfect in that it has communion with, and finds its life in, God. In an earlier chapter we noted that individual human beings were created to reflect God. The church, a community that was created at Pentecost and which is continued wherever Christ's own assemble in his name, was also designed to reflect the Triune God.[94] When the church does not reflect God or participate in the reality of his presence it becomes a mere form. The result is that many within the church often become guilty of ecclesiolatry: the concern with proper form apart from the genuine presence of God.[95]

Gregory Palamas emphasized the corporate nature of the church and taught that it was "a communion of deification."[96] Orthodox ecclesiology, especially concerning the corporate nature of the church and its role in *theosis*, can be understood via two analogic models. The first model is rooted in the doctrine of *perichoresis*:[97] the mutual interpenetration of personalities characterized by the sharing of each other's deepest levels of personhood. When the Orthodox believer, especially through the eucharist and the Holy Spirit's presence, comes into contact with Christ - whether through the sacraments, prayer, worship, or mutual fellowship within the church - she is transformed and becomes like Christ, not in terms of perfection, but in kind. As the believer comes into contact with the Christian community, or is encompassed by it, she is both shaped by

---

[93] Bulgakov, *The Orthodox Church*, 95-99.

[94] Meyendorff, *Byzantine Theology*, 208-209; Zizioulas, *Being as Communion*, 211, 223.

[95] Schmemann, *Church, World, Mission*, 76, 80. Lossky likewise says the Eastern has been less concerned with ecclesiology as a separate dimension of Christian theology, and more as an organism within which the life of the Kingdom of God is experienced. *Mystical Theology*, 174-175. While one empathizes with Orthodoxy in this regard, we must say that here we have theologians speaking, and not historians. If ever there was a overly concerned with precise form it has been the Orthodox.

[96] Mantzaridis, *Deification*, 57.

[97] The term connotes the dynamic activity of the three within the Godhead. Origen was the first to formulate the doctrine of *perichoresis* with regard to the inner-life of the Trinity, but it took on ecclesiological ramifications through the centuries. *Perichoresis* is a "co-penetration of corporal, spiritual and divine qualities." The West has similarly expressed this phenomenon in terms of the "communication of idioms." Lossky, *The Vision of God*, 50, 109.

and shapes the community. The individual persons of the community, when
they are experiencing the life of Christ within (again, this is most commonly
expressed as occurring through the eucharist), will increasingly grow to
resemble one another and Christ. John Zizioulas, in whom we have already seen
Orthodox theology expressed in extremely ontological ways, said, "so
fundamental is the relational character of Church membership, that individuals
disappear as such and become sharers of the eternal and true life only as
members of one another." He continued, "the eschatological fate, therefore, of
any Christian is deeply dependent on his relational existence in the community
of the saints."[98]

The second analogical model is similar to the first in that it represents the
dynamic and mystical interaction involved in Christian ecclesial living. In the
Christian life (alternately expressed as authentic life) there are three concentric
circles: the Trinity, the church, and the individual. At the center resides the
Trinity, within which time and eternity are encompassed, and from which
originate life, truth, beauty, meaning, and personhood. The second circle is
comprised of the community of faith.[99] It finds its existential locus - its *raison
d'être* - in the Trinity. Divorced from its relationship to the Trinity it would
cease to exist authentically, and all that it does is supposed to bear witness to,
and bring glory to, the Triune God. The outer circle is that of the individual. Of
his own volition he can choose to remain isolated, or he can be trapped within
his own circle. But when he comes into contact with the adjacent circle of
community he receives from it that which it receives from the Trinity. Once
inside the community he can indeed move within the inner circle of the Trinity
on his own (that is, through hesychastic prayer - discussed below), but even if
he does so move he will increasingly become like the holy community itself:
imbued by the life, grace, and persons of the Holy Trinity. Ugolnik summarized
this analogical model well, "If we understand identity as a function of our

---

[98] Zizioulas, *Being As Communion*, 232.
[99] The Orthodox are adamant that this community of faith is the eucharistic community,
that is, the local church served by a priest. Criticizing non-Orthodox ecclesial models,
Zizioulas said, "if we say for example that the various communities in the world can
simply unite through the love or faith of their *individual members*, we not only make
unity an abstract matter on the level of subjective emotion or belief, but - what is more
important - we allow for the Christian to be conceived in himself and not as part of his
existential milieu here and now," 237. Emphasis his.

relation with other identities, we have grasped a central principle of the Christian life as the Orthodox live it."[100]

This deifying communion defines its authentic existence not in terms of apostolic succession (more akin to Catholicism) or apostolic formulations of truth (more akin to much of Protestantism), as important as those are, but in the dynamic faith founded upon Christ and experienced in the life of the Holy Spirit within the church.[101] Truth *is* critical to the Christian experience of *theosis* and apart from it the Orthodox teach that one risks being a Christian altogether, but truth is not expressed nearly so much in the juridical-empirical manner which characterizes the Roman Catholics or Protestant Fundamentalists (as the Orthodox hold about the West).[102] Christian truth, Schmemann taught, is not even to be understood as something that has been codified by the Orthodox Fathers, as though one could read the Fathers as the bases for all subsequent theology. Instead, truth is alive, and it changes lives. The truth is not manifested primarily in the abstract formulations of the church, but in her experience.[103] To this understanding of the life of truth, the Orthodox add that apart from the corporate experience of Christ there is no salvation. Meyendorff described the corporate nature of the New Testament church, "Christians gathered together regularly for the celebration of the Lord's Supper and nothing - not even the Roman persecutions - could prevent them from holding their assemblies, because the very nature of their faith implied that God abided not in each of them individually, but in the entire Church, the Body of Christ."[104]

The Russian Orthodox best convey this corporate sense of *theosis*, and the role of the Christian community in *theosis*, in their use of the word *sobornost'*. From *sobor*, meaning both a cathedral and a gathering, *sobornost'* is used to describe and define the sense of community and conciliarity they feel as the

---

[100] Ugolnik, *The Illuminating Icon*, 215.

[101] Mantzaridis, *Deification*, 58-59.

[102] Schmemann, *Church, World, Mission*, repeatedly criticized the West for its juridical understanding (in his perception) of truth and salvation, a fusion he said is part and parcel of the Church's acceptance of the Western juridical understanding of life in general. See Schmemann 33-4, 56-63. Clearly, Schmemann and too many Orthodox are not familiar with either a vast array of Western theologians or the great bulk of modern evangelicals. Bernard of Clairveaux, Martin Luther, and the more recent Pentecostal and charismatic groups provide ample proof that Schmemann's sweeping generalizations about "juridical" Western Christianity are overdone.

[103] Schmemann, *Church, World, Mission*, 84.

[104] Meyendorff, *Catholicity*, 116-117.

church, and believe that church (when she is truly being the church) must manifest. *Sobornost'* dates back to the eleventh century and is the Slavonic rendering of the word 'catholic' in the Nicene Creed,[105] but it was especially formulated by Aleksei Khomiakov (1804-1860), the preeminent theologian of the Slavophile movement.[106] Khomiakov used *sobornost'* with respect to Eastern Orthodox ecclesiology in contradistinction to both the Roman Catholic papal monarchy (which emphasizes authority) and the Protestant ecclesial formulations (which emphasize individuality).[107] Khomiakov believed that the authentic church's central characteristic is neither authority nor individuality, but *sobornost'*. The church's oneness, its *sobornost'*, is sustained via unity and freedom, but never at the expense of one over the other.[108] Khomiakov's communal emphasis did not deny the individual person's importance; the individual's responsibility, freedom, and cooperation in salvation were indeed asserted. He did believe, though, that persons are truly only persons, or more accurately, Christians are truly only Christians, when they are members of a community.

In Russian ecclesiology, as in all Orthodox ecclesiology, the body of Christ is the community of salvation. No person is saved by himself. The icon of Christ's resurrection depicts him victoriously leading a host of saints past the shattered gates of Hades. One of the pedagogical points of the icon is that although Christ is indeed the risen champion over sin and death, his resurrection not only manifests his own vindication, but also that of those who follow him.

---

[105] Sergei Hackel, "Trial and Victory: The Spiritual Tradition of Modern Russia," in *Christian Spirituality, III, Post-Reformation and Modern*, 460.

[106] Lewis Shaw, "John Meyendorff and the Russian Theological Tradition," in *New Perspectives on Historical Theology*. Bradley Nassif (ed.) (Grand Rapids: Eerdmans, 1996), 16. The Slavophiles wanted to return Russia to the 'ideal society' that existed before the reforms of Peter the Great. One reason they supported Russian Orthodoxy was that they believed Russian culture was coextensive with the Church.

[107] Pelikan, *Christian Doctrine and Modern Culture*, 287. Khomiakov believed the Roman Pope, when he allowed the insertion of the *Filioque* clause into the creeds, claimed for himself something which only belonged to the Ecumenical church - infallibility. The Pope thus became the first Protestant because he broke with ecumenical tradition, personally decided a dogmatic question apart from the college of bishops, and usurped infallible authority for himself. The seeds for the Reformation were thus sown centuries before it actually occurred. Aleksei Khomiakov, "On the Western Confessions of Faith," in *Ultimate Questions: An Anthology of Modern Russian Religious Thought*, 31-69.

[108] Shaw, "Meyendorff and the Russian Theological Tradition," 16.

And it is precisely the community of faith that he leads unto life. Anyone who will not enter the *koinonia*, the community of salvation, will not be saved. Khomiakov said, "When anyone falls, he falls alone; but no one is saved alone."[109]

The Unmediated Means of *Theosis*

As central as the ecclesiastical means (the mysteries, the divine liturgy, and the church) are for one's *theosis* they are not the sole means. For all of their emphasis that the Kingdom of God is best experienced at the communal level within an Orthodox church, the Orthodox nonetheless believe Jesus' teaching that "the Kingdom of God is within you," (Lk. 17:21) is something applicable for all Christians. The Kingdom is manifested and experienced in an external manner in the liturgy and sacraments, but because the human person is a living icon of God it is also possible that the Kingdom can be manifested and experienced internally, within one's soul. Accordingly, Orthodox explications of the doctrine are also very much characterized by an unmediated (or, non-ecclesiastical) approach to the divine. This is normally expressed in terms of hesychastic spirituality.[110]

Most Orthodox writers, in teaching about the direct approach to God, often refer directly to Palamas and the mystical fathers. That those Christians lived six hundred, or even sixteen hundred, years ago is of little significance. Despite the fact that the historical milieu changes constantly, human nature is what it has always been: obsessed with serving itself and its own selfish interests. The fathers, guided by the insight of the Holy Spirit, and themselves teaching in agreement with the whole of the experience of Orthodox tradition, rightly

---

[109] Ware, *The Orthodox Way,* 63, quoting Khomiakov, "The Church is One," in *Russia and the English Church in the Last Fifty Years*, W. J. Birkbeck (ed.) (London: Rivington, 1895), 216. So community-oriented are the Russians, so pervasive is community in their world-view, that there is no Russian word for privacy. Svetlana Boym, *Common Places: Mythologies of Everyday Life in Russia* (Cambridge, Massachusetts: Harvard University Press, 1994), 26, 73.

[110] There are manuals on Orthodox spirituality, written primarily for the laity, which describe hesychastic prayer without using the theological or technical language of hesychasm. For example, Anthony Bloom, *Living Prayer* (Springfield, Illinois: Templegate, 1966); Theodora Dracopoulos Argue, *Practicing Daily Prayer In the Orthodox Christian Life* (Minneapolis: Light and Life, 1989).

understood human nature. We point out this historical reliance to evince both the Orthodox' indebtedness to, and appreciation of, tradition, and their historically consistent essentialist view of human nature (something delineated more fully in our earlier chapter on Orthodox anthropology).

The most detailed and orderly presentation of the unmediated approach toward *theosis* was Hierotheos Vlachos' *Orthodox Psychotherapy: The Science of the Fathers.*[111] This book painstakingly detailed the inner-workings of the soul, *nous*, heart, and mind, and then explains how the passions affect each of these dimensions. Because Vlachos manifests the Orthodox essentialist view of humanity, and because he exemplifies the multi-faceted ramifications that the doctrine of *theosis* has for the human person, his book will serve as our main source for noting the ramifications of *theosis* for the existential nature of human existence.[112] As Vlachos presents it, in order to properly practice Orthodox asceticism (hesychasm), one must correctly understand the human person's complex nature. True enough, the human consists of body and soul, but the latter is a complex feature which is little understood.[113]

---

[111] Other classical hesychastic texts include *The Philokalia*, vols. 1-5, Modern Greek translation (Thessaloniki: 1987); John Climacus, *The Ladder of Divine Ascent*, C. Luibheid and N. Russell (tr.) (NY: Paulist Press, 1982); Scupoli, *Combattimento Spirituale,* translated into English as *Unseen Warfare* (Crestwood, NY: St. Vladimir's, 1995); and, *The Way of a Pilgrim*, in George P. Fedotov (ed.), *A Treasury of Russian Spirituality* (Belmont, Massachusetts: Nordland, 1975), 280-345. I have chosen Vlachos' book over all these because it is more purposefully organized and somewhat succinct, whereas the others are rather ad hoc, and some quite voluminous, in structure. While it is true that Vlachos follows a vast array of the fathers, he admittedly wants to organize their ideas in describing the inner relations of the human person's existential composition, 118.

[112] In an earlier chapter I defined this as that dimension of human existence and experience which is not always precisely described or understood in rational terms. This dimension includes, but need not be limited to, the psyche, soul, will, and/or affections.

[113] Vlachos, *Psychotherapy*, 69-71, maintained the aforementioned distinction between image and likeness. A person is created in the image of God, but in order to attain likeness to God one must experience purification, illumination, and deification. These three correspond to Maximus' three stages of practical philosophy (purification of the flesh and avoidance of sin), *theoria* ("illumination of the *nous*" via *apatheia* and a vision of God), and mystical theology (deification).

Hesychasm and the Human Soul

The soul, Vlachos taught, is the "way in which life is manifested in man."[114] It is not only the spiritual element of human existence, but the very life of human existence too.[115] Furthermore, the soul is not the breath of God, or a piece of God (again, pantheism is thus negated). Instead it is something that was created when God breathed into Adam.[116] Thus, both the soul and the body were created in God's image. The soul has the characteristic of *nous*: it can grow, it is intelligent, and it is imaginative. But despite its noetic qualities, the soul refers to the entire person. The soul is not something that merely dwells in a body, but it is true that *the body expresses the soul.* Very importantly, the soul is expressed via the *nous*, the heart, and the intelligence.[117]

THE *NOUS*
The *nous* is simultaneously explained as the eye and the energy (power) of the soul. The *nous* produces thoughts and conceptual images, and as such it is the soul's seat of reason and intelligence. The *nous* can be impacted and influenced by either virtue or vice, angel or demon, sin or godliness. When a person chooses to follow after evil and withdraws from God the *nous* is sickened, darkened, made indifferent, and eventually deadened. Demons arouse the passions which exist in the soul, use those passions to fight and corrupt the *nous*, and force it to assent to sin. The result is that an "idol of sin" is established within the *nous*, and, upon each new sin the *nous* is more deeply wounded and infected so that it itself becomes a cause of new sin.[118] But when a person practices watchfulness, prays the Jesus prayer (which purifies one's mind), observes ascetic practices (vigils, meditation, prayer, self-control, and silence), and keeps Christ's commandments, the *nous* undergoes healing.

---

[114] Vlachos, *Psychotherapy,* 97.
[115] The soul is not the cause, but the bearer of one's life. God is the source of all life. Vlachos, *Psychotherapy,* 98.
[116] Vlachos, *Psychotherapy,* 108, taught that each person is created with a body and soul. Quoting John's Ladder of Divine Ascent he said, "The embryo is endowed with a soul at conception. . . . As the body grows so the soul increasingly manifests its energies." Moreover, the soul pervades the body, and is not located in any one place.
[117] Vlachos, *Psychotherapy,* 97-112.
[118] Vlachos did not say as much, but we can accurately say of his teaching that the human person cooperates synergistically with the devil when we assent to and act upon his temptations.

Through asceticism the *nous* controls itself, is thereby resurrected, and "becomes a temple of the Holy Spirit."[119]

THE HEART

The heart is simultaneously explained as the seat and the essence of the soul. Defining the heart Vlachos specifically meant *the physical organ*, not just the affective dimension of human existence.[120] The heart, in its spiritual dimensions, is difficult to define. It is the center of the soul, but it is not always understood, even by the person. Quoting Archimandrite Sophrony, Vlachos said, "He who enters these secret recesses [of the heart] finds himself face to face with the mystery of being."[121] The heart is where God's grace enters a person. The heart is also the place wherein the Christian is called to center his or her *nous*. The Orthodox Christian is called to learn the depths of his or her heart, to examine it and see whether God indwells it. The heart, like the *nous* (or better, because it is united to the *nous*), is caught between evil and righteousness. When it chooses to follow evil it results in ignorance, hardness of heart, impurity, foolishness, rudeness, and self-indulgence.[122] The heart receives its source of healing in the grace of baptism, but further healing (or the realization of baptism's grace) is aided via the reception of the sacraments[123] and especially via repentance.

In contrast to the bulk of western psychology which seeks to heal broken hearts, the Orthodox Christian is encouraged to live life with a broken heart. A life characterized by a broken heart (repentance, contrition, and tears) will make one sensitive to the Holy Spirit, the attacks of the enemy, and one's own identity.[124] Another writer, I. M. Kontzevitch, described humility as the cement which holds everything together. Christ himself was humble. His followers, if they are to become like him, must also humble themselves.[125]

---

[119] Vlachos, *Psychotherapy,* 119-156. The quote is from p. 149.

[120] Vlachos, *Psychotherapy,* 157, 164.

[121] Vlachos, *Psychotherapy,* 158, quoting Archimandrite Sophrony, *Saint Silouan the Athonite*, trans. Rosemary Edmonds (London: Mowbrays, 1991), 233.

[122] Vlachos, *Psychotherapy,* 156-176.

[123] Though he affirmed their necessity, Vlachos said little about the sacraments and assumed his reader had been baptized into Orthodoxy, *Psychotherapy,* 19. The church, he taught, is indispensable for Christian growth, 29.

[124] Vlachos, *Psychotherapy,* 176-182.

[125] I. M. Kontzevitch, *The Acquisition of the Holy Spirit* (Platina, California: St. Herman of Alaska Brotherhood, 1988), 36.

Along with repentance and humility, the ascetic Christian can also experience fire, warmth, and a leap in his or her heart. Fire, kindled by the Holy Spirit, not only burns up sins and the passions, it also fans the flames of zealous Christian living and transforms one's inner nature. The warmth one feels in hesychastic union with God is a warmth for God. It "gushes up like a spring"[126] and it aids the Christian in prayer, peace, devotion to, and fervor for, God. The leap of heart, Vlachos averred, causes one to love the good and seek the heavenly King.[127] In each of these (repentance, fire, warmth, and leaping of heart) Orthodox asceticism, and the fruits thereof, markedly resembles the affective experiences of Pentecostal Christians. Moreover, despite their desire for *apatheia* (passionlessness), the hesychasts should be by no means characterized as lifeless stoics, as Vlachos' affective language makes clear.

THE INTELLIGENCE AND THE THOUGHTS

Despite the fact that the *nous* and the intelligence (*logistikon*, also called the mind) both pertain to intellection, it is the *nous* and not the intelligence that is the eye of the soul. The mind deals with the sensory and intellectual, it makes the things experienced in the body and the *nous* thinkable and puts them into sentences. But it is the soul by way of the *nous* that encounters God. Before the fall the *nous* accurately perceived God (amid *theoria*, perpetual contemplation) and the mind put those perceptions in order. Because the fall darkened humanity's *nous* and threw it into disarray, the intelligence was elevated above the *nous* and now rules over fallen humanity.[128] Vlachos said, "The intelligence is overnourished, it has been raised to a greater position than the *nous*."[129] Vlachos again quoted Sophrony and said:

> In order to assert its superiority the intelligence points to its achievements, to its creativeness, producing many convincing proofs purporting to show that in the age-old experience of history the establishment or affirmation of truth falls entirely within its province. Intelligence, functioning impersonally, is by nature only one of the manifestations of life in the human personality, one of the energies of personality. Where it is allotted priority in the spiritual being of man, it begins to fight against its source - that is, its personal origin.

---

[126] Vlachos, *Psychotherapy*, 193.

[127] Vlachos, *Psychotherapy*, 188-196.

[128] Vlachos, *Psychotherapy*, 203-206.

[129] Vlachos, *Psychotherapy*, 207.

Rising, as he thinks, to the furthest heights; descending as he believes, to the lowest depths, man aspires to contact the frontiers of being, in order as is his way, to define it, and when he cannot achieve his purpose he succumbs and decides that 'God does not exist.' Then, continuing the struggle for predominance, boldly and at the same time miserably, he says to himself: 'If there is a God, how can I accept that I am not that God?' Not having reached the frontiers of being and having attributed to himself this infinity, he stands up arrogantly and declares, 'I have explored everything and nowhere found anything greater than myself, so - I am God.'[130]

To further counterbalance the human tendency to overemphasize the intellect, Vlachos echoed Orthodox tradition and asserted that the saints in heaven do not know God in the Aristotelian and rational way, but in an experiential manner via the *nous*.[131]

Not only does the lifting up of the mind over the *nous* affect one's perceptions of God, it also perverts one's own self-understanding. The result is that one will examine oneself solely along the lines of intelligence - a method that always falls short of the full truth. Additionally, this exaltation of the mind affects one's attitude toward others. Psychology and psychiatry are employed to make inferences about a person's illness, but they too are limited because of their faulty presuppositions about the existential dimensions (or lack thereof) of human existence.[132]

The Orthodox' understanding of the fall's consequences helps to account for their ambivalence toward the empirical sciences and the humanities. This view of the respective places of the *nous* and the intelligence in Christian epistemology must be emphasized because it is one of the critical issues which confronts Western Christians in their attempts to understand Orthodoxy. "Theology is beyond logic," Vlachos asserted, "it is a revelation of God to man."[133] In a chapter devoted to Orthodox epistemology, Vlachos taught that knowledge of God is not found in words about God but in knowing God himself. In fact, he said, the distinctions in the church are not made pertaining to

---

[130] Vlachos, *Psychotherapy,* 207-208. He quoted from Sophrony, *Saint Silouan,* 165.

[131] Vlachos, *Psychotherapy,* 209. The reader is reminded that the distinction between rational knowing and noetic knowing was the defining feature and the crucible of the debate between Palamas and Barlaam in the fourteenth century.

[132] Vlachos, *Psychotherapy,* 210-213.

[133] Vlachos, *Psychotherapy,* 33.

ethical lines (the moral or immoral), but pertaining to the knowledge of God: there are those who are sick in soul, who have a worldly knowledge and know nothing of the *nous* or heart; there are those who are being cured through Orthodox asceticism, who are acquiring wisdom about the soul; and, then there are the cured, those who throughout their entire being possess knowledge of God (the saints in Christ, among whom are some in this life). Hesychastic asceticism is foundational for all true theology (knowledge of God) because God is most clearly known and experienced in one who possesses a clean and healed soul.[134]

The Orthodox teach that the mind must be made subject to the *nous*. This does not mean the mind must cease to think (something that is impossible), but that it must be quieted (hence *hesychia*) guarded (hence *nepsis*), and controlled for the sake of purity (hence asceticism). Evil thoughts that are not cast away fester, gain power, and spread pollution within the human soul. Evil thoughts not only can cause God to cease revealing himself and his mysteries to a person, they can eventually separate one from God and his fragrant Holy Spirit. Because the human person is a psycho-somatic whole, evil thoughts which are continually entertained can cause anguish, insecurity, physical illness, sleeplessness, and inter-relational problems. When the evil thoughts run unchecked they can cause a loss of self-control and can even eventually cause one to commit suicide.[135]

The cure of these evil thoughts resides with hesychastic asceticism and its various noetic activities. One must first introspectively examine and judge one's ideas, attitudes, and appetites. Second, a person should avoid the causes and environments which provoke evil thoughts. One must thirdly observe fasts, vigils, and even withdraw from society;[136] all in the attempt to quiet ungodly thoughts and appetites. Fourthly, when one recognizes temptation one must acknowledge it as such, battle it, and put it away. That a thief enters a house is not sin, that the thief steals what he finds is. Fifthly, one must understand that the postponement of sinful, or even amoral, actions gives one a greater mastery over oneself. Sixth, one must continue to seek Christ. This is done through

---

[134] Vlachos, *Psychotherapy,* 339-355.

[135] Vlachos, *Psychotherapy,* 225-228. He mentions other symptoms of the passions on 260.

[136] Vlachos was not specific as to what such a withdrawal actually meant. In light of Orthodox teaching he must have had physical solitude in mind (whether anchoritic or cenobitic, or both). But he did go on to instruct that withdrawal from society's values and goals (especially in terms of status, materialism, and sexual impurity) was crucial.

prayer, confession of sin, keeping Christ's commandments, Scripture reading, and the cultivation of virtue. As all of the aforementioned makes clear, *hesychia* is not only outward silence (that is, in one's physical prayer time) it is also inward silence (the silencing of evil thoughts and passions).[137] And while the definition of *hesychia* is literally silence,[138] it by no means implies a quietistic passivity. The Christian life is very much an active one, both as it concerns one's own growth and development as well as one's Christian service.[139]

THE ROLE OF SILENCE

In our earlier discussion of Palamas we noted the Orthodox' understanding of apophatic theology. It deserves clarification that the practice of apophatic theology is not simply listing those characteristics which God is not (finite, physical, mutable, etc.) for the sake of stimulating the mind's apprehension of God's transcendence. Apophaticism has ramifications for *theosis* because of its experiential dimensions. The believer confesses all that God is not in order to better realize and experience - in the depths of one's soul - God's very transcendence. This approach to God is difficult for the Orthodox to express precisely because it involves the inexpressible. But as I will argue later, this experiential dimension of God's transcendence is an important one which the Orthodox and Pentecostals share.

Within apophatic theology (also called the negative way) and amid God's presence, bodily and existential silence are important features. One can variously silence oneself bodily by sitting still, keeping one's mouth closed, closing one's eyes, and by shutting off one's ears from talk and noise. This need for bodily silence is why the Orthodox have revered the desert and monasteries as holy places, but as Vlachos instructed, one can still attain bodily silence even apart from such places. Bodily silence is a precursor to existential silence, or silence of the soul.[140]

The soul is made still by virtue of quieting the thoughts and conceptual images which arise in the mind and the *nous*. Along with the things which stimulate one's bodily senses, the thoughts and reasonings must be quelled and must be prevented from entering into one's heart. If such things enter one's heart they can in turn stimulate the passions which, when aroused, will indeed

---

[137] Vlachos, *Psychotherapy*, 228-241; 345.
[138] It can also be translated as peace, rest, or tranquility. Cuttat, *The Encounter of Religions*, 148.
[139] Vlachos, *Psychotherapy*, 320-331.
[140] Vlachos, *Psychotherapy*, 312-315.

prevent *theoria*, or the vision of God. The practice and acquisition of godly virtues is like medicine for one's soul, but *theoria* is the fruit of virtuous living and silence.[141]

This silent stillness, this *hesychia*, is facilitated not only by a focused guarding of one's heart (*nepsis*) but also by unceasing prayer.[142] As we noted in our study of Palamas, the traditional hesychastic prayer of unceasing is the Jesus prayer, "Lord Jesus Christ, Son of God, have mercy." The form of this prayer can vary so that sometimes "Lord" is omitted, or so that sometimes "have mercy *on me*" or "have mercy on me *a sinner*" are added. The Scriptural bases for this prayer, also called the Prayer of the Heart, reside in Mark 10:47 and Luke 18:13. The Jesus prayer is understood to be a kind of arrow prayer: a prayer which busies the mind (again, we cannot cease to think), but which having fixed itself on the words enables the mind to reach out into the stillness where God resides. It is not an imaginative act where one either attempts to picture Jesus or imagine him in the Gospel accounts. Instead, it is something done with the purpose of focussing oneself upon God's presence, if he chooses to come to one in prayer.[143] The Jesus prayer can be prayed as a prayer of repentance or praise or focus, or all three, depending upon which words in the prayer are emphasized by the supplicant.[144] While sometimes the Christian must, by force of discipline, bring himself or herself to a silent frame of being, the Orthodox deny that hesychasm is merely a mechanical act which, if properly practiced, will produce the desired effects. The hesychastic supplicant must recognize that authentic encounter with Christ will occur only as the result of deep repentance and obedience to Christ's commandments. The recognition of one's sins and sinfulness, together with a sense of God's own holiness will make it so that tears become a way of life.[145]

Not only does *hesychia* have value because it facilitates the divine-human encounter amid prayer, it is also a well of depth upon which one may draw for everyday living, and this in several ways. Firstly, one can seek God amid silence when one is personally agitated. Secondly, the silence of one's passions enables one to more accurately assess and redirect one's own values, goals, and

---

[141] Vlachos, *Psychotherapy*, 315-319.

[142] Based on a literal interpretation of Lk. 18:1 and 1 Thes. 5:17.

[143] Ware, *The Orthodox Way*, 122-123.

[144] Bloom, *Living Prayer*, 85-88.

[145] Vlachos, *Psychotherapy*, 319-20, 328; Bloom, *Living Prayer*, 120.

motivations.[146] Thirdly, because such silence helps the individual to progressively realize God's own desires for his or her character, the hesychastic Christian (whether monk, priest, or layperson) will be enabled to love and serve others more selflessly. Fourthly, *hesychia* enables a person to understand better the world and God's relationship to it. Christos Yannaras marvelously expressed this dimension of asceticism so that he deserves a full quotation.

> Asceticism is the struggle to renounce my egocentric tendency to see everything as neutral objects, subject to my needs and desires. By poverty and submission to the common rules of asceticism, I fight precisely against my egocentric claim, I transpose the axis of my life from my ego to my relationship with the world which surrounds me, because the relationship begins only when in practice I desist from the tendency to subject everything. Then I begin to respect what surrounds me, to discover that it is not simply objective impersonal riches (of objective utility), but *things*, that is, results of activity, what has been done by a creative Person. I discover the personal character of the data of the world, a uniqueness of reason in each something, a possibility of relationship, a ground of loving reference to God. My relationship with the world becomes then an indirect relationship with God, the maker of the world, and the practical use of the world a ceaseless study of the truth of the world, a constantly deeper knowledge inaccessible to 'positive' science.[147]

Finally, while God is indeed revealed in the activity of his created energies, it is also true that God exists within a mystery of unknowing. Vlachos said, "It is not enough to hear His word, but one must also advance towards the unhearing of His stillness."[148]

Hesychasm and Existential Integration

To reiterate an emphasis noted throughout this study, *the Orthodox understand the Christian life not so much in terms of forgiveness* (though that is by no means neglected), *but in terms of healing.* God not only wants to forgive us, he wants to heal us. This theandric healing is not limited to the human will alone, it

---

[146] There is no consensus as to whether the passions can be altogether rooted out or merely silenced.

[147] Yannaras, *Elements of Faith*, 49-50. Emphasis his.

[148] Vlachos, *Psychotherapy*, 324-326. Quote taken from p. 325.

extends down into the core of human existence, into one's soul. Furthermore, God does not only want to heal us so we can be nice, good, or even whole. He wants to heal us so we can best enjoy his presence as those made like him by his grace.[149] This healing, Vlachos taught, is not accomplished through secularism's psychological means. The secularists fail to recognize that the great bulk of human ailments result from "problems of thoughts, a darkened mind, and an impure heart."[150] In contrast to the secularists, authentic healing is not only anthropocentric, it is also theanthropocentric. "Orthodoxy," said Vlachos, "is mainly a therapeutic science." "Every means that it employs," he continued, "and indeed its very aim, is to heal man and to guide him to God."[151] Sin shatters the person's existential core and leaves one struggling against oneself. But hesychasm unifies the soul and presents it to God through what one scholar called an "inner liturgy."[152] When the *nous* has been returned to the heart, and when from there it rightly governs a person's mind and body, the Christian is then able to pray to God without distraction and experience *theoria* (the vision of God).[153]

When the *nous*, heart, and thoughts are united in hesychastic prayer and asceticism - both of which must be aided by the grace of the Holy Spirit - the person's existential core begins to be unified and one begins to gain knowledge of oneself. The human person will thus experience freedom, purity, joy, illumination, and life in Christ.[154] To all of this it must be added that the physical body, too, will benefit, since a person's soul and body are one. This does not mean the body will naturally be free from all illness, but that the body, freed from the sickness of the *nous*, can live in greater wholeness and health.[155]

This ascetic pursuit of God, though there will be dramatic moments wherein the divine will be experienced, is a gradual one. Self-control is not easily gained. Love is not easily manifested in hearts formerly ignorant of God and consumed with themselves. One must cooperate with the grace of the Spirit in

---

[149] Vlachos, *Psychotherapy,*, 354.

[150] Vlachos, *Psychotherapy,* 20. He admitted that people obviously get physically sick and suffer apart from the soul, heart, and mind.

[151] Vlachos, *Psychotherapy,*, 15.

[152] Cuttat, *The Encounter of Religions*, 119.

[153] Vlachos, *Psychotherapy,* 34; 106-110; 144-145.

[154] Vlachos, *Psychotherapy,* 133-156.

[155] Vlachos, *Psychotherapy,* 155, 195. The Orthodox believe that several saints bodies have shined with a divine light and/or smelled of myrrh. Ware, *The Orthodox Church*, 232-4.

order to become like Christ.[156] Like Vlachos' own discussion, the great bulk of contemporary Orthodox writers' teaching concerns the progressive growth in one's *theosis*. In this regard, there are several degrees of *theoria* (degrees of purification and knowledge/vision of God),[157] along the way toward perfect *theoria* (the unencumbered vision of God's uncreated light). While some theologians do describe their experiences of the divine vision, a vision constituting the Orthodox' most narrow definition of theology itself,[158] rarely do they provide precise descriptions of what a person fully divinized will be like in this life, though such a one will indeed be characterized by love and *apatheia*. Palamas taught that deification begins in this life, but is only perfect and irreversible in eternity. Because the final deification includes one's physical body, one cannot be perfectly deified until after the resurrection.[159] Lastly, the unencumbered face to face vision of God is one that will infinitely progress throughout eternity. God himself is infinite, and it will be the saints' privilege throughout eternity to know him (via *theoria*) ever more perfectly.[160]

Hesychasm and Spiritual Guidance

The hesychastic pursuit of God, it is generally taught, is to be done under the guidance of a spiritual physician-confessor (*staretz*, in Russian). This confessor, simultaneously called a priest therapist, not only should know the hesychastic life himself, but should also be gifted to spiritually guide and heal. Unless one can diagnose one's passions and sins, one will be unable to be healed of them. A spiritual guide can help a person diagnose, and fight against sin, and its individualizing tendencies. Sin deceives one into relying only upon oneself and one's own capacity to judge. Sin also goads the human person to make oneself the measure of life and truth. The therapist, like a shepherd, can assist one in pursuing Christ and his virtue.[161]

---

[156] Vlachos, *Psychotherapy,* 117-118.

[157] These are: the remembrance of one's death, inspired obedience, spiritual poverty, and repentance. Vlachos, *Psychotherapy,* 354.

[158] For example *Symeon the New Theologian in Discourses*, C. J. de Catanzaro (tr.) (NY: Paulist, 1980); and, Krivocheine, *In the Light of Christ: St Symeon the New Theologian.*

[159] Vlachos, *Psychotherapy,* 354.

[160] Mantzaridis, *Deification,* 117-125.

[161] Vlachos, *Psychotherapy,* 212-214; 252.

The therapist need not be a bishop (though such an official would be outwardly the most qualified), but he will most likely be a priest. In addition he must be a godly person who manifests the characteristics of Christian leadership and righteous living as outlined in the New Testament.[162] If a therapist is to be effective he will above all be characterized by an holy humility, an humility that is anchored in an acute awareness of not only his own sins but also of the sinful tendencies in those he shepherds. Because of this awareness of sin, he will live a life characterized by repentance and tears.[163] However, because of his high calling and moral-spiritual purity, such persons are quite rare today.[164]

Summary and Analysis

Ecclesiology and Transformation: The Sacramental System

The word mysteries (from μυστήριον) occurs twenty-four times in the New Testament.[165] That μυστήριον connotes all the Orthodox hold about it is doubtful. More likely, it finds its more nuanced definitions in Orthodox tradition. However, it is the case that the notion of participatory acts themselves can be traced to the Biblical witness. As the Orthodox rightly teach, Jesus commanded his followers to both receive the bread and wine (1 Cor. 11:23-26) and baptize new disciples in his name (Mt. 28:19). By obeying Jesus and performing these rites, evangelical scholars admit that the first century Christians not only preached the *kerygma*, they enacted it in visible ways. Together with subsequent generations of Christians, the earliest believers observed these Christian ceremonies in participatory and dramatic ways, and not

---

[162] E.g., a sober spirit, purity, charismatic gifting, indwelled by the Holy Spirit, vigilant, and the willingness to suffer. Vlachos, *Psychotherapy*, 82-84. One's spiritual counselor does not necessarily have to be a priest.

[163] This also implies that total sinlessness in this life is denied in the Orthodox' doctrine of *theosis*. Ware, *The Orthodox Church*, 236.

[164] Vlachos, *Psychotherapy*, 95.

[165] Three times in the Gospels (Mk. 4:11; Mt. 13:11; Lk. 8:10) where Jesus and the disciples discuss his use of parables, and twenty-one times in the Pauline corpus (Rom. 11:25; 16:25; 1 Cor. 2:1,7; 4:1; 13:2; 14:2; 15:51; Eph. 1:9; 3:3,4,9; 5:32; 6:19; Col. 1:26-27; 2:2; 4:3; 2 Thes. 2:7; 1 Tim. 3:9).

merely commemorative ways.[166] It was thus rather inevitable that these rites began to be understood both as visible signs of invisible grace and as physical means to involve the believer in the invisible presence of Christ.[167] Even the great Protestant reformers, Luther and Calvin, asserted the integrity of the eucharist and baptism; the Reformer's protests were directed against the Catholic church's abuses and heterodox manipulations of the sacramental system - such as adoring the eucharist and transubstantiation - and not the sacraments per se.[168]

The above comments clarify two important issues for the broader comparative purposes of this study. Firstly, Christianity has always been a participatory religion. No single Christian tradition would deny this truth, it's just that each goes about it differently, and each emphasizes different dimensions of human existence which ought to be involved; for example, the mind, faith, personal relationships, and/or service are variously emphasized within the different traditions. Some traditions emphasize the participatory nature of Christianity more than others. What Orthodoxy avows, and as we will see later what Pentecostalism avows, is that humankind's soul - the existential dimensions discussed throughout this study - is an integral element in this divine-human *koinonia*. As was noted in this chapter's explication, the Orthodox assert that the life of Christianity must be rooted in one's heart, the center of the soul. A second issue important for our broader comparative purposes is that from the apostolic age through the age of the Reformation - to which our own contemporary era can be safely added - Christians have always believed that God works through physical means. Whether through a preacher's

---

[166] R. S. Wallace, "Sacrament," in *EDT*, p. 965. Zwinglian Protestants need to exhibit at least some degree of tolerance for those who hold to the sacramental model if only because Jesus' words "Take eat; this is my body," and "Drink from it. . . this is my blood," (Matt. 26:26-38) can, in light of the early church's practice, be understood in a participatory manner (that is, sacramentally).

[167] Tertullian (f. 195-220) was the first to use the Latin word *sacramentum* for the Greek *musterion* in referring to the Christian ceremonies themselves, as against the Greek's reference to the shared life that Christians experienced together. Augustine (354-430) was the first to coin the phrase, "the visible sign of an invisible grace." Lambert, "Sacraments," 2636.

[168] Luther held that there were only two sacraments - baptism and eucharist - and that these "aids of grace" were efficacious only for the person with faith. Calvin believed in a special presence of Christ in the Lord's Supper, but that the sacraments were efficacious only for the predestined. Seeberg, *History of Doctrines*, 2:230, 282, 411-418.

voice, a printed text, a hymn, a sacred rite (however variously understood), a sin confessed, or a prayerful moment of silence, Christians have believed that God uses finite things to convey his infinite presence and grace. To believe otherwise is to fall prey to a dualistic divorce of God and his creation.

While the church's founders intended Christianity to be experienced - or better, because they knew that to experience Christianity was to experience life itself - and while the church has always believed that God works through physical means, nowhere is it taught in Scripture that Christian experience is, or that the means of encountering God are, the exclusive domain of any Christian sub-group. The book of Acts exemplifies that apostles and food servers,[169] eloquent orators and simple tent-making married couples,[170] young Gentile disciples and well trained Jewish-Christian rabbis,[171] all participated in the life and ministry of Christianity. That women were receiving religious instruction and prophesying,[172] that Paul repeatedly taught in ways that suggested the egalitarian nature of the body of Christ,[173] and that Peter taught that all Christians are priests unto God,[174] all stand in stark contrast to the institutionalized model of priestly service and mediated communion with God as prefigured in Judaism and later re-established in Christianity's sacerdotal models. All to say, the Orthodox' symbolic and participatory model of the mysteries (sacraments) itself is not so nearly as problematic, on the basis of Scripture, as is Orthodoxy's institutionalized sacramental system. Despite the fact that God uses his church to convey the news and grace of salvation, grace is not the church's possession. The Orthodox' dogmatic position that the sacraments are efficacious only when administered by a priest,[175] or that a Christian community is only authentically Christ's body when served by an Orthodox priest, evinces the sociological axiom that institutions inevitably take on a life and force of their own, even if they were initially begun for benevolent reasons. Clearly, the Orthodox' institutionalization of the sacramental model is rooted in tradition, and not Scripture. And, what is so problematic, in terms of our study of Christian transformation, is that the Orthodox' position makes

---

[169] Stephen and Philip.

[170] Apollos, Priscilla and Aquila.

[171] Titus and Timothy, and Paul himself.

[172] For such instruction see most of the New Testament, for prophesying see Acts 21:9; 1 Cor. 11:5.

[173] Rom. 12:3-8; 1 Cor. 12; Eph. 4:4-13.

[174] 1 Pet. 2:5,9.

[175] Save baptism, which can be performed by a layperson or a non-Orthodox.

one's *theosis*, indeed the bulk of the average layperson's Christian experience, largely contingent upon the office and availability of the priesthood; a priesthood which, for any number of reasons, may be corrupt or non-existent. Apart from that, the institutionalization of Christian transformation is dangerous, and not merely problematic, because it tends to supplant Christ's exclusive mediatory role as it is expressed in the New Testament witness. We do not approach God through Christ "and" priests, saints, buildings, or liturgies. We approach God through Christ himself. Those other elements can indeed be, and often are, beneficial for establishing and facilitating the congregation's attitude, the atmosphere of worship, and the human response to God, but those elements must always be kept as secondary, lest new or syncretistic ideas of salvation result.

The institutionalized model of grace is further problematic because it has the potential to limit how Christians think about themselves, their lives, and their activities as members of God's Kingdom. In other words, if the manifestation and experience of God's Kingdom and grace are only, or primarily, available through the liturgical and sacerdotal means, then Christians are going to be prone to think of Christianity primarily in terms of the church institution and church building. However, such an understanding is inconsistent with the New Testament testimony about God's Kingdom as a dynamic reign which can be manifested variously in groups and individuals, established Christian ceremonies and mundane humanitarian acts, pastoral ministry and faithful lives of integrity lived in a secular and even anti-Christian world.[176]

---

[176] We cannot examine this in detail here, but this church-bound view of Christianity must at least partly account for the Orthodox' inability to break out from its ethnic boundaries, despite their presence for over 175 years in America. That is, most Orthodox churches in America are organized first along ethnic lines. Those Orthodox who establish their churches on the basis of a more aggressive kind of evangelism are comprised of evangelicals who have since converted to Orthodoxy. For a study of Greek Orthodox immigration see Doumouras, "Greek Orthodox Communities in America Before World War I." For examples of evangelicals who have converted to Orthodoxy see Peter Gillquist, *Coming Home: Why Protestant Clergy are Becoming Orthodox* (Ben Lomond, California: Conciliar Press, 1992); and Gillquist's *Becoming Orthodox.*.

Liturgy

Another acute problem facing the Orthodox church, not only as it presents itself to the Christian West, but also as the philosophical-cultural foundations of Eastern Europe are gradually and steadily being transformed, is its emphasis upon a fixed liturgical form. In the previous chapter I criticized the Orthodox for their fixation on a specific historical-cultural milieu, so I will not repeat that. On a positive note, the Orthodox correctly assert that the primary issue for Christian worship is facilitating an experience of God, that God may fill his temple and therein be glorified.[177] Contemporary Western evangelical innovators who would rather talk to their congregations *about* God or principles of godly living rather than teach them how to encounter and glorify God must ask themselves to what are they precisely converting people? Nonetheless, the Orthodox' insistence on using only one form of corporate encounter - the liturgy of Chrysostom - is certifiably stultifying! That the average Eastern European Orthodox believer only sporadically attends the liturgy is ample evidence of how the Orthodox are failing to reach the people in lands traditionally deemed Orthodox. Of those Russians polled in a 1992 survey, 40 per cent professed belief in God. Of those who professed belief in God, 2-8 percent attend church services once a week or once per month, the rest only attend on holidays or once a year. Of this God-believing group, only 17 percent received the Eucharist in the last year, and only 7 percent participated in religious fasting.[178] If Orthodox church attendance is the primary means of receiving the Spirit's energies and uniting one to Christ, it is not only sad that the Orthodox, by virtue of the liturgy's stultifying sameness, continue to keep the people away, it is irresponsible Christian service. If it is true that tradition "is the life of the Church in the Holy Spirit,"[179] then the Orthodox simply must recognize that tradition can, precisely because of human nature, take on a lifeless life of its own. Moreover, creative and Spirit-breathed liturgical variations that more intentionally involve the congregations' minds and affections could invigorate and stimulate Orthodox peoples in fresh and magnetic ways. Such worshipful variations might not only not injure Orthodoxy's theological commitments, they

---

[177] Bulgakov, *The Orthodox Church*, 129.

[178] Sergei Filatov and Liudmila Vorontsova, "New Russia in Search of an Identity," in *Remaking Russia*, 284.

[179] Lossky, *Mystical Theology,* 188.

would also produce a greater level of theological involvement on the part of the laity.[180]

Mystery

The Orthodox assert that the divine-human communion involves ontological ramifications which are not easily comprehended. Rather than viewing this mysterious incomprehensibility as a barrier for Christian transformation and worship, as the West generally sees it today, the Orthodox assert that it touches on the very life of Christianity itself. One is not drawn to Christ because one understands him, one is drawn to Christ, especially in the liturgical setting, because therein one recognizes in the depths of one's soul that Christ is the embodiment of transcendent truth.

This element of mystery is just one element that the Orthodox and Pentecostals share. The Orthodox may be hesitant to admit that the divine mystery is at all being manifested among the Pentecostals. Some Pentecostals, for their part, are growing uncomfortable with God's mysterious presence (because of their increasing demographic affluence and its resultant rationalization), others are attempting to box it up in a package of revivalism (Pentecostals want revival, but they want it in the tried and true forms), but Pentecostalism nonetheless has historically been marked by an element of mystery. These qualifications aside, it is clear that there are indeed vast numbers of people who are spiritually hungry for God's transcendent presence. The Orthodox can indeed facilitate such an experience.[181]

Finally, for all of its power to impact the human soul, the mysterious dimension of Orthodox worship and theology needs to be integrated with a keener sense of precisely what can be known about God and his workings. Clearly I am discussing degrees of emphasis here, and not truth versus falsehood, but the Orthodox liturgy, because of its very structure, does little to

---

[180] The rather recent Charismatic Episcopal , consisting today of over 400 churches worldwide, exemplifies this kind of innovation with their fusion of charismatic and liturgical services. See Paul Thigpen, "Ancient Altars, Pentecostal Fire" *Ministries Today* (Nov.-Dec. 1992), 43-50.

[181] Perhaps a specific demographic cross-section of persons would be more drawn-in by this quality than others. Those who believe that God is, and his ways are, entirely comprehensible, along with those who see life as a simple choice between truth and falsehood, would be less inclined to affirm the mystery of Christianity.

inform the believer's mind about the truths of Christianity. Faith flourishes within the believer not only as a result of affective and existential encounters with God's Spirit, but also from a clear understanding of God's self-revelation. In this regard, apart from vocalizing Scripture, the liturgical ceremony does little, if anything, to explain or expound upon it. One's yearning for existential encounter with God may be sated in the liturgy, but one's hunger for rational knowledge about the Christian faith will go unfed if the liturgy comprises the whole of one's corporate Christian pedagogical experience. As important as the existential elements of human existence are they do not comprise the totality thereof.

The Unmediated Means of Transformation

Ramifications for Christian Spirituality and Anthropology

For all of their emphasis upon encountering the Kingdom of God within oneself, the Orthodox are not religious enthusiasts. As they express it, experiences of God, simultaneously described as visions of the divine light, the acquisition of the Spirit's grace, or the reception of Christ, are not for the sake of experience itself. In fact, they often warn against such religious questing. Instead, their experiential emphasis is always part and parcel of the growth and development of a person's Christ-likeness, one's *theosis*. One disciplines oneself so one can more easily become like Christ, and so that one can better apprehend his presence. When one apprehends the divine presence it is always to be processed with the understanding that God wants to transform the person into his own likeness. Communion with the divine always comes with ethical and existential ramifications. In this regard the Orthodox maintain a healthy middle ground between many emotionally oriented groups which emphasize the intuitive and charismatic elements of Christianity, on the one end, and the staunchly rational groups which emphasize knowledge and ethical behavior, on the other end.

The Orthodox' emphasis upon the existential dimensions of the human person, like that held by Pentecostals, calls for a fresh examination of Christian anthropology among Western Christians. In the West the fall is primarily interpreted as having impacted the human will, the *moral* aspect of human existence. In the West, generally speaking, the result of the fall is that religious and ethical goodness (alternately expressed as love or purity) is difficult, or even unnatural, for fallen persons to choose.[182] However, there is little sense or appreciation that the human person's very existential elements have been impacted, altered, or even perverted, or that these elements themselves impact, alter, or pervert the will. Although Western Christians may confess the sinfulness of their hearts, they nonetheless assume that they *do* rightly understand, that their minds *are* sufficient for a precise comprehension and summation of reality; thus the tremendous emphasis upon the empirical sciences for Western epistemology. But, in light of Orthodoxy's science of the soul, it seems fair to ask whether or how the existential dimensions of human existence have been befouled by sin.

As to hesychastic epistemology, I have a few comments. Firstly, if the Orthodox were more able, and more willing, to discuss Christianity by distinguishing the biblical witness from the later developments of tradition, their own ideas and insights might be more readily considered by Protestant Christians. However, for various reasons the Orthodox cannot and do not so discuss their faith; though, to be fair, this stems from their belief that Scripture and tradition both stem from the life and inspiration of the Holy Spirit. Secondly, their ambivalence about, and disdain toward, the value of the empirical sciences and humanities has caused them to work an anthropological myopia which blinds them to the roles which genetics, social constructs, culture, and economics have in a human being's development. In this regard their open ambivalence and disdain toward the sciences is unfortunate because it appears as being intellectually naive to those Christian outsiders who might otherwise consider the Orthodox' insights. One of these insights is prayerful contemplation.

Hesychastic Prayer

The Orthodox' awareness that Christianity is as much about the quality of existence - the necessity of an encounter with the divine, and the subsequent depths of Christian character such an encounter must eventually produce - as it is about the quantity of those in its existence (that is, the numbers claiming to be Christians) is a little appreciated refrain in the West, even if the Orthodox' hesychastic psycho-somatic techniques are questionable (at best) on the basis of Scriptural foundations. Moreover, there are other problematic issues about the

---

[182] For example see Erickson, *Christian Theology*, 967-971.

hesychastic approach which deserve mention. These are the dangers of quietism, anthropological heterodoxy, and an overemphasis upon apophaticism.[183]

Most Orthodox writers are careful to clarify that hesychastic pursuits of God must always be practiced in concert with the reception of the sacraments. They issue this warning, in part, because they are leery of potential quietists who pursue God by themselves at the expense of authentic Christian living - a kind of living which necessitates life in the Christian community. If it is true that Christianity can be sapped by a busy pragmatism, it is also true that Christianity is not authentic if the believer's entire focus is upon oneself. Certainly Scripture calls the faithful to regular times and seasons of quiet prayer and reflection, but the more normative case is one wherein the believer manifests Christ, and experiences Christ, within community. This warning is especially timely for contemporary North American culture where individualism is heralded as the supreme value within nearly every arena of life - religion included. Christians must never forsake assembling together to worship and fellowship with other Christians. To forsake community is both to live contrarily to God's own ecstatic nature and to live in harmony with Satan's own inspired selfish lifestyle.

A related danger of hesychastic prayer is its potential for anthropological heterodoxy.[184] While it is true that each Christian is a member of Christ's body and a temple of the Holy Spirit, nowhere in the New Testament is it taught that a believer is to seek the Kingdom of God within himself or herself.[185] While it is true that a redeemed person is a new creation, it is also true that one is called to actualize that new status. Because the Christian is being transformed from one who formulates his or her values and identity on the basis of this world's Kingdom into one who formulates his or her values and identity on the basis of God's Kingdom, one must always find the source for said transformation outside of oneself. Put more simply, Luther's doctrine that a Christian is *simul justus et peccator* more accurately reflects the indicative-imperative message of

---

[183] Cuttat, *The Encounter of Religions*, 117-153 provides a detailed critique of Hesychasm, noting both its dangers and its values for Christian spirituality. We will not exhaust his essay here, but we will use him as the foundation for the few comments made at this point.

[184] This issue is addressed here, and not in our earlier chapter on anthropology, because it is within the scope of hesychasm that the Orthodox' anthropology goes askance.

[185] The Orthodox wrongly interpret Luke 17:21, "the kingdom of God is within you." Their own historical-cultural presuppositions cause them to read mystical and philosophical meaning back into the text.

the New Testament. One may indeed encounter God in private prayer and contemplation, and one may even experience heavenly visions, but because one is in process, one will either find oneself terribly frustrated (at rarely experiencing the ecstasy described by the likes of Saint Symeon) or spiritually deceived (in the sense of making oneself the primary focus of religious experience) if one limits one's Christian experience to the internal quests of hesychastic prayer.[186] There is a fine line between accepting the doctrine that humans are microcosms of the universe and the idea that humans can transcend the boundaries of the universe within themselves. It is a fine line, but it must not be crossed.[187]

With a degree of insight and inspiration unfamiliar to the Christian West, the Orthodox recognize the supreme nature of human beings as those created in God's image.[188] Their position that Christians must learn to see God in every human being, and even in every created thing, is a way of looking at life that reflects Jesus Christ's own attitude as reflected in the Gospels. These anthropological strengths notwithstanding, the Orthodox' very doctrine of deification is dangerous for at least one additional reason: human pride. As was noted in an earlier chapter,[189] the doctrine of *theosis* stems as much from Greek philosophy as it does the biblical witness. And, the ancient Greek's very desire to somehow become divine (however one expresses it in Christian terms) too easily plays into the hands of our sinful nature, with the result that self-centeredness and pride result. Jesus warned his audience to consider "whether the light in you is not darkness," (Lk. 11:35). The Orthodox rightly counter such tendencies with their constant teachings about humility, *metanoia,* and the corporate dimensions of salvation. Still, it is clear that one can expend so much time and energy in one's divinizing process that one can begin to believe one is somehow superior to any others who are not so questing. Christians are not encouraged in the New Testament's apostolic witness to become like God so much as they are exhorted to become like Christ. Stated alternately, *our focus should not so much be upon becoming fully divine as it should be upon*

---

[186] Cuttat, *The Encounter of Religions,* 135-142.

[187] Indeed, this is the very line which the aberrant new age religions cross on a regular basis.

[188] Cuttat, *The Encounter of Religions,* 143, clarified that Saint Isaac the Syrian, six centuries before Saint Francis of Assisi, said that the "charitable heart is 'a heart which burns with love for the whole of creation, for men, for birds, for beasts. . . .'"

[189] See my analysis of the Orthodox' anthropology.

becoming fully human. In this light, authentic Christians are the most authentic human beings.

The third critique of hesychastic prayer is its tendency to over-emphasize apophaticism, a tendency which, again, stems from Greek philosophy and not the New Testament witness. I qualify that this criticism is one of emphasis, because on many theological fronts the Orthodox adamantly assert the necessity of Christ's incarnation (an event which tempers apophatic knowledge). Nonetheless, the hesychastic quests for visions of the divine light, quests presupposed by apophatic theology, run contrary to the eminent revelation of God in Jesus of Nazareth. In a positive way, the hesychast is taught to pray a prayer that focuses on the person of Christ (the Jesus prayer); the Orthodox are *not* instructed to attain an unconscious or a conscious-less state of mind such as Hare Krishna teaches. Rather, the purpose is clearing away all distractions for an existential communion with God himself. In an arguably negative way, the hesychast is taught to pray such a prayer, in part,[190] for the sake of experiencing an internal vision of divine and inexpressible light. For sake of clarification, we again refer to the New Testament where we see that the early Christians were not so much instructed to seek communion with the unknown, eternal, and wholly other God, so much as they were instructed to seek communion with the incarnate person of Christ. To say this it is not to deny that God is radically wholly other, but it is to assert that our approach to the divine is always to be conducted through the enfleshed *Logos* of God - Jesus Christ. Apophaticism tends toward unchecked pneumatism.[191] Authentic Christian prayer must always be tethered to, and enlivened by, Christ's incarnation.

---

[190] Along with the practice of *nepsis*.

[191] Cuttat, *The Encounter of Religions*, 143.

6

The Assemblies of God:
Historical and Doctrinal Roots

The origins of the Pentecostal movement are often traced to 1901 and Charles Parham (1873-1929). At his tiny Bible school in Kansas, Parham taught that *glossolalia* (speaking in tongues) was *the* sign of baptism of the Holy Spirit. Others hold that the Pentecostal movement's critical point of origin is more accurately traced to Parham's student, William J. Seymour (1870-1922), the famous black preacher at the Azusa Street Mission in Los Angeles. From Azusa Street preachers took the Pentecostal message and experience around the world. However one resolves the debate about origins one must recognize that Parham and Seymour individually prefigured the fact that, from the onset, the Pentecostal movement was, and is, a sociologically and ethnically diverse phenomenon.[1] Although the movement is widely held to have begun in the United States, today it is experiencing explosive growth, especially in Latin American and Africa.[2] In addition, its adherents are scattered throughout England, Scandinavia, western Europe, and parts of Asia. Important for this comparative study's purposes, the Pentecostals have been present in Eastern Europe since 1909.[3] By the time World War II broke out, there were more than

---

[1] On this discussion see Robeck, "Pentecostal Origins From a Global Perspective," 166-180.

[2] David Martin, *Tongues of Fire: The Explosion of Protestantism in Latin America* (Oxford: Basil Blackwell, 1990); Cox, *Fire From Heaven*, 243-262.

[3] Pentecostal missionaries may have been in Estonia as early as May of 1908. *The Apostolic Faith*, the Azusa Street Mission's newspaper reported that "a half-dozen or more little peasant girls" experienced baptism in the Holy Ghost and spoke in tongues. Robeck qualifies that it is not clear whether this incident occurred as the result of Pentecostal missionary work or simply was an indigenous event. However, it is clear that Pentecostal missionaries were in Latvia and the Baltic states in 1909. Robeck, "A Pentecostal Witness in an Eastern Context," Address given to the "Building Bridges, Breaking Walls" Conference in Prague, September 12, 1997, 1-4.

80,000 Pentecostals in Eastern Europe.[4] Like their Orthodox counterparts, they suffered under the Soviet regime for their faith. Arguably worse, a few of these Pentecostals, in 1911, physically suffered at the hands of their Christian brothers - the Orthodox.[5]

The strength of Pentecostalism is its experiential-charismatic emphasis. Because it is not tied to an historic creedal confession, and because it is less tied to a geographically defined point of origin than other Christian traditions (as, for example, are the Orthodox, who - as we saw in the first half of our study - encourage a kind of cultural as well as religious conversion),[6] this experiential emphasis is extremely pliable, as the above noted world-wide numerical explosion attests. There is little historical connection between Pentecostalism and Orthodoxy,[7] but in ways that will become evident in our explication of Pentecostalism, Pentecostals promote a rather mystical kind of spirituality like that of the Orthodox. Despite this mystical commonality, there are theological distinctions between the two. Whereas the Orthodox believe that the transforming power of Christian spirituality stems directly from formal theology, with few exceptions Pentecostals - although they exhibit an acute sensitivity about the need for a transforming spirituality - depreciate formal theology (systematic and historical)[8] as the field of study which merely safeguards said spirituality.[9] Years ago F. F. Bosworth typified the historical

---

[4] Gary McGee, "Working Together: The Assemblies of God-Russian and Eastern European Mission Cooperation, 1927-40," *Assemblies of God Heritage*, 8:4 (Winter 1988-89), 12.

[5] Robeck, "Witness in an Eastern Context," 14, notes that Orthodox Christians in Urmia City (an Armenian occupied and Russian ruled city in northern Iran) beat, kicked, and whipped two Pentecostal preachers with belts and horsewhips. Robeck notes additional Orthodox-Pentecostal tensions and conflicts in the former Soviet Empire.

[6] Though it may be the case that Pentecostalism is becoming a religious vehicle for spreading North American values and understandings.

[7] See my comments regarding John Wesley and the Greek patristic fathers in the introduction.

[8] An exception to this tendency from early Pentecostalism is Myer Pearlman, an early AG educator, who held that "there would be no Christian experience if there were no Christian doctrine." *Knowing the Doctrines of the Bible* (Springfield, Missouri: Gospel Publishing, 1937), x. A contemporary Assemblies of God theologian who believes a thoroughgoing Christian spirituality must be rooted in theology is Simon Chan, *Spiritual Theology*.

[9] Gary McGee, "Historical Background," in *Systematic Theology, A Pentecostal Perspective*, Stanley Horton (ed.) (Springfield, Missouri: Gospel Publishing, 1994), 21-

attitude of Pentecostals like those in the Assemblies of God toward theology when he said, "I hate theology and I hate botany, but I love religion and flowers."[10] Inasmuch as the Orthodox maintain that theological creeds, especially ecumenically patristic ones, serve to unite and invigorate the church, many Pentecostals, especially the earliest ones, tend to view theological creeds and theological study as both divisive and stifling to the move of the Holy Spirit.[11] This is not to say that Pentecostals had, or have, no concern for doctrinal orthodoxy or theology: they routinely and staunchly defended their own doctrinal distinctives. Yet, it was not until the third and fourth generations of its movement that Pentecostals began to recognize the need for careful and detailed theological endeavor,[12] and it remains the case that the Pentecostals still

---

27, notes three reasons why the AG has drawn doctrinal boundaries over the years: 1) "to protect the integrity of the Church and welfare of the saints;" 2) "because believers require solid answers in the face of erroneous doctrine;" and, 3) "Pentecostals have struggled to balance biblical teaching with their religious experience." McGee's qualifications about AG theologizing are correct, but they nonetheless evince the AG's need to protect its spirituality and not its formal theology. As I said in my first chapter, spirituality is understood here as the subjective and lived response to the perceived reality. Following the Asian-born AG scholar Simon Chan, theology, for its part, is distinguished here as "the systematic reflection and formalization of that reality." Chan, *Spiritual Theology*, 16.

[10] F. F. Bosworth, "The Will of God Boiled Down Into Five Words. 'Be Filled With The Spirit," *The Weekly Evangel*, No. 229 (March 2, 1918), 1.

[11] Stanley H. Frodsham, a first generation AG leader, in *Wholly For God* (Springfield, Missouri: Gospel Publishing n.d.), 49, exemplified this widespread attitude when he said, "There are two kinds of religion. One is a dead assent to a doctrine, whether it be of Confucius or Buddha or Jesus. This is a ghostly religion with no body to it." One can find similar sentiments in every Pentecostal denomination. Donald Gee, "This I Believe: The Use and Abuse of Dogmatism," *RT*, 30 (November 5, 1954), 4-5, more evenhandedly clarified that dogma is essential for Christianity, both on theological and experiential grounds. He also astutely noted that the AG's "Statement of Fundamental Truths" had ironically become a creed, despite the original founders' intentions.

[12] Prior to this time, what little theology Pentecostals received was presented in devotionals, testimonials, poems and hymns. Cf. McGee, "Historical Background," 36. The Pentecostals' second and third generations produced theologies that were largely edited regurgitations of other Protestant theologians' works with the inclusion of Pentecostal spiritual distinctives. For example see Pearlman, *Doctrines*; and, Ernest S. Williams, *Systematic Theology*, 3 vols. (Springfield, Missouri: Gospel Publishing, 1953). The recognition of the need for careful integration of Christian theology with the other practical concerns (missions, spirituality, ecclesiology, evangelism, social praxis, etc.)

have little appreciation for the role of systematic theology, historical theology, or church history in shaping and informing their spirituality.

To make the above observations is not necessarily to fault the Pentecostals - they were (and are) responding to the concerns, perceptions, and impulses of their day - but it does immediately clarify that their vibrant spirituality was (and is) fueled by something other than formal theology. One Assemblies of God minister accurately described Pentecostal theology as "a theology by default rather than by serious study."[13] In 1963 Donald Gee, one of the early Pentecostal movement's guiding lights, recognized the Pentecostals' ambivalence toward theology and said, "It has been a common thing for fervent Pentecostal preachers to hold up theology and theologians to ridicule and obloquy as though they were essentially inimical to the working of the Holy Spirit in revival."[14]

Despite this common ambivalence about theology's value, the Pentecostal movement does have a theological heritage. And, despite many turn-of-the-century Pentecostals' claims that their movement was simply the result of God's providential end-times' outpouring, scholars of Pentecostalism, as Augustus Cerillo stated, have clearly established the continuity between the "nineteenth century religious and social developments" with the rise of twentieth-century Pentecostalism.[15] Firstly, Wesleyan-Holiness beliefs and practices contributed important elements in the theological seedbed for the Pentecostal movement. The Holiness movement began in the latter half of the 1800s, when conservative Methodists began to pull away from their own increasingly liberalized denomination. The Wesleyan-Holiness elements included an emphasis upon experiential religion, the doctrine of entire sanctification and its necessity in a believer's life, a literalist interpretation of Scripture, a belief in a post-conversion experience called the "baptism of the Holy Spirit," the teaching that

---

can be traced to both the 1960s when subsequent generations entered graduate schools and to 1970 with the beginning of the Society for Pentecostal Studies (SPS). The SPS' journal, *Pneuma*, has been published since 1979.

[13] Poloma, *The Assemblies of God at the Crossroads: Charisma and Institutional Dilemmas* (Knoxville, Tennessee: The University of Tennessee Press, 1989), 171, citing an unnamed contemporary Assemblies of God minister.

[14] Donald Gee, "Pentecostal Theology," *The Ministry* (Journal of the British Pentecostal Fellowship), 1:1 (January 1963), 22.

[15] Augustus Cerillo, Jr., "Interpretive Approaches to the History of American Pentecostal Origins," *Pneuma*, 19:1 (Spring 1997), 36. Cerillo provides an incisive encapsulation of Pentecostal bibliography.

the Holy Spirit guided individual believers, and the operation of camp meetings and Bible schools.[16]

Secondly, the Pentecostal movement's theological seedbed was comprised of Reformed and evangelical Higher life elements. These elements were influenced by the British Keswick movement's (primarily Anglican and Calvinist evangelicals who, in 1875, began to hold annual conventions in the mountains of northwest England) teachings. Transported to the U.S. and promulgated by the likes of D. L. Moody (the famous nineteenth century revivalist), R. A. Torrey (a president of Moody Bible Institute in Chicago), A. B. Simpson (the former Presbyterian who, in 1897, organized the initially interdenominational Christian and Missionary Alliance association), and A. J. Gordon (a Boston Baptist who founded Gordon-Conwell Theological Seminary), these elements included the belief that the second work of grace was an enduement of power (and not the holiness doctrine of entire sanctification), the belief that sanctification was a progressive conquering of sin, the doctrine that physical healing was located in Christ's atonement, and the belief in Christ's premillennial return.[17] Despite the distinction about the timing of sanctification's completion, the Wesleyan-Holiness and Reformed-Higher life groups shared a tremendous amount of theological understanding and Christian piety.

As the discussion below will show, the Assemblies of God (AG) is decidedly Reformed-Higher life in orientation regarding sanctification. The AG's spirituality-theology deserves analysis for many reasons, not the least of which are its above mentioned theological heritage, its explosive world-wide growth, and its fresh appreciation for pneumatology. In order best to understand how and why the AG believes what it does about sanctification we will present a brief historical sketch. Later, we will develop some heuristic categories for understanding what it is that fuels the AG's spirituality.

---

[16] Klaude Kendrick, *The Promised Fulfilled: A History of the Modern Pentecostal Movement* (Springfield, Missouri: Gospel Publishing, 1961); Vinson Synan, *The Holiness-Pentecostal Movement in The United States* (Grand Rapids: Eerdmans, 1971), 33-93. C. E. Jones, "Holiness Movement," in *DPCM*, 406-409.

[17] John T. Nichol, *The Pentecostals* (Plainfield, New Jersey: 1971); Edith Waldvogel (Blumhofer), "The 'Overcoming Life': A Study in the Reformed Evangelical Origins of Pentecostalism," Diss. Harvard University, 1977, 1-148; Robert Mapes Anderson, *Vision of the Disinherited: The Making of American Pentecostalism* (Peabody, Massachusetts: Hendrickson, 1979), 39-43, 111-13; Dayton, *Theological Roots*, 104-106.

A Brief Historical Sketch

Organization and Backgrounds

The AG came into being in 1914 at the first general council in Hot Springs, Arkansas. More than three hundred people, coming from Egypt, South Africa, and many parts of the United States (but predominantly from the Midwest), attended the first council. Their reasons for forming a new fellowship were very pragmatic and included: the ostracism of the Pentecostals by other Protestant denominations,[18] divisive partisanship caused by strong personalities, the lack of scrutinized ministerial credentials, the increasing problem of strange doctrines, the need to operate missionary endeavors more effectively, the desire to start Bible training schools, and the growing desire to separate themselves from the already incorporated black Pentecostals of the Church of God in Christ (COGIC), a denomination that was then issuing ministerial credentials to the white Pentecostal preachers.[19] Because many early Pentecostals, following Parham himself,[20] were characterized by anti-organizational sentiments (they believed organization stifled the Holy Spirit's movings),[21] the first several days of the primarily white gathering were devoted to spiritual concerns, rather than issues of polity.[22] Eventually, though, the gathering did produce a declaration of purpose - not a Spirit-stifling doctrinal creed - which asserted that Scriptural principles be followed in the issues of Christian unity, church governance, worship, and doctrine. The assembly also issued a statement calling for legal incorporation so that the practices of business transactions, property ownership,

---

[18] Though, as Blumhofer notes, the distance between the Pentecostals and the other Protestants was probably as much a matter of their not wanting to submit to established authority as it was the Protestants' ostracizing them. *The Assemblies of God: A Chapter in the Story of American Pentecostalism,* 2 vols. (Springfield, Missouri: Gospel Publishing, 1989), 1:199-200. Unless otherwise noted, references to Blumhofer's *The Assemblies of God* will always be from the first volume.

[19] William Menzies, *Anointed to Serve: The Story of the Assemblies of God* (Springfield, Missouri: Gospel Publishing, 1971), 80-91; Blumhofer, *The AG,* 200-202.

[20] Synan, *Holiness-Pentecostal Movement,* 151.

[21] E.g., A. W. Orwig, "Program Versus The Holy Ghost and Vice Versa," *The Christian Evangel,* August 8, 1914, 3.

[22] Blumhofer, *The AG,* 97-211; Menzies, *Anointed,* 97.

and missionary work could be properly and legally carried out. In the legal statement the name "Assembly of God," understood to be "a general scriptural name," was adopted for the fellowship.[23]

The earliest AG leaders' own backgrounds were very important for how the denomination's doctrine of sanctification was formulated. Accordingly we will briefly note a few of these who played pivotal roles in the AG's formulation. Certainly other, and later, leaders could be noted for their theological influence, but we will note those from the earliest era precisely because their own backgrounds eventually determined the denomination's doctrine of sanctification. Each of these noted below was one of the original twelve executive presbyters.[24]

Eudorus N. Bell (1866-1923) was one of the original five ministers to call for the Hot Springs convention.[25] Prior to his turn to Pentecostalism, the first General Council's acting chairman and later the denomination's secretary (1919) and chairman (1920), Bell had been a Baptist minister for seventeen years. He completed his higher education at Stetson University, Southern Baptist Theological Seminary, and the University of Chicago Divinity School. Important for the AG's doctrine of sanctification, Bell turned to Pentecostalism upon hearing William Durham (about whom more will be said later) preach in Chicago. Bell was also quite influential in that he published two denominational magazines, *Word and Witness* and *Pentecostal Evangel*.[26]

J. Roswell Flower (1888-1970) was the fellowship's first general conference secretary and one of the initial twelve executive presbyters. Years later he would also serve the denomination in several key capacities including assistant general superintendent (1931-37). When he was a boy, Flower's parents moved first from a Canadian Methodist church to John Alexander Dowie's Zion City in Illinois, and then to a Christian and Missionary Alliance (CMA) church in Indianapolis. When Flower was about nineteen, the Pentecostal minister Glenn Cook came to town and under his ministry Flower became a Pentecostal Christian. Like Bell, Flower was influential not only as a pastor but also through his writings; he was the first editor of the *Christian Evangel*, later to be called

---

[23] Menzies, *Anointed*, 99-100; Blumhofer, *The AG*, 202-203.

[24] Menzies, *Anointed*, 109, said that the executive presbyters initially served as advisors to those churches seeking self-governance.

[25] The original "call" has been reproduced in *Assemblies of God Heritage*, 8:4 (Winter 1988-9), 8. The other four ministers were M. M. Pinson, A. P. Collins, H. A. Goss, and D. C. O. Opperman.

[26] Menzies, *Anointed*, 133-134; Wayne E. Warner, "Eudorus N. Bell" in *DCPM*, 53.

the *Pentecostal Evangel*. During his time as the superintendent of the AG's Eastern District (New York, New Jersey, Pennsylvania, and Delaware), Flower established a camp meeting site upon which a Bible school was started in 1932.[27] Flower later taught at one of the AG's Bible schools, Central Bible Institute, in Springfield, Missouri. He also played a key role in moving the AG into the National Association of Evangelicals (NAE) and other Pentecostal fellowships.[28]

Like Flower, D. W. Kerr (1856-1927) had a CMA background, except whereas Flower simply had been a member of a CMA church, Kerr was affiliated with the CMA for 23 years and pastored a CMA church in Cleveland for four years. Kerr converted to Pentecostalism in 1907 and his CMA church became a Pentecostal church for the next eight years. Both Kerr and John Welch (noted below) were in their late fifties when the AG began, and as such they were the oldest pastors appointed to the executive presbytery (the movement was then largely comprised of younger leaders). Prior to joining the CMA, he attended an evangelical college in Illinois where he studied theology, church history, and Greek. Clearly, Kerr had a better education than the average AG leader in his day. So equipped, he played a critical role in suppressing the Oneness controversy and developed Scriptural arguments for baptism in the Holy Spirit. Important for our study on sanctification, along with four others Kerr was the primary drafter of the foundational "Statement of Fundamental Truths" in 1916.[29] His acute sense of the need for education is evident both in that he (along with Robert and Mary Craig) helped to establish Glad Tidings Bible Institute (now Bethany College) (1919), and he founded both Southern California Bible School (1920) and Central Bible Institute (1922).[30]

---

[27] Initially this school was situated on the grounds known as "Maranatha Park." Over the years its name was changed from Eastern Bible Institute to Northeast Bible Institute to Valley Forge Christian College, its present name.

[28] Menzies, *Anointed*, 135-136; Gary B. McGee, "Joseph James Roswell Flower and Alice Reynolds Flower," in *DPCM*, 311-313; Blumhofer, *The AG*, 202, 204.

[29] Following the teaching of A. B. Simpson, the CMA held that sanctification was a spiritual refocusing whereby one's mind was set on heavenly things. Sanctification was both the believer's privilege and duty, but for Simpson it was not a "work of grace," as the Wesleyan-holiness proponents held. Blumhofer, *The AG*, 63.

[30] Lewis Wilson, "The Kerr-Pierce Role in A/G Education," *Assemblies of God Heritage*, 10:1 (Spring 1990), 6-8, 21-22; Menzies, *Anointed*, 70, 108, 119, 129, 134; Blumhofer, *The AG*, 236.

The man who proposed the name "Assembly of God" to the burgeoning fellowship was Thomas K. Leonard (1861-1946). Leonard, a farmer who had become a Pentecostal in 1907, had pastored a church in Ohio and operated a ministerial training school there before the AG began. Leonard also helped argue against the Oneness proponents in 1918. Sometimes a contentious leader, Leonard withdrew from the AG in 1929.[31]

John W. Welch (1858-1939) came from the CMA where he had served as an evangelist. He turned to Pentecostalism in 1910 at Muskogee, Oklahoma, where he was serving as the CMA's superintendent. "Daddy Welch," so called because of his age (56) at the AG's beginning, played an important role in helping settle the Oneness controversy. Years later he taught at a Bible school in San Francisco and was president of Central Bible Institute in Springfield.[32]

Other original AG executive presbyters included H. A. Goss, D. C. O. Opperman, A. P. Collins, M. M. Pinson, R. L. Erickson, Cyrus B. Fockler, and John C. Sinclair. Together with F. N. Bell, Goss was one of the chief organizers of the AG in 1914. Opperman, who prior to his association with the AG had had Holiness leanings (in contrast to a Reformed-Higher life background), was a founding member of the AG and was initially made an executive presbyter in the AG.[33] Collins and Pinson were initially persuaded to follow F. F. Bosworth's teaching about Spirit-baptism (noted below), but eventually they returned to the accepted position.[34] Prior to AG's founding, Pinson was the editor of *Word and Witness*, a periodical devoted to the "finished work" of sanctification (noted below).[35] R. L. Erickson had pastored Stone Church in Chicago.[36] Before he joined the Pentecostal movement , Cyrus Fockler was first an assistant to Maria Woodworth-Etter, the famous healing evangelist whose own ministry predated the Pentecostal movement, and then he was a supporter

---

[31] Menzies, *Anointed*, 99, 103-105, 118, 129; Blumhofer, *The AG*, 206; Paul C. Taylor, "T. K. Leonard and the Pentecostal Mission," *Assemblies of God Heritage*, 14:4 (Winter 1994-95), 23-25; Michael G. Owen, "Preparing Students for the First Harvest: Five Early Ohio Bible Schools," *Assemblies of God Heritage*, 9:4 (Winter 1989-90), 16.

[32] Carl Brumback, *Suddenly. . . From Heaven* (Springfield, Missouri: Gospel Publishing, 1961), 165-167; C. E. Jones, "John William Welch," in *DPCM*, 881.

[33] Menzies, *Anointed*, 67; J. L. Hall, "Howard Archibald Goss," in *DPCM*, 343; Edith Blumhofer, "Daniel Charles Owen Opperman," in *DPCM*, 653.

[34] Menzies, *Anointed*, 128-130.

[35] Blumhofer, *The AG*, 426, n. 8.

[36] Blumhofer, *The AG*, 204.

of John Dowie at Zion City in Illinois.[37] Sinclair was a Presbyterian who converted to the Wesleyan-Holiness movement, and was purportedly the first Chicagoan to receive the Pentecostal experience.[38]

Of these twelve original executive presbyters, five left the AG within four years of its inception. Both Goss and Opperman left the AG within three years of 1914 to help start the Oneness Pentecostal movement. Fockler and Sinclair left the AG because of their disdain for organization. Erickson was dismissed, Edith Blumhofer said, "on a morals charge."[39] This brief biographical presentation supplies an useful cross-section of the denomination at its origins: AG constituents primarily came from Reformed-Higher life backgrounds, and not Wesleyan-Holiness backgrounds. As will be developed later below, those backgrounds were critical for the AG's doctrine of sanctification.

The Oneness Controversy

Early in the twentieth century Pentecostals engaged in a Trinitarian controversy known simultaneously as the "Jesus Name", "Apostolic", "Oneness", "New Issue", or "Jesus Only" issue.[40] The Azusa Street Pentecostal revival impacted an independent Baptist pastor named Joshua W. Sykes. Based on a vision in which an angel appeared and instructed him, Reverend Sykes, from late 1906 or early 1907 onward, began to baptize his followers "in the name of Christ."[41] Sykes not only seems to have been the first to so baptize, he also maintained doctrines which seemed aberrant to Pentecostals as a whole. One such oddity was his teaching that the Millennium had begun in 1904 - a position which was strongly resisted by premillennialist Pentecostals like those in the AG. Because of his "questionable doctrinal positions" he was viewed by the Pentecostal constituents in negative terms and avoided.[42]

---

[37] Blumhofer, *The AG*, 34-35, 198, 204.

[38] C. E. Jones, "John Chalmers Sinclair," in *DPCM*, 787-788.

[39] Blumhofer, *The AG*, 422, n. 70.

[40] I will refer to this issue as the Oneness issue out of deference for Oneness adherents like David K. Bernard who feel that "Jesus Only" and "New Issue" are misleading and derogatory phrases. Bernard, *The Oneness of God* (Hazelwood, Missouri: Word Aflame, 1983), 15.

[41] Robeck, "A Pentecostal Perspective on Apostolicity," an unpublished paper presented to Faith and Order of the NCCCUSA in March 1992, 16-17.

[42] Robeck, "Pentecostal Perspective on Apostolicity," 17.

A key event for the Oneness issue occurred in 1913 at the Arroyo Seco camp meeting[43] when R. E. McAlister, a Canadian evangelist, preached that the apostles baptized in the name of Jesus, as is evident in Acts 2:38, and not in the threefold formula of the Father, Son and Holy Spirit, as is found in Matthew 28:19. A preacher sitting on the platform went over to McAlister and whispered to him to "refrain from emphasizing [baptism in Jesus' name] or it would 'associate the camp with a Dr. Sykes who so baptized.'"[44] That warning went unheeded and McAlister's message so impacted the people at the Arroyo Seco meeting that many were rebaptized in Jesus' name, as Cecil Robeck, Jr., said, "to bring them into conformity with what they had come to believe was the apostolic pattern of Christian baptism. "[45]

Present at the Arroyo Seco meeting during McAlister's sermon was Frank J. Ewart. Ewart reflected upon and studied McAlister's sermon for a year and came to the conclusion that the "name" found in Matthew 28:19 - the name in which Christians were to be baptized - was indeed that of Jesus Christ, alone. For Ewart, the God who had revealed himself in history as the Father, in the Son, and through the Holy Spirit "was none other than Jesus Christ. "[46] In support of his position Ewart cited Colossians 2:9 which says, "For in him [Jesus] dwelleth all the fulness of the Godhead bodily," (KJV). In 1914 Ewart set up his own tent meeting in Belvedere, California, in which he and his assistant evangelist Glenn Cook (who had formerly worked with William Seymour) mutually rebaptized one another in the name of Jesus. In 1915 Cook influenced Garfield Haywood, a prominent black pastor of a 500 member congregation in Indianapolis, to accept the oneness baptismal formula and "by the spring of 1915 the new movement was spreading rapidly."[47]

---

[43] For Trinitarian Pentecostals this is simply remembered as the Arroyo Seco Camp Meeting, but for Oneness Pentecostal historian Fred J. Foster, *Think it Not Strange: A History of the Oneness Movement* (St. Louis, Mo.: Pentecostal Publishing, 1965), 51, this is remembered as the "World-Wide Los Angeles Camp Meeting" where there was "fired a shot that sounded around the world."

[44] Menzies, *Anointed*, 111.

[45] Robeck, "Pentecostal Perspective on Apostolicity," 18. Robeck notes that apostolicity was a critical ingredient in the formulation of Pentecostal practice and doctrine. The desire to return to the days of the New Testament church, to turn away from "churchianity", to turn again to God's power was central for Pentecostals.

[46] J. L. Hall, "United Pentecostal Church, International," in *DPCM*, 861.

[47] David Reed, "Oneness Pentecostalism," in *DPCM*, 644.

Not only did the Arroyo Seco meeting of 1913 and the subsequent Oneness teachings promulgated by the likes of Ewart and Haywood cause much discussion among AG constituents, so also did E. N. Bell's own rebaptism in the name of Jesus in 1915. (Bell had been the AG's General Council's first chairman, but in 1915 he was an executive presbyter.) The denomination was involved in much debate about Bell's act, and a biblical solution was sought concerning the entire issue. Important for the AG's discussion was the role and place of Acts 2:38 (supporting the Oneness formula) and Matthew 28:19 (supporting the Trinitarian formula). The AG's Third General Council in 1915 addressed the Oneness issue but concluded with no official position. Instead the Council called for a season of prayer and study toward resolution. Despite having taken no official doctrinal position it is significant that the Council replaced all the Oneness leaders on the executive presbytery with confirmed Trinitarians.[48] That power-play notwithstanding, the Oneness proponents continued to make converts to their new teaching. As a result the AG determined at the Fourth Council (1916) that doctrinal limits must be established. Seventeen articles were drawn up and ratified by majority vote as the "Statement of Fundamental Truths", among them was an article which reaffirmed the traditional western doctrine of the Trinity. The Oneness ministers were forced to accept the Trinitarian statement or leave the AG; some chose the latter and "156 of the 585 ministers were barred from membership and with them many congregations."[49]

Oneness Pentecostals, for their part, held to a literal reading of Acts 2:38, "Repent, and be baptized every one of you in the name of Jesus Christ. . .," and took a somewhat modalistic view of God which challenged the traditional Trinitarian doctrine. The major motivations for those who turned to the Oneness position were primitivism and apostolicity. Like their Trinitarian Pentecostal siblings, the Oneness adherents were eager to return to the apostolic times when the Spirit of God was poured out, when miracles were plentiful, and when scores of people repented and came to Christ.[50] This same primitivistic zeal led the Oneness followers to re-baptize believers with the understanding that one was only truly obedient, and one only had God's full blessing, if one was

---

[48] Hall, "United Pentecostal Church, International," in *DPCM,* 862. Blumhofer similarly recounts this history in *The AG,* 221-223.

[49] Reed, "Oneness Pentecostalism," 646.

[50] Robeck, "Pentecostal Perspective on Apostolicity," 14-17.

baptized in Jesus' name.[51] Moreover, in an attempt to emulate the apostolic church, the Oneness followers advocated the use of wine in the Communion service, a practice which was discouraged by the AG.[52]

Although the AG strongly opposed the formulation of creeds and the strangling forms of organization, they could not allow the Oneness teaching to continue spreading among their ministers. The Third General Council of the AG in 1915 addressed the issue with a conciliatory tone, but concluded with no official position and allowed for a season of prayer and study toward resolution. It was also significant that the Third Council replaced all the Oneness leaders on the executive presbytery with confirmed Trinitarians.[53] Despite this power-play, the Oneness proponents, led by Glenn Cook, continued to make converts to their new teaching. As a result, the AG determined in the Fourth Council (1916), that doctrinal limits must be established. Thus, seventeen articles were drawn up and ratified by majority vote as the "Statement of Fundamental Truths." Among them was an article which reaffirmed Western Christendom's doctrine of the Trinity. Bell was won back to the Trinitarian camp in 1916, and the Oneness ministers were forced to accept the Trinitarian statement or leave the AG. In response, approximately one-quarter of the ministers chose to leave and took with them their congregations.[54]

---

[51] Blumhofer, *The AG*, 235. Just as the AG had done with regard to the predominantly black COGIC, the Oneness movement quickly split along racial lines. The black Oneness adherents, following G. T. Haywood, formed the Pentecostal Assemblies of the World (PAW). Two white Oneness groups joined forces to form the largest Oneness denomination, the United Pentecostal Church (UPC) in 1945. David Reed, "Oneness Pentecostalism," in *DPCM*, 644-651. For a fuller apology of Oneness theology see David K. Bernard, *The Oneness of God* (Hazelwood, Missouri: Word Aflame Press, 1983). Both in his text and his glossary definitions Bernard worked a historical revisionism. He condemned the Nicene Creed as the first Trinitarian statement, favorably remarked on Nestorious as a victim of misunderstanding, and stated that Sabellianism and Modalistic Monarchianism are basically equivalent to modern Oneness theology. Finally, for a history of Oneness Pentecostalism see Foster, *Think it Not Strange*.

[52] Blumhofer, *The AG*, 231.

[53] Hall, "United Pentecostal Church, International," in *DPCM*, 862. Blumhofer, *The AG*, 221-222.

[54] Menzies, *Anointed*, 118-121.

Baptism with the Holy Spirit

Whereas the AG's Oneness Issue, and its Trinitarian resolution, is important for any comparisons between the AG and the Orthodox concerning Christian transformation, to include the AG's doctrine of Spirit-baptism in such an analysis may seem odd. In its official teaching (following the teaching of William Durham, which will be noted in a separate section below) the AG does not view Spirit-baptism as a segment of the *ordo salutis*, but prefers to discuss it as an event of divine empowerment for Christian life and service.[55] However, as our later analysis of the AG's sanctification doctrine will show (see the chapter on sanctification's means), AG constituents consistently discuss Spirit-baptism as a life changing event, even if they do so on an unofficial, or non-theological, level. The AG's original statement regarding sanctification said, "By the power of the Holy Ghost we are able to obey the command, 'be ye holy for I am holy.'"[56] The original paragraph was ambiguous as to whether the power for holy living was synonymous with the power gained in Spirit-baptism or through other means. However, since the time of the original statement the AG has denied that Spirit-baptism is a third work of grace in the *ordo salutis*. That is, Spirit-baptism is not a work of regeneration.[57] One can only surmise as to why the AG argues that Spirit-baptism is not a sanctifying event (it is at least in part due to Luke's book of Acts and the focal point of empowerment), but the fact of the matter is that AG constituents themselves nonetheless routinely discuss the spiritual experience of Holy Spirit-baptism as both a life transforming event and an enablement for holy living.[58]

When one examines the AG's matter-of-fact descriptions of Spirit-baptism from the Orthodox' own view of *theosis* as a lifelong process involving communion with God's Spirit, one can argue that the AG's reluctance to include

---

[55] Cf., AG theologian Stanley Horton said, "the baptism in the Holy Spirit is not itself a sanctifying experience," "The Pentecostal Perspective," in *Five Views on Sanctification*, Melvin Dieter, Anthony Hoekema, Stanley Horton, J. McQuilkin, and John Walvoord (Grand Rapids: Zondervan, 1987), 132. See also Pearlman, *Doctrines of the Bible*, 309.

[56] *Combined Minutes of the General Council of the AG in the USA, Canada, and Foreign Lands* (1914-1917) (St. Louis: Gospel Publishing, n. d.), 14.

[57] Horton, "Pentecostal Perspective," 130-132.

[58] In 1995 the AG printed a tract which does mention the effects of Spirit-baptism on holy living. "Our Distinctive Doctrine: The Baptism In The Holy Spirit," An Assemblies of God Pamphlet (Springfield, Missouri: Gospel Publishing, 1995).

Spirit-baptism in the *ordo salutis* is not theologically necessary.[59] Thus, while the Orthodox do not give baptism with the Holy Spirit[60] a codified role in Christian transformation, AG Pentecostals, if only by virtue of the plethora of matter-of-fact testimonies and articles, do. Regarding Spirit-baptism and the *ordo salutis*, we will briefly note the initial historical division caused by the AG's doctrine of speaking in tongues.

As our earlier historical sketches proved, the religious milieu was a multi-faceted one when the Pentecostal movement came on to the historical scene. Whereas Pentecostalism's distinctive doctrine has always been that speaking in tongues was *the* initial physical evidence of one's baptism with the Holy Spirit,[61] many turn-of-the-century American evangelicals believed one could be, subsequent to conversion, filled with the Holy Spirit without speaking in tongues. A Pentecostal who followed the evangelical position in this regard was F. F. Bosworth.

Bosworth was concerned about the Pentecostal doctrine both because so many great Christians throughout history had no testimony of speaking in tongues and because so many, in Bosworth's own day, had spoken in tongues without the fruit which was supposed to accompany Spirit-baptism. These

---

[59] In a paper, "The Transformation of Sanctification: The Church of God (Cleveland, Tennessee) and its Doctrine of Sanctification," for a doctoral seminar at Fuller Seminary, 1997, I argued that this disagreement about whether the *ordo salutis* is a two-fold or three-fold process no longer exists (generally speaking) between the AG and Holiness Pentecostals in the U.S. From an Eastern Orthodox perspective, the AG was wrong to exclude Spirit-baptism as a transforming work of grace within the *ordo*, and the Holiness Pentecostals were wrong to argue that sanctification was a once-for-all experience of sin's eradication. Sanctification is a process of transformation that incorporates a life-long series of tests and transforming experiences, some more dramatic than others, and many not describable as overtly charismatic. For descriptions of sanctification as a progressive and lengthy process see Myer Pearlman and Frank Boyd, *Pentecostal Truth* (Springfield, Missouri: Gospel Publishing, 1968), 49-50; and, Timothy Jenney, "The Holy Spirit and Sanctification," in *Theology, A Pentecostal Perspective*, 416-420.

[60] The Orthodox do not employ the specific teaching about baptism with the Holy Spirit, but, as our earlier study clarified, they clearly affirm the role that spiritual experiences play in Christian transformation. See also, Emmert, "Charismatic Developments in the Eastern Orthodox Church," in *Perspectives on the New Pentecostalism*, 37-39, who discusses the actualization of the Holy Spirit within the believer.

[61] AG Pentecostals further clarify that one can speak in tongues at one's Spirit-baptism without receiving the charismatic gift of tongues (cf. Paul's rhetorical question, "Do all speak in tongues?", 1 Cor. 11:30).

concerns, coupled with his study of Scripture, caused Bosworth to adopt a position similar to the CMA that tongues was one of the signs of Spirit-baptism. Because of his own forceful personality and the respect he commanded as a speaker, Bosworth's position caused an outcry among the AG's constituency in 1917. At the General Council of 1918, and by the persuasion of D. W. Kerr, a resolution was unanimously passed that both affirmed tongues as the initial evidence of Spirit-baptism and discouraged AG pastor's from disparaging the tongues-as-initial-evidence doctrine. The Council had variously argued that the AG's position was grounded in New Testament teaching, that the church would be "immeasurably impoverished" without the doctrine, and that even the issue of Christian harmony could not stand in the way of full biblical revelation on the matter. Bosworth, aware of his own departure from the AG's position, had turned in his ministerial credentials to the AG prior to the General Council meeting.[62]

Sanctification

Scholars of Pentecostal history usually trace the distinction between the Wesley-Holiness and Reformed-Higher life groups concerning sanctification to 1906-1914 and the teaching of William H. Durham (1873-1912). In order to understand Durham's own teaching more clearly one must understand the position of John Wesley (1703-1791). Methodism's founding father, Wesley was less precise about the nomenclature of the works of grace than were the later Holiness teachers who built upon his foundation.[63] Wesley taught about entire sanctification, but variously called it Christian perfection, and perfect love. He clearly believed in the role of the Holy Spirit in Christian transformation, but he had no neatly defined doctrine of Spirit baptism.[64] Wesleyan-Holiness proponents, the majority of whom were swept up by the growing Pentecostal movement in the early 1900s, took Wesley's ideas and both refined and crystallized them so that entire sanctification - the eradication of the sinful nature that originated with Adam's sin - was held to be a second work of

---

[62] Menzies, *Anointed*, 124-130. The quote is from p. 130.

[63] John Fletcher, Asa Mahan, and Phoebe Palmer were three of the critical teachers in this regard. See Dayton, *Theological Roots*, 51-54, 63-84, 92-100.

[64] W. M Arnett, "The Role of the Holy Spirit in Entire Sanctification in the Writings of John Wesley," 15-30; W. S. Johnson, "Christian Perfection as Love for God," 50-60.

grace. When Pentecostalism began to spread, a third work of grace, baptism with the Holy Ghost, was included in the Holiness *ordo salutis*.[65]

Durham, a member of a Baptist church, experienced conversion in 1898 and for the next three years he earnestly sought the second blessing of entire sanctification. In 1901 this desire was filled with an experience he described as a blessing of entire sanctification, peace, and joy. For the next five years in Chicago, where he pastored at the North Avenue Mission, he taught the Holiness position regarding sanctification. In 1906 Charles Parham came to Dowie's Zion City and preached the Pentecostal message for several weeks. In light of Parham's teaching, fifty members of Durham's church, who had also heard about the Pentecostal outbreak occurring in Los Angeles, experienced the Pentecostal blessing. Prompted by the stirrings in his own church, Durham went to Los Angeles in 1907 and there experienced his own Pentecostal blessing.[66]

As Durham described it, from his Spirit-baptism onward, he vowed to stop teaching the Holiness position regarding sanctification. By 1910, Blumhofer states, Durham's "thought had developed and matured into a systematic presentation of an alternative view" which he called the "finished work" teaching. Like the Keswick and "Higher life" proponents, and consistent with a position akin to that of Finney's Oberlin theology,[67] Durham taught that Christ's atoning work transformed the believer into a new creature who only needed to "abide in Christ, receive and walk in the Spirit, hold fast the faith, grow in grace and in the knowledge of God and of Christ." In contrast to the Holiness position, he taught that baptism with the Holy Spirit was the second work of grace.[68]

---

[65] Holiness-Pentecostals believed that purity (entire sanctification) preceded power (Holy Spirit baptism), and that the Spirit would not dwell in unclean vessels; Menzies, *Anointed*, 74. For a sympathetic analysis of the Holiness-Pentecostal doctrine see David Roebuck, "Sanctification and the Church of God," *Reflections . . . Upon Church of God Heritage*, 2:2 (Fall 1992).

[66] Blumhofer, "The Finished Work of Calvary: William H. Durham and a Doctrinal Controversy," *Assemblies of God Heritage*, 3:3 (Fall 1983), 9-11.

[67] Oberlin was an important evangelical college in the 1800s. Oberlin perfectionism, with its emphasis upon the human role in Christian transformation, was a confluence of Wesleyan and Calvinistic themes. Dayton, *Theological Roots*, 66-72. Synan, *Holiness-Pentecostal Movement*, 148, maintains that Oberlin was an important foundation for Durham's theology.

[68] Blumhofer, "Finished Work," 10. She quoted Durham in his magazine *Pentecostal Testimony*, August 1912.

Despite the bitter excoriation he received from Parham and others for this doctrinal deviation, Durham remained steadfast to his rather Reformed position.

As increasing numbers of Baptists, with their own traditional beliefs about sanctification, began to join the Pentecostals, Durham's views gained force among the Pentecostal movement. Furthermore, Durham's position gained acclamation via his periodical, *The Pentecostal Testimony*.[69] Along with some of the earlier noted AG leaders, Aimee Semple (1890-1944), who would later break away from the AG and start the International Church of the Foursquare Gospel in Los Angeles, attended Durham's Chicago Mission and maintained his views on sanctification. Hundreds of "urban independent and unorganized churches and missions" adopted Durham's position on sanctification, but the established Southern Pentecostals remained steadfast to the Holiness position. And, to no small degree, geographical triumphalism characterized the debate when southerners called those holding to the "finished work" position "deluded Yankees" and antinomianists.[70] Durham conversely taught that those holding to Holiness position were "deluded by Satan." In 1912 Parham, in turn, charged Durham with having "committed the sin unto death" and prophesied that Durham would die within six months (eerily, Durham in fact died within those six months).[71] From Durham's time onward, the doctrine of sanctification has been the theological crucible standing between the Wesleyan-Holiness Denominations and Reformed-Higher life Pentecostals.[72]

As early as 1916, when the AG issued its first "Statement of Fundamental Truths," the AG's position on sanctification was rather vague. It followed

---

[69] Menzies, *Anointed*, 64-65; 74-77; 318. Blumhofer, *The AG*, 128-130. Walter Hollenweger, *The Pentecostals*, English translation of *Enthusiastisches Christentum: die Pfingstbewegung in Geschichte und Gegenwart*, R. A. Wilson (tr.) (Peabody, Massachusetts: Hendrickson, 1988), 24-25.

[70] Synan, *Holiness-Pentecostal Movement*. The first quote was from p. 149, the second from p. 150.

[71] Blumhofer, "Finished Work," 10.

[72] The Wesleyan-Holiness groups include the Church of God (Anderson, Indiana), the Church of God (Cleveland, Tennessee), the Church of God in Christ, the Church of the Nazarene, the Free Methodists, the Pentecostal Holiness Church, and the Wesleyan Church. The Reformed-higher life groups are comprised of the Assemblies of God, the Christian Missionary Alliance, and the International Church of the Foursquare Gospel. Synan, *Holiness-Pentecostal Movement*.

Durham, it mirrored the CMA's own theology,[73] and, in order to mollify those of a stronger Wesleyan-Holiness orientation, it also included in its doctrinal formulations the use of the phrase "entire sanctification."[74] Finally, because of the teaching that Christ's righteousness was imputed to the believer, the phrase "entire sanctification" was omitted from the official statement in 1961. Imputed righteousness, the AG qualified, must result in a life of holiness.[75]

Following Durham's "finished work" teaching on Christ's atonement, the AG believes that sanctification is twofold. Upon one's conversion one is positionally sanctified in Christ. Paul revealed this when he addressed the Corinthian church as "saints" and noted that they were already "sanctified in Christ Jesus" (1 Cor. 1:2; 6:11).[76] In light of the Corinthians' heterodox practices and beliefs, Paul could not have meant that they were sanctified in the sense of full Christian transformation. Instead he meant that they were cleansed and consecrated in Christ upon their conversion. Because St. Paul also went on to exhort them to live as persons who had been so washed and consecrated, sanctification is also understood as being progressive. One is sanctified (and thereby saved) by means of his atoning work on the cross. Yet, together with Christ (by means of faith, obedience, and cooperation with the Holy Spirit) one must live a sanctified life and seek to become like him. Unlike many Wesleyan-Holiness proponents, the AG does not believe progressive sanctification can ever be completed, or perfected, in this life. The Spirit enables the Christian not to sin, but in this life the Christian will never come to the point where he or she will not be able to sin. Moreover, it is not God's purpose in this life to make us perfect, but to bring us to maturity.[77]

---

[73] Charles W. Nienkirchen, *A. B. Simpson and the Pentecostal Movement* (Hendrickson, 1992), 41-50.

[74] The original statement said, "The Scriptures teach a life of holiness without which no man shall see the Lord. By the power of the Holy Ghost we are able to obey the command, 'be ye hold for I am holy.' Entire sanctification is the will of God for all believers, and should be earnestly pursued by walking in obedience to God's Word. Heb. 12:14; 1 Pet. 1:15,16; 1 Thes. 5:23,24; 1 Jn. 2:6." *Combined Minutes of the General Council of the AG in the USA, Canada, and Foreign Lands* (1914-1917), 14.

[75] Menzies, *Anointed*, 117, 318.

[76] There are many other passages the AG cites in this regard, some of these include: 1 Cor. 3:13-14; 2 Cor. 3:18; Eph. 4:22-24; Col. 3:5-10; 1 Thess. 4:3-4; 5:23; Heb. 13:20-21; 2 Pet. 1:4-8; 3:18; 1 Jn. 1:7.

[77] This brief synopsis summarizes Horton, "The Pentecostal Perspective," 109-128. AG theologians do not develop why it is that perfect sanctification awaits completion in the

Representing a watershed era in the development of the Reformed-Higher life stream of Pentecostalism, Durham is best understood as an important individual manifestation of - but not the sole cause of - the inevitable differences that arose between the Wesleyan-Holiness and Reformed-Higher life streams. This manifestation-not-cause analysis of Durham is substantiated in light of the fact that the British Keswick movement had, in the late 1800s, begun to resist the American Wesleyan-Holiness tendencies toward perfectionism.[78] Prior to the rise of Pentecostalism, Keswick proponents had also begun to refer to the post-conversion experience of baptism with the Holy Spirit as an enduement with power, and not as an experience of sanctification.[79]

As the above brief historical and theological sketches have shown, the AG is characterized by the following: a belief that God can, and wants to be, experienced on an individual basis; an understanding of the Godhead that is thoroughly trinitarian; a commitment to the authority of Scripture; and, a position harmonious with the two-millennia old church that sanctification is a progressive growth in godliness. But, as this sketch has also shown, the AG is characterized by each of these primarily because of its own leaders' pre-Pentecostal backgrounds and the historical milieu in which it developed. Again, the AG was initially comprised of persons with similar theological views, views which they brought to their new fellowship from their former Reformed-Higher life backgrounds. Apart from defending its chief doctrinal distinctive (tongues as the initial-physical evidence of Spirit-baptism) the AG has done very little in the way of theological development or exploration. This corporate "theology by default" is presently exemplified in that none of the AG's current U.S. undergraduate institutions of education offers a degree in theology.[80] The

---

afterlife. That is, they do not explain whether our environment (i.e., the world) is the problem (so that we can never be free from external temptations), or whether the soul's absolute transformation can only occur in the afterlife. Albert L. Hoy, "Sanctification," *Paraclete* 15:4 (Fall, 1981), 7, implies that this complete transformation will only occur in heaven where we will enjoy unencumbered communion with God.

[78] Anderson, *Vision*, 40-43.

[79] Synan, *Holiness-Pentecostal Movement*, 142; Dayton, *Theological Roots*, 105.

[80] This lacuna regarding theology aside, the twelve accredited and endorsed AG undergraduate institutions do offer Religion degrees in Biblical Studies and Pastoral Ministries. Of those twelve, some offer additional degrees in Music Ministry, Youth Ministry, Pastoral Counseling, and Urban Ministries. To earn a degree in Religion most of these institutions require the completion of two to four theology courses (of which Pneumatology is a consistent theme), and one Pentecostal History/Theology course. The

pedagogical focus is more pragmatic and less reflective: from the beginning, the AG has trained its pastors and lay-leaders in the areas of evangelism, spirituality, biblical exposition, and local church polity.[81] It has done - and continues to do - little by way of grounding the denomination's thought and praxis in historic Christian reflection. At the expense of being redundant, one reason for this theological lacuna is that the AG mostly assumes its theology from the broader Reformed-evangelical milieu.

The AG's Spiritual Catalysts:
Primitivism, Charisma, and Pragmatism

Primitivism

Scholars have long recognized that something other than the intellectual arena fueled the early Pentecostals' spirituality. Like Robert Anderson in *Vision of the Disinherited,* some have argued that the early Pentecostal spirituality took its point of origin from a powerless and disenfranchised people. Amid the troubling issues of the industrial revolution and an ever increasing sense of mobility, both of which eroded older social constructs, and in the throes of philosophic modernism which was both foreign and threatening, these early disinherited religious bands turned to personal piety, religious ecstasy, and millenarian fantasy. In this analysis, the early Pentecostals were reacting to the cultural machinery by retreating into psychic and physical escape.[82] This analytical framework has its merits, but, as Cerillo has pointed out, it tends to interpret the rise of Pentecostalism solely in naturalistic terms. Such a naturalistic analysis fails to satisfactorily explain, Cerillo said:

Assemblies of God's Seminary itself offers a Master's degree in Theological Studies. This survey was completed by examining numerous college catalogues and internet websites (October 1998).

[81] My analysis in this regard is sustained by McGee, "Historical Background," 28, where he discusses pastoral training in the AG's colleges and correspondence courses.

[82] Anderson, *Vision.* Mark Noll, *A History of Christianity in the United States and Canada* (Grand Rapids: Eerdmans, 1992), 386-388, similarly portrays the early Pentecostals.

how a people who were so culturally marginal and economically deprived managed successfully to utilize the techniques of popular culture and build a worldwide movement, to say nothing about how well these early American Pentecostals did in achieving a modicum of a decent standard of living for themselves and especially their children; for its many interpretations that are based on an uncritical and even ahistorical imposition of questionable modern theories of social and economic deprivation and psychological maladjustment on a very limited historical data base; and for its refusal to recognize, as many other scholars have, that the 'disinherited' folk - farmers, workers and immigrants - were more in control of their lives and better able to cope with life's challenges than once believed, and that a Pentecostal experience in fact may have been a source of liberation and empowerment.[83]

In contrast to Anderson, some scholars have focused on the positive forces enabled the Pentecostals to endure and do those things Cerillo noted above. Many have asserted that restorationism was the fuel which propelled the Pentecostals. Edith Blumhofer defined restorationism as "the attempt to recapture the presumed vitality, message, and form of the Apostolic Church."[84] Tired of the cold and lifeless formalism of the Catholic and mainline churches ("priestcraft and ecclesiasticism," as one AG theologian described them),[85] the early Pentecostals, like their Wesleyan-Holiness and Reformed-Higher life forebears, wanted to return to the pure and simple form of New Testament Christianity and reproduce it.[86] This restorationist impulse variously helps to account for why the Oneness movement stressed the earliest "Jesus only" baptismal formula as noted in Acts 2:38 in lieu of the trinitarian formula as noted in Matthew 28:19, why it was that minorities played an important role in early Pentecostalism (following the New Testament's racially inclusive model); and, why it was that many Pentecostals regularly and officially limited women's

---

[83] Cerillo, "The Beginnings of American Pentecostalism," an unpublished paper presented to the *Society for Pentecostal Studies*, Chicago, 1994, 23.

[84] Blumhofer, *The AG*, 18.

[85] Pearlman, *Doctrines of the Bible*, 50. Anderson, *Vision*, 216-217, notes the initial and continued Pentecostal reaction to Catholicism.

[86] H. Paul Holdridge, "The Pure Stream of Christianity," *Pentecostal Evangel*, May 12, 1968, 3, referred to formalism and said, "Traditions, frills, and rituals have been added in an effort to make it appeal to men's physical senses. But these have not invited any greater favor of God."

ministerial roles. Many Pentecostals thought they could bring such a restoration about themselves, others believed that God would work such a restoration.[87]

Those insights notwithstanding, restorationism falters as an analytical rubric because there were many restorationist groups throughout Christian history and in the early twentieth century who rejected the kind of enthusiasm and disorder (in terms of worship and polity) manifested by Pentecostalism.[88] Though it likely would have been meaningless to them, the early Pentecostals themselves failed to realize that the New Testament church was itself characterized by some of the very liturgical forms of worship they were opposing, so that the early Pentecostal restorationist motives were not entirely in keeping with the actual apostolic setting.[89] For these reasons, restorationism imprecisely defines the Pentecostal spiritual impetus.[90]

Grant Wacker holds that the driving and sustaining forces of the movement were, and are, its primitivistic impulses: philosophical primitivism, historical primitivism, and ethical primitivism.[91] Similar to Wacker, though in arguably cruder terminology, Harvey Cox maintains that Pentecostalism has been both

---

[87] Blumhofer, *The AG*, 15. She further explains restorationism on 18-22.

[88] Cerillo, "The Beginnings," 40.

[89] The mere fact that the Jewish synagogue provided a model for the early Christian worship service implies a borrowing of liturgical order. Furthermore, although the New Testament church could not have believed in transubstantiation, their celebration of the Lord's supper actively encouraged anamnesis and participation in Christ's person and work. Ralph Martin, *Worship in the New Testament* (Grand Rapids: Eerdmans, 1974); R. J. Karris, *A Symphony of New Testament Hymns* (Collegeville: Liturgical Press, 1996).

[90] Admittedly the rubrics of restorationism and primitivism overlap. Cerillo, "The Beginnings," 32, noted that Wacker, who will be followed below, himself initially used restorationism and primitivism interchangeably. Still, for the above noted reasons my preference is not merely a semantic one.

[91] Wacker developed the role of primitivism in four different articles: "The Functions of Faith in Primitive Pentecostalism," *Harvard Theological Review*, 77:3 (1984), 353-75; "Pentecostalism," in *Encyclopedia of American Religious Experience*, Charles Lippy and P. Williams (eds.) (NY: 1988), 2:933-945; "Playing for Keeps: The Primitivist Impulse in Early Pentecostalism," *in The American Quest for the Primitive Church*, Richard T. Hughes (ed.) (Urbana: University of Illinois, 1988), 196-219; and, "Character and the Modernization of North American Pentecostalism," paper read at the Society for Pentecostal Studies meeting, 1991. These themes are woven together in Wacker's recent book, *Heaven Below: Early Pentecostals and American Culture* (Cambridge, Massachusetts: Harvard University Press, 2001).

successful and sustained by primal speech, primal piety, and primal hope.[92] Despite the Harvard theologian's intriguing, and more anthropologically oriented, examination, Wacker's analysis is asserted herein because his terminology is more in keeping with the self-understanding of classical Pentecostals themselves.[93]

Wacker defines primitivism more broadly as, "the dark subsoil in which restorationist visions were nurtured. It was the less rational, more emotive urge not simply to build, but also to escape the allurements of modernity, to swing free of the limitations of historical contingency. It fired a determination to rid oneself of the sin and contamination of finite existence itself."[94]

Rather than hindering the movement's growth, this primitive spirituality enabled it to flourish. Pentecostalism, with its experientially based spirituality, was "an island of traditionalism," Wacker said, "in a sea of modernity."[95] Thus, Wacker recognizes the historical-cultural setting of the era, like Anderson and others, but rather than viewing Pentecostalism as merely a socio-economic phenomenon, he characterizes it as a "both-and" phenomenon. It was both a matter of the early Pentecostals' lot in life together with their specific religious (ahistorical, affective, and experiential) ethos.

By philosophical primitivism[96] Wacker meant that Pentecostals believed they "not only could know but in a very real way possess or lay personal claim to

---

[92] Cox, *Fire From Heaven*. In chapters four through six he delineates these three primal elements. He defines all three on 82-3. Primal speech (*glossolalia*) is "a language of the heart" which is intentionally in contrast to the "ultraspecialized terminologies and contrived rhetoric" of the era. Primal piety is characterized by Pentecostalism's mystical vein (dreams, visions, trances, dances, and the miraculous). Primal hope is the movement's eschatological orientation. For some, "primal" has pejorative connotations implying other than Christian, or even divine, elements. In this regard, one wished Cox would have more carefully established the grounds for his own usage.

[93] That is, Cox does an interesting job of locating the Pentecostal spirituality within a broader comparative- religions framework, but his analysis has little in common with the expressions and descriptions of Pentecostals themselves. Wacker, at the Lewis Wilson Institute for Pentecostal Studies Lectureship, Costa Mesa, California, 2/6/98, noted that early Pentecostals used "primitivism" to characterize their movement.

[94] Wacker, "Character and Modernization," 9.

[95] Wacker, "The Functions of Faith," 363.

[96] Wacker wisely qualified that in using the phrase philosophical primitivism he did not mean to imply that the Pentecostals themselves were necessarily philosophical in their epistemology. Although they assumed the theology written in Protestant theology books,

absolute truth." True enough, other sectarians evinced a similar certitude about their own epistemologies, but the Pentecostals' claim in this regard was specifically in reaction to both the modernistic culture and the growing field of biblical scholarship.[97] Because they believed the Bible was essentially written by God (both the human role in, and the original milieu of, the New Testament were rendered as being entirely secondary), and because the early Pentecostals themselves were living in an age which they described as a kind of bookend to the apostolic era (so that like the apostolic era they were escaping the contingencies of history and finite existence), the Pentecostals did not doubt, Wacker said, "that their own interpretation of the Bible. . . was as inerrant as the Bible itself." These assumptions quite naturally led them to read the Bible literally.[98]

The second form of early Pentecostal primitivism, historical primitivism, Wacker defined as "the special way that pentecostals handled church history and their place in it."[99] While they believed their movement "repristinated apostolic Christianity,"[100] *they believed they owed nothing to the vast expanse of church history.* The Pentecostals generally asserted that most of Christian history was a tale of apostasy and formalism. As such, they rendered it - and the creeds it produced - irrelevant. This ahistorical viewpoint, stemming from the above noted hermeneutical literalism, held that the New Testament provided a "workable blueprint" for twentieth-century Christianity. Those who did not adhere to the blueprint, as the Pentecostals parochially interpreted it, were castigated and cut off. For this reason, the Pentecostals were often characterized by internal divisiveness and doctrinal disputes. Even more, they regularly exhibited disdain and vituperation toward those in other denominations.[101]

---

they had little or no interest in the intellectual arena as such. "Playing for Keeps," 198; "The Functions of Faith," 364.

[97] The AG, too, warily viewed the higher critical methods. E. N. Bell said the scholars who used such methods were radical, modernistic, and infidels. *Questions and Answers* (Springfield, Missouri: Gospel Publishing, n.d.), 75.

[98] Wacker, "Playing for Keeps," the former quote was from p. 197, the latter from p. 198. Based on this literal hermeneutic they would handle snakes and take poison. This literalistic hermeneutic also accounts for the former issues Blumhofer noted (re. baptism, inclusiveness, women's roles).

[99] Wacker, "Playing for Keeps," 199.

[100] Wacker, "Playing for Keeps," 199.

[101] Wacker, "Playing for Keeps,", 199-209; and, "The Functions of Faith," 363-375.

Like the church of Acts, the Pentecostals believed the Spirit's presence among them was the proof that God was in their midst and that he was sanctioning their efforts. Whereas the Spirit's outpouring in the apostolic era signaled the beginning of the church's dispensation, they believed the Spirit's outpouring upon them signified that the church's dispensation was drawing to an end. This eschatological orientation - coupled together with, and stemming from, their doctrine that Spirit-baptism was a sign of the end times - was the primary catalyst in their evangelical and missiological endeavors.[102] Notable for this study, eschatology was an important catalyst regarding personal piety and the issue of personal purity. Like the larger evangelical environment, turn-of-the-century Pentecostals avoided tobacco, alcohol, dancing, and gambling. Yet, because their concern for personal piety was heightened by an acute eschatological sense, these Pentecostals went further and banned the use of, and involvement in, things the broader Christian culture deemed frivolous and amoral. Wacker summarized their views in this regard, "When people expect the Lord's return at any moment, frivolousness is not merely imprudent. It is immoral."[103]

This eschatologically-rooted asceticism is important for understanding the history of the AG's sanctification doctrine. As they consistently expressed it, the earliest AG Pentecostals refrained from frivolous activities, not so much to become more like Christ (though they never would have denied that such facilitated becoming like him) but to cease being like the world.[104] By sheer force of emphasis, the Pentecostal doctrine of sanctification in general (and the

---

[102] Wacker, "Playing for Keeps," 203-207; and, "The Functions of Faith," 368-374. Wacker's analysis in this regard is similarly established by Synan, *Holiness-Pentecostal Movement*, 146; Menzies, *Anointed*, 328-330; and, Blumhofer, *The AG*, 141-169, to name a few.

[103] Wacker, "The Functions of Faith," 371. The frivolous activities they shunned included attending ballgames, playing pool, co-ed swimming, watching parades, going to the theater, enjoying recreational activities on Sundays, reading novels and newspapers, and drinking coffee, tea, or soda pop, and even chewing gum.

[104] The AG's bylaws contain a definition of worldliness that is rather general when compared to the lists of activities which were regularly railed against in sermons and in print, ". . . the Scripture warns against participation in activity which defiles the body, or corrupts the mind and spirit; the inordinate love of or preoccupation with pleasures, position, or possessions, which lead to their misuse; manifestation of extreme behavior, unbecoming speech, or inappropriate appearance; any fascination or association which lessens one's affection for spiritual things." "Minutes of the 47th Session of The General Council of the Assemblies of God, Indianapolis," Indiana, 1997, 150.

AG's doctrine in particular) is a doctrine of negation more than it is a doctrine of affirmation. The Pentecostals wanted to distance themselves from the worldly culture, that domain of Satan soon to be judged at Christ's return. But because their asceticism did not have a positive mooring,[105] their ethical codes too easily transmuted into stark legalism. The historical ramifications of this eschatologically-oriented doctrine of sanctification are noteworthy: 1) because eschatology is decreasingly a topic of contemporary pastoral reflection so too are discussions about sanctification; and, 2) because their eschatology was oriented around God's imminent judgment upon the world, they were more concerned to evangelize and escape the world than transform it.

Wacker's description of the third Pentecostal primitivism - ethical primitivism - was largely a reiteration of the ahistorical and anti-worldly themes he already noted in philosophic and historical primitivism.[106] For this reason we will not trace his presentation of ethical primitivism. This last caveat aside, Wacker' heuristic category of primitivism is helpful for interpreting the early Pentecostals' actions and spirituality. However, primitivism alone neither fully explains the early Pentecostals' spiritual fuel nor does it solely account for the contemporary Pentecostals' spiritual fuel. For a fuller understanding, regarding the past and present, the combustible element of charisma must be included.

Charisma

The early Pentecostals not only wanted to "build a new movement;" they did not only nurture "restorationist visions;" the force of their movement lay not only in the fact that they were often less, rather than more, rational; they were not merely protesting (i.e. Wacker's anti-structuralism), or "escaping," modernity and historical contingency because of their ideological and/or demographic lot in life.[107] As they expressed it, the early Pentecostals were impelled by something else, something little addressed in Wacker's model.

If Wacker's model is preferable to those like Anderson's because it more intentionally and sympathetically includes the Pentecostals' experiential religion together with their ideological, historical, and demographic situation, it still falls short of the full picture. This lacuna of perspective results because it proceeds

---

[105] For example, as either the incarnational or ecclesiological arenas can provide.

[106] Wacker, "Playing for Keeps," 207. In addition he develops the early Pentecostal antistructuralist attitudes toward polity and church worship.

[107] Wacker, "Character and Modernization," 9.

largely as a sociological description. More in keeping with the historical witness, the early Pentecostal spirituality was not only a religion of protest or escape, it was also a religion of communion and celebration. While it is true that the Pentecostals' religious milieu deserves study "from the bottom up," their own descriptions of their origins incorporate a "from the top down" character.[108] The Pentecostals' vibrant and numerical success was as much a fact of their being drawn toward something as it was a matter that they were escaping from something else. As they expressed it, indeed as they continue to express it - though perhaps less vigorously, or in less primitivistic ways - they were both in communion with, and celebrating the presence of, God's Spirit.

For good reason, scholars are right to be wary of attributing God's presence or providence within the study of history. Firstly, it is often an uncritical manner of quenching the thirst for knowledge. The earliest historians of Pentecostalism too easily and uncritically attributed the movement's causes and effects to the hand of God.[109] Secondly, assigning divine providence or the divine presence is a difficult task to validate. The problematic nature of this task is well expressed in psychiatrist Victor Frankl's comment, "The spirituality of man is a thing-in-itself. It cannot be explained by something not spiritual; it is irreducible. It may be conditioned by something without being caused by it."[110]

The dangers of assigning a divine role aside, for too long theologians and church historians have been attracted to secularism's intellectually prideful "glitter" and have accommodated to its epistemological biases. Such scholars have both participated in secularism's "group soliloquy"[111] and have altogether ignored the role of the divine. (Ironically, it has been the historically a-theistic fields of anthropology, sociology, psychology that have begun to study the role of religious experience. Theologians and church historians always seem to be about one generation behind the "harder" sciences in adopting the latter's

---

[108] To clarify, scholars have long distinguished Christological studies by virtue of these categories. Those who seek to understand Jesus in light of his historical and cultural milieu work a Christology from below. Conversely, those who seek to understand him as a divine person work a Christology from above.

[109] For example, Brumback, *Suddenly*; Charles W. Conn, *Like a Mighty Army Moves the Church of God* (Cleveland, Tennessee: Pathway, 1955, rev. ed. 1977).

[110] Poloma, *At the Crossroads*, xx, quoting Frankl, *The Doctor and the Soul*, xviii.

[111] Poloma uses the word glitter and quotes "group soliloquy" from Robert Merton, "Discrimination and the American Creed," in *Discrimination and National Welfare* (99-126), in *At the Crossroads*, 92.

methodologies.)[112] Capitulation to secularism's epistemology aside, because both the Eastern Orthodox and the Pentecostals adamantly assert the necessity of religious experience in Christian transformation, the role that charisma played, and plays, in Pentecostalism's spirituality - and doctrine of sanctification - must be included in any assessment of the movement.

For clarification's sake, charisma is herein defined as both the extraordinary powers that are experienced on a community-wide basis and the individual giftedness which enables a leader - usually a pastor or evangelist - to facilitate the community's experience of said extraordinary powers.[113] The New Testament describes the *charismata* as those gifts of grace (succinctly described by one Pentecostal scholar as God's "gracelets")[114] freely given to the Christian community for its edification and empowerment. The apostle Paul variously described these gifts as spiritual giftings,[115] offices of service,[116] and spiritual ministries.[117] Margaret Poloma limited her survey study of the AG[118] to the charismatic gifts of *glossolalia*, divine healing, prophecy, and paranormal experiences, but it is herein asserted that a fuller panorama of definitions (excepting the apostolic office, which for Pentecostals ceased when the last

---

[112] Some of those working in the "harder" sciences have begun to seriously consider ways to empirically study the presence of the divine in and upon human beings. Cf., Robert Hotz, "Seeking the Biology of Spirituality," *Los Angeles Times*, April 26, 1998, A1 and A28. Hotz noted that scientists at several universities have begun to trace the neural activity of the brain during religious trances and/or ecstatic states. Further bibliography on the study of religious experience is extensive. For starters see André Godin, *The Psychological Dynamics of Religious Experience*, Mary Turton (tr.) (Birmingham, Alabama: Religious Education Press, 1985). Since the Enlightenment, religious scholars' capitulation to anti-religious epistemologies is an unfortunate, if understandable, story.

[113] Poloma, *At the Crossroads*, 88-89.

[114] Russell Spittler coined this term in his 1 Corinthians course at Fuller Theological Seminary.

[115] 1 Cor. 12:8-10: words of wisdom and knowledge, faith, healing ability, powers, the discerning of spirits, and tongues and their interpretation.

[116] 1 Cor. 12: 28: apostles, prophets, and teachers.

[117] Rom. 12:6-8: prophecy, ministry, teaching, exhortation, giving, leadership, and mercy.

[118] Poloma, *At the Crossroads*.

apostle died) was and is maintained by the AG as available, helpful, and in some instances necessary for the whole church.[119]

Poloma rightly noted that no one person can be singled out as the original charismatic individual who conveyed the Pentecostal experience and message.[120] (Our earlier comments about the AG's own history typifies the fact that there were many figures who played important roles in the movement's development.) One of the long-acknowledged sociological drawing features of the Pentecostal movement has been its teaching that the *charismatic giftings and ministries are to be exercised by the entire Christian community*. Just as the apostles were simple, ordinary men whom God used extraordinarily, the subsequent historical sweep of Christians - those open to God's supernatural power and enablement - could also have been used in charismatic and extraordinary ways (again, the Pentecostals fail to recognize that there were indeed many such Christians in the sweep of church history). One AG official revealed the typical Pentecostal belief in this regard when he said that the AG was founded in order to "rediscover that apostolic power and blessing which had been so long absent from the ranks of God's people."[121] The Pentecostals,

---

[119] While the Pentecostal movement is very oriented around apostolicity, it does not limit or root its definition thereof with the apostolic office. The apostles themselves died, but the apostolic nature of the Church has been sustained via the *charismata*. In other words, the *charismata* were not apostolic because they were manifested or possessed by the apostles, the apostles were whom they were firstly because they were eyewitnesses to the incarnate Son of God, and secondly because of their unprecedented and preeminent charismatic giftings (alternately understood as gifts of the Spirit). This is an important distinction between the Catholics and the Pentecostals. The Orthodox, for their part, do not root apostolicity in historical persons as much as do the Catholics. Instead, the Orthodox root apostolicity (a.k.a., apostolic ministry) in Christ himself, so that the contemporary Church is only apostolic when and where it is participating (mystically, ontologically) in Christ via the Spirit (esp. in the eucharist). Cf. Zizioulas, *Being as Communion*, 209-246. The respective ways that the Orthodox and the Pentecostals define apostolicity is a topic deserving further study, and it may be that the two have more in common with each other on this issue than either does with the Catholics.

[120] Poloma, *At the Crossroads*, 89.

[121] J. O. Savell, "Serving God With Purpose of Heart," *PE*, September 5, 1954, 3. Savell was then the AG's Assistant General Superintendent. Decades earlier, E. N. Bell typified the Pentecostal view of Church history. Answering how it was that the post-apostolic Church lost its supernatural power, Bell said, "The church has never entirely lost it. After a few centuries most of the church for most of the time, did truly lose it through the loss of consecration, loss of a close touch with God, loss of full gospel light, and through sin

intentionally open to God's charismatic ways, believe that with them a new era
has dawned in the church age, an era where even society's ordinary people can
be used mightily of God. In all of this, Pentecostals are characterized by a belief
in the "charismatic common man."

Together with their dynamic worship services, the Pentecostals have also
facilitated the communal flow of charisma through their hunger for, and
sponsorship of, revivals. Many individual Pentecostal churches regularly reserve
a period of the calendar year specifically for revival. To this end charismatic
evangelists will be brought in for prolonged periods of preaching. In the attempt
to draw people to the revival meetings, home visitations will be made, tracts
will be handed out, and newspaper advertisements will be run. As has been the
case in the three AG churches I have attended in my own experience, the revival
period itself will have been preceded by a season of fasting and prayer. Along
with the salvation of individual persons, revival, precisely because it is the
evangelistic venue to facilitate charisma, is generally understood to be the
fundamental way God transforms his creation. So that as more people attend the
revival, the more likely a mushrooming effect will occur and eventually
families, entire towns, and even entire nations will be transformed. Conversely,
this charismatic emphasis of transformation, again especially manifested in the
AG's individualistic and revivalistic manifestations, partly accounts for the
AG's historic ambivalence to spread Christ's transforming yeast through
vehicles of a more corporate nature (hospitals, hospices, orphanages, and the
like). In light of their charismatic emphasis, it is not surprising that the great
majority of famous twentieth-century revivalists have been Pentecostals.

This emphasis upon revival is not limited to individual churches alone. As a
denomination, the AG declared that the 1990s would be "The Decade of
Harvest."[122] The AG's weekly magazine, *Pentecostal Evangel*,[123] from its

---

and unbelief." He continued by citing Irenaeus, Chrysostom, Augustine, Luther, Charles
Wesley, Finney, Moody as examples of fully consecrated saints who fully believed in
God and were open to the Holy Spirit's moving. *Questions and Answers* (Springfield,
Missouri: Gospel Publishing, n.d.), 30.

[122] Blumhofer, *The AG*, 2:10, notes that this campaign was undertaken to reverse the
trends of decreasing Sunday School attendance and a slowing of new-church growth.

[123] *The Evangel* began as a weekly publication in 1918. Its current circulation exceeds
275,000 copies. In brief, one to four page, articles which are filled with personal
testimonies, anecdotes, and pastoral reflections, the Evangel is published both to
encourage its readers' devotional walks and to inform its readers about AG news,
missionary activities, church planting, religion and politics in America, and obituaries.

inception, has regularly described and tallied the results of revival campaigns. Especially important because it reflects both what the AG's hierarchy maintains, and what it wants its constituency to maintain, the *Pentecostal Evangel* regularly runs articles harkening its adherents to seek revival as the means to transform the United States and return her to her original glory as God's Christian nation.[124]

In addition to their worship services and revivalistic emphasis, the AG's deep longing and appreciation for charisma can be seen in its historic following after charismatic individuals, both at the local parish level[125] and the broader national level. If its official hierarchy has been either wary of such charismatic persons (because of the potential threats to established power and/or doctrinal orthodoxy), or affirmative of such charismatic persons (because of the derived benefits such persons produced), the AG's laity, by the ten-thousands, has clamored after these persons.[126] To be sure, the denomination's hierarchy has not always been pleased with the bombastic claims and outlandish actions of

---

Unquestionably, the Evangel is not intended to be a scholarly journal, and the denomination's long-standing fears of intellectualism are reflected by the paucity of critically crafted articles; only occasionally does an issue include an article by one of the AG's many college faculty members. The magazine accurately reflects the AG's hierarchy as a practically minded, evangelistically motivated, Christ-serving body.

[124] There is a plethora of examples in each decade of *Pentecostal Evangel*. Just to show this thinking has not ceased, a few contemporary ones are: Don Spradling, "Hope for America," August 14, 1994, 8-9; John Maempa, "Restore Us Again," July 31, 1994, 3; and, Dan Betzer, "If My People Pray - Then Perhaps," October 31, 1993, 22-23. The AG's resource for ministry, *Enrichment*, similarly reflects the AG's emphasis upon revival. E.g., Charles Crabtree, "Preparing for Revival," *Enrichment*, 3:1 (Winter 1998), 76-79.

[125] Poloma, *At the Crossroads*, 76-77, 86-87, cogently argues that the local congregation will only be as charismatic as is its pastor. She quotes an old AG axiom, "no church can rise above its pastor," 76.

[126] To name a few: Carrie Judd Montgomery (1858-1946; a famous healer, she operated an orphanage and a Pentecostal campground, and was an original member of the AG); Aimee Semple McPherson (who, because of her tremendous charisma and ensuing popularity, ultimately grew so powerful that the denomination's officials saw her as a threat. She resigned her credentials with the AG after only three years); and, world-famous healing evangelist Raymond T. Richey (1893-1968). Contemporaries include David Wilkerson, Marilyn Hickey, Jim and Tammy Bakker, Jimmy Swaggart, Paul and Jan Crouch, and Benny Hinn. Throughout its history, the AG's national leaders themselves have manifested a mixture of charisma and pragmatism.

some of these people, but it is unquestionably the case that the more charismatic the person, the more political clout that person will have within the AG's constituency.[127] Even when the charismatic person operates on a more benign level, this case of charisma-equals-power is true if only because within the denomination those pastors of the largest churches tend to be the most charismatic. Pastors of large churches have greater influence at both the district and national levels because it is usually their congregations which contribute the most money toward denominational tithes and missions. Finally, it is very much the case that charismatic AG pastors of prominent churches have further clout because of their impact on a public-relations level.[128] Sadly though, it is not always the case that charisma-equals-character, as recent examples of well-known AG televangelists have exemplified. Because they have taken advantage of the denomination's broader understanding that charisma's presence produces a change of character, such persons are all the more embarrassing in the eyes of the denomination as a whole.

As the above discussion indicates, Pentecostals more broadly, and AG members more specifically, believe that they can and do experience God's charisma. Wacker is right that the early Pentecostals processed the presence of that charisma within a primitivistic context. But if their primitivism "fired a determination to rid [themselves] of the sin and contamination of finite existence itself,"[129] it was because they believed there was a better existence to turn toward. As they expressed it, there was an existing realm of forgiveness, healing (spiritual and physical), peace, love, and ecstasy available to those who would earnestly seek it. The indisputable presence of God's transforming charisma, they believed (and believe today), could only mean that they were experiencing God's Spirit in an apostolic manner.

---

[127] Poloma, *At the Crossroads*, 140-161, assessed the AG's dilemma of power.

[128] For example, when Jimmy Swaggart was asked to surrender his ministerial credentials because of his sexual sins and subsequent cover-ups, his own AG district headquarter's officials (Louisiana) supported his continued ministry if only because his televangelistic ministry raised so much money for the AG's missions program. Blumhofer, *The AG*, 2:189-90.

[129] Wacker, "Character and Modernization," 9.

Pragmatism

An important aim of this chapter is, to return to an earlier metaphor, to describe the fuel that impels the AG's spirituality and theology. While primitivism was an important component of the spiritual fuel's mix in the denomination's early years, and while charisma continues to fuel the denomination's spirituality, those two aspects do not account for the entire propelling mixture. Arising within its own national, historical and cultural matrix, the AG was and is characterized by the "one distinctively American philosophy," pragmatism. In its simplest form pragmatism is exhibited in the axiom, "if it works - do it." It is an attitude one scholar described "as a mood of much of American life."[130]

We can attribute the AG's pragmatic attitude to both the broader pioneer-spirit of the United States which characterized the nineteenth and twentieth centuries' expansionism and the formal philosophy developing at roughly the same time. Wacker, too, described the earliest generation of Pentecostals in terms of pragmatism. He said they were comprised of voluntary immigrants from other countries and ambitious mavericks, both of whom were "considerably less interested in what was said than in what was done." Their pragmatic spirit resulted in a "self-taught inventiveness" which manifested in a "defiant unwillingness to be instructed - much less bound - by the conventions of the past or present." They knew how to obtain the "goal at hand," and they knew that one should refrain from wasting time on "pointless theorizing."[131]

The effects of the broader historical-cultural matrix notwithstanding, we do not mean the AG is pragmatic in the philosophical sense which was being developed by Charles Peirce, William James, and John Dewey in the late nineteenth century and the early twentieth century. The AG does not accept several of philosophical pragmatism's broader epistemological tenets: there is no ideal or supreme truth; meaning only resides in an idea's practical results; only those things which are quantifiable are real, and the concomitant tenet that there is no such thing as divine revelation; logical thinking is always the best approach toward living; and, the notion that humanity is an ever-evolving species. James himself once said, "On pragmatic principles, if the hypothesis of God works satisfactorily in the widest sense of the word, it is 'true.'"[132]

---

[130] Both quotes are from Erickson, *Christian Theology*, 42.

[131] Wacker, "Character and Modernization." The quotes are found on pp. 14-18.

[132] Interestingly, these philosophers used the doctrine of transubstantiation and the world's beginning (creation) as case studies to prove their philosophical assumptions. Erickson, 43, quoted James' *Pragmatism* (NY: Meridian, 1955), 192.

In contrast to their forebears' own disdain for conventional instruction,[133] contemporary AG adherents are considerably more willing to seek instruction,[134] but they are every bit as pragmatic. In the healthiest sense, and often motivated by very Christian impulses, they still want to do what works best for the Kingdom. Their focus is immediate: they stick to the task at hand and spend little time in reflection, intellectual theorizing, or detailed analysis. Like their forebears, they know how to get things done.

These healthier characteristics notwithstanding, several of the above tenets of formal philosophic pragmatism are extant within the AG, though admittedly in a kind of shadowy form. Firstly, there is the AG's practical-utilitarian nature. At both the institutional and pastoral levels their educational enterprises are very much done with utilitarian motives: how best to train the denomination to reach the lost (whether at home or abroad);[135] how AG pastors can most efficiently run a local church;[136] and which strategies AG pastors and lay-leaders should follow in conducting inner-city and "generation X" missions.[137] In all of this, accomplishing the immediate goal is the aim, while careful reflection and long-term analysis are regularly overlooked.

Secondly, a shadow of formal pragmatism can be seen in the AG's fascination with quantifiable data. This is benignly evinced in local churches' simple, and common-place, practice of posting weekly and monthly attendance and tithing figures in their foyers. Insidiously, this fascination with quantifiable data also rears its head in that pastors, local churches, missionaries and state-wide districts unilaterally measure themselves, their spiritual worth, and their

---

[133] E.g., Jonathan E. Perkins, "Higher Education and Lower Infidelity," *PE*, December 6, 1924, 2-3.

[134] Robeck, "Seminaries and Graduate Schools," in *DPCM*, 772-776; Blumhofer, *The AG*, 313-336.

[135] For example, Charles T. Crabtree, "The Secret to Building a Soul-Winning Church," *Enrichment*, 2:4 (Fall 1997), 28-31.

[136] The Southern California district office, in its monthly mailers to AG ministers, routinely includes short articles about how to run one's church effectively like a business. These articles include advice from leading U.S. corporate executives and financial officers.

[137] For example, Tommy Barnett, Matthew Barnett, and Daniel de Léon, "Staking a Claim in the Heart of the Inner City: How two churches have developed urban strategies for reaching thousands in the inner city," *Enrichment*, 2:4 (Fall 1997), 18-22; and, Harvey Herman, Jr., "The Missing Generation in Our Churches: What the church must do if it is to see a harvest among Xers," *Enrichment*, 2:4 (Fall 1997), 56-61.

annual success variously by the number of converts they bring to Christ, the amount of money they raise for foreign missions, and the number of new assets (Sunday school classes, churches, ministry programs, missionaries, building programs, etc.) they generate.[138] This culture-driven hunger for quantifiable data can further be detected in the formerly noted emphasis upon revival. Revivals produce numbers. As such they can be measured and weighed for their viability and worth.[139] At a more problematic level, this shadowy tenet of quantifiability is observable in AG missions reports and/or missionary testimonies which can be intentionally exaggerated (or put in "evangelistic terms," as AG minister's often laugh among themselves) for the sake of local church and/or denominational financial support.[140] The examples of the AG's emphasis upon quantifiable data are nearly endless, so we will not continue further thereon.

Thirdly, the shadowy tenets of formal philosophical pragmatism exist in that the AG generally does believe that meaning only resides in an idea's practical results. To no small degree, AG's ministers' pastoral-emphasis reflects this tenet by commonly ignoring such theological subjects as the Trinity, Creation,

---

[138] For example, in 1950 Kenneth G. Short, an AG missionary wrote, "Dollars Mean Souls," *Pentecostal Evangel*, October 1, 1950, 9-10. Today, at statewide and national conventions award plaques are annually given to those pastors whose churches raised the most money for missions.

[139] To say as much is to ignore altogether the problems of revivalism: the manipulations used to cause such events. Furthermore, although God can earnestly and prayerfully be sought to move in "new" ways, such seeking is always done with the assumption that he will do so in the tried-and-tested historical ways.

[140] This is not a new phenomenon. In 1927 W. T. Gaston asked, "Why is truth strained to the breaking point in the report of revivals?" *RT*, July 1927, 1. In 1997 the AG's Spiritual Life committee reported that whereas between 1986 to 1996 the AG converted 3.4 million people to Christianity in the U.S., only 2.5 million people in the U.S. attend AG churches. "Where are the converts?" the committee asked. The answer was ascribed to attrition and the lack of discipleship. Those two critical issues aside, an equally obvious answer is that the reporting methods themselves are skewed. Every local church wants to report growth and revival in order to be seen as a viable work of God because they know well the adage "growth equals God's favor." Thus, speaking "evangelistically" creeps into the way they think about themselves and report on themselves. The Spiritual Life committee failed to question the very numbers themselves. *Minutes of the 47th Session of The General Council of the AG*, Indianapolis, Indiana, 1997, 41.

Anthropology, Christology, and Ecclesiology.[141] In contrast to the AG's traditional emphases of salvation, Spirit-baptism, and one's personal relationship with Christ, each of which can indeed be more easily quantified,[142] the aforementioned theological topics have little practical or immediate benefit. In the AG's colleges, the study of such topics is only sporadically required, even for religion majors. Those topics are either omitted altogether or substituted with introduction-level courses on Christian living or Biblical study.[143] Because of this practicality-generated neglect of theology, the AG's ministers inadvertently devalue theology as an arena which merely safeguards the issues of spirituality and Christian service.[144]

Moreover, this "ideas have meaning only when they are practical" orientation is also presently manifesting itself on an ecclesiological level. In droves, churches are omitting the AG's name from their own local church's name. Wanting to attract as many people as possible, they no longer want to be burdened by denominationalism, something American culture more broadly views as a broken-down and time-bound characteristic. To include the

---

[141] Obviously, one cannot account for every pastor's teaching, but extensive examinations of Pentecostal *Evangel* and *Enrichment*, together with 30 years of my own experience in the denomination, sustains this analysis.

[142] One can memorialize the date(s) when one accepted Christ into one's heart and/or was filled with the Spirit. One can determine the level of one's relationship with God (in the worst cases) by virtue of his blessings, by the degree of intimacy one experiences with him (in better cases), and by the regularity of one's devotional times (in still other cases).

[143] The aforementioned contemporary survey of eight AG school's catalogues and three college internet websites revealed that whereas Pneumatology (especially classes about Spirit-baptism and the charismatic gifts) and Eschatology are taught regularly in AG institutions, other substantial Christian theological topics such as Christology, the Trinity, and Ecclesiology are regularly omitted.

[144] The trinitarian "New Issue" of 1915 can be accurately understood in this regard. The AG's early defense of the trinitarian doctrine was clearly not a polemic stemming from the belief that correct belief about God facilitated either a keener relationship with him or a more authentic Christian transformation (as say the Orthodox argue). Instead it was primarily a two-fold issue of wanting to remain loyal to authentic apostolic form (that is, regarding water baptism) and not wanting to be heretical in the eyes of the larger sweep of Christendom. Clearly further theological analysis is warranted here, but my analysis is sustained in E. N. Bell, "The Sad New Issue," *The Weekly Evangel*, June 5, 1915, 1 and 3; and, "The Great Controversy and Confusion," *The Christian Evangel* (author not cited), September 6, 1919, 6.

denomination's name is simply no longer practical. Driven by a similar practical impetus, AG ministers and churches are turning to the culture-accommodating, market-driven,"seeker sensitive," models of church life and structure. For proponents of these church models, church is only meaningful when it exhibits practical characteristics (whether felt needs are met, whether homogeneous socialization occurs, or whether pastoral teachings have any benefit for daily living). Because more people attend church when they feel comfortable, and because attendance figures routinely comprise the litmus test as to whether or not God is blessing a church, such accommodation is a rather natural and easy procedure.[145]

To point out that these shadowy tenets of philosophic pragmatism exist in the AG is not necessarily to fault it, any more than one can fault Orthodoxy's accommodation to Greek philosophic and epistemological structures. Both traditions evince the natural historic tendency whereby Christianity and culture are fused together. The crux of the problem is, as it has always been, the degree to which a Christian tradition sacrifices the authentic life of Christianity to the less-than-authentic claims of culture. Moreover, in each area where pragmatic philosophy is notable in the AG, we are really only saying what was noted at the onset of this section: the AG is largely an American religious entity. It is not just "one more" American religious entity, it has its own unique characteristics and features, but it does indeed share some of the broader characteristics of American evangelical Christianity in general. The specific dangers confronting it are located, to no small extent, in the degree to which it uncritically allows its Christian values to become infected with American pragmatic values. To be clear, the AG always was an American entity, but in earlier eras it was more mindful about the dangers of the broader culture's values than it is today.[146]

---

[145] Poloma discusses the AG and cultural accommodation throughout her book.

[146] Stanley Frodsham, an early AG leader, railed against the first World War and patriotism, and the bloodshed those two were producing. Christians, Frodsham taught, were supposed to give their allegiance to the flag of Calvary, and not any nation. *Wholly For God*, 51-54. "Patriotism," he said, "is the selfishness of multitudes of selves. It is an abominable imitation of the kingdom of God," 59. Donald Gee, speaking with reference to World War 2, and the growing nationalism said, "The end and aim of modern political tendency is the worship of the almighty state instead of the worship of Almighty God. . . . In our democratic lands we still enjoy great freedom, but the same spiritual forces [of humankind's autonomy] are at work and steadily working towards the same [ideological] issue." "Simultaneous Praying," *RT*, August 26, 1938, 2.

Lastly, while the AG indeed was initially organized for pragmatic reasons (as noted in the earlier historical sketch), the AG's growing pragmatic emphasis is unquestionably a critical factor in the demise of the denomination's emphasis upon sanctification.[147] My own study of the AG's weekly magazine, *Pentecostal Evangel*, found that while many articles called for both holy living and maturity, between 1967 and 1992 only three articles specifically addressing sanctification were published. One article addressing sanctification was indeed published in 1998, but it was mostly a regurgitation and expansion of the AG's bylaw on the matter and provided no further reflection or application beyond the original delineations.[148] Sanctification requires reflection and introspection and time. When things need to be accomplished and/or when programmatic busy-ness makes heavy demands upon one's time, the quieter activities which can play a role in sanctification (reflection, introspection, reading, confession, prayerful solitude, and the like) are too regularly held to be ways to fritter away precious time. As will be developed later, earlier generations of AG adherents were more willing to employ the aforementioned quieter kinds of activities in their daily lives, and they would even practice such activities in their corporate church gatherings (as against contemporary norms which relegate those activities to the individual believer's personal time).[149] Moreover, the AG's earlier generations, like their Holiness-Pentecostal siblings, were more oriented toward holiness, and they were living in an era wherein the culture itself more widely encouraged and facilitated the virtues of character and integrity; their very context naturally pushed sanctification to the fore. Contemporary AG constituents do not have the benefit of laboring within such a society; accordingly they must be all the more sensitive to cultural and nationalistic accommodation.

---

[147] As early as 1943, E. S. Williams, then the AG's General Superintendent, lamented the lack of emphasis upon sanctification. Cf., P. C. Nelson, *Bible Doctrines* (Ft. Worth: Southwestern Press, 1943), 115. More recently Gary McGee echoed a similar assessment in, "The Quest for Holiness: A lost cause?" *PE*, August 2, 1987, 6. McGee believes this decreased emphasis is because sanctification is regarded as a process rather than an instantaneous moment of experience, and that people have grown disenchanted with the, "lists of don'ts which holiness proponents often developed."

[148] Stanley Horton, "Sanctification," *PE*, September 20, 1998, 20-21.

[149] See Ralph Riggs, *The Spirit Himself* (Springfield, Missouri: Gospel Publishing House, 1949), 181-186, who discusses corporate prayer and corporate prostrations.

Summary

As the above has shown, the AG's historical-cultural milieu and its theological heritage is critical for understanding its sanctification doctrine. It regularly assumed the presuppositions of, and borrowed from, that milieu as it made its doctrinal formulations. But, as will be shown, with its emphasis upon the role of the affections and its view of the human person in more existential terms, it also exerted a rather new emphasis on the doctrine of sanctification for Western Protestant models, a dimension with similarities to the Orthodox' own understanding of Christian transformation. The AG's earliest generations would not have claimed any novelty in their transformational model - they were merely returning Christian experience to its apostolic heritage - but without question the novel emphases they shared with the broader Pentecostal movement went on to transform numerous other Protestant denominations in what has become the charismatic movement.

Our three heuristic categories - primitivism, charisma, and pragmatism - combine together to fuel the AG's spirituality and theology. Depending upon the historical era, the issue at hand, the geographical proximity, the personalities of key leaders, or the specific local church, anyone of these three components can be the dominant catalyst. The denomination is increasingly being assimilated by the broader evangelical milieu, and its adherents are increasingly moving up the economic, intellectual, and political ladders. The more those phenomena occur, the more likely the denomination will move away from the primitivism that especially characterized its early generations. It seems likely, in light of the historical trends noted by sociologists, that charisma too is on the wane,[150] though the denomination would be slow to admit so much. This latter trend would in no way threaten the denomination's existence (the bureaucratic machinery is solidly established), but it would clearly indicate that the AG is becoming something other than it was at its inception. One can only wonder whether revival - in its immutably Americanized forms - can arouse new flows of charisma, or whether an altogether new and unprecedented move of God is the denomination's answer.

Pragmatism, for its part, must be recognized as a double-edged sword. While it has been a boon to the denomination's explosive globalization, it has been

---

[150] Anderson, *Vision*, said, "Those Pentecostals, like the Assemblies of God, that first achieved a modicum of stability and realized some improvement in their social circumstances, were the first in which ecstasy began to subside," 231.

emphasized with expensive losses on several fronts, not the least of which is the doctrine of sanctification. With a keen and prophetic insight, Donald Gee, in 1927, warned against that very process when he said, "It is admittedly possible to achieve a merely numerical enlargement by means the very reverse of spiritual; and the lust for bigness has tempted more than one Christian worker into the pitfalls ending in disaster."[151]

This chapter's broader historical-cultural context and its heuristic categories will be the primary background for our examination of the AG's doctrine of sanctification. That is, while we want to examine the denomination's specific doctrinal elements (i.e., through the avenues of Anthropology, Theological Foundations, and Means), we also want to better understand why it shaped its doctrine the way it did. Not surprisingly, and as we saw with the Orthodox, the broader milieu has had a tremendous impact upon the AG's doctrinal explications.

---

[151] Donald Gee, "Enlargement," *RT*, July 1927, 14.

7

Pentecostalism's Anthropology

Though the curse on all is resting, *dregs of splendor yet remain*,
'gainst the tides of ill contesting, but contending all in vain.
Culture, more than truth desiring, see pedantic spirits grow,
elated by their vain aspiring; filled with pride through what they
know.
For there are avenues of soul, through which some truths must
reach us,
beyond the power of mind's control, *that reason cannot teach us*.
Where every wish and power is brought within divine control,
and not a vain or idle thought, finds audience in our soul.[1]

As was the case in our study of the Orthodox, it is necessary to see precisely what the AG believes about the human person, both at creation and after the fall, in order to fully understand the its doctrine of sanctification. More simply, what the person is has tremendous import for how a person can be and is transformed. Its anti-academic theme aside, the above poem displays the traditional Pentecostal belief that the human person is characterized by more than the rational mind. There are existential dimensions to humans, and if those dimensions are neglected truncated understandings of anthropology and spirituality will result.

Human Beings at Creation

Adam in Eden: Humanity's Preeminence and God's Purpose

Adam and Eve were preeminent among God's earthly creations because only they had the capacity to know God, had the potential for immortal life, could understand wrong from right, and exercised dominion. With regard to humanity's preeminence, AG writers often made careful distinctions between

---

[1] J. T. Boddy, "Divine Rationality," *PE*, May 14, 1921, 1, 3. The italics are mine.

animals and human beings.[2] For example, animals and people both have souls
(the principle of life within), but the human being's soul is characterized by a
spiritual dimension.[3] Animals and human beings both have blood, but people's
blood is valued higher because they bear the image of God.[4] Human beings and
animals both build dwelling places, but the people's homes are built with reason
and imagination, while the animals' dwelling places are built from mere
instinct.[5] Like human beings, animals can learn, but the latter do so from instinct
and not intellect.[6] And, people are preeminent over other creatures as seen in
God's giving animals to human persons for food and sacrificial substitution.[7]

Human beings were created to be what they were because of God's purpose.
AG writers certainly did not openly refute ontological discussions about
creation and anthropology, they just had little reason to consider them. Even
though Myer Pearlman, an AG educator, exhibited an awareness of ontological
issues when he wrote his theology, his predecessors only rarely discussed those
issues.[8] The root issues in AG anthropology have less to do with precisely
"who" created and more to do with precisely "why" it was done.[9] As AG writers
generally discussed it, God's purpose for creating mankind is variously
manifested in that God gave mankind dominion, His image, and the possibility
of fellowship with him. God did not act haphazardly when he began to create,
he had a clear plan in mind which he carefully followed. This plan included the
very sequence by which he created, the organization of the universe, the
manifold variety of creatures with their corresponding characteristics and

---

[2] Throughout my delineation of AG theology I will regularly use the past tense when
citing deceased authors, and the present tense for living ones. The denomination as a
whole will routinely be addressed in the present tense, because for the most part the
theology has not changed much since its inception.

[3] Pearlman, *Doctrines*,102.

[4] Pearlman, *Doctrines,* 113-114. In patristic fashion, Pearlman qualified that Christ's
blood is the most precious because it is united with the divine.

[5] Pearlman, *Doctrines,* 104; William Menzies and Stanley Horton (eds.), *Bible
Doctrines: A Pentecostal Perspective* (Springfield: Logion, 1993), 84-85.

[6] Pearlman, *Doctrines,* 109; E. S. Williams, *Systematic Theology*, 2:94-95.

[7] Williams, 2:110. Another who noted distinctions between humans and animals was E.
J. G. Titterington, "What Genesis 1-3 Teaches About Man," *PE*, June 24, 1956, 26-27.

[8] Pearlman, *Doctrines,* 68-77 regarding the Trinity.

[9] This is true not only of the AG's earlier generations but the most recent as well. Cf.
Timothy Munyon, "The Creation of the Universe and Mankind," in *Theology: A
Pentecostal Perspective*, 215-253. Munyon, an AG Bible instructor, focuses much more
on God's purpose than he does God's person.

instincts, and the providential purpose of humanity's salvation. The entirety of creation was intended to glorify God.[10]

With regard to the biblical creation narratives, and creation in general, the denomination's focus is consistently more historical and less metaphysical, its hermeneutic is far more literal than symbolic.[11] The Scriptural texts rarely delve into the pre-existence of the Logos or the divine ontology. Accordingly, the AG rarely takes up those topics.[12] Sure enough, Adam and Eve were preeminent because of God's initiative, but the AG's interpretations of the Edenic narratives do not take God's own identity as an epistemological foundation. For this study's sake we cannot overemphasize the fact that unlike Athanasius and the stream of Orthodoxy after him AG writers consistently do not hold the Trinity as being foundational for understanding human beings.[13] Adam and Eve were not so much preeminent because they were created to reflect God's identity, they were preeminent because God intended that they should be. God's purpose (reflected in His actions), not His being, is the departure point for the AG's anthropology.

In our analysis of Orthodox anthropology, we saw that Orthodox theologians viewed the natural sciences as having only a minimal role in aiding an understanding of the human person. Some Orthodox writers openly manifested disdain for said sciences. There are a few instances where AG writers reflect the same sentiments. Donald Garlock said, "Science and the machinations of man are nothing in the sight of a sovereign and eternal God."[14] But by and large AG writers hold that the natural sciences truly can be used to increase knowledge about the human race. In recent decades several articles were written to clarify how it is that Scripture's historical record can be substantiated by science, and

---

[10] Pearlman, *Doctrines,* 37-41; Williams, *Systematic Theology,* 1:166-167; Munyon, "The Creation," 220-222.

[11] The AG's 1977 General Presbytery explicitly said this about the AG's hermeneutic. "The Doctrine of Creation," reprinted in *PE,* December 11, 1977, 10-12.

[12] In AG literature on creation there is seldom a discussion about the Logos' pre-existence. That attribute is not denied, its just that it is discussed more often in the AG's Christology and Soteriology, as will be shown later. Russell Spittler, *God the Father* (Springfield, Missouri: Gospel Publishing, 1976), touches upon the divine ontology.

[13] Pearlman, *Doctrines,* 101-102, is the exception to this rule, as is Joseph R. Flower, "How to be a Spiritual Person," *PE,* June 2, 1968, 2-3 (he mentioned that human beings are patterned after the Trinity but did not develop how that is so).

[14] "God had a better idea," *PE,* May 18, 1990, 15.

how it is that the two should not be viewed as necessarily antithetical.[15] As early as 1925 Stanley Frodsham said, "The old Bible is scientifically correct every time."[16] When AG writers struggle with the sciences it is about philosophical bias, and not the veracity of scientific methods per se. Specifically, since its inception the AG has battled the doctrine of evolution. Together with its challenge to the authority of the Scriptural narratives, evolution challenges the cardinal anthropological tenets of humanity's preeminence and God's purpose. One British AG constituent summed up the AG's general attitude regarding evolution when he said, "ALL who believe EVOLUTION DENY CHRIST."[17]

Despite its threatening presence, evolution has been positive for the denomination because it regularly caused its constituents to search the Scriptures regarding creation and anthropology. Apart from the challenge of evolution the topics of creation and anthropology rarely occurred in AG literature.[18] Incidentally, in the past few decades the abortion debate has proved to be another catalyst for the doctrine of anthropology.[19] Additionally, the development of humanity's preeminence and God's purpose are accurately understood as the AG's direct responses to the evolution theory.

Adam in Eden: Defining Characteristics

Unlike Orthodox delineations, there is little discussion among AG writers about Adam and Eve in their pre-fallen state. This silence stems from the AG's commitment to Scripture as the primary theological source, and, as we saw above regarding God's pre-existence, because the Bible is almost entirely silent about Adam and Eve's state of being prior to the fall so also is the AG. AG constituents quite obviously recognize that Adam and Eve were created in God's image (developed further below), but when descriptions of their original

---

[15] E.g., Bruce Williams, "The Story of Creation," *PE*, September 17, 1961, 4-5; "The Doctrine of Creation," rep. in *PE*, December 11, 1977, 10-12; H. Wayne Hornbaker, "Science Supports The Bible," *PE*, September 14, 1980, 8-9; Ronald Cooper, "The Bible, evolution, and science," *PE*, January 18, 1987, 18-19.

[16] "Evolution," (editorial) *PE*, November 7, 1925, 4.

[17] T. Myerscough, "Origin of Man," *RT*, December 1924, 8 (original emphasis).

[18] An example of an evolution-less creation discussion was John Alexander, "Why did God make me?" *PE*, March 11, 1973, 3. Both Pearlman and Munyon in their treatises devote sizeable sections to evolution.

[19] E.g., John C. Katter, "Is the human fetus a person?" *PE*, May 20, 1984, 20-22.

sinless existence are posited the prevalent discussions are those which proceed by negation.[20] Accordingly, the AG primarily makes its anthropological formulations based on humans as they were *after the Fall*. Together with the contrasting emphases between God's person and God's action, this is critical for understanding the differences between the Orthodox' and Pentecostals' anthropologies. Next we will note the predominant defining characteristics of sinless humanity in AG discussions; and, these characteristics will be presented in the order of their preponderance within AG literature. Despite the fact that we will carefully delineate each prominent feature, in their anthropological discussions AG writers clearly understand that the entire human person is valuable.[21]

THE MORAL NATURE

Whereas the *imago dei* was clearly the preeminent dimension of Orthodox anthropology (but a feature which received its greatest delineation with respect to Christ himself), the chief feature in AG explications is humankind's moral nature.[22] Pearlman said, "of all the differences between man and the lower animals, the moral sense or the conscience is by far the most important." "It is," he continued, "the most noble of all the attributes of man."[23] Whenever an AG writer discusses Adam and Eve in the garden, the writer will always note that they were morally innocent. In fact, an important element of the *imago dei* itself was the moral dimension: Adam and Eve knew right from wrong. Because all subsequent humans are likewise created in the image of God, Timothy Munyon said, "even pagans who have no knowledge of the written law of God"

---

[20] In other words, the fall made us sinners, evildoers, haters of God, oppressors of one another and God's creation, and the like. Therefore, prior to the fall we were not any of those things. For example see Donald Gee, "Studies on the Fundamental Truths: The Fall," *RT*, 2:3 (March 1926), 8.

[21] Williams, 2:102. This view was maintained from the denomination's onset. E.g., J. T. Boddy, "Self - Its Authorship And What It Really Is," *The Weekly Evangel*, January 27, 1917, 5.

[22] E. S. Williams, 2:117-128, typifies this emphasis, but the broad sweep of *Pentecostal Evangel* does too. Pearlman, once again, is the single most prominent exception to this emphasis in his discussion regarding the inner-workings of the body, soul, and spirit, *Doctrines,* 101-115.

[23] Pearlman, *Doctrines,* 117.

nevertheless have the moral nature imprinted upon their hearts.[24] In the beginning, Adam and Eve's moral nature was not tainted by sin; the AG's logic rightly argues that if God was sinless, and Adam and Eve were created in His image, then they too were sinless.

Also concerning their moral nature, Adam and Eve were indeed created as adults, but it was God's intention that they should mature and develop. For this reason God placed the tree of the knowledge of good and evil in Eden, and he prohibited them from eating of it. Their obedience to His commandment would facilitate the growth of their moral nature. Although Adam and Eve were created sinless, E. S. Williams held that they were not yet holy, "Holiness. . . and character result from choices and decisions. Man could not develop morally were there nothing to resist. In innocence moral character was undeveloped, because not tested."[25]

For the sake of comparison with Orthodox theology, the AG holds that God's intended growth for Adam and Eve was largely limited to their moral nature. Upon their creation the first couple already enjoyed unencumbered fellowship with God,[26] they did not need to transcend themselves via the participatory knowledge of God which the Orthodox call *theoria*. Additionally, there is little sense among AG writers regarding Adam and Eve's task of presenting God to creation and creation back to God. The relationship between humans and God's creation was stated more simply: just as God sovereignly rules over creation, they were given dominion both to rule and subdue His creation.[27]

The moral nature is additionally emphasized in AG theology in that it was the determining element with regard to humankind's immortality. Because they were placed in Eden "under a covenant of works" they had the capacity to live forever, provided that they "obeyed God's law." Immortality was not so much predicated upon their constitution as God's images on earth (though their souls are definitely understood as being immortal), or something which stemmed directly from their communion with God, as it was conditioned upon their obedience.[28]

---

[24] Munyon, "The Creation," 252. Williams averred the same, *Systematic Theology*, 1:167.
[25] Williams, *Systematic Theology*, 2:123-125; also see 2:119-120. Pearlman, *Doctrines*, affirmed the same on 109.
[26] Pearlman, *Doctrines*, 116.
[27] Pearlman, *Doctrines*, 117.
[28] Pearlman, *Doctrines*, 136.

Human free-willing also falls under the rubric of the moral nature. Humankind does not have intellect simply to choose as it wishes, yet in nearly all of its choosing it incurs moral ramifications and consequences.[29] The great bulk of AG theological discussions on the human free-will concern the contrasting Protestant positions of the Augustinian theologian John Calvin (and his successors) and the Dutch theologian James Arminius (and his successors), and their debate regarding the human role in salvation.[30] Whereas the AG sides with the Reformed in the belief that sanctification is a life-long process of transformation, they argue against the Reformed concerning salvation. Based on several New Testament texts,[31] Calvin believed that God, prior to creation, issued a decree which determined who would and would not be numbered among the elect. The AG agrees with Calvin that no one can save himself or herself, but the AG also holds that God will not save anyone apart from his or her free-willing. Siding with Arminius, the AG maintains that while human beings cannot save themselves, or by themselves choose God without His own aid, they nonetheless have the responsibility of responding to God's convicting, drawing, regenerating, and sanctifying work. We must be clear, God is always understood to be the first mover in salvation, and it is he who enables human persons to respond to himself. Nonetheless, the AG believes both that every person must choose between eternal life and eternal death, and that God's grace can be resisted; both of these beliefs are in contrast to Calvin's teaching.[32] As my own boyhood pastor used to preach, "The Holy Spirit is a gentleman." My pastor's point was that God will not force anyone to submit either to salvation or the subsequent process of Christian transformation.

Although AG discussions on salvation are rooted in the broader juridical framework of Protestantism (whether one's debt[s] with God is [are] atoned for, and/or whether one will go to heaven when one dies), they emphasize Christ's person and work far more than they do God's decree. AG ministers and writers commonly exhort their audiences about the necessity of knowing Christ (giving

---

[29] Williams, *Systematic Theology*, 2:118.

[30] Pearlman, *Doctrines*, 268-276. Nearly one half of Williams' first volume concerns the Calvinistic-Arminian debate on God and salvation; see *Systematic Theology*, 155-278. It appears also in 2:142-3, 145-146. See also Bruce Marino, "The Origin, Nature, and Consequences of Sin," in *Theology: A Pentecostal Perspective*, 261-7; and, Daniel Pecota, "The Saving Work of Christ," in *Theology: A Pentecostal Perspective*, 353-60, 368-372.

[31] 1 Cor. 2:7; Eph. 1:4; 2 Tim. 1:9; Heb. 4:3; 1 Pet. 1:20; 2 Tim. 1:9.

[32] Pearlman, *Doctrines*, 268-76.

him one's life, heart and will), walking in fellowship with him, and serving him faithfully.[33] In all of this, the AG's theology of salvation and spirituality is very much synergistic. As was noted in earlier chapters, synergy is the cooperation of God's energy and effort with our own energy and effort.

EXISTENTIAL FEATURES

The term existential, used here in a broad and non-traditional sense, is intentionally used to describe important elements of the human person. One could discuss the following existential features as the invisible or transcendent qualities of humanity. Similarly, one could forcefully argue that these features are rooted in a person's spiritual (God-breathed) dimension; Christians have believed as much for centuries. Nonetheless, by using the word existential we want to convey the notion that these dimensions of human nature are not just eternal or invisible qualities which merely reside in a temporal-visible being. Because these dimensions can be altered, the word transcendent also implies something too static and too wholly different. Instead, these features are the way the God-breathed dimension of personhood manifests itself. These features reveal, to borrow from an AG writer, "our inner life, our heart life, the springs and fountains of our life."[34] The existential nature of a human characterizes and qualifies the entire person; it is not just a divine spark implanted by God in a physical body.[35]

In more traditional Christian language this existential nature has usually been called the soul. But here we want to convey the notion - again, in a way that is implicit within AG delineations - that the soul is both rooted in, and manifests itself from within, the depths of the human person. Clearly, it is more accurate, in light of Scripture, to say everyone is a soul than it is to say everyone has a soul. With respect to sanctification, God the Father not only wants to pardon the human soul, he wants us to cooperate with His Spirit as he shapes it into the holy image of His Son.

Everyone has an existential core. In holding such, AG writers, like their Orthodox brothers and sisters, affirm an essentialist view of humans (even though AG constituents do not describe it as such). One author evinced the

---

[33] The examples of this are nearly endless. Thus, only a few formal theologians will be cited. Pecota, "Saving Work," 347-348, 361-365; Timothy Jenney, "The Holy Spirit and Sanctification," in *Theology: A Pentecostal Perspective*, 418-420.

[34] W. I. Evans, "Sanctification and the Holy Spirit," *PE*, July 15, 1950, 3.

[35] Pearlman, *Doctrines*, 104, denies that the soul is merely a divine spark. Williams agrees, *Systematic Theology*, 2:111.

common belief in humanity's essential nature when he said, "We all emerge from the same lump of clay."[36] Another similarly stated, "All the differences between the various races, such as the color of the skin or texture of the hair, are merely superficial."[37] Although every human person is born with a similar nature, AG constituents also recognize that this nature also can be shaped, impacted, and altered not only by oneself, but also by family, the social environment, values, belief system, and the like; so that essentialism is also qualified in AG models. We must clarify, AG writers are quite aware that the following features intersect and overlap one another.[38] To speak analogically, the following features are like concentric rings; each helps to distinguish specific features of humanity, but each is integrally united with the others. We will make use of three rubrics which help to describe the mostly indescribable dimensions of humans as clarified in AG documents: the soul, the affections and intuition, and the image of God.

THE SOUL

The soul is the critical feature distinguishing people from animals. Humans beings' souls live eternally, while animals' cease to exist when their bodies die. Moreover, each creature is created with a quality of soul consistent with its own species, animals and human beings each after their kind. This is evident in that people's souls have a greater intelligence than do animals'. Despite the similarity between human souls, each person has his or her own individual soul;[39] more accurately we may say, each person is his or her own soul.[40] Stated differently, in having souls, people do not have a portion of something possessed more broadly by the entire human race. In contrast to Orthodox models, there is an unquestionable emphasis upon individuality in AG anthropology. The Orthodox' premise whereby each human person is an hypostasis of the larger human race is foreign to AG thought. Kerry McRoberts, an AG college religion instructor, understood well the denomination's

---

[36] James Clutter, "Potter and Clay," *PE*, February 24, 1974, 10.

[37] E. J. G. Titterington, "What Genesis 1-3 Teaches About Man," *PE*, June 24, 1956, 26. More recently, Donald Garlock "[God] also knows that man is not subject to the environment and that God gives man his traits. . ." in "God had a Better Idea," *PE*, May 18, 1990, 14.

[38] E.g., Munyon, "The Creation," 239.

[39] Pearlman, *Doctrines*, 104-105; Williams, *Systematic Theology*, 2:94-95, 110-111.

[40] Gordon Fee, *God's Empowering Presence: The Holy Spirit in the Letters of Paul* (Peabody, Massachusetts: Hendrickson, 1994), 568.

theological mindset when he recently remarked that technical Greek and Latin theological terminologies present a frustrating maze for most AG readers.[41] In light of the fact that the denomination emphasizes that every human person is unique (both individuality and in terms of God's specific task or purpose for each individual)[42] far more than it discusses human beings as members of the same species, it seems likely that the concepts of hypostasis/hypostases would be rejected in official anthropological discussions.[43]

Myer Pearlman said the God-breathed soul is, "the life-giving and intelligent principle animating the human body, using the bodily senses as its agents in the exploration of material things and the bodily organs for its self-expression and communication with the outside world."[44] For reasons which are not historically clear, Pearlman's discussion of the human soul and its animation, use of, and operation through, the human body is similar to the Orthodox' own delineations.[45] (This similarity will be further developed below in our discussion of human instincts and the fall.) The soul indwells the body with life, and expresses that life through the body. And, even though the soul's initial source of origin was God's own breath, people cooperate with God in the generation of new souls by producing children. Each soul is not necessarily breathed afresh by God, rather "the normal processes of human reproduction set in motion those

---

[41] "The Holy Trinity," in *Theology: A Pentecostal Perspective*, 154, 166. Furthermore, McRoberts did not use those terms regarding human persons. The foreign nature of such terminology was also noted in that the editor, 176, wrongly posited that there is a "massive conflict between the Eastern and Western Churches" regarding *homoousia* and *homoiousia*. Although the editor attributed the latter to the East, it was specifically the error of Sabellius who was condemned by the ecumenical church in AD 261 and again at the Council of Constantinople in AD 381. Hagglund, *History of Theology*, 73; and, Seeburg, *Textbook of The History of Doctrines,* 1:234.

[42] E.g., James O. Savell (then Asst. General Supt.), "Serving God With Purpose of Heart," *PE*, September 5, 1954.

[43] In a later chapter I will address this issue further, but for now it warrants mention that this view of human person is characteristic of Western philosophy/theology in general. Clearly, Eastern and Western Christianity's contrasting views regarding the human person have dramatic ramifications for how each respective culture developed its doctrine of human rights.

[44] Pearlman, *Doctrines*, 104.

[45] Pearlman never cited his sources, if there were any he was explicitly following. Williams, by way of contrast, interacted with multiple scholars on each individual dimension of theology, but did so more as a survey of theology, and less as an analysis of those scholars' contrasting positions.

Divine laws of life which cause a human soul to be born into the world." The exact way that the soul comes into existence with relation to the parents and God is veiled in a mystery, so that one cannot be dogmatic in one's speculations.[46]

Although they do not express it in ontological terms, AG adherents do affirm that humans are both physical and spiritual in a manner unique among God's creatures. As was noted earlier, they do not describe humans as intermediaries between God and His creation. People are spiritual and "can relate to spiritual reality."[47] But they are also physical and can interact with the physical world. Both dimensions of people are created by God and are therefore good. Unlike the Orthodox who believe that humans are microcosms and mirrors of the entire universe precisely because of their physical-spiritual nature, the AG is generally opposed to describing humans as "little gods,"[48] and would be hesitant to assert that humans are "richer than the angels."[49]

Mankind's unique spiritual-physical composition gives rise to a common question in AG theological writings as to whether the human person is a two-element (body and soul/spirit), or three-element (body, soul, and spirit), being. For AG theologian's this question has more to do with definitional precision than it does with a precise doctrine of soteriology or Christian transformation the likes of which are manifested in Orthodoxy. Thus, there is not a dogmatic position in this regard, and most theologians seem satisfied with simply presenting the arguments for both positions.[50] Williams chose the trichotomist position on the grounds that the universe is comprised of triads. He did little, however, to develop or sustain his argument.[51] Fee reasoned that Paul's use of

---

[46] Pearlman, *Doctrines*, 105-106. The quote is from p. 106.

[47] Munyon, "The Creation," 244.

[48] This opposition stems from the AG's critique of the heterodox Word-of-faith teachers who do describe humans as such. Cf. Munyon, "The Creation," 251, n. 108.

[49] Angels are held as being higher in the created order than people because they are not subject to the same physical boundaries and limitations as are people. Pearlman, 79-94; Williams, *Systematic Theology*, 1:93-108. The AG's position here also stems from its literalistic Scriptural hermeneutic. Ps. 8:5 (KJV) says humankind is, "a little lower than the angels."

[50] Pearlman, *Doctrines*, 101-102; Williams, *Systematic Theology*, 2:102-108; Munyon, "The Creation," 241-245; Menzies and Horton, *Bible Doctrines: A Pentecostal Perspective*, 81-83.

[51] E.g., he described the following items comprised of, or characterized by, threes: the Trinity, the material universe (energy, motion, phenomena), time (past, present, future),

"spirit, soul, and body," (1 Thes. 5:23) was not an anthropological phrase but a statement revealing that he wanted the church to be fully sanctified, even in their physical bodies.[52] What AG adherents *are* clear about, ontologically speaking, is that a human person's entire being sins.[53] In this regard, sin is not a problem merely rooted in the human body, sin affects every dimension of the person.

THE AFFECTIONS AND INTUTION

Stemming from the appetites and yearnings of the soul, but also impacting the soul, the human affections and intuition could well be placed under the rubric of the soul. However, because the affections are prominently discussed throughout AG literature, and because the AG's spirituality is markedly affective, they are treated separately here. For clarification's sake, although AG writers do discuss the affections (the heart) within their anthropology, these topics occur with much greater frequency in their discussions of spirituality (the ramifications of which will be addressed in our next two chapters)To a degree surpassing the evangelicals who comprise an important aspect of their milieu, AG writers emphasize the affective nature of people. While the emotions are definitely incorporated into the affections, they do not wholly define them. Rather, the affections also include the person's conscious feelings and visceral sensations, and how it is that those impact and interact with the will. Summarily stated, the affections are included with the mind in how the soul perceives and experiences life; reflecting AG discussions, one can accurately describe the affections and intuition as comprising the seedbed of visceral knowing and willing. Scripture is full of texts that describe various bodily organs' experiences and emotions. Pearlman believed these texts should not be taken literally, as though the kidneys, heart, belly, or intestines think or feel. Instead, these passages describe how it is that the soul operates through the bodily organs. "These scriptures describe the inward parts as the center of feeling, spiritual experience, and wisdom," he said. These inner parts, together with the traditional five senses

---

human personality (intellect, sensibilities, will), and human mind (imagination, memory, judgment). Williams said, "It is not difficult from these triads to reason that man also is trichotomic or triune in his construction," 108.

[52] Fee, *Empowering Presence*, 63-65.

[53] E.g., Pearlman, *Doctrines*, 103; Fee, *Empowering Presence*, 568; Munyon, "The Creation," 245.

(sight, hearing, taste, smell, and touch) receive information and impressions and transmit them to the brain through the nervous system.[54]

Like the Orthodox, AG constituents emphasize the human heart in their anthropology. Not only is the heart the center of physical life, Pearlman said, "it is also the source and meeting place of all the currents of life, spiritual and soulish." It is the deepest part, the "engine room," of the personality. It is where a person's impulses originate, and the center of a person's character and conduct.[55] The heart's desires - good and bad - spread through the human person and influence the intellect, the will, the affections, and even the body.[56] Describing the heart, one author said, "[it] is a tricky thing - it is the seat of all our affections, our passions, and our appetites," and "[it] is impressionable, it is pliable, it is sensitive, it may be broken and wounded and crushed - and it may be hardened."[57] Still another writer manifested this understanding of human beings when he said, "God is a spiritual Being, so it follows that our communication with Him in worship must be a spiritual exercise. 'Deep calleth unto deep' - the depths of the human spirit respond to the infinite deep of the Spirit of God." That same writer went on to describe how it is that sometimes even words cannot express what the human soul needs to express to God.[58] Without question, the divine-human communion incorporates more than the human mind or intellect.[59]

AG writers frequently express this affective nature in the affective language of poetry. In 1955 an unnamed writer described this divine-human encounter:

Not a sound invades the stillness, not a form invades the scene,
Save the voice of my Beloved, and the person of my King.
Precious, gentle, holy Jesus! Blessed Bridegroom of my heart,
In Thy secret inner chamber, Thou wilt whisper what Thou art.
Wrapt in deep adoring silence, Jesus, Lord, I dare not move,
Lest I lose the smallest saying meant to catch the ear of love.

---

[54] Pearlman, *Doctrines*, 107.

[55] Pearlman, *Doctrines*, 112.

[56] Williams, *Systematic Theology*, 2:130, where he followed the Wesleyan theologian Pope.

[57] Paul H. Pipkin, "Know Your Heart," *PE*, June 17, 1962, 4-5, 17. Respective quotes on pp. 4 and 5.

[58] Arne Vick, "Pentecostal Worship," *PE*, 10-11, 1966. The quotation is on p. 10.

[59] Editorial, "The Spirit of Man and the Spirit of God," *PE*, November 29, 1924, 1 and 5. See also Munyon, "The Creation," 238-239, regarding the bodily organs.

Rest then, O my soul, contented: Thou has reached thy happy place
In the bosom of thy Saviour, gazing up in His dear face.[60]

Although clearly intended to move the reader, this poem was not merely
sentimental. The writer expressed the pervading conviction (itself a term
connoting experiential knowledge) regarding people's affective nature which
characterizes Pentecostal understandings of human beings.

Whereas many evangelical Christians are wary to make much of the
affections' role in Christian spirituality, Pentecostals emphasize that God
created the human nature expressly with an affective dimension.[61] That is, the
affections do not simply reside in the person as an accident of creation, they
were created by God as a means of knowledge and experience. J. T. Boddy's
poem, quoted at this chapter's onset, reflects well the Pentecostal belief
regarding the affections. By affirming that "avenues of the soul" reside beyond
the rational, Boddy did not mean one should eradicate the intellect as a means of
knowing, but he did clarify that one can overemphasize the intellectual means of
knowing. The mind can pridefully overtake the human understanding and usurp
the intellectual-affective integration with which God created men and women.
The heart, the seat of the affections - fairly described as the person's moral and
spiritual compass - was created to rule over a person's being. When the mind
fails or refuses to grasp the things of the Spirit (invisible and the eternal things
which can only be apprehended by the soul), the heart is supposed to bring such
vain (doubting) thoughts under its domain.[62]

To be sure, this affective dimension can lead one astray (in light of their
affective emphasis Pentecostals have regularly had to clarify that emotions
and/or affections ought not comprise one's sole source of decision making),[63]
but it nevertheless was created by God as a good and essential element of the

---

[60] *PE*, November 6, 1955, cover page.
[61] For example, Steven Land, a Church of God (Cleveland, Tennessee) scholar, discussed
the role and importance of the affections in Pentecostal spirituality and theology.
Pentecostal Spirituality: Passion for the Kingdom (Sheffield, England: Sheffield, 1993).
In order more narrowly to focus our study, and because the Church of God officially
disagrees with the AG on the issue of sanctification, Land will not be referred to here,
although much of his discussion is quite applicable for AG theological models.
[62] J. T. Boddy, "Divine Rationality," *PE*, May 14, 1921, 1, 3.
[63] Pearlman, *Doctrines*, 50; Williams, *Systematic Theology*, 1:159. Charles A. Harris
urged his readers to consult Scripture not just their feelings in, "Strength for Each Day,"
PE, August 23, 1964, 5.

human person. Moreover, these senses were created by God as vehicles through which men and women were to experience, and have communion with, God. Indeed, precisely because of the a-rational dimension of intuition the human race has been historically characterized variously by a belief in a Supreme Being (however that belief is expressed), a hunger for spiritual and eternal things, and a sense of right and wrong.[64] Both Ezekiel and Jesus referred to these affective senses, albeit in their fallen state, when they said, "They have eyes but do not see, ears to hear but do not hear."[65] The apostle Paul also referenced humanity's affective dimension when he said, "I pray that the eyes of your heart may be enlightened" (Eph. 1:18).[66]

THE IMAGE OF GOD

Because its anthropological emphasis concerns humankind after the fall (and the concomitant primary issue of how to save fallen humanity), the AG historically has given little thought as to what originally constituted the *imago dei*. That is, apart from citing the creation narratives themselves (where God both creates and commissions Adam and Eve), the denomination has done little to develop why or how its view of the *imago* is true. When it does discuss the *imago*, it regularly follows the work of evangelical theologians.[67]

The primary exception to the aforementioned lacuna regarding the image of God is William Williams. An Old Testament scholar, Williams holds that the image of God is that which separates humans from animals, and which enables humans to have fellowship with God. Developing the poetic parallelism of Genesis 1:27, Williams argues that men and women reflect God's image corporately, not distinctly. That the Hebrew word for man ('adam) has been interpreted solely by focussing on the male, both exemplifies the patriarchal exegesis of church history and ignores the parallelism of the *locus classicus* for the *imago dei*. The only thing pronounced "not good" in the creation narrative was Adam's being alone (Gen. 2:18). Eve is thus not at all inferior to Adam, but

---

[64] Williams, *Systematic Theology*, 1:159, 168.

[65] Ezek. 12:2; Mt. 13:13; Mk. 4:12; *passim*. Richard L. Dresselhaus, "Developing inner senses," *PE*, January 11, 1987, 12-14.

[66] John R. Higgins, "God's Inspired Word," in *Theology: A Pentecostal Perspective*, 111.

[67] E. S. Williams, *Systematic Theology*, 2:117-18, followed Wm. Pope; Munyon, "The Creation," 252, who follows H. Wiley; Pearlman, *Doctrines*, 115-118, did not cite his sources, if he used any.

is instead his "corresponding opposite," the one who reciprocates and complements him. Indeed, she was taken from him.[68]

The AG believes the image of God in humanity is fashioned both after God's personality *and* purpose.[69] Concerning personality, humankind's preeminent nature (moral, spiritual, and intuitive) is oriented toward God. The very word *anthropos*, Pearlman clarified, defines the human race as a species which looks up and prays to God.[70] Reason and intellect, too, are often prominent features regarding personality.[71]

Regarding purpose, the human race was created to have dominion over God's earth as well as to glorify, and become like, God; in this regard both Genesis 1:28-30 and Psalms 8:5-8 (regarding dominion and purpose) are interpreted with significance for the *imago dei*. It must be emphasized, the AG is rather clear that fulfilling God's intent with regard to the *imago dei* requires fulfilling God's purpose for one's life. As shall be developed later in our chapter on the means of sanctification, God's purpose since the fall - and even more since Christ's coming - is to save people, a task to which he calls all Christians.

Human Instincts and Sin

Human beings were created with natural instincts, instincts which are in accord with their biological nature. The instincts of self-preservation, reproduction, acquisition, and the procuring of sustenance help to safeguard the species' perpetuation. The instinct to dominate enables humanity to fulfil God's vocation of dominion and it provides the self-assertion required to fulfil God's requirements. However, these instincts were not the only elements with which

---

[68] William C. Williams, "Human Sexuality" in *Evangelical Dictionary of Biblical Theology*, W. A. Elwell (ed.) (Grand Rapids: Baker, 1996), 727-730.

[69] Protestant theologians are divided as to whether dominion/purpose constitutes a portion of the *imago dei*. Erickson, *Christian Theology*, provides a succinct survey of the history of Protestant theology concerning the image of God on 498-515 and concludes that it does not incorporate the element of dominion.

[70] Pearlman, *Doctrines*, 116.

[71] Munyon, "The Creation," 252.

Adam and Eve were created. They were also given God's law, a conscience, free-will, and reason: features in keeping with their spiritual nature.[72]

Thus, in an important distinction from many Orthodox theologians, AG theologians hold that not only were the original man and woman's bodies created good (in contrast to Zizioulas who views the biological constitution as problematic at best) so were the inner drives (also called "spontaneous inward urgings").[73] These drives were not something Adam and Eve had to endure or suffer. They were created with these drives for their own good. Even their sexual drives were ordained of God, as is evident in that Adam and Eve's bodies were specifically created in physiological correspondence with one another.[74] AG theologians do not overtly express it (again, their more immediate focus is fallen humanity), but it is fair to infer that these instincts existed in harmony with Adam and Eve's spiritual natures; that is, prior to the fall the instincts were not in tension with the spiritual qualities. The AG no longer employs terminology regarding the passions[75] (a root cause for original sin in some Orthodox delineations). AG constituents would reject the assumption that the passions are inherently evil because humankind's created nature was totally beneficent. Furthermore, the AG, in its synergistic model of sanctification, yearns for the complete transformation of the now-fallen natural instincts; it would view the Orthodox' notion of apatheia as a disembowelment of the God-given drives which are specifically to be used in Christian service.

The above difference aside, it is important to note that, like the Orthodox (and virtually every Christian tradition), AG theologians aver that these internal yearnings have been corrupted by sin. The instinct of self-preservation is perverted so that selfishness, jealousy and anger result. The food-seeking instinct has gone awry producing gluttony. Sexual immorality and impurity both evince a twisted instinct of self-preservation. The instinct of acquisitiveness is vitiated until one practices covetousness and theft. Self-assertion and dominion degenerate into quarrelsomeness, injustice, and oppression. These instinctual perversions do not stop at their own natural boundaries. They spread throughout

---

[72] Pearlman, *Doctrines*, 108-9; E. S. Williams, *Systematic Theology*, 2:111-112 (he relies on Pearlman), and "Human Instincts," *PE*, May 18, 1958, 5-6. Pearlman carefully reasoned how these instincts are discernible in the Genesis accounts.

[73] E. S. Williams, *Systematic Theology*, 2:111.

[74] W. C. Williams, "Human Sexuality," 727-730.

[75] When the passions as such are referred to, it occurs in the AG's earliest years. Cf., A. Gregory Wilkinson, "Filled with the Holy Spirit," *The Weekly Evangel*, October 20, 1917, 6.

the person's heart and will, weakening him or her. First they produce ingrained habits contrary to God's intended order. Then they become increasingly malevolent until a person begins to exist according to the law of the flesh (the sinful nature, not the physical body).[76]

Another commonality resides between the AG and the Orthodox regarding the ramifications of the original biological drives: the issue of temptations (although, this is something the two share with the vast sweep of Christendom). The AG is unanimous that temptations are not in themselves sins,[77] but to entertain sinful notions or imaginations concerning perversions of the natural instincts can indeed result in sin. Indeed, Scripture's locus classicus of the kinds of sin (1 Jn. 2:16) is itself a depiction of the corrupted natural instincts. "The lust of the flesh," is a corrupted appetite for sex, food, and/or possessions; in Eve's case it was her desire to eat the forbidden fruit. "The lust of the eyes," pertains to entertaining physical appearances as primary; Eve *saw* that the fruit was pleasant. "The pride of life," is spiritual and/or personal pride; Eve thought the fruit would make her wise. As depicted in 1 John 2:16, sin appeals to the natural instincts - instincts which were in themselves good - with the end result that they become the soul's primary foci, rather than parts of the whole.[78]

Because the human instincts were originally good, Pentecostals like those in the AG consistently place more of the odious nature of the fall upon Satan than do the Orthodox. A creature capable of speaking with great cunning, the serpent took God's words of prohibition and twisted them so as to deceive Eve and then Adam. Satan enticed them to doubt God's own instructions with the result that they sinned.[79] This emphasis upon Satan's own role stands in contradistinction to the Orthodox' emphasis, not only concerning original sin, but also with regard to the whole spectrum of spirituality. Whereas the Orthodox describe spiritual warfare largely in terms of inner warfare, temptations, and resisting the passions, the AG (like their other Pentecostal siblings) regularly describes spiritual warfare in terms of the church's battle against Satanic temptations, plots, and counterforces.

---

[76] Pearlman, *Doctrines*, 110-111, especially developed this position.

[77] E.g., Smith Wigglesworth, "Manifesting the Divine Nature," *RT*, November 1, 1935, 2; Marino, "The Origin," 279.

[78] E. S. Williams, *Systematic Theology*, 2:126-127.

[79] Pearlman, *Doctrines*, 124-28; E. S. Williams, *Systematic Theology*, 1:125-129, and 2:126.

Human Beings After the Fall

Juridical Issues: Guilt and Judgment

Consistent with the aforementioned anthropological emphasis on the moral nature, the AG teaches that the single most injurious result of the fall is humanity's standing with God. The preeminent beings of all God's creations, their orientation toward God was conditioned upon their moral innocence. When they disobeyed God's command, their innocence was lost and with it went their perfect fellowship with God. "Whatever else sin is," Bruce Marino said, "at its heart, it is a breach of God's law."[80] Upon eating the forbidden fruit Adam and Eve realized their physical nakedness and were ashamed. But their nakedness also concerned their conscience: they realized they had violated God's law, and in an act exhibiting psychological guilt they covered their bodies with leaves and hid themselves in the garden. God's response to sin was judgment, and all three parties involved in sinning received God's verdict.[81]

Physical death is not so much presented in AG discussions as the natural ontological consequence of sin (though that is not denied) as it is emphasized as God's judgment. Because God is a just God, he could not overlook their disobedience. Thus, His statement, "in the day that you eat thereof you will surely die," (Gen. 2:17) is not interpreted as a simple cause-and-effect warning, it is understood to be a judgmental warning. Sin makes one guilty, and guilt with regard to God's law results in death. Ultimately, this judgment will result in an eternal separation from God, a separation which will result in a kind of perpetual life of non-life (itself the most horrific of God's judgments). Adam and Eve's immortal nature was predicated upon innocence, and when that innocence was shattered so was the possibility of their immortality.[82]

---

[80] Marino, "The Origin," 273.

[81] The serpent was sentenced to crawl in the dust, the woman was sentenced both to suffer during childbirth and be subject to her husband, and the man was sentenced to laborious and frustrating work. Pearlman, *Doctrines*, 126-128.

[82] Pearlman, *Doctrines*, 136; E. S. Williams, *Systematic Theology*, 2:128-130; Marino, "The Origin," 285-289.

Unless God pardons both one's sinful nature and one's sins (the AG does not distinguish between mortal or venial sins),[83] one cannot enter His kingdom. Death is unquestionably problematic, but the immediate concern and consistent emphasis in AG theology and praxis is the forgiveness of sin and guilt. If one receives divine forgiveness one will escape God's judgment. One must not overstate the case because the AG is indeed aware of other ramifications of sin (noted below), but the critical issues - the primary features which characterize the denomination's hamartiology - are guilt and God's judgment. Since the first sin, human beings have been physical-spiritual persons in need of pardon.

Sin as Ruination

The former moral emphasis aside, sin does not pertain to the human being's will or conscience alone.[84] Sin did enter through human willing (a viewpoint shared with the Orthodox), but its effects were not limited to the will. Sin entered creation upon humankind's fall with the result that not only humanity, but even the non-human creation, was put under its curse.[85] This curse involves an insidious and thoroughgoing process of ruination. Marino said, "Sin shades every aspect of human existence, enticing us from the outside as an enemy and compelling us from the inside as a part of our fallen human nature."[86] The person's moral nature and natural instincts are thrown into confusion (noted earlier), as are the affections. The very way the human soul works within the body is tainted with a process of ruination, so much so that the person can and does eventually sin of one's own volition, and that repeatedly.[87] The unencumbered fellowship which Adam and Eve enjoyed with God and one

---

[83] There are degrees of sin which produce increasingly detrimental results (in terms of personal, familial, and societal structures), but any sin will leave one guilty and deserving divine punishments. Marino, "The Origin," 255, 281, 284-285.

[84] Marino, "The Origin," 258.

[85] Marino, "The Origin," 285, 286. Why or how human sinning affected the entire created order is not addressed in AG literature. Clearly, the Orthodox' ontological position (regarding men and women as creation's microcosms and priests) coheres with this dimension of sin better than does Western Christendom's position in general.

[86] Marino, "The Origin," 255.

[87] W. C. Williams, "Evil" in *Evangelical Dictionary of Biblical Theology*, 222, likens the warping effects of sin to an addict's "fix," or Gollum's ring (addressed as "my precious") in Tolkein's *The Hobbit*.

another is obfuscated by selfishness and oppression. Truth, the feature which characterized the original inter-personal relationship (divine-to-human, and human-to-human), is ignored and/or openly denied. Furthermore, sin's presence prevents a person from fulfilling one's purpose for one's life. The lists of sin's effects can be as lengthy as the virtues one can identify.[88]

Though it is not an emphasis, some AG writers do discuss sin's ontology (though again, the specific word is only rarely employed). They recognize that sin feeds on the good, and that it only exists because of the created order's finitude. Although God is asserted as the sole creator, he is not the author of sin.[89]

With respect to Orthodox formulations like those of Zizioulas,[90] the AG does not maintain that humanity's biological/physical/finite nature was or is the problem, nor does it believe that that nature keeps one from becoming an authentic person. In his monumental book on the apostle Paul and the Holy Spirit, Gordon Fee specifically argues against the teaching that humanity's physical nature is problematic. Describing Paul's use of the word "flesh" Fee said, "[it] denotes not simply humanity in its creatureliness vis-a-vis God, but humanity in its *fallen* creatureliness as utterly hostile to God in every imaginable way."[91] As will be developed more fully below, the AG holds that death resulted from moral transgression, not humankind's biological constitution. Indeed, one of the marvels of the human race is that it was God's original purpose that we live eternally in physical and contingent bodies.[92]

Sin and the Imago Dei

Earlier we noted that the denomination infrequently takes the image of God as a theological topic. Nonetheless, the denomination is clear that this image was not eradicated by the fall. The good and loving things which even bad and hateful

---

[88] Pearlman, *Doctrines*, 129-138; E. S. Williams, *Systematic Theology*, 2:129-133; Marino "The Origin," 255-257.

[89] Marino, "The Origin," 278-279 where he variously describes sin's residence in the heart, sin as a malignancy, and sin's self-reproducing and self-reinforcing qualities.

[90] Zizioulas, *Being As Communion*, 50-53.

[91] Fee, *Empowering Presence*, 819, original emphasis. Fee examines every single passage pertaining to the Holy Spirit in the Pauline corpus and exegetes its meaning.

[92] Again, it is my contention that the very way each tradition views the human person has tremendous consequences for the doctrine of human rights.

people do testifies to this fact, as does the truth that even fallen people have moral consciences. More importantly, some biblical passages are clear that despite the fall people are still created in God's image (Gen. 9:6; 1 Cor. 11:7; Col. 3:10; Jas. 3:9).[93]

Earlier it was noted, following William Williams, that the image of God was to be reflected by men and women together. It then follows that the dominance which Adam asserted over Eve was a result of the fall. It was not until the fall (Gen. 3:20) that he named her using the same naming formula with which he named animals (Gen. 2:20). It was not until after the fall that God told Eve that Adam would rule over her (Gen. 3:16). Based upon the Genesis passages, male dominance was not a part of the original created order.[94] Women have enjoyed ministerial service in Pentecostalism primarily on the basis of the Spirit's empowerment.[95] Nonetheless, concerning the *imago dei*, Williams' view radically contrasts with the Orthodox' own views of male and female relationships, God's intention regarding human sexuality, and the effects of the fall.

With subsequent regard to the *imago dei*, AG writers go to no small effort in rejecting the Reformed doctrine of total depravity; that they do this is evidence of how many affinities there are between themselves and the Reformed. True, people can do nothing to save themselves; here the AG agrees with the Reformed.[96] But this does not mean humans are in and of themselves incapable of good or moral acts (another contrast with the Reformed). Instead the AG holds that humans are depraved. Original sin is a spiritual and moral handicap, "a tendency or bias to sin," as Pearlman said, which makes sin quite natural - and indeed inevitable - for every person.[97] Although some AG writers recognize that various Protestants have taught that the good people do is by virtue of

---

[93] Pearlman, *Doctrines*, 41-43; E. S. Williams, *Systematic Theology*, 1:167-168, and 2:134; W. C. Williams, "Human Sexuality," 727.

[94] W. C. Williams, "Human Sexuality," 729.

[95] Sherilyn Benvenuti, "Anointed, Gifted and Called: Pentecostal Women in Ministry," *Pneuma*, 17:2 (Fall 1995), 229-235. In Pentecostal history women actively served, evangelized, and pastored in important and prominent ways. One must not overstate the case, because women were quickly relegated to (and today fill) subordinate roles in North American and British Pentecostalism. But it is true that during the movement's early years, during the initial charismatic outburst, women had unique and unprecedented opportunities for service.

[96] Pearlman, *Doctrines*, 118.

[97] Pearlman, *Doctrines*, 135.

God's own common grace, the AG consistently roots these good acts in the person's marred, but still extant, *imago dei*.[98] Stated differently, people do not do good because God's grace is moving in, upon, or around them. They do good because it is in keeping with their created identity, fallen though it is. In this regard it must be noted that here the AG manifests its single ontological anthropological tendency: life is not viewed within the philosophical-theological framework of Medieval or Scholastic (Catholic or Protestant) Christendom whereby grace and nature are consistently viewed as being in opposition to one another. In important ways, AG theological and spiritual formulations - like the Orthodox' own - are fashioned in terms of persons (human and divine), and not in the more abstract terminology of nature and grace.[99]

Still another point of contrast with Reformed models is that the AG believes the imago dei provides the human's capacity for redemption.[100] Although Fee limits his theological statements to the Pauline corpus, he nonetheless concludes that the human person's spirit is precisely the place where God's Spirit interfaces in the believer's life. Indeed, as Saint Paul himself expressed it, the believer's own spirit can be suffused with, and moved by, Christ's own Spirit, so that the entire *ordo salutis* is a synergistic interplay between the believer's spirit and the Spirit of God. This interplay Fee denotes as a S/spirit, divine-human, relation;[101] and, in this regard Fee is unequivocally Pentecostal.[102] As

---

[98] E. S. Williams, *Systematic Theology*, 2:147.

[99] The reason for its personalistic anthropology may be as simple as the Pentecostal movement's having developed in the twentieth century, so that contemporary philosophical presuppositions colored the movement. In this regard, existentialism, with its rampant individualistic emphases, may have made subtle inroads. This personalistic anthropology may also be traced back to John Wesley's own emphases (and here it would seem likely that Wesley would, like Durham, probably have been a forceful manifestation of culminating forces, and not the cause of those forces). Much study needs to be done to locate the Pentecostals' anthropology within the modern philosophical context, both for historical and missiological reasons.

[100] E.g., E. S. Williams, *Systematic Theology*, 2:137.

[101] Fee, *Empowering Presence*, 25. In his massive book Fee develops Paul's flexible use of *pneuma*. Fee concludes that in fourteen instances (1 Thes. 5:23; 1 Cor. 2:11; 5:5; 7:34; 14:14; 16:18; 2 Cor. 2:13; 7:13; Gal. 6:18; Rom. 1:9; 8:16; Phlm 25; Phil. 4:23; 2 Tim. 4:22) Paul uses *pneuma* to refer simultaneously to the divine Spirit and the human spirit; something Fee expresses as S/spirit. Thus, in Pauline literature, there is a dynamic interaction between the Spirit of God and a believer's spirit. See p. 15, n. 6.

[102] Fee's own discussion is remarkably like that of earlier Pentecostals like Donald Gee, "A City without Walls," *RT*, March 15, 1934, 1-2. Therein Gee discusses the interplay

noted before, God is always understood to be the prime mover in the work of redemption,[103] but as the AG emphasizes it, God's so moving does not find its point of origin in an eternal decree so much as it does in His love for men and women, His preeminent creations. God lovingly wants to restore the divine image still extant in human beings. To that end he sent His Son, and continually sends His Spirit, to renew us "to a true knowledge according to the image of the One who created him," (Col. 3:10).[104] Following James Arminius' teaching, God's decree was that those who are found "in Christ" would be saved; the decree is thus understood in a more Christocentric, and less juridical, manner.[105] By interpreting the decree Christocentrically, that is "in Christ," Pentecostals are more like the Catholics and the Orthodox than they are like the Reformed.[106]

Summary and Analysis

That human beings are understood primarily (but not solely) in terms of the juridical arena, explains why redemption receives more of an emphasis than sanctification in AG thought and praxis. One can be saved and obtain positional sanctification (that is, be "in Christ"), but one will still go to heaven whether or not one's person, character, and affections are sanctified (that is, having been made "like Christ"). AG ministers and theologians might object to such a stark portrayal of their theology, but practically spelled out in the AG's day in and day out life and ministry, this analysis holds true. In our previous chapter we

---

between God's Spirit and the human spirit concerning the charismatic gifts and grace. See also Gee's, *Concerning Spiritual Gifts* (Springfield, Missouri: Gospel Publishing, 1928).

[103] E.g., Pecota, "Saving Work," 355.

[104] E. S. Williams, *Systematic Theology*, 2:135.

[105] Pecota, "Saving Work," 355-359; see the glossary in *Theology: A Pentecostal Perspective*, 640-641.

[106] Richard Muller, "Arminius and the Scholastic Tradition," in *Calvin Theological Journal*, 24:1, 263-277, argues that Arminius broadened Protestant theology and tradition by incorporating some of the ideas of Catholic theologians like Francisco Suarez and Luis de Molina. Muller holds that Arminius' system was not merely a rejection of the doctrine of supralapsarian predestination but instead was a full-fledged alternative to the Reformed system. For a thoroughgoing study of Arminius and his interaction with Suarez and Molina see Muller's *God, Creation and Providence in the Thought of Jacob Arminius: Sources and Directions of Scholastic Protestantism in the Era of Early Orthodoxy* (Grand Rapids: Baker, 1991), 29, 159-163, 182.

cited some of the reasons for this theological imbalance, but they deserve reiteration here. Firstly, western pragmatism, both in its philosophical and simple forms, tends to spur the denomination toward a numerical standard of measurement; numbers *are not* produced by sanctification, they *are* produced by conversion. The juridical arena dovetails together quite well with pragmatism, not just by force of the cultural context (which cannot help but have an impact), but also in terms of the religious context. That God created humanity to exist within a juridical context naturally pushes the AG to emphasize how it is that one is saved (a crisis-moment wherein one accepts Christ into one's heart). Secondly this theological imbalance is part and parcel to a process of cultural accommodation. Such accommodation has tolerated and produced an erosion of the older values of holiness and integrity, with the result that the doctrine of sanctification has lost both its original emphasis and its original cultural context. Lastly, charisma, in its most authentic manifestations, appears to be on the wane and is being supplanted by revivalism. Charisma's wane results to no small degree from the uncritical embracing of pragmatism and cultural accommodation, but it seems that it also occurs as a normal historical-sociological process. That is, throughout history those generations of Christians who followed initial charismatic eruptions turned to the one characteristic left accessible to them: liturgical and sociological form.

Fortunately, because of its commitment to a biblical foundation, the denomination will not allow the juridical-moral arena to be the sole filter through which its anthropology is processed. It is too aware, and too committed to the conviction, that human beings are comprised of existential components which God yearns to transform and use. Without question, the AG has historically been enticed toward an exclusively juridical model in its anthropology and soteriology. But, as our above explication bears out, a consistent theme in AG theology is that the human person must be understood in more dynamic ways. Expressed musically, if the juridical-moral arena is the denomination's overarching melody, its existential insights and convictions provide the denomination with an invigorating harmonic undercurrent.

AG adherents are acutely aware that human beings are comprised of far more than a moral nature. They believe human beings have deep and mysterious elements which dynamically interact with one another. The fallen moral nature variously pollutes every dimension of the human person: the physical body, the natural and physical instincts (to eat, to reproduce, to exercise dominion, and the like), the heart, the affections and the intuition. These dimensions can further warp and twist a person's identity and soul with the result that the moral nature is itself more deeply injured and rendered ineffective. Although they have not always expressed it well theologically, AG constituents - like all classical Pentecostals - have intuitively understood the importance which these dynamic and existential elements have for Christian spirituality.

Alternately stated, their spirituality reflects their intuitive understanding of the human person. Their members do not traditionally spend time waiting on the Lord in holy reverence in order to experience a sentimental "warm fuzzy." They do so in order to seek God's specific purpose for them individually and corporately. Their members do not lay hands on one another's ailing bodies as an act of emotional or psychological solidarity (although that is not excluded). They touch one another because Scripture tells them that God will touch and heal them through their touching of one another. They do not sing exuberant worship songs or incorporate kinesthetic elements in their celebrations because these provide a release for their otherwise pent up desires (as external observers often project upon them). They know that the entire human person yearns for communion and contact with the divine. They do not fall to the ground, either on their knees or backs, merely because they enjoy mystic and rapturous experiences. They traditionally do so because such acts involve the very core of the human person: will, affections, body, and soul. One could list the various facets of their spirituality at length and scrutinize each one for cause and effect. However, until one realizes that the Pentecostals' spirituality is one which is purposefully shaped with respect to, and one which intuitively responds with regard to, the deepest elements of the human person, one will not fully seize precisely what it is that drives them.

We must be fair: the Pentecostals were not, and are not, simply mystics. Their theology is only occasionally mystical. They do not attempt to transform the Christian believer in the mystical ways of the Orthodox. From their inception the Pentecostals have attempted to present their movement in rational, reasoned, and apologetic terms. In this way, they have used terms attuned to the surrounding historical-cultural milieu where rationalism and science reigned supreme. But - and this is an important qualifier - the divine charisma which so commonly characterized their meetings and their ministers was a presence which they regularly recognized as being something which was larger than themselves. Yet, charisma was also something in their midst which touched the core of their individual identities and urged them to transcend themselves.

It seems that there is not a clear distinction between mystical and charismatic experience. If the broader Christian culture tolerated the latter (which it finally did after roughly fifty years), it was downright opposed to the former. Knowing this, the AG, together with the bulk of Pentecostals, routinely downplayed (and at times even denied) being mystical.[107] This rational-versus-charismatic tension presents Classical Pentecostals like those in the AG with one of their greatest contemporary challenges: to what will they be true? If they forsake their intuitive-charismatic-mystical character, as they seem to be doing, they will become just one more tributary in the larger evangelical stream.

Pentecostal ministers and scholars have long argued that the real attraction to the movement has been its pneumatology, not only for its fresh theological appreciation of, but especially for its evangelical emphasis upon, the person and work of the Holy Spirit. I am convinced that the movement's equally magnetic pull is its anthropology. Pentecostalism - in its authentic manifestations - intuitively understands and impacts the deepest elements of the human soul, and then goes on to encourage each person to seek and fulfil God's specific purpose. This transformational-purposeful divine-human transaction is proving to be incredibly infectious around the globe. And, as I will more carefully argue later, the Pentecostals' understanding that affirms and incorporates the mysterious, the a-rational (not necessarily irrational), and the existentially complex elements of human nature, together with those of the moral and rational realms, is an understanding which Pentecostals share with the Eastern Orthodox, even if these two great cisterns of Christian spirituality have heretofore been ignorant of one another.

---

[107] E.g., Arne Vick, "Pentecostal Worship," *PE*, 10-11, 1966, who clarified that Pentecostalism was not sheer mysticism.

8

Sanctification's Theological Foundations

'Tis Jesus who settles my troubles, 'Tis Jesus who gives me release.
When filled with fear and trembling, 'Tis Jesus who giveth me peace.
Do I love Him? O, ask me not, brother,
For words can n'er truly express My love and affection for Jesus,
Whose name I continually bless.
'Tis Jesus who opens my vision to scenes of all loveliness rare;
'Tis Jesus who made me the promise - His Throne and new name I might share.
And only thro Him I'm o'er coming; Day by day grace enough He provides,
And my heart overfloweth with gladness, For He keeps me whatever betides.
'Tis Jesus who quickens this body, Frail dust in itself,
But His life more abundant imparted, brings healing and strength for each hour of
the strife.
'Tis Jesus - both now and forever, The same strong, compassionate Lord,
Who said "I will leave thee, no never." What a privilege to rest on His word!
Just Jesus - the temple all filling, His power permeating my frame,
Till my soul is transported with glory, And my lips can but breathe His sweet
name.
Just Jesus - the Saviour all-glorious - The message of true Pentecost,
Revealing forever - just Jesus, Through the power of the Holy Ghost.
'Tis Jesus - the One who is coming; He has waited so long for His bride,
That she might be robed and all radiant for her place at His blessed side.
But, somehow, His Spirit is whispering, "Arise now, my fair one, arise,"
And my heart's longing changes to gladness; Soon His beauty shall burst on
mine eyes.

So Alice Flower, wife of the prominent AG leader J. Roswell Flower, wrote in
1914.[1] Not only does this poem provide us with a synopsis of the common four-
fold pattern of Pentecostal Christological doctrines (Jesus as Savior, Healer,

---

[1] Alice Flower, "'Tis Jesus," *The Christian Evangel*, October 3, 1914, 4.

Spirit-Baptizer, and Soon Coming King),[2] it also exhibits Pentecostalism's affective experience of Christ: Jesus did not simply perform an objective or historical work to save and transform people, He continues to work subjectively and contemporarily within and upon people to draw them to, and make them like, himself. In this chapter we will develop the three theological foundations for the AG's doctrine of sanctification: Jesus Christ, the Holy Spirit, and Scripture. As will become apparent, to discuss those three in that order is also to discuss the AG's order of salvation.

Christ

The supreme grounding point for the AG's doctrine of sanctification is Jesus Christ. Jesus is preeminent with respect to the Holy Spirit and Scripture not only because both the Spirit and Scripture testify to him and glorify him, but also because He both preceded the Spirit in the economy of salvation and is the one in whom Scripture finds its authority.[3] In this regard, those outside the pale of Pentecostalism err when the say the movement over-emphasizes pneumatology in its *ordo salutis*.

Evincing the denomination's juridical emphasis, an emphasis very much reflected in the New Testament witness, Timothy Jenney defines sanctification as "the process by which God is cleansing our world and its people. His ultimate goal is that everything - animate or inanimate - will be cleansed from any taint of sin or uncleanness." Continuing, he says, "Sanctification includes all God's work in attempting to save men and women from the judgment to come."[4] Following William Durham's line of teaching, the AG holds that upon one's conversion (the moment of salvation) one is completely cleansed in Christ. As was noted in an earlier chapter, Durham's teaching starkly contrasted with that of Holiness Pentecostals who said that one must have a distinct religious experience (whereby the sinful nature is rooted out) subsequent to one's

---

[2] Pentecostals from a Wesleyan-Holiness background would add a fifth feature to this theological pattern: Jesus as Sanctifier. Dayton, *Theological Roots*, 15-28, describes and notes the development of these four patterns within Pentecostalism.

[3] Pearlman, *Doctrines*, 282-283; Higgins, "God's Inspired Word," in *Theology, A Pentecostal Perspective*, 90, 113-115. Christ as Scripture's authoritative foundation is asserted in that he both affirmed Old Testament teaching and was the catalyst for and within New Testament teaching.

[4] Jenney, "Spirit and Sanctification," 399 and 416, respectively.

conversion in order to be sanctified. To the contrary, Durham taught that one's faith is to be centered "in Christ rather than in an experience of sanctification."[5]

When one accepts Christ as one's savior (as it is regularly stated, in contrast to Reformed Protestant statements wherein God's choosing the human for salvation receives emphasis)[6] one is instantaneously justified. In order to be saved (born-again), one need not undergo a lengthy or eternal process of becoming God-like; at the moment of justification one is freely and graciously declared righteous by God. However, God does not simply pardon the person because He is, as Pearlman said, "big hearted enough" to waive his righteous judgment. Such an act would violate his own holiness and justice. On the contrary, Christ's own righteousness is imputed to the believer at the moment of faith (1 Cor. 1:30; Eph. 5:26; Heb. 2:11). Because of Christ's atoning work, God, Pearlman said, "treats the person as if he had never committed a sin in his life!" This moment of justification effects *positional sanctification*, so that in God's eyes the justified one has a sinless status. Positional sanctification is implied in Scripture where the apostle Paul addressed the carnal Corinthian Christians as "saints" (1 Cor. 1:2). He called them that not because of their moral purity or maturity in godliness, but because they were in Christ.[7]

As the AG develops it, positional sanctification is specifically rooted in Christ's work, not his person. True enough, only the second person of the Trinity, the incarnate Jesus Christ, could do what he did and fulfil the old covenant in the way that he did.[8] But the AG's historical emphasis has been less upon him than upon his work. More specifically, as the AG emphasizes it (both in the United States and Great Britain),[9] it is not Jesus' suffering which provides

---

[5] Horton, "Pentecostal Perspective," 108. Nobud E. Much (the editor?) quoted A. B. Simpson who similarly taught that Christ is the one who should be sought after, not a spiritual experience of sanctification. "Holiness Unto the Lord!" *PE*, June 3, 1956, 6-7.

[6] To make this qualification is not to imply that Pentecostals ignore God's role of election.

[7] Pearlman, *Doctrines*, 227-242, 252-254. The former quotation is from p. 233, the latter is from p. 228. The emphasis is mine. See also E. S. Williams, *Systematic Theology*, 2:230-55; Pecota, "The Saving Work of Christ," in *Theology, A Pentecostal Perspective*, 365-367. E. N. Bell was clarifying the AG's *ordo salutis* for his readers as early as September 4, 1920, 5, "Questions and Answers," No. 870.

[8] Williams, *Systematic Theology*, 2:195-6, 198-199.

[9] This emphasis holds true for the AG's British journal *Redemption Tidings*. The examples are manifold. For example see: Charles S. Price, "The Lord's Broken Body and Shed Blood," *RT*, August 15, 1934, 1-3; Howard Carter, "The Death of Christ: The

for our propitiation so much as it is his shedding of blood and death (his suffering is taken as the grounds for our physical healing, based on a rather literal reading of Is. 53:5). Hebrews 13:12 says that Jesus sanctified us - positionally - through his blood. In the Old Covenant, the blood of animals was offered to God both for humans' sin and as a means of praise, but the offering of animal blood was less than perfect because it did not effect fellowship "between the offerer and the victim." Furthermore, animal blood could not be equated with a human's soul, it could not "effect the spiritual redemption of a soul," and it was not offered by a perfect priest. Christ's shedding of blood variously met the demands of God's holy law, atoned for human sinfulness, and appeased God's wrath for sin and disobedience. Not merely an act of love intended to stir humans toward repentance, Jesus' death was a necessary saving act. His blood blots out sin and casts it into the "depths of the sea" with the result that sin no longer affects God's view of those covered with it. It is by virtue of his death that the doorway to eternal life has been opened up.[10] In all of this, Christ is both the ransom and the Ransomer (Mt. 20:28; Mk. 10:45; 1 Tim. 2:6).[11] He has been made to be our sanctification.[12] Pearlman said, "The outstanding event and central doctrine of the New Testament may be summed up in the words, 'Christ died (the event) for our sins (the doctrine),' 1 Cor. 15:3."[13]

Although the moment of justification is described by the AG primarily in juridical terms, as the above has clarified, it is not understood solely therein. Upon one's salvation one is simultaneously adopted into God's family (Jn . 1:12,13; Rom. 8:15,16; 1 Jn. 3:1). Because of Christ's atoning work, those who repent of their sin(s) and confess their faith in Christ become children of God with the result that a process of inner and spiritual transformation is initiated (2 Cor. 6:16-18; Gal. 4:5-6; 1 Jn. 3:24; 4:13). They become new creatures in Christ (2 Cor. 5:17), and they are made to be partakers of the divine nature (2 Pet. 1:4). They are separated unto Christ, and they begin to be existentially separated from the defilement that characterizes the world. Saint Paul himself noted sanctification's transforming power when he taught that we have been buried in

---

Greatest Event in History," *RT*, March 26, 1937, 1-2; Henry E. J. Jessup, "The Blood of Jesus Christ: The Analogy Between the Blood of Jesus and the Blood in Our Bodies," *RT*, Sept. 25, 1936, 1-2.
[10] Pearlman, *Doctrines,* 191-214. The former quote is from p. 191.
[11] Pecota, "The Saving Work of Christ," 349.
[12] Winston I. Nunes, "Four Aspects of Sanctification," *PE*, March 5, 1949, 3.
[13] Pearlman, *Doctrines,* 171.

Christ's baptism so that we can walk in newness of life (Rom. 6:4).[14] In all of this sanctification involves transforming dimensions, both in terms of our relationship with God and our own appetites and desires.[15] One author summed up this transformational dimension of sanctification when he said, "Sanctification is character by faith."[16] J. T. Boddy clarified that Christians are not just representatives of Christ but partakers of his divine nature. Boddy, with decidedly colorful language, said, "as in the natural the blood, which is the life-giving principle, flows through our veins and arteries, carrying life to every part of our physical, so in the spiritual the life divine flowing, as it does, through our spiritual circulation, carries divine life to every part of our moral nature." Christians, Boddy continued, have the privilege of "being literal, conscious experimental partakers of the divine nature."[17]

Along with being the basis of justification and sanctification, Christ's blood is understood to be the means by which the Christian is forgiven of sins which are committed after the moment of salvation. Sins committed by Christians produce barriers of fellowship between themselves and God. These post-conversion barriers are washed away by Christ's blood when the believer confesses his or her sin (1 Jn. 1:7).[18]

Christ's role in sanctification is evident firstly in that he is the believer's basis of holiness, and secondly that he works inside the Christian to change and cleanse her. As Boddy's above quote revealed, holiness is not described in the ontological categories which characterize the Orthodox' doctrine of *theosis*. Instead, consistent with a literal reading of Scripture, the AG defines holiness as being clean, separated, made righteous, and called according to God's purpose.[19]

---

[14] W. I. Evans, "Sanctification and the Holy Spirit," *PE*, July 15, 1950, 3, suggested that the New Testament's negative emphasis about sanctification as separation from the world is because the world itself is so very contaminated.

[15] Pearlman, *Doctrines*, 247-249. See also Nunes, "Four Aspects of Sanctification," *PE*, March 5, 1949, 3, 12.

[16] Morris Williams, "Sanctified Believer Behavior," *PE*, July 13, 1986, 5.

[17] J. T. Boddy, "Partakers of Christ," *PE*, May 1, 1920, 4. Reprinted, edited in *PE*, July 21, 1963, 15.

[18] Pearlman, *Doctrines*, 255.

[19] AG authors regularly make word studies of both the Old and New Testaments in producing their juridical definition of holiness and sanctification. Pearlman, *Doctrines*, 249-252; Williams, *Systematic Theology*, 2:256-258; Jenney, "Spirit and Sanctification," 404-418.

Lastly, pertaining to Christ as a theological foundation for sanctification, from the onset of this study it was assumed that the AG's traditional eschatological emphasis would provide important grist for its doctrine of sanctification. One expected the AG writers and preachers to have said something like, "Jesus is coming back any moment, sanctify yourselves!" or, "Jesus is coming back soon! Zealously seek to become like Him!" True enough, the AG historically has been characterized - both in its writing and preaching - by its calls for conversion and to repentance (i.e., "getting right with God") in light of Jesus' soon return. However, despite the fact that the most written about topic in eighty years of the *Pentecostal Evangel* was Jesus' second coming, little to nothing has been done by AG writers to root the doctrine of sanctification within an eschatological framework. One can only surmise the reasons for this gaping lacuna, but in light of the pressures of the AG's culture and context it very likely has to do with the denomination's pragmatic orientation and its previously mentioned lack of appreciation for careful and detailed theological study. In terms of pragmatic orientation, eschatology has been largely limited to the practical applications of moving people to crisis decisions. As to theological study, the denomination has been consistently preoccupied with determining how contemporary events fit into the eschatological schemes noted in Scripture.

The above lacuna aside, Gordon Fee, an AG biblical scholar, does make an immediate connection between sanctification and eschatology. We will not unpack Fee's position on sanctification here, precisely because there is indeed variation between his own position and that of the AG. We will note that, like the AG, Fee does not believe sanctification is an experience subsequent to conversion. But, unlike the AG, and closer to a more Reformed position, he believes sanctification is a "metaphor for conversion."[20] Transformation is possible for, and present in, the believer because salvation, for Paul, is an eschatological phenomenon. Those in Christ are set apart (in a manner like the holy vessels of the Jewish religion) as people of the new age. As such, they have been given a pledge of the new age's dawning - the Holy Spirit. In this way they have become *pneumatikoi*, people who belong to the sphere of the Spirit.[21] Additionally, they have been given the privilege of participating with the Spirit in the ministry of the gospel via the *charismata*.[22] As Fee presents it,

---

[20] Fee, *Empowering Presence*, 859.

[21] Fee, *Empowering Presence*, 29-32; 803-826; *et passim*.

[22] Fee, *Empowering Presence*, 859. Cf., 32-5; 93-112.

sanctification is becoming what one already is in Christ: a person of the new age.[23]

The strength of Fee's eschatological mooring notwithstanding, he avoids the inevitable, and indeed necessary, issues of the human's existential elements. That is, not only does Fee believe Paul largely ignored or avoided making existential and/or anthropological delineations, he believes Paul taught that the Christian's struggle is not internal, but eschatological. The Christian is not so much being plagued by conflicting internal urges (fleshly versus spiritual) as he or she is caught between two conflicting ages: the age of this world (fleshly), and that of the Spirit (Spirit-ual).[24] Whether Paul did not recognize that the eschatological conflict has important existential ramifications, or whether Fee did not see that recognition in Paul, is not clear. That Christians East and West have seen and experienced as much for two millennia is irrefutable.

The Holy Spirit

Because Scripture reveals that whereas persons who are pronounced righteous in Christ still sin, and because the AG knows from its debates with the Wesleyan-Holiness groups that those persons who claim to have experienced entire sanctification still continue to sin,[25] its constituents also recognize the need for *progressive sanctification*. One becomes consecrated (chosen and separated) unto God upon one's conversion (Col. 3:3; Heb. 10:14; 1 Pet. 1:2),

---

[23] Fee, *Empowering Presence*, 78-79; 127-132; 135-137; 475-476; 626-627.

[24] Fee, *Empowering Presence*, 820.

[25] E. N. Bell commented favorably upon any experience that helps to sanctify a person, but noted that sin still rises up after such experiences, "The Crucified Life Needed," *The Christian Evangel*, February 13, 1915, 3; E. S. Williams commented favorably on, but also contrasted the AG against, Wesley's teaching in 2:259-261; Joseph R. Flower, then superintendent of the New York District, qualified sanctification with respect to the Holiness teaching in, "Holiness, the Spirit's Infilling, and Speaking with Tongues," *PE*, July 15, 1973, 4-5; Morris Williams in, "Sanctified Believer Behavior," *PE*, July 13, 1986, 4-6 also clarified that Christians sin after their positional sanctification in Christ. We previously noted that the AG only changed its official statement on sanctification (negating the phrase entire sanctification) in 1961. Examples of AG writers who encouraged an experience of entire sanctification were Harriett Gravelle, Letter to the Editor, *PE*, October 27, 1917, 10; J. Narver Gortner, "The Sanctification of the Soul," *PE*, June 18, 1949, 2-3; and, J. H. J. Barker, "A Refiner of Silver," *PE*, January 19, 1958, 4-5.

but because the sinful nature is not eradicated in conversion it remains for the believer to separate herself and live a holy, consecrated, life unto God (Eph. 4:22; Col. 3:8; Heb. 12:14; 1 Pet. 1:15; 1 Jn. 1:8-9). One must live a life in keeping with one's status in Christ. Authentic progressive sanctification - a life of holiness - will witness to the believer's increasing death unto sin and living unto righteousness. Pearlman clarified, "This does not mean that we grow *into* sanctification, but that we progress *in* sanctification."[26]

Whereas Christ is the basis for the believer's sanctification, and provides the righteousness by which the believer is continually being transformed, the Holy Spirit is the person of the Trinity who draws the believer to - and makes the believer become like - Christ in the process of progressive sanctification. Jesus' role in effecting believers' positional sanctification was completed when he died on the cross. But the Spirit continues to apply the benefits of Christ's cleansing blood.[27] Pearlman said, "He makes real *in* believers what Christ has done *for* them." The Spirit has not come to take Christ's place, instead he has come to "make Christ real."[28] Fee similarly explained the roles of Jesus Christ and his Spirit in the believer's life. Conversion has both an objective reality and a subjective dimension about it. The historical reality - Christ's death - effects a *positional* reality. The subjective dimension - the Holy Spirit's presence within the believer - effects an *experiential appropriation* of Christ. For Gordon Fee, the latter produces "some radical changes in the believer."[29]

John 14:16 reveals that both Jesus and the Holy Spirit are *paracletes*, comforters. Jesus is now the believer's advocate in heaven, and the Spirit is the believer's paraclete (comforter, advisor, and helper) on earth.[30] In this regard, a central work of the Holy Spirit is to sanctify the believer.[31] Indeed, Scripture

---

[26] Pearlman, *Doctrines,* 251-4. Quotation taken from pp. 253-254. Emphasis his.

[27] Jenney, "Spirit and Sanctification," 417.

[28] Pearlman, *Doctrines,* 283. His emphasis.

[29] Fee, *Empowering Presence,* 854. Emphases his. It should be clarified that Fee does not limit this experiential appropriation to the event of conversion. He said, "frequently Paul implies there are further, ongoing appropriations of the Spirit's empowering," (Gal. 3:5; 1 Thes. 4:8; Eph. 5:18; Phil. 1:19), p. 863. In this regard, he believes Pentecostals recapture the heart of the New Testament pattern of Christian religious experience, 864.

[30] Pearlman, *Doctrines,* 283-284.

[31] AG writers unanimously recognize that in one's own experience one cannot distinguish between Christ and the Spirit. When God works sanctification in the believer's heart, or more broadly when God works in the course of history, one must hold

identifies the Spirit as Holy because he is one with the Holy Triune God and because, as Pearlman said, "His chief work is sanctification."[32] Jenney similarly said, "The writers of the New Testament used the phrase 'Holy Spirit' so often because they recognized the Spirit's significance for the sanctification of the world."[33]

Whereas both Jesus and the Holy Spirit are paracletes, they are both nonetheless understood to be persons. Alternately stated, Pentecostals are adamant that the Holy Spirit is neither a holy power, a spiritual influence, nor an impersonal presence. He is instead a person - the person - who comes to dwell within and alongside the believer (both prior to her conversion and for her life's duration).[34] The Holy Spirit is God himself who has come to make the believer like her redeemer. We must add, the reason for this belief in the Spirit as a person does not stem as much from historical theology or ancient Christian creeds as it does from a simple literal reading of Scripture. Jesus, especially in John's gospel, spoke of the Holy Spirit as a person. Similarly, in their epistles, the apostles Paul, Peter, and John taught about the Spirit in ways clearly presenting him as a person. In all of this, Pentecostals believe their "personal relationship with Christ" (a phrase nearly turned into a universal slogan by Pentecostals and evangelicals alike) is heightened and intensified precisely because of the intimacy they share with the person of the Spirit.[35]

As the AG discusses it, the Spirit of Christ does not come and re-instill the image of God in a human (the AG rejects Wesley's notion of total depravity,[36] as was previously noted). Instead, he comes to renew and reorganize the person's nature with the increasing result that that person will be opposed to sin and drawn toward righteousness. The Spirit's presence in the believer, if

---

that it is the Triune God who is at work. Even Christ's own ministry was one involving the entire Trinity.

[32] Pearlman, *Doctrines,* 287.

[33] Jenney, "Spirit and Sanctification," 397.

[34] Donald Gee, "Guidance By The Holy Spirit," *RT*, June 1, 1935, 5-6; Riggs, *The Spirit Himself.*

[35] For a contemporary, and more theological treatment, see McRoberts, "The Holy Trinity," in *Theology, A Pentecostal Perspective,* 145-177.

[36] For sake of clarification, Calvin - who is famous among Protestants regarding total depravity - did not hold that fallen people have lost all virtue. Louis Berkhof summarized Calvin on this point and said, "The whole image was vitiated by sin, but only those spiritual qualities were completely lost." Berkhof, *Systematic Theology* (Grand Rapids: Eerdmans, reprinted 1986), 203.

submitted to, will produce an existential order, so that one's desires and affections function according to their created identity.[37] The Spirit is also a seal and a pledge of the believer's salvation. Exegeting the apostle Paul's teaching, Fee said, "the Spirit is the absolute *sine qua non* of becoming a believer in Christ," and, "the Spirit has now replaced the Torah as the new 'identity marker' of God's people."[38] The Spirit comes and imprints the righteousness of Christ's identity within the believer. In this regard, the same breath/Spirit of God which quickened the original human body comes and quickens (energizes and awakens) the believer's soul. Present within the human soul, the Spirit variously strengthens one's faith, assures one of one's status before God, fortifies one's love, corrects sinful tendencies, alters one's spiritual appetites, and empowers the believer to help other Christians become sanctified. The Holy Spirit enables the individual to live in a manner which the unconverted person - the natural person - cannot live of his or her own strength.[39]

The AG is not unanimous as to the extent to which sin's power is broken or rendered ineffectual by the Spirit within the believer. Similarly, AG scholars and pastors are divided as to how Romans 7 should be interpreted. Some, like Gordon Fee, hold that it is describing an unconverted person and his struggle with sin under the Mosaic law. Fee said, "Paul, therefore, contrary to popular - and much scholarly - opinion, does not view life in the Spirit as a constant struggle between the flesh and the Spirit, in which the flesh generally has the upper hand. That may indeed be the experience of many of God's good people, but they can find no comfort in that existence on the basis of Pauline theology."[40] Others hold that it shows that even a person like the apostle Paul struggled with sin's presence. W. I. Evans, in an *Pentecostal Evangel* article, attempted to work a middle ground and argued that in light of Romans 7 we are not immune to the effects of sin in our environment, even though sin's controlling power within us has been broken by the Spirit's renewing presence. Just as unbelievers sin because they are driven to do so, believers only sin when they consent with their wills and yield to temptation. Romans 7 may have been, said Evans, "the experience of a Christian, but it is not Christian experience."[41]

---

[37] E. S. Williams, *Systematic Theology,* 2:262.
[38] Fee, *Empowering Presence,* 469-470.
[39] Pearlman, *Doctrines,* 287-90, 305-308. See also John W. Lackey, "Sanctified by the Spirit," *PE,* August 4, 1963, 20-21; and, Jenney, "Spirit and Sanctification," 399.
[40] Fee, *Empowering Presence,* 817.
[41] W. I. Evans, "Sanctification and the Holy Spirit," *PE,* July 15, 1950, 3-4.

In its teaching about progressive sanctification the AG rightly can be called synergistic. A person can do nothing to save himself (conviction of sin and repentance are themselves works of the Holy Spirit),[42] but he must cooperate with the workings of the Holy Spirit, and obey the Holy Spirit, if he is to increasingly become like Christ. It is the believer's responsibility to yield his or her bodily members unto the Lord's righteousness. This yielding is accomplished via an act of faith, an assent of the heart to God that Christ's work on Calvary is accepted as payment for sin. Addressing the question of whether a person has anything to do in one's sanctification other than accepting God's plan in faith, an official AG publication answered, "No and yes. He merely accepts, but that acceptance involves a fight of faith." That fight of faith involves walking by faith with the Spirit and refusing to allow himself to yield to sin.[43]

Whereas a person knows he or she is justified and has been granted positional sanctification based upon one's salvation experience, the person can know he or she is progressing in sanctification based on the fruit of the Spirit that is being produced within. These Christian virtues (love, joy, peace, patience, kindness, goodness, faithfulness, gentleness, and self-control; Gal. 5:22-3), or marks of Christian character, cannot be produced by one's self-effort, or by one's own ascetic attempts to subdue one's body and/or sinful impulses. Instead they result from one's yieldedness to God, faith, and cooperation with the Holy Spirit's leading.[44] It should also be clarified, the AG has long taught that one's spiritual giftings (the *charismata* of 1 Cor. 12:8-10) do not necessarily make one more spiritual or more sanctified.[45] The same can be said regarding spiritual experiences.[46]

In our explication of Orthodoxy we saw that they believe the entire universe has been, and is being, sanctified on the basis of Christ's incarnation (the archetypal person within whom matter itself has been united to God). AG scholars, when they address the issue of the universe's sanctification (a notion

---

[42] Riggs, *The Spirit Himself*, 42-45; Williams, *Systematic Theology*, 3:31-33.

[43] Riggs, *We Believe: A Comprehensive Statement of Christian Faith* (Springfield, Missouri: Gospel Publishing, 1954), 107.

[44] E. S. Williams, *Systematic Theology*, 2:259; 3:34-35; Pearlman, *Doctrines*, 311.

[45] Gee, *Concerning Spiritual Gifts*, 14, 84-85, 102, 107. See also Pearlman and Boyd, *Pentecostal Truth*, pp. 102-105, where ways to test the gifts' authenticity and Christian character are noted.

[46] Don Mallough, "He That is Spiritual," *PE*, December 3, 1967, 3-4; Richard L. Dresselhaus, "Is radical transformation possible?" *PE*, November 8, 1992, 4-5.

which historically has not been a concern),[47] teach that this is to be accomplished through the Holy Spirit's work. Thus, the Holy Spirit does not isolate his efforts within the church or individual believers alone. Instead, his aims are to convict unbelievers of their sin and need of Christ, and then to cleanse them in Christ.[48]

Scripture

The last theological foundation for the AG's doctrine of sanctification is the written Word of God, Scripture. This position stems from the AG's Scriptural hermeneutic, one that is primarily literal. Several passages are pertinent in this regard. 1 Timothy 4:5 says that everything created by God "is sanctified by means of the word of God and prayer." Similarly, Psalm 119:9 said, "How can a young man keep his way pure? By keeping it according to Thy word." Jesus, in John 17:17, prayed that the Father would "sanctify them in the truth; Thy word is truth." Paul, in Ephesians 5:25-26, taught that Christ loved the church and sanctified her by the word.

As the AG argues it, the Bible is God's revelation in objectified form. As such, it provides the denomination with a sure foundation for its doctrine of sanctification. Pearlman made a one-for-one correlation between the Word of God (his capitalization) and Scripture,[49] as did Stanley Horton. Horton says, "The Word is His primary tool for accomplishing His work in the hearts and lives of individuals. The people He uses are His willing agents, but the means of

---

[47] The traditional eschatological focus of the entire Pentecostal movement tended to cause it to be apathetic regarding the universe's transformation. Convinced of Jesus' imminent return, the thrust of Pentecostal preaching and teaching has been that the church will be taken out of the world (raptured), and that the world's ultimate destiny is destruction. That AG scholars today address the universe's sanctification is itself an indication that the movement is maturing theologically.

[48] Jenney, "Spirit and Sanctification," 397-398, 413, 420.

[49] Other passages referenced in this regard include: Jn. 15:3, "You are already clean because of the word which I have spoken to you." Jas. 1:23-25, "For if anyone is a hearer of the word and not a doer, he is like a man who looks at his natural face in a mirror. . . But one who looks intently at the perfect law. . . and abides by it . . . this man shall be blessed in what he does." 1 Pet. 1:23 teaches that Christians have been born again "through the living and abiding word of God." Cf., Pearlman, *Doctrines,* 256-257.

doing the work is the Word."[50] Apart from its formal doctrinal consensus, the "Statement of Fundamental Truths" (today totaling about five pages),[51] the AG has done little in terms of making official theological pronouncements. However, in the 1970s and 1980s it published position papers which, though they have not received a denomination-wide ratification,[52] have a canon-like status among the denomination's hierarchy.[53] One of these, entitled "The Inerrancy of Scripture," said, "We conceive the Bible to be in actuality the very Word of God."[54]

Scripture is secondly foundational for the AG's doctrine of sanctification because of its clear commitment to the necessity of knowledge. That is, the believer will not only be made to be like Christ through the spiritual and existential workings of Christ and his Holy Spirit, the believer will be made like Christ as she increasingly learns about him, and encounters him, through God's special revelation of Scripture. The Holy Spirit takes the revealed knowledge contained in the Bible and uses it to educate the believer in the truths of Christianity. A first generation Pentecostal writer aptly expressed the necessity of Bible reading for Christians' spiritual growth when he said, "the Holy fire should never go out on the altar of their hearts." "It must be kept burning by the fresh fuel of God's Word day by day," he went on, "and as we muse or meditate upon it, the fire will glow with an ever-increasing and more vehement flame."[55] In all of this, the believer's mind and understanding must be transformed and sanctified, not just her heart and soul.[56]

---

[50] Horton, "Pentecostal Perspective," in *Five Views on Sanctification*, 117-123. The quotation is from p. 120.

[51] Cf., *1997-98 Yearbook of the Southern California District Council of the Assemblies of God, Inc.* (Springfield, 1997), 35-39.

[52] These have never been put before a General Council session in order to be voted upon. Nonetheless, AG ministers can be called before denomination officials and examined *vis-a-vis* the position papers.

[53] Ranging between 15 to 25 pages in length (tract form), these papers address moral issues like abortion, homosexuality, divorce and remarriage, and abstinence, as well as theological issues like creation, eternal punishment, eternal security, the rapture, healing, demon possession, and Spirit-baptism.

[54] *The Inerrancy of Scripture*, Assemblies of God Position Paper (Springfield, Missouri: Gospel Publishing, 1976), 3.

[55] H. M. Turney, "The Baptism of the Holy Ghost," *The Weekly Evangel*, July 1, 1916, 5.

[56] Horton, "The Pentecostal Perspective," 122; Jenney, "Spirit and Sanctification," 418.

The Bible is thirdly foundational for the AG's doctrine of sanctification, and this at a more subjective level. AG constituents are regularly instructed, both in sermons and written discussions, to prayerfully search the Scriptures and allow the Holy Spirit to speak to their hearts regarding very personal issues. Not only can the Spirit give guidance and wisdom for the spiritual matters of sanctification (temptations, one's prayer-life, conviction of sin, and the like), he can also (but does not always) illuminate a passage of Scripture for a believer and thereby provide guidance in how one should respond or act in a specific situation. These Scriptural illuminations wrought by the Spirit are not today understood to be new revelations of God (although early in Pentecostal history such a belief was more widespread),[57] rather, they give the believer new understandings and a new comprehension for his or her own life.[58] Not only does this practice of subjective Bible reading once again make evident the general existential-experiential orientation of Pentecostals, it reveals that Pentecostals believe the Scriptures were written to speak - and not just be pastorally applied - to every individual in every age.[59]

Lastly, the AG's commitment to the Bible as a theological foundation for sanctification stems from its Protestant epistemological heritage of *sola scriptura*. Like Protestants in general, and evangelicals in particular, the AG believes Christian doctrine should be founded upon Scripture, first and foremost. The features of Christian tradition and church authority (whether formal or informal), human reason,[60] the philosophical considerations of the broader culture, and the harder (empirical) sciences are consistently relegated to a lower strata in the AG's epistemological framework. Indeed, each of these features have been seen as antithetical and/or opposed to Christian epistemology

---

[57] Menzies, *Anointed*, 84.

[58] Stanley Horton, *What the Bible Says About the Holy Spirit* (Springfield, Missouri: Gospel Publishing, 1976), 121.

[59] Higgins, "God's Inspired Word," 111-113. Mark McLean insightfully pointed out that many contemporary Pentecostals have uncritically bought into the Fundamentalist Biblical hermeneutic and are thereby forced into the anti-Pentecostal position whereby God does not speak in the same dynamic ways he formerly did, but that he has limited his speaking to the printed word and the church's sermons. McLean, "Toward a Pentecostal Hermeneutic," *Pneuma*, 6:2 (Fall 1984), 49-50.

[60] The AG's original "Statement of Fundamental Truths" admitted that whereas Scripture is superior to human reason, it is "not contrary to reason." *A Statement of Fundamental Truths Approved By The General Council of the Assemblies of God*, October 2-7, 1916, 10.

in the AG's history. In comparison, Scripture provides Pentecostals with a reliable theological foundation. The Bible is variously trustworthy because: 1) it is inspired;[61] 2) it has an internal theological unity; 3) its writers had, and teachings have, a high moral quality; 4) its many prophecies have been fulfilled; 5) Jesus attested to its authority; 6) it has "demonstrated agreement with approved science"; 7) it has been providentially preserved throughout Christian history; and, 8) it is the most widely printed and read book in history.[62]

Summary and Analysis

The AG's Theological Foundations
vis-a-vis its Cultural Context

In our examination of Orthodoxy we saw that the incarnation was viewed as a pivotal event in the economy of salvation. By becoming fully human (yet lacking a human hypostasis) Christ sanctified the entirety of human nature. Through the incarnation, God united himself with his creation and thus became the means by which all of creation is being sanctified. Christ's death is understood to be the means of victory over death, and those found in him will not suffer the second death; his death is not viewed with the penal substitutionary lenses that characterize the great bulk of Western Christendom. *Theosis* - like the whole of Orthodoxy's theology - is an ontological issue. By virtue of passing across (or through) the great divine-human ontological bridge named Jesus Christ, one becomes like God. In all of this, Christ's person is emphasized over his work. By no means is the cross ignored, but because of the emphasis upon the restoration and healing of the *imago dei* the cross receives less emphasis in Orthodox writings on *theosis* than does Christ's person.

---

[61] AG scholars in specific, and Pentecostals in general, have done little to explore the Christian community's necessary role in recognizing the Spirit's inspiration.

[62] Riggs, *We Believe*, 87-88; Higgins, "God's Inspired Word," 84-93. Quotation from Riggs, 88. The AG follows the conservative evangelical position of biblical inerrancy wherein it is maintained that the original manuscripts were without error. Higgins manifests some of the uneasiness produced by radical inerrancy on pages 103-105, and qualifies his definition of inerrancy so that inerrant and infallible are nearly synonymous. Inerrancy, he says on p. 103, is simply "more in vogue" than the term infallibility.

By way of contrast, as the above delineation has shown, AG writers and theologians, together with other classical Pentecostals, emphasize Christ's work generally, and his shedding of blood specifically. In the course of its history, the AG has spent very little time or energy reflecting upon, or making applications with respect to, the *Logos'* incarnation. To no small extent, the AG's emphasis upon Christ's juridical work of atonement also helps to account for the traditional lack of theological and ministerial interest on both Jesus of Nazareth (either as an historical figure, or as the supreme model of ethical or eschatological living) and his favorite topic for preaching, the Kingdom of God; both issues fall outside the purview of a juridically oriented doctrine of salvation.[63] Of the thirty-three years or so of Jesus' life, what has consistently been emphasized in traditional Pentecostal life and theology are the six or so hours he hung on the cross.[64]

This focus on Christ's work *vis-a-vis* his person manifests the degree to which the denomination parallels the pragmatic character of Western and North American culture more broadly. Within that culture, especially since the Industrial Revolution of the late nineteenth and early twentieth centuries (that is, roughly since the origins of the Pentecostal movement), the concerns that have received the greatest emphasis are those of a very pragmatic basis, "what works?" and its twin-sister "what works best?" In light of salvation and Christology, the AG's emphasis is that "Christ works," and more specifically that his blood has worked sufficiently. With only a few exceptions in AG literature and preaching, Jesus' person, life, and teaching are all secondary to his having shed blood for us.[65] To so clarify this emphasis is not at all to fault the Pentecostals, but it helps both to identify them as residents within their own culture and simultaneously contrasts their position and milieu with that of the Orthodox. The Orthodox, located within their own historical-cultural-

---

[63] Gary McGee notes that the AG's interest (like that of evangelicals more broadly) in the Kingdom of God began to arise after World War II. In 1966 AG missiologist Melvin L. Hodges incorporated the theme of God's Kingdom in his teaching. In 1987 Ruth A. Breusch, a retired Pentecostal missionary, wrote a ten-part series on the Kingdom in the AG's missions magazine, *Mountain Movers*. Still later in the 1980s, many AG scholars began to publish articles on God's Kingdom and ethics. See McGee's, "Historical Background," in *Theology, A Pentecostal Perspective*, 33-35.

[64] Pearlman precisely says as much in *Doctrines*, 214.

[65] The single best piece which runs against my analysis is Frank M. Boyd, *The Kenosis of The Lord Jesus Christ* (San Francisco: Frank M. Boyd, 1947). Boyd develops the critical nature of Christ's *kenosis* for our own faith, humility, and life in the Spirit.

philosophical milieu, take God's person as the point of departure for their theology in general, and their *theosis* doctrine in specific. For nearly a millennium in Orthodox lands apologetic defenses of God's existence were largely unnecessary, even their traditional enemies the Muslims believed in God; what needed establishing were the grounds for fellowship with a God that the bulk of civilization understood to be utterly transcendent. Furthermore, by locating each tradition within its respective historical and cultural milieu we are not arguing that each is the simple and natural product of that milieu. Each tradition's theology and practice has been shaped and modified with regard to the context, but neither tradition has entirely capitulated to the culture's epistemology, as has been typified herein by each tradition's resistance to the secular sciences. Like the Orthodox, the AG has assembled its theology in general, and doctrine of transformation in specific, in light of its own surrounding context. That context's demands for empirical evidence has made a tremendous impact on how the denomination has formulated and appealed to, its theological foundations. Responding to the demand for empirical evidence, the denomination has appealed to three Christian epistemological bulwarks: Christ's death on the cross, the Holy Spirit's abiding presence, and God's revelation in Scripture. Christ's death (and resurrection) has been attested to by millions over two millennia: it was *the* historical event - Christianity's *sine qua non* - which provided crucial and necessary evidence of Jesus' authority and teaching; the AG shares this emphasis with Protestants in general, and evangelicals in particular. The Holy Spirit continues to provide proof of God's ongoing presence and work. For the Pentecostals, the proof of the Spirit's presence and work is so manifestly evident as to be replete with physical evidence (*glossolalia*); in this regard the Pentecostals are distinct from evangelicals. Scripture, for its part, is a tangible witness which can be appealed to as an authoritative source for religious belief and practice; this is another feature which Pentecostals share more broadly with evangelicals. Moreover, while it has not been dealt with herein, the Pentecostal emphasis upon physical healings and the frequency of miracles has equally contributed to its empirically successful mission. These theological foundations provide the denomination with the empirical standards, evidence, and/or proofs necessary to present its case to the wider civilization.

Some scholars believe Pentecostalism is a protest against modernity. Characterized by ecstatic religious experiences, the movement is understood as a religious and communal reaction against the overbearing technological and scientific-rational worldview which typifies twentieth-century civilization.[66] However, in light of the way that the AG grounds and presents its *ordo salutis* and spirituality it seems more accurate to hold that the Pentecostal movement has numerically flourished precisely because of its modernistic orientation. Their theological message comes replete with historical proof (Christ's death and resurrection), *physical proof* (*glossolalia*, bodily healings, and miracles), and *tangible-empirical proof* (Scripture). Through these proofs - perhaps better understood as religious avenues - the Pentecostals have an experiential theology which fits quite well the existing worldview which demands verifiable evidence. One must be clear, Pentecostals are not intellectual "talking-heads" who rationalize their faith in deeply philosophical ways. However, because of the modern orientation of their spirituality, and because they know how to impact the human person's deepest existential levels (especially with regard to their dynamic view of the Holy Spirit), they have found it unnecessary to intellectualize their faith in order to gain adherents. Again, even though they take few intentional steps to explain their faith system in intellectual ways, they have an epistemological scheme which powerfully interacts with the broader culture's juridical and empirical biases. Christ died, sent and sends his Spirit, and has left an authoritative and life-transmitting document; the problem for those who cannot make faith-decisions in light of those grounds does not reside with their minds, but with their hearts.[67]

Furthermore, to make this connection between the world's growing epistemological suppositions (the necessity of tangible and/or quantifiable proof) and the Pentecostal movement's success is not to deny the reality of the Spirit's presence in its midst. Rather, like the Orthodox church of Eastern Europe in previous centuries, one can rightly identify Pentecostalism as one of God's powerful and providential tools for the day. Just as the flourishing of Orthodoxy, has for centuries, provided millions with a meaningful worldview, Pentecostalism's epistemological framework and rich narrative tradition work together and enable the movement to construct its own meaningful worldview for millions across diverse cultural and ethnic divides.

---

[66] Anderson, *Vision*, 223-227; Poloma, *At the Crossroads*, xvii, 19, 90.

[67] To say this is to be descriptive, not apologetic.

The Holy Spirit: Synergy and Subordination

The AG's doctrine of sanctification is clearly synergistic. With respect to the AG's distinctions between positional and progressive sanctification, it is more synergistic regarding the latter than the former. That is, whereas God will not save a man without his faith and assent, he absolutely cannot transform him without his continued faith and assent.[68] One is first positionally sanctified in Christ (at conversion), but one needs to experientially appropriate sanctification in a life-long process of growth. In this regard, the Holy Spirit and faith are not only necessary for salvation, they are necessary for the whole of the Christian experience. Put another way, a believer, by faith and the Holy Spirit, may be positionally sanctified in Christ upon his conversion, but that does not mean that he is immediately all that God wants him to be: there is more to being a Christian than being saved. To summarize the way Pentecostals have traditionally expressed it, to be a Christian is to be Christ-like; the latter is a quality which surpasses the issue of being judicially pardoned by God. In all of this, human beings cannot do anything to save themselves; the Spirit himself is understood to be a gift of God.[69] But, by cooperating with the continual work of the Holy Spirit - the divine person who increasingly impels Christians to become like their Lord - human persons truly can be transformed in this life.

The AG's synergistic pneumatological-anthropological (S/spirit) position is based on the belief that the Holy Spirit is sovereignly free to interact with the believer on an individual basis. He does not act apart from the Father or the Son, and he does not act in contrast to the identity or teaching of the Son, but he nonetheless remains the sovereign God. The AG has traditionally interpreted John 3:8 ("The wind blows where it wishes and you hear the sound of it, but do not know where it comes from and where it is going; so is everyone who is born of the Spirit.") to affirm the Spirit's sovereignty both with respect to his dealing

---

[68] This model harkens back to Wesley's own. Describing the dynamics of this Wesley said, "First, God works, therefore you can work: Secondly, God works, therefore you must work." That is, salvation comes by virtue of God's being the first mover, but we must live in cooperation with God's salvific work if we are to grow in grace. *The Bicentennial Edition of the Works of John Wesley*, 36 vols., Frank Baker (ed.) (Nashville: Abingdon Press, 1984-1999), 3:206-209.

[69] Fee said, "Although it does not fit our logical schemes well, the Spirit is thus both the cause and the effect of faith," *Empowering Presence*, 853. That is, not only does the Spirit aid the believer's faith, the result of the believer's faith is the reception of the Spirit (Fee's experiential appropriation of Christ).

with individual persons and the church.[70] True enough, the Spirit consistently works through the church and the Scriptures (here again, God the Spirit is understood to work synergistically, and through means), but he is not bound to them. Pentecostals are well aware of personal testimonies, often from foreign lands, wherein people will recount the gnawing spiritual hunger[71] they experienced prior to learning about, and coming to a saving knowledge of, Jesus Christ. That pre-conversion yearning and conviction, the testifier will later clarify, was unquestionably the drawing work of the Spirit. The same holds true for the Christian's sanctification; once drawn into Christ, the Spirit will consistently and lovingly prompt and call the believer toward Christ-likeness.

If James Dunn's analysis is correct, the Catholic church tends to subordinate the Holy Spirit to the church and its institutionalized sacramental system. Protestants (especially those of a Reformed persuasion), for their part, tend to subordinate the Spirit to the Bible and the preached word.[72] The Pentecostals maintain a much more dynamic view of the Holy Spirit's person and work - a view which even transcends their distinctive doctrine of Holy Spirit-baptism. In the Pentecostal model, the Spirit is free to use any means at his disposal to draw his children steadily into conformity with Christ's image. In my Pentecostal youth, I was taught to be open to the Spirit's presence, guidance, and instruction through nearly any imaginable means: Scripture, the spoken words of a preacher or teacher, another Christian's testimony, devotional materials, or a heartfelt conversation between believers. Moreover, the beauty of nature, music (whether with lyrics or not), silence, a hug or a smile or a shed tear, billboards, and even bumper stickers were fair game for the Spirit's communication to me. (About the only things the Spirit didn't work through were the sacraments of the

---

[70] For example, Frank J. Lindquist, "Heavenly Winds," *PE*, February 3, 1963, 2-3, 22, where he explicitly teaches that the Spirit's moving is both "inexplicable" and "unpredictable." Lindquist also clarified that the Spirit is neither bound to a church's program, ritual, or creed.

[71] In the case of my own Pentecostal boyhood, in our Sunday night services we even heard testimonies about the visions and dreams that unsaved persons had which prompted them toward Jesus Christ. Arne Vick, an evangelist, recounted a similar story in which the Holy Spirit prompted him to pray fervently for some unknown person named Charley. Three weeks later, in a revival meeting a man named Charley testified that three weeks earlier (on the same night Vick was prayerfully interceding) he had climbed up into his barn to commit suicide, but therein had a vision of Jesus Christ and found eternal life. Vick, "The Ministry of Tears," *PE*, September 23, 1951, 15-16.

[72] James Dunn, *Baptism in the Holy Spirit* (London: SCM Press, 1970), 224-225.

historical church!) Whereas I, in my youth, was being taught to be open to the
Spirit's communication to me through nearly any means, some young person in
an Orthodox church was at the same time being instructed to view not only all
other human beings, but the whole universe, in a eucharistic way, "as
sacraments of communion with God." These two approaches, these two
worldviews, are thus surprisingly and coincidentally alike (at least on this
point). The Spirit has not ceased hovering over his creation (Gen. 1:2), he has
not stopped breathing the life of God into those who are willing to take it in
through Christ. And, as our next chapter will demonstrate, he can make use of
the most mundane of means to transform those humans open to his presence.

We will only hint at it here (a more detailed comparison remains for the
conclusion), but this notion of the Spirit's sovereignty is one shared by both
Pentecostals and Orthodox. True enough, some Orthodox theologians and
ecclesiarchs write and teach as though the Spirit is nearly enslaved within the
sacramental system. But, as our explication of Gregory Palamas indicated,
Orthodoxy has historically been characterized by the conviction that God,
through the person of the Holy Spirit, yearns to have intimate, existential, and
mystical fellowship with his supreme creations, human beings. Indeed, God's
very purpose for creating was to facilitate a divine-human *sobornost*.

The Orthodox present their pneumatology, and its specifically Spirit-as-
sovereign character, to Western Christians by rejecting the Western (initially
Catholic) doctrine of *Filioque*. The West, so say the Orthodox, with its *Filioque*
clause, has made the Spirit become a subordinated power rather than a person.
In Orthodox models it is the person of God - the Holy Spirit - who comes to
have fellowship, and who seeks to transform, the human person. Similarly,
Pentecostals have dogmatically insisted that the third person of the Trinity is a
person, not a power, as our above delineation made clear.[73] Only occasionally
do Pentecostals clarify this Spirit-as-Person emphasis *vis-a-vis* the metaphysics
of the Trinity. They know little or nothing about either the *Filioque* controversy
or the language about *hypostasis* and *ousia*. Nonetheless, Pentecostals do know
that when they experience the Spirit's presence, they are experiencing the
person of God himself; this in contradistinction to the Reformed and Wesleyans
who describe God's working in the less personal terminology of grace:
prevenient or common or universal, and saving or regenerating or special.
Strangely resembling the Orthodox' own synergistic model, though expressed
within its own respective theological-contextual milieu, the Pentecostals'

---

[73] See also Riggs, *The Spirit Himself.*

anthropology is inextricably tied together with its pneumatology. Human beings were created for fellowship with God, and that in the most intimate of ways - between persons.

Like the Orthodox' own spiritual-transformational model, the Pentecostals' is largely personal. However, both see Christian transformation occurring within their own framework. The Orthodox' is heavily colored by ontological and communal terminology, but the Pentecostals is largely colored by juridical and individual terminology. The Orthodox believe the Christian is increasingly becoming united to Christ's very being by the person of the Spirit. The Pentecostals believe the Christian is increasingly being transformed and made like Christ through the person of the Holy Spirit. The Orthodox' personalistic emphasis is formed with regard to the ancient Greek philosophical constructs regarding ontology. The Pentecostals' own personalistic and individualistic emphases are formed with regard to contemporary Western constructs, not the least of which is existentialism.

In their best cases, both of these Christian tributaries have qualified and critiqued the broader culture's philosophical and epistemological assumptions. The genius of Orthodoxy is its brilliant interweaving of the saving gospel with Greek philosophy, without capitulating to the Greeks' epistemology. The power of Pentecostalism is its inspired folding together of an individualistic society's emphasis with a gospel directed toward saving and transforming individuals. Whereas the historic and philosophic connections are absent, one clear theological reason for the resultant similarities lies specifically with each's pneumatological formulations: for both, God's sovereign and free Holy Spirit synergistically works with - and in - human persons to make them like Christ.

The Scriptures: AG Epistemology

The Bible provides the AG with an objective basis for its doctrine of sanctification. If a Christian wants to know what God requires him to do and yearns for him to become, he only needs to read Scripture. The Bible's objective nature helps to safeguard the doctrine of sanctification against foreign and/or speculative interpretations. Scripture is also important in that it functions as an anchor, or counterbalance, to the denomination's subjective and experiential character. The Spirit's subjective impressions for guidance and leading are important for an individual's own transformation (or daily living), but those subjective means never replace the inspired Scriptures as an authoritative source for the AG's knowledge and doctrine. This objective-subjective (Scripture versus the Spirit's guidance) tension has characterized the denomination from the onset. Although an over-emphasis of either feature can lead to less than authentic versions of Christian life and thought (an excessive spiritualism and/or emotionalism on the one hand, and a charismatically dry and formalistic traditionalism on the other hand), one of the denomination's great successes (in terms of effecting a vibrant Christian life which in turns produces committed constituents) has been that it treasures the latter (subjective experiences of the Spirit), but then always measures those in light of the former (Scripture).[74]

Another strength of the denomination's commitment to Scripture's role in the sanctification process concerns its beliefs about people. Whereas the Orthodox are less concerned that the Christian person understand his or her faith, AG constituents are unequivocal that the Christian must grow in the knowledge of the Lord. In recent years the AG has been slow to explicitly teach the doctrine of sanctification to its adherents, but it has been more militant than ever in striving to educate them in the Pentecostal faith (concerning both its homeland efforts and its foreign missions programs). Simply stated, Pentecostals hold (evangelicals would agree here) that one's Christian faith will be strengthened, and that one is more likely to manifest a Christ-like nature, when one has an understanding of God's Scriptural revelation.

Whether or not the New Testament writers, when they exhorted their readers toward sanctification, used the term "word" with explicit reference to the written Scriptures is much debated. The AG's own preeminent New Testament scholar, Gordon Fee, believes that Paul, for his part, was referring to the Spirit-empowered preaching (and singing) about the gospel of Jesus Christ. Christian authority is always rooted in the person of Jesus Christ - the person who realized God's promises and manifested God's trustworthy character.[75] That

---

[74] Pentecostals have long been aware of the problems either extreme can cause. In 1930 Donald Gee said, "You never know what may happen next in a live Pentecostal Meeting. Therein lies wonderful attraction and opportunity, but also a constant element of peril. Indeed the danger may drive some to seek refuge back again in the old 'cut-and-dried' methods of conducting a religious service where everything has to run to a pre-arranged programme [sic]; but the loss involved will be irreparable. That the Holy Spirit shall have absolutely unhampered opportunity in our midst is one of the things we have stood. . . for from the beginning of this Movement, and it represents a return to the New Testament standard which we believe is wholly in accord with the Divine Mind." Gee, *Concerning Shepherds and Sheepfolds* (London: Elim, 1952, rev. ed.), 54. See also 58.
[75] Fee, *Empowering Presence*, 258, n. 719; 288-289; 649; 728-729; 848-850.

evangelicals, Fundamentalists, and Pentecostals traditionally appeal to 2 Timothy 3:16 ("All Scripture is inspired by God and profitable for teaching, for reproof, for correction, [and] for training in righteousness.") in order to assert the authority of Scripture, only begs the question as to what constituted Scripture for Paul at the time of his writing (most scholars agree that he was referring to the Old Testament).[76] Similarly, the commonplace argument that if the Old Testament was authoritative, then it logically follows that the New Testament itself is similarly authoritative, only further begs the issue. That is, one must be able to determine who decided which early Christian books were and were not canonical. The answer is obviously the church, but it is an answer which some conservative evangelicals (among them Pentecostals) are hesitant to assert because it seems to give the church more authority than Scripture (it obviously need not).[77]

As our delineation of the AG's theological foundations revealed, even in recent years there is little distinction made among AG writers and theologians between the person of the Word of God and the written Word of God. John

---

[76] Jesus' statement in Matt. 5:18, ". . . until heaven and earth pass away, not one letter, not one stroke of a letter, will pass from the law until all is accomplished," similarly referred to the Old Testament. Higgins, "God's Inspired Word," 95, agrees that Paul in 2 Tim. 3:16 was referring to the Old Testament. However, his argument that Paul (1 Cor. 2:13; 1 Tim. 5:18) and Peter (1 Pet. 1:12-18, and 3:16) both implied that they were writing Scripture (or that they were implying that other early Christian documents were inspired) is questionable. Furthermore, his argument still does not resolve the issue regarding the many other documents which are not referred to in those passages but which are nonetheless in the canon.

[77] Conservative Protestants are wary to grant that it was the church which determined which documents were authoritative and therefore to be canonized because it seems to indicate that Scripture would have no authority apart from that recognition. Such Protestants, for their own epistemological biases, believe Scripture stands authoritative on its own. However, someone first needed to write Scripture. Moreover, someone subsequently needed to collect, preserve, and study the early Christian documents for veracity and apostolicity or else those documents would have fallen into disregard and disuse. Clearly, those who wrote the New Testament were in the earliest church. Those persons who collected, preserved, and studied those documents obviously were post-apostolic Christians in the church. It is the church which recognizes the authority of Scripture, but in its so recognizing it in no way supplants the authority of Scripture. Whereas the church merely testifies to the truth and power of Scripture, Scripture cannot be studied accurately as anything other than the authoritative revelation of God as recognized by the church.

Higgins, in his quotation of Carl Henry sustains this analysis, "It is true that the Christian's authority is more than paper and ink, but 'God's propositional revelation. . . cannot. . . be distinguished from divine self-revelation."[78] We note this personal-propositional fusion to contrast the AG's understanding with that of the Orthodox. The latter's ontological framework - while averring an iconic participation of the inspired Scriptures in God - is more careful about not blurring the identities of Scripture and the *Logos*.

We also note the AG's perception of Scripture to place the denomination within its own milieu. That the AG consistently capitalizes the letter "W" in Word when referring to Scripture is no accident (again, the denomination shares this emphasis with evangelicals more broadly). Its proponents recognize the epistemological quagmire which is perceived to arise if it is admitted that there is an authoritative distinction between God's person and God's written revelation. The denomination's position paper on inerrancy said, "to reject the doctrine of inerrancy transfers the question of truth from the objective into the realm of the subjective."[79] Consistent with the Protestant anthem of Sola Scriptura, the AG believes (rightly, we would resolutely affirm) that Scripture is God's authoritative revelation. But because its own cultural-philosophic milieu demands empirical proof for epistemological formulations (whether for science or religion), AG theologians and ecclesiarchs have been rather forced to staunchly assert that Scripture is on equal footing with the Word (*Logos*) of God, not only for its sanctification doctrine, but its theology in general. (The AG did not begin to use the specific word "inerrancy" until it published a position paper on the topic in 1976. That document noted that "inerrancy" had been adopted by the Executive Presbytery in 1970.)[80]

That is, both in its inner-denominational homiletic discussions and its apologetic discussions with the broader society the AG has been rather forced into interpreting and defending Scripture as a juridical-empirical *res*.[81] This *res*,

---

[78] Higgins, "God's Inspired Word," 83, quoting Carl Henry, *God, Revelation and Authority* (NY: Channel Press, 1964), 3:462.

[79] *The Inerrancy of Scripture*, 9.

[80] *The Inerrancy of Scripture*, 2. It is noteworthy that Harold Lindsell's book, *The Battle for the Bible* (Grand Rapids: Zondervan) was published in 1976.

[81] This is notable in the preponderance of "promise" language in AG devotional materials. E.g., one AG official exemplified this Scripture-as-legal-document mentality when he said, "We are told that there are 32,000 promises in the Word of God, all of which are calculated and designed to meet our every human need." The implication was that since God "promised" these things he (and/or Scripture) was therefore trustworthy.

like any other evidence from history, can be studied for the sake of reaching a verdict.[82] As a *res*, and in light of how these are studied, Scripture is thus argued to be true - first and foremost - because it can be historically proven accurate. That Scripture is God's preeminent, providentially preserved, message of truth and life is consistently secondary in the debate. And we should say, to clarify this juridical-empirical apologetical emphasis is not at all to argue against Scripture's historical accuracy, but it is to point out the degree to which conservative evangelicals have fallen prey to the epistemological presuppositions of the empirical arena in which they find themselves.

We want to reiterate, that although the AG (typifying Pentecostalism in specific, and evangelicals in general) has historically appealed to Scripture as a kind of evidentiary prooftext in its apologetics and theology, it has traditionally encouraged its parishioners to allow Scripture to "breathe" new life into them as the Holy Spirit speaks through the text amid new circumstances and situations. This latter hermeneutic is a much more dynamic view of Scripture[83] and is yet another fascinating dimension that Pentecostals and the Orthodox share. The Orthodox understand the text of Scripture to be a religious "happening," rather than a static transmitter of measurable, or quantifiable, truth. Scripture is a Christian epistemological bulwark and an embodiment of truth because it participates in the very life of God, not because it can be proven accurate by scientific methods (something which the Orthodox are generally ambivalent about anyway). Not unlike the participation in the other-worldly reality (divine, eternal, eschatological) that icons (which participate in the reality of Jesus

---

J. O. Savell, "Believing God," *PE*, February 21, 1954, 4. The evangelical-Pentecostal "promise" language is yet another topic deserving a richer analysis.

[82] A great seller among evangelicals and Pentecostals (although it is understandable in light of their own cultural-philosophical milieu) is Josh McDowell's, *Evidence that Demands a Verdict: Historical Evidences for the Christian Faith* (San Bernardino, California: Campus Crusade for Christ International, 1972).

[83] Several Pentecostal scholars have attempted to define and describe the Pentecostals' dynamic hermeneutic. McLean, "Toward a Pentecostal Hermeneutic"; Richard Israel, D. Albrecht and R. McNally, "Pentecostals and Hermeneutics: Texts, Rituals and Community," *Pneuma*, 15:2 (Fall 1993), 137-161; Timothy Cargal, "Beyond the Fundamentalist-Modernist Controversy: Pentecostals and Hermeneutics in a Postmodern Age," *Pneuma*, 15:2 (Fall 1993), 163-187; Joseph Byrd, "Paul Ricoeur's Hermeneutical Theory and Pentecostal Proclamation," *Pneuma*, 15:2 (Fall 1993), 203-222. See also the Spring 1994 issue of *Pneuma* which is given over to the topic of Pentecostal hermeneutics.

Christ, the saint, or the angel depicted), the eucharist (which participates in and transmits the life of the risen incarnate Christ), and the Liturgy (uniting both heaven and earth, and time and eternity) facilitate; the written word of God is a divine-human "happening" through which God communicates himself. At the minimum, the Orthodox' position protects the word of God from being forced to be something other (for example, a scientific journal) than what it originally was. Nonetheless, the Orthodox' position exalts Scripture as being supreme in the Christian epistemology, though on different grounds than is argued in the Christian West.[84]

Lastly, with regard to its use of and interpretation of Scripture, in the AG's sanctification theology in specific, and its life and practice in general, there is little awareness that the way in which it teaches its constituents to interpret Scripture stems from a larger and often unrecognized meta-framework. This meta-framework is variously informed by: a) church history - both its immediate Wesleyan, Holiness, Reformed, and evangelical backgrounds and the larger sweep of church history; b) the humanistic influence which variously fed the Renaissance, the Reformation (as for example Zwingli and Melanchthon represented),[85] and the Enlightenment ; c) Existentialism, with its individualizing thrust for hermeneutics in specific (as say occurs in Neo-orthodoxy), and religious experience in general; d) the above mentioned reaction to Catholicism and religious formalism; and, e) the aforementioned empirical-juridical framework of Western civilization which demands proof and evidence. For centuries the universal Christian community has referred to its meta-framework as church tradition, but because to no small extent Pentecostals arose on the religious scene as a reactionary movement to the established Christian denominations and their practice (something the Holiness and Pentecostal folks both referred to as "cold formalism") the word "tradition" is unilaterally avoided in AG discussions about Scripture. Because they believe their tradition is the fullest and most accurate representation of Christianity, the Orthodox are proud of theirs, and even appeal to it as "the natural and essential

---

[84] Thomas Torrance, *Divine Meaning: Studies in Patristic Hermeneutics* (Edinburgh: T and T Clark, 1995), 1-10.

[85] The former of whom the AG follows regarding the communion emblems as only being memorials. Humanism is not employed here in the modern and often polemical sense, but in its earliest sense wherein human persons were being increasingly understood in more naturalistic (including the idea of human personality) and less religious (less medieval, less metaphysical) ways. Cf. Copleston, *A History of Philosophy, Vol. 3: Ockham to Suarez,* 17-23, 217-220, 227-228, *et passim.*

'term of reference' in Orthodoxy."[86] Contrastingly, because they are opposed to it on political grounds (in terms of the Catholic church's structure and abuses)[87] and formal grounds (in terms of epistemology), the Pentecostals reject tradition as an authoritative source or framework, even though in 1954 the AG church-leader Donald Gee was pointing out that their theology and practice was being made static because of it.[88]

The AG will better understand its own theology, and its own theological motivations, firstly when it admits to having a larger meta-framework (tradition) for interpreting Scripture. Secondly, it will be better able to critique the larger culture's epistemological assumptions and doctrines when it understands more carefully what those are. As this study is implying, Pentecostals can learn many things from the Orthodox. One of those on a more negative front is that if one is not able to recognize and criticize one's own meta-framework, whether religious or secular, one will eventually become just like it. Worse, one will then impugn all others who do not resemble oneself. In all of this, sanctification - the process of becoming Christ-like - has corporate dimensions. Entire traditions and denominations can lose their Christ-like ability to discern between the world and God's Kingdom. Over time, they can become so pervaded by the broader culture's values and epistemological necessities (sadly, this pervasion occurs amid the very work of Christian mission to and within those cultures) that they lose their single-mindedness for Christ and his Kingdom. Ceasing to be Christ's yeast, they become subsumed by the loaf.

---

[86]Schmemann, *Church, World, Mission,* 87.

[87] For example, James Railey, Jr., and Benny Aker, "Theological Foundations," 43; and, Higgins, "God's Inspired Word," 81-83; both pieces are in *Theology, A Pentecostal Perspective.*

[88] "This I Believe: The Use and Abuse of Dogmatism," *RT,* 30 (November 5, 1954), 4-5. Gee astutely noted that the AG's "Statement of Fundamental Truths" had ironically become a creed, despite the original founders' intentions. Creeds have always been important elements for church tradition.

9

The Means Of Sanctification

> I saw a field where floods had lain,
> I saw the cold dark mire
> But when I passed that way again,
> I saw the emerald fire
> Of grasses shimmering with light,
> And oh! it was a lovely sight!
> I saw a man with anguished face
> Drift on sin's purple flood.
> I saw him find redeeming grace
> And give his life to God.
> And oh! in that transforming hour
> I felt the Master's mighty power!
> More beautiful than grass or light
> Is a human soul, sin-cleansed and bright![1]

Having established the AG's theological foundations for its sanctification doctrine, it remains our task to delineate the denomination's means of sanctification. That is, what specific things or practices does the denomination believe helps facilitate sanctification? For at least three reasons, this task is problematic. Firstly, Pentecostals - like their Orthodox counterparts - believe that all of life can be used by God the Father to bring us into conformity with the image of his Son. This sanctifying transformation is not limited to what occurs within church walls, prayer meetings, or small-group Bible studies. Because the Spirit is able to speak, and convey his charisma, through most any means (provided the believer is open to the Spirit), his work of transformation can take place in a multitude of ways and settings. Not only is the churchly realm an avenue for transformation, so also is the mundane. Life's daily tests and trials can provide grist for the mill of sanctification,[2] as can otherwise

---

[1] Grace V. Watkins, "The Transformed," *PE*, January 18, 1976, 2.

[2] A. G. Ward, "Walking With God," *PE*, December 11, 1920, 3-4; J. H. J. Barker, "A Refiner of Silver," *PE*, January 19, 1958, 4-5; Juanita Stetz, "You Can Profit From

routine acts like walking through a forest,[3] or a walk past a grassy green field, as the above opening poem indicated. Secondly, our task is problematic if only because the denomination does not always discuss Christian transformation under the category of sanctification. We must be clear, throughout its history the AG has regularly taught about how one can and should become more like Christ. But this process of transformation can be described under any number of categories: preparing for Christ's return, how best to accomplish God's purposes, how to have the most spiritual power in one's life, how best to experience God's blessings, and the like. For this study's sake, we will consider those kinds of discussions as fair game, if only because they pertain to growth in Christ-likeness and godliness. Thirdly, our task in this chapter is rendered somewhat problematic because the AG's theologians, while they are clear to explain the doctrine's theological foundations, do little to explain the believer's role in appropriating Christ's sanctifying work. There are two reasons for the silence in this regard: 1) the issue is rather moot for them because they know their readers understand that sanctification occurs through both the churchly modes and one's personal relationship with Christ through the Spirit; and, 2) AG theologians have almost entirely limited their efforts to defending the denomination's core doctrinal issues - sanctification is not numbered among those.[4]

In light of the last characteristic (a specific theological lacuna), our method will primarily be to survey the denomination's magazines, *Pentecostal Evangel* (and its historical antecedents) and its British counterpart, *Redemption Tidings*, in order to present some examples of those means which occur most frequently and/or with the greatest degree of emphasis.

For the sake of delineation, the AG's pastoral teaching on the means of sanctification will be presented as residing in three definitional tributaries. The first tributary has two components: a) those discussions which remarkably reflect the Eastern Orthodox' own ascetic ideas regarding Christian transformation and spirituality; and, b) the codification of moralisms. That the Orthodox-like discussions occurred mainly, but not exclusively, in the earliest era of the Pentecostal movement reveals that the denomination's religious vocabulary (at the minimum) has changed, and that its mind-set (more broadly)

Pressure," *PE*, May 3, 1964, 13; George Wood, "How to Grow Spiritually in 1984," *PE*, January 1, 1984, 8-10.

[3] George Holmes, "Reflections Among the Redwoods," *PE*, July 7, 1985, 4-5.

[4] Those include Spirit-baptism, Eschatology, Christ's atoning work, and physical healing.

has changed. The presence of moralisms has not faded entirely in the AG; this is a fact revealing that the primitivistic impulse of Pentecostalism has not entirely disappeared.[5] In the second contributing tributary, we will show how the various means of personal devotions and revivals can impact one's sanctification process. This second definitional tributary shows that the Pentecostals resemble the broader (and older) evangelical context, a context which defines Christianity largely in terms of individual piety. The third sanctifying tributary displays how the Pentecostals took a very Western and evangelical tenet - God's purpose for one's life - and "Pentecostalized" it with the doctrine of Spirit-baptism. The third tributary's currents have been running deep within Pentecostalism's spirituality and theology since the movement's onset. Not only are God's purpose and Spirit-baptism inter-related in the AG's teaching on sanctification, it is also the case that together they impel the denomination's missionaries and missions programs. As such, they can accurately be described as the denomination's *raison d'être*. This third tributary, as will be argued, especially in contradistinction to the Orthodox, specifically locates the Pentecostals within their own Western cultural-philosophical-epistemological milieu (the second tributary of personal piety could also accurately be analyzed with regard to the larger existential milieu), a milieu characterized by pragmatism.

A word of qualification is in order. By examining the AG's means of sanctification via three tributaries, or definitional rubrics, we do not mean to imply that there was, or is, no intermixing of these various streams. Even though we will look at them separately, one would obviously be taught to exercise *humility* in *prayer*, or that *prayer* is necessary for *revival*, or that *humility* will help to effect God's *purpose* in one's life, or *that Spirit-baptism* is central to *God's purpose* in one's life, and so on. An AG member, whether in 1929 or 1999, could be taught to employ all of these simultaneously, just as an Orthodox parishioner could be encouraged to pursue *theosis* on either sacramental or hesychastic lines, or both. The emphasis upon the specific means, for an AG layperson, would largely be contingent upon the emphasis of his or her own pastor.

---

[5] See my chapter on the AG's historical background for more on primitivism as a means of physical and ethical escape.

The First Tributary: Early Pentecostalism

Parallels with Orthodoxy

The specific similarities with Orthodoxy that we will note have to do with the believer's inner life: guarding against temptation, the practice of silence, and the importance of humility. There are other similarities with Orthodoxy,[6] but these three were the ones most consistently discussed in AG literature.

GUARDING AGAINST TEMPTATION
The single greatest motive for self-examination, throughout the years of AG literature, has not been sanctification itself. Rather, the archetypal reason for self-examination has been the imminence of Christ's second coming. As the AG emphasizes it, one must be ready for Jesus' own return (consistently portrayed as a fearful - not hopeful - event), lest one be left behind. We make this qualification to remind the reader of the Pentecostals' traditional heightened eschatological awareness (something little addressed in this study). Secondary motives for self-examination, as will become evident below, have a consistently pragmatic character. That is, one's sanctification, one's growth in Christ-likeness, is only occasionally an issue that is an end in itself. AG constituents are only occasionally taught to become Christ-like. They are only occasionally taught to be "deep wells" because it is the most authentic way to be Christian. Those qualifications aside, there were in fact discussions of sanctification and spiritual growth which will be delineated herein.

---

[6] Repentance could have been studied separately, but it is subsumed in other categories herein. Still other topics important in Orthodox asceticism that AG proponents rarely treated included the confession of sins and the shedding of tears. While AG readers were regularly exhorted to confess their sins to God, they were rarely instructed to do so to other believers. The shedding of tears was almost exclusively limited to its necessary role in intercessory prayer for the salvation of souls and the spreading of revival. E.g., Donald Gee, "Tears At The Beginning," *Pentecost* (A British Pentecostal Periodical), September 1954, 17; Gee, "Mighty Growth and Many Tears," *PE*, July 13, 1952, 3-4; Arne Vick, "The Ministry of Tears," *PE*, September 23, 1951, 3-4, 15-16. Alternately stated, the topic of shedding tears almost never appeared in treatments on sanctification or personal growth. One exception was an excerpt of Francois Fenelon's writings (a Frenchman who lived in the seventeenth century), "Steps to Perfection," *PE*, February 20, 1966, 32.

Previously we noted that the AG does not believe temptation itself constitutes sin, but in its earliest years it taught that temptation could originate in, or play upon, a person's natural appetites and internal drives. (Again, it would likely aver to believing as much today, it's just that it is no longer an emphasis.) Myer Pearlman taught that a person's spirit (that something which distinguishes humankind from all other creations) can be mastered by any number of forces, forces either good or evil. To the extent that a person allows those forces to master him, he can variously be described as having a "haughty spirit," a "perverse spirit," a "hasty spirit," or a "humble and contrite spirit." Eventually those forces can rule over a person. Pearlman taught that we must examine ourselves and see to it that our spiritual dimension rules over the soul-life, something he referred to as the "self-life or natural life." When the spiritual dimension gives way to unseemly natural appetites, described as "evil passions" by Pearlman, the person will have become a "carnal" person. For the non-Christian, regeneration is the solution to carnality. For the Christian, repentance and renewed commitment to God are the solutions to carnality.[7]

In 1916, *The Weekly Evangel*'s editor taught about temptations in a manner similar to the Orthodox' own introspective way. Although he did not use the word passion in his discussion, he noted that some people are compelled by temptation's power, even to the extent that they are "at a loss to know why." Even those who daily experience God's grace, and even those who are committed to Christian service, can suffer temptations so subtle that they are not recognized. The source for all temptations, this editor continued, resides in each person. Sometimes natural inclinations go awry, at other times an unholy desire is at first entertained and then unrejected. If it is unrejected long enough, eventually one will not be able to escape the unholy desire's drawing power, just as Scripture said, "When lust conceives, it bringeth forth sin." (Another writer similarly said, "God did not intend for our desires to control us; He intended for us to control our desires.")[8] The editor instructed his readers to guard against allowing even apparently good desires to lead them in selfish and sinful directions. There is a clear difference between "God placing something upon one's heart" (a phrase the author rightly noted as being regularly cited by Pentecostals) and something which is already in one's heart. We must not allow

---

[7] Pearlman, *Doctrines,* 103. Another who explicitly spoke of the fleshly passions was A. F. Missen, "Keep Thyself Pure," *RT*, May 7, 1943, 10-11, "Our bodies. . . have passions and appetites which, though in themselves legitimate and healthy, will, if played with, set on fire the whole course of evil desire and practice."

[8] Hardy W. Steinberg, "Control Yourself!" *PE*, September 24, 1972, 2-3.

ourselves to confuse the two. He encouraged his readers to guard against temptation in its earliest stages and to watch and test every desire to see if it be from God.[9]

Others warned of sin's developmental power. People rarely sin unwittingly or simply upon a moment's notice. Rather, a sinful notion will enter a person's thoughts or heart (the two are not always carefully distinguished by AG writers) and fester therein. Hart Armstrong, in 1953, said, "No man sins suddenly. First he conceives the sin in his mind; then by a series of evil thoughts he overcomes the natural repugnance to the deed, the strivings of conscience and training, the influences of the Holy Spirit and of good friends, until at last the evil thoughts succeed in producing a decision to commit an outward sin."[10]

The antidote to the perpetuation of sinful thoughts in one's mind and heart, as Armstrong described above, is not only to know God - as crucial as that is - but also to know oneself and one's environs. One must know one's own weaknesses, one's own interests, and where one is most likely to fall. As one Redemption Tidings author put it, "Points where we have failed in the past should be marked with a danger signal." "We should learn well," he continued, "the weaknesses and the possibilities of our own natures, and not trifle with them."[11] Moreover, one must recognize that sin takes root, Paul Pipkin said, "in the imagination of the heart." Having gained a footing therein, sin gathers energy and begins to move the will. Eventually, Pipkin said, "there is a lurking volcano in every heart that can explode" unless it and its power are "brought into subjection." Having placed the motives of one's heart before God, and having recognized the sin that lurks therein, one must understand God's perspective on the matter: he does not hate the human heart (he created it), but he "hates the evil imaginations that are often entertained" there. Like Daniel, who purposed in his heart not to defile himself, we must purpose not to defile ourselves. That purposing begins with guarding the attitudes and appetites of

---

[9] "Temptations," *The Weekly Evangel*, August 12, 1916, 1. See also A. Gregory Wilkinson, "Filled with the Holy Spirit," *The Weekly Evangel*, October 20, 1917, 6.

[10] Hart R. Armstrong, "The Thought Life of a Christian," *PE*, October 25, 1953, 3. More recently Craig Brian Larson described temptation's, and sin's, existential work, "Dangerous Even When Dead," *PE*, April 23, 1989, 4-6.

[11] Leonard Gittings, "How to Conquer Sin: Our Position With Regard To Self," *RT*, March 1, 1934, 12.

our heart. Daniel's success did not begin with the spectacular event of the lion's den, it began in his beginning years with how he examined his heart.[12]

Not only is such self-examination "absolutely necessary for our sanctification," as Arthur Hedley said, there are many fruits which can result from careful and prayerful examination. When we allow the Holy Spirit to search our hearts and thoughts (Ps. 139:23-4) we are better able, Hedley said, "to see ourselves as we really are in God's sight." Such a vista results in the awareness not only of our need for salvation and forgiveness, but also in the awareness of how unjust it is to judge and condemn others. Humility is another fruit that can grow in prayerful introspection. Said Hedley, "It is deeply humiliating when we examine ourselves and search the innermost recesses of our heart. Then we see that we have no cause for pride, boastfulness, or self-righteousness, and the prayer goes up from the heart, 'God be merciful to me a sinner,' (Luke 18:13).'" Those unwilling to exercise such self-examination will remain "nominal Christians" who "know so little of union and communion with Christ."[13]

Not only overt sins must be guarded against, one's attitudes need to be recognized. Depression, pessimism, cynicism, self-pity and bitterness can all manifest themselves through evil words and actions. Echoing Proverbs 23:7 ("For as he thinks within himself, so he is."), Jesus himself, in Luke 6:45, taught that a person acts and speaks in accordance with the treasure in his heart. In the course of life it is natural to experience tragedy and misfortune, but one can still govern one's attitudes and choose which kind of thoughts one will think. Not only is the believer supposed to examine her attitudes and thought-life and root out the negative, she is also supposed to fill her thought-life, positively, with the

---

[12] Paul H. Pipkin, "Know Your Heart," *PE*, June 17, 1962, 4-5, 17. See also, Leonard Gittings, "How to Develop Spiritually: The Necessity For Concern," *RT*, June 15, 1934, 5-6; and, Hardy Steinberg, "Control Yourself!" *PE*, September 24, 1972, 2-3.

[13] Arthur Hedley, "A Spiritual Checkup," *PE*, March 8, 1964, 6-7. Smith Wigglesworth taught similarly in a reproduction of one of his sermons, "A Living Sacrifice," *RT*, April 23, 1937, 1. The great evangelist Dwight Moody affirmed the same when he said, "Fervency in prayer by the power of the Holy Spirit is a good preservative against thought rushing in. Flies never settle on a boiling pot." Quoted in *The Weekly Evangel*, August 11, 1917, 3.

life and truth of Scripture. Hardy Steinberg said, "the Bible emphasizes getting the Word into the heart," so that one can have a more Christ-like thought-life.[14]

Along with examining one's heart, one must be aware of the broader society's influences. Just because society is becoming lax in its moral stance, just because culture argues that each person is his or her own moral arbiter, and just because society says the outward appearance (clothing and cosmetics) of a person is more important than one's inner state, does not mean such things are true. We need to place our motives, and our whole selves, before God and allow him to cleanse and refresh us with his love. God alone is the standard against which we must measure ourselves.[15]

Although fasting has, in the AG's history, more regularly been encouraged with regard to intercessory prayer (deeply affective and effectual prayer variously made for the unsaved, those in dire crises, national emergencies, spiritual battles, and revivals' preparatory times; prayer understood as wrestling with, or for, God), it has also had a place in discussions about the believer's inner life. One should not fast to manipulate God into doing something. Neither should one equate fasting as a one-for-one source of spiritual power. Instead fasting is a way to focus one's existential self for spiritual purposes. Donald Gee summed up a healthy presentation of fasting:

> The value of fasting for the Christian lies in it being an entirely voluntary act of self-discipline. Since self-indulgence is the natural inclination of all of us, anything that heads us off in the opposite direction has positive value. Discipleship means denying ourselves. This is the essence of fasting. It means far more than going without food. It should include extravagance in dress, housing, cars and all unnecessary ostentation. The opposite extreme of asceticism is to be equally avoided. Our Lord wants His disciples to live normal and balanced lives.[16]

Gee went on to note that whereas the power of God in one's life can be lost through "spiritual carelessness," fasting and prayer exhibits our sincerity to God

---

[14] Hardy Steinberg, "Your thoughts can make or break you," *PE*, April 9, 1972, 2-3, 7. Quote from p. 3. See also, Maurice Allan, "Destroy Evil Thoughts Before They Destroy You," *PE*, August 15, 1965, 9.

[15] Alice Muse, "On Guard," *PE*, March 12, 1967, 5; E. H. Ogier, "Spiritual Adornment," *RT*, May 31, 1940, 7; Frank J. Lindquist, "Resist!" *PE*, January 23, 1966, 2-3.

[16] Donald Gee, "Prayer and Fasting," *RT*, June 12, 1959, 3.

and helps to ready our existential selves for God's purposes. In all of that, fasting "takes its place among all acts of sanctification."[17]

THE PRACTICE OF SILENCE
If some AG constituents recognized the necessity of introspection for sanctification, others recognized the important role which silence can play. J. T. Boddy, in 1920, urged his readers to practice seeking God in silence, "There is a profound stillness produced by the Spirit, which is freighted with life and power divine." Pentecostals, he continued, were well known for their shouts of victory and praise. But they ought also remember that God's presence and direction can be discerned amid silence, something he also called a "holy hush." Furthermore, it is not just an external silence and quiet that he encouraged, but an internal quiet that should be maintained. Using a biblical example, Boddy noted that Elijah did not sense God's presence in the great wind, the earthquake, or the fire, but amid the "divine stillness." The very universe's functions, Boddy argued, reveal that "all power. . . is distilled in silence."[18] Similarly, Howard Carter, a prominent early British Pentecostal leader,[19] taught about the role of inner silence for private and corporate prayer. He said, "I often needed to 'round up' my straying thoughts, and bring my mind to a determined concentration on spiritual things."[20]

Like Boddy years earlier, Ernest Williams in the 1960s addressed the typically exuberant, and even noisy, Pentecostals. Correcting those who believe the Lord is only present amid emotional expressiveness, Williams taught that God can also be found within a believer's inner quiet. Emotional outbursts need not be squelched, as some "staid ecclesiastics with their cold reasoning"[21] would argue, but an inner calm and a quiet soul are also the marks of an inwardly rich Christian. Furthermore, not only is the believer to manifest Christian character outwardly, in terms of Christian service, but also inwardly, in the depths of one's being. In fact, "the interior is more important." The Pentecostal believer

---

[17] Gee, "Prayer and Fasting," *RT*, June 12, 1959, 4.
[18] John Thomas Boddy, "The Value of Stillness," *PE*, November 13, 1920, 4.
[19] Carter exemplifies how much the Pentecostals' have changed over the years in that he "was imprisoned a conscientious objector during World War 1." D. D. Bundy, "Howard A. Carter," in *DPCM*, 109.
[20] Howard Carter, "People Who Love Prayer," *RT*, November 15, 1934, 4.
[21] Ernest S. Williams, "Inner Calm," *PE*, March 24, 1968, 6.

needs to recognize that God can deal powerfully in "silence, quietness of spirit, and self-possession."[22]

In 1943 a British writer urged his readers to seek a silence of the soul. His reason was that amid the soul's silence one variously cease from life's turmoil, hear God whisper, and experience God's glory.[23] Similarly, an American writer, in 1953, described silently waiting upon God in language resembling the Orthodox' own discussions. Because God yearns to love and bless those who love and bless him (Is. 64:4; 1 Cor. 2:9), a person is not supposed to approach God as would a selfish beggar: one is to seek God for himself, and not for the blessings he can give. One must be silent and still in God's presence, but this does not mean one is to be either mentally or emotionally inactive. Instead, one must silently wait for him like a yearning lover. One should "relax from all strain," "abandon all fear," and obtain "a state of objective rest with confident anticipation." This state of anticipatory rest is like a voluntary surrender. God will, the author affirmed, reveal himself in intimate and personal ways, just like a lover who kisses his lover's mouth and shows his lover tender affection. But, one cannot hurry God and one cannot be impatient with him, even if it takes days of silent waiting. "The impatient restlessness of the human spirit is not easily subdued," he said, "yet it must be conformed to the deep calm of God's Spirit before God can manifest Himself." With regard to subduing human impatience, the author reminded his readers that waiting upon God is indeed a spiritual discipline involving constancy. Though the believer may be at times moved by emotional impulse, or even "a shallow sense of duty," the overriding motives for his seeking after God must be "a deep and abiding love" and "a yearning after Him who alone can satisfy."[24]

THE IMPORTANCE OF HUMILITY

The presence of pride in the believer's life has all manner of repercussions for the believer's existential nature. Pride can distance one from God's presence (an affective and existential - experiential - understanding of God's presence is implied), and cause one to be less pliable in God's hands.[25] Pride can cause one to become self-reliant and aloof from God. It can blind one to one's sins and faults while at the same time heighten one's awareness of those things in others.

---

[22] Williams, "God in the Silence," *PE*, March 11, 1962, 4-5.

[23] S. A. Pinchbeck, "The Reward of Stillness," *RT*, April 9, 1943, 6-7.

[24] Walter H. Beuttler, "Waiting for God," *PE*, May 31, 1953, 3-4.

[25] "Transformation," Editorial, *PE*, December 10, 1921, 5.

Pride is, one editor said, "the mother of selfish ambition and is the source from whence comes the desire to be seen and heard." The antidote to pride is humility. Like the supreme example of humility, Christ himself (Phil. 2:8), the believer is to crucify his self-appreciation. Such humility is not a hatred for the self or the body (God created those).[26] Neither is it something Donald Gee called a "studied humility," something outwardly portrayed in order to secure a "good welcome in religious meetings."[27] Instead, it involves putting to death of the selfish nature, choosing the lowly positions in life, and esteeming other people as better than oneself. So important is humility that God will indeed humble the believer with loving discipline, something which is often a bitter experience for the believer. But, if the Christian will humble himself, as Scripture instructs, the bitter nature of humility can be avoided.[28]

The Orthodox, especially the Russians, frequently talk about *kenosis* (Jesus' self- emptying, Phil. 2:5-11) in their spirituality. Pentecostals do not use that precise word, but some of their discussions markedly resemble the Orthodox' kenotic tone.[29] Writing in 1930, Mary Lowe Dickinson noted that it is normal for Christians to be outraged at incidents of personal injustice, "undeserved condemnation, unmerited abuse, misconception of our motives, [and] calling our good evil." In fact, she reminded, these incidents of personal insult are the rule in life, not the exception. The authentically Christian response to these things, she instructed, is to yield to them. Such yielding is neither to be done in a self-congratulatory way, nor should one call attention to one's own humble response. Moreover, the Christian is not to waste time making explanations or vindicating oneself.[30] Gee said, "You can't overcome the man that gets low enough; he wins all the time. There is something invincible in humility."[31] The

[26] "He Humbled Himself and Became Obedient" Editorial, *The Weekly Evangel*, July 8, 1916, 7-8.
[27] Donald Gee, "Mighty Growth and Many Tears," *PE*, July 13, 1952, 3-4.
[28] "He Humbled Himself and Became Obedient" July 8, 1916, 7-8.
[29] One theologian who did study *kenosis* was Frank Boyd, *The Kenosis of The Lord Jesus Christ*.
[30] Mary Lowe Dickinson, "Seeketh Not Her Own," *RT*, June 1930, 1-2. See also, W. J. Thomas, "The Satisfaction of the Meek," *RT*, February 10, 1939, 4-5; and, Melvin L. Hodges, "The Meaning of Discipleship," *PE*, August 25, 1968, 6-7.
[31] Donald Gee, "The Power of Worship," *RT*, May 6, 1938, 2.

truly Christ-like person will recognize that amid insults and injustices God is ultimately forcing one to struggle with one's own character.[32]

If humility is important for the lay Christian's growth and development, it is critical for that of the minister. In order to be genuinely successful - from God's perspective - the Pentecostal pastor must remember that all the good that he or she might do, for all the souls that might be saved under his or her ministry, it is God's grace that is causing the results. In order for the minister to be guided by God most effectively, and concomitantly guide his congregation, he or she must be submissive to God.[33] Those ministers who take selfish pride in their work fail to realize the potential damage they can cause. They ought not be proud about either their office, denomination, scholarship, physical appearance, eloquence, talent, or achievement. So dangerous is pride, said W. T. Gaston, that "there is no soul so holy in which its root will not strike, there is no employment so sacred on which it will not engraft itself. It will even make the Cross of Christ a pedestal on which to erect its deformed image."[34] The minister must allow God to humble himself or herself, which God will do with gentle kindness. Yet, if the minister stubbornly resists God's internal workings, he will, as it were, "put [him] between the mill-stones and grind [him] to powder, until He can mould [him] without any resistance to His purpose."[35]

We saw that the hesychastic strain of Orthodoxy encourages the believer to seek out a *staretz*, a spiritual therapist-confessor, from whom guidance, instruction, and humility could be learned. Even though the AG has historically recognized the need for sage spiritual counselors[36] (a common position is that district officials are pastors to the pastors), the specific notion that one should

---

[32] Mary Lowe Dickinson, "Seeketh Not Her Own," *RT*, June 1930, 1-2. See also, W. J. Thomas, "The Satisfaction of the Meek," *RT*, February 10, 1939, 4-5; and, Melvin L. Hodges, "The Meaning of Discipleship," *PE*, August 25, 1968, 6-7.

[33] Donald Gee, "Meekness: A Pre-Requisite for Guidance," *RT*, April 1, 1935, 4-5.

[34] W. T. Gaston, "Humility," *RT*, July 1927, 1.

[35] Author Unknown, "Subdued," *RT*, February 1928, 1.

[36] In 1930 Donald Gee was already teaching that the movement needed spiritual fathers. Leaders and pastors, Gee taught, are important, but even they need mature and wise counselors. Too often Pentecostal leaders and pastors were measured via their spiritual gifts instead of the depth of their character. *Concerning Shepherds and Sheepfolds,* 5-6, 43.

have a spiritual therapist-confessor is viewed warily by many Pentecostals.[37] Those qualifications notwithstanding, there is one anthem of submission which AG writers sounded with regularity: the issue of loyalty to one's pastor. There are many sociological reasons for such a prevalent anthem (not the least of which concerns power, at both the local church and district-wide levels), but there are instances where this is presented as one more facet of being humble. In 1914 Walter Mortlock instructed his readers not to allow themselves to be coerced by those in authority, but they should still respectfully follow those whom God has gifted with the ability to lead and teach. Those who listen to their pastors only for the sake of contradicting them and denying them will eventually stagnate spiritually. Conversely, those who follow their pastors and spiritual teachers "in the fear of the Lord" will be blessed by the promises of Scripture. The Lord blesses and teaches those who follow him with fear, something which Mortlock defined as "a holy affection, or gracious habit wrought in the soul by God." Submissive love, in the believer's life, is to be offered unto one's leaders, as well as unto God.[38]

The Codification of Moralisms

In keeping with their initial primitivistic impulses, especially in the earliest generations, AG constituents regularly warned one another, both in writing and in sermons, about the evils of the world which surrounded them. Because they believed they were shaping a purer version of Christianity than had existed since the apostolic era, there was a distinct need to distance themselves from anything perceived to be either a clear moral violation or a waste of precious time. This moralizing tendency fits together with the above mentioned Orthodox-like ascetic features as the two primary features of the AG's earliest tributary regarding sanctification.[39] The above ascetic features showed how the denomination internalized the doctrine of sanctification, while the activities and

---

[37] In order to counter the abuses of the Word of Faith movement, and its overemphasis on spiritual shepherds and submissive discipleship, the AG issued "The Discipleship and Submission Movement," Position Paper (Springfield, Missouri, 1976).

[38] Walter J. Mortlock, "The Conditions on Which God Has Promised to Teach Us," *The Christian Evangel*, August 1, 1914, 3.

[39] That is, in discussions specifically about one's process of becoming Christ-like. Again, the reader is reminded that Christian transformation was regularly discussed in AG literature outside the distinct boundaries of sanctification as a topic.

issues noted below demonstrate how the Pentecostals saw sanctification as involving external separation from the larger world's activities and values.

My own boyhood pastor's sermons were regularly colored by exhortations toward separation from the world, a theme that is scattered throughout the New Testament (Jn. 15:19; 2 Cor. 6:17; 1 Jn. 2:15) and which comprised an important dimension to our local church's worldview. In contrast to Orthodox theology, which holds that Christ's presence (via the church) will ultimately transform the world, we were instructed to flee the world, and abstain from its activities at all costs. And, fleeing the world was described in very specific terms. Our pastor, reflecting the denomination's corporate convictions, repeatedly identified and warned us about the world's immoral activities so that over time the specific activities to be shunned were ingrained in our congregation's collective psyche. The world's specific immoralities were thus codified - albeit rather implicitly and unconsciously - in the denomination's sin-lists.[40]

Within these sin-lists there were some things that have been unilaterally understood to be evil: smoking or chewing tobacco, drinking alcoholic beverages, using non-prescription drugs, relying on prescription drugs to deal with life's problems, attending dances or movies or theaters, and gambling of any kind. Other things which have been held to be evil, but with less unanimity than those noted above, include: buying life insurance (a deed betraying one's lack of faith), public swimming (in earlier years this included co-ed swimming), the wearing of cosmetics and jewelry (by women), going to the circus or fairs, bowling, tennis, playing cards or billiards, attending public ballgames or concerts, coffee and soda drinking, chewing gum, golfing, reading comic books or novels or newspapers, watching television (especially soap operas), any leisure activity done on a Sunday, seeing doctors, and even taking medicine.[41] Other, and even more specific, activities to be shunned could be as varied as the constituent's specific geographical location and the era in which one lived.[42]

---

[40] These sin-lists were carried over from the earlier Holiness movement, so that the AG was cut from the same historical-cultural cloth as other Pentecostals and evangelicals. Cf. Synan, *Holiness-Pentecostal Movement*, 190.

[41] E. N. Bell argued that taking medicine presumed an absence of faith. *PE*, January 5, 1918, 7.

[42] For example, for my own rural Oregon church, if one hunted, fished, or waterskied on Sunday one was sinning. There is a plethora of bibliographic sources which evince the denomination's moral codifications. A few include: "Separation," Editorial, *PE*, May 6, 1916, 8-9; E. N. Bell, "Questions and Answers: No. 385. 'Is it wrong for a Christian to

Lest the AG sound entirely severe or legalistic, there were indeed more thoughtful discussions which presented the implications and ramifications of indulging in the kinds of things and activities noted above. For example, one not only did not dance or go to nightclubs because people in the world did, one refrained from such because there was a definite atmosphere of sexual lasciviousness present there which could entice one to make wrong decisions. One ought not only refrain from smoking cigarettes or drinking alcohol because those in the world did, one also excluded such activities both because one knew one's own body was a temple of the Holy Spirit (1 Cor. 3:16; 6:19; 2 Cor. 6:16)[43] and because one did not want such activities to cause oneself to be dependent on others (in the sense of addiction or impaired judgment). Importantly, one did not partake of such things because it would color one's existential orientation with regard to prayer, worship, and ministry; one did not want to grieve the Holy Spirit either regarding one's actions or one's interior life.[44]

In the latter regard the AG quite resembles the Orthodox teaching about the necessity of a unity (perhaps alternately expressed as a correlation) between one's own existential self and God's Spirit. That is, in Pentecostal teaching, the effectiveness of one's prayers, worship, and/or ministry, is to a clear extent dependent upon the degree to which one's existential self is in harmony with God. The anointing of God's Spirit upon oneself - something terribly important in Pentecostalism's spirituality - is in no small way affected by one's existential purity and one's relationship with the Holy Spirit. Observing the AG's moralizing lists did not guarantee one's anointing with the Spirit (for prayer, worship, or ministry), nor did it necessarily mean one would be attuned to God's Spirit, but without scrupulous observance of the moral lists one could be sure to have neither the Spirit's anointing power nor a sense of his presence in one's daily life.

---

use tobacco?" *PE*, March 9, 1918, 9; "Abstinence," Assemblies of God Position Paper (Springfield, Missouri: Gospel Publishing, 1985).

[43] Cf., C. Stacey Woods, "What is Worldliness?" *PE*, May 27, 1956, 14-15; E. S. Williams, "Holiness," *PE*, April 12, 1959, 4-5; Morris Williams, "Sanctified believer behavior," *PE*, July 13, 1986, 4-6; Thomas E. Trask, "Have we changed?" *PE*, April 30, 1989, 8-9; and, Milton Beckett, "Worldliness, where is the line?" *PE*, August 20, 1989, 8-9.

[44] E.g., Frank Lindquist, "Resist!" *PE*, January 23, 1966, 2-3.

The Second Tributary: Personal Piety

As was noted earlier, the second tributary of AG thought on how one progresses in sanctification stems from the larger evangelical context and its emphasis upon personal piety. We will examine the means of having personal devotions and attending revivals. In the two following means, the primary focus is the individual person's own self, but this does not mean to imply that there are no outward, or communal, ramifications.

Personal Devotions

> In the secret of His presence, how my soul delights to hide!
> Oh, how precious are the lessons which I learn at Jesus' side!
> Earthly cares can never vex me, neither trials lay me low;
> For when Satan comes to tempt me, to the secret place I go.

> When my soul is faint and thirsty, 'neath the shadow of His wing
> There is cool and pleasant shelter, and a fresh and crystal spring;
> And my Saviour rests beside me, as we hold communion sweet;
> If I tried, I could not utter what He says when we thus meet.

> Would you like to know the sweetness of the secret of the Lord?
> Go and hide beneath His shadow: this shall then be your reward;
> And whene'er you leave the silence of that happy meeting place,
> You must mind and bear the image of the Master in your face.[45]

THE STRUCTURE AND FORM OF DEVOTIONS

AG ministers and laypersons, since the denomination's beginnings, have regularly been exhorted to set aside a distinct time each day for personal devotions. These devotions can variously consist of praising God, confessing sins, praying, listening in silence for God (also called "waiting on the Lord"), meditative Bible reading, or Bible study. Apart from the fact that one should be alone, there is no set formula. There are no prescribed prayers, there is not a liturgical calendar to direct one, and there are no preferred series of physical prostrations or movements to be made. One should simply be open to what the

---

[45] Ellen Lakshami Goreh, "In the Secret of His Presence," *PE*, February 23, 1964, 3.

Spirit is requiring of one and what he wants to do in and with one. He may only want to hear three words, "Lord, save me!" Or he may want communion lasting hours and requiring verbose intercession. In all of this, the Spirit will guide the believer to the right target and teach him or her how to pray.[46] Speaking from my own personal experience in the AG, it is fine for the believer to have a regular and structured devotion. Generally one begins with praise and confession, dimensions which prepare one's heart for further communion with God. Then one shifts to intercession or Scripture reading, movements which are subsequently followed by silence - in order that one may hear anything the Lord should want to communicate. Obviously the Spirit is not bound to either "show up" (although it is usually taught that he will) or "speak," but even if he should fail to do either of these for a prolonged season one must, because of one's love for Christ, still discipline oneself to seek God regularly.[47]

Whereas the believer needs to have a regularly scheduled devotional period for communion with God's Spirit, she also needs to be open to the leadings of the Spirit. The Holy Spirit may, from his own desire for loving fellowship with the Christian, occasionally impel her into prayer, no matter the time of day. Howard Carter instructed that those who are sensitive to the Spirit's guidance, those who already have a passion to pray, may "feel the promptings of the Holy Spirit." "The overwhelming grace of God revealed to us in the Cross of Calvary, and borne to us by the dove-like Spirit," Carter continued, "moves the deepest passions of our natures, and we seek the face of the Lord." Such Spirit-impelled prayer is like a joyous conversation between friends. People open to the Spirit in this way, he said, "forget the hours as a true lover always does, and they speak about the ONE they love." Eventually, when words begin to fail them in the attempt to "express the deepest longings of their souls, then the Holy Spirit makes intercession for them with groanings which cannot be uttered."[48]

---

[46] Chester I. Miller (Overseer, Pentecostal Church of Christ), "The Holy Spirit in the Believer's Prayer Life," *PE*, June 14, 1964, 8-9. Miller typified the Pentecostal flexibility in all of this by teaching that one could variously pray kneeling, standing, lying down, prostrate on the floor, or sitting. Furthermore, taking examples from numerous Biblical texts, one can pray anywhere.

[47] Dorothy C. Haskin, "Battle For The Quiet Time," *PE*, January 1, 1978, 11, sustains these comments.

[48] Howard Carter, "People Who Love Prayer," *RT*, November 15, 1934, 5. Original emphasis.

THE PURPOSE OF DEVOTIONS

Despite the traditional flexibility as to form, there are critical things the believer should know. The first concerns purpose. The devotional period is not supposed to be primarily a time of petition for needs (either one's own or those of others) or intellectual study,[49] though as the above iterated, both can be included. Instead, the main point is to renew one's existential self through communing with Christ's Holy Spirit. The devotional exercise should renew one's inner senses and help one to stay pliable, perceptive, and in tune with God's Spirit.[50] Richard Champion, a longtime *Pentecostal Evangel* editor, reminded his readers that time spent in secret with God will help one bear the image of Jesus. "Man's soul, like a sensitive photographic plate," he said "takes on the image of that to which it is exposed; and the longer the exposure, the clearer the image."[51]

In one's devotions, one must seek to create an edifying atmosphere, one that is conducive to communion with God. Just as the Orthodox hesychasts warn against mechanistic forms of ascetic prayer, the Pentecostals warn against mere formalism. That is, one will not simply move deeper in Christ by going through the ritual (a word avoided at all costs in describing devotions!). One will progress to the degree in which one's heart, one's passion, is involved in the endeavor. Although it is lengthy and specifically about prayer, the following quote, taken from a 1934 *Redemption Tidings* editorial, so marvelously captures the traditional Pentecostal sentiment regarding the necessity and purpose of devotions and the Pentecostal approach to spirituality - and their impact on one's existential self - that we will quote it in its entirety:

Preaching which is the outcome of wide reading and deep thinking moves the mind; particularly when based on sound Homiletics and backed by a forceful personality. But the mind is then more likely to be affected in favour of the preacher than the Christ. We have seen audiences held by such preaching, but when the preacher went the people went too, and one has afterwards looked in vain for even a residue of real work. *The mind has been gratified but the heart has not*

---

[49] Pentecostals, from their inception, have been wary of rationalism. The human mind is a magnificent creation, but when it runs unchecked and makes itself the rule and measure of existence it becomes guilty of idolatry. Cf. Menzies and Horton, *Bible Doctrines,* 17-18.

[50] Richard L. Dresselhaus, "Developing inner senses," *PE*, January 11, 1987, 12-14.

[51] Richard C. Champion, "Exposed to the Glory," *PE*, June 16, 1963, 4.

been moved, and it is only with the heart that man believes the things which change his life.

The heart can only be moved by an emotional atmosphere, and that can only be produced by the Holy Ghost. He alone, by the nearness of His Presence, can bring conviction. *The mind may be convinced by clever argument, but unless the heart is convicted, no permanent change can be expected.* Convincing preaching, then, is not enough. It must be exercised in the only atmosphere which can make it effective. This can be produced in no other way than by serious prayer. The word serious is used advisedly. There are so many prayer meetings which fail to produce the convincing atmosphere. It is so easy for prayer to become merely conventional, and therefore meaningless. *Unless prayer is the outcome of inward urge, it cannot be expected to produce anything.*

All this is only a word to the heart of those of us who are not, or ever can be, fine preachers. *If we cannot produce mental brilliance, we can produce an Holy Ghost atmosphere; and that will produce real results.* The finest preaching needs to be steeped in prayer. The poorest preaching may be steeped in it, then both can be equally successful. In a word, if we cannot preach we can pray, and if we CAN preach we MUST pray just the same. The pathway to success is therefore clear; let us cease to mourn our lack of talent and tread it with a brave heart. It is a better path than the way of popularity, has not so many dangerous stretches, and leads to more abiding results.[52]

It should also be noted that one's devotional time is not so much for the purpose of changing or directing God's mind or plans (which may in fact happen through intercessory prayer) as it is for the sake of changing and renewing oneself in God's presence. One writer clarified that while one's encounter with God can indeed change one's circumstances, it is more likely that said encounter will change one's own viewpoint and oneself.[53] Although the primary purpose is self-renewal, the AG consistently teaches that this renewal will only occur when one focuses, not on oneself, or even on other remarkable Christians, but on God, through the work and person of Jesus Christ.[54] By focusing on who God is, and the good things he has done and said,

---

[52] Editorial, "Concerning 'Serious' Prayer," *RT*, August 15, 1934, 1. The italics are mine. The caps are in the original.

[53] Albert L. Hoy, "The Passport of Praise," *PE*, June 14, 1964, 2-3, 24.

[54] Arthur H. Graves, "Spiritual Attainment," *PE*, July 26, 1964, 6.

both in Scripture and in one's life, the things that too easily hinder us will more likely fall to the side, including personality differences, clashes of opinions, and doctrinal differences.[55]

The teaching that the devotional time should be oriented around God, rather than around oneself, is one mitigating factor in the AG's rejection of transcendental meditation (the critical factor is that it is rooted in the non-Christian religions of the Far East).[56] The focus of transcendental meditation is to suspend all thought and "'dive' into the great ocean of Creative Intelligence" in order to variously realize one's full mental potential, reach an altered state of consciousness, and obtain a state of bliss. Contrastingly, the Pentecostal believer - even when he or she is praying a-rationally, that is in tongues (about which more will be said later in this chapter) - is specifically to focus upon the Lord Jesus Christ and his Scriptures.[57] Pentecostal meditation is also different from transcendental meditation because it is (as one writer instructed even before transcendental meditation reached the United States) an intentionally "mental reflection on all we know about a subject." It does involve contemplation and introspection, but these are quiet practices whereby one considers the truths and facts of Christianity. Even though one will realize and recognize things about oneself through Christian meditation, it will be because one is measuring oneself against the higher standards of Scripture and Christ.[58]

In contrast to Eastern religions' meditative practices, the intellect, and its comprehension of Christian truths and facts, is emphasized in the AG. But throughout the bulk of Pentecostalism's history the affective and emotional elements (the existential elements) have been understood to be the most important issue for one's devotional and spiritual life. There are (were) at least three reasons for this existential-over-intellectual impulse. Firstly, there was the Pentecostals' own lot in life. Most (not all) early Pentecostals had little or no

---

[55] Stanley Frodsham, "A Practical Word to Those Who Desire a Life of Victory," *PE*, July 23, 1921, 6-7. Similarly, and more recently, was Roger D. Cotton, "New Testament Victory, *PE*, August 6, 1989, 6.

[56] Pentecostals are generally unaware that Protestant history is characterized by a deep appreciation for meditation. John Calvin and the Puritans believed meditation was an important way to experience participation in Christ. Cf., Chan, *Spiritual Theology,* 167-168.

[57] "Transcendental Meditation," Assemblies of God Position Paper (Springfield, Missouri: Gospel Publishing, 1976). Reprinted in *PE*, October 10, 1976, 4-6, 30.

[58] Sylva Doolin, "The Godly Art of Meditation," *PE*, March 15, 1964, 32.

college education (that has changed dramatically in the past few decades).[59]
Thus, their existential emphasis gave them a kind of corporate defense
mechanism with which they could define, and distinguish, themselves against
other, better educated, Christians. Secondly, the perceived cold religious
formalism - "the temple of ecclesiasticism," as one writer put it[60] - of the
Catholics, Lutherans, Episcopalians, and even Methodists, was believed to stem
from those traditions' intellectual thrusts. At all costs, the Pentecostals did not,
and do not, want to be like those traditions.[61] Smith-Wigglesworth, the famous
Pentecostal evangelist, typified this anti-intellectual sentiment when he said, "O
how many people have lost out because the mind and head are too big! If only
God could cut our heads off and get into the heart! The head is too big, the mind
is too active, and the whole thing is too natural, therefore God cannot get His
way."[62] Thirdly, there were the looming threats that the more intellectual strains
of evangelicalism were perceived to pose. That those Christians were dabbling
in the higher critical methods of Biblical study and attempting to incorporate
notions about evolution with their understandings of God as the creator,[63]
proved to be clear indicators for the Pentecostals of the dangers which the
intellect can produce, and fall captive to, when it runs unchecked by the
spiritually attuned and existential elements of humankind.

In an article about spiritual development, British AG author Leonard Gittings
described the perceived milieu of his day and thereby typified the Pentecostal
attitude regarding intellect and the affections when he wrote:

> Intellect is exalted above feeling; indifference is counted a virtue; while
> earnestness in religion is styled old-fashioned. Cold cynicism gazes down
> superciliously upon warm-hearted devotion to Christ. Truth must be handled with
> the icy-cold fingers of criticism, but it must not be allowed to quicken the pulse or
> to warm the heart. It is sometimes very difficult to resist the influence of this cold,
> material, heartless and lifeless religion whose touch is like a winter's night. In
> contrast to the context of the day, the Pentecostal believer should experience a
> lively religious life, one that "glows with holy passion.

---

[59] Cf., Blumhofer, *The AG,* 1:313-336.
[60] James D. Menzie, "Pentecostal Principles," *PE*, October 11, 1953, 2.
[61] Cf., Anderson, *Vision,* 212-217.
[62] Smith Wigglesworth, "Sonship" (edited sermon notes), *RT*, December 24, 1924, 3.
[63] Anderson, Vision, 214-215.

But, Gittings warned, one cannot allow oneself to be given over to emotional excess, mere sentimentality, or the fires of fanaticism.[64]

DEVOTIONS AND FREQUENCY

Still another critical issue for Pentecostal devotions pertains to frequency. Like athletes who improve their skills and gain strength through daily exercise, and like soldiers who awake to reveille in order to discipline themselves for the moment of battle, Christians can only remain strong and healthy through regular times of communion with God.[65] The early morning hours are generally presented as the most beneficial because therein one sets a precedent for one's day. Even before one begins one's busy day, one's attitudes and mindset should be given over to the Lord. Whatever the specific time of day, one must not neglect the devotional period. One writer said that neglect, whether because of one's busy schedule or the cares of this life, "is probably the greatest cause of the loss of spiritual vigor." An established devotional time will help one keep one's spirit hungry for communion with God.[66] Moreover, even when the Spirit of God is moving mightily in church services or revivals the believer must not neglect the devotional time. Kenneth Barney wrote, "We need to keep the tide of spirituality high in our everyday living. There is danger that we may become

----

[64] Leonard Gittings, "How to Develop Spiritually: The Necessity For Development," *RT*, September 15, 1934, 3. Aimee Semple McPherson, the former AG minister who founded the Four Square denomination, railed against the evils of cold rationalism and spiritually eviscerating Modernism. Answering her own question of what was wrong with Seminaries she said, "THEY HAVE TAKEN AWAY the 'Spiritual' and have supplied the 'Material.' They have dethroned the experience of the 'heart and lifted to pre-eminence the experience of the 'head.'. . . By this new method of teaching the worldling and the 'Thinker,' we are told, and the man who otherwise would not be appealed to by 'some-thing he cannot accept because his world-darkened mind cannot understand or grasp it,' is instantly met on his own grounds by something 'reasonable' which he can immediately endorse because it is on his own plane. Thus, the modern Seminary tells the young theological student, he will appeal to the wise of this world." *What's the Matter?* (Los Angeles: Echo Park Evangelistic Association, 1928), 30-31. See also 11-18.

[65] Leonard Gittings, "How to Develop Spiritually: The Pursuit After Godliness," *RT*, June 1, 1934, 2-3; Don Mallough, "Exercise is Vital, In the Spiritual Life as in the Physical," *PE*, October 24, 1965, 2-3.

[66] J. M. Bryan, "Blessed Are They That Hunger," *PE*, January 31, 1965, 6-7. Nathanael Olson, "The Barrenness of Busyness" *PE*, August 10, 1963, 9, sounded a similar refrain.

occupied with the thrill of being caught up in something big and fast-moving and forget to keep our own souls fed."[67]

DEVOTIONS AND PERPETUAL PRAYER

Because they believe life's entirety can and/or must be characterized by a divine-human communion, and because of their literal Biblical hermeneutic, in this case concerning Paul's admonition to "pray without ceasing" (1 Thes. 5:17), Pentecostals have been concerned to distinguish between specific devotional periods and unceasing or perpetual prayer. Some, like my own boyhood pastor, taught that unceasing prayer is best understood as a kind of perpetual human-divine dialogue which the believer is to experience daily. As we went about our activities, jobs, and responsibilities, it was our privilege to have direct and immediate access to God the Father, through Jesus Christ. Unceasing prayer did not mean one was literally to be either continually on one's knees or be perpetually talking to God, but that the whole of one's life could be, and arguably should be, characterized by conversational fellowship and prayer with God.

Occasionally, AG articles addressed the topic of perpetual prayer. Reflecting an affective spiritual orientation, one writer taught that every day of our lives ought to be characterized by prayer, not as a mechanical ritual, but as the release of love and gratitude we feel toward God. In the same Biblical passage about perpetual prayer the apostle Paul exhorted the Thessalonians to 'rejoice evermore' and 'give thanks in everything.' One quite obviously cannot simultaneously and perpetually pray, rejoice, and give thanks. Instead, the apostle was encouraging his readers toward a Godward attitude which ought to characterize every Christian.[68] Another author, having conducted a word study, concluded on the topic by arguing that Paul was exhorting the Thessalonians toward recurring prayer. Like the widow in Jesus' parable, who sought help from an unjust judge, believers ought to repeatedly and insistently be approaching God in prayer.[69] Still another writer displayed Pentecostalism's pragmatic vein when he taught that prayer gives a believer purpose for one's life. "The prayerless life," he said," is like a piece of driftwood, floating wherever wind or tide may take it." Those who pray consistently and energetically make their very existences to be lives of endless prayer.[70]

---

[67] Kenneth Barney, "Strengthen The Stakes," *PE*, August 23, 1959, 3.

[68] Jerry K. Rose, "How To Pray Without Ceasing," *PE*, September 8, 1985, 4-5.

[69] Ora De Von, "Unceasing Prayer," *PE*, July 25, 1954, 4.

[70] Richard Champion, "Pray Without Ceasing," *PE*, April 12, 1964, 4.

Revivals

Down in the human heart, crushed by the tempter,
Feelings lie buried that grace can restore:
Touched by a loving heart, wakened by kindness,
Chords that were broken will vibrate once more.[71]

As Pentecostals generally employ the term, revival is first and foremost a move of God to bring sinners to salvation; although, somewhat unique to Pentecostal revivals are their eschatological flavor, their calls to return to apostolic Christianity, and the role of the charismata operating within in the worship assembly.[72] This bringing-sinners-to-life definition does not square with the literal definition of the term itself - to restore to consciousness or life; to bring back - and instead relies on a historical usage predating Pentecostalism itself. In the eighteenth and nineteenth centuries, the United States was widely impacted by the First and Second Great Awakenings, revival movements toward which the Pentecostals repeatedly harken themselves and the nation.[73] With that historical and primary definition in mind, it may seem odd to include the issue of revivals in the Pentecostal teaching on sanctification; they, in fact, rarely make such an explicit connection. Nonetheless, when one reads year after year of their literature one will be struck by how important revivals are for their understanding of Christian transformation. Given the Pentecostals' traditionally tremendous emphasis upon the human person's affective (existential) nature in Christian experience, and given that the Pentecostals portray this nature as being easily and variously made dormant by everyday life, the cares of the world, religious formalism, and a lack of spiritual vigilance, one begins to understand the reason why Pentecostals insist upon the necessity of revival, for the believer as well as the sinner.

---

[71] This poem's author was not identified. It was quoted by Burt McCafferty, "A Revival Needed," *The Weekly Evangel*, April 29, 1916, 6.

[72] Edith Blumhofer, "Restoration as Revival: Early American Pentecostalism," *in Modern Christian Revivals*, eds. Blumhofer and Randall Balmer (Chicago: University of Illinois, 1993), 145-160.

[73] E.g., William Menzies, "Lessons from Great Revivals," *Paraclete* (Winter 1974); Colin C. Whittaker, "The Fourth R," *PE*, March 18, 1990, 4-5, 30.

Among Wesleyan-Holiness Pentecostals, sanctification was presented as a crisis event which occurs subsequent to conversion. Understanding sanctification as they did, those Pentecostals yearned for revival as a means to bring believers to the necessary and transforming crisis moment. One could not be Spirit-baptized, in the Wesleyan-Holiness Pentecostal model, unless one was first sanctified. "The Holy Spirit will not dwell in unclean vessels," was an adage often cited to sustain their *ordo salutis.*[74] As our initial chapter on the Pentecostals clarified, Reformed-Higher Life Pentecostals, like those in the AG, do not maintain that understanding of the *ordo*. However, they do share the broader emphasis with their Wesleyan-Holiness brothers and sisters that experiences with, and in, God's presence can radically transform and renew the believer. Revivals are thus seen as the necessary venues for that divine-human communion.

The Gospels record instances where Jesus himself was unable to work miracles because of the atmosphere of unbelief. Revivals, because they are steeped in prayer and praise, and the resulting atmosphere of faith and expectation, produce an environment in which the Spirit can more readily work. Revivals open the believer's existential doors so that the divine-human, S/spirit, communion is more easily facilitated. Describing a Pentecostal revival, Thomas Zimmerman, the AG's longtime General Superintendent, said, "When God begins to come into a place, the very air seems to be charged with His presence." "When we come into the holy presence of God," Zimmerman continued, "we sense the glory cloud that begins to settle down, and the fire that begins to burn, creating a wonderful atmosphere."[75]

It deserves qualifying that what takes place in a revival can, and does, regularly take place in the normal Pentecostal church service. "An ideal Pentecostal Meeting," Donald Gee said about Pentecostal church services which facilitate a divine-human communion, "is none other than the gate of heaven."[76] If the Christian were to maintain her spiritual openness amid her own devotions

---

[74] Reformed-Higher Life Pentecostals fail to understand, as a Church of God (Cleveland, Tennessee.) writer said, that, "the old man will have to be crucified [in sanctification] before the Holy Ghost will move into that house [in Spirit-baptism]." W. W. Ball, "Sanctification," *Church of God Evangel*, May 19, 1945, 7. For a more in-depth examination see James Slay, *This We Believe* (Cleveland, Tennessee: Pathway, 1963).

[75] Thomas F. Zimmerman, "Perpetuating Pentecost," *PE*, January 8, 1956, 4. See also, O. L. Harrup, "The Atmosphere in Which God Releases His Power," *PE*, November 15, 1953, 3-4.

[76] Gee, *Concerning Shepherds and Sheepfolds*, 64.

and regular church attendance, she would have no need of a revival. But, because the Pentecostal movement is so keen on facilitating a divine-human (S/spirit) communion, as this section's opening poem typified, even if she were attuned to God's Spirit in a thriving manner, and thereby in the process of becoming Christ-like, she would always be needy of more of God's presence. She would always be open to God's new promptings and whispers. Revivals, as the AG has traditionally presented them, can cause one's existential chords to vibrate with a greater level of resolution than ever.

Throughout the AG's history it has been taught that true and authentic revival will only come about through earnest prayer. Every single AG article on revival maintains this axiom. A Redemption Tidings author exhorted the readers toward such prayer and said, "Multitudes! Multitudes! The day of the Lord is near in the valley of determination."[77] Such determined and heartfelt praying, F. F. Bosworth said, "brings about an atmosphere that makes a real revival possible." That God responds to earnest prayers with powerful revivals is a "law just as workable and dependable as the law of gravitation."[78] The previously noted Redemption Tidings article similarly averred this prayer-necessitates-revival axiom as one of the "natural laws of the spiritual world."[79] That is, since God has already decided that he wants to save the whole earth, and since he has already revealed that he will answer the prayers of those who earnestly seek him, the only thing holding back an authentic revival is the church's failure to pray.[80] Robert Cummings, then employed at the AG's Central Bible Institute,

---

[77] Anonymous Author, "Revival Conditions: Will YOU Pay the Price?" *RT*, October, 1928, 1.
[78] Bosworth, "Nothing Can Hinder A Revival," *The Weekly Evangel*, April 15, 1916, 6. Orig. emphasis.
[79] Anonymous Author, "Revival Conditions: Will YOU Pay the Price?" *RT*, October, 1928, 2.
[80] Bosworth, "Nothing Can Hinder A Revival," 6. Bosworth went on, in typical Pentecostal fashion, by saying, "There are thousands of God's children who have had their sins forgiven, their hearts have been purified through the blood of Christ, and they would not do wrong for anything, but out of this multitude there is only one here and there that is definitely by prayer undertaking any project for God and the salvation of souls. They hope for it; they want it; they go through the form of asking for it in family prayer, but do not 'stir themselves up to take hold of God' and see the thing brought to pass." We will not delve further into the issue of pragmatic prayer here, but it suffices to say that Pentecostals have historically taught about the need to persevere with God in prayer: God delights in those who will wrestle with him and who will incessantly seek

typified the AG's traditional attitude concerning the movement's own role in revival when he said:

> The most important religious body in the world today, I truly believe, is the Pentecostal Movement, provided that we recognize our high calling and our God-given destiny and the day of our visitation. I am sure that if we realized how much our beloved is counting upon us, we would drop the weights that would hinder, and we would hasten to do His bidding. He is attempting to awaken us to seek His face, that He might send a great revival to all our churches and all our mission fields. How shall we escape if we neglect his call?[81]

Other factors which were emphasized as being necessary for revival included personal and congregation-wide humility, repentance, forgiveness, separation from the world (both in terms of actions and attitudes), reverence for God's written word, and a hunger for God.[82] We may summarize all of these factors by saying that whereas the local church (or city, or district, or nation) needs to ready itself for God's move, it also needs to prod God to move by calling upon him through these corporate measures. Generally speaking, God only responds to those Christians who want him to move.

A reason the AG emphasizes revival the way it does, along with the earlier mentioned North-American historical one, has to do with its biblical hermeneutic. The first great Christian revival occurred in Acts 2, when the disciples, who were already praying and waiting upon God (again, necessary conditions for a revival) experienced the marvelous outpouring of the Holy Spirit. Colin Whittaker, a British AG minister, said, "The Book of Acts is the pattern by which all revivals should be judged. Significantly it covers about thirty-three and a half years, roughly the same period as the life of the Son of God on earth." He continued, "As the only unfinished book in the Bible. . . Acts reminds the Church that God's purpose is to present the living Christ to each generation in the power of the Spirit." So critical is revival that Whittaker called

---

his intervention, especially concerning issues like revival and salvation about which he has already stated his will. He's only waiting for someone to earnestly seek him before he will act.

[81] Robert W. Cummings, "What Is True Revival?" *PE*, May 13, 1956, 8.

[82] S. Franklin Logsdon, "The Route to Revival," *PE*, February, 5, 1961, 8-9, 19; A. L. Todd, "Revive Us Again!" *PE*, September 18, 1966, 5; James L. Hennesy, "You can have revival," *PE*, July 19, 1998, 13; M. Wayne Benson, "Revival priorities: repentance and humility," *PE*, July 19, 14-15.

it the fourth "r" of the church (the first three are reformation, renewal, and revelation).[83] This hermeneutic calls to mind the previously noted characteristic of Pentecostalism of primitivism. The Pentecostals not only want to escape the world and its allurements, they want to reproduce New Testament Christianity, something to their minds that can only result with the presence of revivals.

First because two Great Awakenings had a sweeping impact the on the United States and Britain, and secondly because Pentecostals are well aware of the impact that even geographically isolated revivals continue to have on people, revivals are regularly viewed as the panacea for all of society's ills. The United States, as many Pentecostals argue it, is blessed to the extent it is because it is a "Christian nation." God's judgments have variously been visited upon the nation both because of its backslidden Christian nature and its outright wickedness. Because the US has become God's new Israel, and the American church the faithful remnant within the nation, it remains America's task in general, and the American church's task in specific, to bring about God's renewed blessings. The number of *Pentecostal Evangel* articles sounding the various themes of "Christian America," revival as the nation's answer, and the citation of 2 Chronicles 7:14[84] to ratify those issues is legion.[85] Most of these

---

[83] Colin C. Whittaker, "The Fourth R," *PE*, March 18, 1990, 30.

[84] "If my people, which are called by my name, shall humble themselves, and pray, and seek my face, and turn from their wicked ways; then I will hear from heaven, and will forgive their sin, and will heal their land." (2 Chronicles 7:14, KJV).

[85] The following are from *PE*'s recent years: John Maempa, ""Restore Us Again," July 31, 1994, 3; Keith Boudreaux, "Aliens and Citizens," July 31, 1994, 14; Keith Boudreaux, "Reclaiming America for Christ," June 12, 1994; Thomas Trask, "Let's Pray, Church," May 1, 1994, 12; Wayne Hampton, "Are we under God's Judgment?" January 1, 1994; Dan Betzer, "If My People PrayThen - *Perhaps*," October 31, 1993, 22-3; Charles Crabtree, "Lord, Give us America," October 10, 1993, 16-17; Harvey Meppelink, "America has Heart Trouble," February 14, 1993; Raymond Carlson, "A call to Spiritual Renewal and Action," October 25, 1992, 4-5; Everett Stenhouse, "Vote for Christian Values," October 25, 1992, 6-7; "Our obligations as Citizens," August 9, 1992, 7; Lyle Thomson, "Prayer - the key to Europe in 1992," January 5, 1992, 12-13; Richard Champion, "Trials and Victories," September 22, 1991, 3; Champion, "Outpouring of Love," April 14, 1991, 3; Glen Cole, "How to help Miss Liberty," June 30, 1991, 12-13; Champion, "Take Pride in America," May 26, 1991; "Evangelicals warn President of deteriorating relations," December 30, 1990, 27; C. M. Ward, "Don't sell your Birthright," July 1, 1990, 8-9, 14; Glen Cole, "God's formula for a Nation," July 2, 1989, 6-7; Robert Ashcroft, "Let us pray for our Country," July 2, 1989, 7; Champion, "Wrong maps," October 30, 1988, 3; J. C. Holsinger, "God governs in the Affairs of Men,"

exemplify the belief that "if we can just get individual souls saved, then society's 'dark clouds' will roll away." Rarely was any thought given to the notion that the very structures of society - including the church - are corrupted by sin.

The unsaved masses aside, revivals are important for the person who already is a Christian, as has been suggested above, because they can help deepen and refreshen one's relationship with God.[86] Contrary to Pentecostalism's detractors', authentic revivals, even though they can produce emotional and exuberant responses, are neither simply emotional in orientation nor are they simply transient religious-ecstatic states. As one writer succinctly stated it, revivals put one into contact with Christ's resurrection power. Revival, he said, "lifts one to a higher plane, back to heaven's tableland; back where fellowship is once again enjoyed freely with the Father and with the Son." A revival can plunge the believer into "an energy which transcends and outlasts all fleshly effort." A revival's effects can be lifelong; when one undergoes a profound experience of Christ, not only will one's heart be warmed, not only will one's love for Christ and others be rekindled, and not only will one's entire mental attitude be refashioned with the result that one wants to live in accord with God's will, but one will also be filled with the power of the Holy Spirit for ministry. Even more, the revitalized Christian may find that the former valleys of loneliness have disappeared, that his love for Scripture has been renewed, and that his desire to live a holy and pure life is rekindled.[87]

In contrast to Orthodoxy, and its oft repeated theme that one need not understand the mysteries of God in order to participate in them or be changed by them, AG constituents are unequivocal that the Christian has a very definite role in the divine-human encounter if such an encounter is to produce change. In the process of sanctification, and in revivals themselves, Christians should not, as one British writer clarified, simply "Let go, and let God" do the work. They are instead to "Take hold, and let God" by cooperating with Christ's victorious

---

September 13, 1987, 18-19; and, Kenneth Barney, "God, save America," June 29, 1986, 4-5.

[86] Burt McCafferty, "A Revival Needed," *The Weekly Evangel*, April 29, 1916, 6; Robert Cummings, "What Is True Revival?" *PE*, May 13, 1956, 8.

[87] S. Franklin Logsdon, "The Route to Revival," *PE*, February 5, 1961, 8-9, 19. See also, Donald Gee, "Looking Around: Royal Modesty," *Study Hour*, August 15, 1950, 148-149; Elton G. Hill, "Seven Things The Holy Spirit Baptism Will Do For You," *PE*, April 30, 1972, 2-3; Adeline Emery Worthley, "Beyond The Initial Evidence," *PE*, February 12, 1978, 6-7.

power, given through the Holy Spirit. The Christian cannot be spiritually lazy, he must involve himself in the encounter: affectively, intellectually, and practically (in terms of obediently living one's life).[88] The New Testament church's worship service is a pattern for that of the contemporary church in that it modeled this intentionally active participation. Albert Hoy said, "first-century Christians never assumed the role of spectators in their times of worship." "The New Testament Christian was and is," said Hoy, "a contributor to the fellowship."[89] More recently the AG taught about the believer's cooperative and intentional role in spiritual experiences. Believers variously need to understand the biblical bases for this divine-human synergy; they must desire it; they must be "willing to submit to the inner sense that the Spirit is seeking expression;" and, they must "offer to the Holy Spirit [their] heart, emotions, will, and voice. . . ."[90]

Revivals foster an atmosphere of divine-human communion with the result that one can encounter God through vehicles that need not always involve an immediate, or visionary, apprehension: personal prayers, prophetic utterances, the preacher's sermon, the worship music, the congregation's acappella and harmonic praises (in earlier days known as the "heavenly choir"), and personal testimonies. The Spirit of God can use any of those vehicles to illuminate something to one's heart, one's existential nature; one cannot only know in one's mind that God has spoken, one can also know down in one's gut that God has required something from oneself or that he has changed one's affections and inner being so one can more readily live like, and for, Christ.

The above less immediate vehicles aside, revivals also help facilitate divine-human experiences which are more immediate and which also produce an often fantastic degree of transformation. The first and most famous of these is Spirit-baptism. AG theologians and ecclesiarchs qualify that baptism in the Holy Spirit is primarily for empowerment, not sanctification. As was noted in an earlier chapter, this empowerment-versus-sanctification qualification stems from their hermeneutic which reads the experiences of the Spirit in Acts solely in terms of empowerment. Earlier I noted that the older historical arguments have been

---

[88] Bryn Barrett, "Holiness of Life," *RT*, July 23, 1965, 12-14. Quotations from p. 13.

[89] Albert L. Hoy, "Flame In The Sanctuary," *PE*, April 26, 1964, 14.

[90] "Our Distinctive Doctrine: The Baptism in the Holy Spirit," Assemblies of God Pamphlet (Springfield, Missouri: Gospel Publishing, 1995), 9. The authors spoke explicitly about charismatic gifts, but their teaching is equally applicable to the divine-human synergy we are describing.

made a moot issue by the winds of time (many Wesleyan-Holiness Pentecostal theologians today present sanctification similarly to their Reformed-Higher Life counterparts).[91] Regarding the apostles themselves, it is undeniable that they were only willing to die for Christ because of their experience of having been plunged into the Holy Spirit.[92] In Pentecostal language, the apostles were not willing to risk all for Christ and die for him until their existential natures had been radically renewed and transformed by the Spirit. Today, Pentecostal believers (nearly to a person) testify to having been radically changed in a deep and existential manner; what happened to the apostles continues to happen today. Because it receives so much emphasis in Pentecostal teaching and preaching Spirit-baptism will be dealt with in a separate section below.

Another of these more immediate means of transformation is to be "slain in the Spirit": being knocked down or falling backward under the power of the Holy Spirit (in the worst cases, preachers and evangelists physically push people over).[93] Such persons can lay on the floor for several minutes or even several hours in a kind of rapturous experience of the divine. Some people lay on the floor and praise God, others lay like statues in complete silence, and still others weep or laugh uncontrollably. Later they can variously report to having seen visions, having heard God speak to them, having been flooded with Godly repentance, cleansing, or inexpressible joy. Robert Cummings once again typified the AG's reflections on these experiences when he said, "True revival is an atmosphere brought about by the Holy Spirit - a spiritual atmosphere of such intensity that divine realities become the only great realities, and the things of time and space take their proper and minor place."[94]

---

[91] Horton affirms much the same, "The Pentecostal Perspective," 135.

[92] Smith Wigglesworth affirmed exactly as much in, "How To Become A Powerful Christian," *RT*, January 2, 1939, 8. See also, A. A. Wilson, "Be Filled With the Spirit," *PE*, September 9, 1950, 3.

[93] There are at least a couple reasons for such manipulations: to demonstrate one's spiritual charisma and/or authority, and to produce an awed response in the congregation which in turn can spawn greater emotional outbursts. The fact that there are indeed such gross manipulations does not necessitate that the entire phenomenon is wrong and should be banned (on that basis, the whole of Christianity would need to be eradicated).

[94] Robert W. Cummings, "What Is True Revival?" *PE*, May 13, 1956, 8. He was himself quoting W. I. Evans, Central Bible Institute's dean of 25 years.

The Third Tributary:
Twentieth-Century Western Distinctives

The third tributary, or layer of definitional distinction, within the AG's doctrine of sanctification consists of two relatively new emphases in the historical scope of Christendom's teaching on sanctification. Even though we will examine these two features - God's purpose for one's life and Spirit-baptism - separately for the sake of a more careful discussion, they are quite accurately understood as two sides of the same coin. That is, in many ways these two are the most Western of elements in the AG's doctrine of sanctification, and as such they serve to heighten the contrast between Pentecostalism and Orthodoxy. Having clarified that, it also remains true that Spirit-baptism, and the ensuing phenomenon of existential transformation which nearly always accompanies the event, in many ways, is the dialectical linchpin for any comparisons between Pentecostalism and Eastern Orthodoxy. To clarify, to no small extent Spirit-baptism is the most Western of Pentecostal notions, and yet, it is the *sine qua non* for any comparisons between these two great Christian cisterns. From the perspective of this Pentecostal, Spirit-baptism is not the only bridge for comparing the two (many others were suggested in the introduction), but, as the apex of Pentecostal doctrines and experiences, it is the primary and obvious one. First we will examine God's purpose, and then we will conclude with Spirit-baptism.

God's Purpose for One's Life

God has a plan for every life;
We are not here to drift
Through our few years of earthly strife
But love and serve, and lift
Our struggling brother to his feet,
And cheer the drooping hearts we meet.

We're here upon an errand great,
Sent by Divinity;
Our best in life we consecrate
To bless humanity -
That truest life is that which finds
God's thought, and its great dictum minds.

> No better purpose can be born
> Than that which seeks to fill
> Its truest place, and thus adorn
> The beauty of God's will;
> To live successful is to show
> Accomplished good where'er we go.[95]

As the earlier discussions of Pentecostal primitivism and its ensuing moralizing tendencies indicated, remaining pure from the world has regularly been a Pentecostal concern. But as our examination of the AG's (mostly early) ascetic tendencies and practices of piety also revealed, Pentecostals are more concerned to rejuvenate positively their existential natures than they are to guard carefully against sin's encroachment or pare away any of temptation's roots, as say occurs in Orthodox' hesychastic teachings. Having attuned their hearts to God's Spirit, Pentecostals immediately shift their spiritual attention to what it is that God wants them to do. Stanley Horton, an AG theologian, evinced both the AG's qualification of ascetic like activities and how it is that God's purpose plays a role in sanctification when he said, "we believe that the chief object of our Christian life is not to purify ourselves. Growth in grace comes best as we are involved in service. We do not believe that the saint, or dedicated believer should spend every day in nothing but study, prayer, and devotion. Those things are important, but the holy, sanctified life involves much more." Just as the ancient Jew's religious vessels were holy precisely because they were put to use in the tabernacle, Horton reasoned, so also Christian believers are called saints not only by being made holy but also by being used of God.[96]

For some in the AG, the teaching that one is sanctified through Godly service is as simple as the common-sensical approach to life which says that the best way to stay out of trouble is to keep oneself busy doing good. R. H. Boughton, in 1934, said, "Finally, let us be so occupied in actively doing His will in all things, that there may be no passive place for the flesh to gain an advantage."[97] For other AG folks, the more generally pragmatic Protestant work-ethic is grounds for exhorting one another to good works. As Robert Cunningham said,

---

[95] D. Wesley Myland, "Life's Purpose," *The Christian Evangel*, May, 28, 1917, 5.
[96] Horton, "The Pentecostal Perspective," 132.
[97] R. H. Boughton, "Starving the Flesh," *RT*, June 1, 1934, 6. See also, Marlon Jannuzzi, "The Lazy Man Will Lose," *PE*, July 25, 1965, 19.

"Labor strengthens the body, sharpens the mind, and disciplines the spirit."[98] But for still others, God's purpose for one's life has a more intentionally defined place in one's sanctification. J. O. Savell, then the AG's assistant general superintendent, said, "Life should mean more to us than a mere desire to exist." "The Christ-life is intended," he said, "to make each of us realize that God has a plan for each of our lives. We shall never find the best in life until we are willing to live according to God's plan." Savell furthered his argument by noting that everything in God's creation has a purpose. Similarly, because Christians were created for a purpose, it is not their own place to plan their own lives.[99]

In our examination of the Orthodox' *theosis* doctrine, we saw that it had some very corporate and communal dimensions; in their case, those dimensions were rooted in ontology, most specifically involving a mystical participation in the theandric person of Jesus Christ. Pentecostalism, despite the high value it places on corporate worship and public revival, tends to relegate its spirituality and theology to the individual realm.[100] The primary exception to Pentecostalism's individualizing tendency is its deep and unchanging commitment to Christian service. That is, the act of fulfilling God's will for one's life - almost exclusively defined as Christian service[101] - helps not only to sanctify oneself, but others as well. While there are some AG discussions which help root the corporate dimensions of sanctification in God's nature (that is, ontology: to be like God we must do his will),[102] the bulk of these discussions stem from a more pragmatic Biblical hermeneutic, a hermeneutic with two primary foundations. The first of these foundations is, simply, that God

---

[98] Robert C. Cunningham, "Idleness Is Not Happiness," *PE*, August 28, 1966, 4.

[99] J. O. Savell, "Serving God With Purpose of Heart," *PE*, September 5, 1954, 3.

[100] One must not overstate the case here, but together with its traditional reactionary tone to the established church, this individual emphasis helps to account for Pentecostalism's rather minimal theological interest in, or treatment of, ecclesiology. Alternately stated, not only have the Pentecostals traditionally ignored church history and ecclesiology because they see themselves as the epitome of the church age ("why study it when we are it?"), the larger cultural and philosophical individualistic constructs, constructs within which their belief about the church developed, quite naturally led them to view it with ambivalence (or in some cases with outright disdain).

[101] Robert C. Cunningham, "Idleness Is Not Happiness," *PE*, August 28, 1966, 4, was an exception in that he included non-ministerial kinds of employment in the fulfilling of God's purpose for one's life.

[102] E.g., Ralph Riggs, "Partners in Redemption," *PE*, March 29, 1959, 3, 33.

commanded his children to spread the gospel of salvation to all the nations. The unsaved around the world will never hear the gospel, and themselves grow in sanctification, unless believers obey Scripture and spread the Christian message. The second, and equally pragmatic foundation, is that until enough believers are willing to move out on God's behalf and themselves fulfill Christian service (preaching, missionizing, evangelizing, and teaching) the church will have failed in its vocation. Ralph Riggs, another AG General Superintendent, displayed this pragmatic bent when he said, "You cannot separate Christ's resurrection from missions, for each is a link in God's program of redeeming the lost. Our joy in the resurrection of Christ can only be complete as we accept our privilege and responsibility to fulfill our part in the plan of redemption."[103] Similarly, another AG writer taught that it is not enough to acknowledge that Jesus is Lord, one must also, as Saul of Tarsus did, say to him, "what wilt thou have me to do?" The Savior will speak to our hearts, and he does have a plan to use us in sanctifying others.[104]

In our previous chapter we noted the Pentecostals' synergistic understanding of sanctification (concerning progressive sanctification). Earlier in this chapter we demonstrated how that synergistic position manifests itself with regard to the Pentecostals' existential nature (the necessity of attuning oneself to the Holy Spirit, pp. 361-2). Concerning both of those, progressive sanctification and existential orientation (which are really two ways to express the same issue), the synergistic focus concerns the believer. However, as the AG consistently teaches it with regard to God's purpose for one's life,[105] this synergism takes a Godward orientation. That is, whereas the Pentecostal believer needs to cooperate with the Spirit's presence, guidance and promptings, in order to be more fully sanctified, God himself needs the believer's help in order for his own purpose to be accomplished.[106] N. D. Davidson said, "God can grow trees, lift mountains, fill space with singing stars. . . and fill the earth with His glory; but He has so arranged things that He needs our help in the salvation of a lost world." We thus become God's servants, but he, in turn, fills us with joy and makes us to experience the harmony that comes from working with him.[107]

---

[103] Riggs, "Partners in Redemption," 3, 33.

[104] Robert C. Cunningham, "Waiting on the Lord," *PE*, June 9, 1963, 4.

[105] Unquestionably there are ministers who would aver that God's purpose can be fulfilled in other, non-ministerial, ways. It's just that the AG's literature rarely admits so much.

[106] E.g., Jenney, "Holy Spirit and Sanctification," 418.

[107] N. D. Davidson, "Workers Together With God," *PE*, August 30, 1959, 5.

Within the AG's teaching that fulfilling God's purpose for one's life serves to sanctify oneself there is a concurrent belief that being baptized in the Holy Spirit will empower one to satisfy God's plan for one's life more fully. That is, no matter what God has called one to do, one can always do it more effectively if one has been Spirit-baptized, and therefore divinely empowered. Rarely did an AG author teach on God's purpose apart from mentioning Spirit-baptism. The two consistently go hand in hand, and as such serve to manifest the AG's thoroughgoing Western pragmatic character.

Spirit-Baptism

In the following delineation of Spirit-baptism our chief focus will be its role in the sanctification process. Specifically, we want to clarify what AG constituents say the experience does in and to them in their sanctification process. Thus, the issues of Pentecostal hermeneutics, the meaning and role of *glossolalia*, or any comparisons of those against the greater sweep of Christian history are not our immediate concern and will only be touched upon incidentally.[108]

Specifically defined, baptism in the Holy Spirit[109] is that post-conversion moment when the Christian is plunged into the Holy Spirit with the result that he or she speaks in tongues.[110] Just like the apostles on the Day of Pentecost (Acts 2), contemporary believers can be plunged into the Holy Spirit with the

---

[108] An outstanding examination of Pentecostal theology on Spirit-baptism is Frank Macchia's, "Sighs Too Deep For Words: Toward A Theology of Glossolalia," *Journal of Pentecostal Theology*, 1 (1992), 47-73. Macchia not only reiterates standard Pentecostal teaching on *glossolalia*, he also offers new lines of thought through which the doctrine might be freshly and meaningfully processed.

[109] Alternately expressed as baptism with the Holy Spirit (some preachers and writers argue that the doctrine is founded upon using the correct preposition). In former days this was Holy Ghost-baptism, an expression which is decreasingly being used because of its ghoulish and fiction-like overtones.

[110] Other physical manifestations can also result: trembling and shaking, quivering lips, prophetic utterances, an almost uncontrollable zeal to express God's goodness, dancing, shouting, weeping and wailing, trances, falling prostrate, visions or dreams, and charismatic giftings. These were noted by Alice E. Luce, "Physical Manifestations of the Spirit," *The Christian Evangel*, July 27, 1918, 2.

result that they are empowered for ministry, given charismatic gifts,[111] and transformed in their inner (existential) persons. Spirit-baptism, with the spiritual power and divine-human intimacy it provides, is understood to be the long-awaited promise of the Father (Acts 2:33, 39). This experience usually involves an emotional outpouring (some would say in-pouring)[112] that can result in ecstatic outbursts which outsiders frequently misunderstand ("they are drunk," Acts 2:13). However, one should neither seek the experience for experience's sake, nor in order to speak in tongues. Instead one should so seek for the sake of obedience to Scripture, divine empowerment, and greater intimacy with God.[113] An earlier AG writer corrected a frequent misunderstanding and said, "Brother, speaking in tongues is not the Baptism of the Holy Ghost, - speaking in tongues is the OUTCOME of the INCOME."[114] Moreover, one need neither be Spirit-baptized to be saved nor to bear the fruit of the Spirit. The experience does *not* make one spiritually superior to other Christians.[115]

As noted in an earlier chapter, the AG's traditional position is that Spirit-baptism is primarily an enduement with power. It is neither to be interpreted as a segment in the *ordo salutis*, nor as a sanctifying experience.[116] Yet, as AG constituents have expressed it for more than eighty years, when one is plunged into the Spirit of God one is transformed and therefore progresses in

---

[111] Section 7 of the AG's "Statement of Fundamental Truths," holds that it is normative for one to receive one's charismatic gifts in the Spirit-baptism experience. "Minutes of the 47th General Council of the Assemblies of God," 1997, 107-108. That statement aside, Pentecostals are not unanimous as to how or when charismatic gifts are given to believers. For example, spiritual gifts can pertain to one's personality, so that the S/spirit model whereby the Spirit works through the believer and with the believer's cooperation would once again be sustained. For a brief treatment of the S/spirit model see the AG's "Our Distinctive Doctrine: The Baptism In The Holy Spirit," 8-9.
[112] A. A. Boddy expressed well the overwhelming nature of Spirit-baptism when he said, "A jar plunged into a river is not only surrounded, but filled with water." "The Holy Ghost For Us," *The Weekly Evangel*, September 1, 1917, 2.
[113] "Our Distinctive Doctrine," 3-17.
[114] W. Black, "Here and There," *The Weekly Evangel*, January 22, 1916, 9. Original emphases.
[115] "Our Distinctive Doctrine," 10.
[116] Horton, "The Pentecostal Perspective," 132; Menzies, *Anointed*, 74-77, 318; Blumhofer, *The AG,* 1:217-221; Joseph R. Flower, "Holiness, the Spirit's infilling and speaking with tongues," *PE*, July 15, 1973, 4-5, though Flower qualified that the experience, if it is authentic, will cause one to live a holy life.

sanctification.[117] The number of anecdotes testifying to the transforming nature of Spirit-baptism are legion, we will note just a few.

Sarah Haggard, a first generation Pentecostal contributor to *The Weekly Evangel*, described the deeply personal experience of Spirit-baptism and its effect on her soul. Her testimony reveals how ineffable the experience can be:

> I am never afraid in this field of abandonment to the baptism of the Holy Ghost and fire, for the fearful self is dead while I lie in this 'River of Life' and submit to this sweet immersion of the whole of me in the whole of the sweet, beloved will of God. For the first time in my earth life or my spirit life I am led 'beside the waters still,' so still, that there is not an anxious thought about my mother tongue, not caring what people say, for people, with all their opinions and criticisms, good or bad, are forgotten; in fact, all things of earth for this time, at any rate, are forgotten as I sit within the veil, the holy place where the holy fire is, and banquet with my Kingly Lover, at the feast of His real body and real blood, spread before me 'in the presence of my enemies.' Hidden, at last, in the secret place of the Most High, resting under His 'banner of love.' Resting, resting, resting, such joyful rest in the house of the Lord. . . entering into the Sabbath of my soul.[118]

Smith Wigglesworth said, "Beloved, if God lays hold of you by the Spirit, you will find that there is an end of everything and a beginning of God, so that your whole being becomes seasoned with a divine likeness."[119] Zelma Argue similarly testified to what it was like to watch someone be Spirit-baptized, "Some seeker would get 'through' and perhaps spring to his feet, rapturously wanting to hug everybody, his face shining like the sun, and how transported we all were with joy! As we walked home it would seem we walked on air, feeling the tug from on high and wondering if Jesus might not be coming the next minute."[120] Still another testified that Spirit-baptism helped him quit smoking and live a holier life. He was so changed that he wanted to tell others how God is so wonderful.[121]

---

[117] Blumhofer, *Pentecost in My Soul* (Springfield, Missouri: Gospel Publishing, 1989), 18-27, clarifies that early AG constituents described personal transformation and increased piety as two of Spirit-baptism's effects.

[118] Sarah Haggard, "Joy Unspeakable And Full Of Glory," *The Weekly Evangel*, September 1, 1917, 8.

[119] "How To Become A Powerful Christian," *RT*, January 2, 1939, 8.

[120] Zelma Argue, "The Waiting Meeting," *PE*, January 19, 1964, 8.

[121] Billy B. Kinsey, "Baptism Brings Blessing of a Holy Life," *PE*, July 19, 1964, 6.

A Nigerian Christian formerly had been opposed to the Pentecostal doctrine of Spirit-baptism. Having reluctantly attended a Pentecostal meeting, this person described an encounter during the altar call:

I knelt where I was and made the first confession ever of my sins to God. As I was pouring out my heart to Him, I suddenly began to feel the surge of a strange and supernatural power going through my heart and all over my body. I began to speak freely what I could not understand. . . . Previously . . . I was living as any other nominal churchgoer, boasting that I was alright in the church where I was a member. . . . But glory be to God for that night which drew an indelible line of demarcation between my past and present life. . . . I am but a poor mortal. . . but with the wonderful guidance of the Holy Spirit in me, I have been able to leap over the garrisons of the devil in victory after victory.

Even though this experience caused others to cast aspersions at this transformed believer, he or she went on to walk with the Spirit and bring souls to Christ.[122]

Doris Warren, a self-described happy Christian, struggled with what her Pentecostal friends told her about Spirit-baptism. However, when she attended a women's home-fellowship prayer meeting, she was moved by the sense of joy and peace exhibited. Still unsure about the Pentecostal doctrine, she let the women there pray for her. Describing her own baptism in the Holy Spirit she said:

Suddenly Jesus Christ baptized me in the Holy Spirit! I was speaking in a new and beautiful language! The power of God poured over and over me until I felt saturated in the glory and light that flooded my body and my soul! Before this, I had evaded even the thought of any physical demonstration of God in my life; but when the power of heaven fell on me and filled every part of me, the physical demonstration was extremely precious. . . . My new tongue enables me to truly worship Him, and at the same time the inner being is edified and satisfied completely! This filling of love divine has revived my experience of salvation, enhanced the beauty of Jesus, and magnified the Word of God to my heart![123]

---

[122] S. U. Ozoanya, "The Holy Spirit In Me," *PE*, November 7, 1965, 7.
[123] Doris F. Warren, "I received the fullness," *PE*, March 27, 1966, 5.

Not only does the experience of Spirit-baptism itself serve to transform and sanctify a person, so too do the experience's preparatory steps which the AG regularly teaches as being necessary. (Other than the fact that one must first be a Christian, there is no ready-made formula for how to be so baptized; it is a gift of God which cannot be earned.) These steps consistently include repenting of sin, expressing one's desire to be so baptized, understanding the biblical teaching on the doctrine, and being so submitted to God that one even surrenders one's tongue, and therefore coincidingly one's will, to him;[124] *practices which by themselves serve to consecrate the believer.* These preparatory steps, however, are not mechanical necessities. Thomas Zimmerman reminded the Pentecostal Fellowship of North America (a pan-Pentecostal ecumenical organization) that the important issue for baptism in the Holy Spirit was an authentic spiritual atmosphere, not a prescribed or preconceived formula.[125] Like the Orthodox hesychasts, who, in their quests to encounter God in profound and existential ways, deny that the road to such encounters is paved with mechanistic practices, Pentecostals deny that authentic Spirit-baptisms can be mechanically produced. Those who teach believers to repeat one word faster and faster until a babbling sound is produced are setting their flocks up for disappointment and the potential for backsliding.[126]

An older preparatory practice was that of waiting, or "tarrying" as it was called in earlier days. Stemming from their literalistic hermeneutic (in Acts 1:4 and Lk. 24:49 Jesus told the disciples to "wait for the promise of the Father"), Pentecostals often taught that one must obey Scripture and wait upon God before he baptized one with the Holy Spirit. Like revival meetings, waiting meetings served to facilitate the divine-human communion. As late as 1964 Zelma Argue warned the AG against forsaking these meetings. "This exercise of waiting before the Lord," she said, "we cannot do without! If we neglect it we become like a flute with no sound, like a rose with no fragrance. It is in the atmosphere of anticipation and waiting that God meets our faith and heaven comes down!"[127] Because they are often understood to be mechanical and

---

[124] W. T. Gaston said, "If He can get our tongues He has no trouble with the rest of our anatomy." "The New Birth and Baptism in the Holy Ghost," *The Christian Evangel*, July 12, 1919, 1; J. Robert Ashcroft, "Tongues. . . As Of Fire," *PE*, January 3, 1965, 5; "Our Distinctive Doctrine," 16-17.

[125] Thomas F. Zimmerman, "Perpetuating Pentecost," *PE*, January 8, 1956, 4.

[126] E. N. Bell, "Questions and Answers, No. 612," *The Christian Evangel,* February 8, 1919, 5.

[127] Argue, "The Waiting Meeting," *PE*, January 19, 1964, 7.

manipulative practices, and because the AG's hermeneutical methods are subtly changing, and (I would add) because they take precious time and are therefore not very pragmatic, these waiting meetings are rarely employed today.[128] When they are practiced, they are almost always held distinct from the regular Sunday morning service.

As was mentioned earlier, the experience of Spirit-baptism is consistently fused with pragmatic understandings. Nearly every single article about the necessity of Spirit-baptism for each believer reiterates this person-plus-purpose fusion. The reasons for this experiential-pragmatic fusion are numerous. Firstly, as AG writers regularly express it, this fusion is itself attested to in Scripture. Peter, Stephen, James, and John were each Spirit-baptized and thereby empowered for Christian service, just as Jesus had foretold in Acts 1:8 ("You will receive power, after the Holy Ghost comes upon you"). "Jesus Himself," Normand Thompson said, "never attempted a single miracle until the Holy Ghost came upon Him. How much more do you and I need this heavenly power!"[129] Secondly, Pentecostals consistently testify that the experience of Spirit-baptism makes them want to serve God, especially in Christian ministry. The experience heightens one's awareness of God and makes Christ seem incredibly real. Thus, the power of the experience impels one to want others to experience the Spirit's intimate and joyful presence.[130] Indeed, as many ministers and missionaries express it, their calling to Christian service either came simultaneously with the experience, or resulted from it.[131] Thirdly, it is God's specific intent that the experience be given an outlet. That is, not only does the Biblical witness testify to this order, and not only does one quite naturally want to share what is so precious, but God himself intends that the experience have external and outward moving ramifications (to clarify, the Biblical witness and one's existential transformation are both interpreted as revealing God's will on the matter). "If every Spirit-baptized believer would allow God's power to have an outlet through him," George Holmes said, "there

---

[128] An official AG publication said, "Today there is no longer any reason for waiting, except as 'waiting' may relate to the preparation of the heart for the infilling of the Holy Spirit." "Our Distinctive Doctrine," 16.
[129] Again, nearly every Spirit-baptism asserts this. For example see Normand J. Thompson, "You Need The Engine," *PE*, February 2, 1964, 20; F. Nolan Ball, "Three Great Changes in the Spirit-filled Life," *PE*, January 19, 1964, 6-7.
[130] H. M. Turney, "The Baptism Of The Holy Ghost," *The Weekly Evangel*, July 1, 1916, 5; George B. Studd, "My Convictions," *The Weekly Evangel*, July 15, 1916, 4.
[131] Poloma, *At the Crossroads*, 49, 67-70.

would be a tremendous breakthrough of the rivers of salvation throughout the land."[132]

Even Spirit-baptism's outward manifestation, speaking in tongues, has very pragmatic reasons ascribed to it. Pentecostals regularly teach that *glossolalia* has several purposes: to edify the individual believer (1 Cor. 14:4), to edify the church (1 Cor. 12:10; 14:5), to bear witness to the reality of God's presence to unbelievers (1 Cor. 14:22), and to enable the believer to accomplish things in the spiritual realm with the Spirit (1 Cor. 14:2,18). The latter of these is a synergistic concert of prayer involving the Holy Spirit and the human spirit.[133] Amid groanings (Rom. 8:26) and *glossolalic* utterances - avenues transcending the believer's mind - the Spirit prays through the believer about issues which the believer is likely unaware. Pentecostal believers are taught that such heartfelt and *glossolalic* praying not only fulfills apostolic teaching it also edifies and transforms believers as they unite their spirits with God's Spirit in accomplishing his purposes. Albert Hoy iterated the traditional Pentecostal position in this regard. He said, "When a person speaks with tongues, he does not think syllables in his mind before he utters them. Indeed, he does not know what sounds he will utter until he hears them proceed from his own lips." Such utterances and prayers, Hoy taught, reveal that "Christianity is not simply a philosophy of life, but [a] continuous communion with the divine Trinity dwelling in the soul." Adeline Emery Worthley also described *glossolalic* utterances as facilitating the S/spirit encounter:

> We should treasure and nurture that communion. The Holy Spirit does not speak through us while we just sit in 'neutral.' It is as the spirit of the believer is actively communicating with God, as we are in an attitude of love and worship, that this gift profits. We are lifted into the very presence of God in sweet communion, as tongues is the outcry of a spirit that is humbled before God in love, praise, and worship.[134]

Elsewhere, the AG taught that such praying makes evident that the Holy Spirit not only uses people's minds and bodies to accomplish his aims, but that

---

[132] George Holmes, "Dimensions of Divine Power," *PE*, April 19, 1964, 3-4.

[133] Arthur Berg, "The Twofold Purpose of Speaking with Tongues," *PE*, June 14, 1964, 20-1; "Our Distinctive Doctrine," 5-6.

[134] Adeline Emery Worthley, "Beyond The Initial Evidence," *PE*, February 12, 1978, 7.

he also uses their hearts, emotions, wills, and voices - in short, the whole of their existential natures - and that even if they do not always understand it.[135]

As important as the event of Spirit-baptism is, Pentecostals also regularly remind one another to continually walk with the Spirit and remain filled with the Spirit. "Learn to drink deeply," Stanley Frodsham said, "and to get others to drink with you of that which will cause you to be ever singing and making melody in your heart to the Lord."[136] Just because one has experienced Spirit-baptism does not mean one is therefore perpetually walking in the Spirit. "We are like an electric cord," Robert Cunningham said," useless unless plugged in." When Paul exhorted the Ephesians to be filled with the Spirit (Eph. 5:19), he urged a continuous action; Christians need to recharge themselves in the Holy Spirit's presence regularly.[137]

Summary and Analysis

The First Tributary: Parallels with Orthodoxy

Occasionally AG writers discussed transformation and spirituality in ways that were remarkably like the Orthodox' own ascetic and hesychastic ways. It was noteworthy that the numbers of introspective-sanctification articles appeared in greater proportion in the AG's earlier years than in more recent years. At a minimum, this reveals that in earlier days the AG was more introspective and ascetic than it is today.[138] The historical reason for this Orthodox-Pentecostal similarity is unclear, especially since the early AG writers only infrequently

---

[135] Albert Hoy, "Flame In The Sanctuary," *PE*, April 26, 1964, 14, original emphasis; "Our Distinctive Doctrine," 9.

[136] Stanley Frodsham, "Conquering Evil," *The Christian Evangel*, August 24, 1918, 13.

[137] Robert Cunningham, "Four great benefits of the Pentecostal baptism," *PE*, August 14, 1988, 6-7. See also, "The Baptism in the Spirit: Not a Goal but a Gateway," a *PE* reprint of an earlier *RT* article, July 22, 1956, 8-9; Thomas Zimmerman, "Perpetuating Pentecost," *PE*, January 8, 1956, 29; Jimmy Phillips, "Why I Am Pentecostal," *PE*, June 2, 1963, 2-3.

[138] The extent to which the earlier generations were more sanctified than contemporary generations cannot be studied here, and I do not assume that asceticism necessarily produces transformation. What is being asserted is that the earlier generations were more intentionally focused on internal transformation than are recent ones.

noted the sources (if any) they used. Indeed, this similarity may only be coincidental, the simple result of the ascetic language which has characterized segments of Christendom for centuries. Still, I would posit that there is another reason for this Orthodox-Pentecostal similarity: an ardent hunger for God's presence. Both groups have exhibited an incredible desire to involve the entirety of their beings in communion with God. One cannot so desire this communion and limit one's Christian experience to thinking or doing.

Like the Orthodox, Pentecostals are not content to relegate their faith to the intellectual arena. The mind is important, but one's affections, one's existential core, is critical too. Stated differently, in contrast to some more rationalistic branches of Protestantism, Pentecostals believe that sanctification is not just living by faith in the light of one's conversion, but neither is it a works-oriented process. Even more starkly, even though one's entire Christian life is rooted in one's conversion (the Orthodox would insert baptism for conversion), Pentecostals know that the Christian life is comprised of far more than simply being saved. Although they know that salvation is the gracious gift of God, Pentecostals also know that God richly rewards those who seek him (Heb. 11:6), that God is found by those who pant after him (Ps. 42:1), and that such rewarding and finding occurs in this life after the moment of salvation as well as during it. Furthermore, like the Orthodox, Pentecostals believe that this rewarding, although it may manifest itself in material blessings (possessions) or prosperity (including health, status, and responsibility), is not limited to either the physical realm or the heavenly realm (that is, salvation). Other important blessings, blessings which change a person and/or make a person want to live an ever more committed life, are those existential foretastes of glory (2 Cor. 3:18):[139] personal encounters with the living God.

GUARDING AGAINST TEMPATION

In light of their desire for personal encounter with God, Pentecostals - like their Orthodox, early Methodist, and later Keswick and Holiness brothers and sisters - have employed ascetic practices. Certainly there have been abuses, as could be noted regarding the entire historical spectrum of Christendom. But Pentecostals have never taught that asceticism makes one more saved or that it makes one more Christian. Rather, they have taught that it is a tool to focus oneself. If life in the world is characterized by continually saying "yes" to one's appetites and

---

[139] In 2 Cor. 12-18 Paul himself talks about the heart's awakening, softening, and being liberated in the Spirit's presence.

desires, then some Pentecostals have chosen to say "no" to the same appetites and desires through occasional ascetic practices. If the world is characterized by moods that are precisely licentious, greedy, covetous, ostentatious and opulent, then some Pentecostals have chosen to shape their own atmospheres and moods through ascetic practices. Ascetic activities serve to remind them that this world is not the arena whereby a Christian should formulate one's values nor is it their ultimate destiny. In all of this, sanctification is not earned, but it clearly is a process, and even a life-long one involving the deepest levels of the human person.

Whereas the Orthodox hesychasts, in their teaching about *nepsis*, have developed careful and precise ways to examine the heart and guard it against sin's encroachment, the Pentecostals consistently do not. As the earlier discussions revealed, some Pentecostals teach that one must guard one's thoughts, others that one must keep track of one's attitudes, and still others that one must examine one's heart, or affections, or soul, or selfish nature. We do not mean that within Pentecostalism these various features are understood to be identical. Rather, there is less concern to make specific definitional distinctions or to describe the precise bodily locations for such introspection. The important thing in guarding against temptation, to summarize the Pentecostals accurately, is that one be open to wherever the Spirit might shine his existential spotlight. At the risk of being obvious, whereas the Orthodox do make such definitional distinctions because their acutely ontological model demands it, the Pentecostals are more concerned with the "bottom line" nature of the divine-human interaction because their own pragmatic orientation necessitates it.

THE PRACTICE OF SILENCE

While it is true that silence played an important role in Pentecostalism's spirituality, especially in its earliest years; and while it is also true that Pentecostals were quite willing to wait silently upon God - both in their corporate services[140] and personal devotional times - they did not in years gone by, and do not today, employ silence with the precise methods which do the Orthodox hesychasts. As the above examples indicated, the Orthodox' methods of controlled breathing, listening to one's heartbeat, perpetual and systematic praying (like that of the Jesus prayer), and recognition of the Kingdom of God

---

[140] As early as 1953 this was occurring less and less frequently in AG services. Cf., James Menzie, "Pentecostal Principles," *PE*, October 11, 1953, 2. Menzie lamented the spirituality of his own day, "The whole tenor of our worship, at least in former days, was one of waiting."

within are not present in AG discussions. This does not mean the Pentecostals devalue the role which silence can play in one's transformation process, but it does mean that for the Pentecostals silence (whether external or internal) is just one of many avenues through which God's Spirit can shape the believer.

Pentecostals have always been concerned about church growth. Even in the earlier days, they believed the church universal would benefit greatly from experiencing the Spirit's charismatic movement in the same way that they themselves were experiencing it. But it seems clear that the early Pentecostals were less concerned about growth for growth's sake than are the contemporaries. If visitors thought they were strange for waiting silently to hear from God, if outsiders thought they were patently bizarre because they would have entire meetings given over to waiting in silence, the early Pentecostals were largely ambivalent. What was precious about the early Pentecostals, even if it did indeed manifest in odd practices or behaviors, was their willingness to seek God first. All else - even church growth - took a secondary role. Silence can be a virtue, even if it is not pragmatic.

THE IMPORTANCE OF HUMILITY

Another topic whereby the AG can be likened to the Orthodox regarding Christian transformation concerns humility. In this regard there is similarity with Orthodoxy, but there is also distinction. AG Pentecostals do not exhort one another toward humility along ontological grounds. And, whereas they do occasionally aver that God himself is a humble God,[141] and also whereas they would agree with the Orthodox that one is better able to enjoy communion with God when one is humble, they do not argue that one will be somehow more divine by developing humility. Their reasons for humility are more pragmatic. They want the believer to be obedient to Christ and his Scripture. They want one to be better enabled to existentially listen to, and existentially enjoy the presence of, God. They want to please God and they know that humility is a spiritual fruit. Moreover, they know that humility is a critical characteristic if one is to be powerfully used by God.

---

[141] Cf., C. Yesson, "The Poor in Spirit," *RT*, May 15, 1934, 14, who noted both that humility is one of God's essences and that the incarnation was the greatest act of God's humility.

The First Tributary: The Codification of Moralisms

One scholar argued that the early Pentecostals, because of their own socio-economic lot in life as the working poor, specifically railed against those things which they could not financially afford to indulge in.[142] There may be some credence to that observation, but the more sustainable reason for the moralizing tendency was Pentecostalism's primitivistic urge. They sincerely wanted to separate themselves from the world, and their moral codes enabled them to measure (again the pragmatic impulse is evident) the degree to which that separation had occurred. No sincere Christian could do those things, they taught. The result was that they lived a precise lifestyle, one in many ways austere by today's standards.

If the AG has ceased taking specific activities as its moralizing targets (and that could be debated) because of the arguably more mature understanding that one's attitudes and motives are as important as the activity itself, it has also accommodated to the broader culture's lifestyle and values. We will not reiterate how this cultural accommodation has taken place.[143] Tobacco, alcohol, drugs and the like certainly continue to be shunned by the denomination as a whole. But it does deserve clarification that whereas some of the dainties of days gone by (indulgences which perhaps the Pentecostals could not then afford) can be afforded now and are now quite acceptable (public swimming, sports events, billiards, and the like), an entirely new lifestyle has developed, and that without apparent self-evaluation. In AG churches one will rarely hear a sermon warning against the prideful dangers of owning a Mercedes Benz, a BMW, or a Rolex watch; such items, reflecting the wider process of accommodation to secularism, have become simple issues of personal choice, even among the denomination's district and general officials.[144] Some AG ministers even deign to argue that such niceties are the fruit of their labors, the material harvest that God's own children rightfully deserve. In summation, if the AG's earlier generations overstated the case in their critique of the broader culture by transforming frivolous and a-moral activities into gross immoralities, at least they knew that the broader culture needed to be critiqued (most

---

[142] Anderson, *Vision*, 223-225.

[143] Many scholars could be cited on this aspect. A few include: Poloma, *The At the Crossroads*; Robeck, "National Association of Evangelicals," 634-636; and, Grant Wacker, "Character and Modernization."

[144] To be sure, the local pastor also has to pragmatically decide whether the specific battle is worth the potential members who may be lost.

contemporary Pentecostals would be shocked to know the AG officially took a pacifist position in World War 1). Today's generation has mostly limited its cultural critique to issues of public policy (abortion, school-prayer, and homosexuality), issues rightfully deserving dialogue and critique, but which are nonetheless the "easy" targets of conservative Christianity as a whole. Reflecting the same politically conservative (or is it liberal?) milieu of conservative Christianity, the AG is ignoring various sanctification issues such as personal lifestyle, how a Christian worldview should make one live in distinctly different ways, and what role (apart from engendering personal piety) the Christian community should play in the world.[145] The definition of worldliness (in its less absolute forms)[146] may in fact be relative to each generation and each culture. The deeper existential issues of Christian sanctification and character - modesty, humility, prudence, and responsibility - are timeless.[147]

The Second Tributary: Personal Piety

PERSONAL DEVOTIONS AND SANCTIFICATION
Like the Orthodox, Pentecostals teach about the necessity of one's personal devotions. Both traditions see these times of personal piety as times of deep spiritual refreshment, renewal, and transformation. The Orthodox speak specifically about their devotions, and their theology more broadly, as further uniting one's own person to the person of Christ. The Pentecostals describe their devotions in specific, and spirituality in general, as facilitating a relationship with the person of Christ's Spirit.

The Orthodox tend to process their devotions in specific and theology in general using the realm of vision. This is evident in three ways. They employ icons and therein look (by faith) to see, and thereby participate in, the *hypostasis* of the person depicted (Christ, Mary, saint, or angel). The icon is believed to be

---

[145] In this regard, Anderson's comment that "By concentrating upon individual moral character as the source and solution of all problems, personal and social, they reinforced the social system," seems to be sustained. *Vision*, 31. See his chapter "The Rejection of the World" for a lengthier analysis.

[146] That is, beyond the pale of the New Testament's sin-lists which should be maintained as universal and eternal.

[147] One contemporary writer who did caution against an ostentatious lifestyle was Gary McGee, "Will anybody laugh?" *PE*, March 18, 1990, 8-9.

a window into eternity (if not temporally, then eschatologically),[148] and by gazing therein one enjoys communion with that realm. Secondly, especially within hesychastic teachings, the Orthodox seek to have visions of the divine light. Such visions transform the believer into the image of Christ. Thirdly, the Orthodox instruct one another to look for Christ in all of creation; because creation as a whole is iconically understood, its entirety can reflect Christ himself back to those open and willing to see him therein. The Pentecostals, for their part, tend to process their devotions in specific and spirituality in general using auditory characteristics. Encounters with the Spirit are described as facilitating a divine-human conversation. Pentecostal devotions not only provide the Spirit and the believer with an opportunity to converse, they also serve to open and attune the believer's existential channels so that he or she can better hear the Spirit's voice. Like the Orthodox and their use of icons, Pentecostals teach that faith is necessary to enjoy the divine-human conversation. In a manner surprisingly like the Orthodox' own worldview, Pentecostals teach that the whole of life and creation can become a vehicle for the Spirit's speaking, provided the believer is existentially open and willing to listen.

We will say more about this in our conclusion, but it is pertinent to the issue of devotions that both the Orthodox and Pentecostals manifest an anti-intellectual character. For the Orthodox, the intellect - because it has been darkened by the fall - must be made subservient to the soul. The human person was created so that the soul is to rule the mind (indeed, it does in fact so govern, it is just a matter of whether it governs for good or evil), and the hesychast's internal and ascetic activities are supposed to help one focus one's soul in order that it might better enjoy communion with Christ. When the mind begins to usurp the soul's rule the person's entire being is thrown into spiritual disunity. The Pentecostals, too, warn against over-intellectualizing, both pertaining to life in general and one's devotional time. Again, this belief does not so much stem from precise ontological convictions as it does from their own belief that God created the human person to enjoy *koinonia* with him in the deepest regions of the human self. When those regions are supplanted by the intellectual realm, or are simply ignored in the course of one's everyday life, one's entire being suffers the cold and stifling spiritual consequences.

---

[148] Looking into icons does not enable one to see into eternity in a future sense, but into eternity now - this is the intended meaning of eschatological. Since the human *hypostasis* is depicted, icons enable the believer on earth to commune with that eternal dimension of the soul. Again, because of Christ's theandric nature, and his effect on time thereby, the boundaries between heaven and earth are fuzzy in Orthodox thought.

The above internal-existential elements aside, there are notable differences about devotions between Orthodox and Pentecostals. The most obvious has to do with form. The Orthodox use liturgical calendars. They believe the church calendar gives the believer a framework which commemorates important events in Scripture (and subsequent church history) and that the calendar helps to stimulate the believer when he or she might otherwise flounder on his or her own.[149] Not only do the sacraments facilitate Christian *anamnesis* (active remembering and participation in an event), so too does the church's liturgical calendar. Furthermore, the Orthodox believe the liturgical calendar helps the Christian realize and remember that he or she is a member of a larger community; this community does things together, even when they are apart.

In contrast, Pentecostals reject liturgical calendars as stifling. Because spiritual spontaneity is valued over commemorating specific instances in Scripture or church history, the individual believer is instructed to seek what the Spirit has for him or her - now. The Spirit may have specific instructions which can be revealed existentially or through the illumination of Scripture. The Spirit may impel one to pray for lost souls or crisis situations. Or, he may draw one into a-rational and intercessory prayer.

A problematic issue for Orthodox devotions, on a popular-piety level, resides with the belief that because one is obeying the calendar and observing the prescribed fasts or prayers one is thereby necessarily pleasing God or being transformed into Christ's image. This same corporate-oriented mentality dangerously manifests itself elsewhere in the belief that because one is born in a country which is traditionally Orthodox, one is therefore a Christian. The strength of Orthodox devotions, stemming from their Eastern character, is that there is a communal orientation; the New Testament Christians were certifiably members of a community in a way that modern Western evangelicals and Pentecostals are not (this hermeneutically blinds evangelicals and Pentecostals from seeing that communal feature about the first century believers).

Problematic about Pentecostal devotions is that despite their flexibility and spontaneity, human nature being what it is, each Pentecostal believer will likely fall into some kind of routinized form. Pentecostals can too easily become trapped within the devotional circle of their own making. Worse, because their churches lack a more intentionally defined liturgical calendar, Pentecostals (at

---

[149] For example see Anthony Coniaris, *Daily Vitamins for Spiritual Growth: Day by Day with Jesus Through the Church Year,* 2 vols. (Minneapolis, Minnesota: Light and Life, 1994).

least those in the United States) have clearly made secularism's calendar the hub around which their own church life revolves. Instead of actively remembering and commemorating the important events of salvation history (whether in Scripture or since that time), Pentecostals uncritically celebrate national holidays and allow those dates to determine what, and how, the local church's energies and efforts are spent. Pentecostal ministers are more intent on employing Mother's Day and July fourth for religious purposes than they are on commemorating such important Christian dates and seasons as Advent, Lent, and Pentecost (again, there are not altogether unreasonable pragmatic reasons for this, such as appealing to what it is that is at the forefront of society's attention in order to make inroads for the gospel). Still, Pentecostal ministers and officials take no thought as to how this kind of accommodation impacts the way they and their parishioners process their Christian faith. Lastly, in comparison to Orthodoxy, there is another problematic dimension about Pentecostal devotions, and one which stems from their Western character: they tend to make the believer process his or her Christian experience as a solely individual enterprise. Again, this has important dimensions for how the notions of Christian transformation and spirituality are processed.

East or West, Orthodox or Pentecostal, routinization is routinization. One can just as easily and mechanically follow one's own chosen form as one can naturally and mechanically follow a prescribed form. Disorderly or purposeless spontaneity is no more virtuous than is rote ecclesiastical formalism. In its teachings about individual devotions in specific, and the community's life and thought in general, the church must ever guard against routinization and the resulting spiritual petrification which accompanies it. This brings us to revivals.

REVIVALS

In light of the Pentecostals' emphasis upon the human's existential nature and intuitive knowledge, it is not surprising that Pentecostal spirituality and worship are themselves characterized by those features. (Although it should be clarified that worship services and spiritual activities are not intentionally structured with a full understanding of the person as presented in this study. Pentecostals are not generally so reflective, either about planning their worship services or thinking about human persons in specific. Instead, they intuitively follow what seems to shape and impact people.) This chapter's delineation of revivals must not be taken to mean that Pentecostals alone emphasize revivals; evangelicals also employ revivals, and in fact they were doing so before Pentecostalism's advent. What is novel about Pentecostal revivals is the degree to which charismatic elements are manifested, and the extent to which the existential nature of humanity is affected. Phenomena such as words of knowledge, *glossolalic* utterances, prophecies, healings, and miracles - elements best understood as rooted in the human person's existential (S/spirit) nature - are all employed with the understanding that they are the Spirit's gifts for the sake of edifying and transforming people, both Christian and non-Christian. Worship services, along with providing opportunities to glorify God, provide the individual the opportunity to commune with God's Spirit. Amid the assembled Christian host, the individual can experience a heightened sense of the Spirit's presence.

Still, for all of their sermons and articles about revival as the new movings of God, the Pentecostals, like those in the AG, do not thereby imply or hope that something historically new will result. They do not wait for, pray for, or anticipate the arrival of something unprecedented in history (which could accurately be said about Acts 2 itself). Instead, they mean that they want qualitatively new movings of the Spirit to erupt in their presence. That qualitative goodness is by no means denied herein, but the problem is that revival, for the Pentecostals, has taken on a whole series of connotations which has precisely limited and narrowed what God will do and how he can do it. It is not our purpose here to critique either revivalism as a methodology, or the problems which an emphasis upon a perpetual charismatic celebration can produce; those have already been critiqued by others.[150] It does suffice to say that in my study of the AG's literature rarely did a writer caution the denomination against painting God into a prescribed revivalistic box.[151] Donald Gee warned against co-opting revival as one's own product when he said, "Not only an individual but a collective Revival Movement needs to retain a collective humility (if such thing be conceivable) if it is to retain its collective power. Denominational swagger soon forfeits the anointing of the Spirit. Therefore let us beware of boasting in statistics, unless God gets all the glory."[152] But even the sage and prophetic Donald Gee was unable to see beyond the culturally conditioned norms and forms of revivals. If, as AG

---

[150] William McLoughlin, Jr., *Modern Revivalism: Charles Grandison Finney to Billy Graham* (NY: The Ronald Press, 1959), 400-530; Timothy Smith, *Revivalism and Social Reform in Mid-Nineteenth Century America* (Nashville, Tennessee: Abingdon, 1957); Chan, *Spiritual Theology*, 48-49.
[151] James Stewart, "God Has No Push-Button Revival: Is it not an insult to God - dictating the kind of revival we want?" *PE*, February 12, 1965, 3, 27. Stewart mostly argued against trying to tame, or make less emotional, the Holy Spirit's movings.
[152] Gee, "Mighty Growth and Many Tears," *PE*, July 13, 1952, 4.

publications would have us believe, revivals are the answer to the
denomination's lagging growth rate, it seems clear that an historically
unprecedented move of the Spirit - one more sovereignly and uniquely breathed
of God - is required.

The Third Tributary: Twentieth-Century Western Distinctives

GOD'S PURPOSE FOR ONE'S LIFE
Sociologists and other scholars have long argued that human beings need a
purpose in order to exist. Whether that purpose is variously found in child-
rearing and family, one's vocation, public service or the like, human beings
need a reason to live. Lacking purpose, the delicate existential organism that is
the human person begins to unravel and deteriorate. No less is true for
Christians. Lacking some trace of purpose, the Christian life too can become
vapid and sterile. This argument from human nature is important, but it needs a
surer foundation if we are to apply to a Christian epistemology. Fortunately,
Scripture provides us with such.

If the Bible's narratives not only preserve sacred history but also instruct
their readers about faithful living, and clearly the latter seems obvious, the
dimension of God's purpose for Christian sanctification is a necessity. More
specifically, Pentecostals' teaching on the necessity of fulfilling God's purpose
for one's life is a Biblical theme which can no longer be ignored by the bulk of
Christendom. When God called persons to follow him in the Old Testament, or
more specifically when Christ called persons to follow him in the New
Testament, there consistently was a task to which he appointed them. They were
not only called to *become like* Christ, they were also called to *do like* Christ. To
say as much need not at all imply that one is somehow earning one's
sanctification, rather it means that a holistic view of Christ involves both his
person and his work.

One can go even further. Based on the Biblical witness, we may fairly
assume that Christ himself was - and thereby that God himself is - a pragmatist.
God clearly delights not only in existing but in doing. And, if creation and
redemption are exemplary of his doing, he delights in doing it well.
Unquestionably, he is not in a hurry about his doing. One need not study either
Scripture, history, or geology very long before one recognizes that God does
things according to his own patient (often laboriously so!) timetable.

The ramification's of Christ's own "doings" are manifold for the Christian's Kingdom living. However, Pentecostals need to reflect more carefully on how varied the Christian purpose can be. Arguments from cultural diversity, ethnic diversity, and individual uniqueness alone can attest to the manifold expressions of God's being and purpose. Such arguments are indeed arguments "from below" (from creation to God), but they are no less Christian.[153] Such arguments "from below" aside, the apostle Paul's teaching on the body of Christ (1 Cor. 12) powerfully suffices to reveal that God simply has not called everyone to be a mouth, despite the traditional Pentecostal emphasis to the contrary. For example, God's purpose in sanctification may mean he has called one to a life of prayer (such as is fulfilled in both personal "prayer-closets" and monasteries), the work of healing (fulfilled in a plethora of ways), discipling others in their process of transformation, or manual labor (the "hand" of Paul's 1 Cor. 12 analogy). To clarify thusly is not to denigrate the traditional ministerial vocations, but it is a call for a more carefully developed appreciation for the whole enterprise of Christian service. Lastly, Pentecostals need to re-consider how the larger enterprise of living, and not just one's given task, is part and parcel of Kingdom living. As noted previously, the early Pentecostals were critically aware that to live Christianly meant one lived differently. Those same cultural and time-bound expressions of that difference need not be dogmatized, but somehow one's lifestyle ought itself to reflect the purpose of Christ's Kingdom.

SPIRIT-BAPTISM

Earlier I noted that the Pentecostal doctrine of Spirit-baptism evinces its Western character - in contrast to Eastern Orthodoxy - in a way that none of its other practices or doctrines do. The reasons for this are two-fold. First, while Pentecostals are clear that the Spirit can and should come in, upon, and through the corporate worship assembly (a phenomenon about which the Orthodox are equally adamant), the apex of spiritual experience concerns the Spirit coming in, upon, and through the individual. Whereas the surrounding congregation can be edified as they witness a fellow believer being plunged into the Spirit, the critical issue is that the believer herself experiences this apostolic event. God the Spirit, in a way that the Old Testament believers could never have imagined,

---

[153] The Scriptural references and their implications to sustain this argument are voluminous.

comes to make the human person his temple.[154] Whereas the Jews had a physical location (the tabernacle and then the temple) to which they could go to worship God corporately, one of the incredible dimensions of the New Covenant is that he makes *individuals* to become living temples for his residence, and that in the deepest of existential ways.

The second emphasis of Spirit-baptism which reveals the clearly Western emphasis of the doctrine is that the AG's missiology focuses upon Spirit-empowered individuals who go out for the sake of Christ. We must be fair. Pentecostals are well aware that it is the corporate church's task to proclaim the gospel and make disciples; the whole church is involved in that the laity supports the ministers and missionaries with tithes, donations, and prayers. But the way this is accomplished is through individuals, Spirit-baptized and Spirit-empowered individuals.

In Pentecostalism's single distinctive doctrine, in one great religious moment where the person's spirit is suffused with God's Spirit, three great features of contemporary Western life are welded together: individualism, existentialism, and pragmatism. As has been noted repeatedly throughout this study, the Spirit does not just sate the believer with his presence so that the person can taste of the Kingdom or be changed, he does so in order that the believer is empowered to more effectively do the work of the Kingdom. Nearly every single AG article about the necessity of Spirit-baptism for each believer reiterates this person-plus-purpose fusion. Additionally, to clarify the Western character of the doctrine is by no means to render it null or void. If the Biblical record is to be accepted at face-value, the apostles themselves exhibited very individual, existential, and pragmatic manifestations at their Spirit-baptism.[155] I made this point earlier, but it bears repeating that not one of the disciples was willing to die for Jesus of Nazareth, despite their having bodily lived with him for three years, and despite their having seen him perform numerous signs of the Kingdom's power and presence, until *after* their Acts 2 experience. Following that, they were arguably the most existential and pragmatic Jews ever to have walked in the Biblical accounts. In Acts 11 Peter reasoned with the apostles in

---

[154] Again, the AG, like other Pentecostals, does not deny that one is made a temple of the Spirit at conversion.

[155] Some interpreters tame this event's drama so that it little resembles the emotional and religious exuberance Luke conveyed. One thinks immediately of Renaissance artists' depictions of the apostles sitting passively, eyes lifted ever so slightly and piously to heaven, while flames lightly touch their heads. This despite the fact that the witnesses thought these people were drunk!

Jerusalem that because the Holy Spirit had fallen on the Gentiles in Caesarea, just as he had upon the apostles themselves, it was proof-positive that God was including the Gentiles in Christ's saving work. His argument could not have been more "from below." His argument was unequivocally rooted in an existential experience! Yet it was precisely the argument Peter made. As to pragmatism, the apostles did indeed go to Jerusalem, Judea, Samaria, and the ends of the empire, just as Jesus had foretold (Acts 1:8). The result was that within three hundred years an empire which formerly had murdered those Christ-like-ones was itself accepting Christianity *en masse*.

10

Conclusion

Apples and oranges and fruit stands. As the previous chapters have made evident, one cannot fairly compare Western and Eastern Christianity in general, and Pentecostalism and Orthodoxy in specific, without recognizing that the two share many, but not all, of the same theological fruits. Moreover, because each side's fruit stand has been constructed on the basis of markedly different blueprints, each half of Christendom stacks and emphasizes these common fruits in different ways; again, this is evident within even such a narrow topic as Christian transformation. Each side's fruit stand, to continue the analogy, is formed in correspondence to a critical meta-context consisting of history, philosophy, culture, and the way in which those impact epistemology. In any comparative study of Orthodox and Pentecostal theologies, the many doctrinal distinctives for each side are indeed important and must be clarified, but without some inclusion of each side's meta-context only truncated conclusions can be reached.

The Orthodox rely heavily upon, and brilliantly modify, the philosophic suppositions of ancient Greece. Firstly, in that regard, ontology is tremendously important. Metaphysical concerns, which are assumed at best in contemporary Western theology, continue to be critical for Orthodoxy's theology. Anthropology, the theological foundations for Christian transformation, and even the means of transformation, are each ontologically structured. To become like Christ - to undergo *theosis* - is itself an ontological, not juridical, issue. To be a Christian is to experience, participate in, and be transformed by, the life of God himself. This transformation is primarily accomplished through the sacraments, mysteries which enable a participation in the very life and person of Christ. However, on anthropological grounds - because the human person is an icon of God and thereby participates in, to an extent, what God has intended for him or her - this transformation can also occur via immediate and prayerful encounters with the divine. Secondly, regarding ancient Greek philosophic structures, community is important. In fact, so corporate-minded is Eastern Orthodoxy, that individuality - a topic so assumed and emphasized in the West - is itself an ambiguous concept.[1] To be fully human, as we noted earlier, is to

---

[1] Nonna Verna Harrison, "The Maleness of Christ," *St. Vladimir's*, 42:2 (1998), 118.

manifest *ekstasis*, after the fashion of God's own *ekstasis*. *Theosis*, as the Orthodox express it, stems from an eternally ecstatic relationship between the Father and the Son and the Spirit, the holy and infinite community of God. This relational life, this *sobornost'*, has now been extended to the human race through the theandric one, Jesus Christ. This *sobornost'*, moreover, has been characterized from eternity by a humility that has been variously expressed by God's willingness to risk creating beings who would pervert his gift of life by centering it around themselves, the *Logos'* kenotic act of incarnation, and the Holy Spirit's own kenotic work of making the Father and Son known. The believer, within the *sobornost'* of the Christian community, is granted entrance into the very being of the Triune God, and therein is transformed. Because God is infinite, to become like him will involve an eternal process of growth and transformation.

North American and Western Pentecostals, for their part, also have their own meta-context which has dramatically impacted their theology. This meta-context is a complex mixture of the juridical, individual, pragmatic, existential, and empirical arenas; arenas which have preceded the Pentecostals' own history and, like the Orthodox, rather predisposed them to construct their own theology in specific and precise ways. Sanctification is firstly an issue of juridical pardon: one is positionally sanctified, that is in one's standing before God, when one commits oneself to Christ at conversion. In this regard, sanctification pertains exclusively to individuals. However, as we saw with the AG, sanctification as a juridical issue does not solely define the Pentecostals' spirituality. In light of their own existential orientation, Pentecostals secondly assert - with the various empirical proofs of *glossolalia*, affective transformation, charismatic gifts, and prayerful encounter - that God himself can be experienced and known. As I said in an earlier chapter, if the juridical arena around which conversion is oriented provides Pentecostals with an overarching melody, their existential insights and convictions provide them with an invigorating harmonic undercurrent. The Pentecostals' spirituality is also framed in light of their own meta-context in that both Jesus' death and resurrection, and Scripture, are appealed to as further empirical evidence of the Gospel's validity and reality. Still further with regard to meta-contexts, one's Pentecostal experience of God is consistently framed as a pragmatic issue: God has changed the believer so that he or she can in turn fulfill God's plan to transform others. By fulfilling the great commission (Mt. 28:19) one is further progressing in one's own sanctification. Ultimately, Pentecostal spirituality is a complex dynamic reflecting God's own character as a juridical, pragmatic, and existential being.

As I have intimated, especially throughout this study's latter half, despite the fact that the Orthodox and the Pentecostals express their respective theologies within entirely different meta-contexts, the two share two important similarities. The first is that both believe Christian transformation must necessarily incorporate a divine-human communion. The second is that the two share a fascinatingly similar worldview. With specific regard to the latter, the two hold very congruent views of anthropology, God, and creation. In drawing out similarities about those three issues I will not reiterate the depths of each side's position, or restate each side's meta-context for these three features, but a more intentional comparison is nonetheless warranted.

Anthropology

The similarities will be noted shortly, but it deserves immediate clarification that the single greatest anthropological difference between Orthodoxy and Pentecostalism has to do with hermeneutical perspectives, that is, what is it that constitutes the Scriptural norm for understanding human beings? The Orthodox believe Jesus Christ, the ontologically perfect one, is that norm. All that Christ is, by virtue of his incarnation, is read back into the Genesis texts and applied to Adam as he existed before the fall.[2] Adam and Eve were created to enjoy perfect fellowship with God. Had they continued to follow and commune with God, they would have eventually experienced the completion of their own *theosis*, the likes of which was realized by Jesus himself. However, whereas Jesus fulfilled that goal by virtue of his person, human beings could only have, and indeed, can only attain God's goal of *theosis* by virtue of God's grace. God's purpose for humans was that they live out and fulfill the ramifications of their created identities as the universe's microcosms, beings who, as the *hypostases* of the universe, present God to creation and creation back to God. Through them the universe would enjoy the eternal *sobornost'* of the Triune God. In all of this, pre-fallen humans, processed through an iconic understanding of Christ, are normative for understanding what it is that Christians are to aspire. The Image

---

[2] And, this hermeneutic is not at all problematic in the Orthodox' eyes. Because Jesus Christ, the incarnate *Logos*, is the One in whom both material and Spirit are joined, and the One in whom time and eternity intersect, he can be interpreted as the first born of all creation (Rom. 8:29; Col. 1:15, 18), the archetypal human whom the Father predestined from before time to recapitulate the human race (Eph. 1:10).

of God - the incarnate *Logos* - perfectly reflects the Father. Human beings, in turn, were created to reflect the *Logos*.

For Pentecostals, like the bulk of Western Christendom, the normative understanding of human beings rests with what they have been *since the fall*. In this regard, humans are first and foremost sinners in need of redemption. Because the Genesis accounts reveal so very little about their pre-fallen state, Pentecostals, have been hesitant to speculate as to what Adam and Eve might have been like - other than that they were innocent - or the extent to which they enjoyed fellowship with God - other than that it was perfect. Because the force of the Genesis accounts concerns Adam and Eve's obeying God's initial commandments, their Edenic state is naturally processed by Pentecostals within a juridical context. The two sinned and plunged their descendants headlong into sin and destruction. Their sin disrupted God's intended purpose that they exercise dominion over the creation and glorify him.

The issue of hermeneutical perspectives is just one of many issues about which Eastern and Western Christians ought more carefully to reflect. That issue notwithstanding, there are several places where Pentecostals and the Orthodox hold a similar anthropological vista. These concern the *imago dei*, humanity's preeminence, and the existential nature.

The Imago Dei

The Orthodox do not believe the fall caused humans to cease being whom God created them to be. It is just that they ceased being *all* God had initially created them to be. The fall both rendered his task for them impossible - they could no longer attain God's desired goal of *theosis* - and obfuscated their circles of fellowship, both with him and with one another. Vladimir Lossky said, "Man has closed up within himself the springs of divine grace."[3] The fall did not eradicate those springs of grace, instead it corrupted, perverted, and fractured them. It made human beings to be prisoners within mortal and decaying bodies, tragic figures who perpetuate the species but who all the while fail to accomplish the goal of their own *hypostases*.[4] The remedy is not that grace be added to, or granted on behalf of, the human person in order for God to grant

---

[3] Lossky, *Image and Likeness,* 131. Lossky quoted Philaret of Moscow, *Discours et sermons*, I, 5.
[4] Zizioulas, *Being As Communion*, 50-53.

him pardon or life, but that he fulfill and attain what God created him to be. Thus, because the ultimate issue between God and humanity is not juridical but relational, the issue of original innocence is a moot one for the Orthodox. From their theological vista, even if one were morally or religiously innocent, that in itself would not enable one in turn to achieve God's goal of *theosis* and all it implied for the human race and creation. Innocence does not equate with nor necessitate salvation.

Along with the fact that Scripture ascribes God's image to fallen humans (Gen. 9:6; 1 Cor. 11:7; Col. 3:10; Jas. 3:9), Pentecostals follow James Arminius - who himself followed and modified the Catholic theologian Molinas - and also do not believe the *imago dei* was destroyed by the fall. That Scripture describes post-fallen humans as beings created in God's image, that even evil and hateful people still do good and loving things, and that people still interact with their God-given consciences, all testify to the fact that the image was not destroyed. Furthermore, unlike John Wesley, who believed the fall eradicated the *imago dei* and who described the good done by humans as resulting from God's prevenient or common grace, Pentecostals tend to posit the good and loving things done by humans in terms of their own created identity;[5] this even though Pentecostals know that good works can in no way count for salvation. Humans are not totally depraved (again, they can do good and even though they are fallen they reflect something of God himself), but they are depraved. Original sin is a spiritual and moral handicap, "a tendency or bias to sin," as Pearlman said, which makes sin quite natural-and indeed inevitable-for every person.[6] (On a pastoral basis, the horrific doctrine whereby original sin subjects even the unborn and infants to damnation is thus avoided.) Salvation is a juridical matter for Pentecostals, but salvation has implications that reach far beyond the juridical arena. Following Wesley, Pentecostals believe God's pardon is granted for the sake of participation in a divine-human koinonia. Additionally, and rooted in their understanding of the imago, God's purpose for each person is critical. In order to be all that God intends for one to be, one must determine and fulfill the task for which one was created. As AG Pentecostals tend to express it, this task will inevitably involve the salvation and transformation of others. It is a task which can and should be empowered by the Holy Spirit's *charismata*, but it will also stem from one's own unique giftings and character as one created in God's image.

---

[5] E.g., E. S. Williams, *Systematic Theology*, 2:137.
[6] Pearlman, *Doctrines*, 135.

In my introduction I posited that the Pentecostals can fairly be interpreted as a *via media* between Orthodoxy and Protestantism, especially along experiential lines. Because Reformed-Higher Life Pentecostals, like those in the AG, deny the doctrine of total depravity, they are unlike the Reformed and Baptistic Protestants. Because those same Pentecostals believe salvation is indeed a juridical issue, they resemble their Reformed and Baptistic Protestant brothers and sisters. Conversely, because they hold that humans are innately capable of good deeds, deeds which are nonetheless ineffectual for salvation, Pentecostals are like the Orthodox. Pardon? Yes, but not exclusively. Participation? Emphatically, but not without pardon. In all of this Pentecostals represent a kind of middle ground, a kind of *via media*, between Orthodoxy and Protestantism along anthropological lines.

Humanity's Preeminence

Both Pentecostals and the Orthodox believe that of all God's creations humanity is preeminent. Pentecostals consistently root that preeminence in God's purpose; God created humans variously with the capacity to know him, with the potential for immortal life, with an understanding of wrong and right, and with the responsibility of exercising dominion. The single greatest catalyst for the Pentecostals' anthropological discussions has been evolution, a doctrine of existence which relegates humans to being just one more species on the earth. Pentecostals believe that evolution dangerously leads men and women to believe they do not answer to God, and to believe that they are only biological-intellectual beings whose existence ceases at death. Evolution can produce beliefs which result in a truncated and meaningless existence on earth. Ultimately, these beliefs will ultimately can cause eternal damnation. The Orthodox, for their part, root mankind's preeminence along ontological lines. As beings created with physical and noetic (intellectual-existential-spiritual) dimensions, humans alone of all God's creations experience the totality of the universe. As such, they are the ontological high points of creation. They are microcosms of the universe who are able to transcend the physical realm and bring it into fellowship with God himself. The catalyst for their discussions on preeminence is once again Greek ontology. Unlike ancient Greek philosophy, especially in its Platonic forms, the Orthodox by no means affirm pantheism. But, stemming from their *Logos*-theology, they do understand the universe in a

more communal and monistic way than do either Pentecostals in specific, or
Protestants more broadly.

It is important, even if obvious, to note that for both the Orthodox and
Pentecostals, mankind's preeminence stems from its position *vis-a-vis* God. For
the former the definitions of person have ramifications for purpose, and for the
latter definitions of purpose have ramifications for person.[7] Still, there are clear
implications of such a shared anthropology. Firstly, is the arena of praxis. That
is, on the basis of humanity's preeminence, the two can and should work
together concerning human rights issues, and the two ought to seek some level
of tolerance - if not cooperation - about missions. These practical endeavors
ought especially to occur in geographical regions where the two have tended to
view one another warily. If people have been created in light of God's own
ekstasis, as the Orthodox assert, and if Christians are called and commissioned
to transform the lives of others, as Pentecostals assert, the two have a
theological treasure house from which the two can work as practical allies.
Secondly, the two need to explore more intentionally one another at a
theological level. Even if they express it within different meta-contexts, the two
are adamant that anthropology is always a soteriological issue. That is, the
human person can never be considered apart from God. The ramifications for
this belief are legion, and could be applied to nearly every arena of human
existence.

The Existential Nature

Of the anthropological similarities shared by the Pentecostals and Orthodox,
humanity's existential characteristic is the most obvious one, and the one most
unique in contrast to the broader sweep of Christendom. To a degree surpassing
Catholicism and Protestantism, the Orthodox and Pentecostals emphasize the
reality and importance of the human person's nearly ineffable, but nonetheless
real, dimensions. Again, Catholics and non-Pentecostal Protestants do not deny

---

[7] It is also fascinating that each tradition "sees" its own emphasis in the dominion
narrative of Genesis 1:26-28. As was noted in chapter four, the Orthodox explain the
issue of humanity's dominion by including ontological ramifications: to exercise
dominion means one should *be* like God. For their part, as was noted in chapter nine, the
Pentecostals explain the issue of dominion in light of purpose: to exercise dominion
means one should *do* like God.

that those dimensions exist, but they do not hold them as being so critical and necessary in the Christian life as do the Pentecostals and Orthodox. Moreover, whereas specific Catholic and Protestant individuals emphasize humanity's existential dimensions, it cannot be said that either of those traditions emphasize the existential element on a consistent basis, as occurs in Orthodoxy and Pentecostalism. Because this existential similarity is so critical for a mutual understanding, I will summarize and develop three different pertinent issues: existential definitions, anthropological essentialism, and the role of spiritual atmosphere.

DEFINITIONS BRIEFLY SUMMARIZED

Each side's definitions of this existential nature will not be repeated here, but because this element is so central some summary is necessary. The Orthodox are not unanimous as to how this nature should be understood, but it consistently has to do with *nous*: that element of human nature which involves consciousness and understanding; it is also the element especially created to reflect the *Logos* to creation and other humans. This dimension does not preclude the mind, but neither is it limited to it. Instead, it includes the intuitive dimension of human apprehension, a dimension which involves the visceral regions (often, but not exclusively the heart) of the body. In and through one's *nous* one can intuitively experience-commune (something the Orthodox refer to as *theoria*) with God. The *nous* was created, Palamas taught, as an *organ of vision*, which, when it receives divine grace, is able to transcend itself and commune with God.[8] This dimension needs to be disciplined and trained. Through hesychasm's ascetic practices - prayer, obedience, fasting, humility, repentance, and guarding one's heart against the passions, temptation, and sin - one can tune one's inner being so that one can simultaneously better experience God, have a more Christ-like view of life and creation, and live one's own life in a more existentially integrated manner.

For their part, Pentecostals are far less concerned to define mankind's existential nature in precise terminology, or to describe it *vis-a-vis* a divine ontology, but they are no less emphatic that it exists. In AG critiques of evolution, the existential nature (soul-spirit) is regularly discussed as one of the elements which makes men and women preeminent over animals. Unlike animals, human beings were created with existential chords, chords which can be attuned to vibrate in accord with God's own Spirit so that increasingly

---

[8] Meyendorff, *The Triads*, 35. My emphasis.

greater levels of resolution can be reached. However, as the AG expresses it, one can be saved (judicially pardoned; that is, positionally sanctified) without one's inner self having been fully transformed (sanctified; that is, having experientially appropriated one's new identity). One can be in Christ, but still having the need to become fully like him. Also like the Orthodox hesychasts, but not with the same precision or emphasis, Pentecostals have traditionally understood that it is edifying for the Christian believer to exercise a degree of asceticism in order to bring himself or herself to a better existential place.

The two also share a common belief that this existential nature is not just an eternal element residing in a physical body. Instead, this nature constitutes the very personality and eternal uniqueness of each person. The Orthodox describe this uniqueness using the word *hypostasis*, that irreducibly mysterious something which both participates in the nature common to all people, but which remains distinctly itself. A person's *hypostasis* variously shines forth in the way she smiles, her artistic and aesthetic expressions, her mannerisms, the way she relates to and among others, and the like; even though none of those things by themselves constitute her *hypostasis*. The soul, Vlachos taught, is the "way in which life is manifested in man."[9] Like the Orthodox, AG theologians recognize that the soul is not just a divine spark placed within the human person. Instead it is, as Myer Pearlman said, "the life-giving and intelligent principle animating the human body, using the bodily senses as its agents in the exploration of material things and the bodily organs for its self-expression and communication with the outside world."[10] It is an important spiritual organ for communing with God, a fact which Pentecostal theologians explicitly affirm and which Pentecostal ministers and laypersons intuitively understand.

ESSENTIALISM

One of the implications of this existential similarity is that both traditions assert an essentialist view of human persons. Simply stated, there is something with which all human beings are created and have in common, an existential core. Stemming from our having been created in God's image, both traditions affirm that we do "all emerge from the same lump of clay," as one AG writer put it.[11] The world's multitude of religions attest to the fact that human beings, impelled by their very nature, look beyond themselves for life's value and meaning, even

---

[9] Vlachos, *Psychotherapy,* 97.
[10] Pearlman, *Doctrines,* 104.
[11] James Clutter, "Potter and Clay," *PE,* February 24, 1974, 10.

as one AG writer so eloquently said it, '"Deep calleth unto deep' - the depths of the human spirit respond to the infinite deep of the Spirit of God."[12] To assert that the Pentecostal anthropology resembles the Orthodox' own iconic anthropology may seem like I am pushing their position too far, for some. However, it is indeed the case that throughout the movement's history Pentecostal converts have regularly testified that in their pre-conversion, and/or pre-Spirit-baptism state, they were being drawn by, and looking for, something religiously real and powerful, even if they did not know what that something was. It seems quite accurate to hold that they were being prompted and made spiritually hungry firstly by the Spirit of God (God is always the first mover in salvation) and secondly by their own innate natures as beings created in God's nature. E. S. Williams, a former AG General Superintendent, himself argued precisely as much when he said:

'Why then do the heathen have a sense of moral responsibility, for they do not have a Bible?' We answer that 'He left not Himself without a witness.' *The Holy Spirit* which 'moved upon the face of the waters' during the time of chaos before our present world order was brought into *existence has never ceased moving upon the chaos of depraved mankind.* Consciousness of a Supreme Being has been provided in 'that he did good, and gave us fruitful seasons, filling our hearts with gladness' (Acts 14:17). *That man has sought Divine aid when these blessings have been withheld gives evidence of intuitive belief in God.* The traces of moral standards everywhere to be found reveal *that the Holy Spirit has spoken to the conscience of man in all generations,* enlightening conscience concerning what is right and what is wrong. Sin, it is true, has warped the judgment of conscience, but has never erased its action. Man was created in the image of God, and in that image dwelt righteousness and true holiness.[13]

Both the Orthodox and Pentecostals describe the essential human character as one whereby humans mirror and reflect their God given identities. Some people reflect this identity more lucidly than others - especially those whose identities have been fused and pervaded with Christ's own Spirit. We can add that some religions, on a corporate level, reflect this identity in a more authentic manner than do others. For example, the monotheistic religions of Christianity,

---

[12] Arne Vick, "Pentecostal Worship," *PE*, 10, 1966.
[13] Williams, *Systematic Theology*, 1:167-168. My emphasis. Also see Pearlman, 44-46, regarding the universal belief in God.

Judaism, and Islam, respectively, can be said to reflect - and facilitate the reflection of - the God-given nature of humans more accurately than do polytheistic, animistic, or atheistic religions - religions which deny God's true identity and mankind's own preeminent identity. In light of the theology of image, one can say that perhaps those non-monotheistic religions reflect some religious truths not so much because God's Spirit has granted them a degree of religious revelation, but because they share the common existential nature which resides in all humans and naturally impels them Godward.

That latter comment on world-religions and their own fractured iconic character brings us to another issue regarding the Orthodox' and Pentecostals' shared anthropological insights: both groups traditionally have been quite parochial in their willingness to recognize Christ in others claiming to be Christians but whom are not Orthodox or Pentecostal, as the case may be. Stemming from the corrupted nature common to all people, both groups naturally allow meta-context issues to impair their vision of Christ in others claiming to be Christians. We must be fair. Both the Orthodox and Pentecostals are virtuously impelled by their convictions about Christian truth, and neither is - rightly, I might add - willing to sacrifice Christian truth for the sake of spurious fellowship. All is *not* relative. Christ is the only means of salvation. However, an historical examination of both traditions bears out that both groups have allowed race, culture, nationalism, historical myopia, and tradition to obfuscate a recognition of Christ in others - and that even regarding internal debates within both traditions.[14] If it is true that, as the apostle Paul said, "There is no longer Jew or Greek, there is no longer slave or free, there is no longer male and female; for all of you are one in Christ Jesus" (Gal. 3:28), the two must begin to recognize the degree to which meta-contexts predispose them against seeing Christ in the other.

Not only have meta-contextual issues played a critical role in how these two traditions view Christians from other meta-contexts, such issues have also caused a kind of myopia regarding the essential nature of human beings. Both the Orthodox and Pentecostals have been terribly slow to recognize that genetics, heredity, social constructs, economics, and culture each has a tremendous role to play in how the "lump of clay" common to all persons is shaped. To so qualify those issues does not mean that each person is somehow

---

[14] As early as 1947, Donald Gee was warning the Pentecostals about their own self-satisfaction and narrowness. See, "Are we too 'Movement' Conscious?" *Pentecost*, No. 2, December 1947, 17.

not responsible for his or her own standing *vis-a-vis* God. "God does not grade on a curve," as the charismatic leader John Wimber once colorfully put it. (This is a theological issue, and need not even be driven by the winds of popular culture, as perhaps an inclusion of social constructs, economics, and culture might suggest.) But, if it is the case that the existential core both shapes and is shaped by its environs, theologians and ministers within both traditions need to reflect more carefully on the ensuing ramifications. For example, can it be that some people are more naturally predisposed to accept and live in light of the Gospel than others? The ramifications are dizzying. The possibilities are numerous. The solutions may only come from cross-disciplined studies, if at all.

Lastly, with regard to essentialism, there is a very real tension between the communal and individual expressions of Christianity which exist between the Orthodox and the West. Again, the two have many things to learn from one another, things which can be mutually edifying and empowering at the theological and ecclesial levels. As a Westerner, I am utterly fascinated to read about the fall as a move toward individualism. The Orthodox recognize something terribly corrupt within human nature when they so describe the fall: we really do want to be our own gods. As a Pentecostal, I find myself even a bit disconcerted to learn that my very S/spiritual giftings belong not to myself, but the Christian community. Pentecostals have always affirmed so much, it is just that amid the cultural and commercial bombardment of individualism that comprises life in the Western world, it is so easy to forget that we are part of, and responsible to, a much larger organism: the body of Christ. The Orthodox are critically attuned to processing Christian transformation in specific, and Christianity in general, in corporate ways, ways that seem to be presupposed in the Biblical accounts and therefore authentically Christian. As a Western Christian, I find the notion of corporate Christianity - so assumed and emphasized in the East - to be a terribly ambiguous concept. My meta-context quite naturally pre-disposes me against such a mindset, but I am willing to consider it.

The Orthodox' rich and intriguing panorama notwithstanding, I do not know how - even on the basis of the more community-oriented New Testament pattern - God deals with us apart from the fact that we are individuals. This individualizing thrust seems to be one of the clear ramifications of both the new covenant and Pentecost: God no longer establishes his communion with people on the basis of ethnicity, heritage, or class; and, he will indeed make individual persons to be his own Spirit-filled temples. In all of this, he has thrown wide open the door to every individual willing to come to him. My own commitment to Christ may indeed predispose my children and grandchildren to seek Christ out, but as Scripture presents it, they ultimately stand before God on their own. The implications for ecclesiology and missions, again, are multiple. The challenges for an expanding and *ekstasis*-oriented Orthodoxy are voluminous, and they will not likely be overcome by simply insisting that all potential converts adapt a Greek Patristic reading of life and Christ.

SPIRITUAL ATMOSPHERE: AESTHETICS AND KINESTHETICS

Another issue pertaining to the existential nature, and one critically important to both the Pentecostals and Orthodox and their respective doctrines of Christian transformation, is the issue of spiritual atmosphere. As both groups express it, especially but not exclusively with regard to the corporate worship assembly, a Spirit-filled atmosphere is essential for a full encounter with God. The Orthodox believe, together with reasons of historical continuity, that the very church building's architecture must meet specific standards. The Orthodox believe that the "earthly church should be the image of the heavenly Church."[15] It should not only bring glory to God but should signify his presence as well. To this end the building is often shaped in the form of a cross, in the middle of which is a dome. The cross and dome symbolize our need to accept the cross of Christ if are to receive the eternal blessings of heaven which descend through the dome. The altar is always turned toward the East because this is from whence Christ came.[16] In all of this, the Orthodox church building is not only supposed to glorify God, but by its very design is supposed to cause men and women to want to worship and encounter God and thereby be transformed.

Recognizing that the human body has a critical part to fulfill in worship, prayer, and spirituality, the Orthodox are active in stimulating and using it to glorify God. Crossing oneself is, Peter Gillquist said, "a way to physically express [one's] allegiance to Christ."[17] This act is also variously done to invoke the power of the cross against temptation, to glorify God in one's body, and to remind oneself of God's triune nature.[18] The Orthodox burn incense to stimulate

---

[15] Quenot, *The Icon*, 43.

[16] Coniaris, *Introducing The Orthodox Church*, 86.

[17] Gillquist, *Becoming Orthodox*, 121.

[18] To further support the practice of crossing oneself, Gillquist quotes Jack Sparks, "The Sign of the Cross," *New Oxford Review* (January-February, 1982), "We freely use the symbol of the cross atop our church buildings, our lecterns, altars, bulletins, and imprinted on our Bibles. Why not use it on ourselves - the people for whom Christ died -

the olfactory sense - it helps them to focus themselves during the Liturgy, and points them toward Isaiah's vision of the heavenly temple.[19] They kneel on the church floor or use kneelers (if the church has them) as a way to reverence the triune God and Holy Scripture. They light candles during their pre-Liturgy prayers. They use architecture and art as a means to seize their attention, to assist their worshipping of God, and to attempt to circumscribe the indescribable transcendence of eternity.[20] They use music to express their love and worship of the Trinity. They also sing the Scriptures - it helps make the written word come to life in the participants' minds - and to remind themselves that there is, and will be, singing in heaven.[21] In light of both architecture and the human body, the church's corporate worship service, like that of the hesychast's private prayer time, is very much focused on the person's existential nature. Through precise and prescribed means - means in accord with the Orthodox' own meta-context - the Christian believer's existential nature is impacted and opened up to the presence of the Holy Spirit.

Pentecostals, for their part, do not give the church building itself a central role with regard to spiritual atmosphere,[22] and have traditionally de-emphasized both church aesthetics and church architecture (so much so that in former days they prided themselves in communing with God in austere storefront churches and beneath grape arbors). That apathy aside, Pentecostals very much have a sense of sacred space. Pentecostal worship services have been characterized by "waiting on the Lord," a prolonged period of reverent and prayerful silence spent in anticipation of imminent Spirit-baptisms,[23] personal and corporate

as well? . . . . We use our voices and lips to tell others of the cross. Why should we withhold our hands and arms, which God has also given us, from doing the same?"

[19] Gillquist, *Becoming Orthodox*, 86-88.

[20] Quenot, *The Icon*. Though his book is devoted to the subject of icons, he discusses Orthodox architecture on 43-45.

[21] Gillquist, *Becoming Orthodox*, 81-84.

[22] In more recent times the church building has taken on tremendous importance, but this consistently concerns pragmatism (what kind of building best facilitates church growth?) and ego (what kind of building best reflects the pastor/congregation as one blessed by God?).

[23] James Menzie, "Pentecostal Principles," *PE*, October 11, 1953, 2, described the early Pentecostal services, "When we assembled, it was not uncommon to see people waiting upon God at the altar bench, or at their seats. During the service there was that same atmosphere of waiting. There was not the hurried atmosphere that we sometimes find in our services these days. Our services were not programmed. We may have planned

spiritual breakthroughs,[24] and prophetic utterances; the last of these each could potentially be manifested through anyone in the congregation. Traditionally, Pentecostal parishioners have gone to church with the expectation that any of the following can happen. The Spirit can fall and baptize people. Glossolalic utterances accompanied by interpretations can be made - these are usually intended for the entire congregation, but they can be given for specific persons. Calls for corporate repentance and renewal are typical. Words of knowledge and wisdom can be proclaimed publicly, though historically these are spoken primarily by spiritual leaders to specific persons during the altar call. Hands can be laid upon sick and infirm persons for healing. Spontaneous shouts and adoring applause are common, as is the raising of hands; all in accord with Biblical teaching. "Singing in the Spirit" by individuals, or the "heavenly chorus" sung by the congregation, can occur during worship - in their best forms the latter are acappella and harmonious melodies of praise enjoined without a prescribed order of words. Both the preacher and the altar take on a very sacred aura during the service, the former proclaiming God's word, the latter as the physical local for encountering God. Some folks even might be impelled to dance in the Spirit or even start a "Jericho March."[25]

So important are the above items for the Pentecostals and their existential orientation, many would confess that they had really not "had church" unless the Spirit had moved in one or more of the above specified ways. Each of the aforementioned items shape the Pentecostals' spiritual atmosphere. Important for our study, these charismatic activities and manifestations - events which Pentecostals believe facilitates a divine-human, S/spirit, encounter - elicit an affective response among Pentecostals which they believe changes them and how they live their lives.[26] While Pentecostals have historically emphasized

---

certain items but it didn't matter too much if those plans were not carried out; the program was not written, anyway. People were there to wait upon God."

[24] These can pertain to spiritual warfare, emotional and/or relational issues, repentance, needs, or healings.

[25] Gradually the congregation will join a leader, or an instigating group, and begin circling the sanctuary. Singing and shouts of praise typify these marches. Sometimes they can last hours and can replace the sermon. Russell Spittler, "Pentecostal and Charismatic Spirituality," in *DPCM*, 807. For another portrayal of Pentecostal worship and spirituality see Riggs, *The Spirit Himself*, 176-186.

[26] For example, Poloma, *At the Crossroads*, 13, noted that AG constituents pray more frequently, read their Bible's more frequently, attend church more often, and read other

spontaneity in their corporate services - believing the Spirit blows where he wants (Jn. 3:8) - it is very much the case that these services can be routinized until they become their own kind of liturgy.[27]

Like the Orthodox, Pentecostals employ precise and prescribed means - means in accord with their own meta-context - so that the Christian believer's existential nature can be impacted and opened up to the presence of the Holy Spirit. Whereas the Orthodox service is very intentionally aesthetic, the Pentecostals is very intentionally kinesthetic. Nonetheless, both use means which they believe best facilitates a divine-human encounter. Even though Pentecostal and Orthodox corporate services look distinct from one another on the exterior, the two are both very much oriented around the human's existential characteristics.[28]

The theological and spiritual implications of this aesthetic-kinesthetic symmetry are complex and deserve further study. Because of limitations, I will only suggest some possible avenues for exploration. First is the issue of epistemological precedent. That is, what Scriptural foundations are normative, and where do the implications of those begin and end? Can we say there is only one New Testament model for Christian worship?[29] Should the Old Testament models and teachings impinge on Christian worship? Or, to what extent do the Old Covenant's kinesthetic-aesthetic teachings hold for the New Covenant?[30] Secondly, what are the ramifications of Christ's person, life, death and resurrection for not only aesthetics and kinesthetics, but for the human person's

---

religious literature more frequently than do members of mainline Protestant denominations.

[27] See Daniel Albrecht, "Pentecostal Spirituality: Looking through the Lens of Ritual," *Pneuma*, 14:2 (Fall 1992), 107-125.

[28] Again, both traditions would assert that much more is occurring than just a divine-human encounter. Both would assert that whether such an encounter occurs or not God is being glorified and the gospel is being preached.

[29] Or, should the fact that the New Testament Christians did not have cultic edifices (i.e., churches) in which to worship be taken as normative for subsequent ages or as a mere historical fact? A pertinent question for Protestants in general would be, to what extent does the apostolic teaching that believers now constitute the body and temple of Christ qualify, or even limit, architectural expressions of the church?

[30] I am thinking here especially of the notion of sacred space, conversely stated as the church building itself.

transformation as well?[31] Similarly, to what extent can we, or should we, argue that physical matter and time have been impacted by the incarnation? Thirdly, is it simply the case that aesthetics and kinesthetics are non-essentials with regard to the gospel? If so, or if not, what are the implications? There are myriads of other questions and issues which could be addressed and which deserve study, not only for Pentecostals, for whom aesthetics are increasingly important, but for the Orthodox (especially foreigners) who must confront more kinesthetically oriented groups moving into their lands.

We can say also that both traditions ought to learn from the other, and that on a very practical level. Pentecostals need to recognize and affirm that the aesthetic realm is also one that can be employed for God's glory and believers' transformation. The simple fact is that Pentecostals have historically steered clear of using such overtly aesthetic devices precisely because those have for so long been the spiritual property, so to speak, of the established traditions. Because those traditions are perceived to be spiritually and charismatically lifeless - and heterodox - all that they are and do is avoided. Conversely, the Orthodox must recognize that active involvement of the laity is central to arousing spiritual hunger and growth. True, the abovementioned Orthodox physical activities are indeed exercised in their services, but it remains the case that the laity is primarily reduced to being an audience - watching the priest perform the bulk of the rites and allowing him to act vicariously for the assembly.

There are still other ramifications of this aesthetic-kinesthetic symmetry and its impact upon the believer's existential core. Sadly, if understandably, Pentecostalism's anthropological implications have been limited by the Pentecostals' own lot in life. That is, whereas the Pentecostals are rather adamant about the reality of the human's existential nature and its importance within the religious arena (regarding communion with God and one another), they have done little to express the reality of this human characteristic in other ways. Apart from their music (Pentecostal music, in historical and cultural concert with jazz and the blues, has made a tremendous impact on Western

---

[31] Was Jesus' cleansing of the temple, his prophecy that the temple would be destroyed, and the tearing of the temple's veil at his death signifying something important about how the early Christians had begun to think about their experience of God and sacred space? See Samuel Terrien, *The Elusive Presence: Toward a New Biblical Theology* (San Francisco: Harper and Row, 1978), 439.

culture),[32] and some notable personal exceptions regarding drama,[33] Pentecostals have mostly ignored the role which the arts, aesthetics and architecture, the medical professions,[34] or the social sciences[35] play and/or can play in life. One would think it natural for such an existentially oriented group to be at the vanguard of those Christians active in these arenas. However, because of their primitivistic impulse - to escape the allurements of these historically "worldly" arenas - and because of the juridical understanding of Christianity which often characterizes them - they believe God wants to save people, and *that* is how the world will be transformed, in contrast to any notions that changing the world can either help to bring people to salvation or serve as a larger witness of the Kingdom's presence - Pentecostals have shied away from these arenas.[36] One would hope that this gaping lacuna will be spanned, especially as the movement matures along theological lines. Instead what seems to be occurring, at least in the USA, is that Pentecostals are assimilating into the larger Western (rationalistic) Christian culture and altogether abandoning the existential impulses which originally ignited them.

Similarly, the Orthodox have limited their aesthetic expression to ecclesial circles. That is, they intentionally limit their religious art to the confines of the church. Because they believe it to be sacred, they do not allow their own aesthetic inspiration to ecstatically move beyond their churches boundaries. This

---

[32] For an intriguing development in this regard see Cox, *Fire From Heaven*, 139-157.

[33] Aimee Semple-McPherson (1890-1944) was known to have the "best show of all" in *the* town of shows, Los Angeles. Blumhofer, *The AG*, 1:251.

[34] The first generations of Pentecostals were ambivalent about, and even militantly against, the use of medicines on the grounds that to use them exemplified a lack of faith. Even today (though this is indeed changing) there is little appreciation among Pentecostals for how it is that the medicinal sciences can be appreciated as stemming from the life of God's kingdom.

[35] For the better part of their history, Pentecostals have either been wary of or outright opposed to the sciences of psychology and sociology.

[36] H. P. B. Benny marvelously typified this historical antipathy regarding aesthetics when he said, "Older denominations. . . seem to rely upon the entrancing effects of the mystic splendor of architectural awe, the swaying pageantry of colorful ritual, the heady fragrance of incense, and the moving solemnity of the chant, to produce an 'atmosphere of worship.' Pentecostal services, in contrast, *contain little that is calculated to play on the emotions*. Where the Spirit of God is, there is little need for artificial religious effects," (my emphasis!). Benny's primitivism negated the full existential ramifications of his own core convictions. "Pentecostal Ecstasy," A *RT* article reprinted in *PE*, September 19, 1965, 5.

is true not only of their art, but their entire ecclesiological understanding as well: the church is sacred and must not be defiled by secular or external factors. However, as the New Testament so dynamically exemplifies, the life and power of the church was never intended to be land-locked within itself. I've said it before, but Orthodoxy has much to share with Western Christianity, if only the Orthodox can transcend themselves and their meta-contexts to share it.

Furthermore, the Orthodox must begin to recognize that the meta-context is shifting dramatically around the world. They can continue to insist on primarily one prescribed Liturgy where the priest is the main participant, but they will do so to the peril of their churches' growth. Not only Orthodox churches in the West, but those in the East as well, are being encompassed by new forces which are changing the way people think about themselves, their religious involvement, and their religious service. This is not a plea for outright accommodation, such as seems to be occurring in the North American church-growth movement and something which I critiqued in another chapter. Nor do I believe that liturgical variation must necessarily result in theological reductionism. However, unless Orthodoxy allows the same creative Spirit which impelled their theology also to breathe new life into their liturgical constructs, it seems they are fated to remain mostly ethnic-bound and dependent upon the birth of Orthodox babies for the healthy numerical continuance of their churches.

God

The Orthodox and Pentecostals have a great deal in common regarding anthropology. This is because for both groups anthropology is founded upon theology. As I asserted above, neither takes the human person as a topic of study apart from soteriology, that is, apart from humanity's relationship to God. *God as person* is the epistemological point of departure for both traditions. Both earnestly desire to teach how it is that the Christian believer can have fellowship with and become like Christ, the incarnate person of God. Neither takes knowledge for knowledge's sake as its point of departure. For that matter, metaphysics, God's divine substance, the order of the universe, and divine decrees are mostly incidental within Orthodoxy and Pentecostalism. It is not that either is unconcerned about those - they are all topics of discussion within each tradition - but none of those supplant God as person as the ground for all knowledge.[37]

There is no historical bridge for this God-as-person similarity. As I clarified in my introduction, the Pentecostals are not at all familiar with Orthodox theology. One might posit that the Pentecostals' eschatological emphasis has pushed them in directions resembling apostolic and Patristic - and therefore Orthodox - delineations, so that considerations about history's end are equally important to those about its beginning - and both of which are rooted in God. However, it seems far more accurate to hold that this emphasis is a curious historical coincidence. To repeat, Orthodox theological delineations are consistently made within the structures of Greek philosophic considerations while Pentecostal theological delineations are made within Western structures. Despite their juridical definitions of salvation, Pentecostals are quite adamant that it was the person of Jesus Christ who accomplished the work of salvation on our behalf. That is, in contrast to some Reformed scholastic treatises, Christ is far more than the means for accomplishing the divine decree. Both the Orthodox and Pentecostal meta-contexts - paradigmatic bookends for the age of Christendom, at least to the present - have been radically concerned with personhood. To be fair, Scripture clearly reveals God as a person, no matter how transcendent his personhood may be, so that both traditions have good reason to so describe God. But in light of Christian history, divine personhood can be processed within any number of meta-contexts which define and/or limit his personhood in precise ways (the most obvious of which is the juridical meta-context which focuses upon God's decrees as the governing principles of the universe). No, Scripture alone does not account for this mutual emphasis.

In light of the various tributaries of Western Christendom, the Orthodox consistently point to the *Filioque* controversy as the historical point of separation regarding the doctrine of God. To argue, as have many Catholics and Protestants, that the Spirit is an impersonal force or the love shared between, and sent by, the Father and Son, is to depersonalize the Godhead. Better to assert the ineffable nature and personhood of the triune God, even if that mystery cannot be apprehended by the human mind, and thereby seemingly endanger monotheistic understandings of God, than to describe God in less than personal ways (here I generalize, but the point holds). The Pentecostals, for their

---

[37] The Orthodox position in this regard was repeatedly noted throughout this study. A contemporary AG writer who insists that the Trinity is the epistemological starting place is Simon Chan, *Spiritual Theology*, 40-55.

part, having arrived on the historical scene when existentialism began to flourish, quite naturally emphasized the personal encounter with God's Spirit which they were experiencing. This was no impersonal force irrupting in their midst with physical healings, deliverances of various kinds, and charismatic outpourings. In light of their experiential-existential character, Pentecostals would regard Thomist definitions of God as an essence within which three persons exist to be alien (this even though historically they have assumed as much via their having arrived as children of Western Christianity). People were not - and are not - being transformed and leaving behind lives of corruption and disaster, because they felt a divine "something." As this dissertation has demonstrated, God is understood and emphatically discussed as a person by both traditions.

Additionally, the notion of God as person plays a critical role in accounting for both groups' doctrine of Christian transformation. Orthodox hesychasts do occasionally focus on the divine light in their spirituality, but it is consistently done with the understanding that this light is the splendor (created energies) and glory of the person of God. Pentecostals do occasionally focus on power in their spirituality, especially as they discuss evangelism, missions, and healings, but it is consistently done with the understanding that it is the power of the personal God so moving. Both traditions describe Christian transformation as involving encounters with God's person. Sometimes these encounters are deeply emotional and are only approximately expressed in words. At other times they are taken by faith - whether sacramentally oriented by the Orthodox, or faith in God's promises by the Pentecostals. But personhood is always at the fore in the discussions of both groups.

The notion of personhood is also an important element for both tradition's synergistic understandings. Again, to say both are synergistic does not mean that either tradition believes one can do anything to save oneself. For both, synergy is located within the life-long process of becoming Christ-like. The Christian is not simply living by faith in light of his or her conversion, as many Protestants would put it, or in light of his or her water baptism, as many sacramentalists would put it. For both the Orthodox and Pentecostals, to become Christ-like is to be continually transformed into his image. As this study has shown, both the Orthodox and Pentecostals express this transformation in on-going existential ways, even if the two employ different terminologies to express it.

The implications of this personal emphasis are numerous and incorporate the totality of life. One can even posit that both sides' ambivalence toward precise theological systemization stems from the fact that both make personhood - including as it does many and often paradoxical characteristics, on both the divine and human sides[38] - the primary category by which these two process their respective theologies. Simply stated, life is often difficult to comprehend, if only because the categories of personhood are regularly complex and mysterious. This personalistic presupposition does not always facilitate a crystal clear apprehension (perhaps in this regard Pentecostals can be said to exhibit their own apophatic character), but it does help account for the often inexpressible reality which characterizes human existence.

Creation

Still another fascinating similarity between the Orthodox and Pentecostals has to do with how each views God and creation. The Orthodox, for their part, believe that all created things participate (ontologically) in the divine mind by virtue of the divine *paradigmata*, as was noted in my discussion of Palamas. Because all things have this ontological connection to/through God, the Orthodox teach their followers that all created things must be looked upon as avenues for the divine. That is, through the eyes of faith *God can be seen* in every created thing. Creation does not just reflect and participate in God's being through the arbitrarily assigned issues of creation's variety (as reflected in the multitude of God's creations), purpose (as reflected in the order of creation), or beauty (reflected in both magnificent and subtle ways). For those with faith, God himself can be seen through and within the multitudinous forms themselves. Pentecostals, on the other hand, arrive at a similar worldview, though through a different epistemological lense. Because of their emphasis upon the *charismata* (and this is *the* foundation for this specific dimension of their dynamic worldview), Pentecostals believe that *God can be heard* through creation. One does not look for or sense God's energies, in the ontological ways of Orthodoxy. But one can intuit - through a synergistic concert with the Spirit - the expressions of God's purposes and instructions (through creation's order as well as many other avenues), God's delights (through the variety of creation), his sense of humor (look in the mirror!), and his patience; all of which can impact the believer with a sense of the *mysterium tremendum* and thereby

---

[38] God's immanence and transcendence, divine immutability and the incarnation, divine sovereignty and human free-will, to name a few.

change him or her. In all of this, both traditions assert a radically panentheistic worldview. Both understand that creation is a means by which God is apprehended. The Orthodox extend that iconic and sacramental dimension of panentheism into the broad sweep of their theology. The Pentecostals tend to limit their panentheistic implications to the individual's encounter with God.

It is fascinating that whereas the Orthodox emphasize a vision of God - not only in icons, in the liturgy, in religious ornamentation, and the whole of creation - the Pentecostals emphasize an auditory experience of God - not only via their doctrine of *glossolalia*, but also through music, corporate silence, laughter, and the whole of creation. The Orthodox want the soul to "see" God. They believe a visionary experience of God - however one describes that - will produce an ontological change within a person. Thus, it is not surprising that Jesus' transfiguration holds an exalted place in Orthodoxy's theology in general and their *theosis* doctrine in specific.[39] The Pentecostals want the soul to "hear" God. They believe an auditory experience of God - however one describes that - will produce an ethical change within a person. Thus, passages like 1 Kings 19:12, "God was in the still small voice of the wind,"[40] and sermons encouraging the believer to listen for God, hold an important place in their theologies.

Further reflection and analysis is necessary at this point, but it is fascinating to see the visionary emphasis of Orthodoxy and the auditory emphasis of Pentecostalism prefigured through the course of Samuel Terrien's book, *The Elusive Presence.*[41] Through his analysis of the Old Testament, Terrien develops two theologies concerning God's presence: the theology of Name and the theology of Glory. The theology of the Name is a theology which emphasizes an auditory experience of God's presence. Name-theology tends to manifest itself in the ethical, pragmatic and temporal arenas; and in this regard one can foresee Pentecostalism and its regular attention to Terrien's "ethical ear" of Name. The theology of the Glory is a theology which emphasizes a visual/visionary experience of God's presence. Glory-theology tends to manifest itself in religious ceremony and a sense of divine space; and in this regard one can foresee Orthodoxy and its attention to Terrien's "mystical eye" of Glory.

---

[39] This emphasis could deservedly have been covered in this study, but limitative lines had to be drawn somewhere. See Lossky, *The Vision of God*, for an historical-theological examination.
[40] My paraphrase of the King James Version.
[41] Terrien, *The Elusive Presence.*

One must not confuse the issue as though the Orthodox overlook time or ethics, or as though the Pentecostals ignore a sense of ceremony or sacred space. Both incorporate important dimensions of each respective theology of presence.[42]

Terrien argues that in Jesus, both Name and Glory become intertwined.[43] Sadly, the respective spiritual and theological manifestations of Name and Glory seem to be only sporadically manifested across the broad spectrum of Christianity. Because Terrien's Name-Glory analogy provides the church with an insightful model, both the Orthodox and the Pentecostals could employ his model in any trans-traditional conversations.

The way each tradition processes the divine-human encounter aside, both emphasize that the existential elements of the human person are to be transformed in the process of becoming Christ-like. The Orthodox maintain their *a priori* views regarding God and creation in light of Greek philosophy; they tend to begin with the Triune God and work down to humanity. The Pentecostals maintain their own *a posteriori* views about God and creation in light of their pneumatological understandings and experiences, understandings and experiences which meet the Western empirical demands for certifiable proof; they thus tend to begin with anthropology and work upward to God.

If these two groups have looked favorably upon creation as an avenue for experiencing and knowing God, they tend to look disdainfully upon the natural sciences as means for informing their respective epistemologies. This is not because the two are necessarily unwilling to learn from those sciences, rather they are regularly disdained because experts within those arenas have typically worked from presuppositions which run contrary to a Christian worldview. This shared disdain also stems from the fact that those experts often raise their own truth claims to the level of religious dogma. Naturally, such claims are threatening to both groups. Unfortunately, both groups have at times over-reacted to, and dismissed altogether many of, the natural scientists' claims. The result is that both groups are perceived as intellectually narrow by those more sympathetic to scientific interpretations of life.

That these two great Christian cisterns - Orthodoxy and Pentecostalism - share anti-intellectual and anti-scientific sentiments is not only due to the above

---

[42] Robeck argues that Pentecostals have long been characterized by a deep longing for and appreciation of God's glory as the uniting force of Christianity. "Pentecostal Perspectives on the Ecumenical Challenge." An unpublished paper originally presented in 1984 to the American Academy of Religion. Revised in 1989.

[43] Terrien, *Elusive Presence,* 410-447.

negative reasons. The Orthodox' anti-intellectual and anti-scientific attitudes can be partly attributed to the fact that those traditionally Orthodox countries did not experience Western Europe's Renaissance and Enlightenment, but that alone does not account for their anti-intellectual and anti-scientific worldview. There is another impetus for these sentiments. As I noted in my previous chapter on the means of *theosis*, the intellect is not exalted in Orthodoxy the way that it is in the West. The mind must be subdued and rendered a servant to the soul. Only in submission to the soul, when the latter itself has been submitted to Christ, can the mind proffer true knowledge. Science is regularly viewed by the Orthodox as the chief arena where the mind runs rampant in its autocratic quest for knowledge. Science, a device of the West, causes the Orthodox in foreign lands to view Westerners and Western Christians with suspicion.

Regarding the Pentecostals, we cannot solely attribute their similar anti-scientific and anti-intellectual attitudes to a precise demographic lot in life, or a pre-modern worldview, which relegated them to ignorance. Pentecostals may indeed have come from a generally defined demographic milieu, but as our chapter on the AG's theological foundations for sanctification clarified, the AG is as empirically oriented in their *ordo salutis* as any evangelical group. Indeed, with their teaching that *glossolalia* is empirical evidence of Spirit-baptism's reality, they are arguably more empirically oriented in their spirituality than some of their evangelical siblings. Instead, the Pentecostals' conservative belief that Scripture is the filter through which all of life must be processed tends to make them wary of intellectuals and scientists who either want to nuance an understanding of life or transform it altogether. Within their own empirically laden milieu, Pentecostals tend to take Scripture as the measure of proof against which, or through which, all knowledge must be strained. This epistemological presupposition, while preserving the traditional Pentecostal worldview, has rather painted them into an epistemological corner.

One can only suggest here that both traditions need to cease fearing science as a means of knowing, even if the presuppositions of individual scientists themselves need to be scrutinized. Science itself is neither good nor bad, even if there are both carefully grounded and speciously crafted scientific studies which must be sifted.

Tying the Two Together

As I said in my introduction, there is no clear historical connection between Eastern Orthodoxy and North American Pentecostalism. Like a kind of sieve, John Wesley filtered Greek patristic theology so that some of Orthodoxy's experiential thrust was revivified and re-introduced into North American Christianity in the eighteenth century. But by the time of Pentecostalism's advent in the twentieth century, Wesley's own ideas had themselves gone through a process of modification. How then should we best account for the existential and mystical shimmerings of Orthodoxy which are so obviously apparent in Pentecostalism? Together with the issue of historical context - the rise of existentialism and all it implies for the meaning of human personhood, worldview, and religion in North America - there is, I believe, a still older reason for these experiential shimmerings: created human nature itself.

The mystical and existential ways in which both Orthodoxy and Pentecostalism process Christianity are rooted in theological anthropology. That is, as both traditions express it, the human spirit was created in such a way that it longs for eternal communion with God's Spirit. Contrary to the position of some Protestants, this longing is not legalistic-human nature's tendency to add something to the divine-human encounter, as though the human person somehow has a role in saving himself or herself.[44] Rather, it is the soul's natural character both to reach out toward God and to seek communion with him. The human soul, in its Godward yearning, is not simply satisfied with intellectual knowledge about God, neither is it satisfied with obtaining the knowledge necessary for salvation. Instead, the human soul was created with an innate sense that *God himself desires a life-long communion, a communion that is indeed rooted in salvation, but one that by no means perceives salvation to be the epitome of the divine-human interaction.* Indeed, in all of this, it may be most accurate to say that not only do we have spiritual organs which enable our fellowship with God, we are spiritual organs created for eternal fellowship with God. True enough, this element of human nature is only discussed with great difficulty - just as existential encounters with God themselves are only discussed with great difficulty - but that makes it no less real.

Within their own historical contexts, the one informed by Greek ontology, and the other informed by North American existentialism, these two traditions

---

[44] E.g., Hoekema's response to the Pentecostal doctrine of sanctification in *Five Views on Sanctification*, 139.

emphasize a personal encounter with God that not only does not find mystical-existential manifestations embarrassing, both see them as normal and necessary. Indeed, as the two express it, to allow Christ's Spirit to transform the depths of one's being will necessitate mysterious and nearly inexpressible experiences. Moreover, one may fairly aver that both traditions are nearly magnetic in their mystical-existential pull because of their understanding of the divine-human relationship as an acutely inter-personal dynamic. Put differently, the two are as spiritually dynamic as they are because each - within its own meta-context - has developed ways to facilitate an experience of the mystery and transcendence of the infinite God. Each presents that mystery in ways that draw human persons to Christ: the Orthodox through aesthetics, the Pentecostals through kinesthetics. Both emphasize that the human person was created for a transforming fellowship with God.

I do not want to be mistaken. Pentecostals are not Eastern Orthodox believers who, whether consciously or unconsciously, are struggling to break free from their Western moorings. They are quite comfortable with their own spiritual and theological identity. Pentecostals maintain a theological and spiritual tension that is novel among most Christian groups. It is a tension between their existential-affective and empirical (in terms of presenting their *ordo salutis* and spirituality to the epistemological constructs of the wider society) orientations. Without question, the latter element within this tension has led many Pentecostals to practice a kind of fundamentalistic rationalism. Conversely, the existential-affective element has caused many others to embrace a rather uncritically-minded spirituality. Still, this tension is generally maintained all the same. The Orthodox, from their own vista might see the Pentecostal existential-empirical tension in this regard as a capitulation to the vainglorious arena of science, that arena whereby mankind posits itself as the arbiter of all truth. Evangelicals, from their own rationalistic vista, might see the Pentecostal tension between an existential-affective orientation and a modern-empirical orientation as a Western Christian anomaly, proving once again how truly backwards the Pentecostals really are. In truth, what we really have with Pentecostalism is the revivification of the ancient Christian practice of the reality of God's presence formulated within the constructs of a Western, modern, and rational epistemology.

As this delineation has also shown, Pentecostals emphasize a vibrant existential spirituality in their doctrine of sanctification. One need not always be "on the mountain top" of existential experience to progress in sanctification - no

AG writer makes such a crass correlation.[45] But there is a clear connection between the degree of one's existential communion with God and one's sanctification. One need not merely observe and keep precise moralistic codes (although, as has been shown, that has been a traditional Pentecostal feature) to grow in Christ-likeness, one also needs to seek to unite one's spirit with God's Spirit - and that regularly - if one is to become like Christ. In the best cases this existential dimension of the AG's spirituality in general, and teaching on Christian transformation in specific, has transformed and vitalized millions of Christian believers' experiences around the globe for the better part of a century. People *can* experience God in the depths of their being; they *can* have communion with God with the result that they are impelled to forsake the niceties and dainties of this life for God's higher purposes. We should also add that whereas its constituents would never put it in so many words, the Pentecostals' doctrine of Spirit-baptism is a dogmatic anthropological assertion. That is, not only are people comprised of physical bodies and rational intellects, they are also unquestionably comprised of an existential core. Just as people can interact and commune with one another through their bodies, intellects, and existential natures, so also can people interact and commune with God via their bodies, intellects, and existential natures. Indeed, they can become so suffused with the presence of God's Spirit that they "overflow," to put it in the Pentecostal vernacular, and speak in unknown tongues. *Glossolalia* is not unfairly understood as the existential core's attempt to express the fulness of the Spirit within. And, this experience empowers the Pentecostal believer to share Christ's reality with others.

As the above implies, an important reason for Pentecostalism's world-wide growth is that it has captured and transmitted an understanding of the human person which has been missed or altogether avoided by many others within Western Christendom. The human person, to quote an AG writer, "is more than a cool, calculating machine." "The self-expression of a normal, human soul," that writer went on, "ranges over a whole octave of mood and emotion. . . . Were the artist unable to feel the emotion of a crimson sunset; were the poet

---

[45] In some cases the Pentecostals' teaching can - like the Orthodox' own hesychastic tendencies - become overbearing. Under the subjection of a steady stream of preaching and teaching on existential spirituality, believers can too easily equate Christian transformation with emotionalism or mysticism. In that light, one can be led to believe that one is only pleasing God, and that one is only becoming like Christ, when one feels close to God in a visceral and existential sense.

unable to feel the rhythmic balance of adjective against noun; were the composer unable to feel the wonder of God's love: what would life be?"[46]

The Orthodox too affirm as much about the human person, but go further. In light of their metaphysical underpinnings, they seek to unite the believer to Christ in specifically metaphysical ways. The most important of these means of uniting, as we have seen, is the institutionalized sacramental system. Through water baptism one is initiated into both the Kingdom of God and the community of the church, the latter being the archetypal manifestation of the Kingdom. By receiving the eucharist one receives Christ himself. Thus, regular reception of the eucharist is understood by nearly all Orthodox theologians as a necessary element in *theosis*. By participating in the liturgy - that moment which the Orthodox believe unites both time and eternity, and heaven and earth, in Christ - the believer further unites herself or himself to the community of salvation and shares in its participation in Christ.

As important as the institutionalized means of participation are, the Orthodox, like the Pentecostals, are emphatic that the Kingdom of God can be experienced internally, apart from the church's institution. (Whereas the Pentecostals wrestle with and maintain the above noted existential-empirical tension in their theology, the Orthodox wrestle with and maintain a tension between the institutional and immediate means of encountering Jesus Christ.) As our study of Palamas evinced, because of humankind's iconic nature, that is, because the human person iconically participates in the divine *paradigmata*, and because the human person reflects the *Logos* of God, the human person himself is a location for encountering God. The ramifications of such a hesychastic-iconic notion, especially in light of this study's comparison of Eastern and Western mystical Christian expressions of transformation, deserve extensive reflection and exploration. I will raise only one possibility.

Whereas the Orthodox include and/or encourage mystical encounters distinct from the sacramental system (so that the church need not necessarily be understood as the only venue for encountering Christ), and whereas with the ancient church councils the Orthodox admit that water baptism's efficacy is not dependent upon the priest's moral character or apostolic succession (so that communion with Christ is not entirely dependent upon the vehicle or person administering the sacrament), then the Orthodox must either admit that Pentecostalism is an orthodox (small case intended) branch of Christendom or

---

[46] H. P. B. Benny, "Pentecostal Ecstasy," A *RT* article reprinted in *PE*, September 19, 1965, 5.

pronounce it as altogether heretical. If they choose the latter then they must either make the same pronunciation about the most famous of their own existentialists - Gregory Palamas - or admit that their insistence on Orthodoxy's orthodoxy is rooted in culture as much as it is theology. That is, other than arguing that Pentecostals' existential encounters with Christ's Holy Spirit are not authentic because the Pentecostals are not Orthodox, how can the Orthodox any longer dismiss the former's spiritual and life-giving encounters as heterodox? If *an* image of God (the human person) encounters *the* Image of God (Jesus Christ through the person of the Spirit), and if God's eternal longing was indeed for a divine-human *sobornost'*, then the Orthodox must wrestle with the implications of other Christians' existential-mystical encounters with Christ. As I said, there is room for much reflection and dialogue on this point.

This study does not exhaust the range of comparisons and issues pertinent for studies of Orthodoxy and Pentecostalism. I have not delineated or critiqued either tradition's ecclesiology. On the Orthodox front, I have only briefly addressed the theology of the sacramental system. On the Pentecostal side, the lacuna about the corporate nature of the body of Christ has been touched upon, but much room remains for development thereabout. An in-depth examination of both traditions' cultures and nationalistic moorings has only been mentioned, and more than any other issues these may stand as a barrier to any future mutual understandings. Furthermore, questions about the validity of both traditions' spirituality has, for the sake of the immediate doctrinal focus of Christian transformation, been assumed; many commonalities and divergences remain to be clarified. What is clear is that these two traditions - largely distanced though they are by culture, history, and other important ingredients in each's respective meta-context - both recognize that the human person, like the person of God himself, is vastly complex and marvelously mysterious. Both agree, in contrast to reductionistic Christian anthropologies, that God created us as he did in order that we might be transformed into the image of his Son, and that at the very depths of our complex and mysterious selves.

Bibliography

Books and Monographs

Anderson, Robert Mapes. *Vision of the Disinherited: The Making of American Pentecostalism*. Peabody, Massachusetts: Hendrickson Publishers, 1979.

Annas, Julia. *Hellenistic Philosophy of Mind*. Berkeley and Los Angeles: University of California Press, Ltd., 1992.

Argue, Theodora Dracopoulos. *Practicing Daily Prayer in the Orthodox Christian Life*. Minneapolis, Minnesota: Light and Life Publishing Co., 1989.

Arseniev, Nicholas. *Russian Piety*. Trans. Asheleigh Moorhouse. 2nd. ed. New York: St. Vladimir's Seminary Press, 1975.

Assemblies of God Heritage. 2 Vols. Ed. Wayne E. Warner. Springfield, Missouri: Assemblies of God Archives, 1981, 1995.

A Statement of Fundamental Truths Approved By The General Council of the Assemblies of God, October 2-7, 1916.

Barasch, Moshe. *Icon: Studies in the History of an Idea*. New York: New York University Press, 1992.

Bauer, Walter. *A Greek-English Lexicon of the New Testament and Other Early Christian Literature*. Trans. William F. Arndt and F. Wilbur Bauer. The University of Chicago Press, 1979.

Bell, E. N. *Questions and Answers*. Springfield, Missouri: Gospel Publishing House, n.d.

Benz, Ernst. *The Eastern Orthodox Church: Its Thought and Life*. Trans. Richard and Clara Winston. Chicago: Aldine Publishing Company, 1963.

Berkhof, Louis. *Systematic Theology*. Grand Rapids, Michigan: Wm. B. Eerdmans Publishing Company, reprint 1986.

Bernard, David K. *The Oneness of God*. Hazelwood, Missouri: Word Aflame Press, 1983.

Bloom, Anthony. *Living Prayer*. Springfield, Illinois: Templegate Publishers, 1966.

Blumhofer, Edith L. *The Assemblies of God: A Chapter in the Story of American Pentecostalism*. 2 vols. Springfield, Missouri: Gospel Publishing House, 1989.

—. *"Pentecost in My Soul," Explorations in the Meaning of Pentecostal Experience in the Assemblies of God*. Springfield, Missouri: Gospel Publishing House, 1989.

Blumhofer, Edith L. and Randall Balmer, Eds. *Modern Christian Revivals.* Chicago: University of Illinois Press, 1993.

Boyd, Frank Mathews. *The Kenosis of The Lord Jesus Christ.* San Francisco: Frank M. Boyd, 1947.

Boym, Svetlana. *Common Places: Mythologies of Everyday Life in Russia.* Cambridge, Massachusetts: Harvard University Press, 1994.

Bratsiotis, Panagiotis. *The Greek Orthodox Church.* Trans. Joseph Blenkinsopp. London: The University of Notre Dame Press, 1968.

Bruce, F. F. *I & II Corinthians.* The New Century Bible Commentary. Eds. Ronald E. Clements and Matthew Black. England: Marshall, Morgan & Scott, 1971. rpt. Grand Rapids: William B. Eerdmans Publishing Company, 1984.

—.*Commentary on the Epistle to the Colossians.* The New International Commentary on The New Testament. 11th ed. Grand Rapids: William B. Eerdmans Publishing Company, 1980.

Brumback, Carl. *Suddenly. . . From Heaven.* Springfield, Missouri: Gospel Publishing House, 1961.

Brumfield, William C., and Milos M. Velimirovic. *Christianity and the Arts in Russia.* Cambridge University Press, 1991.

Brown, Colin. *Miracles and the Critical Mind.* Grand Rapids: William B. Eerdmans Publishing Company, 1984.

Bulgakov, Sergius. *The Orthodox Church.* Trans. Lydia Kesich. Crestwood, New York: St. Vladimir's Seminary Press, 1988.

Burgess, Stanley M. *The Holy Spirit: Eastern Christian Traditions.* Peabody, Massachusetts: Hendrickson Publishers, 1989.

Burns, J. Patout. *Theological Anthropology.* Sources of Early Christian Thought Series. Philadelphia: Fortress Press, 1981.

Bushkovitch, Paul. *Religion and Society in Russia: The Sixteenth and Seventeenth Centuries.* Oxford University Press, 1992.

Cabasilas, Nicholas. *A Commentary on the Divine Liturgy.* Trans. J. M. Hussey and R. M. French. London: S.P.C.K., 1960.

—. *The Life in Christ.* Trans. C.J. de Catanzaro. New York: St. Vladimir's Seminary Press, 1974.

Campbell, Ted A. *John Wesley and Christian Antiquity: Religious Vision and Cultural Change.* Nashville, Tennessee: Kingswood Books, 1991.

Carmody, Denise Lardner and John Tully Carmody. *Mysticism: Holiness East and West.* New York: Oxford University Press, 1996.

—. *Interpreting the Religious Experience: A Worldview.* Englewood Cliffs, New Jersey: Prentice-Hall, Inc., 1987.

Cavarnos, Constantine. *Orthodox Iconography.* Belmont, Massachusetts: The Institute for Byzantine and Modern Greek Studies, Inc., 1977.

Chan, Simon. *Spiritual Theology: A Systematic Study of the Christian Life.* Downers Grove, Illinois: InterVarsity Press, 1998.

Clendenin, Daniel B. Ed. *Eastern Orthodox Theology: A Contemporary Reader.* Grand Rapids: Baker Book House, 1995.

—. *Eastern Orthodoxy: A Western Perspective.* Grand Rapids: Baker Book House, 1994.

Climacus, John. *The Ladder of Divine Ascent.* Trans. Colm Luibheid and Norman Russell. New York: Paulist Press, 1982.

Coniaris, Anthony M. *Daily Vitamins for Spiritual Growth: Day by Day with Jesus Through the Church Year.* 2 vols. Minneapolis, Minnesota: Light and Life Publishing Company, 1994.

—. *Introducing the Orthodox Church.* Minneapolis, Minnesota: Light and Life Publishing Company, 1982.

Conn, Charles W. *Like a Mighty Army Moves the Church of God.* Cleveland, Tennessee: Pathway Press, 1955, rev. ed. 1977.

Copleston, Frederick. *A History of Philosophy.* 3 vols. New York: Image Books, 1985.

Cox, Harvey. *Fire From Heaven: The Rise of Pentecostal Spirituality and the Reshaping of Religion in the Twenty-first Century.* Reading, Massachusetts: Addison-Wesley Publishing Company, 1995.

Cuttat, Jacques-Albert. *The Encounter of Religions: A Dialogue between the West and the Orient with an Essay on the Prayer of Jesus.* Trans. Pierre De Fontnouvelle and Evis McGrew. New York: Desclée Company, 1960.

Dayton, Donald. *Theological Roots of Pentecostalism.* Peabody, Massachusetts: Hendrickson Publishers, 1987.

de Grunwald, Constantin. *The Churches and the Soviet Union.* Trans. G. J. Robinson-Paskevsky. New York: The MacMillan Company, 1962.

Dulles, Avery. *Models of The Church.* Expanded ed. New York: Image Books, 1987.

Dunn, James D. G. *Christology in the Making: An Inquiry into the Origins of the Doctrine of the Incarnation.* 2nd ed. London: SCM Press, 1989.

—. *Baptism in the Holy Spirit.* London: SCM Press, 1970.

Dvornik, Francis. *The Photian Schism: History and Legend*. Cambridge: At The University Press, 1948; rpt. Cambridge: At The University Press, 1970.

——. *The Ecumenical Councils*. Twentieth Century Encyclopedia of Catholicism. Vol. 82. New York: Hawthorn Books, 1961.

Elwell, Walter A. *Evangelical Dictionary of Theology*. 10th ed. Grand Rapids: Baker Book House, 1994.

Erickson, Millard J. *Christian Theology*. 11th ed. Grand Rapids: Baker Book House, 1994.

Evdokimov, Paul. *The Art of the Icon: A Theology of Beauty*. Trans. Fr. Steven Bigham. Redondo Beach, California: Oakwood Publications, 1972.

Fedotov, George P. *The Russian Religious Mind*. 2 vols. Ed. John Meyendorff. Belmont, Massachusetts: Nordland Publishing Company, 1975.

——. *A Treasury of Russian Spirituality*. 2 vols. Belmont, Massachusetts: Nordland Publishing Company, 1975.

Fee, Gordon D. *God's Empowering Presence: The Holy Spirit in the Letters of Paul*. Peabody, Massachusetts: Hendrickson Publishers, Inc., 1994.

——. *The First Epistle to the Corinthians*. The New International Commentary on The New Testament. Ed. F. F. Bruce. Grand Rapids: William B. Eerdmans Publishing Company, 1987.

Fee, Gordon D., and Douglas Stuart, Eds. *How to Read the Bible for All Its Worth*. 2nd ed. Grand Rapids: Zondervan Publishing House, 1993.

Ferguson, Everett. *Backgrounds of Early Christianity*. 2nd ed. Grand Rapids: William B. Eerdmans Publishing Company, 1993.

Florensky, Pavel. *Iconostasis*. Trans. Donald Sheehan and Olga Andrejev. Crestwood, New York: St. Vladimir's Seminary Press, 1996.

Florovsky, Georges. *Creation and Redemption*. Belmont, Massachusetts: Nordland Publishing Company, 1976.

——. "St. Athanasius' Concept of Creation." *Aspects of Church History*, Vol. 4 in the Collected Works of Georges Florovsky. Belmont, Massachusetts.: Nordland Publishing Company, 1975.

——. *Bible, Church, Tradition: An Eastern Orthodox View*. Nordland Publishing Co., 1972.

Foster, Fred J. *Think it Not Strange: A History of the Oneness Movement*. St. Louis, Missouri: Pentecostal Publishing House, 1965.

Frodsham, Stanley H. *With Signs Following*. Springfield, Missouri: Gospel Publishing House, 1926.

——. *The Life of Joy*. Springfield, Missouri: Gospel Publishing House, n.d.

—. *Wholly for God: A Call to Complete Consecration*. Springfield, Missouri: Gospel Publishing House, n.d.

Gee, Donald. *Concerning Shepherds and Sheepfolds*. rev. ed. London: Elim Publishing Co., 1952.

—. *Concerning Spiritual Gifts*. rev. ed. Springfield, Missouri: Gospel Publishing House, 1947.

Giakalis, Ambrosios. *Images of the Divine: The Theology of Icons at the Seventh Ecumenical Council*. London: E.J. Brill, 1994.

Gillet, Lev. *The Jesus Prayer*. Crestwood, New York: St. Vladimir's Seminary Press, 1987.

Gillquist, Peter E. *Becoming Orthodox: A Journey to the Ancient Christian Faith*. rev. ed. Ben Lomond, California: Conciliar Press, 1992.

—. *Coming Home: Why Protestant Clergy are Becoming Orthodox*. Ben Lomond, California: Conciliar Press, 1992.

Godin, André. *The Psychological Dynamics of Religious Experience*. Trans. Mary Turton. Birmingham, Alabama: Religious Education Press, 1985.

Green, Joel B., Scot McKnight, I. Howard Marshall, Eds. *Dictionary of Jesus and the Gospels*. Grand Rapids: InterVarsity Press, 1992.

Hagglund, Bengt. *History of Theology*. Trans. Gene J. Lund. St. Louis: Concordia Publishing House, 1968.

Harakas, Stanley Samuel. *Living the Liturgy*. Minneapolis, Minnesota: Light and Life Publishing Co., 1974.

Heron, Alasdair. *The Holy Spirit*. Philadelphia: The Westminster Press, 1983.

Hill, Kent. *The Puzzle of the Soviet Church: An Inside Look at Christianity and Glasnost*. Portland, Oregon: Multnomah Press, 1989.

Hilton, Alison. *Russian Folk Art*. Indiana University Press, 1995.

Hoekema, Anthony A. *Created in God's Image*. Grand Rapids: William B. Eerdmans Publishing Company, 1986.

—. *The Bible and The Future*. Grand Rapids: William B. Eerdmans Publishing Company, 1979.

Hollenweger, Walter. *The Pentecostals*. English translation of *Enthusiastisches Christentum: die Pfingstbewegung in Geschichte und Gegenwart*, R. A. Wilson (tr.). Peabody, Massachusetts: Hendrickson, 1988.

Horton, Stanley M., Ed. *Systematic Theology, A Pentecostal Perspective*. Springfield, Missouri: Logion Press, 1994.

—. *What the Bible Says About the Holy Spirit*. Springfield, Missouri: Gospel Publishing House, 1976.

International Standard Bible Encyclopaedia, The. 5 vols. Gen. Ed. James Orr. Grand Rapids: William B. Eerdmans Publishing Company, 1955.

Iswolsky, Helene. *Christ in Russia: The History Tradition and Life of the Russian Church.* Milwaukee, Wisconsin: The Bruce Publishing Company, 1960.

James, William. *Essays in Pragmatism.* 16th ed. New York: Hafner Press, 1977.

Karris, R. J. *A Symphony of New Testament Hymns.* Collegeville: Liturgical Press, 1996.

Kendrick, Klaude. *The Promised Fulfilled: A History of the Modern Pentecostal Movement.* Springfield, Missouri: Gospel Publishing, 1961.

Kesich, Veselin. *The Gospel Image of Christ.* rev. ed. New York: Crestwood, St. Vladimir's Seminary Press, 1991.

Kinnamon, Michael. *Truth and Community: Diversity and its Limits in the Ecumenical Movement.* Grand Rapids: William B. Eerdmans Publishing Company, 1988.

Klibanov, Aleksandr I. *History of Religious Sectarianism in Russia (1860s-1917).* Trans. Ethel Dunn. New York: Pergamon Press, 1982.

Kontzevitch, Ivan M. *The Acquisition of the Holy Spirit.* Platina, California: St. Herman of Alaska Brotherhood, 1988.

Krivocheine, Basil. *In the Light of Christ: St Symeon the New Theologian.* Trans. Anthony P. Gythiel. Crestwood, New York: St. Vladimir's Seminary Press, 1986.

Küng, Hans. *The Church.* Garden City, New York: Image Books, 1976.

Land, Stephen Jack. *Pentecostal Spirituality: Passion for the Kingdom.* Sheffield, England: Sheffield Academic Press, 1993.

Latourette, Kenneth Scott. *A History of Christianity, Volume II: Reformation to the Present.* rev. ed. San Francisco: Harper & Row, Publishers, Inc., 1975.

Lindsell, Harold. *The Battle for the Bible.* Grand Rapids: Zondervan Publishing House, 1976.

Long, A. A. *Hellenistic Philosophy: Stoics, Epicureans, Sceptics.* London: Duckworth, 1974.

Lossky, Vladimir. *In the Image and Likeness of God.* Eds. Erickson, John H. and Thomas E. Bird. New York: Crestwood, St. Vladimir's Seminary Press, 1985.

—. *Orthodox Theology: An Introduction.* Trans. Ian and Ihita Kesarcodi-Watson. New York: Crestwood, St. Vladimir's Seminary Press, 1978.

—. *The Mystical Theology of the Eastern Church*. Crestwood, New York: St. Vladimir's Seminary Press, 1976.

—. *The Vision of God*. Trans. Asheleigh Moorhouse. 2nd ed. Bedfordshire: The Faith Press, 1973.

Lupinin, Nickolas. *Religious Revolt in the 17th Century: The Schism of the Russian Church*. Princeton, New Jersey: The Kingston Press, Inc., 1984.

Maloney, George A. *A Theology of Uncreated Energies*. Milwaukee, Wisconsin: Marquette University Pres, 1978.

Mantzaridis, Georgios I. *The Deification of Man: St. Gregory Palamas and the Orthodox Tradition*. Trans. Liadain Sherrard. Crestwood, New York: St. Vladimir's Seminary Press, 1984.

Marsden, George M. *Reforming Fundamentalism: Fuller Seminary and The New Evangelicalism*. Grand Rapids: William. B. Eerdmans Publishing Company, 1987.

—. *Fundamentalism and American Culture: The Shaping of Twentieth-Century Evangelicalism, 1870-1925*. Oxford: Oxford University Press, 1980.

Martin, David. *Tongues of Fire: The Explosion of Protestantism in Latin America*. Oxford: Basil Blackwell, 1990.

Martin, Ralph P. *Worship in the New Testament*. 2nd ed. Grand Rapids: William. B. Eerdmans Publishing Co., 1974.

Mascall, E. L. *The Triune God: An Ecumenical Study*. West Sussex, England: Churchman Publishing Limited, 1986.

McDowell, Josh. *Evidence that Demands a Verdict: Historical Evidences for the Christian Faith*. San Bernardino, California: Campus Crusade for Christ International, 1972.

McGee, Gary B, Ed. *Initial Evidence: Historical and Biblical Perspectives on the Pentecostal Doctrine of Spirit Baptism*. Peabody, Massachusetts: Hendrickson Publishers, 1991.

McLoughlin, William G., Jr. *Modern Revivalism: Charles Grandison Finney to Billy Graham*. New York: The Ronald Press, Company, 1959.

Meijering E. P. *Orthodoxy and Platonism in Athanasius: Synthesis or Antithesis?*, (Leiden: E. J. Brill, 1968.

Menzies, William W. and Stanley M. Horton, eds. *Bible Doctrines: A Pentecostal Perspective*. Springfield, Missouri: Logion Press, 1993.

Menzies, William. *Anointed to Serve: The Story of the Assemblies of God*. Springfield, Missouri: Gospel Publishing House, 1971.

Meyendorff, John. *Rome, Constantinople, Moscow: Historical and Theological Studies.* Crestwood, New York: St. Vladimir's Seminary Press, 1996.

—. *Christ in Eastern Christian Thought.* Crestwood, New York: St. Vladimir's Seminary Press, 1987.

—. *Gregory Palamas: The Triads.* Trans. Nicholas Gendle. New York: Paulist Press, 1983.

—. *Catholicity and the Church.* Crestwood, New York: St. Vladimir's, 1983.

—. *The Orthodox Church: Its Past and its Role in The World Today.* Crestwood, New York: St. Vladimir's Seminary Press, 1981.

—. *Byzantine Theology: Historical Trends and Doctrinal Themes.* New York: *A Study of Gregory Palamas.* Trans. George Lawrence. The Faith Press, 1974.

—. *St. Gregory Palamas and Orthodox Spirituality.* Trans. Adele Fiske. Crestwood, New York: St. Vladimir's, 1974.

—. *Orthodoxy and Catholicity.* Sheed and Ward, Inc., 1966.

—. *The Orthodox Church: Its Past and Its Role in the World Today.* Trans. John Chapin. Pantheon Books, 1962.

—. *Primacy and Primacies in the Orthodox Church.* Crestwood, New York: St. Vladimir's Seminary Press, 1960.

Meyendorff, John, Alexander Schmemann, Nicolas Afanassieff, and Nicolas Koulomzine. *The Primacy of Peter.* Trans. Katharine Farrer. London: Faith Press, Ltd. 1963.

Migne, I. P., Ed. *Patrologiae Cursus Completus, Series Graecae.* 168 vols. Reprint, Turnholti, Belgium: Typographi Brepols, 1978.

Muller, Richard A. *God, Creation and Providence in the Thought of Jacob Arminius: Sources and Directions of Scholastic Protestantism in the Era of Early Orthodoxy.* Grand Rapids: Baker Book House, 1991.

—. *Dictionary of Latin and Greek Theological Terms.* Grand Rapids: Baker Book House, 1985.

Murray, John. *The Epistle to the Romans.* The New International Commentary on The New Testament. F. F. Bruce, Ed. Grand Rapids: William B. Eerdmans Publishing Company, 1980.

Nelson, P. C. *Bible Doctrines.* Ft. Worth: Southwestern Press, 1943.

Nichol, John T. *The Pentecostals.* Plainfield, New Jersey, 1971.

Nicozisin, George. *Born Again Christians, Charismatics, Gifts of the Holy Spirit: An Orthodox Perspective.* Greek Orthodox Archdiocese of North and South America, undated.

Nielsen, Niels C., Jr., Ed. *Christianity after Communism: Social, Political, and Cultural Struggle in Russia.* Boulder, Colorado: Westview Press, 1994.

Nienkirchen, Charles W. *A. B. Simpson and the Pentecostal Movement.* Peabody, Massachusetts: Hendrickson Publishers, 1992.

Noll, Mark A. *A History of Christianity in the United States and Canada.* Grand Rapids: William B. Eerdmans Publishing Company, 1992.

Ouspensky, Leonid. *Theology of the Icon.* Crestwood, New York: St. Vladimir's Seminary Press, 1978.

Ouspensky, Leonid and Vladimir Lossky. *The Meaning of Icons.* rev. ed. Trans. G. E. H. Palmer and E. Kadloubovsky. Crestwood, New York: St. Vladimir's Seminary Press, 1982.

Outler, Albert C. Ed. *John Wesley.* New York: Oxford University Press, 1964.

Pearlman, Myer. *Knowing the Doctrines of the Bible.* Springfield, Missouri: Gospel Publishing House, 1937.

Pearlman, Myer, and Frank M. Boyd. *Pentecostal Truth.* Springfield, Missouri: Gospel Publishing House, 1968.

Pelikan, Jaroslav. *Imago Dei: The Byzantine Apologia for Icons.* Princeton University Press, 1990.

—. *The Christian Tradition: A History of the Development of Doctrine.* 5 vols. Chicago: The University of Chicago Press, 1989.

Petro, Nicolai N., Ed. *Christianity and Russian Culture in Soviet Society.* Boulder, Colorado: Westview Press, 1990.

Phan, Peter. *Culture and Eschatology: The Iconographical Vision of Paul Evdokimov.* New York: Peter Lang, 1985.

Philokalia, The. Vols. 1-5. Modern Greek translation. Thessaloniki: 1987.

Poloma, Margaret M. *The Assemblies of God at the Crossroads: Charisma and Institutional Dilemmas.* Knoxville: The University of Tennessee Press, 1989.

Praeger, Dennis. *Think A Second Time.* New York: Regan Books, 1995.

Quasten, Johannes. *Patrology.* 3 vols. Utrecht-Antwerp: Spectrum Publishers, 1975.

Quenot, Michel. *The Icon: Window on the Kingdom.* Trans. A Carthusian Monk. Crestwood, New York: St. Vladimir's Seminary Press, 1991.

Randolph, Eleanor. *Waking the Tempests: Ordinary Life in The New Russia.* New York: Simon & Schuster, 1996.

Riggs, Ralph M. *We Believe.* Springfield, Missouri: Gospel Publishing House, 1954.

—. *The Spirit Himself.* Springfield, Missouri: Gospel Publishing House, 1949.

Robeck, Cecil M., Jr. *Prophecy in Carthage: Perpetua, Tertullian, and Cyprian.* Cleveland, Ohio: The Pilgrim Press, 1992.

Robertson, Archibald, Ed. *A Select Library of Nicene and Post-Nicene Fathers of the Christian Church.* Trans. Philip Schaff and Henry Wace. Grand Rapids: William. B. Eerdmans, 1978.

Rusch, William G., Ed. *The Trinitarian Controversy.* Sources of Early Christian Thought Series. Philadelphia: Fortress Press, 1980.

Schmemann, Alexander. *The Historical Road of Eastern Orthodoxy.* Trans. Lydia W. Kesich. Crestwood, New York: St. Vladimir's Seminary Press, 1992.

—. *Church, World, Mission: Reflections on Orthodoxy in the West.* Crestwood, New York: St. Vladimir's Seminary Press, 1979.

—. *Ultimate Questions: An Anthology of Modern Russian Religious Thought.* Tans. Asheleigh Moorhouse. Crestwood, New York: St. Vladimir's Seminary Press, 1977.

—. *For the Life of the World.* St. Vladimir's Seminary Press, 1973.

Scupoli, Lorenzo. *Combattimento Spirituale.* Translated into English as *Unseen Warfare.* Edited by Nicodemus of the Holy Mountain. Revised by Theophan the Recluse. Translated by E. Kadloubovsky and G. E. H. Palmer. Crestwood, New York: St. Vladimir's Seminary Press, 1995.

Seeberg, Reinhold. *Textbook of The History of Doctrines.* 2 vols. Trans. Charles E. Hay. Grand Rapids: Baker Book House, 1954.

Semple McPherson, Aimee. *What's the Matter?* Los Angeles: Echo Park Evangelistic Association, 1928.

Shalin, Dmitri N., Ed. *Russian Culture at the Crossroads: Paradoxes of Postcommunist Consciousness.* Boulder, Colorado: Westview Press, 1996.

Sinkewicz, Robert E. *Saint Gregory Palamas: The One Hundred and Fifty Chapters.* Toronto: Pontifical Institute of Mediaeval Studies, 1988.

Slay, James. *This We Believe.* Cleveland, Tennessee: Pathway, 1963.

Smith, Barbara. *Orthodoxy & Native Americans: The Alaskan Mission.* Occasional Paper #1 for the Department of History and Archives, Historical Society. Crestwood, New York: St. Vladimir's Seminary Press, 1980.

Smith, Timothy L. *Revivalism and Social Reform in Mid-Nineteenth Century America.* Nashville, Tennessee: Abingdon Press, 1957.

Spittler, Russell P. *God the Father.* Springfield, Missouri: Gospel Publishing House, 1976.

Staniloae, Dumitru. *Prayer and Holiness: The Icon of Man Renewed in God.* 4th ed. Trans. A. M. Allchin. Oxford: The Sisters of the Love of God, 1993.

Stavropoulos, Christoforos. *Partakers of the Divine Nature.* Trans. Stanley Harakas. Minneapolis: Light and Life Publishing Company, 1976.

Stephanou, Eusebius A. *Man: Body, Soul and Spirit.* Fort Wayne, Indiana: Logos Ministry for Orthodox Renewal, 1974.

—. *Belief and Practice in the Orthodox Church.* New York: Minos Publishing Company, 1965.

Stylianopoulos, Theodore G. *The New Testament: An Orthodox Perspective.* Vol. 1. Brookline, Massachusetts: Holy Cross Orthodox Press, 1997.

Stylianopoulos, Theodore G. and S. Mark Heim. Eds. *Spirit of the Truth: Ecumenical Perspectives on the Holy Spirit.* Brookline, Massachusetts: Holy Cross Orthodox Press, 1988.

Symeon the New Theologian. Discourses. Trans. C. J. de Catanzaro. Classics of Western Spirituality Series. New York: Paulist Press, 1980.

—. *The Practical and Theological Chapters and the Three Theological Discourses.* Trans. Paul McGuckin. Cistercian Studies, No. 41. Kalamazoo, Michigan: Cistercian Publications, 1986.

Synan, Vinson. Ed. *Aspects of Pentecostal-Charismatic Origins.* Plainfield, New Jersey: Logos International, 1975.

Synan, Vinson. *The Holiness-Pentecostal Movement in The United States.* Grand Rapids: William B. Eerdmans Publishing Company, 1971.

Terrien, Samuel L. *The Elusive Presence: Toward a New Biblical Theology.* San Francisco: Harper & Row, 1978.

The Way of a Pilgrim. Trans. R. M. French. San Francisco: Harper & Row, Publishers, 1952.

Torrance, Thomas F. *Divine Meaning: Studies in Patristic Hermeneutics.* Edinburgh: T & T Clark, 1995.

—. *The Trinitarian Faith: The Evangelical Theology of the Ancient Catholic Church.* Edinburgh: T. & T. Clark, 1988.

—. *Space, Time, and Incarnation.* Oxford University Press, 1969.

—. *The Doctrine of Grace in The Apostolic Fathers.* London: Oliver and Boyd, 1948.

Tsirpanlis, Constantine N. *Introduction to Eastern Patristic Thought and Orthodox Theology.* Collegeville, Minnesota: The Liturgical Press, 1991.

Turning Over a New Leaf: Protestant Missions and the Orthodox Churches of the Middle East - The Final Report of a Multi-Mission Study Group on Orthodoxy. Lynwood, Washington: Middle East Media, 1992.

Ugolnik, Anthony. *The Illuminating Icon.* Grand Rapids: William B. Eerdmans Publishing Company, 1989.

Verbeke, Gerardo, Ed. *Images of Man in Ancient and Medieval Thought.* Louvain, Belgium: Leuven University Press, 1976.

Vischer, Lukas., Ed. *Spirit of God, Spirit of Christ: Ecumenical Reflections on Filioque.* World Council of Churches, Faith and Order Series, 1981.

Vlachos, Hierotheos. *Orthodox Psychotherapy: The Science of the Fathers.* Trans. Esther Williams. Levadia, Greece: Birth of the Theotokos Monastery, 1994.

Von Campenhausen, Hans. *The Fathers of the Greek Church.* Trans. L. A. Garrard. London: Adam & Charles Black, 1963.

Wacker, Grant, *Heaven Below: Early Pentecostals and American Culture.* Cambridge, Massachusetts: Harvard University Press, 2001.

Ware, Kallistos. *The Orthodox Way.* rev. ed. Crestwood, New York: St. Vladimir's Seminary Press, 1995.

Ware, Timothy (Kallistos). *The Orthodox Church.* Baltimore, Maryland: Penguin Books, 1964.

Webster, Alexander F. C. *The Price of Prophecy: Orthodox Churches on Peace, Freedom, and Security.* 2nd ed. Grand Rapids: William B. Eerdmans Publishing Company, 1995.

Williams, Ernest S. *Systematic Theology.* 3 vols. Springfield, Missouri: Gospel Publishing House, 1953.

Winkler, Gabriele. *Prayer Attitude in the Eastern Church.* Minneapolis, Minnesota: Light and Life Publishing Co., 1978.

Yannaras, Christos. *Elements of Faith: An Introduction to Orthodox Theology.* Trans. Keith Schram. Edinburgh: T & T Clark, 1991.

—. *The Freedom of Morality.* Trans. Elizabeth Briere. Crestwood, New York: St. Vladimir's Seminary Press, 1984.

Yearbook of the Southern California District Council of the Assemblies of God, Inc., 1997-98. Springfield, Missouri: Gospel Publishing House, 1997.

Ye'or, Bat. *The Decline of Eastern Christianity under Islam: From Jihad to Dhimmitude.* Trans. Miriam Kochan and David Littman. Fairleigh Dickinson University Press, 1996. First published as *Les Chrétiientés d'Orient entre Jihad et Dhimmitude. VIIᵉ-Xxᵉ siecle.* Paris: *Les Éditions du Cerf,* 1991.

Zernov, Nicolas. *Three Russian Prophets: Khomiakov, Dostoevsky, Soloviev.* 3rd. ed. Gulf Breeze, Florida: Academic International Press, 1973.

——. *Moscow The Third Rome.* 2nd. ed. New York: AMS Press, Inc., 1971.

——. *Eastern Christendom: A Study of the Origin and Development of the Eastern Orthodox Church.* London: Weidenfeld and Nicolson, 1961.

Zizioulas, John D. *Being as Communion: Studies in Personhood and the Church.* Crestwood, New York: St. Vladimir's Seminary Press, 1993.

Articles

Aghiorgoussis, Maximos. "Sin in Orthodox Dogmatics." *St. Vladimir's Theological Quarterly,* 21:4 (1977), 179-190.

Albrecht, Daniel. "Pentecostal Spirituality: Looking through the Lens of Ritual." *Pneuma: The Journal of the Society for Pentecostal Studies,* 14:2 (Fall 1992), 107-125.

Alexander, David A. "Bishop J. H. King and the Emergence of Holiness Pentecostalism." *Pneuma: The Journal of the Society for Pentecostal Studies,* 5:2 (Fall 1986), 159-183.

Allen, Joseph J. "The Inner Way: The Historical Tradition of Spiritual Direction." *St. Vladimir's Theological Quarterly,* 35: 2 & 3 (1991), 257-270.

Allchin, A. M. "The Epworth-Canterbury-Constantinople Axis," *Wesleyan Theological Journal,* 26:1 (Spring 1991), 23-37.

Khaled Anatolios, "The Soteriological Significance of Christ's Humanity in St. Athanasius," *St. Vladimir's,* 40:4 (1996), 265-286.

"Archbishop Calls Pentecostals Non-Christian." *Christianity Today,* 39:1 (January 9, 1995), 42.

Arnett, William M. "The Role of the Holy Spirit in Entire Sanctification in the Writings of John Wesley." *Wesleyan Theological Journal,* 14:2 (Fall 1979), 15-30.

"Ask the Superintendent: An Interview with Thomas E. Trask." *Enrichment,* 3:4 (Fall 1998), 8-10.

Barnett, Tommy, Matthew Barnett, and Daniel de Léon, "Staking a Claim in the Heart of the Inner City: How two churches have developed urban strategies for reaching thousands in the inner city," *Enrichment,* 2:4 (Fall 1997), 18-22.

Barrett, D. B. "Global Statistics," in *Dictionary of Pentecostal and Charismatic Movements*. Stanley M. Burgess and Gary B. McGee, Eds. Grand Rapids: Zondervan Publishing House, 1988, 810-830.

Bavinck, Herman. "Common Grace." Trans. R.C. Van Leeuwen. *Calvin Theological Journal*, 24 (April, 1989), 38-65.

Behr, John. "A Note On The 'Ontology of Gender." *St. Vladimir's Theological Quarterly*, 42:3-4 (1998), 363-372.

Benne, Robert. "The Neo-Augustinian Temptation." *First Things*, 81 (March 1998).

Benvenuti, Sherilyn. "Anointed, Gifted and Called: Pentecostal Women in Ministry." *Pneuma: The Journal of the Society for Pentecostal Studies*, 17:2 (Fall 1995), 229-235.

Blumhofer, Edith. "The Finished Work of Calvary: William H. Durham and a Doctrinal Controversy." *Assemblies of God Heritage*, 3:3 (Fall 1983), 9-11.

Bobrinskoy, Boris. "The Adamic Heritage According to Fr. John Meyendorff." *St. Vladimir's Theological Quarterly*, 42:1 (1998), 33-44.

—. "The Icon: Sacrament of the Kingdom." *St. Vladimir's Theological Quarterly*, 31:4 (1987).

Boudreaux, Richard. "Russians Sift Past to Find Selves." *Los Angeles Times*, 7 March 1997, A1 & A6.

Breck, John. "The Lord is the Spirit: An Essay in Christological Pneumatology." *The Ecumenical Review*, 42 (April 1990), 114-121.

—. "Reflections on the 'Problem' of Chalcedonian Christology." *St. Vladimir's Theological Quarterly*, 33:2 (1989), 147-157.

—. "The Relevance of Nicene Christology." *St. Vladimir's Theological Quarterly*, 31:1 (1987), 41-64.

Brown, Harold O. J. "An Evangelical Appraisal." *Christian History*, 54 (16:2, 1997), 44-45.

Brown, Colin. "Existentialism." *Evangelical Dictionary of Theology*. Ed. Walter A. Elwell. Grand Rapids: Baker Book House, 1984.

Stanley M. Burgess, "Stephanou, Eusebius A.," in *Dictionary of Pentecostal and Charismatic Movements*. Stanley M. Burgess and Gary B. McGee, Eds. Grand Rapids: Zondervan Publishing House, 1988,, 831-832.

Stanley M. Burgess, "Implications of Eastern Christian Pneumatology for Western Pentecostal Doctrine and Practice," in *Experiences of the Spirit: Conference on Pentecostal and Charismatic Research in Europe at Utrecht*

University, 1989 Studies in the Intercultural History of Christianity, 68 (Frankfurt am Main: Peter Lang, 1991), 23-34.

Bundy, David. "Christian Virtue: John Wesley and The Alexandrian Tradition," *Wesleyan Theological Journal,* 26:1 (Spring 1991), 139-163.

Byrd, Joseph. "Paul Ricoeur's Hermeneutical Theory and Pentecostal Proclamation." *Pneuma: The Journal of the Society for Pentecostal Studies,* 15:2 (Fall 1993), 203-222.

Campbell, Ted A. "Wesley's Use of the Church Fathers." *The Asbury Theological Journal,* 50:2-51:1 (Fall 1995 and Spring 1996), 57-70.

Cargal, Timothy B. "Beyond the Fundamentalist-Modernist Controversy: Pentecostals and Hermeneutics in a Postmodern Age." *Pneuma: The Journal of the Society for Pentecostal Studies,* 15:2 (Fall 1993), 163-187.

Cerillo, Augustus, Jr. "Interpretive Approaches to the History of American Pentecostal Origins." *Pneuma: The Journal of the Society for Pentecostal Studies,* 19:1 (Spring 1997), 29-52.

Chan, Simon. "Sharing the Trinitarian Life: John 17:20-26, 1 John 1:1-4." *On the way to Fuller Koinonia.* Eds. Thomas F. Best and Günther Gassmann. Geneva: WCC Publications, Faith and Order Paper no. 166, 1994.

Chryssavgis, John. "The Liturgy as Tradition and Tradition as Liturgy." *Sobornost,* 7:2 (1985), 18-23.

Ciobotea, Dan-Ilie. "The Role of the Liturgy in Orthodox Theological Education," *St. Vladimir's,* 31:2 (1987).

Clendenin, Daniel B. "Why I'm Not Orthodox." *Christianity Today,* 41:1 (January 6, 1997), 32-34.

—. "What the Orthodox Believe: Four key differences between the Orthodox and Protestants." *Christian History,* 54 (16:2, 1997), 32-35.

—. "Did You Know, Little-known or fascinating facts about Eastern Orthodoxy," *Christian History,* 54 (16:2, 1997), 2-3.

Combined Minutes of the General Council of the AG in the USA, Canada, and Foreign Lands (1914-1917). St. Louis: Gospel Publishing, n. d.

Crabtree, Charles T. "The Secret to Building a Soul-Winning Church," *Enrichment,* 2:4 (Fall 1997), 28-31.

Doumouras, Alexander. "Greek Orthodox Communities in America Before World War I," *St. Vladimir's Theological Quarterly,* 11:4 (1967), 172-192.

Dragas, George. "Holy Spirit and Tradition: The Writings of St Athanasius." *Sobornost,* 1:1 (1979).

Dulles, Avery. "The Church as Communion." *New Perspectives on Historical Theology*. Ed. Bradley Nassif. Grand Rapids: William B. Eerdmans Publishing Company, 1996, 125-139.

Emmert, Athanasios F. S. "Charismatic Developments in the Eastern Orthodox Church." In *Perspectives on the New Pentecostalism*. Ed. Russell P. Spittler. Grand Rapids: Baker Book House, 1976.

Fahey, Michael. "Son and Spirit: Divergent Theologies between Constantinople and the West." In *Conflicts about the Holy Spirit*. Eds. Hans Küng and Jürgen Moltmann. New York: The Seabury Press, 1979.

"Faith and Order Commission's Consultation on the Holy Spirit." *Ecumenical Trends*, 15:2 (February 1986), 32-33.

Fatula, Mary Ann. "The Holy Spirit in East and West: Two Irreducible Traditions." *One in Christ*, 19:4 (1983), 379-386.

Filatov, Sergei and Liudmila Vorontsova. "New Russia in Search of an Identity." In *Remaking Russia*. Ed. Heyward Isham. Armonk, New York, 1995, 277-289.

Flogaus, Reinhard. "Palamas and Barlaam Revisited: A Reassessment of East and West in the Hesychast Controversy of 14th Century Byzantium." *St. Vladimir's Theological Quarterly*, 42:1 (1998), 1-32.

Gee, Donald. "The Adventure of Pentecostal Meetings." *Paraclete* (reprint, Spring 1983), 27-29.

——. "One Word—Pentecost." *Pentecost*, 70 (December 1964-February 1965), 2.

——. "Experience and Theology." *Pentecost*, 65 (September-November 1963), 17.

——. "Pentecostal Theology." *The Ministry* (Journal of the British Pentecostal Fellowship), 1:1 (January 1963), 21-22.

——. "This I Believe: The Use and Abuse of Dogmatism." *Redemption Tidings*, 30 (November 5, 1954), 4-5.

——. "Belief and Faith." *The Elim Evangel*, 3:1 (January 1922), 16.

——. "A Plea for Experience." *The Elim Evangel*, 3:5 (May 1922), 76-77.

Glastris, Paul. "An American-born archbishop, Old World values." *U. S. News & World Report*, 123:15 (October 20, 1997).

Hackel, Sergei. "Trial and Victory: The Spiritual Tradition of Modern Russia," In *Christian Spirituality, III, Post Reformation and Modern*. Eds. Dupré, Louis, and Don E. Saliers. New York: Crossroad, 1996.

Harrison, Nonna Verna. "The Maleness of Christ." *St. Vladimir's Theological Quarterly*, 42:2 (1998), 111-151.

—. "Poverty in the Orthodox Tradition." *St. Vladimir's Theological Quarterly*, 34:1 (1990), 15-47.

Henry, C. F. H. "Image of God," In *Evangelical Dictionary of Theology*. Ed. Walter Elwell. Grand Rapids: Baker Book House, 1984.

Herman, Harvey Jr. "The Missing Generation in Our Churches: What the church must do if it is to see a harvest among Xers," *Enrichment*, 2:4 (Fall 1997), 56-61.

Heron, Alasdair. "Filioque." *Dictionary of the Ecumenical Movement*. Eds. Lossky, Bonino, Pobee, etal. Geneva: WCC Publications, 1991.

—. "The Filioque Clause: Questions Raised by Member Churches - Attempt at an Answer." *Reformed World*, 39:8 (1987), 842-852.

Hilton, Alison. "Piety and Pragmatism: Orthodox Saints and Slavic Nature Gods in Russian Folk Art." In *Christianity and the Arts in Russia*. Eds. William C. Brumfield and Milos M. Velimirovic. Cambridge University Press, 1991.

Peter D. Hocken, "Charismatic Movement," in *Dictionary of Pentecostal and Charismatic Movements*. Stanley M. Burgess and Gary B. McGee, Eds. Grand Rapids: Zondervan Publishing House, 1988, 130-160.

Hopko, Thomas. "Ministry and the Unity of the Church: An Eastern Orthodox View." *St. Vladimir's Theological Quarterly*, 34:4 (1990), 269-279.

Horton, Stanley M. "The Pentecostal Perspective." In *Five Views on Sanctification*, Melvin E. Dieter, Anthony A Hoekema, Stanley M. Horton, J. Robertson McQuilkin, and John F. Walvoord. Grand Rapids: Zondervan Publishing House, 1987.

Hotz, Robert Lee. "Seeking the Biology of Spirituality." *Los Angeles Times*, April 26, 1998, A1 & A28.

Houston, Shelly. "Growing Unrest: Greek Church says laity lamentations are groundless." *Christianity Today*, 42:10 (September 7, 1998), 28.

Hoy, Albert L. "Sanctification," *Paraclete*, 15:4 (Fall, 1981), 5-7.

Israel, Richard D., Daniel E. Albrecht and Randal G. McNally, "Pentecostals and Hermeneutics: Texts, Rituals and Community." *Pneuma: The Journal of the Society for Pentecostal Studies*, 15:2 (Fall 1993), 137-161.

Jepson, J. W. "The Unity of the Spirit." *Paraclete* (Winter 1978), 3-5.

Johnson, W. Stanley. "Christian Perfection as Love for God," *Wesleyan Theological Journal*, 18:1 (Spring 1983), 50-60.

Jugie, Martin. "Palamas Grégoire," *Dictionnaire de théologie catholique*, Vol. XI, 2 (Paris, 1932), col. 1735-1776.

Kesich, Veselin. "The Orthodox Church and Biblical Interpretation." *St. Vladimir's Theological Quarterly*, 37:4 (1993), 343-351.

Kreitzer, L. "Apotheosis of the Roman Emperor." *Biblical Archaeology*, 53 (1990), 210-217.

LaCugna, Catherine M. and Killian McDonnell. "Returning from the Far Country: Contemporary Trinitarian Theology." *Scottish Journal of Theology*, 41:2 (1988), 191-215.

Leggett, Dennis. "The Assemblies of God Statement on Sanctification (A Brief Review by Calvin and Wesley)." *Pneuma: The Journal of the Society for Pentecostal Studies*, 11:2 (Fall 1989), 113-122.

Limouris, Gennadios. "The Church: A Mystery of Unity in Diversity." *St. Vladimir's Theological Quarterly*, 31:2 (1987), 123-142.

MacDonald, William G. "Pentecostal Theology: A Classical Viewpoint." In *Perspectives on the New Pentecostalism.* Ed. Russell P. Spittler. Grand Rapids: Baker Book House, 1976.

Macchia, Frank D. "The Tongues of Pentecost: A Pentecostal Perspective on the Promise and Challenge of Pentecostal/Roman Catholic Dialogue." *Journal of Ecumenical Studies*, 35:1 (Winter 1998), 1-18.

——. "Tongues as a Sign: Towards a Pentecostal Theology of Glossolalia." *Pneuma: The Journal of the Society for Pentecostal Studies*, 15:1 (1993), 61-76.

——. "Sighs Too Deep for Words: Toward a Theology of Glossolalia," *Journal of Pentecostal Theology,* 1 (1992), 47-73.

Maddox, Randy L. "John Wesley and Eastern Orthodoxy: Influences, Convergences, and Differences." *The Asbury Theological Journal*, 45:2 (Fall 1990), 29-53.

Martin, Dennis D. "Mysticism," In *Evangelical Dictionary of Biblical Theology.* Ed. Walter A. Elwell. Grand Rapids: Baker Book House, 1996.

Martin, Tory W. "John Wesley's Exegetical Orientation: East or West?" *Wesleyan Theological Journal*, 26:1 (Spring 1991), 104-138.

McCormick, Steve K. "Theosis in Chrysostom and Wesley: An Eastern Paradigm on Faith and Love," *Wesleyan Theological Journal*, 26:1 (Spring 1991), 38-103.

McGee, Gary B. "Working Together: The Assemblies of God-Russian and Eastern European Mission Cooperation, 1927-40," *Assemblies of God Heritage*, 8:4 (Winter 1988-89), 12.

McLean, Mark D. "Toward a Pentecostal Hermeneutic." *Pneuma: The Journal of the Society for Pentecostal Studies*, 6:2 (Fall 1984), 35-56.

Menzies, William. "Lessons from Great Revivals," *Paraclete* (Winter 1974).

Merritt, John G. "'Dialogue' within a Tradition: John Wesley and Gregory of Nyssa discuss Christian Perfection," *Wesleyan Theological Journal*, 22:2 (Fall 1987), 92-116.

Meyendorff, John. "Visions of the Church: Russian Theological Thought in Modern Times." *St. Vladimir's Theological Quarterly*, 34:1 (1990), 5-14.

——. "Christ as Savior in the East," In *Christian Spirituality, Vol. I, Origins to the Twelfth Century*. Eds. Bernard McGinn, John Meyendorff, and Jean Leclercq. New York: Crossroad, 1988.

——. "Les Débuts de la Controverse Hésychaste," *In Byzantine Hesychasm: Historical, Theological, and Social Problems*. London: Variorum Reprints, 1974, 90-102.

Meyendorff, Paul. "Reflections on Russian Liturgy: A Retrospective on the Occasion of the Millennium." *St. Vladimir's Theological Quarterly*, 33:1 (1989), 21-34.

"Minutes of the 47th Session of The General Council of the Assemblies of God." Indianapolis, Indiana, August 5-10, 1997.

Morris, John Warren. "The Charismatic Movement: An Orthodox Evaluation." *The Greek Orthodox Theological Review*, 28:2 (Summer 1983), 103-134.

Muller, Richard A. "Arminius and the Scholastic Tradition." *Calvin Theological Journal*, 24:1 (1989), 263-77.

Mylonas, Efsthathios V. "Towards The Common Expression of the Apostolic Faith Today: An Orthodox Reply." *One in Christ*, 23:1-2 (1987), 131-7.

Nassif, Bradley. "Kissers and Smashers: Why the Orthodox killed one another over icons." *Christian History*, 54 (1997, no. 2).

Nicastro, R. Vito, Jr. "Mission Volga: A Case Study in the Tensions Between Evangelizing and Proselytizing." *Journal of Ecumenical Studies*, 31:3-4 (Summer-Fall, 1994), 223-243.

Outler, Albert C. "John Wesley's Interest in the Early Father's of the Church." *Bulletin of the United Church of Canada Committee on Archives and History*, 29:2 (1980), 5-17.

——. "The Place of Wesley in the Christian Tradition," In Kenneth E. Rowe, ed., *The Place of Wesley in the Christian Tradition*. Metuchen, New Jersey: Scarecrow Press, 1976.

Papademetriou, George C. "N.C.C.C. Consultation on the Holy Spirit." *Journal of Ecumenical Studies*, 23:2 (Spring 1986), 334-335.

Pentecostal Evangel. The Weekly Magazine of the Assemblies of God. Springfield, Missouri: 1918 to Present.

Poloma, Margaret M. "Charisma, Institutionalization and Social Change." *Pneuma: The Journal of the Society for Pentecostal Studies*, 17:2 (Fall 1995), 245-252.

Randall, Claire. "The Importance of the Pentecostal and Holiness Churches in the Ecumenical Movement." *One in Christ*, 23:1-2 (1987), 83-92.

Rhodes, Stephen. "Christ and Spirit: Filioque Reconsidered." *Biblical Theology Bulletin*, 18 (July 1988), 91-95.

Ritschl, Dietrich. "Historical Development and Implications of the Filioque Controversy," In *Spirit of God, Spirit of Christ: Ecumenical Reflections on the Filioque Controversy*. Ed. Lukas Vischer. Geneva: World Council of Churches, 1981.

Robeck, Cecil M., Jr. "A Pentecostal Assessment of 'Towards a Common Understanding and Vision' of the WCC." *Mid-Stream*, 37:1 (January, 1998), 1-36.

—. "The Assemblies of God and Ecumenical Cooperation: 1920-1965." In *Pentecostalism in Context: Essays in Honor of William M. Menzies*. Wonsuk Ma and Robert P. Menzies, Eds. Journal of Pentecostal Theology Supplement Series 11. Sheffield, England: Sheffield Academic Press, 1997, 107-150.

—. "Evangelicals and Catholics Together." *One in Christ*, 33:2 (1997), 138-60.

—. "Evangelism or Proselytism of Hispanics? A Pentecostal Perspective." *Journal of Hispanic Liberation Theology*. 4:4 (1997), 42-64.

—. "Mission and the Issue of Proselytism." *International Bulletin of Missionary Research*, 20:1 (January, 1996), 2-8.

—. "Discerning the Spirit in the Life of the Church." *In The Church in the Movement of the Spirit*. William R. Barr and Rena M. Yocum, Eds. Grand Rapids: William B. Eerdmans Publishing Company, 29-49.

—. "Pentecostal Origins in Global Perspective," In *All Together in One Place: Theological Papers from the Brighton Conference on World Evangelization*. Harold D. Hunter and Peter D. Hocken, Eds. Sheffield, England: Sheffield Academic Press, 1993, 166-180.

—. "The Nature of Pentecostal Spirituality." *Pneuma: The Journal of the Society for Pentecostal Studies*, 14:2 (Fall 1992), 103-106.

—. "National Association of Evangelicals," In *Dictionary of Pentecostal and Charismatic Movements*. Stanley M. Burgess and Gary B. McGee, Eds. Grand Rapids: Zondervan Publishing House, 1988, 634-6.

—. "Pentecostals and the Apostolic Faith: Implications for Ecumenism." *One in Christ*, 23:1-2 (1987), 110-130.

Roebuck, David G. "Sanctification and the Church of God.*" Reflections . . . Upon Church of God Heritag,* 2:2 (Fall 1992).

Sawatsky, Walter. "Visions in Conflict: Starting Anew Through the Prism of Leadership Training." *In Christianity after Communism: Social, Political, and Cultural Struggle in Russia.* Ed. Niels C. Nielsen, Jr. Boulder, Colorado: Westview Press, 1990.

Schmemann, Alexander. "Russian Theology: 1920-1972, An Introductory Survey." *St. Vladimir's Theological Quarterly*, 16:3 (1972), 172-194.

Shaw, Lewis. "John Meyendorff and the Russian Theological Tradition," In *New Perspectives on Historical Theology.* Ed. Bradley Nassif. Grand Rapids: William B. Eerdmans Publishing Company, 1996.

Sheler, Jeffery L. "Discovering Byzantium: Eastern Orthodoxy is no longer a 'stealth' religion." *U. S. News & World Report.* 123:15 (October 20, 1997).

Sherrard, Philip. "The Revival of Hesychast Spirituality," In *Christian Spirituality, III, Post Reformation and Modern.* Eds. Dupré, Louis, and Don E. Saliers. New York: Crossroad, 1996.

Slesinski, Robert. "The Relationship of God and Man in Russian Religious Philosophy from Florensky to Frank." *St. Vladimir's Theological Quarterly*, 36:3 (1992), 217-235.

Snyder, Howard A. "John Wesley and Macarius the Egyptian." *The Asbury Theological Journal*, 45:2 (Fall 1990), 55-60.

Spittler, Russell P. "Spirituality, Pentecostal and Charismatic." *In Dictionary of Pentecostal and Charismatic Movements.* Eds. Burgess, S. M., and G. B. McGee. Grand Rapids: Zondervan Publishing House, 1988.

Staniloae, Dumitru. "The Holy Spirit and the Sobornicity of the Church." *In Theology and the Church.* Trans. Robert Barringer. Crestwood, New York: St. Vladimir's Seminary Press, 1980.

Stout, Maury. "The Holy Spirit in the Life of the Believer." *Paraclete* (Winter 1986), 14-17.

Theosis: Newsletter for Orthodox Charismatic Renewal. East Lansing, Michigan: Service Committee For Orthodox Charismatic Renewal.

Thigpen, Paul. "Ancient Altars, Pentecostal Fire." *Ministries Today* (Nov.-Dec. 1992), 43-50.

Thunberg, Lars. "The Human Person as the Image of God: Eastern Christianity," In *Christian Spirituality, I, Origins to the Twelfth Century.* Eds. Bernard McGinn, John Meyendorff, and Jean Leclercq. New York: Crossroad, 1988.

van Rossum, Joost. "A.S. Khomiakov and Orthodox Ecclesiology." *St. Vladimir's Theological Quarterly*, 35:1 (1991), 67-82.

Wacker, Grant. "The Functions of Faith in Primitive Pentecostalism," *Harvard Theological Review*, 77:3 (1984), 353-375.

—. "Pentecostalism," In *Encyclopedia of American Religious Experience*, Vol. 2, Eds. Charles H. Lippy and Peter W. Williams. New York: 1988.

—. "Playing for Keeps: The Primitivist Impulse in Early Pentecostalism," In *The American Quest for the Primitive Church.* Ed. Richard T. Hughes. Urbana: University of Illinois, 1988.

—. "Character and the Modernization of North American Pentecostalism." Paper read at the Society for Pentecostal Studies meeting, 1991.

Ware, Kallistos. "Ways of Prayer and Contemplation: Eastern," In *Christian Spirituality, I, Origins to the Twelfth Century.* Eds. Bernard McGinn, John Meyendorff, and Jean Leclercq. New York: Crossroad, 1988.

—. "The Human Person as an Icon of the Trinity." *Sobornost*, 8:2 (1986), 6-23.

—. "The Mystery of the Human Person." *Sobornost*, 3:1 (1981), 62-69.

—. "Orthodoxy and the Charismatic Movement." *Eastern Churches Review*, 4 (1973), 182-186.

Watson, Gordon. "The Filioque—Opportunity For Debate?" *Scottish Journal of Theology*, 41:2 (1988), 313-330.

Widdicombe, Peter. "Adoption, Salvation, and Life of Unity," In *The Fatherhood of God from Origen to Athanasius.* Oxford University Press, 1993.

Williams, William C. "Evil." In *Evangelical Dictionary of Biblical Theology.* Ed. Walter A. Elwell. Grand Rapids: Baker Book House, 1996.

—. "Human Sexuality." In *Evangelical Dictionary of Biblical Theology.* W. A. Elwell, ed. Grand Rapids: Baker Book House, 1996, 727-730.

Wilson, Dwight J. "Pentecostal Perspectives on Eschatology," in *Dictionary of Pentecostal and Charismatic Movements.* Stanley M. Burgess and Gary B. McGee, Eds. Grand Rapids: Zondervan Publishing House, 1988, 264-268.

Wilson, Lewis. "The Kerr-Pierce Role in A/G Education," *Assemblies of God Heritage*, 10:1 (Spring 1990), 6-22.

Woodward, Kenneth L. "Friends, Brothers, Heretics: Patriarch Bartholomew labels the Catholics." *Newsweek*, Nov. 3, 1997, 64.

WorldLink. A Quarterly Communique Linking The World Assemblies of God Fellowship, 4:3 (July 1998).

Dissertations, Pamphlets, Theses and Unpublished Papers

Blumhofer, Edith L. (Waldvogel). "The 'Overcoming Life': A Study in the Reformed Evangelical Origins of Pentecostalism." Diss. Harvard University, 1977.

Bundy, David. "Visions of Sanctification: Themes of Orthodoxy in the Methodist, Holiness and Pentecostal Traditions." Paper presented at the Building Bridges, Breaking Walls International Discussion, Prague, September 12, 1997.

Cerillo, Augustus, Jr. "The Beginnings of American Pentecostalism: An Historiographical Overview," Paper presented to the Society for Pentecostal Studies, Chicago, 1994.

Cole, David. "Pentecostal Koinonia: An Emerging Ecumenical Ecclesiology Among Pentecostals." Diss. Fuller Theological Seminary, 1998.

Del Colle, Ralph. "The Pursuit of Holiness: A Catholic-Pentecostal Dialogue." Paper presented to the Society for Pentecostal Studies, Cleveland, Tennessee, 1998.

Johansen, Ernest. "An Alternative View of Baptism in the Holy Spirit." Master of Theology, Thesis. Fuller Theological Seminary, 1994.

"Our Distinctive Doctrine: The Baptism In The Holy Spirit." An Assemblies of God Pamphlet. Springfield, Missouri: Gospel Publishing House, 1995.

Robeck, Cecil M., Jr. "A Pentecostal Witness in an Eastern Context." Paper presented at the Building Bridges, Breaking Walls International Discussion, Prague, September 12, 1997.

——. "A Pentecostal Perspective on Apostolicity." Paper presented to Faith and Order NCCCUSA, American Born Churches, March 1992.

——. "Pentecostal Perspectives on the Ecumenical Challenge." Paper originally presented in 1984 to the American Academy of Religion. Revised in 1989.

——. "Name and Glory: the Ecumenical Challenge." Paper presented to the Society for Pentecostal Studies, 1983.

The Discipleship and Submission Movement. An Assemblies of God Position Paper. Springfield, Missouri: Gospel Publishing House, 1976.

The Inerrancy of Scripture. An Assemblies of God Position Paper. Springfield, Missouri: Gospel Publishing House, 1976.

Transcendental Meditation. Assemblies of God Position Paper. Springfield, Missouri: Gospel Publishing House, 1976.

Wacker, Grant. "Character and the Modernization of North American Pentecostalism," Paper presented at the Society for Pentecostal Studies, 1991.

Ware, Kallistos. "Personal Experience of the Holy Spirit According to the Greek Fathers." Paper presented at the Building Bridges, Breaking Walls International Discussion. Prague, September 12, 1997.

Zeucuch, Stefan. "Building Bridges, Breaking Barriers in the Power of the Holy Spirit." Paper presented at the Building Bridges, Breaking Walls International Discussion, Prague, September 12, 1997.

Index

Paternoster Biblical Monographs

(All titles uniform with this volume)
Dates in bold are of projected publication

Joseph Abraham
Eve: Accused or Acquitted?
A Reconsideration of Feminist Readings of the Creation Narrative Texts in Genesis 1–3
Two contrary views dominate contemporary feminist biblical scholarship. One finds in the Bible an unequivocal equality between the sexes from the very creation of humanity, whilst the other sees the biblical text as irredeemably patriarchal and androcentric. Dr Abraham enters into dialogue with both camps as well as introducing his own method of approach. An invaluable tool for any one who is interested in this contemporary debate.
2002 / 0-85364-971-5 / xxiv + 272pp

Octavian D. Baban
Mimesis and Luke's on the Road Encounters in Luke-Acts
Luke's Theology of the Way and its Literary Representation
The book argues on theological and literary (mimetic) grounds that Luke's on-the-road encounters, especially those belonging to the post-Easter period, are part of his complex theology of the Way. Jesus' teaching and that of the apostles is presented by Luke as a challenging answer to the Hellenistic reader's thirst for adventure, good literature, and existential paradigms.
2005 */ 1-84227-253-5 / approx. 374pp*

Paul Barker
The Triumph of Grace in Deuteronomy
This book is a textual and theological analysis of the interaction between the sin and faithlessness of Israel and the grace of Yahweh in response, looking especially at Deuteronomy chapters 1–3, 8–10 and 29–30. The author argues that the grace of Yahweh is determinative for the ongoing relationship between Yahweh and Israel and that Deuteronomy anticipates and fully expects Israel to be faithless.
2004 / 1-84227-226-8 / xxii + 270pp

Jonathan F. Bayes
The Weakness of the Law
God's Law and the Christian in New Testament Perspective
A study of the four New Testament books which refer to the law as weak (Acts, Romans, Galatians, Hebrews) leads to a defence of the third use in the Reformed debate about the law in the life of the believer.
2000 / 0-85364-957-X / xii + 244pp

Mark Bonnington
The Antioch Episode of Galatians 2:11-14 in Historical and Cultural Context
The Galatians 2 'incident' in Antioch over table-fellowship suggests significant disagreement between the leading apostles. This book analyses the background to the disagreement by locating the incident within the dynamics of social interaction between Jews and Gentiles. It proposes a new way of understanding the relationship between the individuals and issues involved.

2005 / 1-84227-050-8 / approx. 350pp

David Bostock
A Portrayal of Trust
The Theme of Faith in the Hezekiah Narratives
This study provides detailed and sensitive readings of the Hezekiah narratives (2 Kings 18–20 and Isaiah 36–39) from a theological perspective. It concentrates on the theme of faith, using narrative criticism as its methodology. Attention is paid especially to setting, plot, point of view and characterization within the narratives. A largely positive portrayal of Hezekiah emerges that underlines the importance and relevance of scripture.

2005 / 1-84227-314-0 / approx. 300pp

Mark Bredin
Jesus, Revolutionary of Peace
A Non-violent Christology in the Book of Revelation
This book aims to demonstrate that the figure of Jesus in the Book of Revelation can best be understood as an active non-violent revolutionary.

2003 / 1-84227-153-9 / xviii + 262pp

Robinson Butarbutar
Paul and Conflict Resolution
An Exegetical Study of Paul's Apostolic Paradigm in 1 Corinthians 9
The author sees the apostolic paradigm in 1 Corinthians 9 as part of Paul's unified arguments in 1 Corinthians 8–10 in which he seeks to mediate in the dispute over the issue of food offered to idols. The book also sees its relevance for dispute-resolution today, taking the conflict within the author's church as an example.

2006 / 1-84227-315-9 / approx. 280pp

Daniel J-S Chae
Paul as Apostle to the Gentiles
*His Apostolic Self-awareness and its Influence on the Soteriological Argument
in Romans*
Opposing 'the post-Holocaust interpretation of Romans', Daniel Chae com-
petently demonstrates that Paul argues for the equality of Jew and Gentile in
Romans. Chae's fresh exegetical interpretation is academically outstanding and
spiritually encouraging.
1997 / 0-85364-829-8 / xiv + 378pp

Luke L. Cheung
The Genre, Composition and Hermeneutics of the Epistle of James
The present work examines the employment of the wisdom genre with a certain
compositional structure and the interpretation of the law through the Jesus
tradition of the double love command by the author of the Epistle of James to
serve his purpose in promoting perfection and warning against doubleness
among the eschatologically renewed people of God in the Diaspora.
2003 / 1-84227-062-1 / xvi + 372pp

Youngmo Cho
Spirit and Kingdom in the Writings of Luke and Paul
The relationship between Spirit and Kingdom is a relatively unexplored area in
Lukan and Pauline studies. This book offers a fresh perspective of two biblical
writers on the subject. It explores the difference between Luke's and Paul's
understanding of the Spirit by examining the specific question of the
relationship of the concept of the Spirit to the concept of the Kingdom of God in
each writer.
2005 / 1-84227-316-7 / approx. 270pp

Andrew C. Clark
Parallel Lives
The Relation of Paul to the Apostles in the Lucan Perspective
This study of the Peter-Paul parallels in Acts argues that their purpose was to
emphasize the themes of continuity in salvation history and the unity of the
Jewish and Gentile missions. New light is shed on Luke's literary techniques,
partly through a comparison with Plutarch.
2001 / 1-84227-035-4 / xviii + 386pp

Andrew D. Clarke
Secular and Christian Leadership in Corinth
A Socio-Historical and Exegetical Study of 1 Corinthians 1–6
This volume is an investigation into the leadership structures and dynamics of first-century Roman Corinth. These are compared with the practice of leadership in the Corinthian Christian community which are reflected in 1 Corinthians 1–6, and contrasted with Paul's own principles of Christian leadership.
2005 / 1-84227-229-2 / 200pp

Stephen Finamore
God, Order and Chaos
René Girard and the Apocalypse
Readers are often disturbed by the images of destruction in the book of Revelation and unsure why they are unleashed after the exaltation of Jesus. This book examines past approaches to these texts and uses René Girard's theories to revive some old ideas and propose some new ones.
2005 / 1-84227-197-0 / approx. 344pp

David G. Firth
Surrendering Retribution in the Psalms
Responses to Violence in the Individual Complaints
In *Surrendering Retribution in the Psalms*, David Firth examines the ways in which the book of Psalms inculcates a model response to violence through the repetition of standard patterns of prayer. Rather than seeking justification for retributive violence, Psalms encourages not only a surrender of the right of retribution to Yahweh, but also sets limits on the retribution that can be sought in imprecations. Arising initially from the author's experience in South Africa, the possibilities of this model to a particular context of violence is then briefly explored.
2005 / 1-84227-337-X / xviii + 154pp

Scott J. Hafemann
Suffering and Ministry in the Spirit
Paul's Defence of His Ministry in II Corinthians 2:14–3:3
Shedding new light on the way Paul defended his apostleship, the author offers a careful, detailed study of 2 Corinthians 2:14–3:3 linked with other key passages throughout 1 and 2 Corinthians. Demonstrating the unity and coherence of Paul's argument in this passage, the author shows that Paul's suffering served as the vehicle for revealing God's power and glory through the Spirit.
2000 / 0-85364-967-7 / xiv + 262pp

Scott J. Hafemann
Paul, Moses and the History of Israel
The Letter/Spirit Contrast and the Argument from Scripture in 2 Corinthians 3
An exegetical study of the call of Moses, the second giving of the Law (Exodus 32–34), the new covenant, and the prophetic understanding of the history of Israel in 2 Corinthians 3. Hafemann's work demonstrates Paul's contextual use of the Old Testament and the essential unity between the Law and the Gospel within the context of the distinctive ministries of Moses and Paul.
2005 / 1-84227-317-5 / xii + 498pp

Douglas S. McComiskey
Lukan Theology in the Light of the Gospel's Literary Structure
Luke's Gospel was purposefully written with theology embedded in its patterned literary structure. A critical analysis of this cyclical structure provides new windows into Luke's interpretation of the individual pericopes comprising the Gospel and illuminates several of his theological interests.
2004 / 1-84227-148-2 / xviii + 388pp

Stephen Motyer
Your Father the Devil?
A New Approach to John and 'The Jews'
Who are 'the Jews' in John's Gospel? Defending John against the charge of antisemitism, Motyer argues that, far from demonising the Jews, the Gospel seeks to present Jesus as 'Good News for Jews' in a late first century setting.
1997 / 0-85364-832-8 / xiv + 260pp

Esther Ng
Reconstructing Christian Origins?
The Feminist Theology of Elizabeth Schüssler Fiorenza: An Evaluation
In a detailed evaluation, the author challenges Elizabeth Schüssler Fiorenza's reconstruction of early Christian origins and her underlying presuppositions. The author also presents her own views on women's roles both then and now.
2002 / 1-84227-055-9 / xxiv + 468pp

Robin Parry
Old Testament Story and Christian Ethics
The Rape of Dinah as a Case Study

What is the role of story in ethics and, more particularly, what is the role of Old Testament story in Christian ethics? This book, drawing on the work of contemporary philosophers, argues that narrative is crucial in the ethical shaping of people and, drawing on the work of contemporary Old Testament scholars, that story plays a key role in Old Testament ethics. Parry then argues that when situated in canonical context Old Testament stories can be reappropriated by Christian readers in their own ethical formation. The shocking story of the rape of Dinah and the massacre of the Shechemites provides a fascinating case study for exploring the parameters within which Christian ethical appropriations of Old Testament stories can live.

2004 / 1-84227-210-1 / xx + 350pp

Ian Paul
Power to See the World Anew
The Value of Paul Ricoeur's Hermeneutic of Metaphor in Interpreting the Symbolism of Revelation 12 and 13

This book is a study of the hermeneutics of metaphor of Paul Ricoeur, one of the most important writers on hermeneutics and metaphor of the last century. It sets out the key points of his theory, important criticisms of his work, and how his approach, modified in the light of these criticisms, offers a methodological framework for reading apocalyptic texts.

2006 / 1-84227-056-7 / approx. 350pp

Robert L. Plummer
Paul's Understanding of the Church's Mission
Did the Apostle Paul Expect the Early Christian Communities to Evangelize?

This book engages in a careful study of Paul's letters to determine if the apostle expected the communities to which he wrote to engage in missionary activity. It helpfully summarizes the discussion on this debated issue, judiciously handling contested texts, and provides a way forward in addressing this critical question. While admitting that Paul rarely explicitly commands the communities he founded to evangelize, Plummer amasses significant incidental data to provide a convincing case that Paul did indeed expect his churches to engage in mission activity. Throughout the study, Plummer progressively builds a theological basis for the church's mission that is both distinctively Pauline and compelling.

2006 / 1-84227-333-7 / approx. 324pp

David Powys
'Hell': A Hard Look at a Hard Question
The Fate of the Unrighteous in New Testament Thought
This comprehensive treatment seeks to unlock the original meaning of terms and phrases long thought to support the traditional doctrine of hell. It concludes that there is an alternative—one which is more biblical, and which can positively revive the rationale for Christian mission.
1997 / 0-85364-831-X / xxii + 478pp

Sorin Sabou
Between Horror and Hope
Paul's Metaphorical Language of Death in Romans 6.1-11
This book argues that Paul's metaphorical language of death in Romans 6.1-11 conveys two aspects: horror and hope. The 'horror' aspect is conveyed by the 'crucifixion' language, and the 'hope' aspect by 'burial' language. The life of the Christian believer is understood, as relationship with sin is concerned ('death to sin'), between these two realities: horror and hope.
2005 / 1-84227-322-1 / approx. 224pp

Rosalind Selby
The Comical Doctrine
The Epistemology of New Testament Hermeneutics
This book argues that the gospel breaks through postmodernity's critique of truth and the referential possibilities of textuality with its gift of grace. With a rigorous, philosophical challenge to modernist and postmodernist assumptions, Selby offers an alternative epistemology to all who would still read with faith *and* with academic credibility.
2005 / 1-84227-212-8 / approx. 350pp

Kiwoong Son
Zion Symbolism in Hebrews
Hebrews 12.18-24 as a Hermeneutical Key to the Epistle
This book challenges the general tendency of understanding the Epistle to the Hebrews against a Hellenistic background and suggests that the Epistle should be understood in the light of the Jewish apocalyptic tradition. The author especially argues for the importance of the theological symbolism of Sinai and Zion (Heb. 12:18-24) as it provides the Epistle's theological background as well as the rhetorical basis of the superiority motif of Jesus throughout the Epistle.
2005 / 1-84227-368-X / approx. 280pp

Kevin Walton
Thou Traveller Unknown
The Presence and Absence of God in the Jacob Narrative
The author offers a fresh reading of the story of Jacob in the book of Genesis through the paradox of divine presence and absence. The work also seeks to make a contribution to Pentateuchal studies by bringing together a close reading of the final text with historical critical insights, doing justice to the text's historical depth, final form and canonical status.
2003 / 1-84227-059-1 / xvi + 238pp

George M. Wieland
The Significance of Salvation
A Study of Salvation Language in the Pastoral Epistles
The language and ideas of salvation pervade the three Pastoral Epistles. This study offers a close examination of their soteriological statements. In all three letters the idea of salvation is found to play a vital paraenetic role, but each also exhibits distinctive soteriological emphases. The results challenge common assumptions about the Pastoral Epistles as a corpus.
2005 / 1-84227-257-8 / approx. 324pp

Alistair Wilson
When Will These Things Happen?
A Study of Jesus as Judge in Matthew 21–25
This study seeks to allow Matthew's carefully constructed presentation of Jesus to be given full weight in the modern evaluation of Jesus' eschatology. Careful analysis of the text of Matthew 21–25 reveals Jesus to be standing firmly in the Jewish prophetic and wisdom traditions as he proclaims and enacts imminent judgement on the Jewish authorities then boldly claims the central role in the final and universal judgement.
2004 / 1-84227-146-6 / xxii + 272pp

Lindsay Wilson
Joseph Wise and Otherwise
The Intersection of Covenant and Wisdom in Genesis 37–50
This book offers a careful literary reading of Genesis 37–50 that argues that the Joseph story contains both strong covenant themes and many wisdom-like elements. The connections between the two helps to explore how covenant and wisdom might intersect in an integrated biblical theology.
2004 / 1-84227-140-7 / xvi + 340pp

Stephen I. Wright
The Voice of Jesus
Studies in the Interpretation of Six Gospel Parables
This literary study considers how the 'voice' of Jesus has been heard in different periods of parable interpretation, and how the categories of figure and trope may help us towards a sensitive reading of the parables today.
2000 / 0-85364-975-8 / xiv + 280pp

Paternoster
9 Holdom Avenue,
Bletchley,
Milton Keynes MK1 1QR,
United Kingdom
Web: www.authenticmedia.co.uk/paternoster

Paternoster Theological Monographs

(All titles uniform with this volume)
Dates in bold are of projected publication

Emil Bartos
Deification in Eastern Orthodox Theology
An Evaluation and Critique of the Theology of Dumitru Staniloae
Bartos studies a fundamental yet neglected aspect of Orthodox theology: deification. By examining the doctrines of anthropology, christology, soteriology and ecclesiology as they relate to deification, he provides an important contribution to contemporary dialogue between Eastern and Western theologians.

1999 / 0-85364-956-1 / xii + 370pp

Graham Buxton
The Trinity, Creation and Pastoral Ministry
Imaging the Perichoretic God
In this book the author proposes a three-way conversation between theology, science and pastoral ministry. His approach draws on a Trinitarian understanding of God as a relational being of love, whose life 'spills over' into all created reality, human and non-human. By locating human meaning and purpose within God's 'creation-community' this book offers the possibility of a transforming engagement between those in pastoral ministry and the scientific community.

2005 */ 1-84227-369-8 / approx. 380 pp*

Iain D. Campbell
Fixing the Indemnity
The Life and Work of George Adam Smith
When Old Testament scholar George Adam Smith (1856–1942) delivered the Lyman Beecher lectures at Yale University in 1899, he confidently declared that 'modern criticism has won its war against traditional theories. It only remains to fix the amount of the indemnity.' In this biography, Iain D. Campbell assesses Smith's critical approach to the Old Testament and evaluates its consequences, showing that Smith's life and work still raises questions about the relationship between biblical scholarship and evangelical faith.

2004 */ 1-84227-228-4 / xx + 256pp*

Tim Chester
Mission and the Coming of God
Eschatology, the Trinity and Mission in the Theology of Jürgen Moltmann
This book explores the theology and missiology of the influential contemporary theologian, Jürgen Moltmann. It highlights the important contribution Moltmann has made while offering a critique of his thought from an evangelical perspective. In so doing, it touches on pertinent issues for evangelical missiology. The conclusion takes Calvin as a starting point, proposing 'an eschatology of the cross' which offers a critique of the over-realised eschatologies in liberation theology and certain forms of evangelicalism.
2006 / 1-84227-320-5 / approx. 224pp

Sylvia Wilkey Collinson
Making Disciples
The Significance of Jesus' Educational Strategy for Today's Church
This study examines the biblical practice of discipling, formulates a definition, and makes comparisons with modern models of education. A recommendation is made for greater attention to its practice today.
2004 / 1-84227-116-4 / xiv + 278pp

Darrell Cosden
A Theology of Work
Work and the New Creation
Through dialogue with Moltmann, Pope John Paul II and others, this book develops a genitive 'theology of work', presenting a theological definition of work and a model for a theological ethics of work that shows work's nature, value and meaning now and eschatologically. Work is shown to be a transformative activity consisting of three dynamically inter-related dimensions: the instrumental, relational and ontological.
2005 / 1-84227-332-9 / xvi + 208pp

Stephen M. Dunning
The Crisis and the Quest
A Kierkegaardian Reading of Charles Williams
Employing Kierkegaardian categories and analysis, this study investigates both the central crisis in Charles Williams's authorship between hermetism and Christianity (Kierkegaard's Religions A and B), and the quest to resolve this crisis, a quest that ultimately presses the bounds of orthodoxy.
2000 / 0-85364-985-5 / xxiv + 254pp

Keith Ferdinando
The Triumph of Christ in African Perspective
A Study of Demonology and Redemption in the African Context
The book explores the implications of the gospel for traditional African fears of
occult aggression. It analyses such traditional approaches to suffering and
biblical responses to fears of demonic evil, concluding with an evaluation of
African beliefs from the perspective of the gospel.
1999 / 0-85364-830-1 / xviii + 450pp

Andrew Goddard
Living the Word, Resisting the World
The Life and Thought of Jacques Ellul
This work offers a definitive study of both the life and thought of the French
Reformed thinker Jacques Ellul (1912-1994). It will prove an indispensable
resource for those interested in this influential theologian and sociologist and for
Christian ethics and political thought generally.
2002 / 1-84227-053-2 / xxiv + 378pp

David Hilborn
The Words of our Lips
Language-Use in Free Church Worship
Studies of liturgical language have tended to focus on the written canons of
Roman Catholic and Anglican communities. By contrast, David Hilborn
analyses the more extemporary approach of English Nonconformity. Drawing
on recent developments in linguistic pragmatics, he explores similarities and
differences between 'fixed' and 'free' worship, and argues for the
interdependence of each.
2006 / 0-85364-977-4 / approx. 350pp

Roger Hitching
The Church and Deaf People
A Study of Identity, Communication and Relationships with Special Reference to
the Ecclesiology of Jürgen Moltmann
In *The Church and Deaf People* Roger Hitching sensitively examines the history
and present experience of deaf people and finds similarities between aspects of
sign language and Moltmann's theological method that 'open up' new ways of
understanding theological concepts.
2003 / 1-84227-222-5 / xxii + 236pp

John G. Kelly
One God, One People
The Differentiated Unity of the People of God in the Theology of
Jürgen Moltmann
The author expounds and critiques Moltmann's doctrine of God and highlights the systematic connections between it and Moltmann's influential discussion of Israel. He then proposes a fresh approach to Jewish–Christian relations building on Moltmann's work using insights from Habermas and Rawls.
2005 / 0-85346-969-3 / approx. 350pp

Mark F.W. Lovatt
Confronting the Will-to-Power
A Reconsideration of the Theology of Reinhold Niebuhr
Confronting the Will-to-Power is an analysis of the theology of Reinhold Niebuhr, arguing that his work is an attempt to identify, and provide a practical theological answer to, the existence and nature of human evil.
2001 / 1-84227-054-0 / xviii + 216pp

Neil B. MacDonald
Karl Barth and the Strange New World within the Bible
Barth, Wittgenstein, and the Metadilemmas of the Enlightenment
Barth's discovery of the strange new world within the Bible is examined in the context of Kant, Hume, Overbeck, and, most importantly, Wittgenstein. MacDonald covers some fundamental issues in theology today: epistemology, the final form of the text and biblical truth-claims.
2000 / 0-85364-970-7 / xxvi + 374pp

Keith A. Mascord
Alvin Plantinga and Christian Apologetics
This book draws together the contributions of the philosopher Alvin Plantinga to the major contemporary challenges to Christian belief, highlighting in particular his ground-breaking work in epistemology and the problem of evil. Plantinga's theory that both theistic and Christian belief is warrantedly basic is explored and critiqued, and an assessment offered as to the significance of his work for apologetic theory and practice.
2005 / 1-84227-256-X / approx. 304pp

Gillian McCulloch
The Deconstruction of Dualism in Theology
With Reference to Ecofeminist Theology and New Age Spirituality
This book challenges eco-theological anti-dualism in Christian theology, arguing that dualism has a twofold function in Christian religious discourse. Firstly, it enables us to express the discontinuities and divisions that are part of the process of reality. Secondly, dualistic language allows us to express the mysteries of divine transcendence/immanence and the survival of the soul without collapsing into monism and materialism, both of which are problematic for Christian epistemology.

2002 / 1-84227-044-3 / xii + 282pp

Leslie McCurdy
Attributes and Atonement
The Holy Love of God in the Theology of P.T. Forsyth
Attributes and Atonement is an intriguing full-length study of P.T. Forsyth's doctrine of the cross as it relates particularly to God's holy love. It includes an unparalleled bibliography of both primary and secondary material relating to Forsyth.

1999 / 0-85364-833-6 / xiv + 328pp

Nozomu Miyahira
Towards a Theology of the Concord of God
A Japanese Perspective on the Trinity
This book introduces a new Japanese theology and a unique Trinitarian formula based on the Japanese intellectual climate: three betweennesses and one concord. It also presents a new interpretation of the Trinity, a co-subordinationism, which is in line with orthodox Trinitarianism; each single person of the Trinity is eternally and equally subordinate (or serviceable) to the other persons, so that they retain the mutual dynamic equality.

2000 / 0-85364-863-8 / xiv + 256pp

Eddy José Muskus
The Origins and Early Development of Liberation Theology in Latin America
With Particular Reference to Gustavo Gutiérrez
This work challenges the fundamental premise of Liberation Theology, 'opting for the poor', and its claim that Christ is found in them. It also argues that Liberation Theology emerged as a direct result of the failure of the Roman Catholic Church in Latin America.

2002 / 0-85364-974-X / xiv + 296pp

Jim Purves
The Triune God and the Charismatic Movement
A Critical Appraisal from a Scottish Perspective
All emotion and no theology? Or a fundamental challenge to reappraise and realign our trinitarian theology in the light of Christian experience? This study of charismatic renewal as it found expression within Scotland at the end of the twentieth century evaluates the use of Patristic, Reformed and contemporary models of the Trinity in explaining the workings of the Holy Spirit.
2004 / 1-84227-321-3 / xxiv + 246pp

Anna Robbins
Methods in the Madness
Diversity in Twentieth-Century Christian Social Ethics
The author compares the ethical methods of Walter Rauschenbusch, Reinhold Niebuhr and others. She argues that unless Christians are clear about the ways that theology and philosophy are expressed practically they may lose the ability to discuss social ethics across contexts, let alone reach effective agreements.
2004 / 1-84227-211-X / xx + 294pp

Ed Rybarczyk
Beyond Salvation
Eastern Orthodoxy and Classical Pentecostalism on Becoming Like Christ
At first glance eastern Orthodoxy and classical Pentecostalism seem quite distinct. This ground-breaking study shows they share much in common, especially as it concerns the experiential elements of following Christ. Both traditions assert that authentic Christianity transcends the wooden categories of modernism.
2004 / 1-84227-144-X / xii + 356pp

Signe Sandsmark
Is World View Neutral Education Possible and Desirable?
A Christian Response to Liberal Arguments
(Published jointly with The Stapleford Centre)
This book discusses reasons for belief in world view neutrality, and argues that 'neutral' education will have a hidden, but strong world view influence. It discusses the place for Christian education in the common school.
2000 / 0-85364-973-1 / xiv + 182pp

Hazel Sherman
Reading Zechariah
The Allegorical Tradition of Biblical Interpretation through the Commentary of Didymus the Blind and Theodore of Mopsuestia
A close reading of the commentary on Zechariah by Didymus the Blind alongside that of Theodore of Mopsuestia suggests that popular categorising of Antiochene and Alexandrian biblical exegesis as 'historical' or 'allegorical' is inadequate and misleading.
2005 / 1-84227-213-6 / approx. 280pp

Andrew Sloane
On Being a Christian in the Academy
Nicholas Wolterstorff and the Practice of Christian Scholarship
An exposition and critical appraisal of Nicholas Wolterstorff's epistemology in the light of the philosophy of science, and an application of his thought to the practice of Christian scholarship.
2003 / 1-84227-058-3 / xvi + 274pp

Damon W.K. So
Jesus' Revelation of His Father
A Narrative-Conceptual Study of the Trinity with Special Reference to Karl Barth
This book explores the trinitarian dynamics in the context of Jesus' revelation of his Father in his earthly ministry with references to key passages in Matthew's Gospel. It develops from the exegeses of these passages a non-linear concept of revelation which links Jesus' communion with his Father to his revelatory words and actions through a nuanced understanding of the Holy Spirit, with references to K. Barth, G.W.H. Lampe, J.D.G. Dunn and E. Irving.
2005 / 1-84227-323-X / approx. 380pp

Daniel Strange
The Possibility of Salvation Among the Unevangelised
An Analysis of Inclusivism in Recent Evangelical Theology
For evangelical theologians the 'fate of the unevangelised' impinges upon fundamental tenets of evangelical identity. The position known as 'inclusivism', defined by the belief that the unevangelised can be ontologically saved by Christ whilst being epistemologically unaware of him, has been defended most vigorously by the Canadian evangelical Clark H. Pinnock. Through a detailed analysis and critique of Pinnock's work, this book examines a cluster of issues surrounding the unevangelised and its implications for christology, soteriology and the doctrine of revelation.
2002 / 1-84227-047-8 / xviii + 362pp

Scott Swain
God According to the Gospel
Biblical Narrative and the Identity of God in the Theology of Robert W. Jenson
Robert W. Jenson is one of the leading voices in contemporary Trinitarian theology. His boldest contribution in this area concerns his use of biblical narrative both to ground and explicate the Christian doctrine of God. *God According to the Gospel* critically examines Jenson's proposal and suggests an alternative way of reading the biblical portrayal of the triune God.
2006 / 1-84227-258-6 / approx. 180pp

Justyn Terry
The Justifying Judgement of God
A Reassessment of the Place of Judgement in the Saving Work of Christ
The argument of this book is that judgement, understood as the whole process of bringing justice, is the primary metaphor of atonement, with others, such as victory, redemption and sacrifice, subordinate to it. Judgement also provides the proper context for understanding penal substitution and the call to repentance, baptism, eucharist and holiness.
2005 / 1-84227-370-1 / approx. 274 pp

Graham Tomlin
The Power of the Cross
Theology and the Death of Christ in Paul, Luther and Pascal
This book explores the theology of the cross in St Paul, Luther and Pascal. It offers new perspectives on the theology of each, and some implications for the nature of power, apologetics, theology and church life in a postmodern context.
1999 / 0-85364-984-7 / xiv + 344pp

Adonis Vidu
Postliberal Theological Method
A Critical Study
The postliberal theology of Hans Frei, George Lindbeck, Ronald Thiemann, John Milbank and others is one of the more influential contemporary options. This book focuses on several aspects pertaining to its theological method, specifically its understanding of background, hermeneutics, epistemic justification, ontology, the nature of doctrine and, finally, Christological method.
2005 / 1-84227-395-7 / approx. 324pp

Graham J. Watts
Revelation and the Spirit
*A Comparative Study of the Relationship between the Doctrine of Revelation
and Pneumatology in the Theology of Eberhard Jüngel and of
Wolfhart Pannenberg*
The relationship between revelation and pneumatology is relatively unexplored.
This approach offers a fresh angle on two important twentieth century
theologians and raises pneumatological questions which are theologically crucial
and relevant to mission in a postmodern culture.
2005 / 1-84227-104-0 / xxii + 232pp

Nigel G. Wright
Disavowing Constantine
*Mission, Church and the Social Order in the Theologies of John Howard Yoder
and Jürgen Moltmann*
This book is a timely restatement of a radical theology of church and state in the
Anabaptist and Baptist tradition. Dr Wright constructs his argument in dialogue
and debate with Yoder and Moltmann, major contributors to a free church
perspective.
2000 / 0-85364-978-2 / xvi + 252pp

Paternoster
9 Holdom Avenue,
Bletchley,
Milton Keynes MK1 1QR,
United Kingdom
Web: www.authenticmedia.co.uk/paternoster

July 2005